OXFORD WORLD'S CLASSICS

THE DAWN OF THE ROMAN EMPIRE
BOOKS THIRTY-ONE TO FORTY

TITUS LIVIUS (LIVY), the historian, was born in Patavium (modern Padua) in 64 or 59 BC and died in AD 17 in Patavium, surviving therefore into his late seventies or early eighties. He came to Rome in the 30s BC and began writing his history of Rome by the end of that decade. There is no evidence that he was a senator or held other governmental posts, although he was acquainted with the emperor Augustus and his family, at least by his later years. He appears to have had the means to spend his life largely in writing his huge history of Rome, *Ab Urbe Condita* or 'From the Founding of the City', which filled 142 books and covered the period from Rome's founding to the death of the elder Drusus (753–9 BC). Thirty-five books survive: 1–10 (753–293 BC) and 21–45 (218–167 BC).

J. C. YARDLEY was educated at the (former) Cowbridge Grammar School, South Wales, and the universities of St Andrews and Oxford. He has also translated Quintus Curtius' *History of Alexander* for Penguin Classics (1984) and Justin for the American Philological Association Classical Resources series (1994) and (Books 11–12) for Oxford University Press's Clarendon Ancient History series (1997). He is a former President of the Classical Association of Canada

WALDEMAR HECKEL was born in Königshofen i. Gr., Germany, and educated in Canada, where he received his Ph.D. at the University of British Columbia. He is Professor of Ancient History at the University of Calgary and author of *The Last Days and Testament of Alexander the Great* (Stuttgart, 1988) and *The Marshals of Alexander's Empire* (London, 1992). He annotated J. C. Yardley's translations of Quintus Curtius for Penguin Classics (1984) and Justin's Books 11–12 (on Alexander the Great) for the Clarendon Ancient History series.

OXFORD WORLD'S CLASSICS

*For almost 100 years Oxford World's Classics have brought
readers closer to the world's great literature. Now with over 700
titles—from the 4,000-year-old myths of Mesopotamia to the
twentieth century's greatest novels—the series makes available
lesser-known as well as celebrated writing.*

*The pocket-sized hardbacks of the early years contained
introductions by Virginia Woolf, T. S. Eliot, Graham Greene,
and other literary figures which enriched the experience of reading.
Today the series is recognized for its fine scholarship and
reliability in texts that span world literature, drama and poetry,
religion, philosophy and politics. Each edition includes perceptive
commentary and essential background information to meet the
changing needs of readers.*

OXFORD WORLD'S CLASSICS

LIVY

The Dawn of the Roman Empire

Books Thirty-One to Forty

Translated by
J. C. YARDLEY

With an Introduction and Notes by
WALDEMAR HECKEL

OXFORD
UNIVERSITY PRESS

SCHAUMBURG TOWNSHIP DISTRICT LIBRARY
130 SOUTH ROSELLE ROAD
SCHAUMBURG, ILLINOIS 60193

937.02
LIV

3 1257 01362 5545

OXFORD
UNIVERSITY PRESS

Great Clarendon Street, Oxford OX2 6DP

Oxford University Press is a department of the University of Oxford.
It furthers the University's objective of excellence in research, scholarship,
and education by publishing worldwide in

Oxford New York

Athens Auckland Bangkok Bogotá Buenos Aires Calcutta
Cape Town Chennai Dar es Salaam Delhi Florence Hong Kong Istanbul
Karachi Kuala Lumpur Madrid Melbourne Mexico City Mumbai
Nairobi Paris São Paulo Singapore Taipei Tokyo Toronto Warsaw

with associated companies in Berlin Ibadan

Oxford is a registered trade mark of Oxford University Press
in the UK and in certain other countries

Published in the United States
by Oxford University Press Inc., New York

Translation © J. C. Yardley 2000
Introduction, Notes, and other editorial matter © Waldemar Heckel 2000

The moral rights of the author have been asserted

Database right Oxford University Press (maker)

First published as an Oxford World's Classics paperback 2000

All rights reserved. No part of this publication may be reproduced,
stored in a retrieval system, or transmitted, in any form or by any means,
without the prior permission in writing of Oxford University Press,
or as expressly permitted by law, or under terms agreed with the appropriate
reprographics rights organizations. Enquiries concerning reproduction
outside the scope of the above should be sent to the Rights Department,
Oxford University Press, at the address above

You must not circulate this book in any other binding or cover
and you must impose this same condition on any acquirer

British Library Cataloguing in Publication Data

Data available

Library of Congress Cataloging in Publication Data

Data available

ISBN 0–19–283293–X

1 3 5 7 9 10 8 6 4 2

Typeset in Ehrhardt
by RefineCatch Limited, Bungay, Suffolk
Printed in Great Britain by
Cox and Wyman Ltd., Reading

CONTENTS

Introduction   vii

Note on the Text and Translation   xxx

Select Bibliography   xxxi

A Chronology of Events   xxxv

Maps   xxxviii

THE DAWN OF THE ROMAN EMPIRE   1

BOOK THIRTY-ONE   3

BOOK THIRTY-TWO   53

BOOK THIRTY-THREE   95

BOOK THIRTY-FOUR   141

BOOK THIRTY-FIVE   199

BOOK THIRTY-SIX   249

BOOK THIRTY-SEVEN   293

BOOK THIRTY-EIGHT   356

BOOK THIRTY-NINE   423

BOOK FORTY   482

Appendix 1. List of Variations from the Teubner Text   539

Appendix 2. Consuls (Censors) and Praetors
  200–179 BC   540

Explanatory Notes   543

Index of Personal Names   587

General Index   599

INTRODUCTION

Livy's Life and Work

Titus Livius, one of Rome's greatest historians,[1] was born (according to St Jerome) in 59 BC, the year of Julius Caesar's consulship, though there are reasons for supposing that Jerome has postdated Livy's birth by five years, in which case 64 BC would be correct. Livy himself appears to have delayed publishing Books 121–42, which dealt with Augustus, until after the latter's death; hence his life must have extended beyond AD 14.[2] His birthplace is positively identified as Patavium (Padua or Padova), a city in Cisalpine Gaul noted for its old-fashioned morality and commercial wealth. Livy's Transpadane origins will thus have influenced his moral outlook and, at least in the early stages of his career, his political inclinations. Tacitus claims that Livy's treatment of Pompey the Great was so favourable that Augustus himself called him 'the Pompeian';[3] though Asinius Pollio's unkind remarks about Livy's rustic style were probably motivated more by his own rebuff at Patavium when, as governor of Cisalpine Gaul, he failed to win the city for Mark Antony.[4]

As Livy reached maturity, the series of civil wars, initiated by Caesar's crossing of the Rubicon in 49, made conditions unfavourable for a young man wishing to continue his education either in Rome or in Greece. For a sojourn in the latter there is no explicit evidence, and it is significant that Livy nowhere demonstrates firsthand knowledge of Greek geography. Nor is it certain when he came to Rome, though it is probably safe to assume that he arrived during the 30s or, at the latest, before 27 BC. Before he turned to the daunting task of composing his *History*, Livy composed dialogues of a philosophical and historical nature.

---

[1] For Livy's reputation in antiquity see Tacitus, *Agricola* 10. 3; cf. Pliny (*Letters* 2. 3. 8) who claims that a man from Cadiz travelled all the way to Rome just to look at Livy.

[2] *Periochae* 121 contains the heading: *qui editus post excessum Augusti dicitur* ('which is said to have been published after Augustus' death'). St Jerome places Livy's death in AD 17.

[3] Tacitus, *Annals*, 4. 34.

[4] Quintilian 8. 1. 3; Macrobius 1. 11. 22; Cicero, *Philippics* 12. 10.

At some point he married, though we do not know whom, and produced two sons and a daughter. One the sons authored a work on geography, the other inclined towards the study of rhetoric. Probably it was to the latter that he addressed a letter, advising him to read Cicero and Demosthenes, and writers of that ilk. Livy's daughter, we are told by the elder Seneca, married the rhetorician Lucius Magius, who attracted audiences more by the fame of his father-in-law than by his own talents. Although Livy himself played no role in politics or public life, he was nevertheless personally acquainted with Augustus and the future emperor Claudius, whose childhood interest in historical writing he is said to have encouraged.[5] Whether his connections with the Imperial family affected his integrity and independence as a historian is debated: Livy looks back fondly on the days of Senatorial government, and his treatment of Augustus was, as far as we can tell, cautious and untainted by adulation.[6] Before his death he appears to have returned to his native Patavium, where a tomb inscription dated to the Augustan period commemorates him.

Ab Urbe Condita

The work was immense, recounting in 142 books Rome's history from the foundation (hence the title *Ab Urbe Condita*, 'From the Founding of the City') to his own time, a period of about 770 years. For his readers, the process of excerpting began almost immediately. Such was the activity that preoccupied the younger Pliny amid the eruption of Vesuvius![7] And there existed already in Martial's time an epitome of the whole work, which appears to have been consulted by a majority of later writers in preference to the original.[8] Not surprisingly, then, only 35 books have survived more or less intact to the present day—1–10 and 21–45, probably also the most popular in antiquity since their 'heroic' themes appealed to readers more than

---

[5] Tacitus, *Annals*, 4. 34.; Suetonius, *Claudius* 41.

[6] Cf. P. G. Walsh, *Livy* (Oxford, 1974), 7, who characterizes him as 'the Republican traditionalist *par excellence*'. H. J. Mette, in E. Burck (ed.), *Wege zu Livius* (Darmstadt, 1977), 156–66, argues that Livy was critical of Augustus.

[7] Pliny, *Letters* 6. 20.

[8] Martial, *Epigrams* 14. 190–1; cf. C. M. Begbie, 'The Epitome of Livy', *Classical Quarterly*, 17 (1967), 332–8.

the constitutional struggles of later volumes.[9] The current selection (31–40) thus represents a little less than a third of the surviving corpus. The scope and contents of the lost books (with the exception of Books 136–7) are, however, discernible from the *Periochae*, book-by-book summaries of the *Ab Urbe Condita*,[10] and can be summarized as follows (asterisks indicate the extant volumes):

*Books 1–5:	From the founding of the city to the Gallic catastrophe (*c*.386 BC)
*Books 6–10:	Roman expansion in Italy; the Samnite Wars
Books 11–15:	Rome and Italy, including Pyrrhus' campaigns
Books 16–20:	The First Punic War and aftermath (264–219)
*Books 21–30:	The Hannibalic War (218–201)
*Books 31–5:	Rome and Philip V
*Books 36–40:	Rome and Antiochus III
*Books 41–5:	Third Macedonian War
Books 46–70:	From 167 to 91 BC
Books 71–80:	Events to the death of Gaius Marius
Books 81–90:	Civil war; dictatorship and death of Sulla
Books 91–103:	Events from 78 to 62 BC
Books 104–117:	From 62 BC to the death of Caesar in 44 BC
Books 117–133:	From Caesar's death to Actium (31 BC)[11]
Books 134–142:	The early principate (29–9 BC)

The basic structural unit of the work is the pentad (or set of five books), though these combined to form decades, or even pentekaide-cades, of related material. Occasionally, a division was emphasized by a preface (Books 1, 6, 21, 31), but not all pentads had their own prefaces (see Books 26, 36, 41), nor were the latter restricted to the beginnings of pentads (Book 2). The surviving prefaces introduce the regal period, the establishment of the republic, Roman recovery

---

[9] Cf. R. M. Ogilvie, *Livy: Rome and Italy* (Harmondsworth, Penguin. 1982), 12: 'his philosophical detachment enabled him to see history in terms of human characters and representative individuals rather than of partisan politics.' .

[10] These summaries exist in two forms, a 3rd-cent. collection preserved on a papyrus from Oxyrhynchus and a more extensive 4th-cent. compilation, though the latter is perhaps a little too verbose for this period; cf. Begbie, 'Epitome of Livy', 337). See Alfred C. Schlesinger, *Livy*, vol. xiv, Loeb Classical Library (Cambridge, Mass., 1959) for text and translations of the summaries.

[11] There is, of course, a break between 120 and 121. Book 120 dealt with the for-mation of the Triumvirate; 121 represents a new section which was published after Augustus' death in AD 14.

after the Gallic disaster, the Hannibalic war, and the conflict with the Hellenistic East. From Book 91 onwards the division into pentads and decades is less obvious, leading some to suppose that the practice was abandoned. And, although the placement of the prefaces suggests an awareness of historical 'eras', this does not make the task of schematizing Livy's work any easier, since modern perceptions of late republican 'eras' are doubtless different from those recognized by the Romans themselves.

It was once fashionable to characterize Livy as a writer who gave little thought to matters of organization and often stumbled into error precisely because he neither read nor planned ahead. This view of the wooden-headed, moralizing, storyteller has been dispelled by the careful researches of T. J. Luce.[12] Speculation concerning the composition of lost books, based on the limited evidence of the *Periochae* and scattered *testimonia*, has, however, produced mixed results. By contrast, the extant books, and particularly the two pentads translated in this volume, reflect the efforts of a more thoughtful writer than scholars have believed Livy to be. Some have seen hints of Livy's amateurish approach in the Preface to Book 31:

I feel like someone who wades out into the depths after being initially attracted to the water by the shallows next to the shore; and I foresee any advance only taking me into even more enormous, indeed bottomless, depths, and that this undertaking of mine, which seemed to be diminishing as I was completing the earliest sections, is now almost increasing in size.

But Livy's comments, if they are meant to be taken seriously, may reflect the fact that the material, particularly that which he finds in Polybius, is becoming more diverse, much of it less relevant to Roman history proper. Hence, Livy avoids discussing topics which 'cannot really be justified when I am barely capable of providing an account of those relevant to the war fought by the Romans' (33. 20). Nevertheless, Livy is not entirely consistent in differentiating between 'Greek' and 'Roman' material (cf. 35. 40) and occasionally includes or omits things as they lay claim to, or fail to catch, his interest. Sometimes, he simply cannot resist a good story.[13]

Luce demonstrates that the three pentads comprising Books

---

[12] See, particularly, *Livy: The Composition of his History* (Princeton, 1977).
[13] e.g. the fate of Theoxena (40. 4).

31–45 deal specifically with the Roman wars against Philip V, Antiochus III, and Perseus, each pentad treating these wars as the central episodes around which other material (both domestic and foreign) is grouped. The seventh pentad (31–5) begins with the vote to wage war on Philip, and the declaration of the 'Freedom of the Greeks' occupies precisely the middle of Book 33 (the central book of the pentad); after concluding with Antiochus' crossing into Greece in Book 35, Livy begins the eighth pentad (36–40) with the vote concerning war with the Syrian king. Similarly, the final book of this pentad sets the stage for the Third Macedonian War (which culminated in the defeat of Perseus at Pydna in 168 and effectively put an end to the Macedonian kingdom) by providing extensive detail on the last year of Philip V and Perseus' role in the murder of his younger brother, Demetrius.[14]

Livy's Fourth Decade and the Historical Background

In his first pentad, Livy had described the history of Rome from the foundation of the city and the establishment of the Republic to the Gallic catastrophe of 386 BC. That last event proved only a temporary setback to the growth of Roman power, first in Italy and then in the Mediterranean. Dominance in central Italy, confirmed in three bitter wars with the Samnites (343–341; 326–304; 298–290), brought Roman arms to the south, where the Greek colony of Tarentum summoned King Pyrrhus of Epirus to its aid.[15] This first exposure to the Macedonian style of warfare made a lasting impression on the Romans, who—already influenced by the legend of Alexander the Great—imagined the power of his Hellenistic epigones to be more

[14] Livy sets the stage for both the ninth pentad and the Third Macedonian War, which is its 'main event', early on: at 38. 40 there is the suspicion of Philip's complicity in the Thracian attack on the returning army of Gnaeus Manlius; at 39. 23, Livy remarks that the war with Perseus had its origins in Philip's actions, and this view is reiterated at 39. 29; at 39. 24 Philip is shown preparing his economic and manpower base for another confrontation, and at 39. 26 he is made to say that 'the sun had not yet set on all his days'. Furthermore, by emphasizing the goodwill of the Senate to Demetrius (39. 47–8) and repeating the rumour that the heir to the throne, Perseus, was the son of a whore (39. 53; 40. 9), Livy vilifies Rome's next opponent, soon to be further tainted by fratricide (40. 24). The murder was, of course, ultimately Philip's doing.

[15] The Samnite wars are described in the second pentad. Pyrrhus' invasion was treated in the third pentad, but there are numerous references to the Epirote king in the extant books, including the present selection (31. 3, 7, 31; 35. 14; 39. 51).

formidable than it actually was.[16] But that was to be revealed in the future.

The narrative of events upon which Livy embarks at the beginning of Book 31 recounts the tortuous and largely unwilling expansion of Rome from political and military leadership of Italy to 'world power'. Victory over Carthage in the First Punic War had brought Sicily, and then Sardinia, into the Roman orbit; but the Hannibalic War, caused in no small part by Roman bullying, had taken a heavy toll in terms of manpower and economic resources. One is tempted to see Roman expansion as a logical step towards the recouping of losses, but for the Senate the burdens of imperialism will have dampened enthusiasm for such policy. Certainly, the readiness to withdraw from Spain—strategically important during the Second Punic War—suggests that Rome favoured a retraction to older boundaries. Africa was evacuated at the earliest opportunity, secured by the friendship of the Numidian king, Masinissa, and the planned withdrawal from Greece was put into effect, only to be confounded by political complications. If it was truly Rome's intention to seek security and strategic advantage without occupation, the outcome was otherwise. The first quarter of the third century, roughly the period covered by Livy in the fourth decade, thus marked the dawn of the Roman empire.

The First and Second Macedonian Wars

In 217, while Philip was attending the Nemean Games, word reached him of Hannibal's victory at Lake Trasimene. Polybius alleges that the exile, Demetrius of Pharos, planted in Philip's mind the idea of translating Rome's weakness into territorial gains on the Adriatic coast. The opportunity will not have escaped the king, but clearly no alliance with Hannibal and Carthage was made until after Cannae, indeed not until 215.[17] Philip's pact with Hannibal threatened Rome's eastern flank in a time of great crisis. Rome countered by entrusting the affairs of Greece and Macedonia to Marcus Valerius Laevinus, limiting Roman actions to the naval sphere. For-

[16] Even if we allow for bias in the Roman sources, we cannot help but note the poor showing of Philip and his Macedonians. This does not, however, mean that the Romans themselves anticipated easy victory.

[17] Polybius 5. 101. 6–10 for Demetrius' advice at the Nemean Games; Polybius 7. 9 for the terms of the treaty with Carthage; cf. Livy 23. 38 for Roman awareness of the negotiations between Philip and Hannibal.

tunately, the Greek world had its own internal divisions which could be exploited, and in 211 Aetolia—the traditional enemy of both Macedon and the Achaean League, which since the time of Antigonus III Doson had been part of the Hellenic Symmachy—broke with Philip V. Rome was quick to make a pact, but, in the war with Philip, Aetolia was far too often left to her own devices. In 206 Philip captured Ambracia and devastated Aetolian territory up to Thermum.[18] Despite the stipulation that neither would make a separate peace with Macedon, Aetolia was forced to enter into negotiations with Philip. The Peace of Phoenice of 205 ended the matter for all parties.

In 201 Rome made peace with Carthage, marking the end of the life-and-death struggle with Hannibal. The ink had scarcely dried on the peace-treaty with Carthage when the question of war with Macedon was placed before the Roman People in the Comitia Centuriata. Appeals from Pergamum, Rhodes, and Athens, coupled with tales (some true, most exaggerated) of Philip V's aggression, provided a pretext for Roman intervention. What induced Rome to embark upon a new war with Philip so soon after Hannibal's defeat is uncertain.[19] The motives were neither altruistic nor opportunistic. In retrospect Rome's power seems unassailable. But the Hannibalic War had had a destabilizing effect on Italy and its neighbours, and new ventures in the East were a hard sell to the war-weary Roman populace. One looks for economic factors, but the evidence (leaving aside the matter of plunder) is insufficient.[20] Large-scale demobilization remained a concern: laws that prohibited commanders from coercing veterans of the Hannibalic War appear to have been ignored in many cases.

Certainly there was a case to be made for pre-emptive action, even though Philip's 'aggression' was more or less confined to the east, where he and Antiochus III were making territorial gains at the expense of the Ptolemaic kingdom in the aftermath of Philopator's death. Ptolemy IV had died in 204/3, leaving the throne to a mere

[18] Polybius 4. 61; cf Livy 36. 31.

[19] See the discussion in H. H. Scullard, *A History of the Roman World from 753 to 146 BC*, 3rd edn. (London, 1961), 234–7.

[20] F. B. Marsh's comment that 'the victories of the legions abroad exalted the capitalists at home' (*A History of the Roman World 146 to 30 BC* (London, 1971), 5) refers to a later period. Cf. also W. V. Harris, *War and Imperialism in Republican Rome, 327–70 BC* (Oxford, 1979), ch. 2.

boy, Ptolemy V Epiphanes. Antiochus III, who defeated Epiphanes' general at Panion in 200, derived the greatest advantage from the weakness in Alexandria; in 195 he arranged the marriage of his daughter Cleopatra I to the young Ptolemy.[21] But Philip's activities on the Aegean littoral threatened Pergamum and Rhodes, both of whom had diplomatic relations with Rome. Their appeals, coupled with those of Athens, provided the Senate with the pretext for declaring war and punishing Philip for siding with Carthage during the Hannibalic War, perhaps the true motive for Roman involvement in the Greek world.

Stymied in its first attempt to persuade the Roman People to declare war on Philip of Macedon, the Senate directed Publius Sulpicius Galba (consul for 200 BC) to put the case in the strongest possible terms. The speech Livy attributes to the consul reveals Roman anxieties: they should not allow another enemy to land in Italy. If the recent experience of Hannibal were not enough, Pyrrhus had given a good indication of what Macedonian arms could do. Scare-tactics thus played no small part in Sulpicius' address and the assembly voted for war (31. 7–8). While Rome made extensive preparations for the new war and tied up the loose ends from the preceding one (31. 11), Philip V's agents and armies were active in Greece and the Aegean: Abydus was taken and enslaved (31. 17–18) and the environs of Athens ravaged (31. 24–6). Publius Sulpicius had at last crossed the Adriatic to Apollonia, while Roman forces and Attalus of Pergamum campaigned around Euboea (31. 22–3), but at home the Gauls in northern Italy threatened Roman colonies (31. 21; cf. 31. 49–50). After meeting with the Aetolian allies, and winning the support of Athamania, Sulpicius made a successful push into the interior: his victory at Ottolobus (31. 36–8) forced Philip to withdraw deeper into Macedonia and soon the Romans occupied Eordaea (31. 40). With corresponding successes by Attalus in the Aegean (particularly, the capture of Oreus in late summer 200 BC), the Second Macedonian War had started well.

Sulpicius' successor was, however, late in setting out and the gains of 200 were all but negated by Publius Villius' inertia and Philip's energetic counter-offensive in Thessaly (32. 4). New elections brought Titus Quinctius Flamininus to Greece, where he quickly

---

[21] See 35. 13 and note.

crossed from the Adriatic coast to Thessaly, winning an important
victory at the River Aous *en route* (32. 10–13). The consul's brother,
Lucius, was equally successful at sea (32. 16), while Titus managed
to detach the Achaean League from its alliance with Macedon, a
shift induced as much by fear of the Spartan tyrant Nabis as by the
success of Roman arms (32. 19–23). For Flamininus negotiation took
on greater importance as his term of office drew to a close, but news
that his command had been extended allowed him to take a more
aggressive stance, and in 197 Roman forces invaded Thessaly and
confronted Philip not far from Pherae at a place known (from the
peculiarities of the terrain) as Cynoscephalae (33. 3–10).

Compared with the protracted struggle against Hannibal, war with
Philip was a relatively simple affair, unmarred by military disaster.
For the enemy had in practice displayed little of the prowess of his
famed ancestors, Demetrius and Alexander. (Alexander was not, of
course, a true ancestor of Philip V, although Antigonid propaganda
made him so.) Peace proved more difficult, as the complex balance of
power was upset by Macedon's defeat (see below pp. xvii–xix).
Achaean defection from the Hellenic League established by Antigonus Doson had been motivated by fear of a Peloponnesian enemy,
and there was no love of Aetolia south of the Gulf of Corinth. At the
Isthmian Games of 196, Flamininus proclaimed the 'Freedom of the
Greeks' in the shadow of Acrocorinth (33. 31–4) where a Roman
garrison had replaced that of Macedon. Few were convinced that the
occupation would be temporary, and Aetolia openly complained that
it had not been adequately compensated for having assumed what it
considered the lion's share of the burden in the war with Philip. It
soon became clear that Macedon had not been the only obstacle to
Greek freedom. When Flamininus turned to deal with Nabis (34.
22–36; 35. 25–30) he was striking a blow for the Peloponnesian
aristocracy, which feared the social and economic reform based on
redistribution of land far more than the tyrant himself, whose death
(35. 35–6) brought only a short reprieve for Achaea and the Romans.

The Hellenistic World

The jubilation that accompanied the fall of the Athenian Empire and
the destruction of the city's walls in 404/3 was short lived. Spartan
'imperialism' proved harsh and arbitrary, and many of her former
allies—members of the Peloponnesian League—found themselves

alienated by her high-handed conduct. They had gone from sharing the burden of the war against Athens to sharing the indignities of servitude. The fourth century BC thus witnessed a succession of debilitating, internecine wars. The alliance of Thebes, Athens, Corinth, and Argos against Sparta in the Corinthian War (394–387/6) served only to bring the Great King of Persia into the picture as guarantor of the 'Spartan' peace. But the power of Sparta was broken at Leuctra (371 BC) by the Thebans, whose own period of hegemony endured for less than a generation. While the Greek world south of Olympus and the Vale of Tempe dissipated its power, there arose to the north the powerful kingdom of Macedon, formed by the sons of Amyntas III and forged into a military threat by the youngest of these, Philip II (359–336 BC).

The political stability created by Philip II at home, which saw the integration of the semi-independent highland cantons of Upper Macedonia into the Argead kingdom and the annexation of Thessaly and Epirus to the south, was matched and, indeed, facilitated by substantial military reforms. In 338 Philip, with his 18-year-old son, Alexander, leading the cavalry on the right, defeated the combined forces of Athens and Thebes at Chaeronea. In the following year, he created the League of Corinth, which elected him its *hegemon*, or military leader, and empowered him to lead an allied force against Persia. The expedition was pre-empted by the assassination of its leader. But the son was destined to excel the father and, despite Alexander's claim that 'only the name of the king had changed', history's judgement has been otherwise. From 334 to 323 the young conqueror brought the entire Persian empire, and a few adjacent territories, under his rule and, by adding a veneer of Graeco-Macedonian administration and culture to the region, established what nineteenth-century scholarship was to term the 'Hellenistic' world.

Alexander's conquests were, in many respects, superficial. Had he had time to consolidate his work, the story might have been different. But in the event he died before his thirty-third birthday in June 323, without naming an heir. It would have been pointless to do so: Alexander's male relatives comprised only a half-witted brother (Arridaeus, who nevertheless ruled briefly as Philip III), an illegitimate son by his mistress Barsine (Hercules), and an as-yet-unborn son, the ill-fated Alexander IV. Devotion to the royal house waned as Alexander's marshals contemplated the pathetic candidates for the kingship, and there followed very quickly a bitter struggle amongst the most powerful of these generals, known to posterity as the *Diadochoi* ('Successors'). By 306–305, the Argead male line had been eradicated and the *Diadochoi* had openly assumed the titles and trappings of 'Kings'. Antigonus the One-Eyed and his son Demetrius were the first to do so, in the wake of their naval victory at Cyprian Salamis in 306; Ptolemy, Lysimachus, Cassander, and Seleucus all followed suit. The 270s saw the now-familiar map of the Hellenistic world beginning to take shape. Ptolemy II Philadelphus, son of Alexander's general, ruled Egypt; Antigonus II Gonatas had secured Macedon; and Seleucus' son Antiochus I ruled the largest (Asiatic) portion of Alexander's empire and commanded in Asia Minor the allegiance of Lysimachus' former treasurer at Pergamum, Philetaerus. But this man, and his successors, Eumenes I and Attalus I, asserted their independence, forming the fourth major Hellenistic kingdom, Pergamum.

Sparta and the Achaean League

Weakened by the catastrophe at Leuctra and the subsequent foundation of Megalopolis and detachment of Messenia, Sparta declined rapidly as a power in Greece. She played no part in the resistance to Philip at Chaeronea in 338—either from weakness or simply enmity towards Thebes. Certainly, it was not a pro-Macedonian stance, for Sparta refrained from joining Philip's League of Corinth in the following spring. In 331 Agis III's attempt to rid the Peloponnese of Macedonian domination ended in defeat and death at Megalopolis. Alexander the Great's disparaging remarks about 'a battle of mice' (Plutarch, *Agesilaus* 15) disguise the seriousness of the threat. Nevertheless, Spartan fortunes continued to decline: the collapse of the 'Lycurgan' system and the shortage of manpower (*oliganthropia*), which had plagued the *polis* from the beginning, offered scant hope of Lacedaemonian resurgence.

In the northern Peloponnese, the Achaean League constituted a powerful counterweight to Spartan aspirations. Established in 281 as a federation of rather insignificant Achaean towns,[22] the League was revived in 250/49, when Aratus of Sicyon overthrew the tyranny at

---

[22] Patrae, Dyme, Pharae, and Tritaea were the original members.

home and secured membership for his city. Corinth and other cities were added later, and under Aratus' leadership the League resisted Aetolian aggression and the ambitions of Sparta. But the rising power of Cleomenes induced Megalopolis to join the Achaeans in 235/4, and the city soon played no small role in directing the League's policies.

While Aratus was rebuilding the Achaean League, Agis IV, a descendant of the great Agesilaus, embarked upon an ambitious programme of debt-cancellation and redistribution of land. But, before the latter could be effected, Agis IV was dead, the victim of his political enemies. Continuation of his policies came from an unexpected source, Cleomenes III, son of Agis' opponent Leonidas.[23] Cleomenes' 'Revolution' (235–222) paid dividends in terms of Spartan military resurgence. Achaea, in turn, allied itself with Macedon, now ruled by Antigonus III Doson (regent for the young Philip V), whose intervention in the Peloponnese proved too much for Sparta. The decisive blow was struck at Sellasia in 222, and Cleomenes fled via Gytheum to Alexandria.

At the Ptolemaic court, Cleomenes expected to find support for his cause; for it involved opposition to Antigonid Macedon, the common enemy. But he fell victim to the intrigues of Philopator's courtiers and committed suicide after an abortive attempt to incite unrest in Alexandria. Since Cleomenes' departure, the ephors had ruled in Sparta without acknowledging or appointing a king, but soon the state was ruled by a series of 'tyrants': Lycurgus, Pelops, Machanidas, and, eventually, Nabis (207–192). Nabis' policies in the 190s reflect the kaleidoscope of political patterns in Greece. Sparta's hatred for Megalopolis had its origins in the very founding of the latter city, whose sole purpose was the limitation of Lacedaemonian power. In the late third century, Megalopolitan politicians, notably Philopoemen and Aristaenus, dominated the League. Thus it was normal for Sparta to ally herself with Achaea's enemies. Philopoemen advocated an independent course for the League, but the Second Macedonian War opened with Cycliadas, a pro-Macedonian, as *strategos* (200/199). Aristaenus, however, assumed the *strategia* in 199/8, and Achaea inclined towards Rome. There followed a series

[23] Cleomenes was of the Agiad line. Perhaps there is some truth to the story that he was converted to the cause of reform by Agis' widow, Agiatis, whom Leonidas had wedded to his son (Plutarch, *Cleomenes* 1).

of agreements that blurred the boundaries of perfidy and opportunism. Philip attempted to buy Nabis' support by offering him Argos,[24] which the tyrant accepted only to betray Philip's trust and enter into negotiations with Flamininus. Rome's agreement with Nabis (made without consulting Achaea) left him in possession of Argos against the wishes of the League. But in 195, with the threat of Philip eliminated, Flamininus sided with Achaea against Nabis. The inevitable Roman victory deprived Nabis of Argos and restricted his territories.

The Aetolians, who had expected territorial gains in return for their efforts against Philip V, now turned against Rome; Nabis, understandably, gravitated towards Aetolia, which favoured summoning Antiochus III to Greece as a champion against the Romans. But the cauldron of Peloponnesian politics boiled over yet again: a second confrontation with Achaea and Rome resulted in the destruction of Spartan power and, in 192, Nabis' assassination. Agis and Cleomenes were fortunate in having the *History* of Phylarchus as a counterbalance to the slanders of Aratus' *Memoirs*. No sympathetic account of Nabis has survived, although he completed the reforms of Cleomenes. Nor should we be surprised that the negative portrait of Nabis derives from Polybius; Achaeans of his class feared reform as much as they did Sparta itself.

Antiochus the Great

The Seleucid kingdom was by far the wealthiest, largest, and most diverse of the Hellenistic states. It had been consolidated in the east by Alexander's general, Seleucus, whose conquests on the Iranian plateau earned him the epithet Nicator ('Conqueror'), despite the fact that Seleucus was forced to cede the satrapies adjacent to the Indus to Chandragupta Maurya. In the west, it was enlarged from the spoils of the victory at Ipsus in 301. But these spoils brought Seleucus into conflict with Ptolemy (over Hollow Syria, that is, the region between Mt. Lebanon and Antilebanon) and Lysimachus, who acquired much of western Asia Minor. The claim to Syria was suspended, but never relinquished; for Seleucus had not forgotten

[24] Sparta had been an ally of Aetolia, whereas Achaea had been a member of the Hellenic Symmachy, of which the Macedonian king was *hegemon*. Philip's alliance with Nabis involved handing over to him (at least temporarily) control of Argos (Livy 32. 38–40); for Flamininus' command against Nabis see 33. 43–5; 34. 22 ff.

Ptolemy's support between 315 and 312. With Lysimachus, however, there was to be a final reckoning in 281, when the two veterans of Alexander's campaigns (now both septuagenarians) met on the battlefield of Corupedium. There Lysimachus fell, and Seleucus crossed to the Chersonese (Gallipoli peninsula), only to be struck down soon afterwards by Ptolemy Ceraunus, the dispossessed son of Ptolemy I Soter and half-brother of Philadelphus. On this victory over Lysimachus, Antiochus III was later to base his claim to the European side of the Hellespont as 'spear-won land'.

Hollow Syria became the focus of three 'Syrian Wars' before Antiochus III's accession and two more during his reign. The third—sometimes called the Laodicean War—had been particularly costly since it was followed almost immediately by a second conflict between the ruling Seleucus II and his younger brother Antiochus Hierax. In the course of this fraternal war, Hierax formed an alliance with the Galatians, whose marauding in Asia Minor compelled the Greeks of the area to find a new champion of their cause in Attalus I of Pergamum. Hitherto they had sought the protection of the Seleucid kings. Eumenes I of Pergamum had already attained a measure of independence from Seleucid control, styling himself *dynastes* and defeating Antiochus I in battle in 262 or 261. After his victory over the Galatians Attalus openly sported the title *basileus* ('king').

The third century had also witnessed the arrival of the Parni, who drove a wedge into the centre of the kingdom and came to be known as the Parthians after the region in which they settled. But the accession of Antiochus III in 223[25] saw a revival of the central authority in Seleucid Syria. After some initial disappointments,[26] Antiochus overcame a dynastic rival, Achaeus, conducted a successful reconquest of the eastern satrapies, and defeated the forces of Ptolemy V at Panion (200 BC). Now, hailed throughout the kingdom as *Megas* ('the Great'), he also revived Seleucid claims to the Thracian Chersonese and held court at Lysimachia, which he had himself rebuilt.

In the stages leading up to the Second Macedonian War, the

---

[25] Antiochus III was the son of Seleucus II; he became king when his brother, Seleucus III (officially 'Soter', but nicknamed 'Ceraunus') was killed in Asia Minor by some of his own followers.

[26] Antiochus was defeated at Raphia (217) by Ptolemy IV during the Fourth Syrian War.

Romans were careful to secure the neutrality of the Seleucid monarch; but, in the aftermath of Cynoscephalae, the approach was far less respectful (33. 39–40; 34. 57–9). The picture, however, was complicated by the Aetolians, who had fallen out with Rome and with Flamininus (33. 35). The Romans had not entirely forgiven the Aetolians for making a separate peace with Philip during the First Macedonian War, and the Aetolians for their part felt slighted when they failed to receive sufficient compensation in the settlement with Macedon. Soon they summoned Antiochus to Greece as champion of Hellenism against the new barbarians—the Romans.

War with Antiochus the Great

Misled by the Aetolian reports and promises, Antiochus III crossed to European Greece with 10,000 troops in 192 BC (35. 43–50). Each side expected more than the other was prepared to deliver. Rome, on the other hand, was far more decisive, declaring war on Antiochus (36. 1–2) and entrusting its conduct to Manius Acilius Glabrio, the consul for 191. The Seleucid king enjoyed the support of Boeotia and made initial gains in Thessaly (36. 6, 9–10). Over the winter of 192/1 Antiochus, now 50 years old, married the young daughter of Cleoptolemus in Chalcis (36. 11). This is often dismissed as a sign of the king's debauchery and personal weakness, but it is more likely that the taking of a local bride was designed to enhance Antiochus' image as champion of the Greeks;[27] for the Seleucids were, in fact, the most barbarized of the Hellenistic dynasties.[28] Glabrio for his part wasted little time and defeated the Seleucid forces at Thermopylae (36. 15–19), during which engagement Marcus Porcius Cato led the encircling movement over Mt. Callidromus and routed the Aetolians who were on guard there (36. 18). Antiochus himself fled from Euboea to Asia (36. 21), thus bringing to a rapid conclusion his 'liberation' of Greece and leaving the Aetolians to make their own terms with Rome (36. 22 ff.).

Flight from Greece brought Antiochus only temporary relief. There were still the grievances of Pergamum—now ruled by

[27] Cf. E. S. Gruen, *The Hellenistic World and the Coming of Rome* (Berkeley, 1984), 637.

[28] Laodice, the mother of Seleucus IV and Antiochus IV, both of whom succeeded their father, was the daughter of Mithridates II of Pontus, and, in fact, the entire dynasty was established by Seleucus I and his Persian (Bactrian) bride Apame, daughter of Spitamenes.

Eumenes II (for Attalus had died during the Second Macedonian War, 33. 21)—and the Rhodians, who wanted to see Seleucid power in Asia Minor curtailed, with the concomitant redistribution of confiscated territory (cf. 37. 52–5). Furthermore, the Roman nobility sought military glory and political kudos from the defeat of an illustrious foreign enemy. In that respect, the election of Lucius Cornelius Scipio, brother of Africanus, and Gaius Laelius, that acolyte of the Cornelii, assured Antiochus that extrication from the war with Rome would be anything but an easy and inexpensive matter. It was all the more fitting that the Senate should assign command in the east to Lucius Cornelius, on the understanding that Publius would accompany him as the nominal second-in-command (37. 1), since the inveterate enemy of Rome, Hannibal, had taken refuge in the Seleucid kingdom.[29]

When the Cornelii Scipiones arrived in Greece they were quick to arrange a truce with Aetolia (37. 7),[30] in order to avoid being detained by the task of crushing resistance to Rome's conditions of peace. Negotiations with Philip secured passage for the troops to the Hellespont (37. 7, 33), where Antiochus now ventured to discuss terms of surrender (37. 34–6). These, predictably, came to naught, and the issue was decided on the battlefield of Magnesia (37. 37–44). Hannibal, in the event, had proved a non-factor, relegated to the naval sphere and confined to the eastern Mediterranean (37. 22–4).[31] Later, in Bithynia (183 BC—in the same year, Philopoemen was captured and killed in Messene, 39. 49–50), he was forced to cheat his assassins with poison, the victim of Prusias' treachery and to the discredit of Titus Quinctius Flamininus (39. 51).

For Antiochus III, defeat at Magnesia, meant the loss of territories west of the Taurus range under the humiliating terms of the Peace of Apamea (188 BC: 37. 45; 38. 38). Roman forces continued the process of conquest under the consuls of 189, at Ambracia under

---

[29] Fitting in the sense that Africanus had achieved fame as Hannibal's conqueror. It should be remembered that he had opposed those in Rome receptive to those Carthaginians who denounced Hannibal's conduct when he held the suffetate in 196 (Livy 33. 45–7). Livy, at 37. 1, nevertheless depicts the coming struggle as one between Hannibal and Scipio Africanus.

[30] They had, at any rate, been kept under pressure by Manius Acilius Glabrio (at Heraclea: 36. 22–4; at Naupactus: 36. 33–5, 43; cf. 37. 4–6).

[31] Much of Book 37 (esp. chs. 8–32) is devoted to the naval war in the Aegean and eastern Mediterranean, which played no small part in Antiochus' defeat.

Marcus Fulvius Nobilior (38. 4–10) and in Galatia, where Gnaeus Manlius Vulso laid the foundations of a triumph against a perennial but overmatched enemy (37. 60; 38. 12–27). Annexation of territory, in Europe and in Asia, was yet to come, but the cornerstones of Roman imperialism were firmly in place.

Events in Italy and the West

Livy's narrative, reflecting that of his chief source, Polybius (see pp. xxvii–xxviii below), deals primarily with the events of the Hellenistic east. These are, however, supplemented—though generally in a sketchy and disjointed manner—by Rome's wars in Spain and northern Italy (where the Gauls and Ligurians were brought to heel), both, to some extent, the result of disruptions and undertakings begun during the Hannibalic War. For the campaigns in Spain, Livy was often forced to rely on inferior source-material, though Cato's own account will have formed a reasonably factual, if somewhat self-serving, basis for the events described at 34. 9–21. In general terms, we may note that Roman plans for Spain at the end of the Second Punic War were transformed by events that followed, and this was reflected by the addition of two praetors in 197, a measure intended to facilitate the reduction and administration of the two Spains. Previously, commanders had been sent out on an *ad hoc* basis—often, like the young Scipio himself, men without magistracies (*privati cum imperio*)—and for extended periods.[32] In northern Italy, meanwhile, the demands of security and land made the Gallic and Ligurian wars essential, but also convenient opportunities for booty and triumphs (31. 48; 33. 23; 33. 37; 36. 40; 40. 34).

In Rome itself other problems surfaced, as social unrest developed in an age that was at once disrupting everyday life and flooding the capital with new wealth in the form of booty and slaves. The Oppian Law, which had been enacted in 215 BC, soon after the disaster at Cannae and at the height of Roman danger, was brought forward for repeal in 195 by the tribunes of the plebs, Marcus Fundanius and Lucius Valerius. The issue itself was hardly of major import—for it dealt with women's rights to certain personal luxuries—but it was marked by the determination of Roman matrons to recover privileges surrendered during a time of crisis and by the paternalistic,

---

[32] A good, readable discussion of these problems can be found in John S. Richardson, *The Romans in Spain* (Oxford, 1996), esp. 43–59.

indeed, misogynistic, reaction to a justified request by Marcus Porcius Cato (34. 1–8). On this issue, the Roman people (that is, the voting males) were prepared to take a liberal stand.

Very different was the Bacchanalian crisis—or, rather, 'conspiracy', as it came to be labelled—of 186 (39. 8–19). Cato's warnings about a female cabal in 195, when he likened Roman matrons to the Lemnian women (34. 2), seem today, as they no doubt did at the time, to be old-fashioned and paranoid. But the suppression by the Senate and the magistrates of Dionysiac practices, conducted under the cover of darkness by women and young men, whose initiation entailed the swearing of oaths (a *coniuratio*) that threatened the laws and the state itself, was swift and brutal. The informant was a woman of the lower classes, a freedwoman who had engaged in prostitution (Livy 39. 9 describes her as 'too good for that occupation'), and the practitioners of the cult were primarily of the same social status. But the matter aroused fears of 'secret societies', and of corrupting eastern influences, the cultural by-products of imperialism.[33] There followed large-scale interrogations and executions, and the fear of arson put the entire city on alert. But the cult was never entirely eradicated, though investigation and punishment continued for several years. Livy's account, which reveals the danger through the actions of the lovers Hispala Faecenia and Publius Aebutius, displays some of the romantic features of Roman comedy. As a story it lacks nothing by way of entertainment, but it obscures rather than illuminates the problem. Nevertheless this episode, like the controversy surrounding the Oppian legislation, provides a welcome view of the issues that confronted Rome in the absence of the legions.

Roman Politics

Against the backdrop of foreign wars, Livy relates the struggles of Rome's great political families. In true annalistic fashion, he preserves with reasonable accuracy the lists of consuls, praetors, and censors; often we learn the names of curule and plebeian aediles, and some of the tribunes of the plebs. Certain episodes illuminate the niceties of constitutional and religious law, and occasionally we

---

[33] Fear of corruption and Greek influences no doubt influenced the Roman government, but the main concern appears to have been to suppress the organizational aspect of the cult, whence it derived its perceived power to harm the state (cf. M. Beard, N. North, and S. Price, *Religions of Rome* (Cambridge, 1998), i. 95).

see clear indications of factional politics. From the lists of elected officials, scattered references to kinship, and the patterns of office-holding we can perceive family-groupings and their political fortunes. Often, however, it is necessary to read between the lines. Walbank observes that Livy's account of Roman internal politics during this period is idealized and romanticized,[34] but the presentation is far from uniform. Frequently it is simple patriotism that obscures the picture. The unflattering aspects of Titus Quinctius Flamininus' behaviour, apparent in the accounts of Polybius and Plutarch, are omitted or reworked by Livy. Polybius brought with him to Rome his share of Achaean 'baggage', but some of his negativity may derive from Cornelian animus against the Quinctii. Livy's whitewashing is pro-Roman rather than pro-Quinctian. Cato, too, retains his dignity despite episodes that illustrate his pettiness.[35] Even when the rivalry between Marcus Fulvius and Marcus Aemilius Lepidus degenerates into vindictive attacks, Livy presents a speech by Quintus Caecilius Metellus urging the two to work together for the good of the state (40. 46). But by far the most acrimonious events—and most fraught with historiographical problems—were the so-called 'Trials of the Scipios'.

The Trials of the Scipios

Livy gives a confused account of the legal proceedings directed against Lucius and Publius Cornelius Scipio in the period 187–183, based largely on the unsatisfactory version he found in Valerius Antias. Livy himself had access to only limited information. He had learned enough from additional sources that Valerius was in error, especially as far as chronology was concerned, but he did not trouble to correct him. Haywood[36] has argued, with limited success, that the testimony of Valerius was based on some good documentary evidence, but that he made the mistake of dating Africanus' death to 187, thus causing him to bring Publius Cornelius Scipio Nasica to the defence of Lucius in 184. Furthermore, it appears that Valerius Antias conflated the earlier investigation conducted by Terentius

---

[34] F. W. Walbank, 'The Fourth and Fifth Decades', in T. A. Dorey (ed.), *Livy* (London, 1971), 54.

[35] At 37. 57 Livy faults Cato for his attack on Manius Acilius Glabrio at a time when they were candidates for the same office: his moral authority was undermined by the fact that he was running against the individual he was prosecuting.

[36] Richard M. Haywood, *Studies on Scipio Africanus* (Westport, Conn., 1933), 87–9.

Culleo, and instituted by the Quinti Petillii (clearly henchmen of Marcus Porcius Cato) in 87, with the second process carried out by the tribune Minucius Augurinus in 184.

The legal grounds for the charges were at best ambiguous. Arrogant and high-handed the Scipios may have been—Lucius in his handling of the money received from Antiochus before the Peace of Apamea, Publius in his defiance of a Senatorial order to produce the accounts—but it seems that they had merely acted as earlier commanders had, and that there was no legal precedent governing the disposition of payments of this kind. Antiochus had indeed paid Lucius some 3,000 talents, before and separate from the 15,000 that were agreed upon at Apamea in 188, but the Scipios appear to have regarded this as booty and to have distributed at least a portion of it to the army. In point of fact, only 500 of the 3,000 talents were actually used by the Scipios, the remaining 2,500 being the responsibility of Manlius Vulso. Although the accusations were directed in the Senate against Lucius, Publius Cornelius responded in the knowledge that it was merely a thinly veiled attack against himself. And the Senate was prepared to tolerate the defiance of Africanus, who was *princeps senatus*.

There is general agreement that Lucius Scipio was tried and convicted, but that through the intervention of Tiberius Sempronius Gracchus he escaped imprisonment; the fine was paid by Scipio's friends. Whether we should date this trial to 187 or 184 is less certain. It is difficult to imagine how Lucius could have celebrated such a splendid triumph in 186 (Livy 39. 22), if he had been driven to virtual bankruptcy in the previous year. That Scipio Africanus himself was charged seems less certain; at any rate, he withdrew to his estate at Liternum where he died soon afterwards.[37]

Sources for Books 31–40

In his account of the years 200–179 BC, Livy mentions the works of four historians and alludes to that of a fifth. The annalists Valerius

---

[37] For discussions see Haywood, *Scipio Africanus*; H. H. Scullard, *Roman Politics, 220–150 BC* (Oxford, 1951), 290–303; H. H. Scullard, *Scipio Africanus: Soldier and Politician* (London, 1970), 216–24; E. S. Gruen, 'The "Fall" of the Scipios', in I. Malkin and Z. Rubinsohn (eds.), *Leaders and Masses in the Roman World. Studies in Honor of Zvi Yavetz* (Leiden, 1995), 59–90.

Antias and Claudius Quadrigarius are named frequently, the Greek historian Polybius on four occasions, and Publius Rutilius Rufus once; additionally, Livy, in the speech he fashions for the tribune Lucius Valerius (34. 5), refers to the elder Cato's *Origins*.[38]

Polybius, perhaps the most 'scientific' of Greek historical writers after Thucydides, was born late in the third century BC, the son of Lycortas, a prominent Achaean from Megalopolis. From the start, he was well versed in the workings of the Achaean League and, of course, the intervention of Rome in Greek and Macedonian affairs. In 182 he was selected to bear the ashes of Philopoemen to their final resting-place, an auspicious beginning to a political career that seemed scarcely in need of assistance. But Polybius was destined for the role of historian rather than politician, although he acquired a sufficient amount of that practical experience which he regarded as the prerequisite for any good historian. The embassy to Ptolemy V Epiphanes, to which he was named in 181, was aborted on account of the king's death. In 170/69 he was elected one of the hipparchs of the League, but the defeat of Perseus in the Third Macedonian War was followed by harsh measures throughout Greece, and Polybius was among 1,000 Achaeans taken as hostages to Rome in 168/7. There he remained until 150 BC. The time was not wasted, however: Polybius became the mentor and friend of Scipio Aemilianus, son of Lucius Aemilius Paullus (Perseus' conqueror), and adopted son of Publius Cornelius Scipio, the otherwise obscure son of Africanus. And it was from Scipio Aemilianus and his 'circle' (to which Polybius belonged) that he learned the details of Roman politics which, added to his own earlier experience in Greece, made Polybius the foremost historian of Roman expansion and the most valuable of Livy's sources. Much of Polybius' history of eastern affairs is lost or fragmentary, but enough survives to prove the extent of Livy's indebtedness.[39]

For Livy, Polybius' *Histories* brought a wealth of information and misunderstanding. Often it proved difficult to integrate Polybius'

[38] Valerius Antias (32. 6; 33. 10, 30, 36; 34. 10, 15; 35. 2; 36. 19, 36, 38; 37. 48; 38. 23, 50, 55; 39. 22, 41, 43, 52, 56; 40. 29); Claudius Quadrigarius (33. 10, 30, 36; 35. 14; 37. 48; 38. 23, 41); Polybius (33. 10; 34. 50; 36. 19; 39. 52). For Rutilius Rufus see 39. 52; for Cato's *Origins*, 34. 5.

[39] These have been collected and discussed by Hermann Tränkle, *Livius und Polybios* (Basle and Stuttgart, 1977), 29–31, who builds on the work of H. Nissen, *Kritische Untersuchungen über die Quellen der vierten und fünften Dekade des Livius* (Berlin, 1863).

chronology, which employed Olympiad years, into an annalistic framework based on consular years and a Roman calendar that was hopelessly out of alignment with the solar year. Further confusion resulted from attempts to abbreviate or from ignorance of geography and topography; added to that were simple mistranslations of Polybius' Greek.[40]

Less satisfactory, but undoubtedly useful in areas untouched by Polybius, were the annalists, Valerius Antias and Quintus Claudius Quadrigarius, both of whom wrote in the post-Sullan era (*c*.70 BC).[41] Claudius treated the period from the end of the Hannibalic War to the Gracchan crisis in three or four books, virtual proof, as E. Badian notes, that he did not know (or at least did not use) Polybius' history.[42] On the other hand, he may have made use of the account by Gaius Acilius, a Roman senator who wrote (in Greek) in the middle of the second century. The much-despised Valerius Antias is cited by Livy in this portion of his *History* more often than any other author—and not always to expose his errors. Livy is, admittedly, more critical of Valerius than any other source he mentions, but it is clear that he was on some occasions forced to accept his testimony. On others (e.g. the 'Trials of the Scipios') he repeated many details in his account although he knew from other, more reliable, evidence that it was deficient and distorted.[43] There may be some basis to Klotz's view that Livy used Valerius as his primary source—supplementing his information with details from Claudius Quadrigarius—up to the 'Trials of the Scipios' in Book 38 and then reversed the procedure, regarding Claudius as more reliable thereafter.[44] Occasionally, Livy failed to reconcile the conflicting evidence of these sources: hence we have the Carthaginian Hamilcar killed in battle by Lucius Furius Purpureo (31. 10–11, 19, 21) and later captured and paraded in triumph by Gaius Cornelius Cethegus (33.

---

[40] See e.g. Explanatory Notes to pp. 101 and 362.

[41] For Antias' life and work see R. M. Ogilvie, *A Commentary on Livy, Books 1–5* (Oxford, 1965), 12–16.

[42] E. Badian, 'The Early Historians', in T. A. Dorey (ed.), *The Latin Historians* (London, 1966), 18–19.

[43] By accepting Valerius' date for the death of Africanus, Livy is forced to attribute one speech in defence of Lucius Cornelius to P. Scipio Nasica instead.

[44] A. Klotz, in various studies listed by Walbank, 'Fourth and Fifth Decades', 67 n.20.

23).[45] Despite their shortcomings, these annalists were probably Livy's chief source for the details of the annual elections and lists of prodigies; for it was material of this very sort, much of it derived from the *Annales Maximi*, that formed the backbone of the annalistic tradition.[46]

Rutilius Rufus' history is mentioned once (39. 52) and Livy's knowledge of the work may be second-hand.[47] Similarly, although 34. 14 contains a phrase that reflects Cato's usage, it is probable that his information, too, was filtered through the account of one of the annalists.

[45] Livy's account of western affairs is generally weak. Cf. Walbank, 'Fourth and Fifth Decades', 58: 'factually unreliable and hopelessly embroidered'.

[46] Two of the earliest incentives for the production of historical writing in Rome were family tradition—the deeds of illustrious ancestors, rehearsed in the households of the aristocracy, promulgated in the form of funeral eulogy, and in some cases committed to writing—and the records of the pontifex maximus, the so-called *Annales Maximi*. The latter were published in the Gracchan period by P. Muceus Scaevola (consul 133), himself pontifex maximus.

[47] Walbank's comment ('Fourth and Fifth Decades', 51) that 'there is no evidence that Livy used any other source besides Claudius, Valerius, and Polybius' appears to omit Rutilius for this very reason.

NOTE ON THE TEXT AND TRANSLATION

The text used for the translation is Briscoe's Teubner (LIVIUS Ab urbe condita Libri xxxi–xl edidit John Briscoe, Stuttgart, 1991). The very few places where I have decided to accept a reading other than Briscoe's—most of them in Book 40—are gathered together in Appendix 1 ('List of Variations from the Teubner Text'). Account could not be taken of P. G. Walsh's OCT of Livy 36–40, which appeared when the translation was already in proof.

I have tried to make the translation as readable as I can without straying too far from the original, but I suspect I have gone too far for some readers, and not far enough for others. I am aware that a significant number of users of the book will be students in schools or universities following courses in Roman History. For their benefit it seemed to me important to indicate those areas where the text is uncertain, even if the non-specialist may find this a little disconcerting. Accordingly I have used the sigla † and <. . .> to indicate respectively the points where Briscoe thinks that the text is uncertain or lacunose, though I have not indicated that editor's supplements to the text where I feel these are either certain or very close to what Livy must have said. Likewise, where I feel confident of the sense of what is missing in the lacunae indicated by Briscoe, I have occasionally inserted a word or two in order to maintain the flow of the narrative, and I have omitted to translate the Latin obelized by Briscoe where this yields no sense at all.

I have not retained Livy's spelling of place-names where another spelling is familiar and generally accepted (e.g. Samos and Lemnos rather than Samus and Lemnus).

I have consulted numerous other translations, including Sage's Loeb, Bettenson's Penguin, and the various Budé editions, but I must acknowledge a particular debt to John Briscoe's commentaries on Books 31–3 and 34–7, and to P. G. Walsh's editions of Books 36–40 (see Select Bibliography).

J. C. Y.

SELECT BIBLIOGRAPHY

Text

Livius: Ab Urbe Condita, Libri XXXI–XL, ed. John Briscoe (Stuttgart: Teubner, 1991), 2 volumes.

Commentaries

Briscoe, John, *A Commentary on Livy: Books XXXI–XXXIII* (Oxford, 1973)
—— *A Commentary on Livy: Books XXXIV–XXXVII* (Oxford, 1981).
Walsh, P. G., *Livy: Book XXXVI*, edited with an Introduction, Translation, and Commentary (Warminster: Aris and Phillips, 1990).
—— *Livy: Book XXXVII*, edited with an Introduction, Translation, and Commentary (Warminster: Aris and Phillips, 1992).
—— *Livy: Book XXXVIII*, edited with an Introduction, Translation, and Commentary, (Warminster: Aris and Phillips, 1993).
—— *Livy: Book XXXIX*, edited with an Introduction, Translation, and Commentary (Warminster: Aris and Phillips, 1994).
—— *Livy: Book XL*, edited with an Introduction, Translation, and Commentary (Warminster: Aris and Phillips, 1996).

Translations

Rome and the Mediterranean, trans. Henry Bettenson, with an Introduction and Notes by A. H. McDonald (London: Penguin, 1976).
Livy: Books XXXI–XXIV, trans. Evan Sage, Loeb Classical Library (Cambridge, Mass., 1935; revised and reprinted 1936).
Livy: Books XXXV–XXXVII, trans. Evan Sage, Loeb Classical Library (Cambridge, Mass., 1935).
Livy: Books XXXVIII–XXXIX, trans. Evan Sage, Loeb Classical Library (Cambridge, Mass., 1936).
Livy: Books XL–XLII, trans. Evan Sage and A. C. Schlesinger, Loeb Classical Library (Cambridge, Mass., 1938).

Works on Livy

Dorey, T. A. (ed.), *Livy* (London, 1971).
Jaeger, M., *Livy's Written Rome* (Ann Arbor, 1997).
Luce, T. J., *Livy: The Composition of his History* (Princeton, 1977).
Walbank, F. W., 'The Fourth and Fifth Decades', in T. A. Dorey (ed.), *Livy* (London, 1971), 47–72.
Walsh, P. G., *Livy: His Historical Aims and Methods* (Cambridge, 1961).

Works on the Roman Background

Balsdon, J. P. V. D., *Roman Women* (London, 1962).

David, Jean-Michel, *The Roman Conquest of Italy*, trans. Antonia Nevill (Oxford, 1996).

Salmon, E. T., *Roman Colonisation under the Republic* (Ithaca, NY, 1970).

Scullard, H. H., *A History of Rome from 753 to 146 BC*, 3rd edn. (London, 1961).

Works on Roman Politics

Astin, A. E., *Cato the Censor* (Oxford, 1978).

Badian, E., *Foreign Clientelae* (Oxford, 1958).

Broughton, T. R. S., *The Magistrates of the Roman Republic*, 3 vols. (Chico, Calif., 1951–84).

Develin, R., *Patterns in Office-Holding, 366–49 BC* (Brussels, 1979).

—— *The Practice of Politics at Rome, 366–167 BC* (Brussels, 1987).

Eckstein, A. M., *Senate and General: Individual Decision-Making and Roman Foreign Relations, 264–194 BC* (Berkeley, Calif., 1987).

Epstein, D. F., *Personal Enmity in Roman Politics 218–43 BC* (London, 1987).

Harris, W. V., *War and Imperialism in Republican Rome, 327–70 BC* (Oxford, 1979).

Haywood, R. M., *Studies on Scipio Africanus* (Baltimore, 1933).

Mitchell, R. E., *Patricians and Plebeians: The Origins of the Roman State* (Ithaca, NY, and London, 1990).

Rosenstein, N., *Imperatores Victi: Military Defeat and Aristocratic Competition in the Middle and Late Republic* (Berkeley, Calif., 1990).

Scullard, H. H., *Roman Politics, 220–150 BC* (Oxford, 1951).

Stewart, R., *Public Office in Early Rome: Ritual Procedure and Political Practice* (Ann Arbor, 1998).

Vishnia, R. F., *State, Society and Popular Leaders in Mid-Republican Rome 241–167 BC* (London, 1996).

Works on the Roman Army

Keppie, J., *The Making of the Roman Army* (London, 1984).

Scullard, H. H., *The Elephant in the Greek and Roman World* (London, 1974)

Works on the Hellenistic World

Africa, T. W., *Phylarchus and the Spartan Revolution* (Berkeley, Calif., 1961).

Austin, M. M., *The Hellenistic World* (Cambridge, 1981).

Berthold, R. M., *Rhodes in the Hellenistic Period* (Ithaca, NY, 1984).

Bevan, E. R., *The House of Seleucus*, 2 vols. (London, 1902).

Billows, R. A., *Antigonos the One-Eyed and the Creation of the Hellenistic State* (Berkeley, Calif., 1990).

Errington, R. M., *Philopoemen* (Oxford, 1969).

Forrest, W. G., *History of Sparta, 950–192 BC* (New York, 1968).

Grainger, J. D., *Hellenistic Phoenicia* (Oxford, 1991).

Green, P., *From Alexander to Actium* (Berkeley, Calif., 1990).

Griffith, G. T., *The Mercenaries of the Hellenistic World* (Cambridge, 1935).

Gruen, E. S., *The Hellenistic World and the Coming of Rome*, 2 vols. (Berkeley, Calif., 1984).

Hammond, N. G. L., *Epirus* (Oxford, 1967).

—— *The Macedonian State* (Oxford, 1989).

—— and Walbank, F. W., *A History of Macedonia*, vol. iii (Oxford, 1988).

Hansen, E. V., *The Attalids of Pergamum* (Ithaca, NY, 1971).

Larsen, J. A. O., *Greek Federal States* (Oxford, 1968).

Lund, H. S., *Lysimachus: A Study in Early Hellenistic Kingship* (London, 1992).

Macurdy, G. H., *Hellenistic Queens* (Baltimore, 1932).

Mitchell, S., *Anatolia*, vol. i (Oxford).

Piper, L. J., *Spartan Twilight* (New York, 1986).

Walbank, F. W., *The Hellenistic World* (London, 1981).

—— *Philip V* (Cambridge, 1935).

—— *A Historical Commentary on Polybius*, 3 vols. (Oxford, 1957–79).

Works on Religion

Beard, M., North, N., and Price, S., *Religions of Rome*, vol. i (Cambridge, 1998).

Dumézil, G., *Archaic Roman Religion*, trans. P. Krapp, 2 vols. (Chicago, 1970).

Levene, D. S., *Religion in Livy* (Leiden, 1993).

Turcan, R., *The Cults of the Roman Empire*, trans. Antonia Nevill (Oxford, 1996).

Further Reading in Oxford World's Classics

Julius Caesar, *The Civil War*, trans. and ed. J. R. Carter.

—— *The Gallic War*, trans. and ed. Carolyn Hammond.

Plutarch, *Greek Lives: A Selection of Nine Lives*, trans. Robin Waterfield, ed. Philip A. Stadter.

—— *Roman Lives: A Selection of Eight Lives*, trans. Robin Waterfield, ed. Philip A. Stadter.

A CHRONOLOGY OF EVENTS

All dates are BC.

200   Rome declares war on Philip V of Macedon. Philip's attacks on Athens. Publius Sulpicius Galba crosses the Adriatic. Battle at Otolobus. Lucius Furius claims triumph over the Gauls.

199   Publius Villius in Greece.

198   Command in Greece passes to Titus Quinctius Flamininus. Battle at the River Aous. Amynander of Athamania and the Aetolians join Flamininus.

197   Battle at Cynoscephalae. Death of Attalus I, accession of Eumenes II.

196   Peace with Philip V. Flamininus declares 'Freedom of the Greeks'. Roman ambassadors sent to Antiochus III at Lysimachia.

195   Marcus Porcius Cato's campaigns in Spain. Hannibal flees to the court of Antiochus III. Defeat of Nabis in Sparta.

194   Flamininus evacuates Greece.

193   Hannibal's agent Aristo sent to Carthage. Aetolians turn against Rome.

192   Aetolians summon Antiochus to Greece. Nabis assassinated. Sparta annexed by Achaean League.

191   Romans declare war on Antiochus. Manius Acilius Glabrio in Greece. Battle of Thermopylae. Antiochus evacuates Greece. Roman naval victory at Corycus.

190   Publius Scipio grants six-month truce to Aetolians. Battle of Side (keeps Hannibal in Eastern Mediterranean). Battle of Myonessus. Antiochus attempts to gain peace terms from Publius Scipio. Battle of Magnesia.

189   Eumenes and Rhodians present their cases to the Senate. Senate ratifies peace with Antiochus III. Marcus Fulvius Nobilior's campaign in Ambracia. Manlius Vulso's Galatian campaign.

188   Peace of Apamea.

187   Prosecution of the Scipios. Triumphs of Manlius Vulso and Marcus Fulvius Nobilior.

186   Suppression of the Bacchanalia.

185   Renewed hostility to Rome in Macedonia.

184 Cato's censorship.

183 Deaths of Philopoemen, Hannibal, and Scipio Africanus.

181 Murder of Demetrius, son of Philip V.

179 Death of Philip V.

MAP I. Galatia in the time of Gnaeus Manlius Vulso's campaign

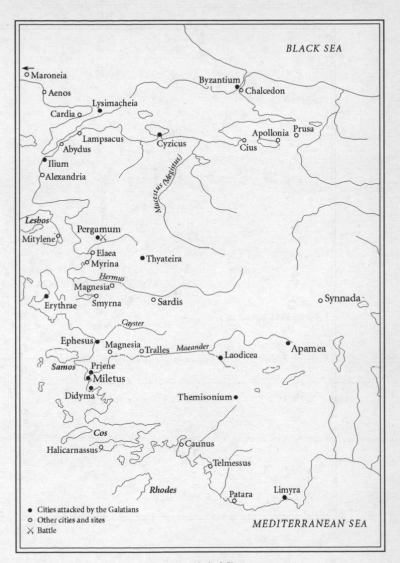

BLACK SEA

o Maroneia

o Aenos

Byzantium
o Chalcedon

Lysimacheia
Cardia o

Apollonia o Prusa
o Lampsacus
Abydus o Cyzicus Cius

Ilium
o Alexandria

Maecestus (Megistus)

Lesbos
Mitylene o

Pergamum
x
o Elaea
o Myrina Thyateira
Hermus
Magnesia o
Erythrae Smyrna Sardis Synnada o

Cayster
Ephesus o Magnesia
o Tralles *Maeander*
Laodicea Apamea
Samos o Priene
Miletus
Didyma Themisonium

Cos
Halicarnassus o Caunus
Telmessus

Rhodes
Patara Limyra

● Cities attacked by the Galatians
o Other cities and sites
x Battle

MEDITERRANEAN SEA

MAP 2. Asia Minor

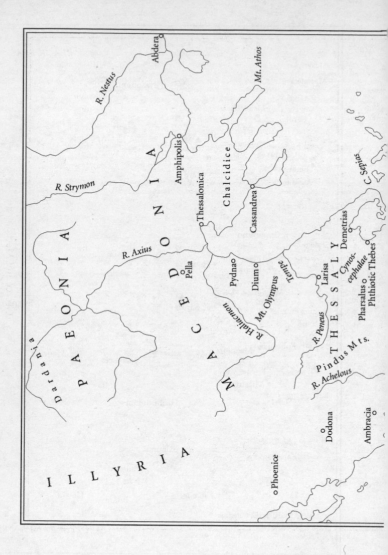

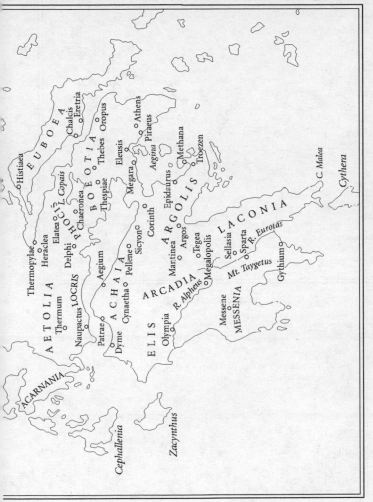

MAP 3. Greece and Macedonia

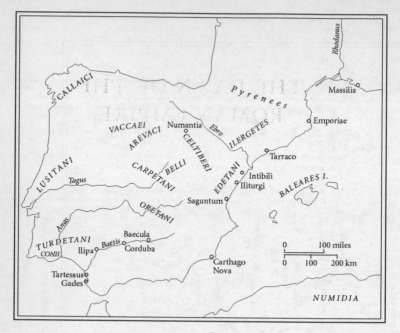

MAP 4. Spain

THE DAWN OF THE
ROMAN EMPIRE

BOOK THIRTY-ONE

1. I too am happy* to have reached the end of the Punic War*—I somehow feel I have personally taken part in its hardships and dangers! I realize that it is most inappropriate for one who has made the rash promise to cover all Roman history to flag in specific sections of such a great work; and yet it does occur to me that the sixty-three years* between the beginning of the First Punic War and the end of the Second have taken up as many rolls as did the four hundred and eighty-eight years* between the foundation of the city and the consulship of Appius Claudius,* the man who began the first war with Carthage. I feel like someone who wades out into the sea after being initially attracted to the water by the shallows next to the shore; and I foresee any advance only taking me into even more enormous, indeed bottomless, depths, and that this undertaking of mine, which seemed to be diminishing as I was completing the earliest sections, is now almost increasing in size.

Peace with Carthage was followed by war with Macedon. Though by no means comparable in terms of the threat it posed, the courage of the enemy commander, or the strength of his forces, the Macedonian war was almost more noteworthy because of the fame of Macedon's kings of old, the ancient repute of its people, and the extent of the empire which the Macedonians had earlier acquired through armed conflict, comprising much of Europe and most of Asia.* The war against Philip had been started some ten years earlier,* but had been discontinued for three years* when the Aetolians had turned out to be the cause of both war and peace.* But the Romans now found themselves unencumbered as a result of the peace made with Carthage, and they were infuriated with Philip because of the treacherous peace which he had made with the Aetolians and his other allies in the region, and also because of the military and financial assistance* which he had recently sent to Africa for Hannibal and the Carthaginians. They were therefore prompted to recommence hostilities with him by the entreaties of the Athenians* whom Philip had driven back into their city after pillaging their farmland.

2. At about this time embassies arrived from King Attalus as well as from the Rhodians. These reported that the city-states of Asia

were also under pressure from Philip. The embassies were told that the Senate would examine the situation; and consideration of the war with Macedon was referred entirely to the consuls, who were at that time involved with their provinces. In the mean time three ambassadors were sent to King Ptolemy of Egypt: Gaius Claudius Nero, Marcus Aemilius Lepidus, and Publius Sempronius Tuditanus. These were to report to the king that Hannibal and the Carthaginians had been defeated, and to thank him for remaining loyal to the Romans at a critical time when even the allies who were their closest neighbours were deserting them. The ambassadors were also to request of Ptolemy that he maintain his former inclinations towards the Roman people* in the event of their being forced by Philip's aggression to commence hostilities against the latter.

At about the same time, in Gaul,* the consul, Publius Aelius, had been apprised that before his arrival attacks had been made on territory of the allies by the Boii,* and he had enrolled two improvised legions to meet the crisis, adding to them four cohorts from his own army. He then instructed the allied commander, Gaius Ampius, to invade the territory of the Boii with this makeshift body through that part of Umbria called tribus Sapinia. Aelius himself led his troops to the same area by the open road through the mountains. On entering enemy territory, Ampius made a number of quite successful raids without exposing himself to danger. But then he selected a spot near the fortified town of Mutilum which was convenient for harvesting grain, the crops being already ripe, and set out without having reconnoitred the area or established armed posts strong enough to afford protection for his unarmed men when they were engrossed in their work. When the Gauls made a sudden attack, Ampius was cut off with his foragers. Even those who were armed then fell prey to panic and flight. Some 7,000 men were cut down as they wandered through the fields, their commander Ampius himself being one of them, and the others were driven in fear back into their camp. The following night, with no recognized leader, the common soldiers came to an agreement amongst themselves, abandoned most of their possessions, and made their way to the consul through mountain ravines that were almost impossible to negotiate. Aelius then returned to Rome, having accomplished nothing of note in his province apart from his raids on the territory of the Boii, and a treaty struck with the Ligurian Ingauni.*

3. When the Senate held its first meeting, the entire membership requested that no item be considered before that of Philip and the grievances of the allies, and the matter was immediately brought up for discussion. A packed house decided that Publius Aelius should send out a man of his own choosing, with imperium,* to assume control of the fleet which Gnaeus Octavius was bringing back from Sicily, and cross with it to Macedonia.* The man sent, with propraetorian* authority, was Marcus Valerius Laevinus,* who took charge of thirty-eight vessels from Gnaeus Octavius in the vicinity of Vibo, and sailed with them to Macedonia. Here the legate Marcus Aurelius* came to Laevinus and briefed him on the size of the armies and the number of ships mobilized by the king, and told of how Philip was rousing men to arms on the islands as well as in all the mainland cities through personal visits or intermediaries. He stressed that the Romans should prosecute the war with increased vigour in case their hesitation led Philip to a venture similar to that which Pyrrhus* had undertaken from a considerably weaker kingdom. It was decided that Aurelius should communicate this information by letter to the consuls and the Senate.

4. At the end of this year the question was brought up in the Senate of land-grants for the veterans who had finished off the war in Africa under the leadership and authority of Publius Scipio. The Senators decided that the urban praetor Marcus Iunius should, if he were in agreement, hold an election for the establishment of a board of ten to measure off and apportion Samnite and Apulian land that was the public property* of the Roman people. Selected for this task were Publius Servilius, Quintus Caecilius Metellus, Gaius and Marcus Servilius (both surnamed Geminus), Lucius and Aulus Hostilius Cato, Publius Villius Tappulus, Marcus Fulvius Flaccus, Publius Aelius Paetus and Titus Quinctius Flamininus.

In elections held at this time by the consul, Publius Aelius, Publius Sulpicius Galba and Gaius Aurelius Cotta were chosen consuls, and then Quintus Minucius Rufus, Lucius Furius Purpureo, Quintus Fulvius Gillo, and Gaius Sergius Plautus were made praetors. That year the Roman dramatic festivals put on by the curule aediles Lucius Valerius Flaccus and Lucius Quinctius Flamininus were impressive and elaborate. The performance was repeated for a further period of two days,* and the aediles distributed amongst the people—at a price of four *asses** per person, and with a consummate impartiality which earned them the people's gratitude—a large amount of grain sent from Africa by Publius Scipio. The Plebeian Games,* too, were three times reproduced in their entirety by the aediles of the plebs, Lucius Apustius Fullo and Quintus Minucius Rufus (who had been elected praetor after his term as aedile). A feast of Jupiter was also put on to celebrate the games.

5. In the five hundred and fifty-first year after the founding of the city,* and in the consulship of Publius Sulpicius Galba and Gaius Aurelius, the war with King Philip was begun, just a few months after peace was granted to the Carthaginians. First of all, on the Ides of March—the day on which one began the consulship at that time*—the consul Publius Sulpicius proposed, and the Senate decreed, that the consuls should use full-grown victims and sacrifice to gods of their choosing, with the following prayer: 'Whatsoever the Senate and People of Rome decide about the welfare of the state and the commencement of a new war, may that turn out successfully and prosperously for the Roman people, their allies and the members of the Latin League.' The Senate also decided that, after the sacrifice and the prayer, the consuls were to confer with it about the welfare of the state and the provinces.

There arrived at that time, at an opportune moment for inflaming passions for the war, letters from the legate Marcus Aurelius and the propraetor Marcus Valerius Laevinus, as well as a fresh deputation from the Athenians. The latter reported that the king was approaching Athenian territory and that in a short while their city, and not just their lands, would be in Philip's hands unless assistance were forthcoming from the Romans. The consuls then announced that the sacrifice had been duly performed and the augurs were reporting that the gods had favourably heard their prayer; that the entrails had turned out to be propitious, and that an extension of Roman territory was predicted, with victory and a triumph.* Then the letter from Valerius and Aurelius was read out, and the ambassadors from Athens were given an audience. After this came a decree from the Senate that the allies be thanked for not having broken faith despite a long period of harassment, and even when there was fear of a siege. On the question of sending of assistance, their decision was that a reply should await the time when the consuls had been assigned their provinces, and the consul who received responsibility* for

Macedonia had brought to the people a motion that war be declared on King Philip of Macedon.

6. The province of Macedonia fell by lot to Publius Sulpicius. He promulgated a bill whereby the people 'wanted and instructed that war be declared on King Philip and the Macedonians* under his rule in view of his offences and aggression against allies of the people of Rome'. The other consul, Aurelius, was allotted the province of Italy. The praetorian sortition* after this turned out as follows:

Sergius Plautus	urban jurisdiction
Quintus Fulvius Gillo	Sicily
Quintus Minucius Rufus	Bruttium
Lucius Furius Purpureo	Gaul

The bill concerning war with Macedon was rejected at the first assembly by almost all the centuries.* This had been the natural reaction of men tired of protracted and relentless warfare—and sick of its dangers and hardships—but the result was also partly due to the tribune of the plebs, Quintus Baebius.* He had resorted to the old practice of recriminations against the Senate, accusing that body of tacking one war onto another so that the plebeians would never feel the advantages of peace. The Senate was indignant at this, and the tribune of the plebs was subjected to cutting reprimands on the floor of the house, with every Senator urging the consul to reconvene the assembly to pass the proposal, reproach the people for their apathy, and make them understand the detriment and humiliation such a deferral of war would entail.

7. The assembly was reconvened on the Campus Martius. Before sending the centuries to vote, however, the consul called the people together in an informal meeting and addressed them as follows:

'Citizens, I do not think you realize that what you are debating is not whether to have war or peace. Philip, who is mounting a vast land and sea offensive, is not going to make that an option for you to take or leave. The question is whether you are to transport your legions to Macedonia, or else admit your enemy into Italy. The difference between these alternatives you have at least learned from experience—even if you had not learned it before—in the last war with Carthage. Suppose we had been prompt in bringing aid to the people of Saguntum* when they were under siege and appealing to us for our protection, as prompt as our fathers had been when they brought aid to the Mamertines—can there be any doubt but that we would have transferred the entire theatre of war to Spain? Our vacillation meant taking the war into Italy, with disastrous consequences for ourselves.

'There can be no doubt of another thing either: this same Philip made a pact with Hannibal through intermediaries and letters to cross to Italy, and we contained him in Macedonia only by sending Laevinus with a fleet to launch a pre-emptive strike against him. We did that at a time when we had Hannibal as our enemy in Italy. Are we hesitating to do it now when Hannibal is driven from Italy, when the Carthaginians are defeated? Let us give the king first-hand experience of our lethargy through his capture of Athens, as we did Hannibal when he captured Saguntum! Philip will not be like Hannibal, arriving here from Saguntum after four months—no, he will reach Italy four days after launching his ships from Corinth! Do not compare Philip with Hannibal or the Macedonians with the Carthaginians. I suppose, however, you will compare Philip with Pyrrhus. "Compare" do I say? There is an enormous gulf between the one man and the other, between the one people and the other! Epirus has always been, and remains today, an insignificant annex of the Macedonian kingdom. Philip has the entire Peloponnese under his sway, including Argos itself, better known these days for Pyrrhus' death* than from its reputation of old. And compare our circumstances at that time and at this. Pyrrhus attacked an Italy that was so much more prosperous; its resources were so much better preserved; its leaders and armies, later wiped out by the Punic War, were still intact—and even so he shattered it, coming in conquest virtually to the city of Rome. It was not just the people of Tarentum who defected from us, along with that coastline of Italy which people call "Greater Greece"—in that case one might have believed in an allegiance to a common language and lineage*—but so did the Lucanian, the Bruttian, and the Samnite. Should Philip cross to Italy, do you think these will stay out of the fight or remain loyal to us? Of course you remember their remaining loyal in the later years of the Punic War! No, there is no occasion on which these peoples will *fail* to revolt—unless they have no one to whom to defect!

'Suppose you had been reluctant to cross to Africa. You would in that case still have Hannibal and his Carthaginians as your enemies in Italy this very day. Let Macedonia have this war, not Italy. Let the cities and the countryside of our enemies suffer the devastation of sword and fire. We already know from experience that our campaigns are more successful and effective abroad than they are at home. Go and vote—may the gods help you—and ratify the decision of the Senate. It is not just your consul who supports this proposal; so now do the immortal gods. For when, offering sacrifice, I prayed for a successful and happy conclusion to this war for myself, for the Senate, for you, for the allies, and for those with Latin rights, for our forces on land and sea—the portents which they sent were uniformly promising and favourable.'

8. After this address the people were dispatched to vote, and, as the consul proposed, they called for war. Acting on a decree of the Senate, the consuls now ordained a three-day period for prayers to the gods, who were during this time importuned at all their couches* to vouchsafe a happy and prosperous conclusion to the war which the people had authorized against Philip. The fetial priests* were also consulted by the consul Sulpicius on the question of whether the declaration of the war on Philip should now go to the king in person, or whether it was enough for the announcement to be made at the first fortress within the bounds of his realm. The priests determined that either option would be proper. The consul was granted permission to send the declaration of war on the king with anyone he liked who was not a member of the Senate.

Then the matter of the allocation of armies to the consuls and praetors was discussed. The consuls were instructed to raise two legions each, demobilizing the veteran armies, and Sulpicius, officially vested with command in this new and momentous campaign, was allowed to draw all the volunteers he could from the force brought back from Africa by Publius Scipio, but he did not have the right to coerce any veteran. To each of the praetors, Lucius Furius Purpureo and Quintus Minucius Rufus, the consuls were to give 5,000 allies and members of the Latin League,* and the praetors were to use these troops to secure their respective provinces, Gaul and Bruttium. Quintus Fulvius Gillo was also instructed to select a complement of 15,000 allies and members of the Latin League from the army formerly under the command of Publius Aelius, choosing those with the shortest period of active service; this force was to form a garrison for the province of Sicily. Marcus Valerius Falto who, as praetor, had been in charge of Campania the previous year,

had his imperium prolonged for a year to enable him to cross to
Sardinia with propraetorian rank. Falto was also to raise from the
army in Sardinia a force of 5,000 allies and members of the Latin
League, choosing those with the shortest period of active service.
Furthermore, the consuls were directed to enrol two urban legions
to be dispatched wherever an emergency required, for many tribes in
Italy had been infected by allegiances with the enemy during the
Punic War, and were simmering with animosity towards Rome as a
result. The state thus intended to put six Roman legions into service
that year.

9. While the Romans were actually involved in preparations
for the war, ambassadors arrived from Ptolemy to report that the
Athenians had requested the king's assistance against Philip.
Although the Athenians were allies both of the Romans and himself,
Ptolemy stated, he would nevertheless send neither sea- nor land-
forces to Greece for defensive or offensive operations without the
sanction of the Roman people. If the Roman people chose to defend
its allies, he would remain inactive in his own kingdom; otherwise, he
would, if the Romans preferred, let them remain inactive while he
himself sent military assistance strong enough to have no difficulty
protecting Athens from Philip. Ptolemy was thanked by the Senate,
who told him the Roman people intended to offer protection to its
allies, adding that they would inform the king of any assistance they
needed for the war and that they were aware that the resources of his
kingdom represented a secure and loyal support for their republic.
Then gifts of 5,000 *asses* per person were sent to the ambassadors by
senatorial decree.

While the consuls were engaged in the conscription and all the
necessary preparations for the war, religious feeling in the city
mounted, as it especially did at the commencement of new wars.
Public devotions were held, and at all the couches of the gods communal prayers were offered. Fearful that any procedure followed in
the past be omitted on this occasion, the people issued orders that
the consul who was allotted the province of Macedonia should make
a vow promising games and a gift to Jupiter. However, the public
votive offering was held up by the pontifex maximus, Licinius, who
asserted that one could not formulate a vow based on an unspecified
sum of money, because such money could not be employed for the
war; it should be immediately set apart and not combined with other

moneys. In the event of the latter happening, the vow could not be duly discharged, he said. The argument and its advocate both made an impact, but the consul was none the less instructed to refer to the college of priests* the question of the possibility of a vow being correctly formulated with its monetary sum unspecified. The priests determined that this was not just possible but was actually the more correct procedure. Following the pontifex maximus' dictation, the consul formulated the vow using the same phraseology as had been traditionally employed in the past for vows to be discharged after the lapse of five years, with the exception that his promise of games and gifts was based on a sum of moneys to be determined by the Senate at the time when the vow was being discharged. On eight previous occasions vows of the Great Games* had been made based upon a specified sum of money, and this was the first time they were made with the sum unspecified.

10. The attention of all was now focused on the war with Macedon when suddenly there occurred the last thing the Romans feared at this time—word was brought of an uprising in Gaul. The Insubres, the Cenomani, and the Boii had been fomenting discontent amongst the Celines, the Ilvates, and the other Ligurian tribes. Then, led by the Carthaginian Hamilcar—a former member of Hasdrubal's army* who had stayed on in the region—they had over-run Placentia. They sacked the city, and in their rage set fire to most of it, leaving behind barely 2,000 men amidst the burning ruins. They then crossed the Po, and headed for Cremona in order to pillage it. The reports of the destruction of the city next to them gave the inhabitants of Cremona time to shut their gates and post garrisons on their walls. They would thus face a siege rather than be taken by storm, and could send envoys to the Roman praetor.

Lucius Furius Purpureo was the governor of the province at that time. He had, following a decree of the Senate, demobilized his entire army with the exception of 5,000 allies and members of the Latin League; and with these latter forces he had taken up a position near Ariminum in that part of the province closest to Rome. He then gave the Senate, by letter, an account of the turmoil in the province: of the two colonies which had avoided the massive calamity of the Punic War, one had been captured and ransacked by the enemy, and the other was now under attack. In his own army he did not have the strength to relieve the colonists' distress, he said—unless he were willing to expose to destruction by the 40,000 enemy troops now under arms his 5,000-strong contingent of allies, and see the confidence of the enemy, already inflated by their annihilation of a Roman colony, further boosted by the calamitous defeat that he would suffer at their hands!

11. The consul Gaius Aurelius had specified a date for the mobilization of an army in Etruria; but after Purpureo's letter was read aloud in the Senate, the Senators decided that the consul should issue orders for the troops to come together at Ariminum on that same day. He should then set off in person, if that were consistent with the best interests of the state, to suppress the uprising in Gaul. Otherwise, he was to inform the praetor Quintus Minucius by letter that when the legions from Etruria should reach him, the praetor should replace these with 5,000 allies, to serve temporarily as a garrison for Etruria, and set out himself to raise the siege of the colony.

The Senate also voted to send an embassy to Africa, both to Carthage and to King Masinissa in Numidia. The ambassadors were to report to Carthage that one of their citizens, Hamilcar, left behind in Gaul—though it was unclear* whether he belonged to Hasdrubal's earlier or Mago's later army—was engaging in warfare in contravention of their treaty, and that he had incited Gallic and Ligurian forces to arms against the Roman people. If peace was what the Carthagians wanted, then they had to bring this man home and deliver him to the Roman people. The envoys were also required to report that not all their deserters had been returned to the Romans, and that most of them were actually living without concealment in Carthage. These had to be arrested and hunted down to be returned to the Roman people in accordance with the treaty. Such were the instructions given to the ambassadors with regard to Carthage. As for Masinissa, the envoys were told to congratulate him on having not only recovered the kingdom of his ancestors but on having also augmented it by adding to it the richest part of Syphax's territory. They were also to report to him the opening of hostilities with Philip because of the assistance the latter had given the Carthaginians and because of his atrocities against allies of the Roman people, which obliged the Romans to commit sea and land forces to Greece when Italy was aflame with war—Philip being thereby primarily responsible, by dividing the Roman forces, for the delay in the crossing to Africa. The ambassadors were also to request of Masinissa that he send Numidian cavalry to assist their war-effort; and they were given generous gifts to bear to the king: vessels of gold and silver, a purple toga, a palm-embroidered tunic with an ivory sceptre, and a toga praetexta with a curule chair.* They were further instructed to make a pledge to Masinissa that the Roman people would, in view of his service to them, take great pains to furnish him with whatever he stipulated as necessary to strengthen or extend the kingdom of Numidia.

At this time the Senate was also approached by envoys from Vermina, son of Syphax. These tried to justify the youthful mistakes of Vermina and put all the blame on Carthaginian duplicity. Masinissa, too, had become a friend of Rome after being its enemy, they said, and Vermina would also make every effort not to fall short of Masinissa or, indeed, of anyone else in his good offices to the people of Rome. They requested, therefore, that the king be given the title 'King, Ally, and Friend' by the Senate. The reply given to the embassy was that Vermina's father, Syphax, had suddenly and inexplicably become a foe of the Roman people after being their ally and friend, and that Vermina himself had devoted his early years to harassing the Romans. He should therefore ask for peace from the Roman people before requesting the title 'King, Ally, and Friend'. Such a title was traditionally an honour which the Roman people conferred as a reward for important services rendered them by foreign kings. There was going to be a Roman embassy to Africa, they continued, and the Senate would dictate to it the terms of the peace-treaty for Vermina, who should leave to the Roman people full authority as to its conditions. Any addition, deletion, or adjustment he wanted should be requested in a fresh application to the Senate. The envoys sent to Africa with these instructions were Gaius Terentius Varro, Spurius Lucretius, and Gnaeus Octavius. Each was granted a quinquereme.

12. Then a letter was read out in the Senate from the praetor Quintus Minucius, whose province was Bruttium. Money had been surreptitiously removed under cover of night, he said, from the treasury of Proserpina* at Locri, and there were no clues as to the guilty party. The Senate was exasperated at the continuing sacrilege and at the fact that even the notorious and recent lesson of Pleminius' crime* and punishment did not serve to deter men from such activities. The consul Gaius Aurelius was assigned the duty of

writing to the praetor in Bruttium. He was to inform him of the Senate's decision that investigation of the matter of the purloined treasure follow the same procedure as had been followed by the praetor Marcus Pomponius three years earlier: any moneys recovered were to be replaced in the treasury, and any shortfall made good, with sacrifices of expiation carried out, if the praetor saw fit, in the manner directed by the priests on that former occasion.

The Senate's concern to atone for the violation of this temple was intensified by simultaneous reports of prodigies in several different locations. In Lucania there were claims that the sky had been on fire; in Privernum that the sun had shone red, in fine weather, throughout an entire day; in Lanuvium that there had been a deafening noise at night-time in the temple of Juno Sospita. In several places there were also reports of sinister births of animals. Amongst the Sabines a child of indeterminate sex was born, and a second child of uncertain sex was found who was already sixteen years old. At Frusino a lamb was born with the head of a pig, at Sinuessa a pig with a human head, and in Lucania, on public land, a foal with five feet. All these appeared to be grotesque and hideous apparitions, indications that nature that was running riot and generating monstrosities, but it was the bisexual creatures which aroused revulsion most of all, and orders were issued for these to be immediately cast into the sea, as had been recently done, in the consulship of Gaius Claudius and Marcus Livius,* with a similar freak that had been born. Even so, the decemvirs were told to consult the Sibylline books* regarding the portent, and these, after examining them, authorized the same observances as had been held immediately after the earlier prodigy. In addition, the decemvirs ordered a hymn to be sung throughout the city by three groups of nine young girls and an offering made to Queen Juno. In conformity with the response of the decemvirs, the consul Gaius Aurelius saw to the implementation of these instructions, and the hymn, of the type composed by Livius,* within the memory of the Senators, was on that occasion composed by Publius Licinius Tegula.

13. Expiatory rites were performed for all these religious phenomena—even the sacrilege at Locri was thoroughly investigated by Quintus Minucius, and the missing moneys, expropriated from the guilty parties, restored to the treasury—and the consuls were ready to leave for their provinces. At this point the Senate was

approached by a large number of private citizens who were due to receive that year the third payment of the money which they had put out on loan in the consulship of Marcus Valerius and Marcus Claudius. Since the treasury had insufficient funds for this new war, the conduct of which required a large fleet and large armies, the consuls had claimed that they were temporarily without the resources to repay the individuals concerned. The Senate could not deny the validity of their complaint, which was that if the state also wished to use for the Macedonian War moneys loaned for the Punic War, the one conflict following hard on the heels of the other, then it was simply a matter of their money, which they had provided as a service, being appropriated by the state as if it were its due.

The request of these individuals was fair, but the state was none the less unable to repay the loan, so the Senate passed a resolution which was a compromise between equity and pragmatism. Since many of these citizens observed that there was, in many areas, land for sale which they needed to buy, the Senate decided that they should be granted the opportunity of using public lands within a fifty-mile radius of Rome. The consuls were to evaluate this land and impose a tax of an *as* per acre to show that it was public land that was involved. The rationale behind this was that, when the public purse was again solvent, anyone preferring cash to land could restore the land to the people. The private citizens were happy to accept this compromise, and the land involved was given the name 'trientabulum' because its granting accounted for one third of the public debt.

14. Then, having made his vows on the Capitoline, Publius Sulpicius set off from the city with his lictors dressed in their military cloaks, and came to Brundisium. Here he enrolled in his legions a number of volunteers who were veterans of the army in Africa, and made a selection of ships from the fleet of Gnaeus Cornelius. With these he crossed to Macedonia, arriving two days after setting sail from Brundisium. There he was met by a deputation from Athens, which asked him to raise the siege of their city. Gaius Claudius Centho was immediately dispatched to Athens with twenty warships and a thousand men. In fact, Philip was not present himself at the siege of Athens; at that moment he was actually mounting his offensive on Abydus, having already made trial of his strength in naval battles against the Rhodians and King Attalus, achieving little success in either engagement. But his confidence was maintained not

only because of his innate truculence but also because of a treaty which he had struck with Antiochus, king of Syria, by which Philip shared with Antiochus the wealth of Egypt, on which both kings had had designs ever since they heard of Ptolemy's death.*

In fact, the people of Athens had not had a sufficiently compelling motive for opening hostilities with Philip, preserving as they did nothing of their former greatness save their spirit. In the days devoted to the Mysteries, two young Acarnanians who were not initiates joined the crowd and entered the temple of Ceres, ignorant of the rites of Eleusis.* Their speech easily gave them away when they asked some bizarre questions. They were taken to the priests of the temple, and although it was evident that they had entered by mistake they were put to death as though guilty of some horrendous crime. The people of Acarnania brought word of this vile and provocative act to Philip, thereby gaining his permission to attack Athens, Macedonian reinforcements being given to them for this purpose. At first the army plundered Attica with fire and the sword, returning to Acarnania laden with all manner of booty. This incursion was the first irritant for the Athenians. Subsequently the war was formalized with a regular declaration made by decree of state.

Philip had now retired to Macedonia, with Attalus and the Rhodians in close pursuit. When the latter reached Aegina, Attalus crossed to Piraeus* to renew and strengthen his alliance with Athens. The entire citizenry, streaming out to meet him along with their wives and children, welcomed him as he entered the city, as did the priests in all their finery and—one might almost say—the gods themselves, summoned forth from their temples!

15. The people were immediately called to a meeting so that the king could publicly state his wishes. But then it was deemed more appropriate to his status for him to write a letter about any matters of concern to him. Rather this, it was felt, than that he be present in person and be put in the embarrassing situation of listing his services to the state of Athens, or receiving applause and acclamation from a crowd that would tax his modesty with extravagant flattery. The letter which was sent to, and read out in, the assembly called attention first to Attalus' good offices to the Athenian community, and then to his military successes against Philip. Finally came an exhortation to undertake a war against Philip while the Athenians had the support of Attalus as well as of the Rhodians and even the

Romans. Hesitate now and they would in future seek in vain this opportunity which they had let slip.

Next the embassy from Rhodes was given an audience. The Rhodians' service to the Athenians was of recent date, and involved the return to Athens of four Athenian warships, lately captured by the Macedonians and then recovered by the Rhodians. So it was that war was declared on Philip by an overwhelming majority. A plethora of honours was showered first on Attalus, then on the Rhodians; and it was at this time that mention was first made of the addition of a new tribe called 'the Attalid' to the ten ancient tribes,* while the people of Rhodes were awarded a golden crown for their bravery and all Rhodians granted Athenian citizenship, just as the Rhodians had previously granted their citizenship to the Athenians. After this Attalus returned to his fleet at Aegina, while the Rhodians sailed from Aegina to Cea and thence to Rhodes by way of the islands, forming alliances with all the latter apart from Andros, Paros, and Cythnos, these being secured by Macedonian garrisons. Attalus was kept inactive for some time in Aegina: he had sent messengers to, and was awaiting envoys from, Aetolia. He was, however, unable to incite the Aetolians to take up arms, happy as they were to have concluded peace with Philip, no matter what its terms. Attalus and the people of Rhodes could have won the remarkable distinction of liberating Greece by their own efforts had they now put pressure on Philip; instead, they allowed him to cross to the Hellespont once more, and to amass his strength by seizing points of strategic importance in Thrace, and thus they kept the war alive and left to the Romans the prestige of conducting it and bringing it to conclusion.

16. Philip revealed a spirit more becoming in a king. Though he had been unable to mount effective resistance to Attalus and the Rhodians, he was still not frightened even by the impending war with Rome. He sent one of his subordinates, Philocles, along with 2,000 infantry and 200 cavalry, to conduct raids on Athenian agricultural land, and assigned a fleet to Heraclides so he could head for Maronea, while Philip himself made for the same town overland with 2,000 light infantry and 200 cavalry. In fact, Philip took Maronea at the first assault, but then had great trouble with the siege of Aenus, which he finally captured only through the treachery of Ptolemy's lieutenant, Callimedes. He then seized other forts,

Cypsela, Doriscus, and Serrheum, afterwards advancing to the Chersonese where he took Elaeus and Alopeconnesus, their populations making voluntary surrender. Callipolis and Madytus also surrendered, along with a number of obscure forts, but the people of Abydus shut their gates on the king, refusing admission even to his envoys. That particular siege detained Philip for a long time and, but for faint-heartedness on the part of Attalus and the Rhodians, the people of Abydus might have been delivered from the siege. Attalus sent a mere 300 men to help with the defence, and the Rhodians a single quadrireme from their fleet even though that fleet was moored at Tenedos. Later on, when the people of Abydus were barely able to hold out against the siege, Attalus crossed to the town in person, but offered only the tenuous hope of assistance from close by without actually helping his allies either by land or by sea.

17. By posting catapults along the walls, the people of Abydus at first succeeded not only in fending off attacks by land but also in putting the enemy fleet at risk as it lay at anchor. Later, when part of the wall had been shattered and the enemy had used tunnels to reach a hastily erected inner wall, they sent an embassy to the king to discuss terms for the town's surrender. The agreement they were seeking from Philip was that they be allowed to send off the Rhodian quadrireme with its crew, and the relief force of Attalus, while they themselves should leave the city with one piece of clothing each.

Philip replied that no terms short of unconditional surrender were acceptable. The report of the embassy was brought back to the people of Abydus, whose resentment and despair roused them to such fury that they resorted to action as insane as that witnessed at Saguntum.* They had all their married women locked in the temple of Diana, and all free-born boys, girls, and even babies, along with their nurses, in the gymnasium. Their gold and silver they ordered to be brought to the forum, their expensive clothing loaded onto two ships in the harbour from Rhodes and Cyzicus respectively. Then they had their priests and sacrificial animals brought forth and altars erected in public. They next selected men who, when they saw their army cut to pieces as it fought before the breached wall, would immediately kill the wives and children, hurl into the sea the gold and silver and the clothing which was on the ships, and set fire to buildings public and private in as many locations in the city as they could. They bound themselves by oath to carry out this monstrous act, the priests dictating to them the formulae of execration;* and the men of military age swore that none would leave the battle alive unless victorious. These men kept the gods in mind, and fought with such tenacity that when nightfall was about to end the fighting the king quit the battle before his enemy, terrified by their furious resistance. The leading citizens of the town who had been charged with the most cruel part of the brutal act could now see that few of their men had survived the battle, and that these were incapacitated from wounds and exhaustion; and so at dawn they sent their priests, wearing fillets,* to surrender the town to Philip.

18. Before the surrender, Marcus Aemilius, the youngest member of the embassy sent to Alexandria, had been told of the siege of Abydus and, with the agreement of his colleagues, he came to Philip. Aemilius lodged a complaint before him over his attack on Attalus and the Rhodians and over his offensive against Abydus which was proceeding at that very time. The king asserted that he himself had actually been the victim of aggression on the part of Attalus and the Rhodians, to which Aemilius replied: 'The people of Abydus are not guilty of aggression against you too, are they?' Philip was not used to hearing the truth, and Aemilius' words struck him as being too arrogant to be used before a king. 'Your age, your good looks and above all the name of Rome make you rather arrogant,' said Philip. 'My own first choice would be for you to observe our treaties and remain at peace with me; but you attack me and you will realize that the realm and name of Macedon—which are as famous as those of Rome—give me courage, too.'

With these words Philip dismissed the ambassador. He then seized the gold and silver that had been amassed, but all human booty he lost. For sheer fury gripped the population of Abydus. They thought the men who had fallen in battle had been betrayed, and they accused each other of perjury. Above all they accused the priests, for these had delivered alive to the enemy the men whom they had by sacred oath marked out for death. They all suddenly ran off to butcher their wives and children, and then committed suicide themselves, seeking every possible path to death. Stunned by such murderous insanity, Philip arrested his men's assault and declared that he was giving the people of Abydus three days to complete their deaths. In that period of time the defeated townspeople inflicted more atrocities on themselves than a bloodthirsty conqueror would have done, and nobody fell into Philip's power alive with the exception of those for whom imprisonment or some other duress made suicide impossible. Philip established a garrison at Abydus and returned to his kingdom. And just as the destruction of Saguntum had stimulated Hannibal to war with the Romans, so now did the massacre of the people of Abydus stimulate Philip to war with Rome. The news came that the consul was already in Epirus, and that he had taken his land-forces to Apollonia, and his naval forces to Corcyra, to pass the winter.

19. In the mean time the deputation sent to Africa had received a reply from the Carthaginians with regard to Hamilcar, commander-in-chief of the Gallic army. The Carthaginians claimed that all they could do was punish him with exile and confiscate his property. As far as deserters and fugitives were concerned, they had restored all they had been able to track down in the process of their investigation, and they would dispatch an embassy to Rome on that very subject to give satisfaction to the Senate. They sent 200,000 measures of wheat to Rome, and 200,000 to the army in Macedonia.

The envoys then set off for the courts of the kings in Numidia. Masinissa was given gifts and issued instructions, and the Romans accepted from him 1,000 Numidian cavalry of the 2,000 he offered. The king had the cavalry embarked on vessels and dispatched them to Macedonia along with 200,000 measures of wheat and 200,000 of barley.

A third call made by the ambassadors was on Vermina. He came right to the frontier of his realm to meet them and allowed them to formulate themselves whatever peace-terms they pleased—any peace with the people of Rome would be good and equitable in his eyes, he said. Terms were given to him, and he was told to send envoys to Rome to ratify the peace.

20. At this time the proconsul Lucius Cornelius Lentulus came back from Spain. In the Senate he gave a detailed account of his achievements and successes over many years, and requested permission to enter the city in triumph. The Senate voted that Lentulus' record merited a triumph, but added that they had no precedent from their ancestors for a triumph being celebrated in honour of the achievements of a man who was not a dictator, a consul, or a praetor, for Lentulus had held command in the province of Spain as a proconsul, not as a consul or praetor. Nevertheless they resorted to the

compromise of his entering the city with an ovation,* although the tribune of the plebs, Tiberius Sempronius Longus, threatened to interpose his veto on the ground that this privilege was no more in conformity with ancestral practice and just as unprecedented. In the end the tribune relented, persuaded by a unanimous Senate, and by Senatorial decree Lucius Lentulus entered the city with an ovation. He brought with him 43,000 pounds of silver and 2,450 pounds of gold, and he distributed from his booty 120 *asses* to each of his men.

21. The consular army had by this time been transferred from Arretium to Ariminum, and the 5,000 allies and members of the Latin League* had marched from Gaul to Etruria. Accordingly Lucius Furius advanced by forced marches from Ariminum towards the Gauls who were at that time besieging Cremona, and encamped at a distance of one and a half miles from the enemy. The opportunity for an exceptional feat was within his grasp, had he but led his men to an attack on the enemy camp immediately after the march; for the enemy were widely scattered and straggling through the fields without having established sufficient protection for themselves. Furius had misgivings about the fatigue of his men, since the column had been taken along at a rapid pace. The Gauls were brought back from the fields by the cries of their comrades; they dropped the plunder which they had in their hands and headed back to camp. Next day they proceeded to battle stations, and the Roman did not hold back from the fight, either. But there was barely enough time to organize the line, so swiftly did the enemy come into battle. Furius had the allied force divided into squadrons, and the right squadron was stationed in the front line, backed up by two Roman legions. Marcus Furius commanded the right squadron, Marcus Caecilius the legions, and Lucius Valerius Flaccus the cavalry, all three as legates.* The praetor kept two legates with him, Gaius Laetorius and Publius Titinius, so that he could survey the battle along with them and counter any unexpected manœuvres by the enemy.

At the start the Gauls hoped that they could overpower and wipe out the right squadron in the front line by attacking in massed force at a single point. Achieving little success with this, they attempted to encircle the wings and outflank their enemy's line, an apparently simple manœuvre, given their numerical superiority. The praetor saw this happen, and added the two back-up Roman legions to the right and left of the squadron fighting in the front in order to extend his fighting line; and he also made a vow to build a temple to Vedio-vis* in the event of his defeating the enemy that day. He issued orders to Lucius Valerius to unleash cavalry on the enemy flanks, that of the two legions on the one side, that of the allies on the other, and not permit the enemy to encircle the line. At the same time, the consul himself could see that the extending of the wings had weak-ened the Gauls' centre, and he ordered his men to attack en masse and break through the enemy lines; and so the flanks were driven back by the cavalry, and the centre by the infantry. Suddenly there was horrendous carnage everywhere, and the Gauls turned tail and headed back to camp in disordered rout. The Roman cavalry chased them as they fled, and presently the legions also followed, attacking the enemy camp. Fewer than 6,000 men made good their escape; more than 35,000 were cut down or captured, along with 70 military standards and more than 200 Gallic waggons loaded with rich booty. The Carthaginian commander Hamilcar died in the battle, as did three Gallic generals of noble birth. Some 2,000 free-born captives from Placentia were restored to their colony.

22. It was a great victory, one that brought joy to Rome; and when the letter arrived a three-day period for religious observances was declared. About 2,000 Romans and allies fell in the battle, most of them from the squadron on the right, which had taken the thrust of the massive enemy assault at the start of the engagement. Hostilities had been virtually brought to a conclusion thanks to the praetor; even so, after finishing all the business required of him in Rome, the consul Gaius Aurelius also set out for Gaul and assumed command of the victorious army from the praetor.

The other consul had reached his province towards the end of autumn and was in winter-quarters close to Apollonia. Gaius Clau-dius and the Roman triremes had been detached from the fleet moored at Corcyra and sent to Athens, as noted above,* and their arrival in Piraeus had brought high hopes to the dispirited allies. For one thing, overland raids on Athenian farmlands, which had been made regularly from Corinth by way of Megara, now no longer occurred; and, secondly, pirate ships from Chalcis, formerly a men-ace to the Athenians not just on the open sea but also in all their coastal farm-land, no longer even dared to ply the sea beyond the strait of Euripus, much less to round Cape Sunium. To supplement these vessels, three quadriremes arrived from Rhodes, and there were three Attic open-decked ships, furnished for the purpose of defending the coastline.

Claudius felt that it sufficed for the moment that the city and its farmland receive protection from this fleet, but then he was offered the chance to bring off an even greater feat.

23. Some exiles from Chalcis, driven from home by atrocities committed by Philip's men, brought word that Chalcis could be taken without a fight. With no fear of an enemy in the vicinity, they said, the Macedonians were drifting aimlessly all over town, while the native townspeople were paying no attention to their city's defences because they relied on the Macedonian garrison. On the basis of this information Claudius set out for Chalcis. He reached Sunium early enough to be able to sail on from there to the opening of the straits of Euboea, but he kept his fleet at anchor till nightfall for fear of being spotted after rounding the promontory. At dusk he moved, and had a smooth crossing to Chalcis, arriving shortly before dawn. He approached a sparsely populated area of town where, with a few soldiers, he scaled and captured the closest tower and the wall adjoining it, finding guards asleep at some points and no guard at all at others. The Romans then advanced to the built-up areas of the city where they killed the sentries, smashed in the gate and let in the main body of their force.

They now ran amok throughout the city, the chaos being further intensified by the torching of the buildings around the forum. The king's granaries as well as the arsenal, with its huge stock of siege-engines and slings, went up in flames, and fleeing men were put to the sword in every quarter along with those offering resistance. When all of military age had either been killed or had fled, and when the garrison-commander, the Acarnanian Sopater, had also fallen, all the booty was first gathered into the forum, then loaded onto ships. The prison was also broken open by the Rhodians and its inmates freed, men whom Philip had incarcerated there in the belief that they were placed in the most secure confinement. The king's statues were pulled down and hacked to pieces, and when the signal for retreat was sounded the Romans took to their ships and returned to Piraeus, their point of departure. Had the Roman numbers been sufficient for Chalcis to be held without the sacrifice of the defence of Athens, the start of the war would have been marked straight away by a momentous achievement, with the king being relieved of Chalcis and Euripus—for just as the pass of Thermopylae controls access to Greece by land, so too does the strait of Euripus by sea.

24. At this time Philip was at Demetrias, and here word was brought to him of the disaster that had befallen the allied city. The battle for Chalcis was lost, and it was too late for assistance; nevertheless, seeking revenge, his consolation prize, he immediately set off with 5,000 light infantry and 300 cavalry and headed at a rapid pace for Chalcis, convinced that the Romans could be caught there. He was frustrated in this hope; all he came to on his arrival was the ugly sight of the allied town half-demolished and still smoking, with few survivors, barely enough to bury those killed in the battle. Philip therefore crossed the Euripus by the bridge as swiftly as he had come and led his troops to Athens through Boeotia thinking that initiative like his enemy's would achieve a not dissimilar outcome. And indeed it would have done but for a scout—these are called 'day-runners' by the Greeks* because they cover huge distances in a day's run—who caught sight of the king's army from a watch-tower. He set off ahead of Philip and reached Athens in the middle of the night.

In Athens there was the same indolence and the same heedlessness that had let down Chalcis a few days earlier. The Athenian praetor* and Dioxippus, the commander of the unit of auxiliary mercenaries, both galvanized to action by the alarming report, called the men to the forum and ordered a trumpet-signal given from the citadel, so all would know that the enemy was at hand. At all points people ran to the gates and to the walls. A few hours later, but still some time before dawn, Philip approached the city, where he saw a large number of lights and heard the clamour of agitated men as one might expect in such an emergency. He halted his troops and ordered the column to pitch camp and rest. He had decided to employ force openly, his stratagem having achieved no success.

He made his approach on the side of the Dipylon, a gate more or less forming the main entrance to the city and considerably larger and wider than the other gates. Inside and outside it ran wide roads. Thus the townspeople could draw up a line of battle from the forum to the gate, while on the outside a road about a mile long which leads to the gymnasium of the Academy gave the enemy infantry and cavalry space to move freely. The Athenians, along with the garrison of Attalus and Dioxippus' unit, drew up their battle-line inside the gate and sallied forth by this road. When Philip saw this he thought he had the advantage of his enemy, that he was going †to satisfy himself† with the bloodbath he had long desired, for none of the Greek city-states was more detested by him. He urged his men to look at him as they fought and to be aware that the standards and battle-line should be concentrated just where the king was to be found. He then spurred on his horse towards the enemy, impelled as much by the promise of glory as by his anger, because the city-walls were already filled with an enormous crowd waiting for the show and he thought he would now be on display putting up a spectacular fight. He rode with a few of his cavalrymen in advance of his battle-line and into the thick of the enemy, inspiring simultaneously great fervour in his own men and great alarm in the foe. In person he followed up large numbers of the enemy whom he had himself wounded at close quarters or at long range, and whom he had driven back to the gate; and after inflicting yet further slaughter on the panicking Athenians in the narrow gateway, he still managed to achieve a safe retreat from this reckless enterprise because the men in the turrets of the gate held back their missiles for fear of hitting their own comrades who were interspersed with the enemy.

Since the Athenians then kept their men back within their walls, Philip sounded the retreat and encamped at Cynosarges, where there was a temple of Hercules and a gymnasium encircled by a wood. In fact, Cynosarges, the Lyceum, and anything else in the vicinity of the city of religious importance or aesthetic appeal were put to the torch, and even graves, and not just buildings, were torn down. Nothing within the divine or human compass survived the king's uncontrollable rage.

25. The following day the city-gates were at first closed, and then suddenly opened again on the arrival in the city of the garrison of Attalus from Aegina and the Romans from Piraeus. Philip therefore withdrew his camp some three miles from the city. He then headed for Eleusis, hoping to take with a surprise assault the temple, and the fort overlooking and surrounding it. He discovered, however, that their defences had been in no way overlooked and also that a fleet was coming with support from Piraeus, and so he abandoned this project and instead led his army to Megara and then straight on to Corinth. Hearing that there was a meeting of the Achaean League at Argos, he took the Achaeans by surprise by turning up at the actual session.

Their deliberations centred on war against Nabis, tyrant of Sparta. Nabis could see that with the transfer of command from Philopoemen* to Cycliadas, who was not in Philopoemen's class as a leader, the Achaeans had declined as a military power, and he had therefore recommended hostilities and was now conducting raids on his neighbours' agricultural lands and even menacing their cities as well. The League was considering the question of each city-state's contribution to a levy of troops to face this enemy, and Philip now undertook to relieve them of all concern with respect to Nabis and his Lacedaemonians. He would not only prevent raids on the territory of his allies, but he also promised to transfer the entire theatre of that frightful war to Laconia itself by immediately taking his forces there. This speech of Philip's found great favour with his audience. 'But', added the king, 'it is only fair that defence of your territory by my forces should not meanwhile leave my own territory bereft of protection. So, if you agree, just assemble an armed force strong enough to defend Oreus, Chalcis, and Corinth, so that I can attack Nabis and the Lacedaemonians feeling sure that my possessions are safe behind me.'

The motive behind such a generous commitment and the offer of help against the Spartans did not escape the Achaeans: the plan was to take the Achaeans of military age from the Peloponnese as hostages in order to embroil their nation in a war with Rome. The leader of the Achaeans, Cycliadas, saw no point in exposing this chicanery. He merely observed that Achaean law did not permit discussion of matters other than those for which the meeting had been convened. A decree was then passed concerning mobilization of an army against Nabis, and Cycliadas adjourned a meeting characterized by moral fortitude and independence of spirit, although till that day he had been regarded as one of the king's lackeys. Frustrated in his great hope, Philip conscripted a few volunteers and moved back to Corinth and then into Attic territory.

26. During the time that Philip was in Achaea, the king's lieutenant Philocles left Euboea with 2,000 Thracians and Macedonians in order to plunder Athenian territory, and crossed the pass of Cithaeron in the vicinity of Eleusis. From here he dispatched half the men to conduct raids at various points in the countryside while he himself covertly encamped with the rest in a location well suited for an ambush. The aim was to make a swift and unexpected attack

on the enemy while they were dispersed, if an attack should be made on his raiding parties from the fortress at Eleusis. Philocles' ambush did not fool the enemy, and so he recalled the men who had gone off to plunder, drew them up in battle-formation and set off to make an assault on the fort at Eleusis. Falling back from there with many wounded, he joined Philip who was now on his return journey from Achaea. An assault was also made on the same stronghold by the king himself, but some Roman ships arrived from Piraeus and a garrison was installed in the city, forcing Philip to abandon the project. Philip then split his forces, sending Philocles to Athens with part of them, and proceeding to Piraeus with the others. His plan was that while Philocles pinned down the Athenians within their city by approaching the walls and threatening to attack, he himself would have an opportunity of storming Piraeus, which would be left lightly guarded. However, the attack on Piraeus he found no easier than the earlier attack on Eleusis since he faced virtually the same defenders. Philip then abruptly led his force from Piraeus to Athens. Here the Athenian infantry and cavalry made a sudden charge through a narrow defile in the partially demolished walls that link Piraeus to Athens with their two arms,* driving back the king who abandoned his assault on the city. Dividing his forces with Philocles once more, he set off to plunder the countryside. Philip had made the object of his earlier marauding expedition the destruction of the tombs around the city; this time, to leave nothing inviolate, he ordered the demolition and burning of the temples of the gods that the people had consecrated in the country villages. And the territory of Attica, richly endowed with monuments of this kind, thanks both to ample resources of local marble and the talent of its craftsmen, provided fuel for Philip's wrath. Nor was he satisfied with destroying the temples themselves and toppling the statues—he even ordered that individual stones be shattered so that they not provide imposing ruins if left whole. And when, rather than sating his fury, he ran out of material on which to vent it, he left the territory of his enemies for Boeotia, and performed no further action worthy of note in Greece.

27. At this time the consul Sulpicius was encamped on the banks of the River Apsus, between Apollonia and Dyrrachium. He summoned to the camp his legate Lucius Apustius and dispatched him with a portion of his troops to conduct raids on enemy territory. Apustius ravaged the outlying areas of Macedonia, captured the

fortresses of Corrhagus, Gerrunium, and Orgessus with his first assault and then came to Antipatrea, a town situated in a narrow gorge. His first approach was to summon the town's leading citizens to a meeting at which he tried to entice them to put themselves under Roman protection; but when confidence in the size, fortifications, and position of their town led them to reject his overtures, Apustius launched an attack and took the place by armed force. He put to death men of military age and awarded his soldiers all the booty; then he tore down the walls and burned the town. Fear of similar treatment prompted the strong and well-fortified town of Codrion to surrender to the Romans without a fight. Apustius left a garrison in Codrion and went on to storm Cnidus, its name better known— thanks to the other Cnidus in Asia—than the town itself. While the legate was returning to the consul with a substantial booty and was fording a river he was attacked from the rear by an officer of the king, one Athenagoras, who threw the end of the column into disarray. On hearing the shouts and panic of the men, the Roman legate swiftly galloped back and made them wheel round. Then, setting the baggage in the centre, he deployed the line of battle. The king's troops failed to stem the attack of the Roman soldiers, and many were killed, with more taken prisoner. The legate brought back the army to his consul unscathed and was immediately sent back to the fleet.

28. Since the war had begun with a relatively successful expedition, chieftains and leading members of the tribes bordering Macedonia came to the Roman camp: Pleuratus, son of Scerdilaedus; King Amynander of the Athamanians; and, from the Dardanians, Bato, son of Longarus (Longarus had already fought a war of his own against Demetrius, the father of Philip). When these pledged support, the consul replied that he would avail himself of the assistance of the Dardanians and Pleuratus when the time came to lead his army into Macedonia; and to Amynander he assigned the responsibility of inciting the Aetolians to the war. To ambassadors from Attalus, who had also arrived at this time, he gave the order that their king should await the Roman fleet at Aegina, where he had his winter-quarters; and after joining the fleet he should apply pressure on Philip by renewing naval operations. The people of Rhodes were also sent a delegation urging them to do their part in the war.

Nor was Philip, now arrived in Macedonia, any less energetic in his preparations for war. Although his son Perseus was just a boy,

Philip sent him with a portion of his forces to seize the passes into Pelagonia, assigning members of his 'Friends'* to hold his youth in check. He destroyed Sciathus and Peparethus, towns of some prominence, so they should not become a source of plunder and gain for the enemy fleet, and he sent a deputation to the Aetolians in case this fractious people changed its loyalties with the coming of the Romans.

29. The council of the Aetolians, which they call 'Panaetolian',* was due to meet on its appointed day, and delegates of the king made special haste to attend the meeting. A Roman envoy, Lucius Furius Purpureo, also came, sent by the consul, and in addition there was a delegation to the council from the Athenians. The Macedonians, with whom the Aetolians had made their most recent treaty, were the first to be heard. They stated that since there had been no fresh developments they had no fresh proposals. They said that the Aetolians had negotiated a peace with Philip, after experiencing the futility of an alliance with Rome, and they had the same reasons for standing by the treaty now that it had been concluded.

'Or do you prefer to follow the model of Roman licence—or should I call it caprice?' asked one of the Macedonian representatives. 'The reply they ordered to be given to your embassy in Rome was "Aetolians, why bother coming to us now after negotiating peace with Philip without consulting us?" And now those same people are asking you to join them in making war on Philip! Earlier they made out that it was for you and in your interests that they took up arms against him—and now they will not let you be at peace with him! They first crossed to Sicily to help Messana; the second time it was to liberate Syracuse when it was under attack from Carthage. These days Messana, Syracuse, and the whole of Sicily are a Roman possession which they have made into a tribute-paying province subject to their axes and rods.* You are holding this meeting at Naupactus under your own rules and presided over by magistrates whom you have elected; and here you are going to choose freely whomsoever you wish to have as ally or enemy, and whether you have war or peace will be your decision. But of course it is the same for the city-states of Sicily—for them too a meeting is called, at Syracuse or at Messana or at Lilybaeum. A Roman praetor holds court. At his command the people are called on to assemble; and they see him on his raised dais handing down imperious judgments, his lictors thronging about him, their rods threatening backs, their axes threatening necks! And every year they are given by lot a different master. They should not, in fact cannot, be surprised at this, not when they see cities in Italy subjected to the same authority—Rhegium, Tarentum, and Capua, not to mention those neighbouring cities whose destruction led to the growth of Rome. True, Capua has survived, necropolis and funerary monument of the people of Campania, its people buried or driven into exile; it is a crippled city, with no senate, no commoners, no magistrates, a bizarre phenomenon whose continued inhabitation is more cruel than its destruction would have been.

'If these territories are occupied by foreigners who are separated from us more by language, culture, and legal systems than by mere distance over land and sea, it is folly to expect anything to remain in the same state. You think Philip's rule some sort of infringement of your liberty; but even when he was, through your own fault, on terms of hostility with you, he asked for nothing from you except peace, and today his only wish is that you stand by the peace treaty which you concluded with him.

'Make these foreign legions feel at home in these lands and accept their yoke! Too late and to no avail will you ask for Philip as your ally when you have a Roman master. Aetolians, Acarnanians, Macedonians, peoples sharing a common language, are driven apart and united by trivial and transient issues; but all Greeks are ever, and ever will be, at war with foreigners, with barbarians. For these are our enemies by nature, which is timeless, not because of disputes which change from one day to another.

'But my speech will end where it began. In this very same spot three years ago, the very same men, namely yourselves, decided on a peace-treaty with the very same Philip, and the people who objected to that treaty were the very same Romans who now wish to disrupt that peace which we negotiated and concluded. With regard to those negotiations, Fortune has brought about no change, and I do not see why you should make any change yourselves.'

30. After the Macedonians, the Athenians were brought forward to speak, with the assent, and in fact at the behest, of the Romans—the Athenians had suffered terrible indignities at Philip's hands and could more legitimately denounce the king's cruelty and ruthlessness. They deplored the destruction and pitiable ravaging of their fields, adding that their complaints were not over their having

suffered the treatment meted out to an enemy by an enemy. For, they said, there were certain conventions in warfare that are legitimately imposed and, conversely, endured by the two sides: the burning of crops; the demolition of buildings; booty taken in the form of people and animals. All of this constitutes a grim experience for the victim but is not unethical. No, what they were complaining about was that the man who was calling the Romans 'foreigners' and 'barbarians' had so desecrated all human and divine laws as to wage an impious war against the gods of the underworld on his first marauding expedition, and against the gods in heaven above on his second. All the tombs and funerary monuments in their territory had been torn down, the shades of all the buried laid bare, the bones of none left with a covering of earth. They had once had shrines, they said, consecrated in the past in the little communities and villages by their forefathers living in the country districts and not left neglected by them even when they were incorporated in a single city. Philip had made the rounds of all these temples, attacking them with his fires; and half-burned, dismembered statues of the gods now lay amongst the shattered temple doors. And what he had made of the land of Attica, once cultivated and affluent, that is what Philip would make of Aetolia and all of Greece if given the opportunity. Their city, too, would have been in an equally hideous condition, they said, but for Roman aid. For Philip had made the same criminal attacks on the city's patron deities and on Minerva, guardian of the acropolis; and the same on the temple of Ceres in Eleusis and on Jupiter and Minerva in Piraeus. He was, however, driven back by armed might not only from the temples of those gods but even from the city walls, and he had then vented his wrath on those shrines whose sole protection lay in the awe they inspired. So, concluded the Athenians, they were begging and pleading with the Aetolians to have pity on them and to undertake the war, in which the immortal gods would be their leaders and, after them, the Romans, second in power to the gods alone.

31. After this the Roman ambassador spoke as follows:

'The whole line of what I had to say has now been revised, initially by the Macedonians and then by the Athenians. The Macedonians first. I came here to protest against the wrongs inflicted by Philip on so many cities allied to us, but by actually denouncing the Romans these men have made me consider self-defence more important than laying charges against him. And in the light of the Athenian account of Philip's nefarious and ruthless crimes against the gods of heaven and the underworld, what further criticism of him have they left me or anyone else? Bear in mind that the very same protests are voiced by the peoples of Cios, Abydus, Aenus, Maronea, Thasos, Paros, Samos, Larisa, and, here in Achaea, Messene; and that they are all the more severe and bitter in these cases because in them he had wider scope to inflict damage.

'As for the allegations levelled against us by Philip, I admit there can be no defence—unless the exploits at issue actually redound to our credit. Rhegium, Capua, and Syracuse were the basis of his criticisms. Rhegium first. In the war with Pyrrhus the people of Rhegium pleaded with us to send them assistance, but the legion sent to garrison the town illicitly took possession of the city* it had been sent to defend. Did we condone this crime? Or did we rather attack the offending legion and bring it back under our control, forcing it to atone to our allies with floggings and executions and then restoring to the people of Rhegium their city, their lands, and all their possessions along with their independence and legal system? Syracuse suffered under foreign tyrants,* making her lot all the more unbearable. We brought assistance and were well nigh exhausted by a three-year land- and sea-offensive* on the city, which was very well fortified. But when the Syracusans themselves expressed a preference for serving their tyrants to being captured by us, we restored their city to them, captured and liberated by the same armed intervention.

'We do not deny that Sicily is our province, and that the city-states on it which sided with the Carthaginians and made war on us in sympathy with them now pay tribute and taxes to us. Quite the reverse, in fact—we want this made known to you, and the whole world as well, that each people's lot is dependent on its services to us. Are we to feel remorse over our punishment of the Campanians, about which they cannot even complain themselves? We had, on their behalf, been at war with the Samnites for almost seventy years,* suffering heavy casualties in the process; and we had forged links with them first by a treaty, subsequently by intermarriage and family ties, and finally by granting them citizenship. Then, in our time of difficulty, they became the first of all the Italian peoples to defect to Hannibal, shamefully murdering our garrison. After this, angry at finding themselves besieged by us, they sent Hannibal to attack Rome. If their very city no longer survived or not a single man of them, could anyone feel indignation, believing that the punishment was harsher than they deserved? More of them actually committed suicide from a guilty conscience than were put to death by us. The rest we deprived of their town and their fields, but not without granting them some land and a place to live and leaving unharmed the city, which had committed no offence, so that anyone seeing it today would find there not a trace of the assault and capture.

'But why mention Capua when we granted Carthage peace and independence after we conquered it? What constitutes a greater danger for us is that by being too ready to forgive those we have vanquished we may by this very tolerance of ours encourage more people to try the fortunes of war against us!

'Let these points suffice in defence of ourselves and against Philip—whose record you, being closer to Macedonia, know better than we: his extermination of family members,* his massacre of kinsfolk and friends, his lust almost more inhuman than his viciousness. As for you, Aetolians, we undertook a war against Philip on your account, and you made peace with him without consulting us. You might perhaps claim that when we were preoccupied with the Punic War you were intimidated into accepting peace-terms from him since he was then more powerful; and that we, encumbered with other more urgent matters, let drop the war which you had abandoned. Now, however, thanks to heaven's favour, we have concluded the Punic War and brought all our might to bear on Macedonia; and you have been offered the lucky opportunity of returning to friendship and alliance with us—unless you prefer perishing with Philip to winning with the Romans.'

32. After this speech from the Roman ambassador the support of the entire assembly inclined towards the Romans. Then the Aetolian praetor,* Damocritus—who was rumoured to have been bribed by the king—without expressing agreement with either side stated that nothing was so prejudicial to decision-making in matters of importance as haste. Regret followed quickly, he said, but came too late and to no avail, since decisions hastily and prematurely reached could not be revoked or reformulated afresh. Even now, he continued, a date could be fixed for discussion of this issue, reflection on which, he personally believed, should be given time to mature.

Their rules stipulated that war and peace could be discussed only in the Panaetolian and Pylaic* councils, and they should therefore decree forthwith that their praetor should duly convene the council when he wished to discuss the matter of war and peace, with all proposals and decrees on that occasion being regarded as legal and binding no less than if these had been debated in the Panaetolian or Pylaic council. The issue was accordingly left up in the air and the delegates dismissed, with Damocritus claiming that their decision was an excellent one for their people since they would now incline towards a treaty with whichever side had the better fortune in the field of battle. Such were the proceedings in the council of the Aetolians.

33. Philip was tireless in his preparations for war on land and sea. He brought together his naval forces at Demetrias in Thessaly and, thinking that Attalus and the Roman fleet would move from Aegina at the start of spring, put his fleet and the coastline under the command of Heraclides, the man whom he had previously held in this position, while he himself proceeded to assemble the land-forces. He believed that he had now taken from the Romans two important sources of assistance, the Aetolians on the one hand and the Dardanians on the other, the passes to Pelagonia having been blocked by his son Perseus.*

As for the consul, by now he was actually at war, not just preparing for it: he was leading his army through the territory of the Dassaretii, taking with him intact the grain that he had brought out of his winter quarters since the countryside supplied enough to meet his men's needs. Towns and villages surrendered to him, some of their own volition, others through fear; some were taken by storm, some were found deserted, the natives seeking refuge in the nearby mountains. At Lyncus, Sulpicius established a stationary camp near the River Bevus, and from here sent out foraging parties around the granaries of the Dassaretii. Although Philip could see the general chaos in the area and the sheer panic in the local population, he had little idea of the direction taken by the consul and he sent out a squadron of cavalry to find out the path followed by his enemy. The consul was equally at a loss—he knew the king had moved from his winter quarters but was unaware of the region for which he had headed—and he, too, had sent out some cavalry to reconnoitre. After a long period of aimless wandering in the territory of the Dassaretii, these two squadrons, approaching from opposite directions, finally converged on the same road. Neither group was insensible to the approach of its enemies, as the commotion of men and horses could be heard at a distance. They had therefore prepared their mounts and their weapons before coming into sight of each other, and at the first glimpse of the enemy the charge was immediate. As it transpired, they were a match for each other both in numbers and in valour, being the élite of both sides, and they fought for several hours on even terms. It was the exhaustion of fighters and horses that broke off the fight, the victory still undecided. Forty cavalrymen fell on the Macedonian side, thirty-five on the Roman. And after that the Macedonians had no more intelligence to report to the king, nor the Romans to the consul, on the whereabouts of the enemy camp. This was ascertained through deserters who, in all wars, are furnished for the gathering of intelligence on the enemy by their unreliable character.

34. Philip thought that seeing to the funerals of the cavalrymen who had fallen in this operation would to some extent win his men's affection and also make them more ready to face danger for him, and he therefore had the dead brought into the camp so that the funeral ceremony could be seen by the whole army. Nothing is so unreliable or unpredictable as crowd-mentality. What the king thought would make them more willing to face all manner of combat instead afflicted them with fear and misgiving.* They had in their frequent clashes with the Greeks and Illyrians seen the wounds produced by spears, arrows, and, on rare occasions, by lances; but now they saw bodies dismembered by the Spanish sword, arms lopped off complete with the shoulder, heads separated from bodies with the neck sliced right through, intestines laid bare, and other repulsive wounds, and there was widespread consternation as they began to comprehend the nature of the weapons and the kind of men they had to face.* The king himself, never yet having met the Romans in pitched battle, was also panic-stricken. He therefore recalled his son and the troops stationed at the defiles of Pelagonia to bolster his own forces with them, and thereby opened a path into Macedonia for Pleuratus and the Dardanians. With 20,000 infantry and 2,000 cavalry, and using deserters as guides, Philip himself set off to meet the enemy. He fortified with a ditch and a rampart a hillock near Ataeum, not much more than a mile from the Roman camp; and they say that as he looked down on the Roman camp below him he was full of

wonder both at its overall appearance and at the arrangement of its
various units, with the tents in rows separated by streets at regular
intervals. Nobody, he is said to have remarked, could think that to be
a camp belonging to barbarians.* Consul and king kept their men
within their fortifications for two days, each waiting for the other to
make a move; on the third the Roman led out his entire force for
combat.

35. Afraid of taking a quick chance on an engagement with all his
forces, the king sent out 400 Tralles (an Illyrian tribe, as I have noted
elsewhere*) and 300 Cretans to harass the enemy cavalry, adding to
this infantry detachment an equal number of cavalry under the
command of one of his courtiers,* Athenagoras. The Romans, whose
line was little more than half a mile distant, sent out skirmishers and
about two cavalry squadrons so as to have numerical parity with the
enemy in cavalry and infantry. The king's men believed the manner
of fighting would be that to which they had been accustomed: the
cavalry advancing and retreating by turns, at one moment employing
their weapons and at the next falling back; the speed of the Illyrians
proving effective for sallies and sudden charges; the Cretans firing
arrows on an enemy making a disordered advance. What ruined this
strategy for the fight was the Roman onslaught, as relentless as it was
savage. It was as if they were engaging with their entire battle-line;
for having thrown their javelins the skirmishers went into close combat with the sword, and the cavalry, after their initial thrust against
the enemy, halted their steeds and joined the fray, either from their
horses, or else by dismounting and linking up with the infantry. As a
result the king's cavalryman, lacking experience in stationary fighting, proved no match for the Roman horseman, nor his skirmisher
(who ranged over the battlefield virtually devoid of any kind of
armour) for the Roman light-armed soldier with his sword and
shield, equally well equipped for defending himself and attacking his
enemy. Unable to keep up the fight, they fled back to their camp with
only their speed to protect them.

36. One day passed and the king was now ready to enter the fight
with all his cavalry and all his light infantry. He had during the
night set in ambush in a suitable location between the two camps
some soldiers with short shields whom they call peltasts,* giving
Athenagoras and the cavalry the order to press their advantage if
things were going well in the pitched battle, but otherwise to retreat

little by little and draw the enemy to where the ambush lay. The cavalry did actually retreat, but the commanders of the unit with short shields did not wait long enough for the signal, and by urging their men to premature action they let slip the opportunity of bringing the operation to a successful conclusion. The Roman went back to camp, victor in the pitched battle and also unscathed by the ambush.

The following day the consul went into battle with all his forces, setting his elephants before the front ranks. This was the first occasion on which the Romans had availed themselves of this type of support—they possessed a number that they had captured during the Punic War.* When the consul saw his adversary cowering within his palisade, he advanced into the hills and even up to the palisade itself, taunting him with cowardice. Not even after that was he given the opportunity to engage, and since foraging would be dangerous if conducted from a base so close to his enemy (whose cavalry was likely to mount sudden attacks on his men while they were dispersed in the fields), he moved his camp some eight miles to a place called Otolobus so that the distance between the two armies would enable him to forage with greater security. While the Romans gathered provisions in a nearby field, the king at first kept his men within his defence-works so that his enemy's carelessness might increase along with his overconfidence. When Philip saw them dispersed, he briskly marched out with all his cavalry and Cretan auxiliaries, at a pace that permitted the swiftest of his infantrymen to keep up with the cavalry, and occupied a position between the Roman camp and the foragers. Then, splitting his troops, he sent one half to hunt down the straggling foragers, with orders to leave none alive, while he himself remained behind with the rest and blockaded the roads by which he thought the Romans would return to camp. Everywhere now the scene was one of slaughter and flight. No word of the débâcle had as yet reached the Roman camp because the fleeing Romans kept running into the king's road-blocks, and more were actually dispatched by the Macedonians blockading the roads than by the soldiers sent out to kill them. Eventually a number of them slipped between the enemy blockades, and in their terror brought to the camp panic rather than reliable news.

37. Ordering his cavalry to give assistance wherever they could to any troops under pressure, the consul then led his legions from camp

and marched in square-formation towards the enemy. Some of the cavalry wandered sporadically through the countryside, misled by cries that arose from different spots, while others met the enemy head-on. Fighting broke out simultaneously at a number of points, but it was the king's blockading detachment which provided the fiercest contest; for from the point of view of sheer numbers involved, both cavalry and infantry, it approximated to a regular army, and since it had been blockading the central road most of the Romans clashed with it. What also gave the Macedonians an advantage was the fact that their king was there in person to encourage them, and their Cretan auxiliary troops inflicted unexpected wounds on many of the Romans because they were fighting as a close-ordered and well-prepared group against a disorganized and scattered enemy. Had they but shown some restraint in their pursuit, their success would have gone beyond a glorious victory in that particular engagement to encompass the entire campaign. As it was, hungry for the kill, they advanced too recklessly and ran up against the Roman cohorts who were pushing forward with their tribunes. The moment they saw the standards of their comrades, the retreating Roman cavalry wheeled about their steeds to face the now-disordered foe, and in an instant the fortunes of the battle changed, with the erstwhile pursuers now turning tail. Many fell in the hand-to-hand fighting, many as they fled. Nor did they die by the sword alone—some were thrown into marshes to be swallowed up by the deep mud, along with their horses. The king, too, faced danger: his wounded horse stumbled, flinging him headlong to the ground, and he was within an inch of being crushed to death where he lay. His salvation was a cavalryman who swiftly dismounted and lifted the terror-stricken king onto his own horse. The man himself, now on foot, was unable to keep up with the retreating cavalry and perished, run through by the enemy forces who rushed to the scene when the king fell. The king, fleeing in panic, rode about the marshes on paths or cross-country, finally arriving in his camp, where most had already lost hope that he would come through alive. Two hundred Macedonian horsemen lost their lives in that engagement, and about a hundred were taken prisoner. Some eighty horses with fine harnesses were taken off by the Romans, and arms were also removed as spoils of war.

38. There were some people who reproached the king with

recklessness and the consul with lack of initiative on that day. Philip, they said, should have remained inactive: with the neighbouring countryside entirely depleted he knew that the Romans would in just a few days face a critical shortage of provisions. On the other side, the consul should have led his men to the enemy camp immediately after routing their cavalry and light infantry and almost taking the king himself prisoner—in their panic the enemy were unlikely to stand their ground and they could have been finished off in no time. But, as usual, this was a case of something being easier said than done. Had the king engaged with all his infantry as well as his cavalry, then it is possible that in the mêlée—with the Macedonians, beaten and panic-stricken, all seeking refuge within the palisade after the battle, and then immediately running from the camp before an enemy that was clambering over their defence-works—he could have been divested of his camp. But since the infantry remained intact within the camp, and sentinels and pickets were posted at the gates, what could the consul have achieved apart from duplicating the recklessness of the king who shortly before had made a disordered pursuit of the panic-stricken Roman cavalry? There could likewise have been no criticism of the king's original strategy of attacking the foragers when they were dispersed through the fields, had he but observed moderation following his success in the battle. Furthermore, this tempting of providence on Philip's part also becomes less puzzling in light of the report that was abroad that Pleuratus and the Dardanians had by this time set off from home with an enormous force and invaded Macedonia. Had Philip been cut off by these forces, one could well have believed that the Roman commander would prevail without taking any action.

Accordingly, after two cavalry engagements had gone against him, Philip thought that remaining in the same camp was by far the more dangerous alternative. Wishing therefore to withdraw and slip away without his enemy noticing, he sent a herald at sunset to the consul to request a truce for the burial of the cavalrymen. Then, giving his enemy the slip, he moved off at the second watch, his column marching in silence, leaving many fires burning throughout the camp.

39. The consul was taking refreshment when word was brought of the herald's coming and his reason for doing so. He replied only that the herald would be allowed to meet with him the next morning, and this gave Philip just what he had wanted, namely that night and part of the following day to cover some ground. He headed for the mountains, a route which he knew the Romans would not take with their heavily armed column. At dawn the consul granted the truce, dismissed the herald and shortly afterwards realized that the enemy had departed. Not knowing where to direct his pursuit he passed several days in the same camp gathering supplies. He then made for Stuberra, and brought in from Pelagonia the grain that was standing in the fields. From there he advanced to Pluinna, still having received no intelligence on the direction taken by the enemy.

Philip had first established his camp near Bruanium; and setting out from there by country roads he struck sudden panic in his enemy, prompting the Romans to move from Pluinna and pitch camp at the River Osphagus. The king also made his camp close to here, constructing a palisade on the banks of a stream the local people call the Erigonus. Confident that the Romans would make for Eordaea, he then moved forward to seize the pass so as to prevent his enemy from penetrating the narrow gorge that formed the entrance to it. He hurriedly fortified the spot by various methods according to the requirements of the terrain or the availability of materials—a rampart here, a ditch there, a pile of stones to serve as a wall or trees as a barrier—and by blocking off every passage with these contrivances he rendered impassable, so he thought, a road which was already difficult by its very nature.

There was extensive woodland around about, and this particularly bothered the Macedonian phalanx* whose effectiveness depended entirely on the use of very long spears to maintain a kind of barrier before the shields—and that required open ground. The Thracians, too, were disadvantaged by their lances,* which also were extremely long, amongst the branches which impeded them at every turn. The Cretan division alone retained its capability, but even that was handicapped. Facing attack, it could shoot arrows at horses and riders who were without protection, but before Roman shields it lacked the power to penetrate and had no target that was exposed. And so, realizing the futility of this type of weapon, the Cretans proceeded to pelt the enemy with the stones that were lying about throughout the valley. Striking the shields (but producing more noise than damage) these held back the advancing Romans for a while. Then, disregarding these missiles, too, some of the Romans made a tortoise-formation* and attacked the enemy head-on. Others made a short deviation to the hill-top, driving the panic-stricken Macedonians from their entrenchments and guard-posts and, flight being difficult amid the obstructions of the terrain, killing most of them.

40. The pass was thus taken with less of a struggle than the Romans had expected and they reached Eordaea. After widespread devastation of farmland here, the consul withdrew to Elimia. Sulpicius next attacked Orestis and marched against the town of Celetrum. This is situated on a peninsula, its walls surrounded by a lake and access from the mainland afforded only by a narrow cause-way. The townspeople, relying on their position, initially shut their gates and rejected the call to surrender; then, seeing the standards brought up, the troops advancing to the gate in tortoise-formation and the causeway blocked by the enemy column, they surrendered in alarm rather than risk a battle. From Celetrum the consul advanced against the Dassaretii and stormed the city of Pelion. He removed from the latter the slaves, along with the rest of the plunder, but let the free townspeople off without ransom. He restored to them their town after installing a strong garrison, for the city was well posi-tioned for conducting incursions into Macedonia. After traversing the countryside of the enemy, the consul now led his troops back to Apollonia—the starting-point of his campaign—in pacified territory.

Philip's attention had been distracted by the Aetolians, the Atha-manians, the Dardanians, and all the wars suddenly breaking out in different places. The Dardanians were already withdrawing from Macedonia, and against them Philip sent Athenagoras at the head of some light infantry and most of the cavalry. Athenagoras had orders to put pressure on the tail-end of the retreating Dardanians and by wearing down their rearguard to make them reluctant to move their troops from home in future. As for the Aetolians, Damocritus, the same praetor who had been responsible for the delay in the declara-tion of war at Naupactus, had incited them to arms at the next meeting of their council. This happened after the news arrived of the cavalry engagement at Otolobus and following the invasion of Mac-edonia by the Dardanians and Pleuratus along with the Illyrians and, in addition, following the arrival at Oreus of the Roman fleet, with the threat of a naval blockade on Macedonia which was already surrounded by so many peoples.

41. These were the factors that had brought Damocritus and the Aetolians back to the Romans. Now, joined by Amynander, king of the Athamanians, they set off and laid siege to Cercinium. The townspeople had shut their gates, though whether they had done so under duress or of their own volition (for they had a royal garrison in town) is unclear. At all events, within a few days, Cercinium was taken and put to the torch; and the survivors of this great catastrophe, free and slave, were hauled off with the rest of the booty. Fear of similar treatment drove all who lived around the Marsh of Boebe to abandon their homes and head for the hills; but, plunder being in short supply, the Aetolians turned aside from the area and proceeded to march on Perrhaebia. Here they stormed and shamefully pillaged Chyretiae, but they accepted the surrender of the inhabitants of Malloea and made them allies.

From Perrhaebia Amynander suggested they make for Gomphi; Athamania lies close to this town and it appeared that it could be taken without much of a fight. The Aetolians headed for the plains of Thessaly, which provided rich opportunities for plunder, and they were followed by Amynander, though he did not approve of the Aetolians' disorganized pillaging or of their randomly pitching camp wherever they happened to be, with no attention paid to security. He feared that their recklessness and negligence might also bring disaster on himself and his men and, when he saw them establishing a camp in the open plains at a point below the city of Pharcadon, he himself seized a hillock a little more than a mile away which even a modest level of reinforcement rendered secure. The Aetolians appeared to be scarcely aware that they were in enemy territory—apart from the fact that they were engaged in looting. Some were drifting about aimlessly and only partially armed, others removed all distinction between day and night as they slept and drank in camp, with no sentries on duty. Philip fell upon them unawares. When news of his approach was brought by men fleeing in terror from the fields, Damocritus and the other officers panicked—it happened to be midday, a time at which most of the men were lying about sleeping and heavy from eating. They tried to rouse one another, telling each other to take up their weapons and sending some of their number to recall the men who were wandering about pillaging in the fields. So great was the panic that some of the horsemen left camp without their swords, and most without their cuirasses. Hurriedly led out in this way, they barely numbered 600, cavalry and infantry altogether, and they ran into the king's cavalry which surpassed them in numbers, weaponry and spirit. The Aetolians were routed with the first charge and they headed back to camp in ignominious flight after barely a taste of battle. Death or capture awaited those cut off from the retreating column by the Macedonian cavalry.

42. As his men were now approaching the enemy defence-works, Philip ordered the retreat to be sounded; for horses and men were exhausted, less by the battle than by the length and, at the same time, the rapid pace of the march. He therefore told his men to fetch water and take food, the cavalry by squadron and the light infantry one maniple* after the other. Some he kept on sentry-duty under arms as he awaited the infantry column which had been brought along at a slower pace because of the weight of its weaponry. When the column arrived, the infantry too were ordered to fix their standards in the ground, set their weapons before themselves, and take a hurried meal, a maximum of two or three men per maniple being sent for water. In the meantime the cavalry and light-armed troops stood drawn up and ready for action in the event of any movement on the enemy's part.

As for the Aetolians, even the large numbers scattered through the countryside had by this time returned to camp, and they now deployed armed men around the camp gates and the rampart to protect their defences, all the while casting fearless glances at their foes, currently inactive, from their position of safety. When the Macedonian forces advanced and their men began to approach the rampart prepared and drawn up for battle, they all suddenly abandoned their posts and fled through the back of the camp to the Athamanian camp on the hillock. Many Aetolians were again captured or cut down in this terror-stricken flight. Had there been sufficient daylight left, Philip had no doubt that he could have taken their camp from the Athamanians; but as it was the day had been used up in combat and then in pillaging the Aetolian camp, and so he took up a position beneath the hillock on an adjacent plain, with the intention of attacking the enemy at first light the following day. The Aetolians, however, prey to the same panic which had prompted them to abandon their camp, scattered and fled that night. Amynander provided them with the greatest assistance; for it was under his leadership that the Athamanians who knew the roads led them back into Aetolia over the mountain tops on tracks unknown to the enemy giving them chase. In their disordered flight some few wandered by mistake into the path of the Macedonian cavalry, sent out at daybreak by Philip to hound the enemy column as soon as he saw the hillock deserted.

43. During this same period the king's officer, Athenagoras, had also overtaken the Dardanians as they were falling back on their own lands. At first he threw the rearguard into disarray; then the Dardanians wheeled round and deployed their battle-line, after which a regular, but inconclusive, pitched battle was fought. When the Dardanians began to advance once more, the king's forces used their cavalry and light infantry to harass them—the Dardanians having no such auxiliary troops and being also encumbered by unwieldy weapons. The terrain also favoured the Macedonians. Very few Dardanians actually lost their lives, more suffered wounds and none was captured, because Dardanians do not recklessly break formation but close ranks both to fight and to retreat.

So it was that Philip had brought to heel two nations by his timely campaigns; and by the energy of his initiative, not just because things turned out well, he had made good the losses sustained in the war with Rome. Then the number of Aetolian enemies facing him was reduced by a fortuitous occurrence. A leading Aetolian, Scopas, had been sent from Alexandria by Ptolemy with a large quantity of gold, and he had hired and transported back to Egypt 6,000 infantry and 500 cavalry. In fact, he would have left behind not a single Aetolian of military age had it not been for Damocritus. The latter had cautioned them about the war that threatened and also about the depopulation they faced in future, and by his strictures had kept some of his younger countrymen at home, though whether he did this from patriotism or to oppose Scopas, from whom he had received insufficient bribes, is debatable.

44. Such were the land-operations conducted by the Romans and Philip that summer. At the start of the same summer the fleet set out from Corcyra under the command of the legate Lucius Apustius. After rounding Malea it joined Attalus off Scyllaeum in the territory of Hermione. It was at this point that the city-state of Athens, in anticipation of the assistance that was at hand, fully indulged the hatred for Philip which it had long kept under control from fear. In Athens, rabble-rousing tongues are never in short supply. This is a phenomenon nurtured by the support of the mob in all free city-states, but especially in Athens where rhetoric is particularly influential. The Athenians immediately formulated a proposal, which the

commons ratified, that all statues and representations of Philip—
their inscriptions too—be removed and destroyed, along with those
of all his ancestors, male and female. They also decreed that the
feast-days, religious rites and priesthoods established to honour
Philip himself or his ancestors be deprived of their religious standing; that a curse be put on the places in which any monument or
inscription had been set up in his honour and that in future no
decision should be made to erect or dedicate in those places anything
which should, according to religion, be erected or dedicated in an
unpolluted place; and that whenever the public priests offered
prayers for the people of Athens and their allies, armies, and fleets,
they should on each occasion also curse and execrate Philip, his children, his kingdom, his land- and sea-forces, and the entire Macedonian race and nation. As an appendix to the decree it was stated that
the Athenian people would ratify in its entirety any proposal apt to
bring discredit and censure to Philip, whereas the slaying of any
person whose words or deeds worked against Philip's discredit, or to
promote his reputation, would be considered justifiable homicide.
A final rider was that all decrees enacted in the past against the
Pisistratids* should remain in force in Philip's case. Indeed, the
Athenians were now waging war against Philip with the weapons
of letters and words, wherein lies their only strength.

45. From Hermione, Attalus and the Romans had first made for
Piraeus. They stayed there a few days and sailed from Piraeus to
Andros after the Athenians had loaded them with decrees as excessive in tributes to the allies as the earlier ones had been in vitriol
towards the enemy. They came to anchor in the port called Gaurion,
and from here sent men to assess the mood of the townspeople, to see
whether they would prefer to surrender their city voluntarily to
facing armed force. The townspeople replied that the citadel was
occupied by a garrison of the king and that they had no control over
their own fate. Attalus and the Roman legate thereupon set ashore
their troops and all equipment necessary for an assault on a city and
moved up to the town from opposite directions. The terror of the
Greeks was considerably increased by the sight of Roman weaponry
and standards, which they had never seen before, and by the spirit of
the fighting men who approached their walls with such alacrity.
There was a sudden flight to the acropolis and the enemy occupied
the town. They held out in the acropolis for two days, more confident

in their position than their weapons, but on the third day the citizens and the garrison reached an agreement with the enemy that they be transported to Delium in Boeotia with one piece of clothing each. They then surrendered the city and acropolis and these were awarded to Attalus by the Romans, who carted off for themselves the spoils and art-works of the city. Not to possess a deserted isle, Attalus persuaded virtually all the Macedonians and some of the Andrians to remain behind. Subsequently, those who had crossed to Delium under the terms of the treaty were also enticed back by promises made by the king, their yearning for their homeland also making it easier for them to feel confidence in him.

From Andros the allies crossed to Cythnus. Here they wasted several days in an assault on the city, eventually abandoning the attempt because it was scarcely worth the trouble. At Prasiae on the Attic mainland twenty light craft* from Issa joined the Roman fleet, and these were dispatched to conduct raids on the territory of the people of Carystus. The rest of the fleet docked at the famous Euboean port of Geraestus to await the return of the Issaei from Carystus. Then they all put out to sea together and, passing in mid-voyage the island of Scyrus, came to Icus. They were detained there for a few days by a furious north wind, but as soon as good weather arrived they crossed to Sciathus, where the city had been recently destroyed and pillaged by Philip. The soldiers roamed through the fields and brought back to the ships grain and whatever else might serve for provisions; but there was no booty, nor had the Greeks here deserved to have their goods plundered. Then, en route for Cassandrea, they headed first for Mendaeum, a coastal village of that city. Next, after rounding the headland, they wanted to bring the fleet right up to the city walls, but a violent storm arose during which they were almost sunk by the waves. Scattered, and with most of their tackle lost, they sought refuge on land.

The storm at sea also served as an omen for their performance on land. After reuniting the ships and setting the troops ashore, the allies assaulted the town, only to be driven back with heavy casualties (the king had a strong garrison there); and after the failure of the operation they withdrew and crossed to Canastraeum in Pallene. From here they rounded the promontory of Torona and set a course for Acanthus. Here they first raided the countryside, and then took the city by storm and pillaged it. Without proceeding further, their ships now being weighed down with booty, they headed back first to Sciathus, their point of departure, and from Sciathus to Euboea.

46. Leaving the fleet in Euboea the allies entered the Malian gulf with ten light vessels in order to discuss strategy for the war with the Aetolians. The head of the delegation that came to Heraclea to formulate plans in concert with the king and the Roman legate was the Aetolian Pyrrhias. Attalus was asked <to supply> 1,000 soldiers according to the terms of the treaty—for this was the number he had been supposed to furnish to those fighting against Philip. The Aetolians were denied their request on the grounds that they had earlier refused to make a plundering excursion into Macedonia at a moment when they could have distracted Philip, who was then burning places sacred and secular around Pergamum, by making him concerned about his own territory. And so, with the Romans making all manner of promises, the Aetolians were sent off with hopes rather than tangible support, and Apustius returned to the fleet with Attalus.

Then an assault on Oreus came under discussion. The city was strong both by virtue of its fortifications and also because, having been attacked in the past,* it had a powerful garrison. After Andros was taken by storm, the allies had been joined by twenty Rhodian vessels, all with decks, and their admiral Acesimbrotus. This detachment they sent to patrol off Zelasium, a promontory of Pthiotis lying in a key position above Demetrias, to guard against any movement by the Macedonian ships from that quarter. Heraclides, the king's lieutenant, commanded the fleet in the area, and his plan of action was to capitalize on his enemy's negligence rather than employ open force. The Romans and Attalus proceeded to assault Oreus from opposite directions, the Romans on the side of the coastal citadel, and the king's forces attacking the valley between the two citadels where the city enjoyed the further protection of a wall. As their points of attack differed, so too did their manner of attack: the Romans brought up to the walls tortoise-formations, siege-sheds, and a battering-ram, while the king's troops used ballistas, catapults, and all other kinds of artillery to shower bolts and rocks of enormous weight on the enemy. They also dug tunnels, and used whatever other contrivances had proved effective in the previous assault. However, not only were the Macedonians who were defending the city and its citadels more numerous than on the former occasion, but they also had firmer resolve, remembering, as they did, the king's reprimand for the mistake they had made before, and his threats, as well as his promises, for the future. More time was thus being spent there than the legate had anticipated, and he now had greater confidence in siege-works than a swift assault. He also felt that some other operation could be attempted in the mean time. He therefore left what he considered a sufficiently large force to complete the siege-works, crossed to the part of the mainland closest to him, and, with a sudden advance, captured Larisa—not the famous city in Thessaly, but the other one, which they call Cremaste—all except its citadel. In addition, Attalus crushed Pteleon whose inhabitants, since an offensive was being mounted on the other city, had no fear of such a manœuvre.

The siege-works around Oreus were now nearing completion, and also the garrison within were exhausted from the unremitting toil, sleepless days as well as sleepless nights, and from their wounds. In addition, sections of the wall had collapsed at many points from the pounding of the battering-ram, and the Romans, making their way through a breach at night, broke into the citadel †above the harbour†. When at dawn a signal was given by the Romans from the citadel, Attalus himself burst into the city through the walls which were now mostly in ruins. The garrison and the townspeople sought refuge in the other citadel, and from this they surrendered two days later. The city was awarded to the king, the prisoners to the Romans.

47. By this time the autumn equinox was drawing near,* and sailors are apprehensive of the Euboean gulf known as Coela.* Wishing, therefore, to quit the area before the onset of the winter storms, the allies headed back to Piraeus, the point from which they had set out for the war. Leaving thirty ships in Piraeus, Apustius then sailed past Malea to Corcyra. The king was detained until the time of the rites of Ceres, since he wished to take part in the ceremony. After the rites, he too withdrew to Asia, sending home Acesimbrotus and the Rhodians. Such were that summer's operations against Philip and his allies conducted on land and sea by the Roman consul and his legate, assisted by Attalus and the Rhodians.

The other consul, Gaius Aurelius, came to his province to find the war over, and he did not hide his anger with the praetor for having fought the campaign in his absence. He sent him to Etruria while he himself led his legions into enemy territory and waged a war of pillage, which brought him more booty than glory. Lucius Furius had nothing to do in Etruria and, at the same time, he was intent on gaining a triumph for his Gallic campaign, which he believed could be more easily achieved in the absence of an irate and jealous consul. And so he arrived unexpectedly in Rome, convened the Senate in the temple of Bellona and, listing his achievements, requested permission to enter the city in triumph.

48. Furius had the support of a large part of the Senate because of his impressive record and also through his personal influence. However, the more senior members opposed the triumph for two reasons: first, Furius had campaigned with an army belonging to another; and, secondly, he had left his province through a wish to avail himself of the opportunity of procuring a triumph for himself (an unprecedented action, they said). The consular members in particular opined that Furius should have waited for the consul. By encamping near the town, they explained, he could have given protection for the colony without fighting a pitched battle, and in this way held out until the consul's arrival. It was incumbent on the Senate, they said, to do what the praetor had failed to do, namely wait for the consul; and their judgment of the issue would be more objective after hearing the consul and praetor in open debate before them.

Most of the Senate reckoned that their body should consider only Furius' accomplishments, and whether these fell within his period of office and under his auspices. Two colonies had been established as barriers to curb Gallic uprisings, they said. What on earth was the praetor to do when one of these was sacked and put to the torch, and the conflagration was about to cross to the other colony which was so close to it, as happens with adjoining houses? If no action was permissible without the authority of the consul, then the Senate was in the wrong to assign an army to the praetor; for if it had wanted the operation carried out by the consul's troops and not by the praetor's, it could have defined by senatorial decree that authority lay with the consul and not the praetor. Either that or the consul was culpable for ordering the transfer of the army from Etruria to Gaul but not then joining it in person at Ariminum to take part in a war which could not be legitimately fought without his participation. The critical moments of warfare did not brook delay, they said, or dilatory commanders; and sometimes one has to fight not because one wants to but under compulsion from the enemy. What should be taken into account was the battle itself and its outcome. The enemy had been routed and massacred, their camp taken and pillaged, a colony relieved of its siege and the prisoners of war from the other colony recovered and returned to their own people, and the war concluded with a single battle. Not only had people been overjoyed with the victory, but a three-day period of devotion to the immortal gods had been held on the grounds that the interests of the state had been competently and successfully—not incompetently and imprudently—handled by the praetor Lucius Furius. Moreover, they said, the Gallic wars had been confided to the family of the Furii* by some kind of destiny.

49. Thanks to speeches of this nature, delivered by Furius himself and by his friends, the prestige of the absent consul was eclipsed by the personal influence of the praetor who was present, and a crowded Senate decreed a triumph for Lucius Furius. The praetor Lucius Furius thus celebrated a triumph over the Gauls during his term of office, and brought to the treasury 320,000 *asses* of bronze and 171,500 pieces of silver.* His chariot was not preceded by captives, there was no display of spoils, and his men did not follow behind. Everything seemed to belong to the consul, save the victory.

After this, the games which he had promised in a vow as consul in Africa were celebrated with great pageantry by Publius Cornelius Scipio, and a decree was issued with regard to land-distribution to his soldiers—each was to receive two iugera for every year of service in Spain or Africa. The decemvirs were to be responsible for the apportionment of the land. A board of triumvirs was also established to strengthen the complement of colonists at Venusia after the attrition of that colony's strength during the Hannibalic war, and this comprised Gaius Terentius Varro, Titus Quinctius Flamininus, and Publius Cornelius Scipio, son of Gnaeus. These men then enlisted colonists for Venusia.

The same year Gaius Cornelius Cethegus, who was proconsular governor of Spain, defeated a large enemy army in the territory of the Sedetani. It is said that 15,000 Spaniards lost their lives in that battle, and that seventy-eight military standards were captured.

When the consul Gaius Aurelius came from his province to Rome for the elections, he did not in fact lodge the grievance that had been expected of him, namely that the Senate had not waited for him and that he had not, consul though he was, been given the chance to debate the issue with the praetor. Instead he complained that the

Senate had proclaimed a triumph without hearing the evidence of any of the participants in the war, apart from the person who would celebrate the triumph. Their ancestors, said Aurelius, had ordained that legates, tribunes, centurions, and even the common soldiers should participate in a triumph, and their purpose was to let the Roman people see the men who had witnessed the feats of the person to whom that great honour was being accorded. Was there, he asked, any member of the army which had fought the Gauls whom the Senate could interrogate on the truth or falsehood of the praetor's version of events—any camp-follower even, if not an enlisted man? Aurelius then fixed a date for the elections. In these Lucius Cornelius Lentulus and Publius Villius Tappulus were elected consuls, and then Lucius Quinctius Flamininus, Lucius Valerius Flaccus, Lucius Villius Tappulus, and Gnaeus Baebius Tamphilus were made praetors.

50. Grain was particularly cheap that year. The curule aediles Marcus Claudius Marcellus and Sextus Aelius Paetus distributed to the people a large amount of wheat imported from Africa at a price of two *asses* per measure. They also staged the Roman Games with great ceremony, repeating one day, and from money taken in fines they placed in the treasury five bronze statues. The Plebeian Games were three times repeated in their entirety by the aediles Lucius Terentius Massaliota and Gnaeus Baebius Tamphilus, who was praetor designate. In addition, funeral games were that year held in the forum over a four-day period, put on to commemorate the passing of Marcus Valerius Laevinus by his sons Publius and Marcus, who also staged a gladiatorial show at which twenty-five pairs of fighters were on the bill. Marcus Aurelius Cotta, a member of the board of ten for sacrifices, died this year and was replaced by Manius Acilius Glabrio.

In the elections it transpired that the two curule aediles elected could not serve immediately. Gaius Cornelius Cethegus had been elected in his absence, during his term as governor of the province of Spain; and Gaius Valerius Flaccus, present for his election, could not take the oath to uphold the laws because he was the *flamen* of Jupiter,* and only a person swearing to uphold the laws could occupy the office for more than five days. Flaccus requested that the legal obligation be waived in his case, and the Senate decreed that if the aedile presented someone who, in the view of the consuls, could take the oath in his stead, then, if the consuls were in agreement, they should discuss with the tribunes of the plebs the possibility of bringing the matter before the plebs. The praetor designate, Lucius Valerius Flaccus, was the man presented to take the oath for his brother. The tribunes then brought the matter before the plebs, who voted that matters should stand as if the aedile had taken the oath in person. There was also a decree passed in the case of the other aedile. The tribunes canvassed the assembly on which two men they wanted to proceed with imperium to the armies in Spain to allow the curule aedile, Gaius Cornelius, to return to enter office and Lucius Manlius Acidinus to leave his province after many years of service,* and the plebs directed that Gnaeus Cornelius Lentulus* and Lucius Stertinius be invested with proconsular imperium in Spain.

BOOK THIRTY-TWO

1. On entering office on the Ides of March,* the consuls and the praetors drew lots for their respective spheres of authority. Italy fell to Lucius Lentulus, and Macedonia to Publius Villius, while amongst the praetors the city prefecture came to Lucius Quinctius, Ariminum to Gnaeus Baebius, Sicily to Lucius Valerius, and Sardinia to Lucius Villius. The consul Lentulus was instructed to enrol fresh legions, and Villius was to take over from Publius Sulpicius command of the latter's army, with permission granted to supplement it by enlisting as many men as he thought appropriate. The legions formerly under the consul Gaius Aurelius were allocated to the praetor Baebius on the condition that he keep them only until he should be replaced by the consul with a new army. On the consul's arrival in Gaul, all soldiers who had completed their service were to be sent home apart from 5,000 allies, a large enough force to secure the province around Ariminum. Gaius Sergius and Quintus Minucius, praetors the previous year, had their terms of office extended: Sergius to supervise the distribution of land to soldiers who had served many years in Spain, Sicily, and Sardinia;* Minucius* so that the investigations into conspiracies could be brought to completion at Bruttium by the same official (for as praetor he had conducted them in a dedicated and diligent manner). Minucius was to dispatch to Locri for punishment the men he had sent to Rome in irons after they were convicted of sacrilege, and see to replacing everything that had been misappropriated from the shrine of Proserpina, adding gifts of atonement.

By decree of the pontiffs the Latin Festival* was repeated. This followed a complaint made in the Senate by representatives from Ardea that the tradition of giving meat on Mt. Alba at the time of the festival had not been followed in their case.

Word came from Suessa that two gates and the section of wall between them had been struck by lightning, and there were reports, brought by representatives from the towns, of the same phenomenon occurring at the temple of Jupiter at Formiae, of Jupiter, too, at Ostia, and of Apollo and Sancus at Velitrae, while hair was said to have grown in the temple of Hercules. A dispatch from the

propraetor Quintus Minucius in Bruttium recorded the birth of a
colt with five feet and of three chicks with three feet, and a letter
was brought from the proconsul Publius Sulpicius in Macedonia
reporting, amongst other things, a laurel tree growing on the poop of
a warship. In the case of the former prodigies the Senate had voted
that the consuls should offer sacrifice of full-grown animals to whatever deities they thought appropriate; in the case of the last one
alone the seers were summoned to the Senate, and on their recommendation an edict was issued enjoining a day of prayer upon the
people and religious ceremonies were conducted at all the couches of
the gods.

2. That year the Carthaginians brought to Rome the first payment
in silver of the tribute* that had been imposed on them. However,
the quaestors reported that the metal was impure and that a quarter
of it had boiled down to dross during the assay; and the Carthaginians made good the shortfall of silver by borrowing in Rome. The
Carthaginians then requested the return of their hostages,* if the
Senate now agreed. A hundred hostages were returned, and the
Carthaginians were led to expect the same for the others if they
continued to respect the treaty. The Carthaginians further requested
that the hostages who were not being returned be transferred from
Norba, where they were not happy, to another place and the hostages
were given leave to go instead to Signia and Ferentinum. The people
of Gades also had their request granted that a Roman official not be
sent to their city; this, they said, contravened the agreement made
with Lucius Marcius Septimus when they came under the protection of the Roman people. Spokesmen from Narnia* lodged a complaint that their colonists were not up to the requisite quota, and that
certain outsiders had infiltrated their number and were comporting
themselves as colonists. Accordingly, the consul Lucius Cornelius
was instructed to establish a board of triumvirs to investigate the
case. Elected to this board were Publius and Sextus Aelius, both
bearing the cognomen Paetus, and Gnaeus Cornelius Lentulus. An
application by the people of Cosa for the same concession granted to
the people of Narnia, namely an increase in the number of colonists,
was unsuccessful.

3. All essential business finished at Rome, the consuls set off for
their provinces. Arriving in Macedonia, Publius Villius faced a horrendous mutiny of the troops. This had been fomented some time

before but not suppressed with sufficient firmness at its commencement. It involved 2,000 men who, after Hannibal's defeat, had been transferred from Africa, first to Sicily and thence as volunteers to Macedonia about a year later. The men claimed that this had been done against their will, that they had been press-ganged aboard the ships by the tribunes. But, they said, whatever the truth of the matter, whether they had served under duress or voluntarily, this was now over, and it was only fair that some limit be set to their military service. They had not seen Italy in many a year; they had grown old under arms in Sicily, Africa, and Macedonia; and they were now exhausted from toil and exertion, and drained of blood from all the wounds they had received. The consul admitted that they appeared to have plausible grounds for seeking demobilization, if these were presented in a reasonable way, but he added that neither this nor any other case was sufficiently strong to warrant mutiny. If they were prepared to remain at their posts and obey orders, he would write to the Senate about their demobilization, and they would more easily gain their end by moderate behaviour than by pig-headedness.

4. At that time Philip was in the process of launching an all-out attack on Thaumaci, using earthworks and mantlets, and he was on the point of bringing the battering-ram up to the walls. He was, however, forced to abandon the effort by the sudden arrival of the Aetolians. Led by Archidamus, these had made their way through the Macedonian guard-stations into the city and now, night and day, there was no end to their counter-attacks on the Macedonian outposts or their siege-works. They were also helped by the very geography of the area. Thaumaci is perched high up, right above a gorge, on the road through Lamia as one comes from Pylae* and the Malian Gulf, and it overlooks the so-called 'Hollow Thessaly'. One passes through rugged terrain, along roads that wend their way through sinuous valleys, and then, on reaching the city, one suddenly finds a limitless plain, stretching out like a vast sea, making it difficult to see where the fields lying below actually come to an end. It is from this marvel of nature that Thaumaci gets its name.* The city owes its security not only to its elevation but also to the fact that it sits on a rocky prominence sheer on every side. These difficulties, and the consideration that the town was a prize hardly worth the effort and danger, made Philip abandon his venture. Winter was also now

approaching* when he left there and took his troops back to winter quarters in Macedonia.

5. In Macedonia, everybody else had used whatever slight repose they were granted for relaxation of mind and body. Not so Philip. The mental release he experienced after the relentless hardship of marching and fighting only served to make him all the more concerned about the final outcome of the war, racking him with anxiety. His fears were not confined to his enemies, who were now applying pressure by land and sea; he worried, too, about the mood of his allies, and even of his own countrymen. The former, he feared, could abandon him in hopes of gaining an alliance with Rome; the Macedonians could be prey to subversive inclinations. He therefore sent a deputation to Achaea. His object was to demand the oath of allegiance from the Achaeans, who had undertaken to swear loyalty to him on an annual basis; and also to restore to them Orchomenos, Heraea, and Triphylia—the last had been taken from the people of Elis—and to give Aliphera to the people of Megalopolis. (The Megalopolitans maintained that this city had never been an appendage of Triphylia, and that it should be restored to them as being one of the cities granted for the founding of Megalopolis* by decision of the Arcadian council.)

In fact, Philip did succeed in strengthening his alliance with the Achaeans by these measures. As regards the mood of the Macedonians, he could see that what especially generated resentment against him was his friendship with Heraclides; and so he laid all manner of charges against him and threw him into prison, to the great joy of his compatriots. He then prepared for war with great diligence, as great as he had ever done before. There was military training both for Macedonians and for mercenaries, and at the beginning of spring Philip sent his entire foreign auxiliary force, plus whatever light-armed troops he possessed, all of them under the command of Athenagoras, through Epirus into Chaonia to seize the gorge at Antigonea (called 'The Narrows' by the Greeks). A few days later he himself followed with the heavier troops. He made a thorough inspection of the topography of the region and concluded that the most opportune spot for a fortified encampment lay beside the River Aous. This flows in a constricted valley between two mountains, called respectively 'Meropus' and 'Asnaus' by the local population, and offers only a narrow pathway along the bank. Philip ordered

Athenagoras and his light-armed troops to hold and fortify Asnaus and he himself encamped on Meropus. The points at which the cliff was sheer were held by pickets comprising only a few armed men; the weaker spots he secured with ditches, or a rampart, or towers. A large battery of slings was also deployed at appropriate points to keep the enemy at bay with their projectiles. The king's tent was positioned on the most prominent hillock before the rampart so that his confidence would inspire terror in the enemy and hope in his own men.

6. The consul had been briefed by the Epirote Charops on the passes the king had occupied with his army; and at the start of spring, after passing the winter at Corcyra, he crossed to the mainland and proceeded to march on the enemy. When he was about five miles distant from the king's camp he fortified a position, left his legions behind and went ahead in person with his light infantry to examine the terrain. The following day he held a meeting to consider whether he should attempt a passage through the gorge held by the enemy despite the enormous hardship and risk to be faced, or alternatively take his troops on the same circuitous route which Sulpicius had used to enter Macedonia the year before. He had spent many a day considering the problem when news arrived that Titus Quinctius had been elected consul, had been allotted Macedonia as his province, and, accelerating his journey, had already made the crossing to Corcyra.

Valerius Antias recounts that Villius entered the gorge but that he could not take the direct route since the whole area was in the king's power. He therefore followed the valley through the middle of which flows the River Aous, hastily constructed a bridge, crossed to the bank on which the king's camp was located, and engaged the enemy in pitched battle. The king was defeated and put to flight, according to Antias, with the loss of his camp; 12,000 of the enemy lost their lives in the battle and 2,200 were captured, along with 132 military standards and 230 horses. Antias adds that, during the battle, Villius vowed a temple to Jupiter in the event of a successful outcome. All the other Greek and Roman authors, at least those whose annals I have read, record no exceptional feat on Villius' part; they claim that the incoming consul, Titus Quinctius, inherited from him a war in which no progress had been made.

7. During the course of these events in Macedonia, the other

consul, Lucius Lentulus, who had stayed behind in Rome, held elections for the censorship,* and from a wide field of distiguished candidates Publius Cornelius Scipio Africanus and Publius Aelius Paetus were elected. In a spirit of close co-operation these two managed to select a list of Senators without censuring anyone, as well as to contract out the collection of sales-taxes at Capua and Puteoli, and transport taxes at Castra (where there is a town today). They also enrolled for Castra 300 colonists (the number prescribed by the Senate) and sold off land belonging to Capua at the foot of Mt. Tifata.

At this time Lucius Manlius Acidinus, on his return from Spain, was refused entry to Rome in ovation by the plebeian tribune Publius Porcius Laeca, although Acidinus had been granted that honour by the Senate.* Acidinus therefore entered the city as a private citizen, and he deposited in the treasury † † pounds of silver and some thirty pounds of gold.

The same year Gnaeus Baebius Tamphilus, having assumed the governorship of Gaul from Gaius Aurelius, consul the previous year, made a reckless incursion into the territory of the Insubrian Gauls where he was cut off with practically his entire army. He lost more than 6,700 men, incurring a terrible defeat in a war which by now had ceased to be a concern. The incident brought the consul Lucius Lentulus from Rome. Arriving in a province full of turmoil, and taking charge of a demoralized army, Lentulus gave the praetor a serious reprimand and ordered him to leave the province and return to Rome.

However, the consul achieved no notable success himself since he was recalled to Rome for the elections.* These were held up by the plebeian tribunes Marcus Fulvius and Manius Curius—they refused to let Titus Quinctius Flamininus stand for the consulship after his quaestorship. The aedileship and the praetorship were now being treated with disdain, they argued; nobles now aimed directly at the consulship without climbing the ladder of successive offices* and giving evidence of their capabilities in them and then, by skipping the intermediate stages, were going directly from the bottom to the top. After being debated in the Campus Martius the issue reached the Senate. Here, members voted that it was fair for the people to have the power to elect anyone they pleased, provided that a candidate was standing for an office which the laws permitted him to hold.

The tribunes accepted the authority of the Senate, and Sextus Aelius Paetus and Titus Quinctius Flamininus were elected consuls. Then the praetorian elections were held, in which the successful candidates were Lucius Cornelius Merula, Marcus Claudius Marcellus, Marcus Porcius Cato, and Gaius Helvius, who had been plebeian aediles. The Plebeian Games were repeated <. . .> by these magistrates, and a feast of Jupiter held to celebrate the games. Furthermore, the Roman Games were celebrated with great ceremony by the curule aediles Gaius Valerius Flaccus, the *flamen* of Jupiter, and Gaius Cornelius Cethegus. The pontiffs Servius and Gaius Sulpicius Galba* died that year, to be replaced by Marcus Aemilius Lepidus and Gnaeus Cornelius Scipio.*

8. When Sextus Aelius Paetus and Titus Quinctius Flamininus convened the Senate on the Capitol after they began their term of office, the members decided that the two consuls should decide amongst themselves, or by lot, which was to receive Macedonia and which Italy as his province, and the one to whom Macedonia fell should engage, to supplement his legions, a force of 3,000 Roman infantry and 300 cavalry plus 5,000 infantry and 500 cavalry from the allies and the Latin League. The other consul was given by decree an entirely new army. Lucius Lentulus, consul the previous year, had his command prolonged, and was ordered not to leave the province himself or demobilize the veteran force before the arrival of the consul and the new legions. The consuls drew lots for their provinces, and Italy fell to Aelius, Macedonia to Quinctius, while amongst the praetors Lucius Cornelius Merula received the city jurisdiction, Marcus Claudius Sicily, Marcus Porcius Sardinia, and Gaius Helvius Gaul. Then began the levy of troops, for, apart from the armies of the consuls, the order was also given for the enlistment of soldiers for the praetors. Marcellus was assigned 4,000 allied and Latin infantry and 300 cavalry for Sicily, and Cato 2,000 infantry and 200 cavalry of the same category for Sardinia. On arrival in their respective provinces, both praetors were to discharge the veteran infantry and cavalry.

The consuls next brought before the Senate envoys from Attalus. These proclaimed that the king was using his fleet and all his land-forces to further Roman interests on land and sea, and that he had to that day actively followed to the letter every instruction of the Roman consuls. Now, however, he feared that Antiochus' conduct would not allow him to continue this service, since Antiochus had overrun Attalus' kingdom when it was bereft of naval and land defences. Attalus was therefore entreating the Senators to send a defensive force for the protection of his realm, if they wished to avail themselves of his fleet and his support for the Macedonian war; and if they refused this they should permit him to withdraw with his fleet and the rest of his forces to defend his own territory.

The Senate ordered the following reply to be given to the envoys: The Senate was gratified by the support King Attalus had provided by means of his fleet and his other troops. It would not, however, send Attalus assistance against Antiochus, who was an ally and friend of the people of Rome; but no more would it hold on to Attalus' assistance longer than was convenient for the king. The Roman people always employed the resources of others only at the discretion of those others: the people who wished the Romans to enjoy their assistance had it in their power to determine the commencement and termination of that assistance. The Senate would, however, send a delegation to Antiochus to report to him that the Roman people were profiting from the assistance of Attalus, his navy, and his land-forces in the fight against Philip, their common enemy, and that he would earn the Senate's gratitude if he kept his hands off Attalus' realm and eschewed conflict with him. Kings who were allies and friends of the Roman people, the delegates would say, should by rights also maintain peace with each other.

9. The consul Titus Quinctius made his levy in such a way as to limit his choice almost exclusively to men of proven courage who had served in Spain or Africa. In a hurry now to reach his province, he was delayed in Rome by news of prodigies and by the expiatory rites for them. A public road had been struck by lightning in Veii, as had the forum and the temple of Jupiter in Lanuvium, the temple of Hercules in Ardea, and the wall, towers, and the temple called the 'White Temple' in Capua. In Arretium the sky appeared to be aflame, and at Velitrae the earth had subsided over an area of three iugera, leaving an enormous chasm. There were reports of the birth of a two-headed lamb at Suessa Aurunca and of a pig with a human head at Sinuessa. In view of these prodigies a one-day period of public prayers was held, and the consuls devoted themselves to the necessary religious ceremonies, setting out for their provinces only after appeasing the gods. Aelius went with the praetor Helvius to Gaul and here transferred to the praetor the army which he had taken over from Lentulus and which he was supposed to disband—his intention was to use the new legions which he had brought with him to conduct the war. In fact, he achieved no notable success.

The other consul, Titus Quinctius, had crossed from Brundisium earlier than had been the practice of former consuls, and he reached Corcyra with 8,000 infantry and 500 cavalry. He made the passage from Corcyra to the closest part of Epirus by quinquereme, and hastened by forced marches to the Roman encampment. After relieving Villius of command, he waited there a few days for his troops to catch up with him from Corcyra, and then held a meeting to consider whether to take the direct route, and try to force a passage through the enemy camp, or alternatively, without even attempting such a strenuous and risky undertaking, to enter Macedonia by a safe detour through the Dassaretii and through Lyncus. The latter viewpoint would have won the day but for Quinctius' fear that by moving further away from the sea he might let the enemy slip through his fingers—if the king decided to seek protection in the wilds and forests as he had done earlier—and the summer would be dragged out fruitlessly. And so, no matter how it might turn out, they decided on a direct attack on the enemy despite the difficulty of the position. But the decision to take this action was firmer than their explanation of how to do it was clear; 10. and the Romans had now spent forty days sitting in sight of the enemy without making a move.

This gave Philip hope that negotiations for peace could be attempted through the agency of the people of Epirus. A meeting was held at which the general Pausanias and the master of the horse, Alexander, were selected for the task, and these two brought consul and king to parley on the banks of the River Aous, where its channel is at its narrowest. The consul's terms were essentially as follows: the king was to withdraw his garrisons from the city-states, and restore to those peoples whose land and cities he had pillaged any retrievable assets, the value of the rest to be estimated through non-partisan arbitration. Philip's response was that the status of the various city-states differed from one to another. Those which he had captured himself he would liberate, but in the case of those passed down to him by his ancestors he would not relinquish possession because they were legitimately his by right of inheritance. In the case

of grievances lodged by states with which he had been at war over
damage suffered during the conflict, he would defer to any arbiter
whom they might choose from amongst the peoples with whom both
parties were at peace. The consul replied that there was no need for
an arbiter or judge in this matter, since it was clear to anyone that
responsibility for injury lay with the aggressor, and Philip had in
every case been the first to resort to force, without provocation.
Then, when discussion arose of which states were to be liberated,
the consul first of all named the Thessalians. At this the king was so
incensed that he cried out: 'What heavier condition could you
impose on a defeated enemy, Titus Quinctius?' and with that
charged from the meeting. It was only with difficulty that the two
were dissuaded from a duel on the spot with projectiles (since they
were separated from each other, with the river between them).

The following day there were at first sallies from the outposts
leading to numerous skirmishes on the plain, which was broad
enough to accommodate them. Then the king's forces fell back on
ground that was constricted and rugged, and the Romans, fired with
enthusiasm for the fight, also entered this terrain. In favour of the
Romans were their orderliness, their military training, and the
nature of their armour, made to protect the body; in favour of the
enemy were the terrain, and the catapults and slings deployed on
almost all the cliffs as if on a wall. Many wounds had been dealt on
both sides with some loss of life, too, as in a regular engagement,
when night brought the battle to an end.

11. Such was the situation when a shepherd was brought to the
consul, sent to him by Charops, a leading member of the Epirote
community. This man claimed that he usually grazed his flock in the
valley now occupied by the king's camp, and that he knew every
winding track and pathway in those mountains. If the consul were
prepared to send some men with him, he said, he would lead them by
a path that was not hazardous or excessively difficult to a point above
the enemy. When the consul heard this, he sent a message to Charops
to inquire whether he thought the peasant could be trusted in a
matter of such importance. Charops had a message sent back that he
should trust the man, but added the proviso that overall control of
the operation should rest in Flamininus' hands, not the shepherd's.
It was more a case of Flamininus wishing to trust the man than of his
taking a calculated risk, and his feelings were a mixture of elation

and apprehension; but, persuaded by the recommendation of Charops, he decided to test the prospect set before him. To avert the king's suspicions, he kept up a relentless attack on the enemy during the two days that followed, deploying his forces in every quarter and bringing up fresh troops to relieve the weary. He then assigned 4,000 hand-picked infantry and 300 cavalry to a military tribune, telling him to take the cavalry as far as the terrain permitted. When these reached an area that a horseman could not negotiate the cavalry should be installed on level ground while the infantry went ahead following the route indicated by the guide. On reaching the point above the enemy promised by the guide, the tribune was to send up a smoke-signal but not raise the shout until, in his judgment, the signal had been received and the battle begun. Flamininus ordered him to make the journey at night—and there happened to be a full moon—and use the daytime for eating and resting. As for the guide, he heaped extravagant promises on him, in the event of his proving reliable, but handed him over to the tribune in irons. Having despatched the troops on their mission, the Roman commander pressed the attack with all the more fervour in all quarters, harrying the king's outposts.

12. Two days later the Romans were sending up the smoke-signal to indicate they had taken and were holding the bluff which had been their objective. At this point the consul split his forces into three parts and made his way up the middle of the valley with the main strength of his army, bringing the right and left wings to bear on the king's camp. The enemy were no less spirited in coming to face them. They surged forward in their eagerness for combat and fought outside their fortifications, but the Roman soldiers enjoyed no small advantage in terms of their courage, expertise, and the nature of their weapons. After suffering many wounds and much loss of life, however, the king's men withdrew to positions that were either fortified or protected by natural features, and the danger recoiled upon the Romans who had thoughtlessly advanced into rough terrain and cramped spots that afforded no easy means of retreat. Indeed, they would not have pulled back from that position without paying for their recklessness but for a loud shout from the rear, followed by fighting breaking out, which drove the king's men out of their senses with sudden panic. Some took to flight. Others stood their ground, less because they had sufficient mettle for the fight, than because of

the lack of anywhere to run, and these were surrounded by an enemy bearing down on them front and rear. The entire army could have been annihilated had the victors pursued the fleeing Macedonians, but the cavalry were hampered by the restricted and rugged terrain, the infantry by the weight of their weapons. At first the king ran wildly and without a backward glance. Then, after five miles, suspecting what was in fact the case, that his enemy could not keep up because of the rough ground, he halted on a knoll and sent off some of his men through all the hills and valleys to bring his scattered troops together in one spot. No more than 2,000 had been lost; all the remainder assembled in one spot as though responding to a signal, and then headed for Thessaly in a dense column. The Romans followed as far as they could in safety, killing stragglers and stripping their bodies. They looted the king's camp, difficult to get at even in the absence of defenders, and then spent the night in their own.

13. The following day the consul tracked his enemy along the gorge through which the river snakes down the valley. As for the king, he reached the Camp of Pyrrhus on the first day (the area bearing this name is in Triphylia, in the territory of Molottis), and the next he made it as far as the Lyncus mountains—an enormous march for an army, but they were being driven on by fear. These mountains are in Epirus, lying between Macedonia and Thessaly, their eastern flank facing Thessaly and their northern abutting Macedonia. They are thickly-forested with broad plateaux and year-round springs at their crests. Here the king encamped for several days, in two minds as to whether he should immediately retreat into his kingdom or whether he could possibly reach Thessaly before his enemy. Deciding finally to take the army into Thessaly, he made for Tricca by the most direct roads and then swiftly marched through the towns on his route. Those men who were able to follow him he called from their homes, and burned the towns. He granted owners the right to take with them from their houses all the possessions they could, the remainder becoming the booty of the common soldier. They suffered everything—no cruel treatment inflicted by an enemy could have surpassed what these people endured at the hands of their allies. Philip found these steps repugnant as he was taking them, but he wanted at least to rescue his allies as living beings from a land that was soon to belong to his enemies. As a result the towns of Phacium, Piresiae, Euhydrium, Eretria, and Palaepharsalus were

destroyed. Philip then made for Pherae, where he was shut out from the town; since storming it meant halting and he had no time, he dropped the idea and crossed into Macedonia, for there was also talk of the approach of the Aetolians.

The Aetolians had heard of the battle fought at the River Aous and had at first pillaged the areas closest to them, around Sperchiae and Macra (the one called Macra Come). Then, passing into Thessaly, they took Ctimene and Angeiae at the first assault. They were driven from Metropolis, as they ravaged the fields, when the townspeople hurriedly assembled to defend the walls. Attacking Callithera next, they put up a stouter fight against a similar counter-attack from the inhabitants; driving those who had made the sortie back into the town, they contented themselves with this measure of victory and left because there was simply no hope of taking the town by assault. They went on to storm and pillage the villages of Teuma and Celathara, and accepted the surrender of Acharrae. Xyniae was deserted by its inhabitants who feared similar treatment. Here, the column of refugees fleeing their homes fell in with a contingent of troops which was being taken to Thaumaci to offer protection for the foraging operations there. The disorderly, unarmed crowd, including the usual group of non-combatants, was cut down by the armed soldiers, and deserted Xyniae was ransacked. The Aetolians then captured Cyphaera, a fortress of tactical importance overlooking Dolopia. Such was the swift progress made by the Aetolians in the course of a few days. But, after receiving word of the Romans' successful engagement, Amynander and the Athamanians did not remain inactive either.

14. Having little confidence in his own men, Amynander requested a modest squadron of troops from the consul. He then headed for Gomphi and straight away took by assault a town called Phaeca, which lies between Gomphi and the narrow pass separating Thessaly from Athamania. Next he attacked Gomphi. For several days the inhabitants defended their city with all their might, and it was only by setting up scaling-ladders on the walls that Amynander eventually frightened them into capitulation. The surrender of Gomphi struck sheer terror into the Thessalians, prompting the submission of the inhabitants of Argenta, Pherinium, Timarus, Ligynae, Strymon, Lampsus, and other fortified towns of little importance close by.

Their fear of Macedon removed, the Athamanians and the Aetolians were now gathering the plunder of another's victory, while Thessaly was simultaneously suffering devastation at the hands of three armies, without knowing which to believe an enemy or which an ally. The consul meanwhile slipped into the region of Epirus by means of the pass left open by his enemy's flight. He was well aware of which side the Epirotes favoured (with the sole exception of their leading citizen, Charops), but he could see that, from a desire to gratify him, they were making every effort to carry out his bidding. He therefore set more store by their present than by their past conduct, and simply by his readiness to forgive he won over their support for the future. Flamininus then sent messengers to Corcyra to give the order for cargo vessels to come into the Ambracian Gulf. He himself advanced by short stages, and three days later pitched camp on Mt. Cercetius. He summoned Amynander to this spot with his auxiliaries, not because he needed the reinforcement but to have guides for the march into Thessaly. It was the same thinking that led him to accept several Epirote volunteers as members of his auxiliary forces.

15. The first city which Flamininus attacked in Thessaly was Phaloria which had a garrison of 2,000 Macedonians. Initially these resisted with all their might, protecting themselves to the maximum with their weapons and defensive walls, but the continuous assault, night and day without respite, crushed the Macedonians' resolve— the consul believed that it would be crucial for the morale of the other Thessalians if the enemy he first encountered failed to withstand the Roman onslaught. When Phaloria was taken, deputations came from Metropolis and Cierium to surrender these towns; they asked for, and were shown, mercy, but Phaloria was burned and pillaged. Flamininus then made for Aeginium, but when he saw the place was secured and rendered virtually impregnable even by a small garrison, he redirected his army towards the region of Gomphi after merely hurling a few projectiles at the closest outpost.

He then went down into the plains of Thessaly, but by now his army was running short of all provisions because he had spared the farmlands of Epirus. He therefore sent ahead to find out if the transport ships had put in at Leucas or the Ambracian Gulf, and then sent his companies out one by one to Ambracia to gather supplies. The road from Gomphi to Ambracia is awkward and difficult, but it is also short. Thus, within a few days, thanks to supplies transported from the coast, the camp was replete with all manner of provisions. From here Flamininus set out for Atrax, which is about ten miles from Larisa, a city on the River Peneus, whose people hail originally from Perrhaebia. The Thessalians felt no alarm at the arrival of the Romans; and Philip, who would not venture into Thessaly himself, established a base inside Tempe and, as need arose, sent out military assistance to any point under enemy pressure.

16. The consul's brother, Lucius Quinctius, who had been assigned charge of the fleet and command of the coast by the Senate, crossed to Corcyra with two quinqueremes at about the time that the consul first encamped opposite Philip in the gorge of Epirus. Told that the fleet had left Corcyra, and thinking he should waste no time, he followed it to the island of Same. Here he dismissed Gaius Livius,* whom he had succeeded, and came at a slow pace from Same* to Maleum, for most of the voyage towing the ships that were following him loaded with supplies. Instructing the rest of his fleet to follow him as speedily as they could, he himself went ahead from Maleum with three light quinqueremes to Piraeus, where he assumed command of the ships left there by the legate Lucius Apustius for the defence of Athens. At the same time two fleets set off from Asia. One, comprising twenty-four quinqueremes, was under Attalus, and the other, under the command of Acesimbrotus, was a Rhodian fleet made up of twenty ships with decks. These fleets joined up with each other off the island of Andros and crossed to Euboea, which is separated from Andros by a narrow strait. At first they raided the farmland of the Carystians; but when it seemed that Carystus was well-protected, a relief force having been swiftly dispatched from Chalcis, they moved on to Eretria. After he heard of Attalus' arrival here, Lucius Quinctius also came to Eretria with the ships from Piraeus, having left orders for each vessel of his fleet to head for Euboea on reaching Piraeus.

Eretria was now being subjected to a full-scale attack, for the ships of the three combined fleets were carrying on board all manner of slings and contrivances designed to smash cities, and the countryside provided an abundance of wood for building new siege-engines. At first the townspeople mounted a vigorous defence of their walls. Later, exhausted and with a number wounded, and observing, too, that a section of their wall had been demolished by the enemy's siege-engines <. . .> they were more disposed to surrender. There was, however, a Macedonian garrison in the town, which they feared as much as they did the Romans; and the king's prefect, Philocles, kept sending them messages from Chalcis to say that he would arrive with help at the appropriate moment if they could but hold out against the siege. This mixture of hope and fear prolonged their resistance beyond their wishes or their powers, but then, receiving the news that Philocles, defeated and in panic, had fled back to Chalcis, they immediately sent spokesmen to Attalus to seek his pardon and protection. Meanwhile, their attention focused on hopes of peace, they were remiss in the performance of their military functions and, neglecting all other areas, stationed armed patrols only at the spot where the wall lay in ruins. Quinctius accordingly made a night attack at a point where it was least expected, and took the town by means of scaling-ladders. The occupants fled *en masse* with their wives and children to the citadel, and then capitulated. Not a lot was found in terms of coined money, or of gold and silver, but there were more statues, pictures by old masters, and art-works of that kind than one would have expected, given the size of the town and rest of its assets.

17. The combined forces then went back to Carystus. Here, before the troops could disembark, the entire population abandoned the town and sought refuge in the citadel, from which they sent spokesmen to ask protection of the Romans. The townspeople were straight away granted their lives and freedom, but a ransom of 300 *nummi** per person was established for the Macedonians, who were also permitted to leave on condition that they lay down their arms. After paying this ransom the Macedonians crossed unarmed to Boeotia. The naval forces, which had now taken two famous Euboean cities in a matter of days, rounded Sunium, the promontory of Attica, and made for Cenchreae, a commercial port of Corinth.

In the mean time, the consul's assault on Atrax turned out to be longer and more ferocious than anyone had anticipated, with the enemy resisting in a manner he had not at all expected. He had believed that all his efforts would be focused on demolishing the wall; once he had opened up a path into the town for his soldiers, he thought the enemy would be put to flight and butchered, the usual sequence of events when towns are captured. However, when a part of the wall had been shattered by the battering-rams and the soldiers then climbed over the debris into the town, that proved to be the start of a new effort, in which all was to be done over again. For the Macedonians in the garrison, hand-picked men and a lot of them, thought it would be a spectacular and glorious feat to defend the town with their weapons and courage rather than by fortifications. They moved closer together and strengthened their fighting-line by introducing more ranks; then, when they perceived that the Romans were clambering over the ruins of the wall, they drove them back across a space that was obstructed and from which retreat was difficult.

This infuriated the consul. He saw the ignominious setback not only as prolonging the siege of a single city but as affecting the outcome of the entire war, which is very often contingent upon the impact of minor events. He cleared the area which was filled with the rubble of the half-demolished wall and brought forward a tower of enormous height, carrying a large number of soldiers on its multiple storeys. He also sent out his cohorts one after the other, and in regular formation, in order to smash by the violence of their charge, if they could, the Macedonian wedge, called the 'phalanx' by the Macedonians themselves.* But besides the restricted space—the gap where the wall had been broken down was not wide—the type of weapons employed and the nature of the fighting favoured the enemy. The Macedonians, in close order, held out before themselves their lances of extraordinary length, while the Romans hurled their spears to no effect against the solid mass of their shields, built up into what was virtually a tortoise-formation. Then they drew their swords, only to find they could neither engage in hand-to-hand fighting nor lop off the ends of the Macedonian lances (and if they did manage to sever or break the odd one, the broken tip itself was sharp and the shaft, standing amid the heads of the unbroken lances, still played its part with them in forming a sort of palisade). Furthermore, the as yet intact sections of the wall on either side sheltered the flanks, while the Romans had little open space for falling back or making a charge, the tactic which usually throws the enemy's ranks into disorder. In addition to this a chance occurrence also served to encourage the enemy. The tower was being manœuvred over a piece of loosely-packed soil when one of its wheels sank into a deep rut, and this made the tower slant at such an angle that it gave the enemy the impression that it was toppling over and filled the soldiers standing on it with †insane† panic.

18. The consul was having no success, and he was not at all happy at comparisons being made between the soldiers of the two sides and the types of weapons involved. At the same time he could see neither any prospect of quickly taking the town nor any means of spending the winter far from the sea, in a region laid waste by the ravages of warfare. He therefore raised the siege. There was no port on the entire coastline of Acarnania and Aetolia capable of harbouring all the cargo vessels carrying supplies for the army and at the same time providing accommodation for the winter for the legions. Anticyra in Phocis, which faced the Corinthian Gulf, seemed best situated for this: it was not far from Thessaly and the territory of his enemies; the Peloponnese was opposite, separated by a narrow stretch of sea; Aetolia and Acarnania lay to the rear; and Locris and Boeotia were on its flanks. Flamininus captured Phanotea in Phocis with his first assault and without a struggle, and the attack on Anticyra did not long delay him, after which Ambryssus and Hyampolis were both taken. Because Daulis occupied a position on a lofty prominence it could be captured neither by scaling-ladders nor siege-works. Flamininus' men therefore enticed the members of the garrison to make sorties by provoking them with projectiles. Then, alternating retreat and pursuit, and engaging the enemy in inconsequential skirmishes, they induced in them such slackness and disdain that the Romans were able to infiltrate their ranks as they withdrew to the city-gate and thus launch their attack. Other Phocian strongholds of slight importance also fell into Flamininus' hands more from fear than as a result of battle. Elatia, however, closed its gates, and it looked as though its inhabitants would receive neither the Roman leader nor his army within their walls unless compelled to do so by force.

19. As he was blockading Elatia, the hope of a greater accomplishment flashed through the consul's mind, namely that of turning the Achaean nation from its alliance with the king to a treaty with Rome. The Achaeans had driven out Cycliadas who had led the faction urging support for Philip, and their praetor was Aristaenus who wanted his people allied to Rome. The Roman fleet, along with Attalus and the Rhodians, was at anchor at Cenchreae where they were all formulating a joint plan of action for an assault on Corinth. Flamininus therefore thought the best plan was to send envoys to the Achaean nation, before the allies proceeded with the assault, with an

undertaking to bring Corinth back into the ancient league of their people on condition that they go over from the king to the Romans. At the urging of the consul, envoys were dispatched to the Achaeans by his brother, Lucius Quinctius, and by Attalus, the Rhodians, and the Athenians; and a council to hear these was held at Sicyon.

However, the state of mind of the Achaeans was not at all straight-forward. They were terrified by the Spartan Nabis, a formidable and relentless foe; they were daunted by Roman arms; they felt obligated to the Macedonians for their services of early as well as of recent date; the king himself they regarded with suspicion because of his ruthlessness and treachery and—an assessment not based on his present actions, which were merely designed to meet the needs of the moment—they could see that after the war he would be a more severe master. Not only were the Achaeans unaware of what each individual would express as an opinion in the legislative assembly of his own city-state or in the common councils of their nation, but it was not really clear to themselves what their own wishes or aspirations were when they reflected on the situation. Such was the indecision of the men whom the envoys were brought before and given permission to address. The Roman envoy, Lucius Calpurnius, had the floor first, then the envoys of Attalus and, after these, the Rhodians. Philip's representatives were permitted to speak after that, and the Athenians were heard at the end, so that they could rebut the arguments of the Macedonians. Because no people had suffered more than they or received such cruel treatment, the Athenians launched what amounted to a scathing attack on the king. When the day had been consumed by the speeches of all these representatives, delivered one after the other, the meeting was adjourned at sunset.

20. The following day the assembly was reconvened, but when, following the Greek practice, the magistrates made available through a herald the opportunity for anyone who wished to present a motion, nobody came forward to speak. For a long while there was a hush, and those present simply looked at each other. In fact, it is not surprising that men who found their intellects somehow paralysed when they merely reflected on conflicting points of view were even more confused by speeches—given on both sides over the course of an entire day—that presented and supported claims that were difficult to assess. Eventually, in order not to adjourn the meeting with nothing said, the praetor of the Achaeans, Aristaenus, declared:

'Men of Achaea, what has become of those clashes of emotions that make you barely able to refrain from physical violence in your dinner-parties and social gatherings whenever there is mention of Philip and the Romans? Now you have a meeting exclusively dedicated to this subject; you have heard speeches made by the delegates on both sides; the magistrates are laying the matter before you; and the herald is inviting proposals from the floor—and you are mute! If concern for our collective security can elicit no response from any of you, cannot this be done even by those personal feelings which have drawn your support to one side or the other? Especially when none of you is so obtuse as to be unaware that now is your opportunity to speak and advocate the policy which you as individuals want or think to be the best—now, before we reach a decision. For the decision once made, it behoves us all, even those earlier opposed to it, to uphold it as being a good and practical one.'

Not only did this prompting from the magistrate fail to induce anyone to make a proposal—it did not even elicit agitation or murmuring from an assembly of such a size and made up of so many peoples.

21. The praetor Aristaenus then addressed them once more:

'Leaders of the Achaeans, you are no more devoid of ideas than you are of the power of speech! Yet, individually, you are reluctant to take a personal risk in offering advice for the common good. Perhaps I, too, would remain silent were I a private citizen. As it is, I am your praetor and I can see that I should not have granted the deputations an audience in the first place—or, having done so, should not now send them off without a reply. But how can I give them a reply without a resolution from you? And since not one of you invited to this meeting has either the wish or the spirit to make any kind of suggestion, let us review the speeches delivered yesterday by the delegates, looking at them simply as suggestions—just as if the delegates had made to us not appeals that served their interests, but proposals they deemed profitable for us.

'The Romans, the people of Rhodes and Attalus are asking for an alliance with us and our friendship, and they think it right that we should assist them in the war they are prosecuting against Philip. Philip reminds us of our alliance with him and the oath we swore; at one moment he asks us to stand alongside him, at the next he claims to be happy if we remain neutral. Does it not occur to any of you to wonder why men not yet our allies ask more of us than one who *is* our ally? It is not Philip's reserve or Roman forwardness that is responsible for this, men of Achaea—no, the actual circumstances give or remove confidence when people are making a request. Of Philip we see nothing but his representative, whereas the Roman fleet is anchored off Cenchreae, with its spoils from the cities of Euboea on display, and we see the consul and his legions, a narrow stretch of sea away from us, overrunning Phocis and Locris. Are you surprised at the bashfulness of Philip's representative, Cleomedon, when he discussed just now our taking up arms against the Romans on Philip's behalf? Suppose we invite Cleomedon to comply with that same treaty and the oath which he kept trying to make us respect, and ask that Philip defend us against Nabis, the Spartans, and the Romans. Apart from finding no troops to protect us, he would not even find an answer for us—no more, for heaven's sake, than Philip did last year. On that occasion Philip tried to draw away our young soldiers from here to Euboea with an undertaking that he would prosecute a war against Nabis; but, when he saw that we were unwilling to vote him this military assistance, or become embroiled in a war with Rome, he forgot about that alliance, which he now plays up, and left us to be pillaged and plundered by Nabis and the Spartans.

'I for one find very little consistency in Cleomedon's address. He made light of the war with the Romans, and kept saying the result would be the same as in the last war they fought with Philip. So why is Philip now absent from here asking for our help instead of being here giving us, his old allies, protection against both Nabis and the Romans? *Us?* I say *us?* Why did he allow Eretria and Carystus to be captured as they were? Why so many of the Thessalian cities? Why Locris and Phocis? Why is he now tolerating the siege of Elatia? Why did he retreat from the passes of Epirus and those unassailable barricades on the River Aous? Why did he abandon his hold on the gorge and withdraw deep into his kingdom? Either he was forced, or he was afraid, or he did so voluntarily. If he did so of his own volition, leaving so many of his allies to be despoiled by his enemies, how can he object to his allies also looking after their own interests? If it was from fear then he should pardon us if we are also afraid. If he withdrew after military defeat, then, Cleomedon, are we Achaeans going to resist the Roman arms which you Macedonians failed to resist?

'Are we to believe your claim that the Romans are not prosecuting this war with more troops and greater resources than they did the last one? Or should we rather face the reality of the situation? On the last occasion* they assisted the Aetolians with their fleet; they did not fight the war with a leader who was a consul or with a consular army. At that time the coastal cities of Philip's allies were in a state of panic and disarray, but the regions of the interior were so secure from Roman arms that Philip plundered the Aetolians as they pleaded in vain for assistance from Rome. Now things are different. The Romans have terminated the Punic War which they coped with for sixteen years within the guts of Italy and, instead of simply sending assistance to the Aetolians when they were at war, have made themselves the leaders in that war, mounting attacks on Macedonia by land and sea simultaneously. Already a third consul is devoting all his energies to the war. Sulpicius has defeated and put to flight the king after engaging with him right inside Macedonia, and has laid waste the richest part of his kingdom. Now Quinctius has driven him from his camp, although Philip held the passes of Epirus and was confident in his geographical position, his fortifications and his army; he has chased him as he fled into Thessaly and has stormed the royal garrisons and the cities allied to Philip virtually before the eyes of the king himself.

'Just suppose there is no truth in what the Athenian delegate said a moment ago about the king's brutality, greed and lust. Suppose that we are indifferent to crimes he has committed in Attic territory against the gods of the upper and lower worlds, and much less concerned about the sufferings of the people of Cios and Abydus, who are far removed from us. If you like, let us forget the wounds we have suffered ourselves. Let us dismiss from our minds the murders and robberies he committed in Messene in the heart of the Peloponnese; the killing of his host at Cyparissia, Chariteles,* virtually at the dinner-table, in contravention of all law human and divine; the assassination of the Sicyonian father and son, both called Aratus* (despite the fact that it had even been his custom to call the hapless old man 'father'); his carting off to Macedonia the son's wife* to satisfy his lust. And let all the other instances of rape of young girls and matrons be consigned to oblivion. Let us pretend we are not even dealing with Philip, fear of whose brutality has struck you dumb— for what other reason can there be for your silence after you have been summoned to this meeting? Let us suppose instead our debate is with Antigonus,* a most compassionate and fair-minded king who has deserved well of us all. He would not demand of us what could not be done, would he? The Peloponnese is a peninsula, joined to the mainland by the narrow tongue of the Isthmus, and is exposed and vulnerable to naval attack more than any other kind of assault. Suppose a hundred decked ships, fifty lighter open-decked vessels and thirty Issaean cutters begin to conduct raids on our sea-coast and attack the cities which are exposed to them, practically right on the shore-line. We shall retreat into our inland cities, shall we—as though we were not burning with an internal war, one clinging to our vitals? When Nabis and the Spartans put pressure on us by land, and the Roman fleet by sea, from where and how can we appeal to the king's treaty and for Macedonian help? Are we ourselves going to use our own arms against the Roman enemy to protect the cities that will be attacked? A fine job we did of protecting Dymae in the last war! The misfortunes that have befallen others offer enough in the way of object-lessons for us; let us not seek a way for us to be a lesson to others!

'Because the Romans are taking the initiative in seeking your friendship, do not spurn an offer you should have been wishing for and using all your resources to gain. For of course it is under the compulsion of fear and because they are pinned down in a foreign land that they come running to you for the protection of your alliance! They want to lurk in the shade of your assistance! Their aim is to gain shelter in your harbours, and have access to supplies! No! They have the sea in their power, and whatever lands they come to they immediately bring under their control. What they are asking of you they can force out of you. Because they wish to spare you, they are not allowing you to commit a self-destructive act. Think of the approach indicated a moment ago by Cleomedon as being the middle course and the safest one for you, namely neutrality and avoidance of war. That is not the "middle course"—it is a non-existent course. For apart from the fact that an alliance with Rome must either be accepted or rejected outright by you, what else will accrue but failure to win good will in any quarter—we shall be seen as having awaited the outcome so that we could shape our policy in the light of events—and our becoming the prize of the victor?

'If you are actually offered something that you should be asking for in your every prayer, do not look down on it. You will not always have the choice of alternatives that is open to you today; an opportunity does not often return, and it does not last long. You have long wished to free yourselves from Philip but have not had the nerve to do so. Men have crossed the sea with powerful fleets and armies to champion your independence, with no suffering or risk for you. If you reject these men as your allies, you must be mad—but either allies or enemies of yours they have to be!'

22. A commotion arose after the praetor's address, some expressing approval and others severely criticizing those agreeing with him, and soon the altercation involved not just individuals but entire member-states. Then a dispute began amongst the magistrates of the Achaean nation (the so-called *damiurgi*,* elected officials, ten in number) which was no less acrimonious than that amongst the general assembly. Five declared themselves ready to present the motion on the alliance with Rome and put the matter to a vote; five claimed there was a legal provision against the magistrates presenting a motion or the council making a decision on any matter prejudicial to the alliance with Philip. That day, too, was entirely taken up with internal squabbling.

There remained a single day in the regular programme of the meeting, for the law stipulated that a decision must be reached by the third day. Partisan feelings flared up so much for that day that parents had difficulty in keeping from doing physical violence to their children. Pisias of Pellene had a son called Memnon who was a *damiurgos* and a member of the group that was holding out against the reading of the motion and the taking of the vote. He long entreated his son to allow the Achaeans to take measures for their collective protection and not destroy their nation by his intransigence. But his entreaties were of no avail. Pisias then swore he would kill Memnon with his own hands and consider him an enemy of the people rather than as his own son, finally inducing him by his threats to join, the following day, the group who were for reading the motion. The latter were now in the majority, but when they put the proposal forward, and nearly all the member-states were clearly in approval and openly demonstrated how they would vote, the representatives from Dymae and Megalopolis, and some of the Argives, rose and left the meeting before a decision was reached. Nobody was surprised and nobody voiced disapproval. This was because the people of Megalopolis had, in the days of their grandfathers, been driven out by the Spartans but then restored to their native land by Antigonus; while in the case of the people of Dymae, recently captured and pillaged by a Roman army, Philip had ordered them ransomed wherever it was that they were in servitude and restored to them not only their freedom but their homeland. As for the Argives, apart from their belief that the Macedonian kings were descended from them,* most of them were also attached to Philip by individual ties of hospitality and close personal friendships. For these reasons they took their leave from a meeting which had been disposed to sanction a treaty with Rome, and they were pardoned for this departure as being beholden for the important services they had received in the recent past.

23. When they were asked for their votes, all the other Achaean member-states approved by immediate decree a treaty with Attalus and the Rhodians; the treaty with the Romans could not be ratified without the authorization of the Roman people and so it was postponed until such time as envoys could be sent to Rome. For the time being it was decided that three envoys be dispatched to Lucius Quinctius and the entire army of the Achaeans be taken to Corinth where Quinctius, who had now captured Cenchreae, was already laying siege to the city itself.

The Achaean army pitched camp in the area of the gate on the Sicyon road. The Romans were concentrating their attack on the part of the city facing Cenchreae, and Attalus, who had brought his army across the Isthmus, was attacking from the direction of Lechaeum, a port on the other sea. At first the attack was conducted in a rather desultory manner, the allies hoping for internal conflict between the inhabitants and the king's garrison. It transpired, however, that the enemy were all of one mind: the Macedonians were defending Corinth as though it were their communal fatherland, and the Corinthians allowed the garrison commander, Androsthenes, to wield his authority over them just as if he were a Corinthian citizen elected by them. Thereafter all hope for the besieging parties lay in duress, weapons, and siege-works. On every side the mounds were being advanced towards the walls, though access was difficult. The battering-ram had demolished a section of the wall on the side under attack from the Romans, and because it was denuded of protection the Macedonians hurriedly converged on that point to defend it with their arms, which gave rise to a ferocious battle between them and the Romans. Initially, the Romans were easily beaten off by superior numbers; but when they enlisted support from the Achaeans and Attalus they made it an even fight and, in fact, there was no doubt that they were easily going to drive back the Macedonians and Greeks from the position. There were, however, large numbers of Italian deserters present. Some had been in Hannibal's army and had followed Philip from fear of retribution from the Romans; others had been ships' crews who had lately left their fleets and gone over to the enemy in the hope of finding more prestigious service. These men had no hope of salvation in the event of a Roman victory, and this incited them to frenzy rather than reckless defiance.

There is a promontory, sacred to Juno (titled 'Acraea'*), jutting out into the sea opposite Sicyon, from which it is about seven miles' journey to Corinth. Philocles, who was also an officer of the king, brought 1,500 men through Boeotia to this spot, where boats from Corinth were waiting to receive these troops and take them across to Lechaeum. Attalus advocated burning the allied siege-works and immediately abandoning the siege, but the Roman commander persevered all the more stubbornly with the operation. When he saw the king's forces deployed before all the gates, however, and became aware that stemming their counter-attacks would not be easy, he conceded that Attalus was right in his opinion. And so, their enterprise aborted, the allies discharged the Achaeans and returned to their ships. Attalus made for Piraeus and the Romans for Corcyra.

24. During the period of these operations by the navy, the consul established camp in Phocis near Elatia and, at first, tried to achieve his goal by negotiation, engaging the help of the town's chief citizens. He was given the reply that any decision was out of their hands, that the king's soldiers were more numerous and stronger than the townspeople. Flamininus then assaulted the city from all directions at once with siege-engines and with weaponry. He brought up a battering-ram which caused the section of the wall between the towers to collapse with a tremendous crash and rumbling, laying bare the city. A Roman cohort then moved into the city through the passage opened up by the recent collapse, and at the same time the defenders all left their posts in every sector of the town and quickly converged on the spot that was under pressure from the enemy attack. The Romans were simultaneously clambering over the ruins

of the wall and also applying scaling-ladders to the ramparts that were still standing; and while the conflict diverted the gaze and attention of the enemy, the wall was taken by means of the scaling-ladders at several points and soldiers climbed over into the city. Hearing the uproar, the enemy were terror-stricken. They abandoned the spot they had been defending *en masse*, and all sought refuge in the citadel, a crowd of unarmed civilians going with them. Thus the consul occupied the city, and after sacking it he sent men to the citadel to promise the king's soldiers their lives, if they agreed to leave unarmed, and the citizens of Elatia their freedom. Guarantees were given on these terms and Flamininus took possession of the citadel a few days later.

25. In fact, the arrival in Achaea of Philocles, the king's lieutenant, had an effect beyond the raising of the siege of Corinth; it also led to the betrayal to Philocles of the city-state of Argos. This was done by certain prominent citizens who had first sounded out the feelings of the common people. It was an Argive custom for the magistrates to avert evil omens on the day of an assembly by calling upon Jupiter, Apollo, and Hercules at the start of the proceedings, and by a legal rider King Philip had been appended to this list. After the treaty was struck with the Romans, the herald failed to add Philip's name to the others, whereupon there was at first a murmuring amongst the crowd, and then an outcry as people supplied Philip's name and insisted that he be accorded the honour legally his, until finally the name was read out to deafening applause.

Confident in the support for Philip demonstrated in this way, the prominent citizens summoned Philocles, who by night seized a hill overlooking the city, a citadel which they call Larisa. Leaving a garrison in place there, Philocles proceeded at dawn in battle-formation to the forum which lies beneath the citadel. Here he was met by a line of men drawn up for battle. This was the recently installed Achaean garrison, some 500 young soldiers, hand-picked from all the member-states and commanded by Aenesidemus of Dymae. A spokesman was sent to these men by the king's officer with orders for them to leave the city. They were no match for the Macedonian sympathizers amongst the citizens of Argos, even if these latter stood alone, said the spokesman; much less could they match them when they were joined by the Macedonians, whom even the Romans had failed to withstand at Corinth. At first the spokesman's words had no effect either on the commander or his men; shortly afterwards, however, they saw the Argives approaching in a large column, also under arms, from the opposite direction, and they could see they were facing certain death. Even then it appeared that they would have been ready to meet any eventuality—had their leader been more resolute. Unwilling to face the simultaneous loss of the city and the pick of the fighting men of the Achaeans, Aenesidemus struck a bargain with Philocles which allowed the men to leave; but then, accompanied by a few clients, he personally refused to leave the spot where he had taken up a position under arms. A man was sent by Philocles to inquire what the point of this was. Without changing his position, Aenesidemus stood there with his shield held out before him and replied that he would die under arms defending the city that had been put in his charge. At this the king's officer issued an order, the Thracians hurled their spears and the Achaeans were all killed. And so, after a treaty struck between the Achaeans and the Romans, the two most famous cities, Argos and Corinth, remained in the power of the king. Such were the land and sea operations of the Romans in Greece that summer.

26. In Gaul nothing of particular note was achieved by the consul Sextus Aelius. He had two armies in the province: the first, which should have been demobilized, he had retained—it had been under the command of the proconsul Lucius Cornelius, but Aelius put the praetor Gaius Helvius at its head—and the second he brought with him into the province. Even so, he spent almost the entire year on the enforced repatriation to their colonies of the peoples of Cremona and Placentia who had been scattered abroad by the tribulations of war.

If Gaul that year was surprisingly peaceful, the environs of Rome almost saw a slave revolt. Hostages for the Carthaginians were being kept under guard at Setia, and with them, since they were the children of dignitaries, was a large body of slaves. The total of the latter was being further enhanced, as was to be expected in the aftermath of the recent African war, by numbers of prisoners-of-war of African stock who had been bought as slaves from the booty by the people of Setia themselves. <. . .> They hatched a plot and sent some of their number to incite to rebellion slaves in the territory of Setia first of all, and later around Norba and Cerceii. With everything now well prepared, they had decided to launch their attack on the people of Setia when these were engrossed in watching games that were forthcoming in the town. In the bloody and unforeseen uproar Setia was captured; the slaves <then tried> to capture Norba and Cerceii. Word of this appalling incident was brought to the urban praetor, Lucius Cornelius Lentulus,* in Rome—two slaves came to him before dawn and gave him a comprehensive account of what had taken place and what was likely to happen in the future. The praetor ordered the slaves to be kept under guard at his home, convened the Senate and reported the information brought by the informers. Lentulus was instructed to undertake a mission to investigate the conspiracy and crush it. Setting off with five legates, he compelled men whom he came across in the fields to swear the oath of allegiance, take up arms and follow him. With this makeshift force, some 2,000 armed men, he reached Setia without anyone knowing his destination. There he swiftly arrested the ringleaders of the conspiracy, precipitating a flight from the town by the slaves, and then sent men through the countryside to hunt down <fugitives>. Sterling service had thus come from two slave informers and one free man. The Senate ordered that the latter be awarded 100,000 *asses*, and the slaves 25,000 *asses* each plus their freedom (their masters were reimbursed for them from the public purse).

Not long after this there was a report that slaves still at large from the same conspiracy were going to seize Praeneste. The praetor Lucius Cornelius set off for the town and executed some 500 men who were guilty of involvement. There was fear in the state that the Carthaginian hostages and captives were responsible for these events, and for that reason street-patrols were instituted at Rome, with the junior magistrates instructed to make the rounds of these. Furthermore, the triumvirs were ordered to keep a particularly close watch on the quarry-prison, and a letter was circulated amongst the Latin allies by the praetor to the effect that the hostages should be confined to private houses and not be permitted access to public places, while prisoners-of-war should be shackled with chains weighing at least 10 pounds and be kept under guard in the public prisons and nowhere else.

27. The same year a deputation from Attalus placed a golden crown weighing 246 pounds on the Capitol and gave thanks to the Senate for the fact that Antiochus had been induced by the authority of the Roman embassy to withdraw his army from the territory of Attalus.

That same summer 200 cavalry, 10 elephants, and 200,000 measures of wheat reached the army campaigning in Greece from Masinissa. Large quantities of supplies and clothing for the army were likewise sent from Sicily and Sardinia. Sicily was under the governorship of Marcus Marcellus, and Sardinia under Marcus Porcius Cato. The latter was a man of high principles and integrity, but was considered too severe in his suppression of usury. Money-lenders were driven from the island, and allowances given by the allies for the entertainment of the praetors were curtailed or discontinued.

On his return from Gaul for the elections, the consul Sextus Aelius pronounced Gaius Cornelius Cethegus and Quintus Minucius Rufus elected consuls.* Elections for the praetorship were held two days later, and that year, for the first time, six praetors were elected,* to meet the increase in the number of provinces and the expansion of the empire. The following were elected: Lucius Manlius Vulso, Gaius Sempronius Tuditanus, Marcus Sergius Silus, Marcus Helvius, Marcus Minucius Rufus, and Lucius Atilius, of whom Sempronius and Helvius were plebeian aediles* (the curule aediles being Quintus Minucius Thermus and Tiberius Sempronius Longus). The Roman Games were that year repeated four times.

28. When Gaius Cornelius and Quintus Minucius assumed the consulship, the very first piece of business transacted was that of the provinces for the consuls and praetors, and the matter of the praetors, which could be decided by lot, was settled first. Jurisdiction of urban affairs fell to Sergius, that of affairs of resident aliens to Minucius; Atilius was allotted Sardinia, Manlius Sicily, Sempronius Hither Spain, and Helvius Farther Spain. As the consuls were preparing to draw lots for Italy and Macedonia, the plebeian tribunes Lucius Oppius and Quintus Fulvius interposed an objection, arguing that Macedonia was a distant province and that down to that time nothing had proved more of an obstacle to the administration of the war than the recall of a consul already in the field at a point when hostilites had barely commenced and when his conduct of the compaign was now well under way. It was already three years since war had been declared on Macedon, they argued. During that time Sulpicius had spent most of *his* year looking for the king and his army; Villius had been recalled just when he was coming to grips with the foe and before he had achieved anything; and Quinctius had been kept back in Rome most of his year for the conduct of religious

ceremonies—but had nevertheless achieved such success that he could have finished off the war had he arrived earlier in his province or had winter come later. Now, despite the fact that he had virtually retired into winter-quarters, it was reported that his preparations for the war were such that he seemed likely to bring it to an end the next season, if no successor got in his way.

With such arguments the tribunes of the plebs persuaded the consuls to agree to abide by the wishes of the Senate if the plebeian tribunes themselves did the same. The two sides agreed to give the Senate complete freedom to decide the issue, and the Senators determined that both consuls should be given Italy as their province, while they prolonged Titus Quinctius' tenure of command until the arrival of a successor appointed by senatorial decree. The two consuls were each assigned two legions and given the responsibility for conducting a war against the Cisalpine Gauls who had defected from the Roman people.

Quinctius was formally assigned a supplementary force for service in Macedonia, and this comprised 6,000 infantry, 300 cavalry, and 3,000 seamen. Lucius Quinctius Flamininus was instructed to continue as admiral of the fleet which he had been commanding. For the two Spains each of the praetors was granted 8,000 infantry, drawn from the allies and the Latin League, and 400 cavalry, so that they could demobilize the veteran troops who had been serving in the Spanish provinces. They were further instructed to define the administrative boundary between the farther and hither provinces. The Senate also appointed Publius Sulpicius and Publius Villius, former consuls in the province, as additional legates for Macedonia.

29. Before the departure of the consuls and praetors for their provinces, it was decided that expiatory sacrifices be held for certain prodigies. At Rome the temples of Vulcan and Summanus had been struck by lightning, as had a wall and a gate at Fregenae. At Frusino daylight had shone out in the middle of the night. At Aefula a lamb had been born with two heads and five feet. At Formiae two wolves had entered the town and mauled some people they chanced upon, and at Rome a wolf had made its way not just into the city but even into the Capitol.

The plebeian tribune Gaius Atinius proposed a bill for the establishment of five colonies on the coast—two at the mouths of the Rivers Vulturnus and Liternus, one at Puteoli, and one at Castrum

Salerni, with Buxentum added to these as the fifth—and 300 families were to be dispatched to each of these colonies. Marcus Servilius Geminus, Quintus Minucius Thermus, and Tiberius Sempronius Longus were elected triumvirs for a three-year term in order to found these colonies.

After completing the conscription and performing all the religious and secular duties for which they were responsible, the two consuls set off for Gaul. Cornelius took the direct route to the Insubres, who had taken the Cenomani as their allies and were now in armed insurrection. Quintus Minucius headed up the left side of Italy to the Tyrrhenian sea where, having led his army to Genoa, he chose the Ligurians as his first adversaries in the war. Clastidium and Litubium, both Ligurian towns, and the Celeiates and the Cerdiciates, also communities of the same people, surrendered, leaving everything this side of the Po under Roman control, apart from the Gallic Boii and the Ligurian Ilvates. Fifteen towns and 20,000 men were reported to have surrendered. Minucius then led his legions into the territory of the Boii.

30. Not long before this the army of the Boii had crossed the Po and joined up with the Insubres and the Cenomani. They had received word that the consuls had put their legions together to mount their campaign, and they too wanted to strengthen their forces by consolidation. Then a report came that one of the consuls was burning the lands of the Boii, and this immediately precipitated dissension. The Boii insisted that the combined forces bring aid to those in distress, but the Insubres refused to abandon their own property. Their troops accordingly separated: the Boii left to protect their farmlands while the Insubres encamped on the bank of the River Mincius along with the Cenomani.

Two miles downstream from that point the consul Cornelius pitched camp on the same river. From here he sent scouts to the Cenoman villages and to Brixia, the tribal capital, and ascertained that the armed uprising of the young warriors had not been sanctioned by the elders and that it was without public consultation that the Cenomani had joined the uprising of the Insubres. Cornelius summoned their chieftains and proceeded to do all he could to detach the Cenomani from the Insubres, make them break camp and either go home or transfer their allegiance to the Romans. That end he did not achieve, but the consul was nevertheless given a solemn pledge by the Cenomani that in the battle they would either remain inactive or, if an opportunity arose, help the Romans. The Insubres were ignorant of this compact, and yet they had some suspicion that the loyalty of their allies was flagging. Accordingly, when they led out the troops to battle-stations, they did not dare confide either of the wings to the Cenomani in case they altered the entire fortunes of the encounter by treacherously giving ground, and instead they positioned them in reserve behind the standards.

At the start of the battle the consul made a vow of a temple to Juno Sospita in the event of a defeat and rout of the enemy on that day, and a shout went up from his men to the effect that they would oblige him to discharge the vow. Then the assault was launched on the enemy. The Insubres failed to withstand the first onslaught. Some authorities have it that they were also suddenly attacked in the rear by the Cenomani when the battle was under way and were thrown into chaos on two fronts; that there were 35,000 killed between the two lines and 5,200 taken alive (including Hamilcar, the general of the Carthaginians,* who had been responsible for the war); and that 130 military standards and more than <. . .> wagons <were captured. . . . towns> of the Gauls which had joined the uprising of the Insubres surrendered to the Romans.

31. The consul Minucius had at first swept through the lands of the Boii, making raids far and wide, but when the Boii left the Insubres and fell back to protect their own territory he stuck to his camp in the belief that he ought to meet his enemy in the field. In fact the Boii would not have refused battle had the report of the defeat of the Insubres not arrived to break their spirit. At this report they abandoned their leader and their camp, and dispersed through the towns in order to defend their individual properties, thus forcing on their enemy a change of strategy for the war. For Minucius now abandoned hope of deciding the issue with a single encounter and went back to ravaging the fields, burning buildings and storming towns. During this period Clastidium was burned. From the Boii Minucius led his legions against the Ligurian Ilvates, the only tribe refusing submission. But when they heard that the Insubres had been defeated in the field and that the Boii were so intimidated that they dared not pin their hopes on a battle, this people also submitted to the Romans. Dispatches from the two consuls regarding their respective successes in Gaul were brought to Rome at about the same

time. The urban praetor Marcus Sergius read them out in the Senate and later, on the authority of the Senate, to the people. Four days of public prayers were enjoined by decree.

32. It was already winter, and after the capture of Elatia Titus Quinctius had his winter-quarters established at various points in Phocis and Locris. Meanwhile civil discord broke out in Opus. One faction called upon the Aetolians, who were closer, the other on the Romans. The Aetolians arrived first, but the wealthier faction shut them out, sent a message to the Roman commander and held the city until his arrival. The citadel was held by a garrison of the king, which could be constrained to leave it neither by the threats of the people of Opus nor by the authority of the Roman general.

An immediate attack was forestalled by the arrival of a herald from Philip requesting a place and date for a meeting, and this was granted to the king with some reluctance. It was not that Quinctius was loath to be seen as having terminated the war by a mixture of armed force and diplomacy; the fact was that he did not yet know whether one of the new consuls was being sent out to succeed him or whether his command would be extended, a goal which he had instructed his friends and relatives to do their utmost to attain. Still, he felt the meeting would be opportune, giving him latitude to incline towards war if he were staying, or a peace-settlement if he were leaving. They chose as a site a beach in the Malian Gulf near Nicaea, and the king came to this spot from Demetrias with five cutters and a warship. With him were leading citizens of Macedonia and a distinguished Achaean exile, Cycliadas. With the Roman commander were: Amynander; Dionysodorus, a representative of Attalus; Acesimbrotus, admiral of the Rhodian fleet; Phaeneas, chief of the Aetolians; and two Achaeans, Aristaenus and Xenophon.* Surrounded by these the Roman went forward to the edge of the shore, and the king advanced to the prow of his ship which lay at anchor.

'We could more conveniently talk and listen to each other at close quarters if you disembark,' observed the consul. When the king refused to do this, Quinctius added 'Whom do you fear, then?', to which Philip replied with the pride of a king: 'I fear no one apart from the immortal gods, but I do not have confidence in the integrity of all the men I see around you, least of all the Aetolians'. 'As far as that is concerned, if trust is lacking, all men who meet to parley with an enemy are exposed to the same danger,' said the Roman. 'But if treachery is afoot, Titus Quinctius,' replied the king, 'Philip and Phaeneas do not come as equal rewards for duplicity—it would not be as difficult for the Aetolians to find another magistrate as for the Macedonians to find a replacement for me as king.'

33. After this there was silence, the Roman thinking it appropriate for the man who had requested the meeting to speak first, and the king that the opening words belonged to the party dictating the terms of peace, not the one being given them. The Roman then said that the statement he had to make was simple, that he would specify only the minimum requirements, without which there could be no peace accord. The king, he continued, had to withdraw his garrisons from all the city-states of Greece, return captives and deserters to the allies of the Roman people, give back to the Romans the regions of Illyricum which he had occupied subsequent to the peace-treaty struck in Epirus, and return to Ptolemy of Egypt the cities which he had seized after the death of Ptolemy Philopator. Such, he said, were his conditions and those of the Roman people, but it was right that Philip listen also to the demands of the Roman allies.

Attalus' representative demanded the return of ships and prisoners taken in the naval engagement off Chios and the restoration to their original state of the Nicephorium and the temple of Venus, both of which Philip had pillaged and reduced to ruin. The Rhodians sought the return of the Peraea (an area on the mainland, facing their island, that had been under their sway since days of old) and also made the following demands: the withdrawal of the garrisons from Iasus, Bargyliae, and the city of Euromus, as well as from Sestus and Abydus in the Hellespont; the restitution of Perinthus to Byzantium, with restoration of their ancient rights; and the liberation of all the markets and ports of Asia.

The Achaeans requested the return of Corinth and Argos. The Aetolian praetor, Phaeneas, made much the same demands as had the Romans, namely Philip's withdrawal from Greece and the restoration to the Aetolians of the cities formerly under their jurisdiction and control. Phaeneas' address was followed by an intervention from a leader of the Aetolians, Alexander, who was thought eloquent for an Aetolian. He had been silent a long while, he said, not because he felt the meeting was serving any purpose, but so as not to interrupt any of his allies while he was speaking. Philip, he continued, did not conduct peace negotiations with honesty, nor had he ever fought wars with pure courage. In discussion he was always laying traps and scheming; in war, instead of fighting in the open field and engaging his enemy, he would retreat, burning and sacking cities and, conquered himself, ruining the prizes of the conquerors. This was not <the way of> the Macedonian kings of old. These would fight regular battles and do their best to spare the cities so as to have a richer empire. For what was the sense in destroying what one was fighting to possess and leaving oneself nothing but the act of warfare? Philip had destroyed more cities of his allies in Thessaly in the course of the previous year than all the enemies of Thessaly had ever done in the past. He had also taken more from the Aetolians themselves as an ally than as an enemy: he had seized Lysimachia after driving out its praetor and the Aetolian garrison; he had reduced Cius, also a city under Aetolian control, to a state of total devastation and ruin; and by similar duplicity he now had in his power Thebes of Phthia, Echinus, Larisa, and Pharsalus.

34. Provoked by Alexander's words, Philip brought his ship closer to shore so that he could be clearly heard. He began to speak, aiming his remarks primarily at the Aetolians, but Phaeneas cut him off sharply, saying that it was not a matter of words—Philip either had to win in the field of battle or do the bidding of his superiors. 'That, at least, is clear even to a blind man,'* answered Philip, poking fun at Phaeneas' eye-condition (Philip was, in fact, of a wittier disposition than was appropriate for a king, and he did not refrain from joking even in the midst of serious business). Then he proceeded to wax indignant that the Aetolians, like the Romans, were calling for a withdrawal from Greece though they could not specify what the boundaries of Greece actually were. Even in Aetolia, he said, the Agraei, the Apodoti, and the Amphilochi, though they represented a large section of the region, were not part of Greece.

'Are the Aetolians justified in their complaint about my not keeping my hands off their allies,' he asked, 'when they themselves have been observing as a rule, from days of old, the practice of allowing their men of military age—though without official sanction—to fight against their own allies (and it often emerges that on both sides opposing armies have Aetolian auxiliaries)? And it was not I who captured Cius—I helped my ally and friend Prusias when he attacked it. I was the champion of Lysimachia against the Thracians, but the Thracians now hold it because the urgency of my situation diverted my attention from its defence to this particular war. That suffices for the Aetolians. To Attalus and the Rhodians I have no real obligation—the war began with them, not me—but as a mark of respect to the Romans I shall restore both the Peraea to the Rhodians and also the ships to Attalus, along with such captives as come to light. As far as the Nicophorium is concerned, and renovations to the temple of Venus, all I can say to those demanding their restoration is the following: I shall see to, and pay for, replantation—the only means by which woods and groves that have been felled can be restored—since such are the demands and responses that kings like to make amongst themselves.'

The final part of his address was an attack on the Achaeans. After a preamble on the kindnesses shown to that people, first by Antigonus and then by himself, he had their decrees read out containing all manner of divine and human honours that had been paid to him, and he berated them for their recent decree by which they broke with him. After a bitter criticism of their disloyalty he none the less said that he would restore Argos to them. As for Corinth, he would discuss the matter with the Roman commander and would at the same time ask him whether he thought it right that the king should leave only the cities which he had captured himself, and which he now occupied by the rules of war, or whether he should also withdraw from those which had been passed down to him by his ancestors.

35. The Achaeans and Aetolians were preparing to respond to his remarks, but since it was close to sunset the meeting was adjourned till the following day. Philip returned to the naval base from which he had come, and the Romans and their allies to their camp. The next day Quinctius came to Nicaea, the rendezvous on which they had agreed, at the pre-arranged time, but Philip was nowhere to be seen, nor did any messenger come from him over a period of several hours. They were all losing hope of his coming when his ships suddenly appeared. Philip's explanation was that the demands being made of him were severe and unreasonable, and so, at a loss what to think, he had spent the whole day in deliberation. It was generally believed that Philip had purposely put off the matter until late in the day so that the Achaeans and Aetolians could not be given time to make their reply to him; and he actually corroborated this view himself by requesting a private discussion with the Roman

commander, with the other representatives excluded, so that time would not be wasted in wrangling, and some closure could be set on the business. At first his request was not entertained, so that the allies should not seem excluded from the debate. Philip, however, kept insisting, and so with everybody's approval the Roman commander, along with the military tribune Appius Claudius, advanced to the edge of the shore, apart from the others, while the king disembarked with the two men he had had with him the previous day.

There they conversed in private for some time. The version of the proceedings that Philip took back to his people is not known, but the account Quinctius gave to the allies was this: to the Romans Philip was ceding the entire coastline of Illyricum, and he was also giving back to them deserters and any prisoners he had; to Attalus he was restoring the ships and the crews he had captured along with them; to the Rhodians he ceded the region called the Peraea, but he would not leave Iasus and Bargyliae; to the Aetolians he returned Pharsalus and Larisa, but not Thebes; in the case of the Achaeans he was prepared to withdraw not only from Argos but from Corinth as well. Not one person was satisfied with the areas identified by Philip as those which he would or would not leave. Everyone reckoned that more was being lost than gained, and that unless the king withdrew all his garrisons from Greece causes for friction would always remain.

36. This was the view expressed by the entire meeting, everyone trying to shout louder than the other, and the noise reached Philip standing in the distance. He therefore asked Quinctius for a postponement of the whole question to the following day, saying that he would surely win over the delegates or allow himself to be won over by them. The beach at Thronium was settled on as the venue, and here they assembled early in the day. At the start of this meeting, Philip asked Quinctius and all present not to upset their hopes of peace, and finally he requested time to send a deputation to the Senate in Rome—either he would gain peace on the conditions already proposed, he said, or he would accept whatever peace-terms the Senate dictated. All were entirely opposed to this—Philip was only seeking to delay and postpone matters in order to gather forces, they said. Quinctius, however, stated that there would have been some truth in this had it been summer and the campaigning season but, as it was, winter was coming on, and nothing was lost by

granting Philip time to send his deputation. No item of any agreement they reached with the king could be ratified without Senatorial authorization, he said, and while winter imposed a necessary lull in the fighting the possibility of the Senate's granting authorization could be explored. All the other allied leaders supported this view; and so a two-month truce was granted, and it was decided that they, too, should send one ambassador each to give intelligence to the Senate in case it be taken in by the king's chicanery. A rider, that the king's garrisons be immediately withdrawn from Phocis and Locris, was added to the terms agreed upon for the truce. To give the deputation a higher profile, Quinctius himself sent Amynander, king of the Athamanians, along with the delegates of the allies, as well as Quintus Fabius, son of a sister of Quinctius' wife, plus Quintus Fulvius and Appius Claudius.

37. When they arrived in Rome, the ambassadors from the allies were granted an audience before those from the king. All of their presentation was taken up with vituperation of the king, but what especially impressed the Senate was their elucidation of the geography of the area in question, of the sea and the land. This made it clear to everyone that if the king held Demetrias in Thessaly, Chalcis in Euboea, and Corinth in Achaea, Greece could not be free, and Philip himself, the ambassadors noted, used to refer to these cities as his 'fetters of Greece', a term as accurate as it was impudent. After this the king's representatives were brought in. They launched into a long harangue, only to have their speech cut short by a brief question—would Philip withdraw from these three cities? For the representatives admitted that they had no specific instructions with regard to them. And so the king's delegation was discharged with no peace-terms concluded, and Quinctius was given a free hand to negotiate peace or make war. It was now quite clear to him that the Senate had not grown weary of the war, and he personally wanted victory more than he wanted peace. Accordingly he did not, after that, grant Philip a meeting, and he said that he would entertain no deputation from him that did not announce complete withdrawal from Greece.

38. Philip could see the issue had to be decided in battle and that he needed to concentrate his forces from all quarters. He was concerned above all about the cities of Achaea, (an area far separated from him) and more about Argos than he was about Corinth. He

concluded that the best idea was to hand over Argos to Nabis, tyrant of Sparta, as a kind of security—Nabis would restore the city to him if the king were victorious, but retain it himself in the event of any mishap befalling him. Philip therefore wrote to Philocles, who was in command of Corinth and Argos, asking him to meet the tyrant in person. Philocles, who was already coming with what was a gift for Nabis, also added the statement that the king wished to give his daughters in marriage to the sons of Nabis* as a guarantee of the friendship between king and tyrant in the future.

At first, the tyrant claimed the only condition on which he would accept the city of Argos was if he were invited to give it help by a decree of the Argives themselves. Later he heard that his title 'tyrant' had been uttered not only with disrespect, but with hatred, in a crowded assembly and, thinking he now had found a reason for dispossessing the Argives, he told Philocles to hand over the city whenever he wished. The tyrant was let into the city at night without anyone knowing, and at dawn all the more elevated areas of the town had been seized by him and the gates closed. A few of the most important citizens had slipped away in the initial commotion, and their valuables were pillaged in their absence; those who remained found themselves despoiled of their gold and silver and subjected to huge fines. Those who unhesitatingly brought out their property were let off without abuse and physical maltreatment, but people suspected of hiding or holding back anything were thrashed and tortured like slaves. Nabis then called an assembly at which he proposed two bills, one on the cancellation of debts and a second on redistributing land to individual citizens—thereby providing two torches for revolutionaries to inflame the proletariat against the nobles.

39. After the city of Argos was in his hands, the tyrant gave no thought whatsoever to the man from whom he had received it and the conditions on which he had done so. He sent a delegation to Quinctius in Elatia and to Attalus, who was in winter-quarters at Aegina, to report that Argos was now in his control. If Quinctius came to parley with him there, he said, he was sure they would reach full agreement. Wishing to deprive Philip of this stronghold, too, Quinctius agreed to come, and he sent word to Attalus, asking him to come from Aegina to Sicyon to meet him. He then crossed from Anticyra to Sicyon with ten quinqueremes which his brother, Lucius

Quinctius, had happened to bring with him during those very days from his winter-quarters in Corcyra.

Attalus was already in Sicyon. He expressed the view that the tyrant should come to the Roman commander, not the Roman to the tyrant, and he won Quinctius over to his opinion, persuading him not to go to the city of Argos itself. A place called Mycenica lies not far from the city, and it was agreed that the meeting be held there.

Quinctius arrived with his brother and a few military tribunes; Attalus with his royal train of attendants; and Nicostratus, praetor of the Achaeans, with a few auxiliary soldiers. They found the tyrant awaiting them there with all his troops. Nabis, in armour himself and attended by armed bodyguards, advanced close to the mid-point of the field separating the parties. Quinctius, accompanied by his brother and two of the military tribunes, was unarmed; and the king, with the praetor of the Achaeans and one of his courtiers at his side, was also unarmed. The conversation opened with an apology from the tyrant for coming to the meeting armed himself and encircled by armed men, when he saw that the Roman commander and the king were unarmed. It was not them he feared, he said; it was the Argive exiles. Then discussion of the terms of alliance began, and the Roman demanded two things of Nabis: first, cessation of hostilities with the Achaeans; and secondly that the tyrant send auxiliary troops with him against Philip. The latter Nabis agreed to send, but instead of peace with the Achaeans Flamininus gained from him a truce until the time that the war with Philip should be finished.

40. The Argive question was also raised by Attalus. He asserted that the city had been betrayed to Nabis through treachery on Philocles' part, and was now being held by him under duress. Nabis defended himself by saying that he had been called upon by the Argives themselves. The king insisted upon a meeting of the Argive assembly so that this could be established, and the tyrant did not object. However, the king asserted that Nabis' garrison should be withdrawn from the city, and the Argives given the opportunity of a free assembly—with no Spartans present—which would reveal the true wishes of the people of Argos. The tyrant refused to withdraw his men, and further discussion proved ineffectual. The meeting then adjourned, with the Roman granted 600 Cretan soldiers by the tyrant and a truce of four months' duration arranged between

Nicostratus, praetor of the Achaeans, and the tyrant of the Lacedaemonians.

Quinctius then set off for Corinth and came up to the gate with his Cretan battalion to make it clear to Philocles, in command of the city, that the tyrant had abandoned Philip. Philocles also came to confer with the Roman commander, who urged him to desert Philip immediately and deliver the city to him. Philocles so worded his reply as to give the impression of having postponed a decision rather than refused outright. Quinctius crossed from Corinth to Anticyra, and from there he sent his brother to try to win over the support of the people of Acarnania.

Attalus headed for Sicyon from Argos. Here the city added fresh honours to the former ones they had made to the king; and Attalus, who had in the past paid an enormous sum of money to redeem the holy precinct of Apollo for the people of Sicyon, did not wish to lose this second occasion to show his generosity to a city-state that was his ally and friend. He made the city a gift of ten talents of silver and 10,000 bushels of grain. After this he returned to his fleet at Cenchreae.

Nabis for his part strengthened the garrison at Argos and returned to Sparta. He had already despoiled the men of Argos himself, and now he sent his wife* back to the city to despoil the women. She brought the ladies of note into her presence, either individually or in family groups, and, by a combination of flattery and menaces, deprived them not only of their gold but eventually even of their clothing and all their feminine accessories.

BOOK THIRTY-THREE

1. Such were the events of the winter. At the beginning of spring*
Quinctius summoned Attalus to Elatia and, wishing to bring under
his control the Boeotians who to that point had been wavering in
their sympathies, set off through Phocis and established his camp
five miles from the Boeotian capital of Thebes. The next day he
proceeded on his march to the city, taking with him the soldiers of a
single maniple, along with Attalus and the numerous deputations
that had come to him from all parts; but he had previously ordered
the *hastati* of a legion, numbering 2,000 men,* to follow him at a
distance of a mile. At about the half-way mark of his journey he was
met by Antiphilus, praetor of the Boeotians;* the rest of the population was watching the arrival of the Roman commander and the king
from the city-walls. Around these two could be seen only the odd
weapon and a few soldiers—the *hastati* who were following at a
distance were hidden by the winding roads and valleys separating the
two detachments.

As Quinctius approached the city, he proceeded at a slower pace as
though to greet the crowd coming from the city to meet him, though
in reality he was delaying to allow the *hastati* to catch up. Since a
crowd of people had been massed before the lictor,* the townspeople
did not catch sight of the column of soldiers that was speedily following before it arrived at the commander's quarters. At this point
they were all taken aback, suspecting that the city had been betrayed
and captured through the treachery of their praetor, Antiphilus. The
Boeotians now seemed to be left with no opportunity for open discussion at the council which was scheduled for the following day, but
they concealed their chagrin, which they would have displayed to no
purpose and not without risk to themselves.

2. At the council Attalus was the first to speak. He opened with an
account of the various services rendered by his ancestors and by
himself both to Greece as a whole and to the people of Boeotia in
particular. But, too old and frail* now to cope with the stress of
public speaking, he fell silent and collapsed. The meeting was
temporarily suspended while they carried the king out and tried to
bring him round (he had suffered a partial paralysis). Thereupon

Aristaenus, praetor of the Achaeans,* was given the floor, and he had all the more impact because the advice he had for the Boeotians was no different from what he had given to the Achaeans. A few remarks were added by Quinctius himself, lauding the dependability of the Romans rather than their military strength or material resources. There followed a motion, proposed and read aloud by Dicaearchus the Plataean, regarding the establishment of a pact with the Romans, and since no one presumed to speak against it this was accepted and carried by the votes of all the city-states of Boeotia. When the council broke up Quinctius stayed on in Thebes only as long as he was obliged to by Attalus' sudden affliction. When it emerged that it had not been a life-threatening attack, but one which had disabled him, the consul left him there to undergo the requisite treatment and returned to Elatia, his point of departure for Thebes. He had now enlisted the Boeotians as allies, as he had earlier the Achaeans, and, with territory to his rear now left secure and pacified, his entire attention had been brought to focus on Philip and what remained of the war.

3. Philip, too, was active at the beginning of spring. When his delegation returned from Rome with no peace settlement, he proceeded with a muster of troops throughout all the towns of his realm since he faced a severe shortage of younger men—uninterrupted warfare over many generations had reduced the Macedonian population, and during his own reign, too, large numbers of men had fallen in wars fought at sea against the Rhodians and Attalus, and on land against the Romans. Accordingly he began to enrol recruits from the age of sixteen, and men whose service was over but who still possessed a modicum of strength were also recalled to service. With his army brought up to strength in this manner, Philip assembled all his troops at Dium after the spring equinox. There he established a base camp and began his wait for the enemy, drilling his men every day.

At about this time, too, Quinctius left Elatia and, passing by Thronium and Scarphea, came to Thermopylae. He was detained in the area by an assembly of the Aetolians, convened at Heraclea, at which members were discussing the number of auxiliary forces they would take when they followed the Romans to war. Learning the decision of the allies, he advanced from Heraclea to Xyniae two days later, pitched camp on the Aenian-Thessalian border, and waited for his Aetolian auxiliaries. The Aetolians wasted no time, and 6,000 infantry and 400 cavalry arrived under the command of Phaeneas. To leave no doubt about what he had been waiting for, Quinctius immediately struck camp. Passing into Pthiotic territory he was joined by 500 Gortynians from Crete under the command of Cydas, and 300 similarly armed troops from Apollonia, and not much later by Amynander with 1,200 Athamanian infantry.

On learning that the Romans had left Elatia, Philip felt he should give encouragement to his men, facing as he was a decisive struggle. After a long harangue on the timeworn themes of their ancestors' glorious exploits, and the military reputation of Macedon, he then came to the items which were at that moment striking terror into them and those which could inspire them to some degree of hope.

4. To counterbalance the defeat suffered in the gorge at the River Aous, Philip referred to the rout inflicted on the Romans †on land† at Atrax* by the Macedonian phalanx. And even at the Aous, he said, where the Macedonians had failed to maintain their grip on the passes of Epirus which they had seized, responsibility lay primarily with the men who had been negligent in guard-duty, and after that, in the battle itself, with the light-armed and mercenary troops. The Macedonian phalanx, he claimed, had stood firm on that occasion, and would always remain invincible in pitched battle on level ground.

Philip's phalanx comprised 16,000 men, and represented the essence of the kingdom's strength. He also had 2,000 soldiers carrying small shields (men known as 'peltasts') and an equal number—that is 2,000 from each nation—of Thracians and Illyrians, these latter coming from a tribe called the Tralles. There was also an assortment of some 1,500 mercenary auxiliaries of various nations and 2,000 cavalry. Such were the troops with whom the king was awaiting his enemy. As for the Romans, they had roughly the same numbers; only in cavalry were they superior, because of the Aetolian supplement.

5. Quinctius had now moved his camp to Pthiotic Thebes. Here he entertained the hope of the city being delivered to him through the intrigue of Timon, a leading citizen of the community, and so he came up to the walls with only a few cavalry and light infantry. His hopes were dashed, however, to such an extent that he faced not only a battle with counter-attacking forces but danger that might have been critical but for the timely arrival of his infantry and cavalry, which had been speedily called to action from the camp. When his

incautiously conceived hopes came to nothing, Quinctius put a temporary halt to his efforts to take the city. Well aware, however, that the king was already in Thessaly, but with no information as yet on the area into which he had come, he sent his men through the fields with orders to cut and prepare palisade-stakes.

The Macedonians and Greeks also used stakes, but they did not modify their practice so as to facilitate transportation of them, or strengthen their defence-capability. They would cut down trees that were too big, and had too many branches, for a soldier to be able to carry them in addition to his weapons and, when they had formed a circle of these around their camp, breaking down the palisade was easy. This was because the trunks of the great trees rose from the ground at wide intervals, and their numerous and sturdy branches enabled one to get a firm hold on them. Thus two, or at most three, young men would, after some effort, pull up one of the trees, and when it was torn out, an open space like a doorway was immediately created, with nothing easily available to block it. The Romans, however, cut stakes that are light and usually forked, bearing three or at most four branches, so that a soldier can easily carry a number of them at a time, with his weapons hanging behind his back. Further, they plant these so close together, and interlace the branches so well, that one cannot tell which branch belongs to a particular trunk nor <. . .>; and the branches are so sharpened and so tightly intertwined as to leave no room for inserting a hand, with the result that it proves impossible to grasp anything that can be pulled out or indeed to pull anything out, since the interlaced branches bond together to form a barrier. And if by chance one stake *is* pulled out, the space that is left is small and it is easy to make a replacement.

6. The following day Quinctius advanced a short distance, his men carrying with them the palisade, so as to be ready to pitch camp in any location. About six miles from Pherae he halted and sent out a scouting party to find out where in Thessaly the king was positioned and what he was doing. The king was in the neighbourhood of Larisa. He had already been informed that the Romans had moved from Thebes to Pherae, and since he, too, wished to have done with the battle as soon as possible, he proceeded to march towards his enemy and pitched camp about four miles from Pherae. The next day light infantry from the two sides went forward from their positions to seize the hills overlooking the city and, when both were

about the same distance from the ridge which they were to take, they caught sight of each other. They sent messengers back to camp to seek advice on what to do now that they had unexpectedly come across the enemy, and halted, quietly awaiting their return. That day they were called back to camp without engaging the enemy; but the following day there was a battle between the cavalry in the area of those same hills, and the king's troops were put to flight and driven back to their camp, thanks not least to the Aetolians.

What seriously hindered both sides in their functioning was the fact that the countryside was covered with closely planted trees, that there were gardens, as was to be expected in districts close to the city, and that there were walls restricting the roads and, in places, blocking them off entirely. Accordingly the two commanders both decided to quit the area, and as if they had prior intelligence both made for Scotusa, Philip hoping to acquire provisions from the place, and the Roman intending to get there ahead of his foe and destroy the crops. The two armies marched an entire day without catching sight of each other at any point, because an unbroken chain of hills lay between them. The Romans encamped at Eretria, in Pthiotic territory, and Philip on the River Onchestus. The following day Philip pitched his camp at a place called Melambium in the area of Scotusa, while Quinctius pitched his in the neighbourhood of Thetideum in Pharsalian territory, and even at that point neither side was certain of the location of its enemy. On the third day there was a downpour, followed by fog dark as night, and this pinned down the Romans who were afraid of being ambushed.

7. In order to accelerate his progress Philip gave the order to advance, undaunted by the clouds which had come down to ground level after the rainstorm. But so thick was the mist that had blotted out the daylight that the standard-bearers could not see the road, nor the soldiers the standards, and the column, floundering around and following indistinct shouts like people lost in the night, was thrown into disarray. After crossing the so-called Cynoscephalae* Hills and leaving there a strong garrison of infantry and cavalry, the Macedonians pitched camp. The Roman commander had remained in the same encampment at Thetideum, but he did send out a scouting detachment of ten squadrons of cavalry and 1,000 infantry to locate the enemy, warning them to be on their guard against an ambush, which the poor daylight would hide, even in the open. When this

detachment reached the hills occupied by the enemy, each side struck panic into the other, and both froze in their tracks. They then sent messengers back to their respective commanders in camp, and after the initial alarm prompted by the unexpected visual contact had abated, they no longer held back from the fray.

The fighting was first provoked by just a few men who rushed ahead of the others, but it then escalated as support arrived for defeated comrades. The Romans, no match for the enemy, sent messenger after messenger back to their commander to tell him they were under pressure. Then 500 cavalry and 2,000 infantry, Aetolians for the most part, were swiftly dispatched under two military tribunes, and these restored the flagging situation for the Romans. With the change of fortunes the hard-pressed Macedonians now proceeded to send messages to implore the king's assistance. After the widespread darkness that had fallen, however, the last thing the king expected on that day was a battle, and he had sent out a large section of his forces of every category on a foraging expedition. For a time he was in a panic, not knowing what to do. The messages became insistent, however, and the cloud had now dissipated to reveal the hilltops, bringing into sight the Macedonians driven together on a prominence that towered above the others and defending themselves more by virtue of their position than with their weapons. Philip thought that, come what may, he had to throw everything into the fight so as not to sacrifice part of his army by failing to come to its defence, and he sent out the leader of his mercenary troops, Athenagoras, with all the auxiliaries—save the Thracians—along with the Macedonian and Thessalian cavalry. With their arrival the Romans were dislodged from the hilltop, and they offered no resistance until they reached the more level part of the valley. It was support provided by the Aetolian cavalry that was mainly responsible for their not being driven off in a complete rout. These were by far the best cavalry in Greece at the time, though as far as infantry was concerned the Aetolians were inferior to their neighbours.

8. The report of the action was more optimistic than was justified by Macedonian success in the encounter, as men came running back from the battle in waves calling out that the Romans were fleeing in terror; but it constrained Philip to lead out all his troops to the line, reluctant and hesitant though he was—it was a reckless manœuvre <. . .>, he declared, and he liked neither the locale nor the timing.

The Roman general did the same, prompted more by the exigencies of the situation than because circumstances favoured combat. Leaving his right wing in reserve, with the elephants positioned before the standards, he attacked the enemy on the left wing with all his light infantry. At the same time he reminded them that the Macedonians they would be fighting were the ones they had dislodged and defeated in battle at the gorges of Epirus where, though the enemy had the protection of mountains and rivers, the Romans had surmounted the natural obstacles of the area. They were, he said, the ones they had defeated when they fought earlier under Sulpicius, and the Macedonians were holding the pass to Eordaea. It was on reputation not real strength that the kingdom of Macedon rested, he continued, and that reputation, too, had finally faded away.

By now the Romans had reached their comrades making their stand in the lower reaches of the valley, and these, with the arrival of the army and their general, renewed the fight, attacking and again throwing back the enemy. With his peltasts and the infantry right wing called the 'phalanx' (which constituted the strength of the Macedonian army), Philip now charged his enemy, almost at a run, ordering Nicanor, one of his courtiers, to follow at a rapid pace with the rest of the troops. On reaching the hilltop, Philip could see from the few weapons and enemy corpses lying around there that the battle in that spot was finished and that the Romans had been driven back, and he could also see a fight going on near the enemy camp. His initial reaction was sheer delight. Soon, however, as his own men came running back and the terror changed sides, he panicked, unsure for the moment whether or not to take his troops back to their camp. The enemy kept coming closer, and now the king's men were being cut down as they turned to run, their deliverance impossible unless they were brought support. Not only that, but there was no longer any way even for Philip himself to retire in safety. And so, although a section of his force had not yet joined him, he was obliged to risk a decisive engagement. He †placed† his cavalry and light infantry who had participated in the engagement on the right wing and †having placed the peltasts† he ordered the men of the Macedonian phalanx to lay down their spears (the length of these proving an encumbrance) and fight with their swords.* At the same time he took measures to prevent penetration of his fighting-line. He took half of the front of the phalanx and with that doubled the depth of the formation, extending the line inwards, so that the battle-line was deep rather than wide. He also ordered the ranks closed up so that men stood shoulder to shoulder, and weapons were touching weapons.

9. After taking in between the ranks the men who had been involved in the battle, Quinctius gave the signal on the trumpet. Rarely, they say, has there been a war-cry at the start of a battle as loud as this one; for as chance would have it both armies shouted at the same time, and not just those who were actually fighting but also the reservists and those arriving for the battle at that very moment. On the right wing the king had the upper hand, aided by his position more than anything else, fighting as he was from the higher hills. On the left, at that instant, the part of the phalanx which had formed the rear was coming up, and this was causing confusion and turmoil. The centre, positioned closer to the right wing, was stationary, the men engrossed in watching the battle as if it did not involve themselves. The phalanx, which had arrived in the form of a column rather than a battle-line, and which was more appropriately drawn up for marching than combat, had barely reached the brow of the hill. While these men were still in confusion Quinctius made his attack, first sending in the elephants against his enemy. He did this despite the fact that he could see his own men retreating on the right wing, for he surmised that if some of the enemy's forces were crushed they would drag the rest along with them. There was no doubt about the outcome. The Macedonians immediately turned tail, their initial terror on seeing the beasts sending them running; and the others did indeed follow their defeated comrades. Then one of the military tribunes made an impromptu decision. Leaving behind that section of his men that clearly had the upper hand, he took the soldiers of twenty companies, made a short encircling manoeuvre and attacked the rear of the enemy right wing. No battle-line would have escaped being thrown into disorder by an attack from behind; but in addition to the alarm any might feel in such circumstances, there was the further problem that the Macedonian phalanx, cumbersome and unmanoeuvrable, was unable to wheel about, an operation that was also inhibited by those Romans who, though earlier pulling back from the front of the phalanx, were at that moment bearing down on the terrified Macedonians. Furthermore, the latter were handicapped by their position: while chasing

the defeated Romans down the slope, they had ceded the ridge from which they had been fighting to those of the enemy who had been brought around to their rear. For a short while they were cut down between the two fronts; then most of them threw down their weapons and took to their heels.

10. Taking a few infantry and cavalrymen, Philip seized a hillock higher than the others <. . . to> observe how his men were faring on the left flank. When he saw them in disorderly flight, with standards and weapons glinting all around the hills, then he too quit the field. Quinctius had been putting pressure on the retreating Macedonians, but then he saw them raising their spears. He was unsure of their intentions, and the strange movement suddenly prompted him to bring his troops to a brief halt. On being told that this was the Macedonian convention for indicating surrender, he had it in mind to show mercy to his defeated foes; but his men, not realizing the enemy had given up the fight, and unaware of their commander's wishes, attacked them and killed those at the front, after which the others scattered in flight.

The king headed for Tempe at breakneck speed, and there halted at Gonni for a day to gather in any who survived the battle. The triumphant Romans, hoping for spoils, <. . . came> into the enemy camp, only to find that it had already been for the most part ransacked by the Aetolians. On that day 8,000 of the enemy lost their lives and 5,000 were captured, while about 700 of the victors were lost. If one can believe Valerius, who is guilty of gross exaggeration of numbers of all kinds, 40,000 of the enemy were killed that day, and 5,700 taken prisoner (a more reasonable fabrication), with 249 military standards captured. Claudius' account* also gives the enemy dead as 32,000, with 4,300 taken prisoner. As for me, it is not simply a case of my accepting the lowest figures, but I have followed Polybius,* no unreliable authority on Roman history in general, and particularly on that concerned with Greece.

11. Philip brought together the fugitives who had followed in his path, after being dispersed by the various hazards of the battle, and he sent men to Larisa to burn the royal archives, so they should not fall into enemy hands. He then withdrew to Macedonia. As for Quinctius, he divided the prisoners-of-war and the booty, selling some and giving some to the men, and set off for Larisa, though he did not yet know the area for which the king had headed or what his

intentions were. At Larisa a herald of the king came to him, ostensibly to seek a truce so that the casualties of the battle could be picked up for burial, but really to ask permission to send ambassadors. Both requests were granted by the Roman general, who added that the herald should tell the king to take heart. This was particularly vexing for the Aetolians, already aggrieved and complaining that victory had altered the commander: before the battle he used to involve his allies in everything, great or small, they said, but now these took no part in planning, and Flamininus did everything on his own initiative. He was, they said, seeking a way to make Philip personally grateful to him, so that while the Aetolians would have had their fill of the hardships and tribulations of the war, the Roman would be deflecting to himself the gratitude for the peace and the resulting profits. It was quite clear that the Aetolians had lost a measure of their prestige; but they had no idea why they were being ignored. They actually believed that a man whose character was not at all susceptible to such avarice had his sights set on the king's largesse. In fact, Quinctius was incensed with the Aetolians, and with good reason, because of their voracious appetite for plunder and their arrogance in appropriating to themselves the credit for the victory,* their boasts of which grated on everyone's ears. He could see, too, that with Philip removed and the power of the kingdom of Macedon shattered, it was the Aetolians who would have to be considered the masters of Greece. For these reasons Quinctius was methodically taking several measures to ensure that their standing and influence be diminished, and be seen to be diminished, in every quarter.

12. The enemy had been granted a fifteen-day truce and a meeting had been scheduled with the king himself. Before the time of that meeting arrived, however, Quinctius called the allies to a conference at which he brought up the matter of the peace-terms they wished to have established. Amynander, king of the Athamanians, stated his position in a few words: peace must be arranged on such terms as rendered Greece strong enough to preserve her independence as well as to keep the peace, even in the absence of the Romans. The speech of the Aetolians was sharper in tone. After a few prefatory remarks, they said that the Roman commander's action in consulting those who had been his allies in the war on the question of peace was right and proper. But, they added, he was quite wrong if he thought

he would be putting peace for the Romans or independence for Greece on a secure footing without Philip being either killed or deposed. Both ends, they said, were easily attainable if he chose to follow up his success.

In answer Quinctius said that the statement of the Aetolians took no account of Roman practice and was also at odds with their earlier views. In all previous councils and meetings the Aetolians had discussed terms of peace, not fighting to the point of extermination; and the Romans, who had a long-established custom of sparing the defeated, had given a notable demonstration of their clemency in granting a peace-treaty to Hannibal and the Carthaginians. But, to say nothing of the Carthaginians, on how many occasions had there been discussions with Philip himself? And there had never been a question of his leaving the throne. Or was it simply that war had become an unpardonable crime now that he had been defeated in battle? One should confront an armed foe with hostility, he said, but with a defeated enemy it is the most humane victor who demonstrates the greatest character. The kings of Macedon seemed to pose a threat to the liberty of Greece, he continued, but if that kingdom and that people were eliminated, Thracians, Illyrians, and, after them, Gauls would come pouring into Macedonia and Greece— barbarous and ferocious peoples. The Greeks, he concluded, should not tear down the states nearest to them and thereby leave themselves exposed to others more powerful and dangerous.

At this point Phaeneas, praetor of the Aetolians, interrupted, declaring that if Philip gave them the slip on that occasion he would soon rise again with a more serious war. 'Stop your blustering when we have matters to discuss,' replied Quinctius. 'Such will be the conditions binding the king that he could not possibly start a war.'

13. The council adjourned, and the following day the king arrived at the pass leading to Tempe, the venue set for their meeting. On the third day following that he was introduced to a crowded assembly of the Romans and allies. At this Philip very wisely conceded of his own accord all items indispensable for negotiating peace, rather than have them forced out of him in argument; and he declared that he accepted all the terms laid down by the Romans or insisted upon by the allies at the previous meeting, and would leave all else to the discretion of the Senate.

It seemed that he had now silenced all his critics, even the most hostile, but when everyone fell silent the Aetolian Phaeneas said: 'So, Philip, are you finally returning to us Pharsalus, Larisa Cremaste, Echinus, and Phthian Thebes?' When Philip said he saw no objection to their retrieving them, an argument broke out between the Roman commander and the Aetolians on the matter of Thebes. Quinctius' position was that it had fallen to the Roman people by the rules of war. Before the conflict, he said, when he had brought the army to the city, the Thebans had been invited to form an alliance and, though they had the clear opportunity to break with the king, they had preferred a treaty with him over one with Rome. Phaeneas was of the opinion that, in the light of the alliance formed to prosecute the war, it was fair that the Aetolians be given back what they had held before the war, and he added that the terms of the original treaty had provided for spoils of the war, in the form of goods and chattels, going to the Romans, and land and captured cities going to the Aetolians. 'You yourselves broke the terms of that particular treaty at the time when you left us to make peace with Philip,' replied Quinctius. 'Even if it were still in force, that clause in it would still only apply to captured cities, and the city-states of Thessaly voluntarily accepted our authority.'

These arguments won the support of all the allies; but for the Aetolians, as well as being unpleasant to listen to at the time, they later proved to be the cause of a war that had disastrous consequences. An agreement was reached with Philip that he give his son Demetrius and a number of his friends as hostages, and pay an indemnity of 200 talents, and that he send a delegation to Rome on the other items (for which the king was granted a truce of four months). Should peace not be granted by the Senate, an assurance was given that the hostages and money would be returned to Philip. They say that the prime reason for the Roman commander's haste to make peace was that it was now certain that Antiochus was making preparations for war and for an invasion of Europe.

14. At this same time, and according to some accounts on the very same day,* the Achaeans defeated the king's general Androsthenes in pitched battle at Corinth. Philip intended using this city as a fortress against the city-states of Greece, and after summoning the leading citizens from there, allegedly to discuss the number of cavalry Corinth could supply for the war, he had detained them as hostages.

Moreover, in addition to the earlier contingent that he had maintained in the city, comprising 500 Macedonians and 800 auxiliaries of various kinds, he had sent a further 1,000 Macedonians, 1,200 Illyrians and Thracians, and 800 Cretans (Cretans were to be found fighting on both sides). Apart from these there were 1,000 Boeotians, Thessalians, and Acarnanians, all shield-bearers, and 700 men of military age from amongst the Corinthians themselves, to make a total of 6,000 men under arms, which gave Androsthenes the confidence to decide matters in the field.

Nicostratus, praetor of the Achaeans, was at Sicyon with 2,000 infantry and 100 cavalry but, since he could see he was at a disadvantage both in numbers and in the quality of his troops, he would not venture beyond the ramparts. The king's troops, made up of infantry and cavalry, were roaming around making raids on the countryside of Pallene, Phlius, and Cleonae. Finally, they passed over into the territory of Sicyon, taunting their enemy with cravenness, and they also used their ships to sail along the entire coast of Achaea, which they routinely plundered. Since the enemy were engaging in these operations in a sporadic and, as happens with over-confidence, even a remiss manner, Nicostratus conceived the hope of attacking them unawares. He quietly sent messages around the neighbouring states with orders for armed men to assemble at Apelaurum, an area in Stymphalian territory, and specifying the date and the numbers from each state. When all the preparations for the appointed day had been made, he forthwith set off by night through the land of Phlius and reached Cleonae with nobody aware of his plans. With him were 5,000 infantry, including <. . .> light infantry and 300 cavalry. With these forces he began his wait, having dispatched scouts to observe the direction in which the enemy were spreading out.

15. Unaware of all this, Androsthenes set out from Corinth and encamped on the Nemea, a stream flowing between the lands of Corinth and those of Sicyon. At this point he disengaged half his army, divided it into three parts, and ordered these and all his cavalry to conduct simultaneous raids on the farmlands of Pellene and Sicyon, and on those of Phlius. These three columns marched off in different directions. When news of this reached Nicostratus at Cleonae, he immediately sent ahead a strong detachment of mercenaries to seize the pass which afforded access to the territory of

Corinth. Then, positioning the cavalry before the standards as an advance guard, he himself swiftly followed the mercenaries with his army split into two columns, the mercenary troops and light infantry marching in one, and the shield-bearers*—at that time the strength of the army for those nations—in the other.

By now the infantry and cavalry were not far from the Macedonian camp, and a number of the Thracians had attacked the enemy who were roaming in disorder through the countryside, when consternation suddenly struck the enemy camp. The general panicked; he had not seen his enemy at any point, apart from an occasional glimpse in the hills before Sicyon—and then they would not venture to send down their column into the plains—and he had never believed they would come to Cleonae. He gave orders for those who were scattered in various places outside the camp to be recalled with a trumpet-signal. Then, ordering his men to take up arms at the double, he went out through the gate with an undermanned column of soldiers and deployed his line of battle on the river-bank. All these troops, apart from the Macedonians, could only with difficulty be brought together and put into formation, and they failed to withstand the initial assault of the enemy. The Macedonians had assembled for the fight in by far the greatest numbers, and they long kept the prospect of victory for either side in doubt. Finally, left unprotected when the others fled, and with two enemy battle-lines bearing down on them from different directions—the light infantry from the flank, the shield-bearers and peltasts from the front—they, too, could see the battle was lost. They gave ground at first and then, under pressure, took to their heels. Most of them threw away their weapons, and with no hope left of holding on to the camp, they headed for Corinth.

Nicostratus sent his mercenaries to pursue them, and his cavalry and Thracian auxiliaries he dispatched against the troops ravaging the farmland of Sicyon, causing a great bloodbath in all quarters, almost greater even than in the battle itself. Then there were the soldiers who had pillaged Pellene and Phlius. Returning to camp out of formation, and unaware of all that had happened, some of these came amongst the enemy outposts which they took to be their own; others suspected from the turmoil what had happened and took to flight, becoming so dispersed as to be surrounded as they wandered about even by the local peasants. On that day 15,000 men lost their lives, and 300 were captured; and all Achaea was delivered from a terrible dread.

16. Before the battle at Cynoscephalae, Lucius Quinctius summoned to Corcyra the leaders of the Acarnanians, the only people in Greece to have remained within the Macedonian alliance, and here he made a start on changing their allegiance. Two major factors had kept the Acarnanians loyal to their treaty of friendship with the king: first, the inbred fidelity of their race, and secondly their fear and hatred of the Aetolians. An assembly of the Acarnanians was called at Leucas, but not all their constituent peoples came, and those who had come were not in agreement. However, their leading men and magistrates succeeded in getting a private decree passed which authorized an alliance with Rome. This enraged all who had been absent, and at this time of national unrest Philip dispatched to Leucas two prominent Acarnanians, Androcles and Echedemus. These were able not only to have the decree sanctioning the Roman alliance rescinded, but also to have Archelaus and Bianor, both notable members of their people, condemned in the council on a charge of treason for having proposed the decree. They also had the praetor Zeuxis' appointment annulled for having introduced the motion.

The condemned men followed a course of action that was impetuous, but which proved successful. Although their friends urged them to accept the situation and join the Romans in Corcyra, they decided instead to present themselves before the crowded assembly, and either assuage its anger by this gesture or accept whatever came to them. When they entered the packed meeting, there was at first a murmuring and buzz from the surprised audience, but silence soon fell, from respect for the men's former status as much as pity for their present misfortune. Granted permission to speak, they began in suppliant tones; but, as their speech progressed and they came to the point of vindicating themselves against the charges, they spoke with the confidence that their innocence gave them, finally even going so far as to make complaints and criticisms about the unjust and cruel treatment to which they had been subjected. Such was the impression they made that the crowded assembly reversed all the decisions that had been taken against them, while still voting to return to the alliance with Philip and reject a treaty with the Romans.

17. Such were the decisions taken at Leucas. This was the capital

of Acarnania, and the place where all its peoples came for their assembly. So when news of this sudden change of heart was brought to the legate Flamininus in Corcyra he immediately set sail with his fleet for Leucas, anchoring off the so-called Heraeum. From here he advanced to the city-walls, taking along artillery and siege-engines of all kinds used for storming towns, in the belief that the towns-people's feelings could change with the initial panic. When there was no indication of readiness for peace, the legate proceeded to erect siege-sheds and towers and to bring the battering-ram towards the walls.

Situated in its entirety between Aetolia and Epirus, Acarnania faces west towards the Sicilian sea. Leucadia, which is now an island, separated from Acarnania by a shallow, man-made strait, was at that time a peninsula, attached to Acarnania at its western end by a narrow isthmus, some 500 paces in length and no more than 120 in width. Leucas lies on the narrow strait, set on a hill that faces east towards Acarnania. The lower reaches of the city are flat, lying beside the sea that divides Leucadia from Acarnania. At this point both land and sea render it vulnerable, for the shallow waters here resemble a pool more than a sea, while the plain is made up of soft earth, easy to dig. As a result the walls were collapsing at several points simultaneously, either undermined or else knocked down by the ram. But if the city itself was an easy proposition for its assail-ants, the spirit of the enemy was indomitable. Day and night they applied themselves to rebuilding the shattered portions of the wall, to blocking the gaps left where it had collapsed, to joining battle with vigour, and to protecting their walls with their weapons rather than themselves with their ramparts. In fact, they would have drawn out the siege longer than the Romans had anticipated but for some exiles of Italian stock, living in Leucas, who came down from the citadel to admit the Roman soldiers. Even so the Leucadians, who drew up their battle line in the forum, held the Romans for some time in pitched battle as they came swooping down with a great commotion from their higher position. In the meantime the fortifications were taken by scaling-ladders at several points, and the Romans clam-bered into the city over the stones strewn on the ground and the fallen walls, while by now the legate himself, at the head of a large column of men, had surrounded the battling Leucadians. Then some were cut down, encircled by their foes; others threw down their arms and surrendered to the victor. A few days later, when news came of the battle that had been fought at Cynoscephalae, all the peoples of Acarnania capitulated to the legate.

18. At this same time, as Philip's fortunes waned everywhere simultaneously, the Rhodians also intended reclaiming from him part of the mainland called the Peraea, which had belonged to their forefathers. To effect this they sent out the praetor Pausistratus in command of 800 Achaean infantry and some 1,800 auxiliary troops drawn from different races—Gauls, Mniesutae, Pisuetae, Tarmiani, and Theraei from the Peraea, and Laudiceni from Asia. With these troops Pausistratus seized Tendeba, which was strategically situated in the territory of Stratonicea, without the knowledge of the king's forces, who were stationed at Thera. He was joined at this opportune moment by an auxiliary force, which he had requested specifically for this operation, 1,000 Achaean infantry along with 100 cavalry, all under the command of Theoxenus. To recover this fortified town, the king's prefect Dinocrates first moved his camp towards Tendeba itself, and from there to a second stronghold called Astragos, also in Stratonicean territory. He then recalled to that place all the widely scattered Macedonian garrisons, as well as the Thessalian auxiliaries from Stratonicea itself, and proceeded to Alabanda, where his enemy were situated. The Rhodians did not refuse the fight, and so, with their camps established in close proximity to each other, the two sides immediately came forward for battle.

Dinocrates set 500 Macedonians on his right wing and the Agrianes on the left, bringing into the centre the men drawn from the garrisons in the fortified towns, Carians for the most part, and placing cavalry and Cretan and Thracian auxiliaries about the wings. The Rhodians had Achaeans on the right wing, and mercenaries, a hand-picked body of infantry, on the left. Their centre was made up of an assortment of auxiliaries drawn from several races, while the cavalry and such light infantry as they had covered the wings. On that day the battle-lines of each side merely took up a position on the banks of a torrent which flowed between them, at that time with low water-level, and after hurling a few javelins retired to camp. The following day, drawn up in the same formation, they fought a battle considerably more fierce than one would have expected, given the numbers participating; for there were on each side no more than 3,000 infantry and about 100 cavalry, but in the fight they were not

just evenly matched in numbers and equipment, but had equal fortitude and similar hopes of victory. The Achaeans initiated the action,
crossing the torrent and attacking the Agrianes, after which the
entire line crossed the stream, almost at a run. For a long time it was
an even fight. By virtue of their numbers the Achaeans, who totalled
1,000, forced their 400 adversaries to give ground; then, when the
left wing buckled, they all put pressure on the right. The Macedonians could not be budged for as long as the ranks and their com-
pressed phalanx, as it were, held firm. But when their left flank
became exposed, they attempted to bring their lances round to face
the enemy coming at them from the side, which immediately dis-
oriented them. At first there was chaos in their ranks; then they
turned tail; and finally they threw down their weapons and took off
in headlong flight. They ran in the direction of Bargyliae, which was
where Dinocrates also fled.

The Rhodians pursued them for the remainder of the day and
then retired to camp. It is widely accepted that, if the victors had
immediately headed for Stratonicea, that city could have been taken
without a struggle. The opportunity for this was lost while time was
wasted on the recapture of fortified towns and villages of the Peraea.
In the mean time those holding Stratonicea with a garrison regained
their spirit, and soon Dinocrates also entered the town with the
troops which had survived the battle. From that point on besieging
and attacking the city proved fruitless, and it could not be taken until
considerably later when it fell to Antiochus.

Such were events in Thessaly, Achaea, and Asia, occurring at
roughly the same time.

19. Philip had heard that, from disdain for his now badly shaken
empire, the Dardanians had crossed his frontiers and were completely laying waste the upper stretches of Macedonia. He was under
pressure almost the world over, as fortune dogged him and his
people at every turn; even so, he felt that being dispossessed of the
throne of Macedonia would be a fate worse than death. He therefore
conducted a hurried levy of troops throughout the cities of Macedonia, and, at the head of 6,000 infantry and 500 cavalry, overpowered
his enemy with a surprise attack in the area of Stobi in Paeonia.
Large numbers of men were massacred in the battle, even more as
they roamed through the fields, hungry for booty. Those who had
the opportunity to flee returned to their countries without even

risking a fight. Philip retired to Thessalonica, the confidence of his people restored by that single campaign, which was at variance with his fortunes elsewhere.

The timely ending of the war with the Carthaginians, which saved the Romans from having to fight them and Philip at the same time, was not as opportune as Philip's defeat at a point when Antiochus was already fomenting war from his base in Syria. Apart from the fact that it was easier for Rome to fight these enemies separately than if the two had joined forces, there was also in that same period an armed uprising and great upheaval in Spain.

The previous summer, Antiochus had wrested from Ptolemy's control, and brought into his own power, all the city-states in Coele Syria, and had then retired to Antioch for the winter, which proved no less active a season for him than the summer had been. Exploiting all the resources of his kingdom, he had amassed huge land- and sea-forces; and at the beginning of spring he sent ahead his two sons, Ardys and Mithridates, overland with an army, ordering them to wait for him at Sardis. He then set out himself with a fleet of a hundred ships with decks, plus two hundred lighter vessels, Cyprian cutters, and pinnaces. His aim was to strike at the cities under Ptolemy's control all along the coast of Cilicia, Lycia and Caria, and at the same time to assist Philip (for the war against Philip was not yet finished) with his army and his ships.

20. The people of Rhodes have performed many exceptional exploits on land and sea out of loyalty towards the Roman people and on behalf of the entire Greek community, but none more glorious than their feat of that summer. Undaunted by the tremendous war that threatened, they sent envoys to the king to warn him not to pass beyond Chelidoniae, a promontory in Cilicia famous for the treaty concluded in days of old* between Athens and the kings of Persia. If Antiochus did not keep his fleet and land-forces behind that line, they said, they would march against him, not from any animosity towards him, but to prevent him joining up with Philip and obstructing the Roman liberation of Greece.

At that time Antiochus was investing Coracesium with siege-works. He had already taken Zephyrium, Soli, Aphrodisias, Corycus, and (after skirting around Anemurium—also a promontory in Cilicia) Selinus; but though all these and other fortified towns on that coastline had submitted without a fight, either from fear or by choice, Coracesium had unexpectedly shut its gates to him and now kept him bogged down there. Here he gave an audience to envoys from Rhodes and, though the embassy's mission was such as to infuriate the king, he none the less controlled his anger and replied that he would send representatives to Rhodes. These he would instruct to renew the ancient bonds* that existed between himself, and his ancestors, and that state, and tell the Rhodians not to feel apprehensive about the king's coming, that there would be no harm or treachery involved, either for the Rhodians or their allies. For, he said, he would not violate his alliance with Rome, and he cited in support of this commitment his recent delegation to Rome,* and the decisions and answers made by the Senate which redounded to his credit. It so happened that his ambassadors had at that point returned from Rome. They were heard, and sent back, with courtesy, as the situation demanded, for it was as yet uncertain how the war with Philip would turn out.*

While the king's envoys were discussing these matters in the assembly of the Rhodians, word came that the war had been terminated at Cynoscephalae. On receiving the news, the Rhodians, who now were freed from fear with regard to Philip, abandoned their plan of confronting Antiochus with their fleet, but they did not abandon their other purpose, that of preserving the independence of the cities allied to Ptolemy, which were then facing the threat of war with Antiochus. Some of these they helped with military aid, others with advance warnings and intelligence on the movements of the enemy, and they were responsible for maintaining the independence of the peoples of Caunus, Myndus, Halicarnassus, and Samos. A detailed report of military operations in these spots cannot really be justified when I am barely capable of providing an account of those relevant to the war fought by the Romans.

21. In this same period Attalus fell ill at Thebes and was taken back to Pergamum, where he died at the age of seventy-one after a rule of forty-four years.* Apart from his wealth, fate had given this man nothing to encourage any hopes of becoming a king, but by a judicious, and at the same time generous, use of his riches he made himself appear fit for a throne,* first in his own eyes, and then in others'. Later he vanquished the Gauls in a single battle, a race all the more feared in Asia at that point for having only just arrived. He then assumed the title 'king', and consistently revealed a disposition

in keeping with the title's majesty. He ruled his subjects with consummate justice; he demonstrated a unique loyalty towards his allies; he was easygoing in his relationship with his wife and children (four of whom survived him*); and he was tolerant and generous with his friends. He left his kingdom on such a firm and solid footing that his family's sovereignty over it lasted to the third generation.*

Such was the state of affairs in Asia, Greece, and Macedonia when the war with Philip was only just finished or, at least, peace had not been concluded. Meanwhile a momentous war broke out in Farther Spain. Marcus Helvius, governor of the province, informed the Senate by letter that two minor kings, Culchas and Luxinius, had taken up arms, and that seventeen towns had joined Culchas, while the powerful cities of Carmo and Bardo had joined Luxinius. On the coast, he said, the Malacini, the Sexetani, all Baeturia, and the tribes which had not yet revealed their sympathies would join the uprising of their neighbours. This letter was read out by the praetor Marcus Sergius, who had jurisdiction in cases between citizens and foreigners,* and the Senators then decreed that, after the elections for the praetorship, the praetor to whom the province of Spain was allotted should bring the question of the war in Spain before the Senate at the earliest opportunity.

22. In this same period the consuls reached Rome. They convened the Senate in the temple of Bellona, and made a request for a triumph in recognition of their military achievements, only to be faced with a counter-request from the plebeian tribunes, Gaius Atinius Labeo and Gaius Afranius, that the consuls hold separate debates on their triumphs. They would not, they said, permit a joint motion on the issue in case equal credit be accorded when the merits were not equal. Quintus Minucius made the point that both consuls had been allotted the province of Italy, and that he and his colleague had conducted the campaign with shared purpose and strategy; and Gaius Cornelius added that when the Boii advanced against him over the Po with the intention of aiding the Insubres and Cenomani, it was only his colleague's plundering of their villages and fields that made them turn back to protect their own property. The tribunes acknowledged that Gaius Cornelius' achievements in the war were so significant that a triumph for him could no more be in doubt than could the honours to be paid to the immortal gods. Even so, they added, neither he nor any other citizen had so much influence or

power as to bestow, after gaining a well-earned triumph for himself, the same distinction, when it was *not* well-earned, upon a colleague with the impertinence to request it. Quintus Minucius had fought some inconsequential battles, barely worth the mention, amongst the Ligurians, and in Gaul he had lost a large number of men. They also mentioned the military tribunes of the fourth legion, Titus Iuventius and Gnaeus Ligurius. These, they said, had lost their lives in Minucius' defeat, along with many other brave men, both citizens and allies. As for the capitulation of the small number of towns and villages, this was all concocted and fabricated on the spot, and without corroboration.

This wrangling between the consuls and the tribunes took up two days, after which the consuls, frustrated by the doggedness of the tribunes, referred their requests separately to the Senate.

23. The decision to award Gaius Cornelius his triumph was unanimous, and the people of Placentia and Cremona lent their support to the consul. They offered him their thanks, and reminded the Senate that it was Cornelius who had raised their siege, most of them adding that he had also delivered them from slavery when they were in the hands of the enemy. As for Quintus Minucius, he merely tried out his motion and then, seeing the Senate entirely opposed to him, declared that he would celebrate a triumph on the Alban mount,* which was within the rights of his consular authority and also sanctioned by the precedent of many distinguished men.

Gaius Cornelius celebrated his triumph over the Insubres and Cenomani in the course of his magistracy. He had many military standards put on display, large quantities of Gallic spoils transported on captured wagons, and many Gallic noblemen led before his chariot, amongst them, some say, the Carthaginian general, Hamilcar.* But what attracted most attention was the troop of colonists from Cremona and Placentia who followed the chariot with freedman caps* on their heads. Cornelius had 237,500 bronze *asses* carried along in his triumphal parade, and 79,000 silver coins stamped with the *biga*.* Seventy bronze *asses* were distributed to each of the soldiers, twice that amount to each cavalryman and centurion.

The consul Quintus Minucius celebrated his triumph over the Ligurians and Gallic Boii on the Alban mount, a less exalted affair by virtue of its location, the reputation of the accomplishments involved, and the fact that everyone knew the expenses for it were not covered by the public purse. In terms of military standards, wagons and spoils, however, it almost rivalled the other. Even the sums of money involved were roughly equal: 254,000 bronze coins and 53,200 silver coins stamped with the *biga* were carried in the procession, and the common soldiers, centurions, and cavalrymen were each given the same amount as Minucius' colleague had given to his men.

24. After the triumph, the consular elections were held, in which Lucius Furius Purpureo and Marcus Claudius Marcellus were elected. The next day the following were elected praetor: Quintus Fabius Buteo, Tiberius Sempronius Longus, Quintus Minucius Thermus, Manius Acilius Glabrio, Lucius Apustius Fullo, and Gaius Laelius.

Towards the end of the year, a letter arrived from Titus Quinctius with the news that he had fought a pitched battle with Philip in Thessaly, and that the enemy army had been vanquished and put to flight. This letter was read out by the praetor Marcus Sergius, in the Senate first of all, and then, later, on the authorization of the Senate, in a public assembly; and five days of public prayers were prescribed in thanks for the successful campaign. Shortly afterwards envoys came from both Titus Quinctius and King Philip. The Macedonians were taken out of the city to the Public Villa where they were housed and officially entertained, and then they were granted a meeting with the Senate at the temple of Bellona. The proceedings here were not long, the Macedonians stating that the king would abide by any decision of the Senate. In accordance with ancestral custom, a board of ten commissioners was appointed in consultation with whom the general Titus Quinctius was to formulate peace-terms for Philip, and a rider was added that Publius Sulpicius and Publius Villius, former consular governors of Macedonia, be amongst these.

†That day† the people of Cosa requested an increase in the number of their colonists. The enrolment of a thousand was authorized, with the condition that none be included who had been an enemy of Rome in the period following the consulship of Publius Cornelius and Tiberius Sempronius.*

25. The Roman Games* were that year held in the circus and theatre by the curule aediles, Publius Cornelius Scipio and Gnaeus Manlius Vulso. The performances were more lavish than on other occasions, and were also watched with greater pleasure because of the military successes, and they were repeated three times in their

entirety. The Plebeian Games were repeated seven times. These were put on by Manius Acilius Glabrio and Gaius Laelius, who erected three bronze statues—of Ceres, Liber, and Libera—from the money taken in fines.

When Lucius Furius and Marcus Claudius Marcellus began their consulship, the question of their provinces arose. The Senate was resolved to assign Italy to the two of them, but the consuls insisted that they draw lots for Macedonia along with Italy. Marcellus was the more ambitious to gain the province, and he declared that the peace was bogus and a sham, that the king would go to war again if the army were removed from there. This had made the Senate think twice about their recommendation, and the consul might possibly have won the day but for the tribunes of the people, Quintus Marcius Ralla and Gaius Atinius Labeo. These said that they would use their veto unless they themselves had first brought before the people the issue of whether peace with Philip was in accordance with the people's wishes and instructions. The motion was put to the people on the Capitol, and all thirty-five tribes voted in favour of it.

In addition, the arrival of bad news from Spain actually served to increase public jubilation over the conclusion of peace in Macedonia; a letter was published announcing the defeat of the proconsul Gaius Sempronius Tuditanus in battle in Hither Spain. The letter stated that Tuditanus' army had been vanquished and put to flight, that many eminent men had lost their lives in the field, and that Tuditanus was carried from the fray with a serious wound, only to die shortly afterwards.

The two consuls were assigned Italy as their province and given the legions that had been commanded by the previous consuls. They were also instructed to enrol four new legions, two city legions and two to be sent wherever the Senate decided. Orders were also issued for Titus Quinctius Flamininus to govern his province with the same army, and it was decided that the earlier extension of his imperium appeared sufficient.

26. In the praetorian allotment of provinces which followed, Lucius Apustius Fullo gained the urban jurisdiction and Manius Acilius Glabrio citizen-foreigner affairs; Quintus Fabius Buteo received Farther Spain, Quintus Minucius Thermus Hither Spain, Gaius Laelius Sicily and Tiberius Sempronius Longus Sardinia. It was decided that the consuls should give to Quintus Fabius Buteo

and Quintus Minucius—to whom the Spanish provinces had fallen—one each of the four legions which they had raised (the consuls selecting these legions), along with 4,000 infantry and 300 cavalry of the allies and Latin League. These praetors were instructed to leave for their provinces at the earliest possible opportunity. War now broke out again in Spain four years after it had been last brought to an end, along with the Punic War.

This was almost a new war because it was the first time the Spaniards had commenced hostilities on their own initiative, without Carthaginian forces or a Carthaginian leader; but before the two praetors could set out for it, or the consuls leave Rome themselves, they received orders to undertake the customary ritual of expiating the prodigies that were being reported. A Roman knight,* Publius Villius, had been killed by lightning, along with his horse, while starting a journey into Sabine territory; the temple of Feronia in the area of Capena had been struck by lightning; the tips of two javelins had ignited near the temple of Moneta; and a wolf had entered Rome by the Esquiline Gate, had run into the forum through the most populous part of the city, and made its way through the Vicus Tuscus and then the Cermalus before escaping almost untouched by way of the Porta Capena. Full-grown victims were used for the expiation of these prodigies.

27. In this same period Gnaeus Cornelius Blasio, governor of Hither Spain before Gaius Sempronius Tuditanus, entered the city celebrating an ovation which had been authorized by Senatorial decree. Carried before him were 1,515 pounds of gold, 20,000 pounds of silver, and 34,500 denarii in coin. Returning from Farther Spain, Lucius Stertinius did not even investigate the prospects of a triumph, but he deposited in the treasury 50,000 pounds of silver, and from the proceeds of the spoils erected two arches in the Cattle Market—before the temples of Fortuna and Mater Matuta respectively—and one in the Circus Maximus. He set gilded statues on all three arches. Such, more or less, were the events of the winter.

During this time Titus Quinctius was spending the winter at Elatia. He received numerous petitions from the allies, including the Boeotians, who asked for (and were granted) the restitution of those of their people who had fought on Philip's side. This request was readily granted by Quinctius, not because he believed the Boeotians merited it but because he was now suspicious of Antiochus, and needed to win support for the Roman cause among the city-states. When the men were returned it quickly became apparent just how little appreciation there was amongst the Boeotians. It was to Philip that they sent a deputation to offer their thanks for the return of the men, as if this had been a concession made to them directly rather than to Quinctius and the Romans. They also made a certain Brachylles Boeotarch at the following elections, for the sole reason that he had been general of the Boeotians who fought on the king's side,* and they passed over Zeuxippus, Pisistratus, and others who had fostered the alliance with Rome. These latter took umbrage at this for the moment, and also harboured anxieties for the future. When that sort of thing happened with a Roman army sitting practically at their gates, they thought, what was their situation going to be when the Romans had departed for Italy and Philip was still close at hand, helping his partisans and ill-disposed to those who had been in the other camp?

28. These men therefore decided to eliminate Brachylles, chief supporter of the king, while they still had Roman armed forces in the vicinity. The time they picked for the coup was when he was on the way home after a public banquet, drunk and in the company of some effeminate men who had been at the dinner—which was attended by many people—to provide entertainment. Brachylles was waylaid by six armed men, three Italians and three Aetolians,* and assassinated. Brachylles' companions fled, there was a call for help, and pandemonium broke out as men with torches ran to and fro throughout the city. The assassins slipped away through the nearest gate.

At dawn there was an assembly in the theatre, as well-attended as if it had been convened by prior edict or called by a herald. In public, people angrily claimed that Brachylles had been murdered by the lewd men in his retinue, but in their hearts they had Zeuxippus singled out as the man responsible for the assassination. For the moment they decided Brachylles' companions should be arrested and interrogated. While the search for them was in progress, Zeuxippus coolly made an appearance at the assembly to deflect incrimination from himself. People were wrong, he said, to believe such a heinous murder to be linked to these effeminate men, and he produced many plausible arguments to support his case. With these he convinced some people that if he had felt guilty he would never have presented himself to the crowd, or made mention of the murder, when he was under no pressure to do so. Others, however, were sure that brazenly exposing himself to the charge was simply a way of averting suspicion.

Shortly afterwards Brachylles' innocent companions were tortured. They knew nothing but, taking as evidence what everybody believed, they named Zeuxippus and Pisistratus, without adding anything to suggest that they actually had some knowledge of the incident. Even so, Zeuxippus fled by night to Tanagra with one Stratonidas, more from fear of his own conscience than of the evidence supplied by men with no knowledge of the episode. Pisistratus remained in Thebes, with scant regard for the informers.

Zeuxippus had a slave who was a go-between and accomplice in the whole affair. Pisistratus feared that he might denounce them, and that very fear induced him to bring his name forward as an informant. He then sent a letter to Zeuxippus to tell him to get the slave-confederate out of the way—he seemed less capable of keeping the affair secret than of perpetrating it, he said. The man bearing the letter had been instructed to deliver it to Zeuxippus on the earliest possible occasion but, not having the opportunity to see him immediately, he passed it to that very slave, believing that he, of all Zeuxippus' slaves, was the one most faithful to his master. He added that it was a letter from Pisistratus on a matter of particular concern to Zeuxippus. Stricken by conscience, the slave swore to deliver it immediately but, instead, he opened the letter and, after reading it, fled in panic to Thebes where he put his statement before the magistrates. Worried by the flight of his slave, Zeuxippus moved to Anthedon, which he felt was a safer location for his exile. As for Pisistratus and the others, they were interrogated under torture and put to death.

29. The assassination provoked venomous hatred of the Romans amongst all Thebans and Boeotians. They believed that, as a leader of their people, Zeuxippus could not have embarked on such a crime without consultation with the Roman commander. They were without the strength or a leader to mount a revolt, and turned instead to the next best thing to war, terrorism. They surprised some Roman soldiers at inns, others as they moved around during the winter season on various everyday commissions. Some were killed by their ambushers right on the highways, at well-known concealment points, others after being lured into isolated stopping-places.

Eventually, such crimes were committed not simply from enmity but also from greed for spoils, because the soldiers were on their journeys to do business with money in their belts. Initially, only a few were lost but, as casualties increased day by day, all of Boeotia began to gain a bad reputation, with soldiers leaving the camp in greater fear than if they were in enemy territory.

At this point Quinctius sent out envoys amongst the city-states to inquire into the terrorist activities. Most of the assassinations were found to have been in the area of Lake Copais—here corpses, with rocks or amphoras attached to them to draw them into the depths with their weight, were pulled out of the slime and dragged from the marsh—and many crimes, it was discovered, had been perpetrated at Acraephia and Coronea. At first, Quinctius issued orders for the guilty parties to be handed over to him, and for the Boeotians to pay him 500 talents for the 500 soldiers that had been murdered. Neither instruction was acted upon, the states merely offering the verbal excuse that nothing that had taken place had official sanction. Quinctius therefore sent envoys to Athens and Achaea to call upon his allies to witness the fact that the war he was going to fight with the Boeotians was a just and righteous one. He then ordered Appius Claudius to make for Acraephia with part of his forces, while he personally besieged Coronea with the rest, having first laid waste the farmlands on the route taken by the two separate columns from Elatia. Taken aback by this catastrophic turn of events, and with panic and flight everywhere in evidence, the Boeotians dispatched ambassadors. These were being refused admission to the camp when the Achaeans and Athenians arrived. The intercession of the Achaeans carried more weight because these had already taken the decision to fight alongside the Romans, in the event of their failing to secure a peace for the Boeotians, and it was thanks to the Achaeans that the Boeotians were given the chance to meet and speak to the Roman commander. They were ordered to hand over the guilty men and pay a sum of 30 talents as a fine, after which they were granted peace and the siege was raised.

30. A few days later the ten commissioners arrived from Rome, and on their advice Philip was granted peace on the following terms:*

All Greek city-states, in Europe and Asia alike, were to have their independence and their own laws.

In the case of those states which had been under Philip's control, Philip was to withdraw his garrisons from them and, before the period of the Isthmian Games, hand them over to the Romans unoccupied by his forces.

Philip was also to withdraw his garrisons from the following cities in Asia: Euromus, Pedasa, Bargyliae, Iasus, Myrina, Abydus, Thasos and Perinthus, since their freedom was also desired. As for the freedom of the people of Cius, Quinctius was to write to Prusias, king of Bithynia, to communicate the decision of the Senate and the ten commissioners.

Philip was to return prisoners-of-war and deserters to the Romans, and surrender all his decked ships, except for five and a single royal galley of almost unmanœuvrable proportions, propelled by sixteen banks of oars.

He was to keep no more than 5,000 soldiers and not a single elephant.

He was not to wage war outside the confines of Macedonia without the authorization of the Senate.

He was to give the Roman people 1,000 talents, half immediately and half in instalments over ten years. (Valerius Antias records that the king was subjected to an annual tribute of 4,000 pounds of silver for ten years; Claudius that it was 4,200 pounds over thirty years, plus 20,000 payable immediately. Claudius also mentions a clause expressly forbidding him to go to war with Eumenes, son of Attalus, the new king of Pergamum at that time.)

Hostages were taken, including Philip's son Demetrius,* to ensure implementation of these conditions. Valerius Antias adds that Attalus was, in his absence, given the island of Aegina and Philip's elephants; the Rhodians were awarded Stratonicea and other cities in Caria that Philip had held; and the Athenians were given the islands of Lemnos, Imbros, Delos and Scyros.*

31. This peace-treaty met with the approval of all the city-states of Greece, apart from the Aetolians, who secretly grumbled and criticized the decision of the ten commissioners as being nothing more than words, a fraud giving only the illusion of independence. Why, they asked, were some cities being passed over to the Romans without being specified by name, when others were actually named and told to accept their independence, without being handed over in this way? Obviously because the cities in Asia, safer by virtue of their

very remoteness, were to be liberated, while those in Greece were to be taken over without even being designated by name—Corinth, Chalcis, and Oreus, along with Eretria and Demetrias.

The charge was not entirely without foundation, for the position of Corinth, Chalcis, and Demetrias was not clear. In the Senatorial decree under which the ten commissioners had been sent from Rome, all the other cities of Greece and Asia were clearly granted their freedom. In the case of the three in question, however, the commissioners had been instructed to take such actions and decisions as were required by the situation in which the state was placed, being guided by the interests of the state and by their own integrity. And there was Antiochus. As soon as he was satisfied that his forces were adequate, he would, they were sure, cross to Europe, and they did not want to leave favourably situated cities open for him to seize.

Setting off from Elatia, Quinctius and the ten commissioners came to Anticyra, and crossed from there to Corinth. Here, in meetings of the ten commissioners, the days were spent almost entirely on discussions of the independence of Greece. Time and again Quinctius reiterated that they had to free Greece as a whole if they wished to make the Aetolians hold their tongues, if they wanted to inspire in everyone genuine affection for the Roman people, and respect for its dignity, and to convince people that they had crossed the sea to liberate Greece rather than merely to transfer power over it from Philip to themselves. The others did not oppose his arguments *vis-à-vis* the independence of the cities, but they argued that it was safer for the Greeks themselves to remain a short while under the protection of a Roman garrison rather than accept Antiochus' overlordship in place of Philip's. In the end the following decision was made: Corinth was to be restored to the Achaeans, but with the retention of a garrison in the Acrocorinth; and Chalcis and Demetrias should remain occupied until the concern about Antiochus had passed.

32. The date fixed for the Isthmian Games was now approaching. This was invariably a well-attended event, even on other occasions, for two reasons: first, the inborn Greek enthusiasm for spectacles involving all manner of competitions in the arts, in physical strength, and in fleetness of foot; and, secondly, the favourable location which, since it provided all manner of goods for the human race, thanks to

its two different seas, made this commercial centre a gathering-place for Asia and Greece. But on this occasion people had assembled from all parts of the world not just for the usual purposes; they were eager to find out what the position of Greece was going to be in the future, and what lay in store for themselves. Not only did they have their different private thoughts on what the Romans would do, but they would bring it up in their conversations, and hardly anyone could be persuaded that they would withdraw from all parts of Greece.

The spectators had now taken their seats for the pageant. Following normal practice, a herald came forward with a trumpeter to the middle of the grounds, from which point the games are customarily opened with a ceremonial hymn. When silence fell after the trumpet-call, the herald made the following announcement:

'The Senate of Rome and the commander Titus Quinctius, having defeated King Philip and the Macedonians, declare that the following peoples are to be free, exempt from taxes, and living under their own laws: the Corinthians, the Phocians, all the Locrians, the isle of Euboea, the Magnesians, the Thessalians, the Perrhaebians and the Achaeans of Pthiotis.'

The herald had listed all the peoples who had been under Philip's control, and when his announcement had been heard the elation was too great for people to take in everything at once. They could all scarcely believe their ears, and they looked at each other in amazement, as though they were witnessing a fleeting dream. With regard to their own situation, they kept putting questions to those next to them, totally unwilling to accept the evidence of their own ears. The herald was called back—everyone was eager not just to hear but to see the harbinger of their liberty—and he repeated the announcement. At this, the reason for their rejoicing being now confirmed, such applause and cheering went up, and was so often repeated, that it was readily apparent that of all possible blessings none is more gratifying to the crowd than freedom. The games were then performed so hurriedly that nobody's mind or eyes were focused on the spectacle—so far had this one delight pre-empted the awareness of all other pleasures.

33. When the games were terminated, nearly everybody ran towards the Roman commander. As the crowd rushed forward, eager to approach this one man and touch his hand, and showering him with garlands and ribbons, he was almost in danger; but he was about

thirty-three years of age, and the vigour of his youth and his pleasure over the remarkable celebrity which he was enjoying added to his strength. Nor was this outpouring of joy just a thing of the moment; it was revived over many days, as people reflected on and talked about their gratitude. There was, then, a nation on earth that waged war for the freedom of others, at its own expense and itself facing the hardship and danger; and it did this not for its neighbours or for people geographically close or on the same land-mass, but actually crossed seas to prevent an unjust empire existing anywhere in the world and to assure the primacy of rectitude, divine justice, and the law of man. With a single announcement from a herald, all the cities of Greece and Asia had been set free; only an intrepid soul could formulate such an ambitious project, only phenomenal valour and fortune bring it to fruition.

34. After the Isthmian Games, Quinctius and the ten commissioners gave audiences to deputations from kings, peoples, and city-states, and the first to be called were the envoys of Antiochus. They made more or less the same declarations as they had at Rome, mere verbiage with no substance to inspire confidence, but this time there was nothing unclear about the response they were given, as there had been earlier when the situation was fluid and Philip's position still intact. They were quite explicitly told that Antiochus was to withdraw from the cities of Asia which had belonged to Philip or Ptolemy, and not touch the city-states that were free, or resort to armed aggression against any city—all Greek cities everywhere were to have both peace and independence. Above all, Antiochus was forbidden either to cross to Europe himself or to send his troops there.

When the king's envoys were dismissed, a meeting of cities and peoples got under way, at which business proceeded all the more briskly because the decrees of the commissioners were delivered to each of the states by name. The Orestae, a people of Macedonia, had their autonomy restored for having been the first to defect from the king. The Magnesians, Perrhaebians and Dolopians were also pronounced free. Apart from being awarded their independence, the people of Thessaly were also granted the Pthiotic Achaeans, with the exception of Pthiotic Thebes and Pharsalus. The Aetolians claimed that Pharsalus and Leucas should be restored to them under the terms of their treaty, and the commissioners referred this to the

Senate. The commissioners did, however, keep the Phocians and Locrians annexed to the Aetolians as before, but with the authority of a decree now added. Corinth, Triphylia, and Heraea (also a city in the Peloponnese) were restored to the Achaeans. The ten commissioners were for giving Oreus and Eretria to King Eumenes, son of Attalus, but Quinctius disagreed and this one issue was referred to the Senate for a decision. The Senate granted these states their independence, along with Carystus. Pleuratus was given Lychnidus and the Parthini (both these Illyrian peoples had been under Philip's control). Amynander they told to retain the strongholds he had captured from Philip during the war.

35. When the meeting was adjourned, the ten commissioners divided their responsibilities and each went off to liberate the city-states in his region. Publius Lentulus went to Bargyliae; Lucius Stertinius to Hephaestia, Thasos, and the cities of Thrace; Publius Villius and Lucius Terentius to Antiochus; and Gnaeus Cornelius to Philip. After delivering to the king the instructions he had been given on the less important matters, Cornelius asked Philip if he could bear to listen to advice that was not just serviceable but truly to his advantage. The king replied that he would even demonstrate his gratitude if the Roman furnished any advice to improve his position. Cornelius then strongly urged him, since he had now gained his peace accord, to send a deputation to Rome to ask for an alliance and a treaty of friendship. Otherwise, he said, should Antiochus make a move, Philip could be thought to have simply been biding his time, on the look-out for suitable occasions to resume the war. The meeting with Philip took place at Tempe in Thessaly. When the king replied that he would send a deputation immediately, Cornelius moved on to Thermopylae where, at fixed dates, there is a plenary council meeting of the Greek peoples called the Pylaic Council.*

Here Cornelius advised the Aetolians in particular to remain scrupulously loyal to their alliance with the Roman people. Some of the leading Aetolians meekly complained that since the victory the attitude of the Romans towards their people was not the same as during the war. Others were more outspoken in their criticisms and reproaches, saying that the Romans could not even have crossed to Greece, much less defeated Philip, without the Aetolians. The Roman stopped short of responding to this in order to avoid a quarrel, and merely said that the Aetolians would obtain complete satisfaction if they sent a delegation to Rome. And so, following Cornelius' advice, envoys were selected. Such was the conclusion of the war with Philip.

36. During the course of these events in Greece, Macedonia, and Asia, Etruria was almost turned into hostile territory by a slave-revolt. Manius Acilius Glabrio, praetor with jurisdiction over citizen-foreigner affairs, was dispatched with one of the two city legions to investigate this and put it down. Some <. . . others> he defeated in battle when they had already assembled. Of these many were killed, and many taken prisoner. Some—those who had been ringleaders in the conspiracy—he had flogged and crucified, others he returned to their masters.

The consuls then set out for their provinces. Marcellus entered the territory of the Boii, but his men were exhausted after spending a whole day on the march; and as he was pitching camp on a hill he was attacked by a certain Corolamus, a prince of the Boii, who fell on him with a large force, killing about 3,000 of his men. Some distinguished men also fell in the mêlée, including the allied commanders Titus Sempronius Gracchus and Marcus Iunius Silanus, as well as Marcus Ogulnius and Publius Claudius, military tribunes from the second legion. Even so, the camp was established and defended with determination by the Romans, and an attack from the enemy, elated by their successful encounter earlier, came to nothing. Marcellus remained within his encampment for a number of days, giving himself the time to tend to his wounded and also restore the men's confidence after such a daunting episode. The Boii, a people with little patience for wearisome delays, dispersed in all directions to their strongholds and villages.

Marcellus swiftly crossed the Po and took his legions into the area of Comum where the Insubres, who had called the people of Comum to arms, had their encampment. Ebullient after the fight put up by the Boii a few days earlier, the Gauls joined battle while they were still in marching-formation, and their initial attack was fierce enough to throw back the Roman front ranks. Seeing this, Marcellus feared that his men might be driven back in defeat by this first shock, and he set a Marsian cohort* in the enemy's path and then unleashed all his squadrons of Latin cavalry against them. The first and second cavalry charge checked the spirited advance of the enemy, and this gave confidence to the rest of the Roman line, which first held its ground and then made a fierce attack. The Gauls, no longer able to keep up the fight, turned tail in scattered flight.

In the battle, according to Valerius Antias' account, more than 40,000 men lost their lives, and 87 military standards were captured, along with 732 wagons and many gold necklaces, including a very heavy one which Claudius states was placed in the temple on the Capitoline as a gift to Jupiter. The camp of the Gauls was taken and sacked that day, and the town of Comum was captured a few days later. After this, twenty-eight fortified towns went over to the consul. A matter of dispute amongst historians is whether the consul led his army in the first place against the Boii or against the Insubres— whether by the successful engagement he obliterated the memory of the earlier reverse, or whether the victory gained at Comum was then sullied by defeat among the Boii.

37. Soon after these operations of varied success, the other consul, Lucius Furius Purpureo, came against the Boii through the tribus Sapinia. He was already approaching the stronghold of Mutilum when, fearful of being cut off simultaneously by the Boii and the Ligurians, he led his army back along the same route by which he had brought it, and reached his colleague by a long detour through open, and therefore safe, country. Combining their armies, the consuls first moved through the territory of the Boii, plundering as they went, as far the town of Felsina. That city, and all the other strongholds in the neighbourhood, surrendered, as did almost all the Boii, apart from their men of military age, who had taken up arms in order to plunder and at that point had fallen back deep into the woods.

The Ligurians were the army's next objective. The Boii now followed the Roman columns, taking pathways hidden from view, with the idea of making a surprise attack—the columns would be carelessly organized, they assumed, because they themselves would be thought to be a long way off. Failing to overtake the Romans, they suddenly crossed the Po in boats and conducted raids on the Laevi and Libui. As they were returning along the borders of Ligurian territory, carrying their spoils from the fields, they ran into the Roman column. The battle that ensued was more spirited and ferocious than if the two sides had been prepared for the confrontation, with time and place for the engagement arranged. Here the potency of anger as a stimulant to courage was made apparent; for the Romans craved bloodshed more than victory, and fought so aggressively that they scarcely left the enemy a survivor to report the débâcle.

When the consuls' dispatch reached Rome, a three-day period of public prayer was decreed in thanks for their success. Shortly afterwards the consul Marcellus arrived in Rome, and was awarded a triumph by a large majority in the Senate. During his term of office, Marcellus celebrated a triumph over the Insubres and Comenses, but left to his colleague the prospect of a triumph over the Boii; for he had personally suffered defeat against that people, but gained victory co-operating with his colleague. Large quantities of enemy spoils and many military standards were carried along on captured wagons. In the procession, 320,000 pieces of bronze were transported, and 234,000 pieces of silver stamped with the *biga*. Infantrymen were granted eighty bronze *asses* apiece, cavalrymen and centurions three times that amount.

38. In that same year Antiochus, after spending the winter at Ephesus, attempted to bring all the states of Asia under his control, as they had been before. He could see that, apart from Zmyrna and Lampsacus, they would all readily accept the yoke, either because of their location in the plains or through lack of confidence in their fortifications, weaponry, and fighting men. Zmyrna and Lampsacus, however, were laying claim to their independence and, if their demands were met, there was a risk of other cities in Aeolis and Ionia following the lead of Zmyrna, and others in the Hellespont following Lampsacus. Antiochus therefore sent a force directly from Ephesus to besiege Zmyrna, and he also instructed his troops in Abydus to leave a small garrison in place and advance to attack Lampsacus. Nor did he simply try to intimidate the cities by force; he also made friendly overtures to them through his envoys, and upbraided them for their foolhardiness and obstinacy, all the time trying to raise their hopes that they would soon attain their objectives—but only when it was evident, to everybody else as well as themselves, that they had achieved their independence as a favour granted by the king, not because they had taken the opportunity to seize it. Their response to this was that Antiochus should be neither surprised nor angry if they could not calmly accept their hopes of freedom being postponed.

At the beginning of spring Antiochus himself set off from Ephesus with his fleet and made for the Hellespont, giving orders for his land-forces to be taken across from Abydus to the Chersonese. He brought his naval and land-forces together at Madytus, a city in the Chersonese, where he surrounded the walls with his soldiers because the people had shut their gates to him. He was already moving up his siege-engines when the town capitulated. Fear of similar treatment prompted the inhabitants of Sestus and other cities of the Chersonese to surrender. From there Antiochus came to Lysimachia with all his naval and land-forces together. Finding the place deserted and almost completely in ruins—it had been captured, looted, and burned by the Thracians a few years earlier—he was overtaken by a desire to restore the famous city which was also strategically located. And so, taking all possible care, he proceeded with the simultaneous implementation of the necessary measures: the restoration of buildings and walls; the ransom of citizens of Lysimachia who were in slavery; the searching out and bringing together of residents who had scattered in flight throughout the Hellespont and Chersonese; the enrolment of new colonists with the prospect of betterment—in fact, everything that could be done to repopulate the city. At the same time, to remove the threat of the Thracians, he personally set off with half his land-forces to plunder the closest regions of Thrace, leaving the other half and all his naval crews to work on the rebuilding of the city.

39. Lucius Cornelius had been sent by the Senate to settle the differences between Antiochus and Ptolemy, and at about this time he halted at Selymbria. Meanwhile certain members of the ten-man commission made for Lysimachia, Publius Lentulus coming from Bargyliae, and Publius Villius and Lucius Terentius coming from Thasos. Lucius Cornelius also arrived from Selymbria, and a few days later Antiochus came from Thrace. Antiochus' first meeting with the commissioners and the reception that followed it were cordial and sociable, but when discussion began of the commissioners' assignments, and the current situation in Asia, tempers flared. The Romans made no secret of the Senate's displeasure with all of Antiochus' activities from the point when he set sail from Syria, and they opined that all the states formerly under Ptolemy's control should by rights be restored to him. Then, they said, there were the cities which had belonged to Philip and which Antiochus had filched from him by a stroke of opportunism when Philip's attention was distracted by his war with Rome. It was quite unacceptable that the Romans should have experienced such perils and hardships over all those years only to see Antiochus reaping the profits of the war. Even if the Romans could overlook his arrival in Asia as being of no concern to them, there was the fact of his now having also crossed to Europe with all his naval and land-forces—how far did that fall short of an open declaration of war on Rome? Of course, Antiochus would deny this even if he should sail to Italy; but the Romans were not going to wait for him to have the capability to do that.

40. In reply, Antiochus said he was amazed that the Romans were making such a thorough investigation into what Antiochus ought to have done, or how far he should have advanced on land and on sea. He was surprised, he said, at their failure to see that Asia was none of their business and that they should no more be inquiring into the activities of Antiochus in Asia than Antiochus should into the activities of the Roman people in Italy. As for Ptolemy, he continued, the Romans protested that city-states had been taken from him, but Antiochus actually had an alliance with him and, moreover, was taking measures for that to be strengthened by family ties* in a little while. He had not, in fact, sought to profit from Philip's misfortunes, and it was not to challenge the Romans that he had crossed into Europe. Rather, he thought that he had authority over all the lands that formerly constituted the kingdom of Lysimachus,* for when the latter was defeated all his possessions passed into the hands of Seleucus by the rules of war. When his ancestors had been preoccupied with concerns elsewhere, some of these lands had been taken over first by Ptolemy, and then by Philip, from a simple wish to appropriate another's possessions. Who could doubt that the Chersonese and the closest parts of Thrace in the neighbourhood of Lysimachia had belonged to Lysimachus? It was to re-establish his former authority over these that he had come, and also to re-found Lysimachia (which had been destroyed by a Thracian attack), so that his son Seleucus* might have it as the seat of his government.

41. This wrangling had lasted a number of days when a rumour* was reported—though it could not be verified—that Ptolemy had died, and this meant that the discussions reached no conclusion. Both sides in fact pretended not to have heard the rumour. Lucius Cornelius, charged with the mission to the two kings, Antiochus and Ptolemy, requested a short interval to meet Ptolemy, his intention being to reach Egypt before there could be any upheaval at the time of the new king's succession. Antiochus for his part thought that

Egypt would be his if he overran it at that time. He therefore dismissed the Romans, left his son Seleucus and the land-forces to continue his planned reconstruction of Lysimachia, and himself sailed to Ephesus with his entire fleet, having first sent envoys to Quinctius to discuss their alliance and thereby give him assurance that the king would do nothing to change it.

Skirting the coast of Asia, Antiochus reached Lycia and, on learning at Patara that Ptolemy was still alive, he abandoned his plan of sailing to Egypt. Even so, he headed for Cyprus. After rounding the promontory of Chelidoniae, however, he was held up for a short time in the area of the Eurymedon river in Pamphylia by a mutiny of his oarsmen. When he had moved forward from there, a terrible storm arose around the so-called 'mouths' of the River Sarus, which almost sank him and his entire fleet. Many of his ships were disabled, and many driven ashore; many were so completely swallowed up by the sea that no one managed to swim to shore. Large numbers of men perished in this incident, not just a nameless herd of rowers and common soldiers, but some illustrious courtiers of the king as well. After he brought together what remained after the wreck, Antiochus was in no position to launch an expedition to Cyprus, and so he returned to Seleucia with a retinue far less grand than at his departure. There he ordered the ships to be drawn up on land, since winter was already coming on, and he himself withdrew to winter quarters in Antioch. This was how matters stood with the kings.

42. In Rome, this was the first year that the *triumviri epulones** were elected and Gaius Licinius Lucullus, the plebeian tribune who had proposed the law regarding their election, Publius Manlius, and Publius Porcius Laeca were chosen. This triumvirate was given the legal right, also accorded the pontiffs, to wear the toga praetexta. That year, however, the urban quaestors, Quintus Fabius Labeo and Lucius Aurelius, were involved in a bitter struggle with all the priests. Money was needed because it had been decided that private individuals should be paid the last instalment of the money they had contributed towards the war, and the quaestors were dunning the augurs and pontiffs for the taxes they had not paid during the period of the war. The priests pleaded in vain with the tribunes of the people, and an amount was collected to cover all the years of non-payment.

The same year two pontiffs died and were replaced by new ones: the consul Marcus Marcellus succeeded Gaius Sempronius Tuditanus who had died while holding the praetorship in Spain, and Lucius Valerius Flaccus succeeded Marcus Cornelius Cethegus. The augur Quintus Fabius Maximus also died at a very young age and before he could hold any magistracy, but no augur was chosen to replace him that year.

The consular elections were then conducted by the consul Marcus Marcellus, and Lucius Valerius Flaccus and Marcus Porcius Cato were elected. The following were then chosen as praetors: Gnaeus Manlius Vulso, Appius Claudius Nero, Publius Porcius Laeca, Gaius Fabricius Luscinus, Gaius Atinius Labeo* and Publius Manlius.

That year the curule aediles, Marcus Fulvius Nobilior and Gaius Flaminius, distributed a million measures of grain to the people at a price of two *asses* per measure. The grain had been brought to Rome by the people of Sicily in homage to Gaius Flaminius and his father,* and Flaminius had shared the credit for the distribution with his colleague. The Roman Games were celebrated with great ceremony, and were repeated three times in their entirety. The plebeian aediles, Gnaeus Domitius Ahenobarbus and Gaius Scribonius Curio, arraigned a large number of cattle-breeders before the people. Three were found guilty, and from the fines exacted from them the aediles built a temple of Faunus on the Island. The Plebeian Games were repeated over a second two-day period, and a banquet was held in honour of the games.

43. On the Ides of March, the day of their entry into office, the consuls Lucius Valerius Flaccus and Marcus Porcius Cato referred to the Senate the matter of their provinces. The Senators took account of the war in Spain, escalating at such a rate as to require both a consular general and a consular army, and decided that the consuls should have as provinces, by mutual agreement or by allotment, Hither Spain and Italy respectively. The man receiving Spain as his province was to transport with him two legions, 15,000 infantry of the allies and the Latin League and 800 cavalry, and also take 20 warships. The other consul was to enrol two legions, sufficient to hold the province of Gaul since the spirit of the Insubres and Boii had been broken in the previous year.

Cato drew Spain as his province and Valerius Italy, and then the praetors drew as follows:

Gaius Fabricius Luscinus	city jurisdiction
Gaius Atinius Labeo	jurisdiction of foreigners
Gnaeus Manlius Vulso	Sicily
Appius Claudius Nero	Farther Spain
Publius Porcius Laeca	Pisae (so the praetor could be to the rear of the Ligures)

Publius Manlius was made consular aide for Hither Spain.

Since there were now concerns about the Spartan tyrant Nabis, as well as about Antiochus and the Aetolians, Titus Quinctius' imperium was extended for a period of a year, with the command of two legions. The consuls were authorized to enrol and send to Macedonia any forces that might be needed to supplement these. Apart from having command of the legion formerly under Quintus Fabius, Appius Claudius was also permitted to enlist 2,000 infantry and 200 new cavalry. The same number of new infantry and cavalry was also assigned to Publius Manlius for service in Hither Spain, and he was further given the legion that had been under the command of the praetor Quintus Minucius. Publius Porcius Laeca was also officially allocated 10,000 infantry and 5,000 cavalry from the army in Gaul for service around Pisae. In Sardinia Tiberius Sempronius Longus had his imperium prolonged.

44. Such was the allocation of the provinces. Before the consuls could leave the city, they were instructed, following a decree by the pontiffs, to carry out the 'Sacred Spring' that the praetor Aulus Cornelius Mammula had promised in a vow during the consulship of Gnaeus Servilius and Gaius Flaminius,* in accordance with a decision of the Senate and a vote of the people. The rite was performed twenty-one years after the vow was made. In the same period Gaius Claudius Pulcher, son of Appius, was elected and installed as augur as a replacement for Quintus Fabius Maximus, who had died the previous year.

While the public was now expressing surprise over the indifference that was being shown towards the war started by Spain, a letter arrived from Quintus Minucius with the news that he had fought a successful pitched battle with the Spanish commanders, Budares and Baesadines, near the town of Turda. Twelve thousand of the enemy had been killed, Minucius said, with Budares the commander taken prisoner and the others defeated and put to flight. After the letter was read out, there was less alarm regarding Spain, where a momentous war had been expected. All concern was now focused instead on King Antiochus, especially after the arrival of the ten commissioners. The latter first reported on their dealings with Philip, and the terms on which he had been granted peace, and then explained that the Romans were threatened with a war no less serious with Antiochus. The king had crossed to Europe with a mighty fleet and a first-rate land army, they said, and had he not been distracted by a flimsy hope, arising from an even flimsier rumour, of invading Egypt, he would soon have brought the flame of war to Greece. For the Aetolians would not remain inactive, either—they were by nature an unruly people and they also bore a grudge against the Romans. There was also another great cancer fixed in the entrails of Greece—Nabis, currently tyrant of the Spartans, but soon to be tyrant of all Greece, if given the chance, a man who rivalled all the notorious tyrants in greed and brutality. If he were allowed to hold Argos—which dominates the Peloponnese like a citadel—when the Roman armies have been taken back to Italy, then the liberation of Greece from Philip will have been for nothing. Instead of a king— who, if nothing else, was far removed—the Greeks would be ruled by a tyrant close at hand.

45. When they heard this from the lips of such authoritative witnesses—men who were †then† bringing reports entirely based on their own inquiries—they felt that the major problem was that of Antiochus, but that discussion focused on the tyrant was now more urgent since the king had, for some reason, withdrawn into Syria. There was a long debate on whether they appeared to have sufficient grounds for declaring war, or whether they should give Titus Quinctius the authority to do what he felt was in the interests of the state with regard to the Spartan Nabis. They did give Quinctius this authority because they thought it not of great importance to the highest interests of the state whether action on the matter came sooner or later. Of greater concern was what the reaction of Hannibal and the Carthaginians would be to war breaking out with Antiochus.

Men belonging to the faction opposed to Hannibal had been writing time and again to their respective friends amongst the leading Romans to say that messengers and letters had been sent to Antiochus by Hannibal, and that envoys had come secretly to Hannibal from the king. Some wild animals could not be tamed by any means, they said, and this man's disposition was equally fierce and recalcitrant. He would complain that his city-state was atrophying in listless inactivity, was drowsing in inertia, and that only the noise of weaponry could wake her up. What gave plausibility to these statements was the recollection of the last war, of which Hannibal alone was prosecutor as well as instigator. In addition to this, he had ruffled the feelings of many of the important people by his recent conduct.

46. At that time power in Carthage lay with the order of judges,* mainly because judges had life-tenure of office. Everybody's material well-being, reputation, and survival rested in these men's hands. Anyone falling foul of a single member of that order had them all against him, and there was no shortage of people to bring a charge against him before these unsympathetic judges. While these men were enjoying their absolute authority—for they did not exercise their exceptional powers as citizens should—Hannibal, who had been elected praetor,* ordered a quaestor summoned to him. The quaestor completely ignored him, for not only was he a member of the faction opposed to Hannibal but he was also in the process of being promoted from the quaestorship to the supreme order, that of the judges, and was already adopting the arrogance in keeping with the power soon to be his. Hannibal found this behaviour totally unacceptable, and sent an officer to arrest the quaestor. He then brought the man before the assembly where he launched an attack not so much on the individual concerned but on the order of judges—before their arrogant manipulation of power, he said, neither the laws nor the magistrates counted for anything. Observing that his speech was falling on willing ears, and that the judges' arrogance infringed the liberty of the lower orders as well, he immediately promulgated and carried a law limiting the election of judges to a period of a single year, and barring anyone from being a judge for two years in succession. The appreciation this move won for him with the masses was commensurate with the offence he gave to most of the nobility. Another of his actions also stirred up personal animosities against him, though it was taken in the public interest. The public revenues were trickling away, partly through poor administration and partly because they were divided up as spoils amongst certain noblemen and the magistrates. There was,

accordingly, a shortage of money to pay the annual tribute to the Romans, and private citizens seemed to be faced with heavy taxation.

47. Hannibal turned his attention to the amount of taxes collected on land- and sea-transportation of goods, and the items on which these taxes were disbursed, noting the portion of them consumed by normal expenses of state and how much was diverted by misappropriation. He then announced before the assembly that, if all moneys that were now due were collected, the state would be sufficiently solvent to pay the tribute to the Romans without having to tax private citizens, and he made good his assurance of this.

At this point the men who had grown fat on embezzlement of public funds over a number of years became furiously angry, feeling they were being deprived of their own property rather than relieved of loot gained by theft, and they began to incite the Romans—who were looking for an excuse to vent their hatred on him anyway—to take action against Hannibal. For a long time Publius Scipio Africanus opposed this, feeling as he did that it was not in keeping with dignity of the Roman people to put the seal of approval on the antipathies of Hannibal's accusers, and link official support with the factions of Carthage. It was as if they were dissatisfied with having defeated Hannibal in war, he thought, if they now had to act as accusers, swearing to the legitimacy of the allegations and bringing charges against him. Eventually, however, Hannibal's accusers persuaded the Senate to send a delegation to Carthage to lay before the Carthaginian Senate their accusations that Hannibal was plotting war along with Antiochus. Three envoys were sent: Gnaeus Servilius, Marcus Claudius Marcellus, and Quintus Terentius Culleo. Arriving in Carthage, these followed the advice of Hannibal's enemies and, when people asked the reason for their visit, had the answer given that they had come to settle the differences that the Carthaginians were having with Masinissa, king of Numidia. This gained general acceptance, and only Hannibal was not fooled—he could see that it was he who was the real target of the Romans, that the granting of peace to the Carthaginians was dependent on a relentless war continuing against him alone. He decided accordingly to yield to circumstances and fortune. He had already prepared everything in advance for his escape, and now he spent the day in the forum to avert suspicion. At dusk he proceeded to one of the city-gates, dressed in his city-clothes, with two companions who had no idea of what he had in mind.

48. Horses were waiting at the spot where he had instructed, and he crossed by night the area in this region known as Byzacium, arriving the following day at his castle on the sea between Acylla and Thapsus. There a ship was awaiting him, fitted out and manned with a crew, and on this Hannibal left Africa, bemoaning his country's fate more often than his own. That same day he crossed to the island of Cercina. Here he found in port a number of Phoenician merchant-vessels loaded with cargo, and when he disembarked a crowd gathered as people came to greet him. When people asked about him, he had the answer given that he was on a diplomatic mission to Tyre. Even so, he was afraid that one of these ships might set off at night and take the news to Thapsus or Hadrumetum that he had been spotted on Cercina. He therefore gave orders for a sacrifice to be prepared, and had the ship captains and traders invited to it. He also issued instructions for the sails and spars to be gathered from the ships to form a sunshade (it happened to be midsummer) for his guests, who were dining on the shore. On that day the banquet was held with all the lavishness permitted by the circumstances and time, and the party was drawn out till late at night with heavy drinking. As soon as Hannibal found the occasion to give those in the port the slip, he set sail. The other diners were asleep, and when the next day they finally awoke from their slumber, still well under the influence of the drink, not only was it late but they spent several hours carrying the rigging back to the ships and then setting it up and adjusting it.

In Carthage the large numbers of people who usually visited Hannibal's house gathered at the entrance to the building, and word spread that he was nowhere to be found. A crowd then converged on the forum demanding their leading citizen. There were loud murmurings, some saying that he had escaped, which was actually the case, but others—and these were the majority—that he had been treacherously murdered by the Romans. One could see the various expressions that one expects to find in a community where loyalties are divided between different parties and which is split by factions. Then finally word was brought that Hannibal had been sighted on Cercina.

49. The Roman envoys declared in the Carthaginian Senate that the Roman Senators had learned that Philip had earlier made war on the Roman people mainly because he had been incited to do so by Hannibal.* They had also learned that dispatches and messages had of late been sent by Hannibal to Antiochus and the Aetolians. Hannibal had, they said, developed plans for provoking Carthage to rebellion, and the destination of his present journey was undoubtedly Antiochus' court—he would not rest until he had fomented war the whole world over. His action should not go unpunished, they said, if the Carthaginians wished to satisfy the Roman people that none of his activities had their approval or were officially sanctioned. The Carthaginians replied that they would do whatever the Romans considered fair.

Hannibal had a good journey to Tyre where he was welcomed by the founders of Carthage* as a man of distinction crowned with all manner of honours, and coming from their second fatherland. He remained a few days in Tyre and then sailed on to Antioch. There he was told that the king had already left for Asia, and he met Antiochus' son, who was engaged in the seasonal celebration of the games at Daphne.* Hannibal was given a warm welcome by him, but did not retard his voyage. At Ephesus he overtook the king. The latter was still vacillating and ambivalent about the war with Rome, but Hannibal's arrival was no minor influence in bringing him to a decision to act. At this same time the Aetolians also abandoned their alliance with Rome: their envoys had been asking for the return of Pharsalus, Leucas, and certain other states in accordance with the terms of their original treaty,* only to be referred by the Senate to Titus Quinctius.

BOOK THIRTY-FOUR

1. Amid the concerns over serious wars that were either barely terminated or else looming on the horizon there occurred an event which is trivial as far as the historical account is concerned, but which led to acrimonious debate with the passions it aroused. The plebeian tribunes Marcus Fundanius and Lucius Valerius brought a bill before the popular assembly to annul the Oppian law. The law had been enacted by the plebeian tribune Gaius Oppius* in the consulship of Quintus Fabius and Tiberius Sempronius,* when the flames of the Punic War were burning fiercely; and its provisions were that no woman was to own more than a half-ounce of gold, wear multi-shaded clothes,* or ride a horse and carriage in any city or town, or within a mile of a town, exception being granted on the occasion of public religious rites. Marcus and Publius Iunius Brutus, who were plebeian tribunes, defended the Oppian law, stating that they would not permit its repeal, and many eminent men came forward to speak for or against its annulment. The Capitol thus was filled with hordes of supporters and opponents of the law. As for married women, there was no authority, no feelings of modesty, no order from their husbands that could keep them at home. They blocked all the roads in the city and the approaches to the Forum, and made earnest entreaties to their husbands when they went down to the Forum. The Republic was prospering and everybody's private fortune was increasing day by day, they said, so married women, too, should be granted the restoration of the finery they once enjoyed. This large gathering of women kept growing every day, for they were even starting to come in from the country towns and administrative centres, and they were already presuming to accost consuls, praetors, and other magistrates with their appeals. But they continued to find one of the consuls, at least, adamantly opposed to them. This was Porcius Cato,* who spoke as follows about the law whose repeal was under consideration:

2. 'My fellow citizens: had each of us, individually, resolved to preserve our rights and standing as a husband with his own wife,* we should now be having less of a problem with women as a whole. As things are, our autonomy has been ground down in our own

homes by female emotionality, and here, too, in the Forum it is
being crushed and trodden under foot. Because we have not been
able to control our women on an individual basis, we are now
frightened of them as a body. Frankly, the notion of the entire male
sex on some island being utterly wiped out by a female cabal* used
to strike me as mere fable and a complete fabrication; but there is
extreme danger with any group of people if one permits them to
hold gatherings, meetings, and clandestine discussions. I personally
have difficulty deciding in my own mind which is worse, the conduct itself or the precedent it sets—one of which is more the concern of us consuls and the rest of the magistrates, while the other
pertains more to you, my fellow citizens. For whether what is being
proposed to you is or is not in the interests of the state is for you to
judge—you who will be voting on the matter. But this riotous
behaviour of the women, whether it be spontaneous or occasioned
by you, Marcus Fundanius and Lucius Valerius, must certainly be
blamed on the magistrates, and I do not know if it is more dis-
creditable to you as tribunes, or to us the consuls. It is more to *your*
discredit if you have drawn the women to stir up your tribunician
revolts, and more to *ours* if legislation is to be accepted because of
a secession of our women, as once it was because of a secession of the
plebs.

'To be honest, I was blushing somewhat a moment ago when I
came into the Forum through the midst of a crowd of women. I was
held back by my respect for their status and for their modesty, as
individuals rather than as a group—they should not be seen being
taken to task by a consul—or else I would have said: "What sort of
conduct is this, all this running out into public view, blocking the
streets and accosting other women's husbands? Could you not all
have asked your own husbands the very same thing at home? Have
you more seductive charms in public than in private, and with other
women's spouses more than your own? And yet not even at home
should the proposing or repealing of laws in this place have been any
concern of yours, not if their modesty kept married women within
their proper limits."

'Our ancestors' will was that women should conduct no business,
not even private business, without a guardian to act as their spokesman; they were to remain under the protection of fathers, brothers,
or husbands. But we, for God's sake, now allow them even to engage

in affairs of state and almost to involve themselves in the Forum, in our meetings and assemblies. For what are they doing at this moment in the streets and at the crossroads if not urging acceptance of the bill of the plebeian tribunes and voting for the repeal of the law? Give free rein to their emotional nature, to this unbroken beast, and hope that they themselves will impose a curb on their licence! If you do not impose it yourselves, this curb on them is merely the least of the restraints which women resent having imposed upon them by convention or the law. If we are willing to speak the truth, what they want is freedom—no, complete licence—in everything. If they win on this point, what then will they not try?

3. 'Consider all the laws pertaining to women which the ancients employed to curb their licence and make them subject to their husbands—though they are restricted by all of these you are still barely able to keep them in order. Suppose you allow them to pick away at these laws one by one, to tear them from you, and finally to put themselves on a par with their husbands. Do you believe you will be able to tolerate them? As soon as they begin to be your equals they will immediately be your superiors.

'But, you may say, they are protesting so that no new measures be taken against them; it is not the law they object to but injustice. Not true! What they want is for you to rescind a law which you have accepted and passed with your votes, a law which has met with your approval after your many years of experience of living with it; which is to say, they want you to weaken all the other laws by removing this one. No law satisfies everybody; all one asks is that it benefit the majority and the state as a whole. If a person is to smash and overthrow any law that inconveniences him as an individual, what will be the point of society enacting laws which can be shortly afterwards rescinded by those against whom they are directed?

'I should like to hear, by the way, what it is that has brought these married ladies to run in an uproar into public places and why they find it difficult to keep out of the Forum and public assemblies. Is it so that their captive fathers, husbands, children, and brothers might be ransomed from Hannibal? Such dire fortune is far removed from our state, and may it ever be! And yet, when that misfortune *was* ours, you refused to accede to the dutiful entreaties of the women. But, I suppose, it was not family duty or concern for their dear ones that brought the women together—it was religion. They are going to welcome the Idaean Mother,* coming from Pessinus in Phrygia. And what is the reason offered for this female revolt—one that is, at least, truthful? "So we can shine in gold and purple," she says. "So we can ride our carriages through the city on holidays and ordinary days alike, in triumph, as it were, after the defeat and annulment of the law, and after the capture and seizure of your ballots. And so there will be no limit to expenditure, no limit to extravagance."

4. 'You have often heard my complaints about the lavish spending of women, and of men as well, and not just private citizens but magistrates, too. You have heard me complain that our state is plagued with two antithetical vices, greed and extravagance, afflictions that have been the downfall of all great empires. The fortunes of our republic are improving and advancing on a daily basis, and our empire is expanding—now we are crossing into Greece and Asia, which are replete with all manner of seductive pleasures, and we are even handling the treasures of kings. The more this happens, the more I shudder at the possibility that these things may have captured us rather than we them. Those statues from Syracuse were enemy standards brought against the city, believe me. Already I hear too many people praising and admiring the artefacts of Corinth and Athens, and ridiculing the earthenware antefixes of the Roman gods. But I prefer to have these gods smiling on us, and I hope they will, if we allow them to remain in their abodes.

'In our fathers' day Pyrrhus used his envoy Cineas* to solicit the support not only of our men, but of our women too, with gifts. The Oppian law, intended to curtail female extravagance, had not yet been enacted, and yet no woman accepted the gifts. Why do you think that was? For the same reason that your ancestors had no need for legal sanctions in such matters—there was no extravagance to be curtailed. Diseases must be diagnosed before cures are found; and in the same way desires appear before the laws to curb them. What brought about the Licinian law of the 500 iugera* but the unconscionable greed for extending one's lands? What gave rise to the Cincian law* regarding emoluments and honoraria but the fact that the commons were becoming tribute-paying subjects of the Senate? Little wonder then that neither the Oppian nor any other law was required to limit expenditure by women at a time when women independently refused to accept gold and purple offered to them as gifts. If Cineas were doing the rounds of the city with those gifts today, he would already have found women standing in the streets in order to take them.

'And yet where some appetites are concerned I personally cannot fathom the rhyme or reason for them. Perhaps your not being allowed something that another is allowed might cause some understandable shame or annoyance; but if everybody's level of personal adornment is standardized, what is it that each of you fears may be conspicuous in her case? The deepest embarrassment one feels is over penny-pinching or one's lack of means, but the law removes that from you in both cases when you do not have precisely what you are not allowed to have. "It is just this kind of levelling I cannot stand," says the rich woman. "Why can I not be admired for the splendour of my gold and purple? Why is other women's lack of means hidden and excused by this law, which makes it appear that they would have had, if it were lawful, just what they cannot have?"

'My fellow citizens, is this the kind of rivalry you want to incite amongst your wives, with rich women wanting to have what no other woman can, and poorer women extending themselves beyond their means in order not to be looked down upon for not having it? Indeed, let them begin to be embarrassed about the things that should not embarrass them and they will stop being embarrassed about the things that should. The woman able to buy from her own means will buy; the one who cannot will ask her husband. And what a sorry man that husband is—whether he accedes to her wishes or whether he refuses—for then he will see what he has not given himself given to her by another man! At the moment they are petitioning other women's husbands in public and, what is worse, petitioning them for a law and for their votes, in some cases with success. Acceding, you are as an individual working against yourself, your own interests, and your children: once the law ceases to curb your wife's expenditure, you will not curb it yourself.

'Do not think, my fellow citizens, that matters will stand where they did before the enactment of the law on this problem. It is safer for a criminal not to be charged than for him to be acquitted, and it would have been easier to bear extravagance left unchallenged than it will be now when it has been provoked by its shackles, as wild beasts are, and then set free. It is my opinion that the Oppian law should not be repealed under any circumstances, but whatever your decision may be I would wish it to have the blessing of all the gods.'

5. After this the plebeian tribunes who had declared that they would interpose their veto added a few words in the same vein. Then Lucius Valerius spoke as follows on the motion which he had himself proposed:

'Had it been only private citizens who had come forward to speak for and against the proposal which is before us, I too should have awaited your vote on the matter in silence, believing, as I would have, that enough had been said on both sides. As it is, a most eminent man, the consul Marcus Porcius, has made an attack on our proposal, using not merely his authority, which itself would have carried enough weight even without a word being spoken, but also a long and diligently prepared oration. I must therefore make a brief response.

'The consul, however, has spent more words on a criticism of married women than on rebutting our proposal, to the point of making it unclear whether the behaviour for which he was reproaching the women was natural or prompted by us. I shall defend the proposal, not us personally, against whom the consul directed insinuations rather than an accusation based on facts.

'Cato has used the words "gathering", "revolt", and sometimes "secession" of women, because married women had asked you in public to rescind at a time of peace, when the republic was flourishing and prosperous, a law which had been passed against them in the cruel moments of war. I know the emotive words chosen to exaggerate the case—those he has used and others—and we all know Marcus Cato to be an orator who is not only stern but on occasion even brutal, though he is by nature compassionate. For, in fact, what is strange about what the married women have done in coming forward publicly in large numbers over a matter that is of concern to them? Have they never appeared in public before? Let me open your own *Origins** to contradict you. Listen to how often they have done it, and always, you will see, for the common good.

'Right at the beginning, when Romulus was king, when the Capitol had been captured by the Sabines, and a pitched battle was going on in the middle of the Forum, was not the battle halted by the married women running between the two lines?* All right? After the expulsion of the kings, the legions of the Volsci, led by Marcius Coriolanus,* had encamped at a point five miles from Rome. Was not this army, which would have overwhelmed this city, turned away by our women? When the city had been taken by the Gauls,* how was it ransomed? The women, of course, with everybody's consent, gathered together their gold for public use. In the last war*—to avoid going into ancient history—did not the widows help out the treasury with their money when there was a financial problem? And when new gods were also brought in to give us aid in a time of crisis, did not all the married women go the sea to welcome the Idaean mother? Ah, you say, these cases are different. It is not my intention to put these cases in the same category—if the women have done nothing new, that is sufficient vindication for them. Nobody was surprised at the action they took in matters concerning the whole population, men and women alike, so are we surprised at their taking the same action in an affair of special concern to themselves? But what have they actually done? Good heavens, masters do not spurn the entreaties of slaves, and we have proud ears if we are annoyed at requests made of us by respectable ladies.

6. 'I come now to the matter at issue. On this the consul had two positions in his oration. For he was indignant at the rescinding of any law whatsoever, and at the same time at the rescinding of that particular law enacted to curb women's extravagance. The first position, the one defending the laws in general, seemed fitting for a consul, while the second, the attack on extravagance, was in keeping with the man's strict principles. There is therefore some danger that unless I demonstrate the speciousness of both standpoints you may be deluged in misconception.

'There are indeed laws which are not temporary measures but enacted to stand for ever because of their continued practicality. I myself grant that none of these should be repealed, unless it is demonstrated by experience to be ineffective or some political situation renders it impractical. But I also see that there are some laws that have been required by temporary emergencies, mortal laws, as it were, which can change as circumstances themselves change. Measures passed in peacetime are often annulled in time of war, and those passed in war are often annulled in peace. It is like steering a ship, for which some manœuvres are useful in fair weather, others in foul.

'Legal measures falling by nature into two categories, to which class then does this law which we wish to repeal belong? †. . .† Is it a law of the kings,* born when the city itself was born? Or, next best, was it inscribed on the Twelve Tables* by the board of ten that was appointed to establish our legal code? If this was a law that our forefathers felt was indispensable for the protection of the dignity of married women, then we should also be concerned that in annulling it we might be annulling the modesty and purity of womanhood. But everybody knows that the law is a new one, passed twenty years ago in the consulship of Quintus Fabius and Tiberius Sempronius. For many years our married women lived without it and had the highest morals. What danger is there then that they will lapse into extravagant living if it is repealed? For if the purpose of that legislation had been specifically to repress female passions, then we ought to fear that its annulment would actually kindle them; but its real purpose will be shown by the date of its passing. Hannibal was in Italy, victorious at Cannae.* He now held Tarentum, Arpi, Capua. It looked as if he was going to move his army up to the city of Rome; the allies had deserted us and we had no soldiers in reserve, no sailors to maintain the fleet, and no money in the treasury. Slaves were being bought up to be put under arms,* on the understanding that their masters would be paid for them when the war was finished. With that same date fixed also for payment, contractors offered to provide wheat and the other provisions needed for the conduct of the war. We provided at our own expense slaves to act as oarsmen, their number being dependent on our tax assessment. We contributed all our gold and silver to the public weal, following the lead of the senators, and widows and orphans contributed their money to the treasury. There was a provision against our having at home more than a fixed quantity of wrought gold and silver and of coined silver and bronze. In a period like that were married women preoccupied with extravagant living and clothing, making an Oppian law a requirement to repress this tendency? At a time when the ceremonies in honour of Ceres were suspended because all the married women were in mourning, and the Senate decreed that the period of mourning be limited to thirty days? It is clear to everyone that it was financial exigency and the miseries our state was experiencing that drafted that law, because the moneys of all private individuals had to be diverted to public use, and that the law would last only as long as the reason for its drafting remained with us. If measures at that time decreed by the Senate or dictated by the people to meet a temporary crisis must be kept in force for ever, why then do we repay loans to private citizens? Why do we tender public contracts on the basis of cash payments? Why are slaves not purchased to serve as soldiers? Why do we not, as private citizens, supply oarsmen as we did in those days?

7. 'All the other classes, all other people will feel that the republic's condition has changed for the better. Is it only to your wives that the rewards of the common peace and tranquillity are not to permeate? Shall we men wear the purple? Shall we be purple-fringed as magistrates and priests? Will our sons wear purple-fringed togas? Are we going to grant the right to wear the toga praetexta* to magistrates in the colonies and municipal towns, along with even the lowest category of administrators here in Rome, the overseers of the wards? And not only allow them to wear such distinguished insignia in their lifetime but also to be cremated with it when they die? Is it only to women that we shall forbid the wearing of purple? You, as a husband, are permitted to use purple as a coverlet for your bed.* Are you going to refuse your wife a purple cloak, and will your horse have trappings more impressive than your spouse's clothing? And yet in the case of purple, which deteriorates and wears out, I suppose I can see some sort of justification, unfair though it be, for inflexibility. But in the case of gold, where the only financial loss is in the workmanship, what kind of stinginess is this? In gold there is rather security for both private and public needs, as experience has taught you.

'Cato kept making the point that there was no rivalry between individual women because each woman had nothing. But, heavens above, they all as a class feel hurt and vexed when they see that the wives of our allies of the Latin League have been granted the accessories that have been taken from themselves! They are hurt when they see those women resplendent in gold and purple, when they see them riding through the city while they themselves follow on foot— just as if empire lay in those women's communities, not in their own! This could wound the sensibilities of men; how do you think it affects those of our little women on whom even trivial things make an impression? Women have no access to magistracies, priesthoods, triumphs, insignia, or to gifts or spoils that come from war. Elegance, grooming, fine appearance—these are the insignia of women. This is their pride and joy. This is what your ancestors called "woman's embellishment". In time of mourning what do they put aside but purple and gold? What else do they take up when their time of mourning is finished? In periods of public thanksgiving and public prayer what do they take up that is special if not finer beautification?

'I suppose that, if you do repeal the Oppian law, forbidding any part of what the law now forbids will be out of your hands! Daughters, wives, even sisters will for some of you be less under your control! No, never can the subservience of women be removed while their kinsmen are alive—and yet they themselves hate the independence granted them by losing husbands or fathers. They prefer their refinements to be under your control rather than the law's, and you on your side should keep them under your care and protection, not servitude, preferring to be called fathers and husbands rather than masters. The consul used pejorative terms just now when he referred to "female revolt" and "secession". For there is real danger of their seizing the Sacred Mount, as the plebs once did in their anger, or the Aventine! No, as the weaker sex they must abide by whatever it is that you decide, and the more power you have the more lenient you should be in exercising it.'

8. On the day after these speeches for and against the law were delivered, a somewhat larger crowd of women flooded the public places. In a single column they all surrounded the doors of the Bruti, who were for vetoing the proposal of their colleagues, and refused to release the pressure until the threatened veto was withdrawn by the tribunes. After that there was no question but that all the tribes would repeal the law and, twenty years after it was passed, the law was withdrawn.*

After the repeal of the Oppian law, the consul Marcus Porcius immediately took twenty-five warships, including five belonging to the allies, and set off for the port of Luna, ordering the army to meet at the same destination. By an edict relayed along the coastline he also assembled here ships of all kinds, and setting out from Luna he issued instructions for these to attend him to the port of Pyrenaeus, indicating that he would proceed against the enemy from there with his fleet *en masse*. These ships sailed past the Ligurian mountains and the Gallic Gulf, and met him on the day he had fixed. From Pyrenaeus they moved on to Rhoda where they forcibly expelled a Spanish garrison installed in the stronghold, and from Rhoda they came with a favourable wind to Emporiae where the entire force, with the exception of the crews, were set ashore.

9. Even in those days Emporiae comprised two towns separated by

a wall, the one belonging to Greeks from Phocaea (mother country also of the Massiliots*), the other to Spaniards. The Greek town, however, was exposed to the sea and had a wall whose entire compass was less than 400 yards, while the Spaniards' wall, lying further back from the sea, had a circumference of three miles. A third category of inhabitant, Roman settlers, were added by the deified Caesar after the defeat of the sons of Pompey. These days they are all integrated into a single body, with first the Spaniards, and then the Greeks, granted Roman citizenship. Anyone seeing them in those days— open sea facing them on one side, the barbarous and aggressive race of Spaniards on the other—would wonder just where their protection lay. What safeguarded them in their weak position was discipline, which is best preserved by fear when one is surrounded by stronger peoples. The landward part of the wall they would keep well defended, with only a single gate facing that direction which was constantly guarded by one of the magistrates. During the night one third of the citizen body kept watch on the walls, and this was not just a matter of routine or law—they posted guards and did the rounds of them with as much care as if an enemy were at the gates. They allowed no Spaniard in the city, and would not even go out of town themselves without good reason. All had freedom of exit on the side facing the sea; but they would go out from the gate facing the Spanish town only in large numbers, that usually meaning the third of the citizens who had provided the watch on the walls the previous night. And their reason for going out was the fact that the Spaniards, who had no experience of the sea, enjoyed trading with them— wishing to purchase themselves the foreign goods imported by ship and at the same time to dispose of the produce of their lands. Desire for such reciprocal advantages rendered the Spanish city open to the Greeks.

The latter were also more secure from the fact that they lived in the shelter of an alliance with Rome which they preserved with a loyalty equal to that of the Massiliots, though with fewer resources than theirs. On this occasion, too, they gave the consul and his army a courteous and warm welcome. Cato waited there a few days until he could find out about the location and size of the enemy forces, and spent the whole period drilling his soldiers so as not to be idle even at a time of enforced delay. It happened to be the time of year when the Spaniards had their grain on the threshing-floor, and Cato therefore forbade the purveyors to buy wheat, sending them back to Rome with the words: 'The war will be self-supporting.' He set off from Emporiae and burned and razed the fields of the enemy, spreading flight and panic throughout the area.

10. At this same time Marcus Helvius was withdrawing from Farther Spain with a detachment of 6,000 men that had been accorded him by the praetor Appius Claudius when he was met by a massive column of the Celtiberians at the town of Iliturgi. According to Valerius' account,* the latter numbered 20,000 under arms; 12,000 of these were killed, he says, the town of Iliturgi was captured, and all males of fighting age were put to death. Helvius then came to Cato's camp. The area was now out of danger from the enemy, and so he sent his detachment back to Farther Spain and set off for Rome where, thanks to his successful operation, he entered the city with an ovation. He brought to the treasury 14,732 pounds of unwrought silver, 17,023 pieces of silver stamped with the *biga*,* and 119,439 silver coins with the Oscan stamp. The reason for the Senate's refusal to award him the triumph was that he had fought the battle under another man's auspices and in another man's province.* He had in fact come home two years later than scheduled; after handing over his province to his successor Quintus Minucius, he had been detained there during the following year by a long and severe illness. It therefore transpired that Helvius entered the city with an ovation a mere two months before his successor Quintus Minucius celebrated his triumph. Minucius also brought to Rome 34,800 pounds of silver, 73,000 pieces stamped with the *biga*, and 278,000 pieces of Oscan-stamped silver.

11. In Spain, meanwhile, the consul had his camp pitched not far from Emporiae, and here three envoys came to him from Bilistages, chieftain of the Ilergetes, including one of Bilistages' sons. These complained that their fortresses were under attack and that they had no hope of mounting resistance unless the Roman commander sent help. Three thousand men would suffice, they said, and if such a force arrived the enemy would not stay to fight. The consul's response was that, while he felt for their predicament and their fears, he had nothing like sufficient forces for him to be able to diminish his strength without risk by dividing his army—not when there were large enemy numbers in the vicinity and he was each day waiting to see how soon he would be forced into pitched battle. On hearing this

the envoys flung themselves at the consul's feet in tears, begging him not to abandon them when they were in such dire straits—where were they to turn if they were rebuffed by the Romans? They had no allies, they said, and no other hope anywhere in the world. They could have avoided this danger had they decided to abandon their loyalties and join the other tribes in their machinations, but no threats and intimidation had swayed them, expecting as they did that they would find sufficient support and assistance with the Romans. If this proved not to be the case and if they were refused help by the consul, then they called on gods and men to be their witnesses that they would join the uprising unwillingly and under compulsion, so as not to suffer the same fate as the people of Saguntum, and that they would perish along with the other Spanish tribes rather than do so in isolation.

12. That day the envoys were dismissed with no response. During the night that followed the consul was tormented by two concerns— he was unwilling to abandon the allies, but unwilling, too, to weaken his army, a move which could retard his decisive encounter with the enemy or prove dangerous in that encounter. He remained determined not to reduce his troops, fearing that the enemy in the mean time might inflict some ignominious defeat on him. The allies, he thought, should be given confidence rather than tangible aid—often, especially in warfare, impressions have been as effective as reality, and a man believing he had support has often saved himself as well as if he really did have it, the assurance he feels giving him hope and mettle.

The next day the consul gave the envoys his answer. Although he feared that lending some of his forces to others would weaken them, he said, he nevertheless took more account of his allies' perilous situation than his own. He then issued orders for one-third of each cohort to be instructed to cook food swiftly to put aboard the ships, which were to be made ready for sailing in two days. He commanded two of the envoys to take word of this to Bilistages and the Ilergetes, but kept with him the chieftain's son, entertaining him and giving him gifts. The envoys set out only after seeing the soldiers embarked on the ships, and when they reported this as a certainty they saturated the enemy as well as their own people with rumours of the forthcoming Roman assistance.

13. When enough of a performance had been mounted, the consul

had the men recalled from the ships, and as the time was approaching when campaigning was possible he established winter-quarters three miles from Emporiae. From here he would lead the men into enemy territory on raiding parties, varying the direction on each occasion and leaving a small detachment in the camp. They usually set off at night, which would enable them to proceed the greatest distance from camp and also fall upon the enemy unawares. This practice provided training for his raw recruits, and large numbers of the enemy were also taken prisoner (in fact, the enemy no longer dared proceed beyond the fortifications of their strongholds).

When the consul had fully tested the mettle both of his men and of the enemy, he had the tribunes, prefects, and all the cavalrymen and centurions called to a meeting. 'The time that you have often longed for has arrived,' he told them, 'the time when you could have the opportunity to demonstrate your courage. So far your mode of fighting has been more that of robbers than warriors, but now you will meet in regular battle, one enemy against another—and then you will be able to go beyond raiding fields to draining the wealth of cities! Our fathers, when the Carthaginians had both generals and armies in Spain and they themselves had not a single soldier there, still wanted a clause added to the treaty stating that the River Ebro should be the boundary of their empire.* Today we have two praetors, a consul, and three Roman armies in Spain, and no Carthaginian has set foot in these provinces for almost ten years—and still our empire on this side of the Ebro is lost to us. This you must recover by your courage under arms, and you must compel a race of people engaged in a headstrong revolt, rather than a determined struggle, to accept once more the yoke it has thrown off.'

Such was the tenor of Cato's exhortation. He announced that he would lead them that night against the enemy camp, and with that he sent them off to rest themselves.

14. After attending to the auspices, Cato set off at midnight. In order to take up a position at a point of his choosing and before the enemy became aware of it, he made a detour around the enemy camp and at first light drew up his line, sending three cohorts right up to the enemy rampart. The barbarians, shocked to see the Romans to their rear, themselves ran to arms. Meanwhile the consul addressed his men, saying: 'Men! Your hope lies in your courage and nowhere else, and my actions have been deliberately taken to ensure this. The

enemy sit between our camp and ourselves, and to our rear lies
enemy territory. The noblest plan is also the safest, to have your
hopes centred on your valour.'

With that he ordered the cohorts to retreat in order to draw the
barbarians out with a simulated flight. It turned out as he had anticipated. Thinking the Romans had lost their nerve and were in retreat,
the Spaniards burst forth from the gate, filling the area between their
camp and the enemy line with armed men. As these scrambled to
deploy their line, the consul, who had his men ready and in order,
attacked their disorganized ranks. He first of all led the cavalry into
the fight on both wings. On the right, however, the Romans were
immediately repulsed, and as they gave ground in alarm they struck
fear into the infantry as well. Seeing this, the consul issued orders for
two hand-picked cohorts to be taken around the right flank of the
enemy and for these to let themselves be seen at the rear before the
infantry lines engaged. The terror that this struck into the enemy
redressed the balance of the fight, which the panic in the Roman
cavalry had upset. But the infantry and cavalry on the right wing
were thrown into such disorder that the consul grabbed a few of
them with his hands and turned them back towards the enemy. So it
was that, as long as the battle was being fought with projectiles, the
contest was even, and on the right flank, where the panic and flight
had started, the Romans were finding it difficult to put up resistance.
On the left, and in the centre, it was the barbarians who were under
pressure, looking back with anxiety at the cohorts bearing down on
their rear. When the javelins and darts had been thrown, however,
and the combatants drew their swords, then the battle was virtually
renewed; for now they were not being dealt unforeseen wounds randomly delivered from afar, but with foot set against foot, their hopes
all lay in their courage and their physical strength.

15. His men were now tiring, and the consul revitalized them by
bringing into the battle reserve cohorts from the second line. A new
battle-line was thus constituted, and fresh troops attacked a weary
enemy with weapons as yet unused, at first pushing them back with a
spirited charge in wedge-formation, then scattering them and driving them off in flight. The enemy ran in confusion through the
fields, heading back to camp. When Cato saw them in flight in every
quarter, he himself rode back to the second legion, which had been
kept in reserve. This legion he ordered to advance their standards

and follow them at full speed to attack the enemy camp. Any man running forward and breaking ranks from an excess of enthusiasm he personally struck with his short spear as he rode between the lines, and he also ordered the tribunes and centurions to punish him. The attack on the camp now commenced, and the Romans were being pushed back from the palisade with stones, stakes and all manner of projectiles. Then, with the arrival of the fresh legion, the spirits of the attacking force were raised while the enemy fought more aggressively to defend their palisade. The consul surveyed the entire field, intending to burst through at the point of least resistance. Seeing a shortage of defenders at the left gate he led the *principes* and *hastati** of the second legion to that point. The sentinels stationed at the gate failed to hold off their charge, and the rest of the Spaniards, seeing the enemy inside their palisade, proceeded to throw down their standards and their arms, the camp now lost to them. They were massacred in the gateways, wedged in by their own numbers, and the men of the second legion cut them down from the rear while the rest pillaged the camp. Valerius Antias reports enemy dead that day to be in excess of 40,000, but Cato himself, who certainly does not underestimate his own achievements,* says that many were killed, but does not specify a number.

16. [Cato is reckoned to have performed three commendable acts that day. In the first place he led his army around the enemy far from his own ships and camp, and proceeded to fight in the midst of the foe, where his men's hope lay entirely in their valour. Secondly, he brought in the cohorts to the enemy's rear. And thirdly, when all the others had broken ranks to pursue the enemy, he ordered the second legion to move forward to the camp gate at full speed, but in proper formation under the standards.]* There was no cessation of activity after the victory. When the signal to retire had been given, Cato led his men, all laden with spoils, back to camp where he gave them a few hours of the night to sleep before leading them to conduct raids on the countryside. The raids were more wide-ranging now that the enemy were scattered in flight. This, no less than their defeat the day before, brought the Spaniards of Emporiae and their neighbours to capitulate. Many inhabitants of other states, who had sought refuge in Emporiae, also surrendered. Cato addressed these politely, and sent them home after entertaining them with wine and food.

Cato then swiftly moved camp, and wherever his army advanced he was met by delegates from states offering submission. When he reached Tarraco, all Spain this side of the Ebro had been brought to heel, and prisoners-of-war, Romans as well as allies and members of the Latin League—men who had fallen victim to various mischances in Spain—were brought to the consul by the barbarians as a gift. Then word spread abroad that the consul was going to lead his army into Turdetania, and a false report that he had already begun his march reached remote mountain peoples. In response to this empty and groundless rumour seven fortified towns of the state of the Bergistani rebelled, but the consul brought his army to the area and subdued them once more without significant fighting. Shortly afterwards the same peoples revolted again, after the consul's return to Terracona and before he left again. Once more they were subdued, only this time the conquered were not shown mercy as before. All were put up for auction to put an end to their frequent breaking of the peace.

17. In the mean time the praetor Publius Manlius set off for Turdetania. With him went the veteran army which he had taken over from his predecessor, Quintus Minucius, and to which he had added the army—also a veteran force—that had been commanded by Appius Claudius Nero in Farther Spain. Of all the Spanish peoples the Turdetani are considered the least aggressive; even so, they confronted the Roman column, relying on their numbers. The cavalry were unleashed against them and these immediately threw the Spanish line into disarray. The infantry engagement was almost no contest: the Roman veteran troops, well acquainted with both the enemy and the art of war, left the outcome of the battle in no doubt. And yet that battle did not constitute the end of the war. The Turduli* hired 10,000 Celtiberians, and were preparing to fight with weapons belonging to others. Meanwhile the consul, shocked by the uprising of the Bergistani and thinking the other communities would seize the opportunity to do the same, disarmed all the Spaniards this side of the Ebro. The Spaniards were so humiliated by this that many took their own lives—they are a headstrong people, feeling a life without weapons to be meaningless. When news of this was brought to the consul, he had the Senators of all the communities summoned to him and said: 'Not to rebel is as much in your interest as it is ours, for up to now this course has proved more a disaster for the Spaniards than it has a hardship for the Roman army. I

think there is only one way of safeguarding against it, and that is to see that the opportunity for rebellion is removed from you. I want to attain this end in the smoothest possible way, and you, too, must help me in the matter with your advice. There is no suggestion I would more willingly follow than the one you bring to me yourselves.' The Spaniards remained silent, and Cato said he would give them a few days to think it over. When they were called back they remained silent at this second meeting as well. In a single day Cato tore down all their city walls, and then set out against those who still refused to submit, accepting the surrender of all the neighbouring peoples in each area through which he passed. Only for the capture of Segestica, an important and wealthy city, did he use siege-sheds and mantlets.

18. Cato had greater difficulty in bringing his enemies to heel than did the Romans who had originally arrived in Spain, and for the following reason. The Spaniards went over to the original colonists because they were tired of Carthaginian rule, but Cato virtually had to reclaim mastery over the natives after they had already seized their freedom; and he inherited a situation so turbulent that some were already up in arms while others were being forced into rebellion by siege, and these would not have held out any longer had not help been promptly brought to them. But so dynamic in temperament and character was the consul that he would personally approach and undertake every chore, great or small, not simply formulating and presiding over measures appropriate to the situation but for the most part seeing them through himself. Nor was the rigour and severity of his authority brought to bear on anyone in the entire army more than on himself; and in simple living, vigilance, and hard work he was on an equal footing with the lowest of his men—indeed, in his army he enjoyed no special privilege apart from his rank and his imperium.

19. As was noted above, Celtiberian mercenaries had been hired by the enemy, and these were making the war in Turdetania more difficult for the praetor, Publius Manlius. Accordingly the consul, whom the praetor sent for by letter, brought his legions to the area. When he arrived, the Celtiberians and Turdetani were in two separate encampments. The Romans immediately had some minor skirmishes with the Turdetani, against whose outposts they launched attacks, and always departed victors no matter how imprudent their engagement. As for the Celtiberians, the consul ordered the military

tribunes to go and discuss matters with them, offering them the choice of three options. First, they could go over to the Romans and be given twice the pay agreed upon with the Turdetani; secondly, they could go home after being given an official guarantee that they would not be punished for having joined the enemies of Rome; or, thirdly, if they wanted war at all costs, they could fix a day and a location to decide the issue with him in the field. The Celtiberians requested a day to consider the matter. A meeting was then held, which the Turdetani attended and at which there was such disorder as to render a decision impossible. It was now unclear whether a state of war or peace existed with the Celtiberians, but the Romans continued the transportation of provisions from the countryside and the fortified towns of the enemy just as in peacetime, frequently entering the enemy's fortifications in groups of ten men under private truces, as if commercial intercourse had been formally sanctioned. When the consul found himself unable to entice his enemy out to fight, he first of all led out in order a number of light-armed cohorts on a raiding expedition into countryside that was as yet untouched. Then, hearing that all the baggage and accoutrements of the Celtiberians had been left at Saguntia,* he proceeded to march in that direction in order to attack the town. When the enemy could be moved by no provocation, he paid off not only his own men but the praetor's troops as well, and then returned to the Ebro with seven cohorts, leaving all the other forces in the praetor's camp.

20. With this force, small as it was, Cato captured a number of towns, and the Sedetani, Ausetani, and Suessetani went over to him. The Lacetani, an isolated tribe living in the woods, remained under arms because of their natural belligerence. In addition they were aware that they had plundered the Roman allies with sudden raids when the consul and his army were occupied with the war against the Turdetani. Therefore, the consul led against their town not only Roman cohorts but also the men of military age from amongst their allies, who had good reason to be hostile to them. The Lacetani lived in a town that was long but not correspondingly wide. Cato halted some 400 yards from it. Leaving some hand-picked cohorts on guard at this point, he instructed them not to move from there before he came back to them in person, and then he took the rest of his troops around to the other side of the town. Soldiers of the Suessetani made up the largest of all his auxiliary detachments, and Cato ordered

these to move up to attack the wall. When the Lacetani recognized their armour and standards, they recalled how often they had run about in the territory of this people with impunity, and the number of occasions on which they had beaten them in pitched battle and routed them. Suddenly they threw open their gate and burst forth in a body against them. The Suessetani barely withstood their battle-cry, much less their charge. When the consul saw that matters were progressing as he had predicted, he rode at a gallop beneath the enemy wall back to his cohorts. Taking charge of these he led them into the city, now silent and deserted since all the townspeople had poured out in pursuit of the Suessetani, and before they could return he took it over completely. Soon afterwards Cato accepted their surrender, for they now had nothing left apart from their weapons.

21. The victor swiftly led his army from there to the fortress of Bergium, which was for the most part a hide-away for robbers, with raids conducted from it on the pacified country areas of the province. The chieftain of the Bergistani slipped away from there to see the consul, and proceeded to make excuses for himself and his fellow-townspeople. Their government, he said, was not under their control—the robbers whom they had received had brought the fortress entirely into their power. The consul told him to invent some plausible reason for his absence and go home. He added that, when the chieftain saw him approach the walls and the robbers preoccupied with the defence of their battlements, he was to be sure to seize the citadel with the men belonging to his party.

This order was put into effect, and the barbarians were overtaken by a twofold fear as they saw the Romans climbing the walls on one side and the citadel already lost on the other. Taking charge of the place, the consul issued instructions for the men who had taken control of the citadel to be set free, along with their relatives, and for them to be granted continued possession of their property. The rest of the Bergistani he ordered the quaestor to sell into slavery, and he executed the robbers. With peace restored to the province, he imposed heavy taxes on the iron and silver mines, and on the basis of these the province grew richer by the day. The Senators decreed three days of public prayers in thanks for these achievements in Spain.

22. That same summer the other consul, Lucius Valerius Flaccus, fought a successful pitched battle against a contingent of the Boii near the Litana forest in Gaul. Eight thousand Gauls are reported

to have lost their lives, and the others abandoned the fight and slipped away to their villages and farms. The consul kept his army at Placentia and Cremona, close to the Po, for the rest of the summer, rebuilding the sections of those towns destroyed in the war.

Such was the state of affairs in Italy and Spain. In Greece, meanwhile, Titus Quinctius' handling of affairs over the winter had ensured that the whole country was reaping the fruits of peace and independence together, and thoroughly enjoying its new status—as full of admiration for the Roman commander's restraint, fairness, and moderation in victory as it had been for his courage in war. All of Greece, that is, apart from the Aetolians, who had not gained the rewards of victory as they had hoped, and could not long be happy with a state of peace, either. Such were circumstances when the Senatorial decree declaring war on Nabis the Lacedaemonian was brought to Flamininus. After reading it, Quinctius called for a meeting of delegations from all the allied states to be held at Corinth on a specified date. On this day the leading citizens came together from all over Greece in large numbers, with not even the Aetolians failing to appear, and the commander addressed them as follows:

'The Romans and Greeks fought against Philip with a spirit and policy as unified as their motives for the war were different. Philip had violated his treaty with the Romans by, at different times, aiding our enemies the Carthaginians and attacking our allies here; and his conduct towards you was such that, even were we to forget the wrongs done to us, those done to you would have been sufficient grounds for war. But today's question is to do with you and you alone. I am bringing before you the issue of whether you wish Argos, occupied by Nabis, as you well know yourselves, to remain under that man's control, or whether you think it fair that this state, of great repute and antiquity, situated in the centre of Greece, should have its liberty restored and be on an equal footing with the other cities of the Peloponnese and Greece. This question, as you can see, is entirely about a matter that is your concern—it has nothing to do with the Romans, except to the extent that the servitude of a single city does not allow the glory of Greece's liberation to be full and complete. But if you are not moved by concern for this city, the precedent set, or by the danger of contamination from this foul disease spreading further, then we are quite content. I am consulting you on this matter and I intend to accept the majority decision.'

23. After his address the Roman commander proceeded with a review of the opinions of the others present. The Athenian representative, in his vote of thanks to them, was as fulsome as he could be in extolling the services performed for Greece by the Romans—they had lent their assistance against Philip when an appeal was made to them, he said, and now they were actually offering help against the tyrant Nabis without being asked. He expressed anger that such great services were nevertheless denigrated in the talk of certain people critical of what was to come when they should be expressing gratitude for the past. He was clearly attacking the Aetolians. Accordingly, the leading spokesman of the Aetolians, Alexander, first launched into an attack on the Athenians—once the leading advocates and champions of independence, these were now traitors to the common cause by virtue of their self-seeking obsequiousness. He then proceeded with protests against the Achaeans' recovery of Corinth and their efforts to take possession of Argos. The Achaeans, he said, had formerly been soldiers of Philip, finally deserting him when his fortunes turned. The Aetolians, by contrast, had been the earliest opponents of Philip, and had always been allies of the Romans, and yet they were being cheated out of Echinus and Pharsalus* despite the agreement in their treaty that the cities and lands would be theirs on Philip's defeat. Alexander further accused the Romans of duplicity. They were occupying Chalcis and Demetrias with their garrisons after bandying about the empty term 'freedom'—these men who had made a practice of criticizing Philip when he was slow to withdraw his garrisons from those towns and saying that Greece would never be free as long as Demetrias, Chalcis, and Corinth were occupied. And finally, he said, they were making Argos and Nabis a pretext for staying in Greece and keeping an army there. Let them take their legions back to Italy, he concluded; the Aetolians gave their word that Nabis would either withdraw his garrison from Argos on their terms, and according to their wishes, or they would oblige him by force of arms to accept the authority of a united Greece.

24. This blustering prompted a response first of all from Aristaenus, praetor of the Achaeans.

'May Jupiter Optimus Maximus not permit this to come to pass, nor Queen Juno in whose protection Argos lies, that the city be a prize set between a Spartan tyrant and Aetolian bandits, in danger of suffering more from being recovered by you than it did from capture by Nabis! Although a sea lies between us, it does not protect us from those freebooters, Titus Quinctius—what will be our fate if they establish a citadel for themselves in the heart of the Peloponnese? The only Greek feature they possess is the language, just as their only human one is their shape! Their morals and practices are more barbaric than those of any foreigners—no, more barbaric than those of beasts of the wild. We therefore ask you, Romans, to take back Argos from Nabis and also to settle matters in Greece in such a fashion as to leave these areas untroubled by the depredation of the Aetolians.'

Faced on every side with unanimous criticism of the Aetolians, the Roman commander declared that he would have given them a reply had he not seen everybody so opposed to the Aetolians that they required to be mollified rather than provoked. He was, he said, content with the opinions voiced on the subject of the Romans and the Aetolians, and he was now laying before them the question of what their pleasure would be with regard to a war with Nabis if he refused to return Argos to the Achaeans. When they all decided on war, Flamininus urged them to send him auxiliary forces, each state according to its resources. He even sent an envoy to the Aetolians, more to bring their intentions into the open (in which he was successful) than from a hope that his request could be granted.

25. Flamininus then ordered the military tribunes to have the army brought from Elatia. During these same days he also made a reply to an embassy from Antiochus which had come to discuss an alliance. In the absence of the ten commissioners, he said, he could not express an opinion, and they would have to approach the Senate in Rome. He then proceeded to lead the forces that had been brought from Elatia towards Argos and was met in the vicinity of Cleonae by the praetor Aristaenus at the head of 10,000 Achaeans and 1,000 cavalry. The two joined forces and pitched camp not far from Cleonae. The next day they went down into the Argive plain and chose a spot for their camp about four miles from Argos. In command of the Spartan garrison was Pythagoras who was the tyrant's son-in-law and also the brother of his wife.* At the approach of the Romans, Pythagoras reinforced with strong detachments of guards both citadels (Argos has two) and other points of vantage or of weakness. But even as he was doing this he was totally unable to hide the panic inspired by the arrival of the Romans.

In addition to the threat from without there was also an uprising within the town. There was a young Argive, Damocles, of greater courage than judgment, who initiated discussions with some prospective supporters, after they had taken an oath, about driving out the garrison. In his enthusiasm to strengthen the plot, however, he showed himself a poor judge of trustworthiness. He was in conversation with his confederates when he was summoned by an attendant sent by the garrison-commander. He realized that his plan had been betrayed, and he encouraged his confederates there with him to join in taking up arms rather than die under torture. So it was that he proceeded into the forum with a few accomplices shouting encouragement for all who wished to save the state to follow him as the champion and prime vindicator of their freedom. He persuaded none of the people, who saw not the least chance of success in the short term, and certainly no firm support for the conspiracy. Damocles was still shouting out his appeals when he was surrounded by the Spartans, who killed him along with his accomplices. Then a number of the other conspirators were arrested. Most of these were executed, but a few who were thrown into prison managed to use ropes to let themselves down the wall the following night and make good their escape to the Romans.

26. The fugitives assured Quinctius that the uprising would not have been abortive had the Roman army been at the gates and that the Argives would not sit idly by if his camp were moved closer to the city. Flamininus therefore sent forward his light infantry and cavalry. These fought a battle near Cylarabis (a gymnasium not 300 paces from the city) with some Spartans who sallied forth from the gate, and drove them back into the city with no great effort. The Roman commander then pitched his camp in the spot where the encounter had taken place, and spent one day watching from there for any fresh developments. Seeing the city paralysed with fear, he called a meeting to discuss an assault on Argos. All the Greek leaders, apart from Aristaenus, were agreed: since this city was the sole reason for the campaign, the campaign should start right there. Quinctius was not at all happy with this, and he listened with evident approval to Aristaenus when he expressed an opinion which was at variance with the general view. He also added the point that, since the war had been undertaken on behalf of Argos and against the tyrant, nothing could make less sense than that Argos should be

under attack and the enemy passed over. He was going to attack Sparta and the tyrant, he said, the source of the war. The meeting was then adjourned and Quinctius sent his light-armed cohorts on a foraging expedition. All the ripe grain in the area was harvested and brought in, and the unripe was trampled under foot and spoiled to deny the enemy use of it later on.

Flamininus then struck camp, and two days later, after crossing Mt. Parthenium and passing by Tegea, he encamped at Caryae. Here he awaited auxiliaries from the allies before entering his enemy's territory, and 1,500 Macedonians came from Philip, along with 400 Thessalian cavalry. At this point the Roman commander was no longer held back by lack of auxiliaries, with which he was abundantly supplied, but by provisions requisitioned from nearby cities which he was expecting. In addition, large naval forces were beginning to assemble there: Lucius Quinctius had already arrived from Leucas with forty ships; there were eighteen decked vessels from Rhodes; and Eumenes was now off the Cyclades with ten decked ships, thirty cutters and an assortment of other craft of smaller dimensions. There also converged on the Roman camp large numbers of exiles from amongst the Spartans themselves, driven out by the wrongs of the tyrants and hoping to be restored to their native land. There were many of these, men who had been driven out by one tyrant or another over the several generations since the tyrants had held sway in Sparta. The leader of the exiles was Agesipolis, to whose family the throne of Sparta rightly belonged. He had been expelled in his infancy by the tyrant Lycurgus after the death of Cleomenes, first tyrant of Sparta.

27. Although a war of such great proportions on land and sea engulfed the tyrant on all sides, and although a realistic appraisal of his own forces and those of his enemy showed that he had practically no hope of victory, he nevertheless did not abandon the fight. He sent for 1,000 hand-picked fighting men from Crete (he already had 1,000) and he also kept under arms 3,000 mercenaries and 10,000 of his own countrymen, along with a number of the inhabitants of the rural strongholds. He fortified the town with a ditch and a rampart, and, to prevent any internal upheaval, he cowed the spirits of the citizens by intimidation and callous punishments, since he could not expect them to wish a tyrant well.

Since he harboured suspicions about a number of his compatriots,

Nabis led his troops out into the plain which the local people call the Dromos. There he gave orders for the Spartan citizens to be summoned to a meeting, after laying down their weapons, and threw a cordon of armed attendants around that meeting. He then made a few prefatory remarks, explaining why allowances should be made for him in the circumstances if he was anxious and taking all manner of precautions. It was in their own best interests, he said, that any people rendered suspect in the current state of affairs be prevented from mutinous activity rather than punished for engaging in it. He was, therefore, going to hold a number of people in custody until the storm that threatened them passed; and when the enemy were driven back—and these would pose less of a threat if only sufficient precaution could be taken against treachery from within—he would immediately release them.

After this the tyrant ordered the names of about eighty of the leading young Spartans to be read aloud, and as each answered when his name was called had him put under lock and key. During the night that followed all were put to death. Next a number of the Ilotae* (a country people, living in fortified towns from early times) were accused of planning to desert and were executed after being driven through all the streets with lashes. By intimidation of this kind Nabis had numbed the spirits of the commons, effectively deterring them from any attempt at revolution. He would also keep his forces confined to their fortifications: he thought himself no match for the enemy if he wished to decide the issue in the field, and he was also afraid to leave the city when the general mood was so volatile and unstable.

28. When all was satisfactorily prepared Quinctius set out from his base camp and the following day reached Sellasia on the River Oenus, the place where the Macedonian king Antigonus was said to have fought a pitched battle with the Spartan tyrant Cleomenes.* Told that the way down from here was by a difficult and narrow path, he sent men ahead by a short detour through the mountains to construct a road and arrived by way of a rather broad and open route at the River Eurotas which flows practically at the foot of the city-walls. The Romans were laying out the camp and Quinctius had gone ahead himself with the cavalry and light-armed troops when they were attacked by the tyrant's auxiliary forces, which created panic and consternation amongst them—they had not been expect-

ing anything like this because they had come across no one the whole length of the march and had been passing through what seemed to be peaceful countryside. For some time there was confusion as infantry appealed for help from cavalry and cavalry from infantry, neither having great confidence in their own capabilities. Eventually the legionary standards came on the scene, and when the cohorts at the head of the column were brought into the fray the men who had a moment earlier been causing the alarm were driven back in terror into the city. The Romans moved back far enough from the wall to be out of javelin-range and then, forming a regular battle-line, waited a short while. When none of the enemy ventured forth against them they returned to camp.

The following day Quinctius drew up his troops and proceeded to lead them along the river and past the city towards the foot of Mt. Menelaus, the legionary cohorts at the front and the light-armed troops and cavalry bringing up the rear. Nabis kept his mercenaries—in whom he had placed all his confidence*—within the wall, drawn up and ready for action under their standards, intending to make an attack on the enemy from the rear; and after the end of the column had passed these burst forth from the town at several points simultaneously and with the same frenzy as they had the previous day. Appius Claudius, who was bringing up the rear, had prepared his men for what was likely to happen so it would not catch them unawares, and now he immediately wheeled around, bringing his entire column to face the enemy. And so there was a regular engagement for a time, just as if two lines in battle-formation had clashed, but finally Nabis' men turned to flee, which might have involved less panic, had not the Achaeans, who knew the ground, kept up their pressure on them. The Achaeans inflicted enormous casualties, and deprived most of them of their weapons as they scattered in flight in every direction. Quinctius pitched camp close to Amyclae, from which point he conducted devastating raids on all the well-populated and attractive country areas around the city. When none of the enemy now ventured forth from the gate he moved camp to the River Eurotas. He then laid waste the valley below Taygetus and the fields stretching down to the sea.

29. At about the same time Lucius Quinctius accepted the surrender of the towns along the coastline, some of whom capitulated voluntarily, others after intimidation and force. Quinctius was then

informed that the town of Gythium served as a depot for the Spartans for all their naval supplies and that the Roman camp lay not far from the sea, whereupon he decided to mount an attack on the town with all his forces. At that time Gythium was a powerful city, home to a large population of citizens and resident foreigners, and furnished with all manner of military equipment. Quinctius was embarking on this difficult venture when King Eumenes and the Rhodian fleet made a timely arrival on the scene. A huge force of sailors, drawn from the three fleets, completed in a matter of days all the preparations that had to be made for an assault upon a city defended by land and sea. The tortoise-formations were brought up, and soon a start was made on undermining the wall, which was also being pounded by the battering-rams. Under the repeated pounding one of the towers was demolished, and as it collapsed it brought down the adjacent section of the wall. The Romans thereupon attempted to break through from the direction of the harbour (from which access was along more even ground) in order to divert the enemy from the more vulnerable spot, and at the same time to burst in where a path had been opened up by the breach. They were not far from gaining entry at the designated point, but their push was slowed down when they were offered hope of the city's surrender, a hope which was then frustrated.

Dexagoridas and Gorgopas had joint command of the city. Dexagoridas had sent word to the Roman legate that he would deliver the city, and after an agreement had been struck on the timing and means of doing this the traitor was killed by Gorgopas and the city was now defended with greater energy by the one commander. In fact, the assault on Gythium would have been more difficult had not Titus Quinctius appeared with 4,000 select troops. When he had exposed to view his battle-line, drawn up on the brow of a hill not far distant from the city, while on the other side Lucius Quinctius was pushing forward from his siege works by land and sea, then despair forced Gorgopas also to adopt the strategy for which he had punished the other commander with death: after bargaining for permission to take from there the soldiers he had as a garrison, he delivered the city to Quinctius. Before the surrender of Gythium, Pythagoras, left as commander in Argos, consigned safekeeping of the city to Timocrates of Pellene and came to Nabis in Sparta at the head of 1,000 mercenaries and 2,000 Argives.

30. Nabis had been panic-stricken when the Roman fleet first arrived and the towns along the coast capitulated, but he could still feel some slight reassurance as long as Gythium was in the hands of his troops. Now he was told that this, too, had been delivered to the Romans, and that in addition to having no hope on land (since everything around him was under enemy occupation) he had been entirely cut off from the sea. He thought he should make concessions to fortune, and he first sent a message to the Roman camp to investigate whether his enemies would permit a delegation to be sent to them. When this was granted, Pythagoras came to the commander with a single assignment, to gain permission for the tyrant to parley with the commander. A meeting was called, at which opinion was unanimous that Nabis be given the interview, and a date and venue were arranged. The two leaders came to some hills in the country lying between them with a few troops in attendance. Here they left their cohorts on guard, the one visible to the other, and came down to the meeting. Nabis was accompanied by a select group of bodyguards, Quinctius by his brother, and by Eumenes, Sosilas the Rhodian, Aristaenus the Achaean and a few military tribunes.

31. At the meeting the tyrant, given the choice of speaking first or of hearing the others, opened the proceedings as follows:

'Titus Quinctius and the rest of you here present: if I could on my own fathom the reasons for your declaring war on me in the first place or waging it now, then I should have quietly waited to see what fate had in store for me. As it is, I have been unable to suppress my longing to know, before I am destroyed, just why I am to be destroyed. If you were the sort of people the Carthaginians are said to be—there is nothing sacred about an oath of alliance for them—then I should not be surprised at some lack of concern on your part about how you deal with me, too. As things are, when I look at you, I see that you are Romans, men who reportedly hold treaties as the most inviolable of things in the divine sphere, and loyalty to one's allies as the most inviolable on the human level. Looking at myself, I can flatter myself as being a man who, on the public level, has enjoyed, along with all other Spartans, a treaty of great antiquity with you, and on the private level has also enjoyed a personal relationship of friendship and alliance with you, one recently renewed in the war with Philip.

'But, you are going to say, I have violated and destroyed this relationship by holding on to the state of Argos. How am I to defend myself against this charge? By appealing to the specific facts of the case, or to the timing? The facts offer me two lines of defence. For it was a case of my accepting control of the city, not seizing it—the inhabitants actually appealed to me to take it and offered it to me—and I accepted the city when it was on Philip's side, not in alliance with you. The timing also exonerates me because my alliance with you was struck at a point when I was still in possession of Argos, and your provision was that I should send you auxiliary forces for your campaign, not remove my garrison from Argos. Heavens above, as far as the Argive question goes, I have the edge both from the equity of the case—I accepted a city which was in the enemy's hands, not yours, one which came to me of its own volition, not under duress—and also on your own admission inasmuch as you left Argos with me in the terms of our treaty.

'But what weighs against me is the title "tyrant" and my record of summoning slaves to freedom and establishing the destitute common people on the land. As for the title I can make this point in response: whatever my qualities, I am the same man that I was, Titus Quinctius, when you yourself concluded the treaty with me. At that time, as I remember, the title "king" was applied to me by you, and now I see I am called "tyrant". In fact, had I myself altered the title which gives me power, I should have been obliged to account for my inconsistency; since it is you who are changing it, you must account for yours. As for my increasing the numbers of the proletariat by freeing slaves and distributing land to the impoverished, I can in fact use the plea of timing to defend myself on this score, too. For these measures, whatever we think of them, I had already taken at the time when you concluded the treaty with me and accepted my assistance in the war against Philip. But suppose I had taken them only recently. I would not be saying to you "How could I have harmed you or violated the treaty with you by that?" but rather I should be arguing that I acted in accordance with the ways and institutions of our ancestors. Do not gauge what happens in Lacedaemon by the measure of your own laws and institutions. There is no need for a detailed comparison between the two. You choose your cavalry and your infantry by assessment of wealth, and you want a few to transcend the others in riches, with the commons subject to these. Our lawgiver* did not want the state to rest in the hands of a few men—

the body you call the Senate—and he did not want one or another class to be pre-eminent within the community. Instead he believed that a levelling of affluence and rank would lead to a large number of men bearing arms for the fatherland.

'I have, I confess, spoken at greater length than is in keeping with our native succinctness,* and a brief summing-up could have gone as follows: since entering a compact of friendship with you, I have done nothing to make you regret that compact.'

32. To this the Roman general replied:

'Our treaty of friendship and alliance was made not with you, but with Pelops, rightful and legitimate king of the Spartans. His title to the throne was usurped by tyrants who subsequently held power in Lacedaemon by force because we were preoccupied with wars—with Carthage at one time, Gaul at another, and then with other nations, one after another. You too have held your power thanks to this recent war with Macedon. What, I ask you, could make less sense than for us—a people who fought a war against Philip for the freedom of Greece—to enter into a compact of friendship with a tyrant? And with the most ruthless tyrant †in history† at that, and the most violent towards his own people? Let us suppose you had not taken Argos by duplicity and were not now occupying it. Even so we should have been obliged, as liberators of the whole of Greece, to restore Sparta as well to her ancient liberty and to her own laws—to which you referred a moment ago as if you were trying to be Lycurgus' equal! Are we going to see that Philip's garrisons are withdrawn from Iasus and Bargyliae and then leave under your feet Argos and Sparta, two illustrious cities that were once the eyes of Greece—to besmirch our reputation as liberators of Greece by their continued servitude? But the Argives sympathized with Philip, you will say. We release you from the obligation to be angry with them on our behalf! We have it on good authority that two or at most three people were to blame in this affair, not the whole community—in the same way, good heavens! that in the case of inviting and welcoming you and your garrison into the citadel no action †was taken† with public authorization. We know that Thessalians, Phocians, and Locrians sided with Philip with the agreement of all their respective peoples, and yet we have liberated them along with the rest of Greece. So what do you think we are going to do in the case of the Argives who are guiltless of giving public authorization for their action?

'You said that you were accused of calling slaves to liberty and distributing land to the poor. These are of themselves not inconsequential charges, but what are they in comparison with the crimes committed one after the other, day after day, by you and your supporters? Convene a free assembly in either Argos or Sparta if you want to hear genuine charges made against a brutal dictatorship. To pass over all the other, older, atrocities, think of the bloodbath created at Argos, almost before my own eyes, by the infamous Pythagoras, your son-in-law. And the one for which you yourself were responsible when I was almost on the borders of Lacedaemon. Come on, have those prisoners brought out—the ones you arrested at the assembly, when in the hearing of all your fellow citizens you proclaimed that you would keep them in custody. Let their poor parents know that the sons for whom they mistakenly grieve are still alive! But, you will say, supposing that all this is true, what business is it of yours, Romans? Can you say such a thing to the people who are liberating Greece? Can you say such a thing to men who have crossed the sea to be able to effect this liberation, and who have fought wars on land and sea?

' "But," you say, "strictly speaking, I have been guilty of no contravention against you, or against my pact of friendship and my alliance with you." How many instances do you want me to cite where you have been guilty? But I do not wish to go on at length. Let me sum up the whole thing. What are instances of violation of friendship? Surely there are these two above all: if you treat my allies as enemies, and if you join my enemies. Both of these things you have done. Take the case of Messene, which was welcomed into an alliance with us with exactly the same treaty rights as Sparta. You, an ally yourself, captured by force of arms this city that was allied to us. Moreover, you not only concluded a treaty with our enemy Philip but—for heaven's sake!—you even used his prefect Philocles to establish a family bond.* As though you were waging war on us, you made the waters off Maleum a dangerous area for us with your pirate vessels, capturing and killing more Roman citizens almost than did Philip, so that the shoreline of Macedonia was safer than the Malean promontory for the ships transporting supplies to our armies.

'So please refrain from bandying about the words "loyalty" and "treaty rights". Cut out this vocabulary of the demagogue and speak like a tyrant and our enemy.'

33. After this Aristaenus proceeded to alternate warnings and pleas to Nabis, telling him to take thought for his position and his circumstances while he could and still had the opportunity. He then began to list by name tyrants of neighbouring city-states who had laid down their power and restored liberty to the people, and who went on to spend their old age amongst their fellow citizens not just in safety but with honour as well. After these viewpoints had been passed back and forth, the debate broke off just before nightfall.

The following day Nabis said that he was retiring from Argos and withdrawing his garrison, since such was the Romans' pleasure, and that he would return prisoners and deserters. He requested that they give him in writing any further demands they had so that he could discuss them with his 'friends'. In this way the tyrant was granted time to think things over, while Quinctius held a meeting to which the leaders of the allies were also invited. The majority opinion was that they should press ahead with the war and remove the tyrant. Only in this way, they said, would the freedom of Greece be guaranteed, and not starting a war against him in the first place would have been far preferable to abandoning it once begun. With his tyranny virtually given approval, Nabis would be in a stronger position through having gained the support of the Roman people for his lawless rule; and the precedent set would spur on many men in other city-states to scheme against the liberty of their fellow-citizens.

The Roman commander himself felt more inclined towards peace. He could see that after the enemy were driven back within their walls there was no alternative to a siege, which would take a long time. For it would not be Gythium that they would be besieging—and even this had been delivered to them, not captured—but Sparta, which had great strength in manpower and weaponry. There had been one hope, he said, and that was the possibility of internal conflict and dispute being stirred up amongst the Spartans as the Romans brought up their forces; but no one had shown any agitation when they saw the standards all but brought to their gates. He added that Villius, returning from an embassy to the king, reported that the peace with Antiochus was precarious—the latter had crossed to Europe with larger land and sea forces than previously. If a blockade of Sparta tied up his army, what other troops would Flamininus use to conduct a war against such a powerful and redoubtable monarch? Such were the arguments he used openly; but there also lurked in his mind the unspoken worry that the new consul might receive the province of Greece in the allotment and Flamininus would be obliged to pass onto his successor a military victory* on which he had made a start.

34. Presenting the opposing case was making no impression on the allies, and Flamininus therefore brought them round to accepting his strategy by the pretence of going over to their opinion.

'I pray it proves successful,' he said. 'Let us then lay siege to Sparta, since this is your decision. But blockading cities is a long process, as you yourselves know, and one which often exasperates the besiegers before those under siege. You should therefore get this into your minds right now: you have to spend the winter around the walls of Sparta. If spending that time here involved only hardship and danger, I would be giving you encouragement to prepare yourselves mentally and physically for this. As it is, though, considerable expense is required for siege-works, for the engines and catapults needed for an assault on a city of this size, and for acquiring provisions for the winter for you and us. So, to avoid any sudden anxieties on your part or the shameful abandonment of an operation already under way, I feel you should first write to your respective city-states and investigate each one's inclinations and resources. Auxiliary forces—I have enough and more than enough. But the more numerous we are, the more provisions we shall need. Already, the countryside of the enemy has nothing to offer us beyond bare soil, and, in addition, winter will be coming on to make long-distance transportation difficult.'

It was this speech that first focused the minds of all on consideration of the problems each had in his own state: apathy, the jealousy and disparagement of those remaining at home towards men serving in the field, the individual liberty hindering general agreement, lack of public funds and the reluctance to contribute on the part of the individual. They suddenly had a change of heart and allowed the Roman general to take whatever action he thought to be in the interests of the Roman people and their allies.

35. Quinctius then convened a meeting which was limited to his officers and military tribunes, and drafted the following terms on which peace was to be made with the tyrant:

There was to be a six-month truce between Nabis on the one hand, and the Romans, Eumenes, and the Rhodians on the other.

Titus Quinctius and Nabis were both to send envoys immediately to Rome so that the peace could be ratified by Senatorial authority.

The day marking the start of the truce was to be the day on which the drafted peace-terms were issued to Nabis, and all garrisons in Argive territory were to be withdrawn from Argos and the other towns within ten days from that day. These towns were to be handed over to the Romans liberated of troops and under no constraint, and with no slave removed, whether he belonged to the tyrant, the state or an individual (and with any slaves formerly removed by state or individual being duly restored to their owners).

Nabis was to return the vessels he had appropriated from the coastal communities and himself retain no ship apart from two cutters which were to be propelled by no more than sixteen oars.

Nabis was to restore deserters and prisoners-of-war to all city-states allied to the Roman people, and also give back to the Messenians any property that was found and recognized by its owners.

He was also to return to Spartans in exile their children and wives, but only those wives willing to follow their husbands, with no woman involuntarily attending an exile.

All possessions were to be duly returned to mercenaries of Nabis who had deserted either to their own city-states or to the Romans.

Nabis was to hold no city on the island of Crete, and he was to hand over to the Romans those which he had occupied.

He was to enter into no alliance and wage no war with any of the peoples of Crete or any other people at all.

With respect to those city-states which he had himself surrendered or which had delivered themselves and their possessions to the protection and authority of the Roman people, Nabis was to withdraw all his garrisons from all of them, and keep his own hands, and those of his confederates, off them in future.

He was to establish no town and no fortress on his own or other people's territory.

To guarantee implementation of these conditions, he was to supply five hostages of the Roman general's choosing, including his own son, plus 100 talents of silver immediately and 50 talents every year for eight years.

36. These terms were drafted and delivered to Sparta after the camp had been moved closer to the city. Nothing in them pleased the tyrant except for the unexpected lack of mention of a restitution of

the exiles. But most galling of all was the condition by which both his ships and coastal cities had been taken from him. The sea had proved very lucrative for him, for he had the entire coastline from Cape Malea at the mercy of his pirate vessels, and in addition the men of military age from these city-states furnished him with auxiliary forces of outstanding quality. Although his discussion of the terms with his 'friends' had been confidential, they nevertheless became the subject of general gossip; for royal courtiers are as naturally unreliable in keeping secrets as in other areas of trust. But it was less a case of general criticism of the whole package of terms as of individuals criticizing those terms affecting themselves. Some had married the wives of exiles or appropriated some of their assets— and these were upset as if they were facing dispossession rather than returning property. Slaves who had been freed by the tyrant pictured to themselves not only the future cancellation of their liberation but an enslavement far more oppressive than it had been before, since they would be returning to the authority of indignant masters. The mercenary troops were displeased that payment for their services would fall off in peacetime, and they could also see no chance of returning to their own city-states which felt as much hostility to the abettors of tyrants as to the tyrants themselves.

37. At first they grumbled amongst themselves like this in small groups: then they suddenly rushed to arms. When the tyrant saw from the unrest that the common people were of themselves sufficiently exasperated, he ordered that an assembly be called. He then presented the Roman demands, falsely representing a number of them as being harsher and more demeaning than they really were. Each item was met with cries of disapproval from the whole audience or from parts of it, and Nabis then asked what response they wanted him to make to the terms, or what action they wished him to take. With almost one voice they all told him that no answer should be given, and the war should go on. And, as usual with crowds, they all told him to take heart and have confidence, and said that fortune favoured the brave. Stirred by these exclamations, Nabis declared that both Antiochus and the Aetolians would help and that he had more than sufficient troops to withstand a siege.

Any idea of peace had now vanished from the minds of all, and, no longer willing to stand idly by, they ran off to their various stations. When a few of them ran out to harry the enemy and immediately hurled their javelins, all doubt about having to continue the war was removed from the Romans as well. The first four days after that saw only light skirmishing with no clear result, but on the fifth there was what was almost a regular battle, and in this the Spartans were driven back into their town in such panic that certain Roman soldiers, as they continued to hack at the backs of the retreating enemy, entered the city through the gaps that then existed in the wall.

38. By the fright given them on that occasion Quinctius arrested the counter-attacks of the enemy, and now he thought he had no option but to blockade the city. He sent men to bring all the marines from Gythium, and in the mean time he rode around the walls with the military tribunes to take stock of the lay-out of the city. Sparta had once been without a wall; only recently had the tyrants erected a defensive-wall* in the exposed and flat areas, while the more elevated spots and those where access was difficult were protected by outposts of armed sentinels rather than a rampart.

After a thorough inspection of the whole site, Flamininus thought he should attack by means of a military cordon, and he threw all his forces around the city—there were Romans and allies, infantry and cavalry, land-forces and naval forces, about 50,000 men. Some were carrying ladders, others torches; some had various other implements for intimidating as well as attacking the enemy. All were ordered to raise a shout and advance from every direction so that the Spartans, in total panic everywhere, should have no idea where first to confront the enemy and where to bring assistance.

The main strength of the Roman army was divided into three. Flamininus ordered the attack mounted with one division advancing in the direction of the Phoebeum, a second towards the Dictynneum, and the third towards the so-called Heptagoniae, all these areas being open and without walls. The city was now faced with a terrifying danger from every direction. At first the tyrant responded to sudden outbursts of shouting and hysterical reports by rushing in person to the points most under pressure or by sending men there. But, as the panic spread all round, he was so paralysed as to be unable to offer, or listen to, any useful information: not only was he incapable of formulating strategy, but he was scarcely in control of his faculties.

39. Initially, the Spartans kept the Romans at bay in the narrow passages, and the three battle-lines were in combat at the same time

in different locations. Then, as the conflict became more intense, the battle did not remain at all even. The Spartans were fighting with javelins, and the Roman soldier could easily protect himself against these by virtue of the large dimensions of his shield, and also because some were off target and others fell with very little impact. The reason for this was that, because of the cramped space and the large numbers packed into it, the Spartans not only lacked the room for hurling their weapons with a run—from which they get the most momentum—but even for attempting their throw with a footing that was unrestricted and solid. As a result, none of the spears dispatched from directly in front of them penetrated Roman bodies, and only a few stuck in their shields. A number were wounded by Spartans standing about them on higher ground, and as soon as they advanced they even began to sustain unexpected injuries from tiles, and not just spears, thrown from the roofs of buildings. They now raised their shields above their heads and interlocked them so tightly as to leave no room for a spear to be thrust in from close at hand, much less from random shots, and then they advanced in their tortoise-formation.

The first narrow streets they encountered, filled with large numbers of their own men and the enemy's, checked their progress for a while, but after they reached one of the wider roads of the city, keeping up gradual pressure on the enemy, the violence of their onslaught was no longer to be resisted. When the Spartans had turned tail and were heading for higher ground in disordered flight, Nabis panicked, thinking the city already lost, and cast about for an escape-route. It was Pythagoras, valiantly carrying out the duties of a general in all respects, who was also single-handedly responsible for the city not being taken, for he ordered the buildings next to the wall to be set on fire. These flared up in an instant, the flames being stoked by men who on other occasions usually bring help to put them out. The buildings collapsed on the Romans; charred beams as well as pieces of tile fell on the soldiers; flames spread far and wide; and the smoke generated greater terror than the danger itself. The result was that the Romans outside the city, who were at that moment making their major assault, fell back from the wall, while those who had entered also retired, afraid of being cut off from their comrades by the fire springing up to their rear; and Quinctius, seeing what was happening, ordered the signal given for retreat. And so, recalled at the point when the city had almost been taken, the men returned to camp.

40. Quinctius placed more hope in the enemy's panic than he did in the operation itself. For the three days that followed he terrorized them, provoking them alternately with attacks and siege-engines, and also sealing off escape-routes. Cowed by these acts of intimidation, the tyrant once more sent Pythagoras as his spokesman. At first, Quinctius rejected his petition and ordered him to leave the camp, but when Pythagoras resorted to abject entreaties, and fell at the Roman's knees, he finally granted him a hearing. In his first address, Pythagoras submitted entirely to the will of the Romans, but he made no headway with this since it was considered an empty and useless offer. Matters then reached the stage where a truce was concluded on the terms which had been given in writing a few days earlier, and the money and hostages were received.

While the tyrant was under attack, the Argives felt encouraged themselves, first because they were receiving message after message saying that Sparta was on the point of capture, and also because Pythagoras had left the town with the strongest part of the garrison. With disdain for the slight numbers left in the citadel, and led by one Archippus, they drove out the garrison. Timocrates of Pellene they let go alive with a guarantee of safe conduct because his regime had been easy-going. During the ensuing jubilation Quinctius arrived; he had now granted peace to the tyrant and sent Eumenes, the Rhodians, and his brother Lucius Quinctius back to the fleet from Lacedaemon.

41. The most popular of Argive feast days, the famous Nemean Games, had not been observed at the regular time because of the difficulties of the war. The joyful city now announced that the celebration would coincide with the arrival of the Roman army and its commander, and further declared the general himself president of the games. A number of factors combined to increase the Argives' exuberance. Their fellow-citizens recently seized by Pythagoras, and by Nabis before him, had been brought home from Sparta; those who had fled when the conspiracy was discovered by Pythagoras, and when the bloody reprisals had already started, had now returned; and after a long interval the citizens could again experience their freedom, and set eyes on those responsible for it—the Romans, whose reason for going to war with the tyrant had been the

Argives themselves! On the very day of the Nemean Games the freedom of Argos was also proclaimed out loud by a herald.

The return of Argos to the common council of Achaea certainly brought pleasure to the Achaeans; but, at the same time, the fact that Sparta was still in bondage, and that they still had a tyrant at their side, would not allow this joy to be complete. The Aetolians for their part excoriated the arrangement at all their council meetings. War was not brought to an end with Philip, they said, until he withdrew from all the cities of Greece; but Sparta had been left to a tyrant while its rightful king, who had been in the Roman camp, and other Spartan citizens of the highest rank were to live in exile. The Roman people had become a tool of Nabis' oppression, they said.

Quinctius led his troops back from Argos to Elatia, the point from which he had set out for the war with Sparta.

Some authorities claim that the tyrant did not fight the war by counter-attacking from the city. Rather, they say, he pitched his camp opposite that of the Romans, and waited a long while because he expected support from the Aetolians. He was finally obliged to commit himself to battle when an attack was made on his foragers by the Romans. Defeated in that battle, and driven from his camp, he sued for peace after 14,000 of his men had fallen, and more than 4,000 had been taken prisoner.

42. At about the same time dispatches arrived from Titus Quinctius—concerning his Spartan campaign—and also from the consul Marcius Porcius in Spain. Three days of thanksgiving were decreed by the Senate in recognition of both.

After the defeat of the Boii near the forest of Litana, the consul Lucius Valerius had peace in his province. He returned to Rome for the elections, and declared Publius Cornelius Scipio Africanus and Tiberius Sempronius Longus elected consul (Scipio for the second time). The fathers of these men had been consuls in the first year of the Second Punic War.*

The praetorian elections were then held, at which the following were elected: Publius Cornelius Scipio, the two Gnaei Cornelii (Merenda and Blasio), Gnaeus Domitius Ahenobarbus, Sextus Digitius, and Titus Iuventius Thalna. At the end of the elections the consul returned to his province.

That year the people of Ferentinum attempted to secure a new legal prerogative: the awarding of Roman citizenship to Latins who had merely submitted their names for membership in a Roman colony. Those who had submitted their names for Puteoli, Salernum, and Buxentum were enrolled as colonists, and because of this they comported themselves as Roman citizens. The Senate adjudged that they were not Roman citizens.

43. At the beginning of the year when Publius Scipio Africanus and Tiberius Sempronius Longus were consuls (Scipio for the second time) envoys came to Rome from the tyrant Nabis. These were given an audience with the Senate outside the city in the temple of Apollo. They asked for ratification of the peace treaty that had been concluded with Titus Quinctius, and their request was granted.

When the matter of the provinces was raised, a full house of the Senate decided that the two consuls should have Italy as theirs, since the wars in Spain and Macedonia were now finished. Scipio's opinion was that one consul was sufficient for Italy, and that Macedonia should be officially mandated to the other. A momentous war with Antiochus was impending, he said, and Antiochus had already himself crossed to Europe on his own initiative. What did the Senators think the king was going to to do, he asked, when he had the Aetolians, unquestionable enemies of Rome, calling him to war on the one side, and Hannibal, a general famous for his Roman conquests, inciting him on the other? While the consular provinces were still being discussed, the sortition taken by the praetors was as follows:

Gnaeus Domitius	city jurisdiction
Titus Iuventius	foreigners' jurisdiction
Publius Cornelius	Farther Spain
Sextus Digitius	Hither Spain
Gnaeus Cornelius Blasio	Sicily
Gnaeus Cornelius Merenda	Sardinia

It was decided that no new army be transported to Macedonia, and that the army already there be brought back to Italy by Quinctius and demobilized. The army with Marcus Porcius Cato in Spain was likewise to be disbanded. The two consuls were to have Italy as their province and were authorized to enrol two city legions so that, after the demobilization of the legions decreed by the Senate, there should be a total of eight Roman legions.

44. A Sacred Spring* had been conducted the previous year in the consulship of Marcus Porcius and Lucius Valerius. The pontifex

Publius Licinius reported, first to the college of priests, and afterwards—on the college's authorization—to the Senators, that the correct procedure had not been followed, and the Senators accordingly voted that the ceremony be repeated to the satisfaction of the priests. They also voted that the Great Games, which had been promised in a vow at the same time as the Sacred Spring, be celebrated with the usual level of expenditure. It was further decided that the Sacred Spring applied to all animals born between 1 March and 30 April in the consulship of Publius Cornelius and Tiberius Sempronius.

The election of the censors came next. Elected were Sextus Aelius Paetus and Gaius Cornelius Cethegus, and these chose as the *princeps senatus* the consul Publius Scipio* (who had also been the choice of the previous censors). They rejected, in all, three Senators, none of whom had held a curule office. They won enormous gratitude from the Senatorial class by ordering the curule aediles to separate Senatorial seating from the public at the Roman Games—for prior to that there was no segregation for spectators. Very few knights had their horses confiscated, and no class was severely treated. The Hall of Freedom and the Public Villa were restored and extended by these same censors.

The Sacred Spring and the games which Servius Sulpicius Galba had vowed as consul were both celebrated. There was a man, Quintus Pleminius, who had been thrown into prison for many crimes that he had committed against the gods and men at Locri,* and while people's attention was focused on watching the games he had gathered together men to set fires simultaneously at numerous locations in the city. His plan was that the prison could be broken open while the whole community was startled by the uproar during the night. The scheme came to light and was reported to the Senate when Pleminius' associates denounced him. Pleminius was sent down to the lower prison and executed.

45. Colonies of Roman citizens were that year established at Puteoli, Volternum, and Liternum, with 300 people assigned to each. Salernum and Buxentum likewise received colonies of Roman citizens. The triumvirs establishing the colonies were Tiberius Sempronius Longus, consul at the time, Marcus Servilius, and Quintus Minucius Thermus. Land that had belonged to the Campanians was divided amongst the colonists. A second board of triumvirs,

comprising Decimus Iunius Brutus, Marcus Baebius Tamphilus and Marcus Helvius, also founded a colony of Roman citizens at Sipontum, on land that had belonged to the Arpini. At Tempsa, too, and at Croton colonies of Roman citizens were founded. The land at Tempsa had been captured from the Bruttii, who had themselves driven out the Greeks, while Croton had been inhabited by Greeks. The founding triumvirs for Croton were Gnaeus Octavius, Lucius Aemilius Paullus,* and Gaius Laetorius; for Tempsa they were Lucius Cornelius Merula, Quintus <. . .>, and Gaius Salonius.

That year prodigies were seen at Rome and also reported from elsewhere. Droplets of blood were observed in the Forum, in the comitium and on the Capitol. There were occasional showers of earth, and the head of Vulcan caught fire. There was a report that the River Nar had flowed with milk; and that freeborn children had been born in Ariminum without ears and noses, and one in the district of Picenum without feet and hands. These prodigies were expiated by decree of the pontiffs. In addition, there was a nine-day sacrifice because the people of Hadria had reported that stones had fallen as rain in their territory.

46. In Gaul the proconsul Lucius Valerius Flaccus fought a decisive pitched battle close to Milan against the Insubrian Gauls and against the Boii who, led by Dorulatus, had crossed the Po to incite the Insubres to rebellion. Ten thousand of the enemy were killed in the engagement.

In the same period Flaccus' colleague, Marcus Porcius Cato, celebrated a triumph for his Spanish campaign. Carried along in the procession were: 25,000 pounds of unwrought silver, 123,000 silver coins stamped with the *biga*, 540 coins of Oscan stamp, and 1,400 pounds of gold. From the booty Cato distributed 270 *asses* to each of his infantrymen and three times that amount to each cavalryman.

Setting off for his province, the consul Tiberius Sempronius led his legions first into the territory of the Boii. The chieftain of the Boii at that time was Boiorix who, along with his two brothers, had incited the entire tribe to rebellion. Boiorix pitched camp in an open area, to make it clear that he would resist an enemy incursion into his lands. When the consul perceived how strong his enemy's forces were and how great his confidence, he sent word to his colleague to ask him to come quickly, if he saw fit—Sempronius would take evasive action to draw matters out until his arrival. Their enemy's hesitation encouraged the Gauls, and in addition they had the same reason for accelerating the action as the consul did for delaying, namely to bring the campaign to a conclusion before the forces of the two consuls could be combined. Nevertheless, for two days the Gauls did nothing more than stand ready for action in the event of an enemy attack. On the third day, however, they moved up to the Roman fortifications and assaulted the camp from every side at the one time. The consul immediately ordered his men to take up their weapons, but held them back under arms a short while in order to boost the enemy's recklessness, and also to deploy his troops at the gates through which they would be making their counter-attack.

Two legions were given the order to advance from the camp by way of the two main gates, but in fact the Gauls stood before them right at the exits, so densely packed as to block the roads. Fighting continued in the two confined spaces for a long while. But the issue now depended less on the strength of the arm and on the sword than on the use of the shield and on pure bodily force as both sides surged forward, the Romans trying to break out, and the Gauls trying either to enter the camp themselves or prevent the Romans from getting out. The battle-lines were unable to move in one direction or the other, until a senior centurion, Quintus Victorius, and a military tribune, Gaius Atinius*—these belonged to the fourth and second legion respectively—resorted to a tactic frequently attempted in critical moments of battle. They took the standards from the bearers and hurled them into the enemy ranks. There was a determined effort to retrieve the standards, and the legionaries of the second legion were the first to burst through the gate.

47. These soldiers were now engaged outside the palisade, while the fourth legion was still bogged down inside the gate. Then another commotion arose on the other side of the camp. The Gauls had broken in through the quaestorian gate and, in the face of furious resistance, had managed to kill the quaestor Lucius Postumius (surnamed Tympanus), and the allied commanders, Marcus Atinius and Publius Sempronius, along with some 200 regular soldiers. On that side the camp was in enemy hands, until the arrival of a crack company, sent by the consul to cover the quaestorian gate. These men killed some of the Gauls within the fortification, drove the others from the camp, and withstood further attack on it. At about the same time the fourth legion also burst out through the gate with

two crack companies. So it was that there were three battles taking place around the camp in three different localities, with the confused shouting diverting the attention of the combatants from the battle in hand to the unclear fortunes of their comrades in the others. The conflict went on until midday, each side displaying as much vigour and almost as much confidence as the other. Then fatigue and the heat forced the Gauls, who are physically soft and weak, with little tolerance of thirst, to quit the field, and the Romans mounted an attack on the few who remained, routed them, and drove them back into their camp. The signal for retreat was now given by the consul, at which most of his men fell back, but some, in their ardour for the fight and hoping to seize the enemy camp, forged ahead to the rampart. With contempt for their small numbers the Gauls made a concerted attack from their camp. The Romans were put to flight and, driven by their own panic and terror, they headed back to the camp to which they had refused to retire on the consul's order. Thus on both sides there was an alternation of flight and victory, but some 11,000 Gauls were killed, and 5,000 Romans. The Gauls withdrew to the interior of their lands, and the consul led his legions to Placentia.

48. According to some historians, Scipio united his army with that of his colleague and advanced on a raiding expedition through the territory of the Boii and Ligurians, as far as the forests and marshes would allow him to progress. Others claim that he returned to Rome for the elections without achieving anything of note.

This same year Titus Quinctius spent all winter dispensing justice at Elatia, to which he had brought back his troops to winter-quarters. He also spent that time countermanding the capricious measures taken in the city-states by Philip himself or by his lieutenants—for these infringed the rights and freedoms of others by bolstering the strength of the men of Philip's party. At the beginning of spring Quinctius called a meeting and came to Corinth. There he addressed delegations from all the city states, positioned around him as in a public assembly. He started with the earliest times of the Roman treaty of friendship with the Greek people, and continued with the exploits of the generals who had preceded him in Macedonia and with his own exploits. Everything was received with great approval, except when it came to the mention of Nabis—it seemed to make no sense at all for the liberator of Greece to have left a tyrant sticking in the vital organs of a city of great renown when he was not only a plague to his own land but a threat to all states in the area.

49. Quinctius was aware that this was how they felt, and he declared that it would have been his duty not to listen to any suggestion of peace with the tyrant had that been possible without it entailing the destruction of Sparta. As it was, he said, Nabis could not be crushed without the ruin of a very important city-state, and it therefore seemed better for the tyrant to be left in place, crippled and with almost all his power to harm anyone wrested from him. Rather that than allow the state to perish from being administered remedies too drastic for her to bear, and see her destroyed in the very act of claiming her freedom.

To his disquisition on the past Flamininus added the comment that he intended to leave for Italy and take all of his army with him. Within ten days they would hear of the withdrawal of the garrisons in Demetrias and Chalcis, he said, and he would immediately hand over Acrocorinth to the Achaeans, evacuated before their very eyes. From this all would know whether lying was a practice of the Romans or of the Aetolians—the Aetolians who had put about defamatory rumours to the effect that it had been a mistake to entrust the independence of Greece to the Roman people, and that it had meant only a change of masters, Roman instead of Macedonian. But the Aetolians had never been much concerned about what they said or what they did, he continued, and he advised all the other states to appraise their friends on the basis of their actions, not their words, and to use their judgement as to whom they should trust and whom they should regard with suspicion. Liberty was something they should use judiciously. Kept in control, it was salutary both for individuals and for communities as a whole; unchecked, it was an affliction for others, and it led those possessing it to reckless and unruly behaviour. He urged leading citizens and the various classes in the states to direct their policies towards concord, and all of the states as a whole to consider their common welfare. Facing a united front, no king and no tyrant would have the strength to challenge them; but disharmony and internal dissension furnished all manner of opportunities for fifth-columnists since the loser in a domestic conflict preferred to support an outsider rather than to capitulate to a fellow-citizen. Their liberty, concluded Flamininus, had been won by the arms of others and restored to them through the loyal support of foreigners; they should now use their own energies to protect and preserve it, to make the Roman people aware that they had bestowed that liberty on men who deserved it and that their gift was well placed.

50. The Greeks heard these words almost as if they came from a father. Tears of joy streamed from the eyes of all, to the point of actually causing the consul himself distress as he spoke. For a moment there was a muttering as they expressed approval for what he had said, and told each other to let these words that seemed to have been sent from an oracle sink into their hearts and minds. Then silence fell, and Flamininus asked them to seek out any Roman citizens in slavery* amongst them and send them to him in Thessaly within the following two months. That liberators of their country should be slaves in the land they had liberated was a disgrace for the Greeks as well, he said. All the delegates loudly proclaimed their gratitude to him for, amongst everything else, having reminded them to discharge such a solemn and urgent duty. In the Punic War there had been an enormous number of Romans taken prisoner whom Hannibal had sold off when they were not ransomed by their families. One may gain an idea of their number from Polybius' comment* that the transaction cost the Achaeans a hundred talents after they had fixed the amount of compensation for the masters at 500 denarii per head. On that reckoning Achaea contained 1,200, and you can calculate on the basis of that the number likely to have been in the whole of Greece.

Before the assembly had even been adjourned the delegates caught sight of the garrison coming down from Acrocorinth, heading straight for the gate and leaving. The commander followed the column, all the delegates streaming after him and hailing him as their saviour and liberator. He then saluted them and took his leave, returning to Elatia by the same road by which he had come. From Elatia he dispatched his legate Appius Claudius with all his troops, instructing him to march through Thessaly and Epirus to Oricum and wait for him there, since he intended to take his army across to Italy from there. He also wrote to his brother, Lucius Quinctius, his legate and navy commander, ordering him to bring together in that same location transport vessels from all along the Greek coastline.

51. Flamininus then set off for Chalcis where, after removing the garrisons not only from Chalcis, but from Oreus and Eretria as well, he held a meeting of the states of Euboea. He pointed out to the representatives the circumstances in which he had found them and those in which he was now leaving them. He then adjourned the meeting and made for Demetrias. He removed the garrison here and, with all the citizens escorting him as at Corinth and Chalcis, he then left for Thessaly. Here his task was not only to liberate the states but also to re-establish some kind of reasonable order from the whole mess and disorder existing there. For the Thessalians were in a chaotic state not just because of the problems of that time, or the king's violent and wayward behaviour, but also because of the turbulent character of their race—from their very beginnings down to our own times they have been able to hold no elections, no meeting or assembly without dissension and mayhem. Flamininus selected both a Senate and judges for them on the basis of property more than anything else, giving greater power to that segment in the city-states more interested in maintaining overall stability and tranquillity.

52. After making this review of Thessaly, Flamininus came through Epirus to Oricum, the point from which he was to make his crossing. From Oricum all his troops were transported to Brundisium. Then they came right through Italy to the city virtually in a triumphal procession, the line of captured goods before the general being as long as his own column of men. Arriving in Rome, Quinctius was granted an audience with the Senate outside the city so that he could give an account of his achievements, following which the Senators gladly accorded him a well-deserved triumph.

His triumph went on for three days. On the first day, Flamininus put armour, weaponry, and statues of bronze and marble on display in his procession—most of this had been confiscated from Philip rather than captured from the states. On the second he displayed gold and silver, wrought, unwrought and coined. There were 18,270 pounds of unwrought silver, and in wrought silver many vessels of every shape and size, most of them with carvings in relief, and some of superlative workmanship. There were many vessels made of bronze, and ten silver shields, as well. In coined silver there were 84,000 'Attic' coins (these are called 'tetrachms';* and each has a weight of silver equivalent to about three denarii). There were 3,714 pounds of gold, a shield made of solid gold, and 14,514 gold Philippics. On the third day 114 golden crowns which had been gifts from the city-states were carried in the procession; and sacrificial animals were paraded, and before the triumphal chariot there were many prisoners and hostages of noble birth, including Demetrius, son of Philip, and Armenes the Spartan, son of the tyrant Nabis. Behind these Quinctius himself entered the city, his chariot attended by a large crowd of soldiers, the entire army having been brought back from the province. The distribution to these men was: 250 *asses* for the infantry, double that for each centurion, and triple for each cavalryman. What provided a spectacular sight in the triumph was the men who had been brought out of slavery marching along with shaved heads.

53. At the end the year the plebeian tribune Quintus Aelius Tubero, following a directive of the Senate, proposed to the plebs the establishment of two Latin colonies, one in Bruttium and a second in the territory of Thurii, and the plebs ratified the proposal. Triumvirs, with a three-year mandate, were elected to establish the colonies and these were: Quintus Naevius, Marcus Minucius Rufus, and Marcus Furius Crassipes for the Bruttium colony; Aulus Manlius, Quintus Aelius, and Lucius Apustius for that in the territory of Thurii. The two elections were presided over by Gnaeus Domitius, the urban praetor, on the Capitol.

A number of temples received formal consecration that year. One of these was the temple of Juno Matuta in the vegetable market. This had been vowed, and its building contracted out, four years earlier during the Gallic War, by the consul Gaius Cornelius, who also now had it consecrated in his capacity as censor. A second was the temple of Faunus, the construction of which, financed by money from fines, had been contracted out two years earlier by the aediles Gaius Scribonius and Gnaeus Domitius, the latter of whom now saw to its consecration in his position as urban praetor. A temple to Fortuna Primigenia was also consecrated on the Quirinal hill by Quintus Marcius Ralla, a duumvir elected for that express purpose, and this had been vowed ten years previously during the Punic War by the consul Publius Sempronius Sophus,* who had also, as censor, contracted out its construction. Furthermore, the duumvir Gaius Servilius saw to the consecration on the Island of a temple of Jupiter which had been vowed six years earlier during the Gallic war by the praetor Lucius Furius Purpureo who had subsequently, as consul, also contracted out its construction. Such were the events of the year.

54. Publius Scipio came from his province of Gaul to appoint the next consuls. In the consular elections Lucius Cornelius Merula and Quintus Minucius Thermus were chosen, and the next day the following praetors were elected: Lucius Cornelius Scipio, Marcus Fulvius Nobilior, Gaius Scribonius, Marcus Valerius Messala, Lucius Porcius Licinus, and Gaius Flaminius. The curule aediles for that year, Aulus Atilius Serranus and Lucius Scribonius Libo, were the first to stage dramatic performances at the Megalesia.* It was at the Roman Games presided over by these aediles that the Senate was segregated for the first time from the public as spectators, and this, as is usually the case with any innovation, made people talk. Some thought that the distinguished order had now been accorded a privilege long overdue; others surmised that any extension of the prestige of the Senators detracted from the standing of the common people, and that any such divisions that separated the classes must entail a weakening of the harmony and balance of freedoms within the community. For 558 years they had had mixed seating to watch the games, they said—what had suddenly happened to make the Senators reluctant to have the common people rub shoulders with them in the audience? Or to make a rich man now disdain his impecunious neighbour? This was a strange and arrogant fancy, they said, neither wished for nor set in place by the Senate of any people in the past. In the end they say even Africanus himself regretted having been the consul to propose the idea. So true is it that no change in time-honoured practice wins approval; people prefer to stick with the old ways unless practice clearly finds them wanting.

55. At the start of the consular year of Lucius Cornelius and Quintus Minucius, earthquakes were reported so often that people grew tired not just of the phenomenon but also of the holidays declared on the occasion. Meetings of the Senate could not be held and no public business conducted because the consuls were busy with sacrifices and expiatory rites. Eventually, the decemvirs were ordered to have recourse to the books, and on their ruling public prayers were held over three days. People made supplication at the gods' couches with garlands on their heads, and a proclamation was made that all members of the same household should worship together. Furthermore, on the authorization of the Senate, the consuls issued a decree forbidding the further reporting of an earthquake on a day on which a holiday had been proclaimed following a previously reported earthquake.

There followed the provincial sortition, the consular first, then the praetorian. Gaul fell to Cornelius and the Ligures to Minucius, and the praetors drew as follows:

Gaius Scribonius	city jurisdiction
Marcus Valerius	foreigners' jurisdiction
Lucius Cornelius	Sicily
Lucius Porcius	Sardinia
Gaius Flaminius	Hither Spain
Marcus Fulvius	Farther Spain

56. The consuls were expecting no hostilities that year, but a letter arrived from Marcus Cincius, prefect at Pisae, with the news that the whole tribe of the Ligurians had formed a conspiracy throughout their hamlets, and that 20,000 of them had risen in arms, ravaged the countryside around Luna first of all, and then passed through the lands of Pisae to overrun the whole coastline. In response to this the consul Minucius, to whom the province of Liguria had fallen, mounted the rostra, with the authorization of the Senators, and ordered the two urban legions enrolled the previous year to present themselves at Arretium nine days later. He added that he would raise two urban legions to replace these. He also ordered the allies and members of the Latin League (that is, the magistrates and representatives of those under obligation to furnish fighting men) to come to him at the Capitol. From these he requisitioned a total of 15,000 infantry and 5,000 cavalry, according to the number of military-aged men each possessed. He then ordered them to leave the Capitol, go immediately to the city gate, and—to speed things along—proceed with the conscription. Fulvius and Flaminius were each assigned a supplementary force of 3,000 Roman infantrymen and 100 cavalrymen, as well as 5,000 infantry and 200 cavalry of the allies and the Latin League, and the praetors were bidden to discharge the veterans when they reached their provinces.

The men in the urban legions approached the plebeian tribunes in large numbers requesting that they examine the cases of those who had either completed their service or had poor health as grounds for exemption from it. The issue, however, was forestalled by a letter from Tiberius Sempronius. Sempronius had written that 10,000

Ligurians had invaded the lands of Placentia, and had plundered them as far as the very walls of the colony and the banks of the Po, slaughtering and burning as they went. Sempronius added that the tribe of the Boii was also contemplating rebellion. In the light of this, the Senate declared a state of emergency, and announced that it was not their wish that the plebeian tribunes consider the soldiers' grounds for disregarding the edict to mobilize. They also added orders for allies and members of the Latin League who had served in the army of Publius Cornelius and Tiberius Sempronius, and had been discharged by these consuls, to muster in Etruria on the day, and at the spot, announced by the consul Lucius Cornelius. Further, the consul Lucius Cornelius, who was leaving for his province, was to enrol any men he thought fit in the towns and countryside he would pass through on his way; he should arm these and take them with him, and have the right to discharge any of them whensoever he pleased.

57. The consuls conducted their levy of troops and left for the provinces. At this point Titus Quinctius requested that the Senate listen to the settlement that he and the ten commissioners had put together and ratify it by their authority if they thought fit. He added that they would the more readily do this if they heard the statements of the ambassadors who had arrived from all over Greece, most of Asia, and from the kings. These delegations were ushered in by the urban praetor, Gaius Scribonius, and they were given courteous replies.

Since the dispute with Antiochus was a longer affair, it was referred back to the ten commissioners, a number of whom had met the king in Asia or in Lysimachia. Titus Quinctius was instructed to listen, along with the commissioners, to what the king's ambassadors had to say, and give whatever response he could that befitted the dignity and served the interests of the Roman people.

Leading the king's embassy were Menippus and Hegesianax, one of whom—Menippus—declared that he could not fathom what was complicated about their mission, since he had come simply to ask for the Romans' friendship and to forge an alliance with them. There were, said Menippus, three types of treaty by which city-states and kings could cement alliances amongst themselves. The first was when terms were dictated to a party which has been defeated in war—for when everything has been surrendered to the party who was superior in the field, it is the victor who has the right to decide what property the vanquished party is to retain, and what he is to lose to confiscation. The second was when the two parties, evenly balanced militarily, entered a pact of non-aggression and friendship on equal terms. In this case requests for restitution of property and the actual restitution are a matter of mutual agreement, and in the case of possession of property rendered indeterminate by the war the matters are settled by recourse to time-honoured legal prescriptions or by the mutual convenience of the parties. The third type was when parties who have never been enemies come together to forge an alliance of friendship on equal terms, and then there is no imposition or acceptance of terms, for that belongs in the context of victorious and defeated parties. Since Antiochus was in the last category, said Menippus, he was surprised that the Romans thought it reasonable to dictate terms to him, specifying which cities of Asia they wanted left free and non-tributary, which they wanted to be tribute-paying, and which they forbade the king's troops and the king himself to enter. For this, he said, was how peace should be concluded with Philip, an enemy, but not how a treaty of alliance should be struck with Antiochus, their friend.

58. Quinctius' reply to this was as follows: 'Since you wish to be precise and to list different ways of contracting alliances, I shall for my part set down two conditions, without which, you can report to your king, there can be no alliance contracted with Rome. First, he must keep his hands off Europe completely if his wish is that we pay no attention to the affairs of the cities of Asia. Secondly, should he not stay within the boundaries of Asia but pass into Europe, then the Romans too would have the right both to safeguard their alliances which they currently have with the Asian states and to contract new ones.'

At this point Hegesianax retorted that this was an insulting proposition for them to listen to, excluding Antiochus from the cities of Thrace and the Chersonese as it did. These were areas that Antiochus' great-grandfather, Seleucus, had won with supreme honour—defeating Lysimachus in war and killing him in the field—and then bequeathed to his descendants. When they were later occupied by the Thracians, Antiochus had matched his great-grandfather's glorious achievement by recovering some of them with armed force; and by repopulating others that were deserted, like Lysimachia itself, and restoring their inhabitants; and by rebuilding at enormous expense what had been ruined and burned. What parallel was there, then, he asked, between Antiochus being deprived of possessions won, and recovered, in such a manner, and the Romans staying out of Asia, which had never been theirs anyway? Antiochus was seeking a treaty of friendship with the Romans, but only on condition that gaining it brought him honour, not disgrace.

Responding to this, Quinctius said: 'Since we are weighing up honour—which should be the only, or at least the prime, consideration for the leading people of the world and so great a king—which seems the more honourable, wanting all Greek cities everywhere to be free, or making them tribute-paying slaves? If Antiochus thinks the noble course for him is to reduce to slavery the cities held by his great-grandfather by the rules of war—but which his grandfather and father never treated as being their possessions—then the Roman people also feel that their sense of loyalty and constancy obliges them not to abandon the championship of the independence of the Greeks which they have taken on. As they freed Greece from Philip, so they intend to free from Antiochus the cities of Asia that are of Greek stock. For colonies were not sent out to Aeolis and Ionia in order to be slaves of a king, but rather to increase the Greek race and spread this ancient people throughout the world.'

59. Hegesianax was baffled; he could not deny that a more honourable cause was served by the title 'freedom' than by the title 'slavery'. 'Enough of all this beating about the bush', said Publius Sulpicius, eldest of the ten commissioners. 'Choose one of the two conditions eloquently laid down by Quinctius just now, or else stop talking about a treaty of friendship. In fact,' replied Menippus, 'we have neither the wish nor the power to make any agreement tending to diminish Antiochus' regal authority.'

The next day Quinctius brought before the Senate all the deputations from Greece and Asia so these could see the attitude of the Roman people, and that of Antiochus, with regard to the Greek city-states, and he presented the demands of the king as well as his own. The envoys were to report back to their governments that, unless Antiochus quit Europe, the Roman people would champion their liberty from him with the same courage and loyalty as they had from Philip. At this Menippus proceeded to entreat both Quinctius and the Senators not to rush into a decision which would shake the entire world. He should allow both himself and the king time to reflect, he said, and the king would indeed reflect when the conditions were reported to him, either gaining some concessions or else making some for the sake of peace. And so the whole question was deferred. It was decided that the same envoys be sent to the king that had been with him at Lysimachia: Publius Sulpicius, Publius Villius, and Publius Aelius.

60. Barely had these envoys started their journey when ambassadors brought word from Carthage that Antiochus was clearly making preparations for war with the assistance of Hannibal, and the news gave rise to fears of a war with Carthage being fomented concurrently. Fleeing his country, Hannibal had come to Antiochus, as noted above,* and was held in great esteem by the king, for the sole reason that Antiochus had long been considering plans for a war with Rome and nobody was more fit than Hannibal to participate in his discussions of such a move. Hannibal had always had the same unwavering opinion on the subject: the war should be fought in Italy. Italy, he claimed, would furnish both provisions and men for an enemy from abroad, but if no initiative were taken in the country and the Roman people were permitted to wage war outside Italy with Italian manpower and troops neither the king nor any nation would be a match for the Romans. He requested for himself 100 decked ships, 10,000 infantry, and 1,000 cavalry. With the fleet he would head first for Africa where he had every confidence that the Carthaginians could also be brought to rebel through his efforts. If the Carthaginians held back, he said, he would foment war against the Romans somewhere in Italy. The king should cross to Europe with the rest of his forces, and keep his troops based somewhere in Greece, not making the crossing but being at the ready to cross, which would suffice to create the impression, and spread rumours, that war was imminent.

61. After Hannibal won the king over to this point of view, he felt he should mentally prepare his countrymen for what was to come, but he dared not write a letter in case it was somehow intercepted and his project thereby disclosed. He had come across a certain Tyrian, Ariston, at Ephesus, and had put the man's ingenuity to the test by sending him on some minor errands. Now Hannibal showered him with gifts as well as promises of rewards, which the king had personally approved, and sent him to Carthage with a set of

instructions. He supplied Ariston with the names of people he had to meet, and also provided him with secret codes from which his people would clearly recognize that the instructions came from Hannibal himself.

When this Ariston appeared in Carthage, Hannibal's enemies found out the reason as quickly as his friends for his coming. At first it was a widespread topic of conversation in social gatherings and dinner-parties, but then some people declared in the Senate that Hannibal's exile had served no purpose if he could orchestrate revolution in his absence and cause civil unrest by inciting men to intrigue. A Tyrian stranger, one Ariston, had arrived in town with instructions from Hannibal and Antiochus, they said, and certain individuals had been engaging in clandestine discussions with him on a daily basis. Some secret scheme was being concocted which would soon erupt to bring destruction on them all.

There was a general outcry that Ariston should be brought in and asked the reason for his coming, and that he should be sent to Rome with a deputation if he would not talk. They had been punished enough for the reckless conduct of one man, it was said; private citizens could transgress in future at their own risk, but the state must be kept free not only of guilt but of any whisper of guilt.

When he was summoned, Ariston protested his innocence and resorted to his strongest line of defence, that he had brought no letter to anyone. But his explanation of why he had come was not satisfactory, and he was particularly disconcerted when they made the point that he had been in conversation only with members of the Barca faction.* A dispute then broke out, with some declaring that Ariston should be arrested as a spy, and imprisoned, others saying that there was no reason for extreme measures. Arresting foreigners for no reason set a bad precedent, these people said, for the same thing would happen to Carthaginians in Tyre as well as in other mercantile centres that they frequently visited. On that day the issue was shelved.

Ariston now employed some Carthaginian ingenuity on the Carthaginians. As evening fell, he hung a written tablet in the most crowded part of the city, above the place where the magistrates sat each day, and then, at the third watch, he boarded his ship and fled. The next day, when the *sufetes*★ took their seats to dispense justice, the tablet was noticed, taken down, and read. It said that Ariston had been carrying no private message to any individual, but a public one for the elders (the name they had for their Senate). Since the charge was now made to apply to everybody, the enquiry into the few suspects lost its intensity. Even so, it was decided that a deputation be dispatched to Rome to bring the affair to the attention of the consuls and the Senate and, at the same time, to lodge a protest about the injuries they had received from Masinissa.

62. Masinissa had become aware that the Carthaginians had been discredited at Rome and were also at each other's throats, the leading citizens being distrusted by the Senate because of their discussions with Ariston, and the Senate being distrusted by the people because of the information supplied by the same Ariston. Thinking he had an opportunity to hurt them, he raided their coastal farmlands and also forced a number of cities that paid tribute to the Carthaginians to remit their taxes to him. The area in question is called the Emporia; it is the coastline of the lesser Syrtis and is a fertile area. One of the city-states here is Lepcis, which paid taxes to the Carthaginians at a rate of a talent a day. Masinissa had at this time brought disorder into the whole region, and raised doubts as to the territorial rights to part of it—creating uncertainty over whether it was under him or the Carthaginians. He also discovered that the Carthaginians were about to go to Rome to clear themselves of the charges against them as well as to complain about him; and so he, too, sent a deputation to Rome to lend weight to the charges by fostering suspicion and to raise an argument about the tribute-rights.

The Carthaginians were granted a hearing first, and their account of the stranger from Tyre fired the Senators with anxiety that they might have to fight wars with Antiochus and with the Carthaginians at the same time. The charge against them was particularly aggravated by the suspicious circumstances: the Carthaginians had decided that the man should be arrested and sent to Rome, and yet they had not kept a guard either on him or his vessel.

Then discussion of the territory began with the envoys of the king. The Carthaginians defended their position by reference to their boundary rights—the area in question was, they said, within the limits defined by their conqueror Publius Scipio for the lands under Carthaginian jurisdiction—and by reference to the king's own words. For when he was pursuing Apthir, a fugitive from his kingdom who was circulating in the area of Cyrene with a group of

Numidians, Masinissa had asked the Carthaginians, as a favour, for permission to pass through the very land in question, thus indicating that it was quite clearly under Carthaginian jurisdiction.

The Numidians claimed that the Carthaginians were lying about the Scipionic boundary, and added the question of what territory in Africa was in any case genuinely Carthaginian, if one wished to examine the true beginnings of the property-rights involved. As new immigrants, the Carthaginians had been granted as a kindness, in order to build a city, as much ground as they could encompass with a bull's hide cut in strips. Whatever they now possessed beyond their original settlement, the Bursa,* they had acquired unlawfully by force. As for the territory in question, the Carthaginians could not even prove long-term possession of it since their occupation, much less continual possession. The Carthaginians and the kings of Numidia had alternated claim to it as the opportunity arose, and possession had always rested in the hands of the one who was stronger militarily. The Numidians therefore asked the Romans to let matters stand as they were before the Carthaginians had become Rome's enemy and the king of the Numidians her ally and friend, and not obstruct possession of the territory by the person capable of holding it.

It was decided that the embassies of both sides be given the answer that the Senate would send a commission to Africa to arbitrate on the spot between the people of Carthage and the king. The commissioners sent were Publius Scipio Africanus, Gaius Cornelius Cethegus, and Marcus Minucius Rufus. After hearing both sides and making an inspection, these decided in favour of neither party and left everything in the air. Whether they reacted spontaneously or under orders is not clear; but it *is* clear that leaving the parties with the dispute unresolved suited the needs of the moment. Otherwise, from his expertise in the matter, or through the authority he had acquired by his services to both parties, Scipio could, all on his own, have brought closure to the dispute with a nod of his head.

BOOK THIRTY-FIVE

1. At the start of the year in which these things occurred, Sextus Digitius, who was praetor in Hither Spain, fought with the communities who had rebelled in large numbers after the departure of Marcus Cato. The battles were more numerous than they were worthy of record, and most went so badly for him that Digitius passed on to his successor barely half the men he had himself been given. There is no doubt that the whole of Spain would have been encouraged by this, but for the other praetor, Publius Cornelius Scipio, son of Gnaeus Scipio, for he had fought many successful battles beyond the Ebro, intimidating no fewer than fifty towns into joining him.

Such was Scipio's achievement as praetor. As propraetor,* he also made an attack on the Lusitanians when they were actually on the road homeward, carrying enormous spoils, after ravaging the farther province. He fought them from the third to the eighth hour of the day in an inconclusive engagement; for while he was no match for them numerically, he had the advantage in other respects. In joining battle he had had his soldiers in a close-formed line which faced a column that was drawn out and encumbered by a herd of animals, and these were fresh troops facing men fatigued by a long march. For the enemy had set out at the third watch, and in addition to the journey during the night there had been the three hours of daytime travel, and then the exertion of the march had been immediately followed by the battle, without a moment's respite. As a result, although the Lusitanians began the fight with a measure of energy and determination, and though they had initially thrown the Romans into disorder, it gradually became an evenly matched struggle. At this critical juncture the commander made a vow of games to Jupiter, contingent on his driving back and cutting down the enemy. Eventually the Romans pushed ahead with greater ferocity, while the Lusitanians gave ground and then actually turned tail. As the victors pressed their advantage against the fleeing Spaniards, some 12,000 of the enemy were cut down, 540 taken prisoner—almost all of them cavalry—and 134 military standards captured. Losses from the Roman army totalled 73. The battle was fought not far from the city of Ilipa, and it was to this town that Publius Cornelius brought back his conquering army with its ample spoils. These were all set out in front of the town and owners were given the opportunity to identify what was theirs. The remainder was given to the quaestor to be sold, and the takings were distributed amongst the soldiers.

2. When these events were taking place in Spain, Gaius Flaminius had not yet left Rome, and so conversations between him and his friends centred more on the failures rather than the successes there. Since a serious war had flared up in the province, and since he was to take over from Sextus Digitius the little that remained of the latter's army, which itself was full of fear and dejection, Flaminius had tried to have the Senate formally assign him one of the urban legions. To this he would add the soldiers he had enrolled following the Senate's decree, and then select from the entire body a force of 6,200 infantry and 300 cavalry. This, he said, was the legion with which he would go into action, for little confidence could be placed in Sextus Digitius' army.

The senior members replied that decrees of the Senate should not be passed in response to rumours foolishly concocted by private citizens to suit the purposes of magistrates, and insisted that no news could be considered official without written statements from praetors in the provinces, or reports from their legates. If there was a state of emergency existing in Spain, they said, then it was the Senate's decision that emergency troops be enrolled by the praetor outside Italy. What the Senate actually intended was that emergency troops be recruited in Spain. Valerius Antias records that Gaius Flaminius sailed to Sicily to raise troops, and that as he headed from Sicily to Spain he was blown off course in a storm to Africa, where he swore in some stragglers from the army of Publius Africanus. To these levies made in the two provinces, says Antias, Flaminius added a third undertaken in Spain.

3. In Italy the war with the Ligurians was escalating just as quickly. Pisae was now under siege by 40,000 men, their numbers increasing every day as word of the war spread and hopes of plunder rose. The consul Minucius reached Arretium on the day on which he had ordered his men to muster. From there he led them to Pisae in regular formation, and since the enemy had moved their camp to a point across the river and no more than a mile from the town, the consul entered a city that unquestionably owed its salvation to his

arrival. The next day Minucius also crossed the river, pitching his camp about half a mile from the enemy. From this position he fought some minor skirmishes, which protected the farmlands of the allies from plundering expeditions, but he would not risk a pitched battle—his men were raw recruits, drawn from different tribes, who were not well enough acquainted to be able to rely on each other. The Ligurians, who had confidence in their numbers, offered pitched battle, and were ready for a decisive confrontation; and, since they had so many men, they also kept sending out numerous raiding parties in all directions along the borders of their territory. And when large quantities of animals and other plunder had been assembled, armed guards were at the ready to take them to their strongholds and villages.

4. The Ligurian war had thus come to a halt around Pisae. The other consul, Lucius Cornelius Merula, now took his army along the borders of the Ligurians into the lands of the Boii, and here the tactics employed in the conflict differed greatly from those used with the Ligurians. It was now the consul who would offer battle, and the enemy who would decline. And when no one came out to face them, the Romans would split up to plunder, the Boii preferring to see their lands pillaged without resistance than join battle protecting them. After effecting wholesale devastation by fire and the sword, the consul left enemy territory and led his men towards Mutina, the column proceeding without caution, as if passing through pacified territory. When they became aware that their enemy had left their lands, the Boii proceeded to follow them, marching without noise and looking for a place to waylay them. During the night they passed by the Roman camp and occupied a ravine through which the Romans had to proceed. They employed insufficient stealth in doing this, however, and the consul, who made a practice of striking camp in the dead of night, now waited for dawn so that the darkness would not intensify the men's panic in the disorderly engagement. Moreover, although he was moving camp at daybreak, he still sent ahead a cavalry squadron to reconnoitre. When a report of the size of the enemy force and its position came back, Merula gave orders for the baggage of the entire column to be brought together in one spot and for the *triarii* to build a defence work around it. He then advanced on the enemy with the rest of his army drawn up for battle. The Gauls did the same after they saw that their ambush had been exposed, and

that they were obliged to fight a regular, open battle in which honest courage would win the day.

5. The sides clashed about the second hour. The allied left wing and the irregular contingent were fighting in the front line under the command of two consular legates, Marcus Marcellus and Tiberius Sempronius, of whom the latter had been consul the previous year. The new consul would at one moment be at the front standards, and at the next he would be holding back the legions in reserve, preventing them from charging before the signal was given from eagerness for the fight. Merula ordered the military tribunes, Quintus and Publius Minucius, to lead the cavalry of these legions outside the line to an open area, and to attack with them from the unimpeded ground when he gave the signal. While the consul was making these arrangements, word reached him from Tiberius Sempronius Longus that the irregulars could not hold out against the charge of the Gauls; large numbers of them had been cut down, said Longus, and the survivors had lost their ardour for the fight through exhaustion or fear. He suggested the consul send help in the form of one of the two legions, if he saw fit, before they were dealt an ignominious defeat. The second legion was sent in, and the irregulars withdrawn. With fresh troops joining it and a legion with a full complement of companies arriving, life was now restored to the battle. The left wing was also withdrawn from the engagement, and the right replaced it in the front line.

The sun now beat down with a fierce intensity on the Gauls who were physically incapable of coping with heat, but with ranks closely ordered and leaning on one another, or on their shields, they kept on parrying the Roman assaults. When the consul saw this, he instructed Gaius Livius Salinator, commander of the allied cavalry, to send in his horsemen at full gallop to break their ranks, and ordered the legionary cavalry to give support. This squall of horsemen at first unsettled and disrupted the battle-line of the Gauls, and then broke it up, but without making the enemy turn in flight. The Gallic officers kept trying to prevent this, striking the backs of their panicking men with their spear-shafts and forcing them back into line, but the allied cavalry rode amongst them and would not let them reform. The consul earnestly appealed to his men to put on a little more pressure, since victory was in their hands. They should press the attack as long as they saw the enemy in disorder and panic;

allowing their ranks to be reformed would mean once more fighting the battle from the start, and its outcome would be uncertain. With that he ordered the standard-bearers to take their standards forward. There was then a concerted effort by everyone which finally turned the enemy. After the Gauls turned and scattered in flight in all directions, the legionary cavalry were sent out to pursue them.

There were 14,000 Boii killed that day, and 1,092 were taken alive, plus 721 horsemen and three of their officers; 212 military standards were captured, and 63 wagons. But it was no bloodless victory for the Romans either. More than 5,000 soldiers, Romans and allies, were lost, plus 23 centurions, four allied officers, as well as Marcus Genucius and Quintus and Marcus Marcius, military tribunes of the second legion.

6. Dispatches arrived at about the same time from the two consuls, one from Lucius Cornelius who gave an account of the battle with the Boii at Mutina, and a second from Quintus Minucius at Pisae. Minucius stated that it had fallen to him to preside over the elections, but the whole situation in Liguria was so precarious that he could not leave without such an action bringing destruction on the allies and damage to the interests of the state. If they concurred, the Senators should send a message to his colleague telling him to return to Rome for the elections, since he had almost brought his campaign to a finish. If Cornelius objected to this on the grounds that the responsibility had not been allotted to him, he said, then he, Minucius, would comply with whatever decision the Senate reached. But, he continued, he entreated them to think long and hard on the question of whether resorting to an interregnum might not be more in the interests of the state than having him leave his province in such a condition.

The Senate entrusted to Gaius Scribonius the task of sending two commissioners of Senatorial rank to the consul Lucius Cornelius. The commissioners were to pass on to Cornelius the letter that his colleague had sent to the Senate and report that, if he did not come to Rome for the selection of the new magistrates, they would permit an interregnum rather than call Quintus Minucius away from an unfinished war. The commissioners on this mission brought back the answer that Lucius Cornelius would come to Rome for the selection of the new magistrates,

The letter from Lucius Cornelius, which he had written after the battle with the Boii, provoked controversy in the Senate. Cornelius' legate, Marcus Claudius, had written personal letters* to a number of Senators saying that thanks for the success in Cornelius' campaign were due to the good fortune of the Roman people and the courage of their soldiers, but that the consul had been responsible both for heavy Roman losses and the escape of the enemy army, which he had been given the chance of destroying. Losses had risen, he said, because of the time taken in bringing up men kept in reserve to relieve those who were under pressure; and the enemy had slipped through the consul's fingers because the legionary cavalry had been given the signal too late, and thus had lost the opportunity to pursue the fugitives.

7. It was agreed that no hasty decision be made on the matter, and discussion was postponed to a time when more members would be present. In fact, there was another pressing concern at the time: the citizens were in difficulties with interest payments. Although profiteering had been checked by numerous laws relating to interest on loans, a loophole had been used to circumvent the rules, by the transfer of debts to allies not covered by these statutes and, with no restrictions on interest, debtors were being crushed by their burden. A way of ending this was now sought. It was decided that the day of the Feralia,* which had just passed, be set as a limit; allies who had loaned money to Roman citizens after that date would have to make a declaration of it, and from that day the creditor would be legally bound, with regard to money on loan, to abide by the rules of whichever judicial system the debtor selected. After this, thanks to the declarations made, the size of the debt accumulated by this fraudulent practice was uncovered, and a plebeian tribune, Marcus Sempronius, made a proposal to the plebs which had been authorized by the Senate—and which the the plebs now ratified—that allies and members of the Latin League be subject to the same laws dealing with loans as Roman citizens.

Such were affairs in Italy, military and political. In Spain the war was nothing like as serious as the exaggerated reports had suggested. Gaius Flaminius took the town of Ilucia in the territory of the Oretani in Hither Spain, after which he led his men to winter-quarters. Throughout the winter there were a number of engagements, none worth putting on record, fought in response to attacks made by marauders rather than by enemy forces, though the results were uneven and not without Roman casualties. More was achieved by Marcus Fulvius who fought a pitched battle with the Vaccaei, Vettones, and Celtiberians near the town of Toletum, defeating and putting to flight the army of these tribes and taking alive their king, Hilernus.

8. The day of the elections was approaching as these events were taking place in Spain, and so the consul Lucius Cornelius left his legate, Marcus Claudius, in charge of the army and came to Rome. Discussing before the Senate his own achievements, and the situation in his province, he lodged a complaint with the Senators—they had failed to pay the honours due to the immortal gods after a war of such proportions had been so successfully terminated with a single victory. Cornelius then requested that the Senators decree a time of public prayer as well as a triumph. However, before the question was formally put, Quintus Metellus, a former consul and dictator, said that conflicting letters had arrived at the same time, one from the consul Lucius Cornelius to the Senate as a whole, and another from Marcus Marcellus addressed to most of the Senators. For this reason, said Metellus, discussion of the matter had been deferred so the debate could take place in the presence of the authors of those letters. The consul, he continued, was aware that negative comments had been made about him in his legate's correspondence, and he, Metellus, had therefore expected him to bring the lieutenant to Rome with him, since he had to come himself. And besides, it was more proper for the army to be confided to Tiberius Sempronius, who already held imperium, than to a legate. As matters now stood, it appeared that Cornelius had purposely kept away from the city a man who might articulate before the house the statements he had put in writing, and who could thus make his charges publicly, and face charges himself if his statements were at all misleading, until the truth of the matter had been thoroughly investigated and brought to light. It was accordingly his view that none of the consul's requests should be officially granted for the moment, he said. When Cornelius continued with no less persistence to push his proposal for the authorization of public prayers, and for permission to enter the city in triumph, the plebeian tribunes, Marcus and Gaius Titinius, declared that they would use their veto in the event of a Senatorial decree on the question.

9. The censors elected the previous year had been Sextus Aelius

Paetus and Gaius Cornelius Cethegus, and Cornelius performed the census-purification.* The census of the citizens totalled 243,704.

There were torrential rains that year, and the Tiber inundated the level areas of the city, even causing some buildings to collapse in ruins around the Porta Flumentana. The Porta Caelimontana was struck by lightning, and so too was the city-wall in the vicinity, at several points. Showers of stones fell at Aricia and Lanuvium, and on the Aventine, and news came from Capua of a huge swarm of wasps that had flown into the forum and settled in the temple of Mars (these, it was reported, had been carefully collected and incinerated). Because of these prodigies the decemvirs were instructed to consult the Books. A nine-day sacrifice was performed, public prayers ordained, and the city was purified. In this same period Marcus Porcius Cato dedicated a shrine to Victoria Virgo near the temple of Victoria, two years after he had promised it in a vow.

That same year a Latin colony was installed at Castrum Frentinum by the triumvirs Aulus Manlius Vulso, Lucius Apustius Fullo, and Quintus Aelius Tubero (it was the latter's law which had been responsible for the settlement). Three thousand infantrymen and 300 cavalrymen went there, a small number in view of the quantity of land available. Infantrymen could have been awarded thirty iugera per head, and cavalrymen sixty, but on the proposal of Apustius a third of the land was set aside to be used to enlist new colonists if that was wanted. The infantrymen were then given twenty iugera, the cavalry forty.

10. The year was now at an end, and campaigning for the consular elections had become more intense than ever in the past. Many powerful men, both patrician and plebeian, were candidates. The patricians were Publius Cornelius Scipio (son of Gnaeus Scipio),* who had recently returned from his province of Spain with great achievements to his credit; Lucius Quinctius Flamininus, who had been admiral of the fleet in Greece; and Gnaeus Manlius Vulso. Plebeian candidates were Gaius Laelius, Gnaeus Domitius, Gaius Livius Salinator and Manius Acilius. But the eyes of all were focused on Quinctius and Cornelius; for they were both patricians seeking the same seat,* and recent military achievements lent lustre to each. But more than anything else it was the brothers of the candidates,* the two most famous commanders of their time, who added excite-

ment to the race. Scipio had the greater distinction, but that also left him more exposed to envy, and Quinctius' distinction was of more recent date, since he had celebrated his triumph that year. There was also another factor. The former man had been constantly in the public eye for almost ten years now—which decreases the respect felt for great men simply because of the over-exposure—and had served as consul for the second time after the defeat of Hannibal, and as censor, too. As for Quinctius, he could win popularity because his whole record was fresh and recent; he had asked for nothing of the people since his triumph, and had been accorded nothing. He kept making the point that he was canvassing for a brother, not a cousin, and for one who had been his legate and partner in the conduct of the war—he himself had campaigned on land, his brother at sea. With these assertions he brought about victory for his brother over a candidate who had the support of Africanus (his cousin), and of the Cornelian family (with a Cornelius presiding over the election as consul*), and the advantage of a great vote of confidence from the Senate, which had judged him the best man in the community to welcome the Idaean mother when she came to the city from Pessinus.*

Lucius Quinctius and Gnaeus Domitius Ahenobarbus were elected consuls, demonstrating how little influence Africanus had even in the selection of the plebeian consul, for he had been supporting Gaius Laelius' candidacy. The next day the following praetors were elected: Lucius Scribonius Libo, Marcus Fulvius Centumalus, Aulus Atilius Serranus, Marcus Baebius Tamphilus, Lucius Valerius Tappo and Quintus Salonius Sarra. The aedileship of that year,* occupied by Marcus Aemilius Lepidus and Lucius Aemilius Paullus, was noteworthy for its holders' prosecution of many cattle-breeders. From the money raised by this they set up some gilded shields on the pediment of the temple of Jupiter, and they constructed one portico outside the Porta Trigemina, adding a wharf on the Tiber to the end of it, and a second which extended from the Porta Fontinalis to the altar of Mars, on the way down to the Campus Martius.

11. For a long while there had been no activity worthy of note amongst the Ligurians, but at the end of that year two situations arose that were fraught with danger. An attack was made on the consul's camp, and only with difficulty beaten off; and not much

later, when a Roman army was being taken through a narrow defile, Ligurian troops occupied the actual opening of the pass. Since there was no way through, the consul turned the column round and proceeded to march back. To the rear, too, the mouth of the pass had been seized by a number of the enemy, and the disaster of the Caudine Forks,* which they now recalled, was not only present in their thoughts but almost danced before their eyes.

The consul had approximately 800 Numidian cavalry amongst his auxiliary troops. The commander of these promised him that he would break through with his men at whichever end the consul wished—he merely had to indicate which end had the more villages. For the Numidians would attack these, and before anything else would set light to their buildings. The panic generated by this would force the Ligurians to quit the pass which they were blockading, and run off to bring help to their respective peoples. The consul applauded the man and showered him with promises of reward.

The Numidians mounted their horses and rode towards the enemy outposts, but without attacking anyone. At first there could not have been a more sorry sight. Horses and men were puny and scrawny; the riders had no body-armour or weapons apart from the javelins which they carried; the horses had no bridles, and their very gallop was unsightly, racing along as they did with neck stiff and head outstretched. The Numidians purposely enhanced the derision of the enemy by falling from their mounts and making themselves look ridiculous. As a result the men in the outposts, who had been at first attentive and prepared for any attack, were now for the most part sitting around unarmed watching them. The Numidians would ride forward, then go back, but little by little they were approaching the mouth of the pass, looking like men carried off unwillingly by mounts which they could not control. In the end they put their spurs to the horses, broke through the midst of the enemy outposts and rode out into more open country, setting fire to all the buildings bordering the road. Next they set light to the nearest village and destroyed everything with fire and the sword. First the smoke was sighted, then shouts from panic-stricken villagers could be heard, and finally old men and children running in flight caused uproar in the camp. So it was that, with no plan of campaign, and on no order, the Gauls all hurried off on their own to protect their own property. In a moment the camp was left deserted, and the consul, delivered from the blockade, reached the destination for which he had been bound.

12. But neither the Boii nor the Spaniards, with whom there had been war that year, proved as hostile and threatening to the Romans as did the people of Aetolia. After the armies were shipped from Greece, the Aetolians had initially entertained two hopes: first, that Antiochus would come to take possession of a now-vacated Europe, and, second, that neither Philip nor Nabis would remain inactive. When they saw nothing happening in any quarter, they thought they should agitate and cause some trouble so their schemes should not waste away through procrastination, and they called a meeting at Naupactus. At this their praetor, Thoas, protested about the injuries the Romans had inflicted on them and about the plight of Aetolia— of all the Greek peoples and city-states, he said, the Aetolians had been shown the least respect following the victory for which they had been directly responsible. He moved that envoys be sent around to the kings, not merely to test their inclinations but actually to incite them to war with Rome with incentives appropriate to each. Damocritus was sent to Nabis, Nicander to Philip, and Dicaearchus, brother of the praetor, to Antiochus. Damocritus told the Spartan tyrant that his realm had been debilitated through his being divested of his maritime states, which had been the source of his soldiers, ships, and seamen. Nabis was practically confined within his own walls, said Damocritus, watching the Achaeans exercise control in the Peloponnese. If he let slip the opportunity now on offer of recovering what was his, he would never have another, for there was no Roman army operating in Greece, and the Romans would not consider Gythium or other coastal towns of Laconia a good reason for sending their legions into Greece once again. These statements were designed to provoke the tyrant. The aim was that, when Antiochus crossed to Greece, Nabis would be aware that he had violated his friendship with the Romans by his mistreatment of their allies and this would lead him to join Antiochus.

Philip, too, was being egged on, with arguments not unlike these, by Nicander, and here there was even more scope for persuasive argument inasmuch as the king had been brought down from a higher position than the tyrant, and had suffered greater loss. Furthermore, there were references made by Nicander to the time-honoured renown of the kings of Macedonia, and the victorious campaigns of that race throughout the world. The advice he was giving would be risk-free both at the outset and when it was carried through, said Nicander. In the first place, he was not suggesting that Philip make any move before Antiochus crossed to Greece with his army. Secondly, Philip had over a very long period sustained a war against the Romans without Antiochus' help, and when Antiochus now joined him, and he now had as his allies the Aetolians—who had been a more formidable enemy than the Romans on that occasion—where could the Romans possibly find the strength to resist him? Nicander added a word about Hannibal's leadership; he had been born a foe of the Romans, he said, and had cut down more of their officers and men than now survived.

Such were Nicander's comments to Philip, but those of Dicaearchus to Antiochus were of a different tenor. The very first thing he said was that the booty taken from Philip had gone to the Romans, while the victory was secured by the Aetolians, for it had been the Aetolians and no one else who had given Romans access to Greece, and furnished them with the strength to win their victory. He next enumerated the infantry and cavalry forces that the Aetolians would provide to Antiochus for the war, and the land bases for his armies and ports for his navies. He then resorted to a bare-faced lie with regard to Philip and Nabis, claiming that both were ready to restart hostilities and would seize the first possible opportunity to recover what they had lost in war. So it was that the Aetolians were simultaneously fomenting war against the Romans throughout the world.

13. The kings, however, either did not react, or else reacted too late. Nabis immediately sent men around all the villages on the coast to instigate rebellion, winning a number of important men over to his cause by bribery, and putting others to death when they obstinately stood by the Roman alliance. The Achaeans had been assigned the responsibility of protecting all Spartan towns on the coast by Titus Quinctius, and they at once sent envoys to the tyrant to remind him of his treaty with Rome, and to warn him against upsetting the peace he had so fervently sought. They also dispatched relief forces to Gythium which was by now under attack from the tyrant, and sent envoys to Rome to report on the situation.

That winter Antiochus gave his daughter in marriage* to Ptolemy, king of Egypt, at Raphia in Phoenicia, after which he retired to Antioch; then, crossing the Taurus range at the end of winter, he came through Cilicia to Ephesus. From here, at the start of spring, he sent his son Antiochus* into Syria to oversee the most remote areas of his kingdom, so there should be no unrest at his rear while he was away, and then set off in person at the head all his land-forces to make an attack on the Pisidians, who live in the area of Side. Publius Sulpicius and Publius Villius, the Roman commissioners who had been sent to Antiochus, as mentioned above, had been instructed to see Eumenes first, and they came to Elaea at this time. From there they went up to Pergamum, site of Eumenes' palace. Eumenes was eager to go to war with Antiochus. He believed that, if there were peace, a king with so much more power than himself would make a worrisome neighbour and, if war broke out, the same king would prove no more a match for the Romans than Philip had been. Antiochus would either be totally destroyed or, if he were given peace terms after his defeat, much of what would be taken from him would go to Eumenes, so that he could thereafter easily defend himself against Antiochus without any assistance from Rome. Even if something went wrong, he reasoned, it was better to face whatever fortune had in store for him with the Romans as his allies than to resign himself to Antiochus' domination in isolation, or be obliged to do so by armed force if he refused. For these reasons Eumenes was using all his influence, and every argument he could think of, to goad the Romans into war.

14. Sulpicius, who had fallen ill, stayed on at Pergamum, but Villius headed for Ephesus on hearing that the king was involved in a war in Pisidia. While he was spending a few days in the city, he made a point of having regular meetings with Hannibal, who happened to be there at the time, in order to sound out his attitudes and, if he possibly could, allay his fear that he faced some threat from the Romans. Nothing was achieved by these discussions, but an incidental result of them—which might have appeared intentional—was that Hannibal began to lose his credit with the king and to become generally regarded with suspicion.

Claudius, who is following the Greek account by Acilius, records that Publius Africanus was on that delegation, and that he conversed with Hannibal at Ephesus. Claudius gives an account of one of the topics of these conversations. Africanus asked who Hannibal thought had been the greatest general, and Hannibal replied that it was Alexander of Macedon, because with a small force he had defeated armies of immense proportions and penetrated to the ends of the earth, which human beings had never expected to visit. When Scipio then asked whom Hannibal would put second, his answer was that it was Pyrrhus: it was he who first taught the technique of laying out a camp and, in addition, no one had selected his terrain and deployed his troops with more finesse. He also had a way of gaining men's support, so that the peoples of Italy preferred to be ruled by a foreign king than by the Roman people, despite the latter's long hegemony in the land. Scipio went on to ask whom he considered third, and Hannibal replied that it was obviously Hannibal himself. Scipio burst into laughter, and retorted: 'What would your answer be if you had defeated me?'. 'In that case', Hannibal replied, 'I should have said that I was ahead of both Alexander and Pyrrhus, and all the other generals in the world.'

The cryptic answer with its Punic ingenuity and this unexpected mode of flattery had a profound effect on Scipio, according to Claudius—Hannibal had set him apart from ordinary commanders as being of incalculable worth.

15. Villius went ahead to Apamea* from Ephesus, and Antiochus also came to this city after hearing of the arrival of the Roman commissioners. The discussion at their meeting in Apamea was almost identical to that which had taken place at Rome between Quinctius and the king's ambassadors. The proceedings were adjourned when news arrived of the death of Antiochus, son of the king, who, as I noted a little while ago, had been sent into Syria. There was intense grief in the palace and the young man was sorely missed. For he had already given an indication of his character, to the point of making it clear that he had the makings of a great and righteous king, had he been granted a longer life-span. The extent to which he was loved and esteemed by everybody made the circumstances of his death all the more suspicious; it was thought that the father had used the agency of certain eunuchs—individuals who endear themselves to monarchs by performing such criminal services—to have him done away with by poison, because he believed that having such a successor waiting in the wings would be a threat to him in his old age. People also adduced the following as a motive for his treacherous act: the king had given Lysimachia to his son Seleucus, but had not had a similar capital to give to Antiochus as a means of keeping him, too, at a distance by apparently showing

him honour. Even so, for several days there was a display of deep mourning at court, and so as not to make a nuisance of himself at this awkward time the Roman delegate repaired to Pergamum.

The king abandoned the war he had started and returned to Ephesus. There, with the court closed in mourning, he engaged in secret discussions with a certain Minnio, who was his leading courtier.* Minnio had no knowledge of foreign affairs, and he based his appraisal of the king's strength on his successes in Syria or Asia. He thought the king had the superior cause because the Roman demands were totally unjustified, but he also believed he would prevail in combat. Since the king was now avoiding discussion with the commissioners—either finding it unproductive or still dazed from his recent bereavement—Minnio assured him he would produce the requisite arguments to support his case, and persuaded him to have the commissioners invited from Pergamum.

16. By now Sulpicius had recovered, and so both commissioners came to Ephesus. Minnio apologized for the king's absence, and the meeting began without him. Minnio then began, speaking from a carefully prepared text:

'Romans: I see that you are using the specious pretext of liberating the Greek states. But your actions do not square with your claims and, while you have established one set of rules for Antiochus, you are following another yourselves. For in what way are the people of Smyrna and Lampsacus more Greek than those of Naples, Rhegium, and Tarentum, from whom you exact tribute and ships under the terms of a treaty? Why do you send a praetor every year to Syracuse and other Greek cities in Sicily with imperium, the rods and the axes? The only possible reason you could give would be that you have imposed these terms on them after military victory. You must accept from Antiochus the argument that the same condition obtains in the case of Smyrna, Lampsacus and the cities that lie in Ionia or Aeolia. These were defeated in war by his ancestors and made into tribute- and tax-paying states, and now Antiochus is reclaiming his erstwhile rights to them. And so I would like a response from you on these points, if this is a fair discussion and not simply a search for an excuse for war.'

Sulpicius replied as follows: 'Antiochus has behaved with propriety. No other arguments being available to support his case, he has chosen to have anyone other than himself to present these ones.

For what resemblance is there between the cases of the states which you have chosen to compare? We demand of the people of Rhegium, Naples, and Tarentum what is owing to us by the terms of our treaty with them, and have done so ever since they came into our power, exercising our rights uninterruptedly and continuously without a break. These peoples have never, through their own actions or anyone else's, effected any change in their treaty. Can you say that the communities of Asia have similarly remained continuously the property of your realm, since the time when they first came under the control of Antiochus' ancestors? Can you say that some have not been under Philip, and others under Ptolemy, and that yet others have not reclaimed their independence, without resistance, over a number of years? Will the fact that people have been once in subservience, disadvantaged by the iniquity of a particular period of history, give others the right to enslave them when so many generations have passed? For, if so, that is tantamount to saying that we accomplished nothing in liberating Greece from Philip—and that his descendants may reclaim Corinth, Chalcis, Demetrias, and the entire Thessalian people. But why am *I* pleading the cause of these city-states when it is more appropriate that both we and the king himself should hear it from their own presentations?'

17. Sulpicius then had a summons issued to embassies from the city-states. These had been given prior coaching and instruction by Eumenes, who assumed that whatever strength was lost to Antiochus would accrue to his own realm. Several were given an audience, and as each added its own protests and demands, combining valid ones with invalid, they turned the discussion into a squabble. And so, with no concessions made or gained, the commissioners returned to Rome unsure of anything, no further forward than when they had come.

When the commissioners had left, the king held a council to discuss the war with Rome. At this each speaker tried to outdo the others in vitriolic denunciation of the arrogant Roman demands, for they all thought that the more abusive their criticism was the more they could hope to ingratiate themselves with the king. The Romans, they said, were imposing terms on Antiochus, the greatest king in Asia, as if he were a defeated Nabis. Yet even Nabis had been left with sovereignty in his own country †and the country of Sparta†,* while it was regarded as intolerable for Smyrna and Lampsacus to be ruled by Antiochus! Others argued that these states were of slight

importance and hardly worth mentioning as reasons for so great a
king to go to war, but that unscrupulous demands always began with
insignificant ones—unless they really were to believe that the Persians needed a lump of turf and a drink of water when they asked the
Spartans for earth and water!* The Romans were now trying the
same sort of tactic with the two states in question, they said, and
other states would go over to the liberating nation as soon as they saw
that these two had thrown off the yoke. Even if independence were
not of itself a preferable state to servitude, everyone still finds the
prospect of a change of circumstances more attractive, no matter
what his present situation.

18. An Acarnanian called Alexander was at this meeting. He had
earlier been a friend of Philip's, but he had recently abandoned him
to latch onto the wealthier court of Antiochus. Knowing Greece
well, and having no small acquaintanceship with the Romans,
Alexander had established such a close relationship with the king as
to be party to all his secret plans. For him the question was not so
much whether or not to go to war but rather where and how to
conduct it; and he would declare that he foresaw certain victory if
the king crossed to Europe and established the theatre of war in
some area of Greece. Antiochus would first of all find that the
Aetolians, who inhabited the central point of Greece, were already up
in arms—these were his forward troops, ready to face the greatest
hardships of the war. On the two flanks of Greece, as it were, there
would be Nabis, who would wreak sheer havoc in the Peloponnese
trying to recover the city of Argos and the maritime states from which
the Romans had driven him, before they shut him up within the walls
of Sparta; and there would be Philip in Macedonia, who would take
up arms immediately on hearing the clarion call to war. He was personally acquainted with Philip's dynamism, and with his temperament, said Alexander; he knew that he had long been churning over
fierce resentment in his heart, like wild animals that are caged or
chained. He remembered how often during the war Philip would pray
to all the gods to give him Antiochus as a partner. If Philip now had
that prayer answered, he would not put off rebelling for a moment.
Only Antiochus must not hesitate or hold back, for victory depended
on forestalling their enemy in seizing strategic positions and in
securing allies. He finished by saying that Hannibal should also be
sent immediately to Africa to create a diversion for the Romans.

19. Hannibal was not invited to this meeting—he had aroused the king's suspicions because of his conversations with Villius, and was subsequently shown no respect by the king. Initially, he suffered this indignity in silence, but later thought it better to ask why the king had suddenly turned from him, and also try to clear himself of suspicion. Choosing an appropriate moment, he bluntly asked the king the reason for his displeasure. On being told the reason, he said:

'When I was just a little boy, Antiochus, my father Hamilcar was performing a sacrifice. He brought me to the altar, and bound me under oath never to be a friend of the Roman people.* I have campaigned observing this oath for thirty-six years. It was this oath that drove me from my country in time of peace, and this that brought me, an exile from that country, to your court. If you frustrate my hopes, I shall hold to this oath and go wherever I know power and military strength exist, searching the whole world over for enemies of Rome. So if any of your friends want to advance in your esteem by making allegations against me, let them find other ways of advancing at my expense. I hate, and am hated by, the Romans. My father, Hamilcar, and the gods are witness to the truth of what I say. So when you reflect on war with Rome, regard Hannibal as one of your foremost friends; but if something disposes you towards peace, look for someone else with whom to discuss *that* course.' These words not only impressed the king but actually reconciled him with Hannibal. The council broke up with a decision for war.

20. In Rome people certainly had Antiochus marked out as an enemy in their conversations but so far they were preparing nothing except their spirit for the oncoming conflict. Both consuls were assigned Italy as their province, on the understanding that they arrange by mutual agreement, or by lot, which of them should preside over the year's elections. The one to whom that responsibility did not fall was to be ready to take the legions wherever necessary outside Italy. This consul was given permission to mobilize two new legions, along with 20,000 infantry and 800 cavalry from the allies and the Latin League. The other was assigned the two legions which had been under the command of Lucius Cornelius, consul the previous year, plus, from the same army, 15,000 infantry and 500 cavalry of the allies and the Latin League. Quintus Minucius, commanding an army in Liguria, had his imperium extended, and his forces were to be supplemented by the enlisting of 4,000 Roman infantrymen and 150 cavalrymen, and by 5,000 infantry and 250 cavalry to be requisitioned for him from the allies.

The responsibility of leaving Italy for wherever the Senate decided fell to Gnaeus Domitius, Gaul and administration of elections to Lucius Quinctius. The praetorian sortition of provinces then proceeded as follows:

Marcus Fulvius Centumalus	city jurisdiction
Lucius Scribonius Libo	foreigners' jurisdiction
Lucius Valerius Tappo	Sicily
Quintus Salonius Sarra	Sardinia
Marcus Baebius Tamphilus	Hither Spain
Aulus Atilius Serranus	Farther Spain

However, the provinces of the latter two praetors were changed, first by Senatorial decree, and then by a resolution of the plebs, with Atilius being assigned the fleet and Macedonia, and Baebius given Bruttium. Flaminius and Fulvius had their imperium in the Spanish provinces extended. Atilius was allocated, for operations against the Bruttii, the two legions stationed in the city the previous year, plus 15,000 infantry and 500 cavalry that were to be requisitioned from the allies. Baebius Tamphilus was ordered to construct 30 quinqueremes, to bring from the dockyards any old vessels that were still serviceable, and to enlist sailors. The consuls were also instructed to furnish him with 2,000 infantry from the allies and the Latin League, and 1,000 Roman infantry. It was claimed that these two praetors with their two armies, a land-force and a navy, were being held in readiness for operations against Nabis, who was now openly attacking allies of the Roman people; but in fact it was a matter of awaiting the return of the ambassadors who had been sent to Antiochus, and the Senate had forbidden Gnaeus Domitius to leave the city until these came back.

21. The praetors, Fulvius and Scribonius, whose area of responsibility was the administration of justice in Rome, were assigned the task of making ready 100 quinqueremes, in addition to the fleet which Baebius was to command.

Before the consul and the praetors left for their provinces, public prayers were held because of a number of portents. There was a report from Picenum of a goat having given birth to six kids in one delivery, another of the birth at Arretium of a baby boy with only one hand, and at Amiternum there were said to have been showers of earth. At Formiae a city gate and wall were said to have been struck by lightning, and—most frightening of all—an ox that belonged to the consul Gnaeus Domitius was reported to have spoken the words 'Rome, be on your guard'. Prayers were held with regard to the other portents, but the soothsayers ordered that the ox be attentively looked after and fed. The Tiber made a more violent attack on the city than on the occasion of the previous flood, destroying two bridges and numerous buildings, particularly in the area of the Porta Flumentana. A huge rock, which had been loosened by rainwater, or else by an earthquake too slight to be otherwise perceptible, fell from the Capitol into the Vicus Iugarius, crushing many people. Cattle were swept away in various parts of the flooded countryside, and farmhouses were destroyed.

Before the consul Lucius Quinctius reached his province, Quintus Minucius fought a pitched battle with the Ligurians in Pisan territory. He killed 9,000 of the enemy and drove the rest in scattered flight back to their camp, over which attackers and defenders fought a furious battle until nightfall. During the night the Ligurians slipped furtively away, and at dawn the Romans attacked an empty camp. The amount of booty found was disappointing because the Ligurians had been intermittently sending to their homes the spoils taken from the fields. Minucius then gave the enemy no respite. He advanced against the Ligurians from Pisan territory, and razed their strongholds and villages with fire and the sword. Here the Roman soldiers took an abundance of spoils from Etruria which had been sent from there by the Ligurian raiding parties.

22. It was at about this time that the commissioners returned to Rome from the kings. They brought no information to justify opening hostilities in the near future, except against the Spartan tyrant who—a report confirmed by the Achaean delegation—was breaking his treaty by attacking the Spartan coastline. The praetor Atilius was then sent to Greece with a fleet to offer protection to the allies. With no immediate threat from Antiochus in view, it was decided that the two consuls should leave for their provinces. These came into the land of the Boii, Domitius taking the most direct route from Ariminum, and Quinctius traversing Liguria, and the armies of the two consuls, coming from different directions as they were, laid waste the enemy's farmlands over a wide area. At first a few enemy cavalrymen

with their officers went over to the consuls, to be followed by the entire Senate and, finally, by all people of any means or status, some 1,500 in all.

That year saw successes in both Spanish provinces. Gaius Flaminius reduced the heavily fortified and wealthy town of Licabrum by means of siege-sheds, taking alive the famous chieftain Corribilo. The proconsul Marcus Fulvius also fought two successful engagements with two enemy armies, and took by storm two Spanish towns, Vescelia and Helo, plus a large number of fortresses. Other towns went over to the proconsul of their own accord. Fulvius then advanced against the Oretani, and after capturing two towns in their territory, Noliba and Cusibi, proceeded towards the River Tagus. In this area lay Toletum which, though a small city, enjoyed natural defences. While Fulvius was assaulting the town, a large force of Vettones came to support the Toletani. Fulvius successfully engaged these in pitched battle, and after routing them took Toletum by siege.

23. In fact, the wars in progress at this time disquieted the Senators less than the prospect of war with Antiochus, which had not yet begun. Although the entire situation was under repeated investigation by the commissioners, wild and unsubstantiated rumours would still arise and these were a mixture of truth and falsehood. One such was the report that Antiochus would send a fleet to Sicily immediately after reaching Aetolia. The Senate had already sent the praetor Atilius to Greece in command of a fleet, but because an authoritative presence, and not merely armed forces, was needed there to retain the loyalty of the allies it also sent a delegation consisting of Titus Quinctius, Gnaeus Octavius, Gnaeus Servilius, and Publius Villius. There was, moreover, a Senatorial decree ordering Marcus Baebius to advance his legions from Bruttium to Tarentum and Brundisium, and cross from there to Macedonia if the situation so required. The praetor Marcus Fulvius was also ordered by the decree to send a fleet of 20 ships to give protection to the coastline of Sicily, and the man who was to be the admiral of this fleet—in fact, the admiral turned out to be Lucius Oppius Salinator, plebeian aedile the year before*— was to have imperium. Furthermore, the praetor was to write to his colleague, Lucius Valerius, to alert him to the danger of Antiochus' fleet crossing from Aetolia to Sicily, and tell him of the Senate's decision, in the light of this, that he raise an emergency force of

about 12,000 infantry and 400 cavalry, to add to the army which he already had. With such a force, Valerius would have the capability to protect the coast of the province that faced Greece. These troops the praetor raised not only in Sicily itself but also from its offshore islands, and he reinforced with garrisons all the coastal towns on the side facing Greece. The rumours were fuelled yet more by the arrival of Eumenes' brother, Attalus, who reported that Antiochus had crossed the Hellespont with his army, and that such was the state of preparedness of the Aetolians that they would be under arms by the time of his arrival. Both men were thanked, Eumenes in his absence and Attalus in person. Attalus was also officially awarded state housing and entertainment, and given presents—two horses, two sets of horseman's armour, silver vases weighing 100 pounds and gold vases weighing 20.

24. Since messages kept arriving one after the other that war was imminent, it seemed advisable that the election of the consuls take place at the earliest possible opportunity. A Senatorial decree was thus passed authorizing the praetor, Marcus Fulvius, to send a letter immediately to the consul. Fulvius was to inform him that it was the Senate's decision that he hand over his province and army to his officers and return to Rome, sending ahead an edict while he was on his way by which he announced the consular elections. The consul obeyed the instructions in the letter, and came to Rome after sending ahead the edict.

There was intense competition that year as well, with three patrician candidates vying for one position: Publius Cornelius Scipio, son of Gnaeus Scipio, who had been defeated the previous year, Lucius Cornelius Scipio, and Gnaeus Manlius Vulso. The consulship was awarded to Publius Scipio, so that it appeared that a man of his distinction had merely had the honour deferred, not refused. As his colleague from the plebs, Scipio was given Manius Acilius Glabrio. The next day the following were elected praetors: Lucius Aemilius Paullus, Marcus Aemilius Lepidus, Marcus Iunius Brutus, Aulus Cornelius Mammula, Gaius Livius, and Lucius Oppius, the latter two both surnamed Salinator* (it was this Oppius who had commanded the fleet of twenty ships that went to Sicily). In the time before the new magistrates were to draw lots for their provinces,* Marcus Baebius was instructed to cross from Brundisium to Epirus with all his troops, and keep them in the vicinity of Apollonia, and the urban praetor, Marcus Fulvius, was given the responsibility of constructing fifty new quinqueremes.

25. In this way the Roman people were preparing themselves for every possible move by Antiochus. By now Nabis, too, was no longer postponing hostilities; he was devoting all his might to the siege of Gythium and to laying waste the fields of the Achaeans, resentful at their having sent assistance to the town's beleaguered inhabitants. The Achaeans for their part dared not commit themselves to war before the return of their envoys from Rome, since they wished to know the will of the Senate. After the envoys returned, they called a council-meeting at Sicyon and also sent a deputation to Titus Quinctius to ask his advice. At the council-meeting everybody was inclined to support an immediate opening of hostilities, but a letter from Titus Quinctius recommending that they wait for the Roman praetor and the fleet gave them second thoughts. Since some of the prominent citizens remained firm in their opinion, while others thought that they should follow the guidance of the man whose advice they had sought, the majority waited for Philopoemen to express his opinion. Philopoemen was then praetor, and he was the pre-eminent man of the time in sagacity and influence.

He prefaced his remarks with the comment that the Achaeans had established a wise practice in forbidding a praetor to express his opinion at a council of war, and he bade them reach as speedy a decision as possible on what they wanted done. He assured them that their praetor would faithfully and scrupulously execute their decrees and do all he could to see that they did not regret their decision, whether it be for war or peace, to the extent that human reason could effect this. Philopoemen's words did more to influence them to commence hostilities than if he had shown a desire to lead the campaign by openly advocating it. As a result, a decision was made for war, with a huge majority, but the praetor was given a free hand with regard to the timing and strategy of operations. Apart from the fact that this was also what Quinctius wished, Philopoemen was himself of the view that they should await the Roman fleet, which could protect Gythium by sea; but he feared that the situation would not brook delay, and that not just Gythium but even the garrison sent to defend the city might be lost, and so he launched the Achaean navy.

26. The tyrant had also put together a small fleet to prevent assistance being sent by sea to the besieged populace. This comprised

three decked ships and a number of pinnaces and cutters, his old fleet having been surrendered to the Romans under the terms of the treaty. Wishing to put the manœuvrability of these new vessels to the test, and also to have everything well prepared for the forthcoming struggle, Nabis had his crews and fighting men put out to sea each day and gave them training in mock naval battles—he thought his prospects for the siege depended upon his cutting off relief that might arrive by sea. The Achaeans' praetor was, in experience and talent, a match for any of the famous generals in the tactics of fighting on land, but he was not familiar with naval warfare. He was an Arcadian, a man from inland who, apart from his service as commander of some auxiliary troops in Crete, was ignorant of everything outside his country.

There was an antiquated quadrireme that had been captured †eighty years†* earlier when it was carrying Nicaea, wife of Craterus,* from Naupactus to Corinth. The reputation of this vessel, which had once been a famous ship in a royal fleet, made an impression on Philopoemen, who ordered it brought from Aegium, despite the fact that it was rotten and decomposing with age. The flotilla had the quadrireme as its flagship, with Piso of Patras, the admiral of the fleet, aboard, when it was met by the Spartan ships coming from Gythium. At the first collision with a new and sturdy vessel, the old ship, which was already taking in water at every joint, immediately shattered, and all aboard her were taken prisoner. The flagship lost, all the other ships fled as quickly as their oars could take them. Philopoemen himself made his escape in a light spy-boat, and did not arrest his flight until he reached Patrae. The event in no way crushed the spirit of Philopoemen, a true soldier with a breadth of experience. Quite the reverse, in fact. This failure in the unfamiliar sphere of naval operations only gave him greater hope of success in an area in which he had competence, he said, and he repeatedly declared that he would see to it that the tyrant's jubilation would be of short duration.

27. Elated by his success, and also confidently expecting to face no further peril from the sea, Nabis now decided to use strategically placed guard-posts to shut off access by land as well. He withdrew a third of his troops from the blockade of Gythium and pitched camp at Pleiae, a spot overlooking both Leucae and Acriae, the direction in which it seemed likely his enemies would bring up their forces.

Nabis had a stationary camp here, but few of his men had tents, and most of them had fashioned huts of intertwined reeds which they had covered with leafy branches just to provide shade. Before he came into the enemy's view, Philopoemen decided to take him by surprise with a novel kind of military manœuvre. He brought together some small boats to a secluded anchorage in Argive territory and manned them with light-armed soldiers, *caetrati*** for the most part, who carried slings, javelins and other light weaponry. Then, hugging the coastline, he sailed to a promontory close to the enemy camp, marched from the shore, following paths that he knew, and came by night to Pleiac. Finding the Spartan sentinels asleep— they thought they had nothing to fear in the vicinity— Philopoemen's men tossed firebrands on the huts from every side of the camp. Many were swallowed up by the flames before they realized the enemy had come, and those who had realized it could bring no help. Fire and the sword caused total destruction, with very few men escaping the two deadly options to reach the larger camp at Gythium. The enemy thus thrown into disorder, Philopoemen immediately marched ahead to raid Tripolis in that part of Spartan territory next to the border of the Megapolitans. Here he seized a large number of cattle and men, and left the area before the tyrant could send assistance to the country districts from Gythium.

Philopoemen then assembled his forces at Tegea, and convened in the city a meeting of the Achaeans and their allies, which was also attended by the leaders both of the Epirotes and Acarnanians. Since †his own men's confidence had now† been restored after the shame of their naval fiasco, and since the enemy were in a state of panic, he determined at this meeting to march on Sparta, considering this the only way the enemy could be diverted from the siege of Gythium. He first pitched camp in enemy territory at Caryae, but on that very same day Gythium was taken. Philopoemen was unaware of this, and he moved his camp further on to Barbosthenes, a mountain ten miles distant from Sparta. As for Nabis, after recapturing Gythium he set off from the town with a force of light infantry, swiftly marched past Sparta and seized a place called the Camp of Pyrrhus,* certain that this was the Achaeans' objective. From there he went on to meet his enemy. Because of the narrowness of the road, the Achaeans were in a long column stretching nearly five miles. The rear was brought up by cavalry, and by the majority of the auxiliary troops, because

Philopoemen believed the tyrant would attack his force from behind with his mercenaries, in whom he had most confidence.* But two unexpected factors meeting him together threw him off balance. First, the position for which he was making had already been taken; and, secondly, he could see that the enemy had come to meet his column head-on. Since his path lay over rough terrain, he could not visualize how any advance could be made without light-armed cover.

28. Philopoemen, however, was a man of extraordinary skill and experience when it came to leading a marching army and selecting positions, and he had trained himself in this in times of peace as well as war. Whenever he was on a journey anywhere and he had reached a defile where passage was difficult, he would examine the lie of the land from every angle. He would mull over with himself, when he was travelling alone, or ask his companions, when he had people with him, what strategy should be employed in the event of an enemy appearing in this particular spot—what strategy if the enemy attacked head-on, or on one flank or the other, or at the rear. The enemy, he hypothesized, could be met with the men in a regular battle-line, or grouped as a column which was not in battle-order and suited only for marching. By reflecting on the problem, or by posing questions, he would work out what vantage point he would take, how many soldiers he would employ and (a most important consideration) what kind of weapons. He would investigate where to put equipment and baggage, where to position the crowd of non-combatants, and what size and what kind of guard to use to protect them. He would ask if it was preferable to continue along the path on which he had started, or to retrace his steps; what site he should choose for a camp and how great an area its palisade should enclose; where there was a suitable water-supply, and where food and wood were to be found; where lay the safest route when he struck camp the next day, and how his column should be organized. Philopoemen had preoccupied himself with such problems and reflections from his early years, to the point that in a situation of this kind there was nothing that he had not considered.

On this occasion he first of all brought the column to a halt. He then sent up to the front his Cretan auxiliaries and the so-named Tarentine cavalry,* each of whom took with him a pair of horses. Then, ordering the regular cavalry to follow, he seized a rock on the banks of a torrent from which they could provision themselves with water. There he placed an armed guard around all the equipment and the camp-followers, whom he brought together into a single group, and established a camp as well as the nature of the terrain permitted—setting up tents on rough ground and a surface that was not level was a difficult matter. The enemy was half a mile away. Both sides, protected by some light infantry, drew water from the same stream, but before battle could be joined—as one would expect to happen when camps are close together—night fell. It was clear that the following day they would have to fight on the river-bank to defend their respective water-bearers, and during the night Philopoemen stationed in a valley out of the enemy's view as large a group of *caetrati* as the place could conceal.

29. At dawn the Cretan light infantry and the Tarentine cavalry opened the fighting on the banks of the stream. The Cretan Telemnastus was in command of his compatriots, the Megapolitan Lycortas* of the cavalry. On the enemy side, too, there were Cretan auxiliaries and the same kind of cavalry—Tarentine—providing cover for the water-carriers. For some time the battle was in doubt, since each side was fielding the same class of troops and using similar weapons. As the fight progressed, the tyrant's auxiliaries got the upper hand; they were numerically superior, and Philopoemen's officers had also been ordered by him to put up only a half-hearted fight and then to fall back, drawing the enemy to the spot where the ambush was set. Nabis' men were in complete disorder as they chased the fugitives along the valley, and several were wounded or killed before they caught sight of the concealed enemy. The *caetrati* had remained immobile, drawn up in such a way, to the extent that the width of the valley permitted, that they could take in their fleeing comrades easily between their ranks. Then they themselves rose up, fresh, vigorous, and in formation, to attack an enemy that was disordered and dispersed, and exhausted from fatigue and wounds. There was no doubt about the victory. The tyrant's men immediately turned tail, and were driven back to camp in a flight no less rapid than their earlier pursuit had been. Many were cut down or captured in the rout, and there would have been panic in the camp, too, had not Philopoemen ordered the retreat to be sounded, fearing the terrain, which was broken and uneven in those parts through which he had recklessly advanced, more than he feared the enemy.

Philopoemen then imagined from the outcome of the battle, and from the temperament of the enemy leader, the state of alarm the latter was in at the moment, and he sent to him one of his auxiliaries posing as a deserter. This man was to report to Nabis as a certainty that the Achaeans had decided to move forward the next day to the River Eurotas, which flows close to the very walls of Sparta. Their purpose, he was to say, was to cut his line of communication, so that the tyrant had no way of retiring to the city when he wished, or of having supplies brought from the city to his camp; and also to test his men's sympathies, in the hope that some could be induced to desert the tyrant. It was less a case of the deserter carrying conviction with his story than his giving the terror-stricken Nabis a reasonable excuse to abandon camp. The following day Nabis commanded Pythagoras to stand guard with the auxiliaries and cavalry before the rampart, while he himself left with the main body of his army as if for battle, and ordered a swift advance towards the city.

30. On seeing the rapidly moving column being hurried along the steep and narrow road, Philipoemen sent forth all his cavalry and the Cretan auxiliaries to charge the enemy on guard before the camp. When these men saw their enemies approaching and themselves abandoned by their comrades, they first tried to retreat into the camp. Then, with the entire Achaean force moving up on them in battle-formation, they feared that they might be taken along with the camp, and proceeded to follow their compatriots' column, already some way ahead.

The Achaean *caetrati* immediately attacked and pillaged the camp, and the rest of their men went off in pursuit of the enemy. The road was such that it could hardly be negotiated by a column of men, even if they had no fear of an enemy, but when fighting broke out at the rear and the spine-chilling cry from the panic-stricken men at the back reached those at the front, they all threw down their weapons and scattered into the woods bordering the road. In a trice the way was barred by a pile of weaponry, spears for the most part, the majority of which fell point-backwards, making a kind of rampart that blocked the road. Philopoemen told his auxiliaries to press ahead and continue the pursuit as best they could—flight would not be easy for the enemy, he said, especially the cavalry—and he himself took the heavier-armed troops by a more open road to the River Eurotas. Here he pitched camp at sunset, and proceeded to wait for the light infantry that he had left behind to pursue the enemy. These arrived at the time of the first watch, bringing word that the tyrant had made it back to the city with a few of his soldiers, but that the remainder, a large body of men, had scattered and were wandering unarmed throughout the woods.

Philopoemen told these men to take food and rest. The others, having arrived earlier in the camp, had already taken food and a short rest to recuperate. Philopoemen immediately led out a hand-picked group of these, carrying nothing but swords, and positioned them on roads leading from two of the city gates, towards Pharae and Barbosthenes respectively, thinking that this was the way the enemy would return after their flight. He was not wrong in his judgment. While there was still some light, the Spartans made their way back by trails secluded in the depths of the forest and, when evening fell and they caught sight of the lights in the enemy camp, they kept away from the area where these were by following concealed paths. When, however, they were beyond the camp, and they thought all was safe, they went down to the open roads. There, at many points, they were cut down or taken prisoner by an enemy lying in wait for them, in such great numbers that scarcely a quarter of the whole army escaped. With the tyrant confined to his city, Philopoemen spent some thirty days after this incident laying waste the countryside of the Spartans, returning home only when he had weakened and almost broken the tyrant's power. The Achaeans now ranked him equal to the Roman commander in greatness, and even above him as far as the war with Sparta was concerned.

31. While the war between the Achaeans and the tyrant was in progress, the Roman commissioners were making the rounds of the allied cities, concerned that the Aetolians might have induced some of them to join Antiochus. They made very little effort to approach the Achaeans, thinking that because these were on hostile terms with Nabis they could be confidently relied upon in other respects as well. They went to Athens first, then Chalcis, and from there to Thessaly. After addressing the Thessalians at a crowded assembly, they then took the road to Demetrias, where a council of the Magnesians had been called. At this they had to be somewhat more diplomatic in what they said, since some of the leading Magnesians had turned against the Romans and were wholeheartedly supporting Antiochus and the Aetolians. This was because when news was brought that Philip's son, who was a hostage, was being returned to him, and that

the tribute imposed on the king was being suspended, there were a number of false rumours in circulation, including one that the Romans were also going to restore Demetrias to Philip. Rather than see this happen, one of the leading Magnesians, Eurylochus, and some of his supporters preferred to have the Aetolians and Antiochus come on the scene to change the whole situation. The arguments employed against these people had to be such that they would allay their groundless fears but not alienate Philip by destroying his hopes—he was in every respect more important to the Romans than the Magnesians. Thus all that was said was the following: that the whole of Greece was in the Romans' debt for the gift of liberty, and Demetrias more than others, since not only had a Macedonian garrison been installed there but a palace had also been built to make sure the people had the master ever present before their eyes; but that what had been done counted for nothing if the Aetolians installed Antiochus in Philip's palace, and the people of Demetrias were obliged to recognize a king who was both new and unfamiliar to them instead of the old one whom they knew.

The Magnetarch—the title the Magnesians give their chief magistrate—was at that time Eurylochus. Confident in the authority vested in him by the office, he declared that neither he nor other Magnesians ought to feign ignorance of the rumour that was abroad that Demetrias was being restored to Philip. The Magnesians, he said, should try anything and risk anything to stop that. But carried to the point of indiscretion in the fervour of his address, Eurylochus tossed out the comment that even at that moment Demetrias might look free but in fact everything was done in accordance with the will of the Romans. At these words there was murmuring in various parts of the crowd, some expressing agreement and others anger that he had dared say such a thing. Quinctius was so beside himself with rage that he held his hands up to heaven, and called the gods to witness the ingratitude and perfidy of the Magnesians. These words struck terror in them all, and one of their leading citizens, Zeno, a man of considerable influence both because he led a respectable life and also because his support of the Romans had always been beyond question, begged Quinctius and the other commissioners, with tears in his eyes, not to attribute one man's lunacy to the whole state—an individual was responsible for his own idiotic behaviour. The people of Magnesia, he said, were indebted to Titus Quinctius and the

Roman people not only for their liberty, but for everything that human beings hold sacred and dear, and thanks to them there was nothing that a person could ask of the immortal gods that the Magnesians did not have. Sooner would they furiously lacerate their own bodies, he concluded, than violate their treaty with Rome.

32. Zeno's words were followed by entreaties from the crowd, and Eurylochus fled from the council, making for the city gate by some backstreets and then heading straight for Aetolia. For by this time the Aetolians were revealing their intention to rebel, and were doing so more and more with every passing day; and it so happened that at that time one of their leaders, Thoas, whom they had sent to Antiochus, had returned from his mission, bringing with him Menippus, a representative of the king. Before these men were granted an audience, they had filled everybody's ears with reports of land- and sea-forces, saying that a mighty host of infantry and cavalry was on its way, with elephants brought from India and above all—something they thought would impress the crowd more than anything—as much gold being transported as could buy the Romans themselves.

It was clear to Flamininus what effect such words would have in the council (for detailed intelligence of the men's arrival and their activities was being relayed to the Roman commissioners). Although hope was all but cut off, Quinctius still thought it was worthwhile for some representatives of the allies to attend that meeting, men who would remind the Aetolians of their alliance with Rome and dare to speak freely against the king's envoy. It was the Athenians who seemed best suited for this purpose, both because of the regard in which their state was held, and also because of their long-standing alliance with the Aetolians, and Quinctius asked them to send ambassadors to the Panaetolian council.

At the council, Thoas opened the meeting with a report on his embassy. Menippus was introduced after him, and he declared that it would have been best for all the inhabitants of Greece and Asia if Antiochus' intervention could have come when Philip's power was still intact. Then, he said, everyone would have retained what was his, and all would not have been subject to the approval and authority of Rome. 'Even now', he continued, 'if you are simply resolute in carrying through to their conclusion the policies you have embarked upon, Antiochus will still be able, with the help of the gods and with the Aetolians as his allies, to restore the fortunes of Greece to their former position of respect, no matter how far they have declined. But this position depends on freedom, and a freedom which stands through its own strength and is not subject to the will of another.'

The Athenians were the first after the king's ambassadors to be given permission to state their view. They avoided all mention of the king, and simply reminded the Aetolians of their alliance with Rome and the advantages conferred on all Greece by Titus Quinctius. They cautioned the Aetolians against recklessly destroying that alliance with plans too hastily conceived, saying that impetuous and foolhardy policies looked appealing at first, but were difficult to execute and dire in their outcome. The Roman commissioners, Titus Quinctius included, were not far distant and, while the situation remained unchanged, they should discuss contentious issues with them rather than arm Asia and Europe for a deadly conflict.

33. The mass of those present, eager for change, were totally committed to Antiochus. They voted against even admitting the Romans to their assembly, and it was principally the older men amongst their leading citizens who by their influence ensured that these be given a hearing. When the Athenians reported this decision, Quinctius thought he should go to Aetolia. Either he would effect some change in the situation, or the whole world would be witness to the fact that blame for the war lay with the Aetolians, and that the Romans would be taking up arms with justice and almost from necessity.

When he arrived, Quinctius began his address in the council with a reference to the beginnings of the Aetolian–Roman alliance, and to the number of times the Aetolians had reneged on their treaty-obligations. He then dealt briefly with the rights of the city-states in dispute. If these thought they had a fair claim, he said, how much better it was to send a delegation to Rome, either to argue their case or to petition the Senate, than to see the Roman people in a fight with Antiochus, with the Aetolians as its promoters, a struggle that would have serious repercussions for all humanity and spell ruin for Greece. And, he added, no one would face the ruin brought by that war sooner than its instigators.

The Roman's prophetic utterance served no purpose. Thoas and the others in his camp were heard next, to universal applause, and they managed to get a decree passed—without even adjourning the council or waiting for the Romans to absent themselves—by which

Antiochus was requested to liberate Greece and arbitrate between the Aetolians and the Romans. On top of the arrogance of this decree, there was also a personal insult delivered by the Aetolian praetor, Damocritus. Quinctius asked him for the text of the decree, and Damocritus, with no regard for the dignity of the man, said that for the moment he had to attend to more urgent business. He would soon give him the decree and his answer, he said, in Italy, from a camp pitched on the bank of the Tiber.* Such was the lunacy that seized the Aetolian people and their magistrates at that time.

34. Quinctius and the commissioners returned to Corinth; and to appear to be doing nothing themselves †about Antiochus† and to be quietly awaiting the king's arrival, the Aetolians held no meeting of the whole people after they let the Romans go. However, by means of their *apocleti*—such is the name of their venerable executive body, which is composed of select individuals—they did consider ways of fomenting revolution in Greece. The universally held view was that, in the city-states, the leading citizens and the aristocrats were for the Roman alliance, and happy with the current state of affairs, while the masses and those who were dissatisfied with their circumstances wanted radical change.

The Aetolians formulated a plan †one day† that was not just bold but downright brazen in its ambition—to seize Demetrias, Chalcis, and Sparta. Some of their leading men were sent out individually to the individual cities: Thoas to Chalcis, Alexamenus to Sparta, and Diocles to Demetrias. Diocles was aided by the exiled Eurylochus (whose flight, and the reason for it, was related above) because he had no hope of returning to his homeland by any other means. Eurylochus' relatives, friends, and partisans, briefed by a letter from him, brought his children and his wife into a crowded assembly, in clothes of mourning and carrying the olive-branches of suppliants; and they begged those present, as individuals and as a body, not to let an innocent man, who had not been condemned, grow old in exile. Honest men were moved by compassion, scoundrels and subversives by the hope of stirring up trouble with an uprising spearheaded by the Aetolians; and they all, for their own reasons, demanded the recall of Eurylochus.

The groundwork thus completed, Diocles took all the cavalry (he was the cavalry commander at that time) and set out, ostensibly on the mission to take the exile home. He covered an enormous amount of ground, travelling day and night and, when he was six miles from the city, he went ahead at daybreak with three crack squadrons, ordering the main body of cavalrymen to follow behind. Approaching the gate, he told all his men to dismount and lead their horses by the reins. They were also not to keep ranks, appearing thus to be on a journey more than anything else. In this way, they would seem to be simply accompanying the commander rather than acting as his armed guard. Diocles then left one of the squadrons at the gate, so the cavalrymen who were following could not be shut out, and conducted Eurylochus, whom he took by the hand, to his home, passing through the town centre and the forum, as many people rushed up to congratulate him. Soon the city was full of horsemen, and the key points were occupied, after which men were sent into the houses to put to death the leaders of the opposing party. So it was that Demetrias fell to the Aetolians.

35. At Sparta the plan was not to apply force to the city but to catch the tyrant with a trap. He had been stripped of his coastal towns by the Romans, and at that moment was confined within the walls of Sparta by the Achaeans. It was supposed that the man who was first to assassinate him would be sure to earn nothing but gratitude from the Lacedaemonians for the act. The Aetolians had good reason to send men to Nabis—he had been plaguing them with entreaties for help to be sent since, he said, it was they who had been responsible for recommencing the war. Alexamenus was given 1,000 infantry and 30 cavalrymen, hand-picked from the young men of Aetolia. These men were briefed by the praetor Damocritus in the privy council of the nation which was referred to above, and told not to imagine that their mission was the Achaean war, or anything else each of them might deduce for himself. Whatever emergency plan Alexamenus might be prompted by circumstances to adopt, that plan, no matter how surprising, adventurous, or audacious it be, they must be prepared to carry out to the letter, and they must accept that this was the sole objective for which they had been sent from home.

The men thus primed, Alexamenus came with them to the tyrant, who was immediately filled with hope by his arrival. Antiochus had already crossed to Europe and would soon be in Greece, Alexamenus told him, and he would fill land and sea with armaments and soldiers. The Romans were going to understand that they were not dealing with a Philip, he said; Antiochus had incalculable numbers of infantry and cavalry, and just the sight of his elephants would bring victory to his army. The Aetolians were ready to come to Sparta with their entire army, when the situation should call for it, but they had wanted to demonstrate the strength of their troops to the king when he arrived. Nabis should himself also take steps not to allow the troops under his command to languish in idleness in their barracks, Alexamenus continued; he should lead them out and make them undertake military exercises, sharpening their spirit and at the same time training their bodies. Practice would lighten the toil, which might even become enjoyable because of the commander's geniality and kindness.

After that the soldiers were frequently brought out to the plain before the city, close to the River Eurotas. The tyrant's bodyguards would stand at about the middle of the line, and the tyrant himself would ride before the standards, inspecting the wings, with no more than three cavalrymen accompanying him, Alexamenus usually being one of them. The Aetolian troops would be on the right wing, both those that had been earlier serving as auxiliary troops of the tyrant and the thousand who had come with Alexamenus. Alexamenus had now made it his practice to go around a few of the ranks with the tyrant, giving him seemingly useful advice. He would then ride over to his men on the right wing and return from there to the tyrant after apparently issuing some order required by the circumstances. On the day which he had fixed for bringing off the coup, he rode with the tyrant for only a short while before going over to his own men. He then said to the cavalrymen who had been sent from home with him: 'My young warriors, the action which you have been ordered to execute with energy is now to be done and dared. Be ready in your hearts and with your hands, so that none of you hangs back from the deed which he sees me commence. If anyone falters or follows his own course instead of mine, let him know that for him there will be no going home.' All shuddered with dread, remembering the orders with which they had left.

The tyrant was returning from the left wing. Alexamenus told his horsemen to put down their spears and keep their eyes on their leader, and even he had to pull himself together, disconcerted as he was by pondering the magnitude of the deed before him. When Nabis came near, Alexamenus attacked, running his horse through and flinging off the tyrant. The horsemen thrust at him as he lay on the ground and, though many of their blows fell ineffectually on his cuirass, eventually their stabbing reached his unprotected body. Before help could be brought from the middle of the line, he breathed his last.

36. At the head of all the Aetolians, Alexamenus now moved off at a rapid pace to seize the palace. While the murder was taking place before their eyes, Nabis' bodyguards were at first terror-stricken; later, after they saw the Aetolian column leaving, they ran to the tyrant's forsaken corpse, and the men who should have defended him in life and avenged his death became merely a crowd of onlookers. There would have been no opposition had Alexamenus immediately put down his weapons, called the populace to an assembly, and delivered a speech appropriate to the occasion, keeping a large force of Aetolians under arms but without injuring anybody. Instead, as was only right in a project begun with treachery, everything that was done combined to hasten the downfall of the guilty. The leader spent a day and a night cooped up in the palace, searching through the tyrant's treasure, while the Aetolian soldiers turned to looting, as though they had captured the city they wished to appear to have liberated.

The enormity of the Aetolians' conduct, and at the same time Spartan contempt for them, gave the Lacedaemonians the courage to take concerted action. Some said they should expel the Aetolians, and reclaim the liberty that was cut off just when it seemed to be in the process of being restored, others that they should take some member of the royal family as their figurehead, to have a leader for their enterprise. There was one Laconicus, a mere boy, who was of royal stock; he had been brought up with the tyrant's children. They put him on a horse, took up their weapons, and massacred the Aetolians as they drifted through the city. Next they stormed the palace, killing Alexamenus who resisted with a few of his men. The Aetolians congregated around Chalcioecus, the bronze temple of Minerva, but were cut down, with only a few throwing down their arms and escaping either to Tegea or Megalopolis. These were arrested by the magistrates in these towns and auctioned off as slaves.

37. On hearing that the tyrant had been killed, Philopoemen set off for Sparta where he found everything full of confusion and trepidation. He summoned the leading citizens and gave the kind of address that Alexamenus should have given, thus bringing the

Spartans into the Achaean League. This was helped by the fact that
Aulus Atilius happened to reach Gythium at that same time with 24
quinqueremes.

Meanwhile, at Chalcis, Thoas had nothing like the success which
attended Eurylochus' taking of Demetrias. He had been assisted by
Euthymidas (a prominent citizen who, after the arrival of Titus
Quinctius and the commissioners, had been driven out of the city by
the authority wielded by the group supporting the Roman alliance)
and also by Herodorus, a merchant who, though from Cius, was
powerful at Chalcis because of his wealth; and he had with the help
of these men primed the supporters of Euthymidas to betray the city
to him. Euthymidas went from Athens, which he had chosen as his
place of residence, first to Thebes, and then to Salganeus, while
Herodorus proceeded to Thronium. Not far from Thronium, in the
Malian Gulf, Thoas had 2,000 infantry, 200 cavalry, and about thirty
light transport vessels. Herodorus was instructed to take the ships
and 600 of the infantry over to the island of Atalante, so that he
could advance from there with them to Chalcis on learning that the
land-forces were approaching Aulis and Euripus. Thoas himself proceeded to take the rest of the troops as quickly as he could to Chalcis,
marching mostly at night.

38. After Euthymidas' expulsion, supreme authority at Chalcis lay
with Micythio and Xenoclides, who either themselves suspected
what was happening, or had the plot betrayed to them. At first they
panicked, and placed no hope in any course of action other than
flight. Then, as their fear abated, and they came to see that it was not
simply their country that they were letting down and abandoning,
but also the alliance with Rome, they fastened upon the following
plan. The annual festival of Diana Amarynthis happened to be
taking place in Eretria at that time, and this is observed not only by a
band of local devotees but by others from Carystus as well. Micythio
and Xenoclides sent men to this festival to beg the Eretrians and
Carystians to have compassion on their misfortunes—they were,
after all, born on the same island—and also to have respect for the
Roman alliance. They asked them not to allow Chalcis to fall to the
Aetolians, who would possess all Euboea if they took Chalcis. The
Macedonians had been hard taskmasters, they said, but the Aetolians
would be much harder to bear. It was consideration for the Romans
that more than anything else carried weight with the two states,

which had recently been witnesses to their valour in war as well as their fairness and generosity in victory. They both therefore put under arms their best men of military age, and sent them into action.

The citizens of Chalcis entrusted the defence of their walls to these troops and themselves crossed the Euripus with all their forces, encamping at Salganeus. From there the Aetolians were sent first a herald, and then ambassadors, to ask what it was the people of Chalcis had said or done to justify their allies and friends coming to attack them. The leader of the Aetolians, Thoas, replied that they were coming not to attack them but to liberate them from the Romans, for they were now bound with fetters more ornate, but much more weighty, than when they had a Macedonian garrison in their citadel. The Chalcidians, however, declared that they were slaves to no one, and that they had no need of anyone's protection. With that the ambassadors left the meeting and returned to their people. Thoas and the Aetolians had placed all their hopes on taking them with a surprise attack, and since they were in no position to mount a conventional campaign, and invest a city that had land and sea defences, they went home. On hearing that his countrymen were encamped at Salganeus, and that the Aetolians had left, Euthymidas himself went back from Thebes to Athens. Herodorus, who had been eagerly but vainly awaiting a signal from Atalante for a number of days, sent out a spy-vessel to find out what was delaying matters and, after he saw that the operation had been abandoned by the allies, he headed back to Thronium, his point of departure.

39. As for Quinctius—who was coming from Corinth by sea— when he heard what had transpired he met Eumenes in the Euripus of Chalcis. It was there decided that 500 men should be left at Chalcis by Eumenes to form a garrison, and that the king himself should proceed to Athens. Quinctius continued to Demetrias, his original destination. He believed that the liberation of Chalcis would, to some extent, favourably dispose the Magnesians towards resuming their alliance with Rome and, to ensure that his supporters there had some protection, he wrote to the chief officer of the Thessalians, Eunomus, asking him to put his fighting men under arms. He also sent Villius ahead to Demetrias to sound out the sentiments of the people, determined not make a move unless some portion of them were in favour of respecting the old alliance. Villius sailed to the harbour-mouth in a quinquereme and, when all the Magnesians

poured out in a mass to the spot, he asked them whether he had come to friends or to enemies—it was their choice. The Magnetarch Eurylochus replied that he had come to friends, but he added that Villius should keep away from the harbour, allowing the Magnesians to live in harmony and liberty and not using the pretext of a meeting to inflame the masses. It then became a slanging-match rather than a discussion, with the Roman berating the Magnesians as ingrates and predicting imminent disaster, and the Magnesian populace hurling strident accusations variously at the Senate and at Quinctius. His initiative a failure, Villius beat a retreat to Quinctius, who then sent a message to the practor to take his forces home, and himself returned to Corinth with his fleet.

40. I have as it were been taken off-course by these events where Greek and Roman history converge, and not because the narration of them was worthwhile of itself but because they represented the causes for the war with Antiochus.

When the new consuls had been designated (which was the point at which I began my digression), the consuls Lucius Quinctius and Gnaeus Domitius left for their provinces, Quinctius going to the Ligurians, and Domitius against the Boii. The Boii remained pacified; even their Senate, together with their children, and their cavalry commanders, along with their troops, surrendered to the consul, a total of 1,500 people. The Ligurian countryside was plundered far and wide by the other consul, and several fortresses were captured. These not only yielded booty of all kinds, and captives along with it, but also saw the recovery of a number of Roman citizens and allies who had been in the hands of the enemy.

In that same year a colony was established at Vibo following a decree of the Senate and its ratification by the plebs. This comprised 3,700 infantry and 300 cavalry, under the direction of the triumvirs Quintus Naevius, Marcus Minucius, and Marcus Furius Crassipes. Infantrymen were each given 15 iugera of land, a cavalryman receiving twice that amount. The land had most recently belonged to the Bruttii, and the Bruttii had taken it from the Greeks.

In this period there were two particularly terrifying incidents at Rome, one of which lasted longer than the other but was not as damaging. There were earth tremors for thirty-eight days, and these suspended business for the same number of days, which were spent in an atmosphere of anxiety and fear. A three-day period of public prayer was held because of the phenomenon. The other event was not a false alarm, but represented actual destruction for many people. A fire broke out in the Cattle Market, and buildings along the Tiber-bank burned for a day and a night, with all the shops in the district and expensive merchandise going up in flames.

41. It was now almost the end of the year, and every day rumours of war with Antiochus were mounting, as were the concerns of the Senate. Accordingly, the assignment of the spheres of duty to the newly elected magistrates began to be mooted, so that these could all apply themselves more diligently to them. The Senators decided that the areas of the consuls should be Italy and 'wheresoever the Senate voted'—and everyone knew that this meant the war against Antiochus. The consul who should find himself allotted this area was allocated 4,000 Roman infantrymen and 300 cavalry, plus 6,000 infantry and 400 horse from the allies and the Latin League. The consul Lucius Quinctius was instructed to raise these troops, so there would be nothing to delay the new consul's immediate departure for whatever destination it was that the Senate voted for him.

A decision was likewise made on the areas of responsibility of the praetors. The first of these was to be a twofold jurisdiction, city affairs and citizen-foreigners affairs; the second was Bruttium; the third the fleet (which was to sail wherever the Senate decided); the fourth Sicily; the fifth Sardinia; and the sixth Farther Spain. The consul Lucius Quinctius was also given the order to raise two new legions of Roman citizens, and 20,000 infantry and 800 cavalry from the allies and the Latin League. The Senate allocated this army to the praetor to whom the province of Bruttium should fall.

That year two temples of Jupiter were dedicated on the Capitol. They had both been promised in vows made by Lucius Furius Purpureo, the first when he was praetor in the Gallic War, the second when he was consul, and they were dedicated by the duumvir Quintus Marcius Ralla. A large number of harsh judgements were passed on usurers that year, with private citizens being prosecuted by the curule aediles, Marcus Tuccius and Publius Iunius Brutus. The fines imposed on those condemned paid for some gilded four-horse chariots which were installed on the Capitol, and twelve gilded shields which were placed in the inner chapel of the temple of Jupiter above the pediment. The same aediles were also responsible for building a portico outside the Porta Trigemina in the carpenters' quarter.

42. While the Romans were busy with preparations for the new war, Antiochus was not wasting his time either, but three city-states were holding him back: Smyrna, Alexandria Troas, and Lampsacus. Up to that point he had been unable to take them by assault, or inveigle them into an alliance by offering terms; and he did not want to leave them to his rear as he himself crossed over into Europe. He was also detained by the question of Hannibal. First of all, there was a delay with the open-decked ships which Antiochus had been going to send to Africa with him, and then there had been some questions raised, principally by Thoas the Aetolian, as to whether Hannibal should be sent at all. Thoas brought the news that there was total chaos in Greece, and that Demetrias was in his hands; and just as he had raised the expectations of many in Greece by lies about the king, and by greatly overestimating the size of Antiochus' forces, so he now used the same routine to build up the king's hopes. Everyone was praying for Antiochus to come, he said, and people would rush to the beaches from which the royal fleet had been sighted. Thoas even made so bold as to challenge the king's decision on Hannibal, by now almost settled in his mind. He opined that the king should not detach a number of ships from his fleet, and further suggested that, if ships had to be sent, then the last man to be put in command of that fleet was Hannibal. He was an exile and a Carthaginian, said Thoas, and a man whose circumstances or character could conjure up for him a thousand new schemes a day. Further, that military reputation of his which, like a dowry for a woman, made Hannibal a real catch—that was too great for a king's officer. It was the king who should have centre-stage, the king who should be seen as the sole admiral and sole commander. If Hannibal should lose the fleet or the army, the damage would be just the same as if these were lost by another general but, in the event of success, the glory would go to Hannibal, not Antiochus. In fact, if they were fortunate enough to inflict defeat on the Romans in the war as a whole, what hope was there of Hannibal living under a king, subject to one individual, when he had scarcely tolerated the authority of his native land? His behaviour from his early years, with his hopes and ambitions embracing world-wide supremacy, had not been such as to suggest that he would tolerate a master in his old age. The king had no need

of Hannibal as a commander, but he could use him as a courtier and
adviser for the war. A limited employment of such a talent would do
no harm and be not unprofitable, but if the greatest services were
requested of Hannibal, these would be detrimental both to the giver
and the receiver.

43. No personalities are as susceptible to jealousy as those of men
whose strength of character does not measure up to their pedigree or
status, because these people hate quality and merit in another. The
project of sending Hannibal—the one sound plan that had been
devised at the start of the war—was immediately abandoned. Particularly encouraged by Demetrias' defection to the Aetolians from
the Romans, Antiochus decided to put off no longer his advance into
Greece. Before setting sail, he went inland from the coast to Ilium in
order to sacrifice to Minerva. Then, rejoining his fleet, he set off
with forty decked and sixty open-decked ships; and two hundred
transport vessels, carrying all manner of provisions as well as military equipment, followed behind. He first put in at the island of
Imbros, and crossed from there to Sciathos. Here he brought
together the vessels that had been scattered at sea and then sailed on
to Pteleum, his first landfall on the mainland. At Pteleum he was met
by the Magnetarch Eurylochus and by leading Magnesians from
Demetrias. He was delighted to see so many of them, and the following day he sailed with his fleet into the harbour of their city, disembarking his forces close by. These comprised 10,000 infantry, 500
cavalry, and six elephants—an armament barely sufficient to seize an
undefended Greece, let alone sustain a war with Rome.

On receiving the news that Antiochus had reached Demetrias, the
Aetolians convened an assembly and passed a decree inviting him to
join them. By now the king had left Demetrias, because he knew the
Aetolians would pass the decree, and had advanced into the Malian
Gulf to Phalara. After receiving the decree, he came from Phalara to
Lamia, where he was given a very warm welcome by the populace,
with clapping and cheering and other displays of extravagant
rejoicing typical of the common mob.

44. When they came to the assembly, it was only with difficulty
that the king could be ushered in by the praetor Phaeneas and the
other leading Aetolians. Then silence fell and Antiochus began to
speak. He began his address with an apology for having come with
forces so much smaller than everybody had been hoping for and

expecting. That, he said, should be taken as the best testimony to the strength of his good will towards them: unprepared in all respects, and at an unseasonable time of year for sailing, he had promptly acceded to the appeal of their envoys, and had believed that when the Aetolians saw him they would consider that in his person alone lay all they needed for their protection. Nevertheless, he would amply fulfil the hopes of those whose expectations seemed temporarily frustrated. As soon as the early months of the year made the sea navigable, he would fill the whole of Greece with men, arms, and horses, and the entire coastline with his fleets; and he would spare no expense and shirk no effort or danger, until the yoke of Roman domination had been removed from their shoulders and he had made Greece truly free and made the Aetolians leaders within it. Provisions of all kinds would also come from Asia with his armies, he said, but for the moment the Aetolians should see to it that his men were furnished with grain supplies, and other commodities, at a reasonable price.

45. After speaking to this effect, and receiving loud applause from all his listeners, the king departed; and after he left an argument broke out between two of the principal Aetolians, Phaeneas and Thoas. Phaeneas expressed the view that, rather than make Antiochus commander-in-chief in war, they should use him to restore peace and arbitrate their differences with the Roman people. His coming, and his regal presence, said Phaeneas, would be more effective than armed might in winning the Romans' respect—to avoid the necessity of going to war, men freely make many concessions which war and force of arms could not wring from them. Thoas claimed that Phaeneas was not really after peace, but merely wished to obstruct the preparations for war; he wanted the king's drive to peter out through ennui, and the Romans to have time to prepare themselves. Experience had shown clearly enough, he said, after all their delegations to Rome and all the discussions with Quinctius himself, that no justice could be obtained from the Romans. The Aetolians would not have asked for Antiochus' help, he said, had not all hope been cut off for them. This help had now been offered them sooner than anyone had expected, and they must not slacken their efforts; rather, because the king had come to them in person as the champion of Greece—the most important point—they should ask him to send for his land- and sea-forces as well. In arms the king would gain some concessions; without arms he would have no influence at all to further the Aetolian cause, or even his own interests, with the Romans. This was the view that won the day. They voted that the king should be appointed commander-in-chief, and chose thirty leading Aetolians that he could consult on any matter he wished.

46. With that the council adjourned and the assembled members dispersed to their various city-states. The next day the king began consultation with the *apocleti* on where hostilities should begin. The best option seemed to be to start with an attack on Chalcis, object of the recent unsuccessful manœuvre by the Aetolians, and for that speed was what was required rather than a powerful drive and extensive preparations. The king therefore set off through Phocis with 1,000 infantry, which had followed him from Demetrias; and the Aetolian leaders, calling up a few of their soldiers, took another route, met him at Chaeronea, and then followed him in ten decked ships. The king pitched camp at Salganeus and, together with the Aetolian leaders, crossed the Euripus by ship. When he disembarked not far from their port, the Chalcidean magistrates and leading citizens came out before the gates of the city. A small number from both sides met to discuss the situation. The Aetolians made a serious effort to persuade the Chalcidians to accept the king as their ally and friend while at the same time preserving their alliance with Rome. The king, they said, had crossed to Europe not to make war, but to effect the liberation of Greece, a genuine liberation and not one that was all talk and show, such as the Romans had provided. In fact, he said, there was nothing more advantageous for the city-states of Greece than to espouse friendships with both parties, for in this way they would always be assured of the protection of one against aggression on the part of the other. They should consider the immediate consequences of not receiving the king, when Roman assistance was far away, and Antiochus, whom they had not the strength to resist themselves, was at their gates as an enemy.

In answer to this one of the leading citizens of Chalcis, Micythio, said he wondered for whose liberation it was that Antiochus had left his realm and crossed to Europe. There was not a single state in Greece that he was aware of which had a garrison or paid tribute to Rome, or which endured laws it did not want through the obligations of a one-sided treaty. The people of Chalcis therefore needed no one to win their freedom for them, for they were free, and needed no protection since, thanks to the Roman people of whom they spoke, they had peace and their freedom. It was not a question of their rejecting friendship with the king or with the Aetolians themselves. The latter's first gesture of friendship, he said, would be to quit their island and withdraw. For, he concluded, the Chalcidians were determined not to welcome them within their walls, and not even to conclude any alliance without the approval of the Romans.

47. The king had remained at the ships and this discussion was reported to him there. Since he had not come with sufficient forces to take forceful action, he made the decision to return to Demetrias for the time being. Here, since their first endeavour had come to nothing, the king conferred with the Aetolians on what the next step should be. They decided to approach the Boeotians, the Achaeans, and Amynander, king of the Athamanians. They believed that the Boeotian people had been at loggerheads with the Romans ever since the death of Brachylles and its aftermath, and that Philopoemen, the leading Achaean, was ill-disposed to, and hated by, Quinctius because the two had been rivals for honour and glory in the Spartan campaign. As for Amynander, he had a wife, Apama, daughter of a certain Alexander of Megalopolis, who claimed descent from Alexander the Great, and who had given the names Philip and Alexander to his two sons, and Apama to his daughter. The daughter had gained fame through her royal marriage, and her elder brother Philip had gone with her to Athamania. This man happened to be an egotistical character, and the Aetolians and Antiochus had led him to hope to succeed to the throne of Macedon—he was, indeed, of royal stock, they said—if he brought Amynander and the Athamanians to join Antiochus. And these empty promises of theirs carried weight not only with Philip, but with Amynander, as well.

48. In Achaea, the ambassadors of Antiochus and of the Aetolians were granted a hearing at a council in the presence of Titus Quinctius, and Antiochus' ambassador was heard before the Aetolians. Like most men whose living comes from a king's resources, he simply blustered, making out with empty rhetoric that seas and lands would be filled with troops. A countless force of horsemen was crossing into Europe by the Hellespont, he said. Some of these were men wearing breastplates, the so-called *cataphracti*,* others were warriors who fired arrows from horseback and—something against which there was no effective defence—found their mark more accurately

when they had turned their horses in flight.* Even if the armies of
the whole of Europe were brought together, they could be crushed by
these cavalry forces, but the ambassador nevertheless kept adding to
the list troops of infantry, one after the other, trying to intimidate his
audience with the names of races hardly ever heard in conversation,
referring to 'the Dahae', 'Medes', 'Elymaeans', and 'Cadusians'.
Then there were the naval forces, which none of the Greek harbours
was large enough to accommodate. On the right wing were sailors of
Sidon and Tyre, on the left Aradians and Sidetans from Pamphylia,
races that no others had ever matched in skill or prowess at sea. It
was, he said, unnecessary by now to talk of money, or of other
resources for the war—the Achaeans well knew themselves that the
kingdoms of Asia had always been awash with gold. So the Romans
would be dealing not with a Philip or a Hannibal, one the leader of a
single city-state, the other limited merely to the territory of the kingdom of Macedonia. No, they would be dealing with a great man who
was king of all Asia and part of Europe. Even so, although he was
coming from the farthest bounds of the East to liberate Greece,
Antiochus made no demand on the Achaeans that would compromise
their loyalty to the Romans, their earlier allies and friends. He was
not asking them to take up arms with him against the Romans, but
simply to join neither side. The Achaeans, said the ambassador,
should wish for peace for the two parties, as was appropriate for
friends standing between the two, and not take part in the war.

The request of Archidamus, the representative of the Aetolians,
was much the same, namely that the Achaeans follow the easiest and
safest course and remain at peace, watching the conflict and waiting
to see how the fortunes of others turned out without putting their
own at risk. Then his outspokenness ran away with him, as he descended to insults both of the Romans in general, and of Quinctius in
particular. The Romans, he said, showed no gratitude, and he sneer-
ingly claimed that not only their victory over Philip but even their
survival was achieved through the courage of the Aetolians, that it
was by them that Quinctius himself and his army had been saved.
What responsibility of a commander had Quinctius ever discharged,
he asked. He had seen him in the battlefield taking the auspices, said
Archidamus, and making offerings and uttering vows like some little
priest at sacrifice, while Archidamus was throwing his body in the
way of the enemy's weapons on his behalf.

49. In reply Quinctius commented that Archidamus had taken into account those present at his address more than those to whom the address was directed. For, he said, Achaeans were well aware that all the pugnacity of Aetolians lay in talk, not action, and was more apparent in their meetings and assemblies than on the battlefield. As a result, Archidamus had not been much concerned with the opinion of the Achaeans, aware as he was that he and the Aetolians were well known to them—it was at the envoys of the king, and through them at the absent king, that his ranting had been directed. If anyone had been unaware earlier of what it was that had brought Antiochus and the Aetolians together, it could have been easily seen in what their delegates said. By lying to each other, and boasting of strength that they did not possess, they had managed to fill each other with false expectations.

'These men maintain that it was they who were responsible for Philip's defeat, that it was by their courage that the Romans were protected', Quinctius continued. 'And, as you heard just now, they say that you, and the other states and peoples, will subscribe to their views. The king, on the other hand, boasts of his "clouds of infantry and cavalry" and of "seas covered with his fleets". It very much reminds me of a dinner-party to which I was invited by a Chalcidian friend of mine, a good man and a refined dining companion. It was the summer solstice and we were given a cordial welcome by him, but we expressed our surprise at where he had been able to find such a variety and such an abundance of game at that time of year. The man†, not boastful like them,† smiled and said that all those different meats that looked like wild game were, thanks to the seasonings, actually made from domesticated pig.' This, he said, could be appropriately said of the king's troops, the subject of boasting a little earlier. The different kinds of arms, the many names of nations they had never heard of—the Dahae, the Medes, the Cadusians, and the Elymaeans—these are only Syrians, all of them, who made much better slaves than soldiers because of their servile nature.

'And, Achaeans,' he continued, 'I wish that I could set before your eyes the picture of this great king running from Demetrias, at one time to the council of the Aetolians at Lamia, at another to Chalcis. In the king's camp you would see what was scarcely the equivalent of two undermanned legions, and you would see the king in various poses—practically begging the Aetolians for grain to distribute to his troops, or requesting a loan (with interest) to pay them, or standing at the gates of Chalcis and then, shut out of the city, returning to Aetolia, having done no more than take a look at Aulis and Euripus! They both made a mistake, Antiochus in trusting the Aetolians, and the Aetolians in believing the king's empty promises. All the more reason for you not to be taken in. Rather, you should trust to the good faith of the Romans, which you have already experienced and put to the test. For the course which they maintain is the best, namely non-intervention in the war—nothing, in fact, is so contrary to your best interests. Earning no gratitude and no consideration, you will become the prize of the victor.'

50. Quinctius' response to the two delegations seemed to be on the mark, and since his comments were delivered before supporters they won easy acceptance. Without debate or hesitation the participants unanimously voted that the Achaean people would regard as their enemies and their friends those whom the Roman people had judged as such themselves, and they authorized a declaration of war on Antiochus and the Aetolians. Furthermore, they immediately sent auxiliaries to the destinations specified by Quinctius, 500 men to Chalcis and 500 to Piraeus. For there was almost a state of civil war at Athens, where some people were trying to win over to Antiochus members of the proletariat, who are easily bought, by holding out the hope of enrichment. Eventually, Quinctius was sent for by the pro-Roman faction, after which Apollodorus, the man responsible for the disaffection, was condemned and driven into exile, the charges against him being brought by a certain Leon.

The delegation returned from the Achaeans to the king with the unfavourable reply, and the response of the Boeotians was vague— they would consider what action was appropriate for them when Antiochus came to Boeotia.

When Antiochus had been told that the Achaeans and Eumenes had both sent assistance to Chalcis, he thought he should move quickly so that his men could get a head start to the city and, if possible, surprise the enemy *en route*. He sent off Menippus with about 3,000 men, and Polyxenidas with the entire fleet, and a few days later he himself led to Chalcis 6,000 of his own men and a rather small number of Aetolians taken from a force that could be quickly raised at Lamia. Since the roads had not yet been blockaded, the 500 Achaeans and a small auxiliary force sent by Eumenes safely crossed the Euripus, led by Xenoclides the Chalcidian, and reached Chalcis. The Roman soldiers, who also numbered about 500 themselves, came at a time when Menippus already had his camp set up before Salganeus near the shrine of Hermes, the crossing-point from Boeotia to the isle of Euboea. Micythio, who had been sent as an envoy from Chalcis to Quinctius to request these very reinforcements, was with them, and when he saw the pass was held by the enemy, he abandoned the march towards Aulis and headed instead for Delium, with the intention of crossing to Euboea from there.

51. Delium, which overlooks the sea, is a temple of Apollo. It is five miles from Tanagra, and less than four miles by sea to the closest parts of Euboea. The Romans were in the shrine and its grove, which are venerable and sacrosanct, enjoying the same religious status as the temples which the Greeks call 'asyla';* war had not yet been formally declared, nor had there been any military brushes serious enough for there to be reports of swords drawn or blood shed in any quarter; and the soldiers were very much relaxed as they wandered about, some visiting the temple and the grove, others strolling unarmed on the beach, while a large number had slipped off to look for firewood and food in the countryside. Suddenly Menippus attacked the widely scattered force, killing †them† and taking some fifty of them alive. A very small number made good their escape, including Micythio, who was rescued by a small merchant vessel. The incident was distressing for Quinctius and the Romans because of the loss of manpower it entailed, but it did also seem to have provided further justification for opening hostilities against Antiochus. The latter now moved his army up to Aulis. He then once more sent spokesmen to Chalcis, a number of his own men and some Aetolians, to raise the same issues as had been recently discussed, only with the addition of more serious threats; and despite opposition from Micythio and Xenoclides, he easily attained his object of having the gates opened to him. The members of the pro-Roman party left the city with the approach of the king.

The troops of the Achaeans and Eumenes were now in possession of Salganeus, and a few Roman soldiers proceeded to build a fortress on the Euripus to defend the spot. Menippus then began an assault on Salganeus, and the king himself on the fortress on the Euripus. The Achaeans and Eumenes' men were the first to abandon their defensive position, striking a bargain that allowed them to depart in safety, but the Romans were more resolute in defending the Euripus. However, facing a blockade by land and sea, and seeing the engines and slings being brought up, they too failed to withstand the siege.

The king now held what was the most important position of Euboea, and the other cities of the island did not reject his authority. He felt he had made an important start to the war, in that an island of such importance and so many strategically positioned cities had fallen into his hands.

BOOK THIRTY-SIX

1. The consuls Publius Cornelius Scipio, son of Gnaeus Cornelius, and Manius Acilius Glabrio had started their term of office when they were told by the Senate to see to the offering of sacrifices before attending to the question of their spheres of command. They were to use full-grown victims, and sacrifice at all the shrines in which the *lectisternium** was normally practised for most of the year; and they were also to offer prayers asking that the Senate's plans with regard to the new war have a prosperous and successful outcome for the Senate and people of Rome. All the sacrifices proved auspicious, and a favourable omen was obtained with the first victims. The opinion of the interpreters was that the bounds of the Roman people would be extended by the war, and that victory and triumph were presaged. This report freed the Senators' minds from religious obligations, and they accordingly issued orders for the question to be formally put to the commons whether it was their wish and command that war be initiated with Antiochus and those who had followed his lead. Should the proposal be passed, the consuls, if they agreed, were to refer the entire matter back to the Senate.

Publius Cornelius saw the proposal through the commons, and then the Senate decreed that the consuls should proceed with the sortition of the areas of responsibility of Italy and Greece. The consul drawing Greece was to command those troops which Lucius Quinctius had as consul levied or conscripted for the province on Senatorial authority. He was also to be given the army which the praetor Marcus Baebius had taken across to Macedonia the previous year, in accordance with a Senatorial decree. He was, in addition, permitted to take auxiliary forces from the allies outside Italy, if the situation warranted, but no more than 5,000 men. It was further decided that the previous year's consul, Lucius Quinctius, should be sent to the war as a legate. The other consul, to whom Italy fell as his province, was to conduct the war against the Boii with whichever army he preferred of the two that had been commanded by the previous consuls. The other army he was to send to Rome to form the city legions, and these should be ready to move to wherever the Senate decided.

2. These decisions were taken in the Senate while it was still undecided which consul would have which sphere of command, but eventually it was determined that the consular sortition should be held. At this, Greece fell to Acilius and Italy to Cornelius. Then, the sortition decided, there was a Senatorial decree to the effect that, inasmuch as the Roman people had ordered that a state of war exist with King Antiochus and those under his command, the consuls should enjoin public prayers for success therein, and the consul Manius Acilius should promise great games to Jupiter in a vow, and gifts at all the couches of the gods. That vow, dictated by the pontifex maximus Publius Licinius, was pronounced publicly by the consul in the following words: 'In respect to the war which the people have ordered undertaken with King Antiochus, should this be concluded as the Senate and people of Rome desire, then the Roman people will celebrate great games for ten successive days in your honour, Jupiter, and gifts will be presented at all the couches, finances for them being drawn at the discretion of the Senate. Whichsoever magistrate celebrate these games, and whensoever and wheresoever he do so, let it be deemed that the games have been celebrated and the gifts duly presented.' After this, a two-day period of public prayer was proclaimed by the two consuls.

The sortition of the consular provinces completed, the praetors immediately drew lots for theirs. The double jurisdiction* fell to Marcus Iunius Brutus, Bruttium to Aulus Cornelius Mammula, Sicily to Marcus Aemilius Lepidus, Sardinia to Lucius Oppius Salinator, the fleet to Gaius Livius Salinator, and Farther Spain to Lucius Aemilius Paullus.

To these men the armies were officially distributed as follows: Aulus Cornelius was given the new recruits that had been conscripted the previous year by the consul Lucius Quinctius in compliance with a decree of the Senate, and he was instructed to protect the entire coastline around Tarentum and Brundisium. For Farther Spain, Lucius Aemilius Paullus was not only to assume command of the army of the proconsul Marcus Fulvius but was further authorized by decree to take there 3,000 new infantry and 300 cavalry, two-thirds of whom were to be allies and members of the Latin League, and one-third Roman citizens. Gaius Flaminius, whose imperium was extended, was sent the same supplementary force for service in Hither Spain. Marcus Aemilius Lepidus was instructed to take over both the province and its army from Lucius Valerius, whom he was to succeed. If Lepidus agreed, he was to retain Lucius Valerius as propraetor in the province, which he should divide in two, one section running from Agrigentum to Pachynus, and the other from Pachynus to Tyndaris (and Valerius should protect the coastline of the latter section with twenty warships). The same praetor was also ordered to commandeer two tithes of grain, and see to its being transported to the sea, and then ferried to Greece. Lucius Oppius was given the same order in respect of a second set of two tithes in Sardinia, only in this case it was decided that the grain should be taken to Rome, not Greece. The praetor Gaius Livius, to whom the fleet had been allotted, was instructed to prepare thirty ships and cross to Greece at the earliest possible moment. There he was to assume command of the ships that had been under Atilius. The praetor Marcus Iunius was assigned the task of repairing and equipping the old vessels in the dockyards, and he was to enlist freedmen as sailors to man that fleet.

3. Envoys were sent to Africa to ask for grain which was to be transported to Greece (and for which the Roman people would pay), three to the Carthaginians and three also to Numidia. So absorbed was the whole community in arrangements and careful preparation for the war that the consul Publius Cornelius issued a proclamation to all Senators, to all with the right to vote in the Senate, and to all minor magistrates. None of these could go so far from the city of Rome that he could not return in one day, and no more than five Senators should be simultaneously absent from the city.

The praetor Gaius Livius was now busily engaged in getting the fleet together, but an argument arose with members of the maritime colonies which distracted him for a short while. These men were pressed into service in the fleet, and they appealed to the plebeian tribunes, by whom the case was referred to the Senate. The Senate then decided, with complete unanimity, that the colonists should have no exemption from naval duty. The colonies in dispute with the praetor over the exemptions were Ostia, Fregenae, Castrum Novum, Pyrgi, Antium, Terracina, Minturnae, and Sinuessa.

The consul Manius Acilius, following a decree of the Senate, then consulted the college of fetial priests, asking whether the declaration of war should be delivered to Antiochus in person, or whether it sufficed for an announcement to be made at one of his military outposts. He also asked if the fetial priests enjoined a separate declaration of war for the Aetolians, and whether the alliance and friendship with them should be formally renounced before that declaration was made. The answer of the fetial priests was as follows. They had already declared* when consulted about Philip, they said, that it was immaterial whether the declaration were made directly to the person or to a military outpost; and the friendship was evidently renounced because, despite the repeated requests for restitution of property by Roman ambassadors, the Aetolians had decided against restitution or equitable compensation. The Aetolians had themselves declared war on the Romans, they said, by forcefully seizing Demetrias, a city of their allies, by launching an attack by land and sea on Chalcis, and by bringing Antiochus to Europe to make war on the Roman people.

All the preparations now completed, the consul Manius Acilius issued a proclamation for a general mobilization at Brundisium, on 15 May, of the troops raised by Lucius Quinctius, or requisitioned by him from the allies and the Latin League—that is, the troops which were to go with him to his province—as well as the military tribunes of the first and third legions. Acilius himself set out from the city wearing his cloak of command on 3 May, and the praetors also left for their provinces at about the same time.

4. It was around this time that embassies came to Rome from the two kings, Philip, and Ptolemy of Egypt. Philip promised to supply reinforcements, money, and grain for the war-effort, and from Ptolemy there actually arrived 1,000 pounds of gold and 20,000 pounds of silver. None of this money was accepted; and the kings were both thanked for their offers. Both kings also made a pledge to come to Aetolia with all their forces and to participate in the war, but Ptolemy was spared such an obligation, while the reply given to Philip's envoys was that the king would gratify the Senate and people of Rome people by simply supporting the consul Manius Acilius.

Envoys also came from the Carthaginians and Masinissa. The Carthaginians gave an undertaking to bring <500,000> measures of wheat and 500,000 of barley to the army, and half that amount to Rome. They were asking the Romans to accept this as a gift, they said, adding that they would also put together a fleet at their own expense and, with a single payment, discharge in full the indemnity which they were under obligation to pay in several instalments over a number of years. The envoys of Masinissa claimed that their king would send 500,000 measures of wheat and 300,000 of barley to the army in Greece, 300,000 measures of wheat and 250,000 of barley to Rome, and 500 cavalry plus thirty elephants* to the consul Manius Acilius. With respect to the grain, both parties were given the answer that the Roman people would avail themselves of the offer if payment were accepted. With regard to the fleet, the Carthaginians' offer was declined, except in respect of such ships as they were obliged to provide under their treaty, and the response regarding the money was likewise that the Romans would not accept any before the due date.

5. While this was happening at Rome, Antiochus was at Chalcis. Not to waste the wintertime, he kept trying to win support among the city-states himself by sending embassies to a number of them, but he was also approached by others who came to him on their own initiative. This was the case with the Epirotes, who came to him with the support of the people as a whole, and with the Eleans, who arrived from the Peloponnese. The Eleans were seeking his help against the Achaeans who, †after declaring war on Antiochus without their approval, would attack their city-state first†. They were sent 1,000 infantry, under the Cretan general Euphanes.

The embassy from Epirus was not at all forthright or honest in its support for either side, its members wishing to win the king's goodwill while at the same time trying to avoid giving offence to the Romans. They asked Antiochus not to drag them heedlessly into the dispute, since their position opposite Italy and at the forefront of Greece meant that they would face the first onset of the Romans. If the king could himself protect Epirus with his land- and sea-forces, they said, all the Epirotes would give him an enthusiastic welcome in their cities and ports. If he could not do that, then they entreated him not to expose them, unprotected and vulnerable as they were, to a war with Rome. The rationale for the Epirote embassy was evident. If, as they were inclined to believe, Antiochus avoided Epirus altogether, their situation with regard to the Roman armies would be unchanged, while they would have won the king's goodwill because they had shown themselves ready to receive him had he come. On the other hand, should he actually come, they could in that case, too, hope for indulgence on the part of the Romans because, not anticipating help to come from them at such a great distance, they would simply have buckled before the might of an enemy on the spot. Unable to come up with an immediate response to an embassy with such a complex agenda, Antiochus stated that he would send a delegation to the Epirotes to discuss the matters of common concern to them and himself.

6. Antiochus himself left for Boeotia. The Boeotians had the pretexts which I gave above for resentment towards the Romans, namely the assassination of Brachylles,* and the attack made by Quinctius on Coronea in retaliation for the massacre of Roman soldiers. In fact, over a period of generations the discipline for which this people was once noted had already been in decline,* in both public and private life, and many were in circumstances that they could not long maintain without political upheaval.

Leading citizens streamed out to meet Antiochus from all over Boeotia when he came to Thebes. He had already taken significant initiatives that established clearly that he was at war, both by his attack on the Roman garrison at Delium and by his offensive at Chalcis, but in the council of the Boeotian people at Thebes he still opened with the same remarks that he had used in his first address at Chalcis, and which he had made through his representatives in the council of the Achaeans: he was asking that a treaty of friendship be established with himself, and not that war be declared on the Romans. No one was under any delusion as to what was really at issue, but a decree was passed, couched in inoffensive language, which supported the king and was unfavourable to the Romans.

With this people also won over, Antiochus returned to Chalcis. From there he sent ahead letters instructing the Aetolian leaders to assemble at Demetrias so that he could discuss with them the general strategy for the war, and he arrived by ship on the day fixed for the meeting. Amynander also attended this conference, having been sent for from Athamania to take part in the deliberations, as did Hannibal the Carthaginian, who had long been excluded from discussions of policy. The issue under consideration was the Thessalian people, whose support all present felt should be enlisted. Opinions diverged only over modalities. Some urged immediate action, and others that they postpone matters for the winter, which was then about half-way through, and wait for the start of spring. Some voted that only an embassy be sent to the Thessalians, and others that they go in full force and intimidate them with threats if they showed reluctance.

7. The discussion was focused almost entirely on this issue, but Hannibal, when he was invited by name to state his opinion, used the following speech to bring the king and all present to think about the war in general:

'Had I been invited to take part in your deliberations from the point when we first crossed to Greece, and when discussion centred on Euboea, the Achaeans, and Boeotia, I would have presented to you the very same opinion that I shall present today, when the subject is the Thessalians. Above all, in my view, we must use any means available to us to bring Philip and the Macedonians into a military alliance. For there can be no doubts as far as Euboea, the Boeotians, and the Thessalians are concerned. They have no strength of their own, and are always ingratiating themselves with powers close at hand; and they will use that same faint-heartedness that they demonstrate in their present policy decisions as an argument for gaining pardon for their actions. So, as soon as they see a Roman army in Greece, they will revert to support of the imperial power to which they have become habituated. Nor will it harm them at all that, when the Romans were far off, they were unwilling to tackle your power and that of your army, which were on the spot.

'So how much more desirable and advisable is it to have Philip rather than these people join us? The moment he has espoused our cause, he would find himself with no way back, and would bring with him a strength that would not merely be extra support for the war with Rome, but one which was recently able to withstand the Romans all on its own. With Philip enlisted, how can I doubt the outcome (I hope I may say it without offence!)? For I can see the Romans themselves will be under attack from the men whose assistance actually gave them success against Philip. It was the Aetolians, everybody agrees, who defeated Philip, and they will now be fighting alongside Philip against the Romans. Amynander and the Athamanian people will stand with us—and their contributions in that war were the greatest after the Aetolians'. At that time you were a nonparticipant and Philip bore the whole weight of the war. This time you will be two great kings employing the strength of Asia and Europe to fight a war against a single people, and a people who (not to speak of my mixed fortunes against them) could not, at least in the days of our fathers, show themselves a match even for a single king of Epirus—and in what way will he possibly stand comparison with you?

'What then makes me confident that Philip can be brought to join us? First of all, that strongest bond in an alliance—common interest. And, secondly, the assurances you have given, Aetolians. For your representative here, Thoas, used to have a number of things to say in favour of summoning Antiochus to Greece, but the reason that he would always put forward before all the others was that Philip was foaming at the mouth, and incensed that the terms imposed on him, ostensibly peace-terms, reduced him to serfdom. Thoas would paint a verbal picture in which the enraged Philip was like a wild beast that had been chained or caged, and was longing to burst its bonds. If that is how Philip feels, let us untie his shackles and break his chains so that he can let his long-restrained fury burst forth against our common enemy. But suppose our delegation fails to persuade him. In that case let us at least make sure that, even if we cannot enlist him in our cause, he cannot be enlisted by our enemies. Your son Seleucus is at Lysimachia. If he advances through Thrace with the army which he has with him, and proceeds with raids on the adjacent areas of Macedonia, he will easily see to it that Philip turns from bringing assistance to the Romans to defending his own possessions, his highest priority.

'You have my thoughts on Philip, and from the very beginning you have not been unaware of my opinion on the strategy for the war as a whole. Had I been listened to at that point, the Romans would not now be hearing of the capture of Chalcis in Euboea, and the storming of a fortress on the Euripus; no, they would be hearing reports of Etruria and the coast of Liguria and Cisalpine Gaul being engulfed in the flames of war, and—their greatest dread—of Hannibal present in Italy. Even at this point I think you should send for all your land- and sea-forces, and have the fleet followed by transports loaded with supplies. Our numbers here are small for all the operations of the war, but too large for the meagre provisions at our disposal. When you have brought together all your forces, split your fleet and keep part on patrol off Corcyra to deny the Romans a free and secure crossing. The rest you must send over to that part of the Italian coastline facing Sardinia and Africa. You personally should move forward with all your land-forces into the territory of Byllis. From that vantage-point you must stand guard over Greece, and at the same time give the Romans the impression that you are going to cross—and, if circumstances require it, you will in fact do so. These are my recommendations, those of a man who may not be an expert in every kind of warfare, but who has at least learned from his successes and failures how to fight the Romans. With respect to the plans I have suggested to you, I promise my loyal and energetic support in carrying them through, and may the gods show their favour to whichever proposal you find the best.'

8. Such was the tenor of Hannibal's remarks, for which his audience expressed immediate approbation but without actually following them up. Apart from the fact that Antiochus sent Polyxenidas to fetch his fleet and land-forces from Asia, not one of Hannibal's recommendations was implemented. Envoys were sent to the council of the Thessalians at Larisa, and a date was set for the Aetolians and Amynander to meet †the army† at Pherae, to which city the king also came post-haste with his troops. While Antiochus was waiting for Amynander and the Aetolians at Pherae, he sent Philip of Megalopolis at the head of 2,000 men to gather up the bones of the Macedonians at the site of the decisive battle with Philip at Cynoscephalae.* Antiochus had perhaps been advised to do this by the Megalopolitan, who wished to ingratiate himself with the Macedonian people, and generate resentment towards their king for having left his soldiers unburied, or else it was the natural vanity of royalty that turned his thoughts to a scheme that looked impressive but was in fact futile. A mound is now there, formed by the bringing together of the bones strewn around the area, but this engendered no feelings of gratitude amongst the Macedonians, while it provoked deep resentment in Philip of Macedon. The result was that the man who, to that point, was going to let fortune guide his policy, now, on the spur of the moment, sent a message to the propraetor Marcus Baebius to inform him that Antiochus had attacked Thessaly, and that Baebius should, if he thought fit, move from his winter-quarters. Philip would advance to meet him to discuss a plan of action.

9. Antiochus was encamped at Pherae, where he had now been joined by the Aetolians and Amynander. Here envoys came to him from Larisa to ask what the Thessalians had done or said to prompt him to open hostilities against them, and to appeal to him to withdraw his army and conduct discussions with them through

ambassadors on anything he considered pertinent. (At the same time the people of Larisa sent 500 soldiers under Hippolochus to protect Pherae, but they were denied access since the king's troops now blocked all the roads, and they fell back to Scotusa.)

The king gave the envoys of the people of Larisa a mild response. He had entered Thessaly, he said, not to make war, but to protect and consolidate the liberty of the Thessalians. A messenger was also sent by Antiochus to make a similar declaration to the people of Pherae, but the latter gave him no reply and sent to the king their chief magistrate, Pausanias, as their spokesman. Pausanias presented much the same arguments as had been made in the conference at the strait of Euripus on behalf of the people of Chalcis, who were in similar circumstances, and some he made even more emphatically. The king let the Larisans go only after bidding them to consider the matter very, very carefully, so they would not adopt a policy which, though devised with extreme caution and foresight for the long-term, might cause them immediate regret.

When the results of this embassy were reported at Pherae, the people had not the slightest doubt but that they should from loyalty to the Romans face whatever the fortunes of war might bring. They therefore proceeded to devote all their energy to defending their city, and the king mounted an attack on their walls from every direction at once. He also realized—what was unquestionably true—that, this being the first city he had attacked, what happened here would determine whether he would be met with derision or fear by the entire Thessalian people. He therefore used every possible means to intimidate the beleaguered inhabitants.

The initial thrust of the attack the Pheraeans withstood with a firm resolve; but then, as the defenders were killed or wounded in large numbers, their spirit began to weaken. Inspired once more to stick to their resolve by the rebukes of their officers, they abandoned the outer encircling wall of the city, which their forces were now too thin to hold, and withdrew to the inner part of the town which had a defence-work of shorter circumference. Eventually, crushed by their adversities, and frightened that they would lose all chance of the victor's mercy if they were taken by force, they capitulated.

Then, without delay, the king sent 4,000 soldiers to Scotusa while the panic was still fresh. Surrender there was immediate, for the Scotusans looked at the recent example of the people of Pherae, ultimately forced by adversity into doing what they had at first obstinately refused to do. Hippolochus and the Larisan garrison were also surrendered, along with the city itself. All were released unharmed by the king because he believed that the gesture would be of great importance for winning the sympathies of the people of Larisa.

10. These successes had been achieved within ten days of Antiochus' arrival at Pherae. He next set off with his whole army for Crannon, which he took immediately on his arrival. After this he seized Cierium and Metropolis, and the forts around these towns, and by now everything in the region was under his control, with the exception of Atrax and Gyrton. Antiochus then decided to mount an attack on Larisa. He thought its inhabitants would not continue their obstinate resistance—they would be too afraid after his storming of the other cities, or would feel grateful for his release of their garrison, or would consider the example of all the other states that had voluntarily surrendered. He ordered elephants to be driven before the standards to intimidate the foe, and marched on the city in battle-formation. As a result, the feelings of most of the inhabitants of Larisa wavered between fear of the enemy before them and shame at letting down their absent allies.

At about this time Amynander, at the head of his Athamanian troops, seized Pelinnaeum, and Menippus set off for Perrhaebia with 3,000 Aetolian infantry and 200 cavalry, taking Malloea and Chyretiae by force, and laying waste the farmland of Tripolis. These objectives were swiftly attained, and the two leaders returned to the king at Larisa, where they found him in conference on the question of what should be done about the town. In that meeting opinions were divided. Some were for using force, thinking that the king should lose no time in making a simultaneous assault on the city walls from all directions by means of siege-works and engines; for the town lay on a plain, exposed and easily approachable on every side over level ground. Others observed that the strength of this city was of a very different order from that of the Pheraeans, and also that it was now winter, a time of year not suited for any kind of military activity, least of all for besieging and assaulting cities. The king was wavering between hope and fear when delegates chanced to arrive from Pharsalus to surrender their city, and this raised his spirits.

Meanwhile, Marcus Baebius met Philip in the land of the Dassareti, and following a plan drafted with him sent Appius Claudius to defend Larisa. Claudius traversed Macedonia with forced marches, and arrived on the crest of the mountains overlooking Gonni, a town twenty miles from Larisa and right at the entrance of the pass called Tempe. There he laid out a camp of proportions greater than his forces warranted, and lit more fires than they really needed, giving the enemy the impression he had actually sought to give, namely that the entire Roman army was there, and Philip, too. As a result, the king made the excuse of the †onset† of winter to his men, and waited only a single day before leaving Larisa and returning to Demetrias, while the Aetolians and Athamanians withdrew to their respective territories. Appius could see that the siege had been raised—the purpose of his mission—but he nevertheless went down to Larisa to give the allies reassurance for the future. These had two reasons to feel overjoyed—their enemy had left their lands, and they could also see a Roman garrison within their walls.

11. The king left Demetrias for Chalcis and here fell in love with a young Chalcidian woman, the daughter of Cleoptolemus.* He kept badgering the father, first sending intermediaries and then presenting his suit in person. Cleoptolemus was averse to involvement in a marriage at a level too uncomfortable for him, but Antiochus finally had his way and proceeded to celebrate a wedding, as though peace were established all around. Forgetting the importance of the two causes which he had taken up together, the war with Rome and the liberation of Greece, the king abandoned responsibility for everything, and spent the rest of the winter in dinner-parties, and the pleasures that go along with drinking, and then in sleeping, exhausted by these activities rather than sated with them. All the king's officers in charge of winter-quarters in all areas, but especially in Boeotia, fell victim to the same excesses. Even the rank and file fell into the same ways, with none putting on armour, doing guard duty, keeping the night-watch, or performing any of the regular military duties or responsibilities. So it was that, at the start of spring, when Antiochus came through Phocis to Chaeronea, where he had ordered his entire army to muster from their various quarters, he had no difficulty in recognizing that the men had spent the winter in no stricter discipline than had their commander-in-chief.

Antiochus ordered Alexander the Acarnanian and Menippus the

Macedonian to take the troops from Chaeronea to Stratus in Aetolia;
and he himself, after sacrificing to Apollo at Delphi, advanced to
Naupactus. He held a meeting of the Aetolian chieftains, and then
met his men, who were taking the route along the Malian Gulf, on
the road which leads to Stratus by way of Calydon and Lysimachia.
Here, a leading Acarnanian, Mnasilochus, who had been bought at
the price of numerous bribes, not only used his own influence to try
to win the support of the people for the king, but he had also converted to his own point of view the praetor Clitus, who held the
highest office at the time. Clitus could see that inciting the Leucadians to rebellion against Rome—their city was the capital of
Acarnania—would not be easy, because of their fear of the Roman
fleet, †both the component that was under Atilius and the part† off
Cephallenia. He therefore set out to trick them. He declared in
council that the interior of Acarnania needed protection, and that all
who bore arms should march to Medion and Thyrreum to prevent
these being captured by Antiochus or the Aetolians. There were
some, however, who argued that a disorganized general levy served
no purpose, and that a force of 500 men would suffice. On being
given that contingent of soldiers, Clitus stationed a garrison of 300
at Medion and 200 at Thyrreum, and began to take steps to have
them fall into the king's hands, to be used as hostages later on.

12. In this same period envoys of the king came to Medion and,
after they were granted an audience, the question of the reply to be
given to Antiochus was discussed in council. Some were of the opinion that they should remain faithful to the alliance with Rome, others
that they should not reject the king's overtures of friendship. Clitus
was apparently advocating an intermediate position—which was
therefore adopted—that they send an embassy to the king, asking
him to allow the people of Medion to discuss such an important
matter in the council of the Acarnanians. Mnasilochus and some of
his adherents were deliberately included in this embassy. These sent
secret messages to the king to tell him to bring up his forces, and
then simply played for time. And so, no sooner had the delegation
left than Antiochus was in their country, and shortly afterwards at
their gates. Those having no part in the duplicity panicked and, in
consternation, called the men to arms. Meanwhile Antiochus was let
into the city by Clitus and Mnasilochus. Some flocked to join the
king of their own volition, and even those unsympathetic to him

were driven by fear to throw in their support. Antiochus allayed their fears with conciliatory words, and a number of the peoples of Acarnania went over to him, their hopes aroused by his widely publicized clemency.

Antiochus set off towards Thyrreum from Medion, sending Mnasilochus and some envoys ahead to the town. However, the treachery that had been brought to light at Medion instilled more caution than fear in the people of Thyrreum. They gave the king the forthright answer that they would undertake no fresh alliance without the authorization of the Roman generals, shut their gates and placed armed guards on their walls. By a stroke of very good fortune, Gnaeus Octavius arrived in Leucas to bolster the resolution of the Acarnanians, filling the allies with hope by reporting that Manius Acilius had already crossed the sea with his legions and that a Roman camp had already been established in Thessaly. (Octavius had been sent by Quinctius and had received a body of troops and a few ships from Aulus Postumius, who had been put in charge of Cephallenia by the legate Atilius.) This rumour was given credence by the fact that it was now a seasonable time of year for sailing. The king, therefore, established a garrison at Medion and in a number of other towns in Acarnania, left Thyrreum, and went back to Chalcis by way of the cities of Aetolia and Phocis.

13. Marcus Baebius and Philip had already met in the wintertime in the land of the Dassareti—the time when they had sent Appius Claudius into Thessaly to raise the siege of Larisa—but because it was still too early in the year for military operations they had returned to their winter-quarters. Now, at about this time, since it was beginning of spring, they joined forces and came down into Thessaly. At that point Antiochus was in Acarnania. On their arrival, Philip assaulted Malloea in Perrhaebia, and Baebius attacked Phacium. Capturing Phacium with his first onslaught, Baebius then took Phaustus with equal swiftness. Turning back to Atrax from there, he next seized Chyretiae and Ericinium and, after placing garrisons in the captured towns, rejoined Philip who was besieging Malloea. At the approach of the Roman army, the inhabitants of Malloea capitulated, either fearing the strength of the enemy or hoping for clemency, and the two leaders went ahead in a single column to recover the cities which the Athamanians had seized. (The cities in question were: Aeginium, Ericinium, Gomphi, Silana, Tricca, Meliboea, and

Phaloria.) The two next surrounded Pelinnaeum, where Philip of Megalopolis was in command of a garrison of 500 infantry and 40 cavalry, and before making their assault, they sent a delegation to Philip to caution him against resisting to the last. He made the truculent reply that he would have entrusted himself to either the Romans or the Thessalians, but he would not put himself in Philip's hands. It was clear that forceful action had to be taken and, because a simultaneous attack on Limnaeum seemed a possibility, it was decided that the king should proceed to Limnaeum while Baebius stayed behind for the assault on Pelinnaeum.

14. The consul Manius Acilius had now completed his sea-crossing with 10,000 infantry, 2,000 cavalry, and 15 elephants, and it so happened that at about this time he ordered the military tribunes to lead his infantry to Larisa, while he himself came with the cavalry to Philip at Limnaeum. At the consul's approach the town capitulated without hesitation, and the king's garrison, along with the Athamanians, surrendered to him. From Limnaeum the consul advanced to Pelinnaeum. There the Athamanians were the first to surrender, followed by Philip of Megalopolis. As the latter was leaving the garrison, King Philip happened to meet him. To poke fun at him, he ordered him be saluted as a king,* and he personally came up to him and addressed him as 'brother', a quip truly inappropriate to his royal station. The Megalopolitan was then brought before the consul, who issued orders for him to be kept under guard, and shortly afterwards he was sent to Rome in irons. The horde of remaining prisoners—Athamanians and soldiers of Antiochus who had garrisoned the towns that surrendered in that period—was delivered to Philip, some 3,000 men. The consul then set off for Larisa to hold discussions on general strategy for the war, and on the journey he was met by delegations from Cierium and Metropolis, come to surrender their cities.

Philip was especially indulgent with the Athamanian prisoners-of-war, in order to win the support of their people through them; and having conceived the hope of gaining control of Athamania, he now led his army there, after first sending ahead the prisoners to their various city-states. The prisoners did have a profound influence on their compatriots with their talk of the king's clemency towards themselves and his open-handedness. Amynander might perhaps have kept some of them loyal by his authoritative presence had he remained; but, frightened that he would be delivered to Philip, an enemy of long standing, or to the Romans, justly angry with him because of his desertion, he left the kingdom with his wife and children, and went into Ambracia. Thus all Athamania fell under Philip's authority and control.

The consul waited a few days at Larisa, mainly for the purpose of resting the pack-animals, exhausted from the sea-voyage and the land-journeys that followed. He then advanced towards Crannon with an army which he now judged restored by its brief repose. While he was on his way, Pharsalus, Scotusa and Pherae surrendered, along with the garrisons of Antiochus stationed in them. Acilius asked which prisoners chose to remain with him, and handed over to Philip 1,000 who wished to do so; the others he disarmed and sent to Demetrias. He next took Proerna and its surrounding strongholds, and then began to march towards the Malian Gulf. As he was approaching the gorge above which Thaumaci lies, all the men of military age armed themselves, left the town, took up positions for ambush in the woods and along the roads, and from the higher ground made attacks on the Roman column. At first the consul sent intermediaries to speak to them face to face to dissuade them from such lunacy; but when he saw they were determined to continue, he sent a tribune around them with the soldiers of two maniples, shut off access to the city to the enemy soldiers, and captured the now-undefended town. When they heard the shouting from the captured city to their rear, the men in ambush fled in all directions from the woods and were slaughtered. The next day the consul came from Thaumaci to the River Spercheus, and then raided the farmlands of Hypata.

15. At the time of these events, Antiochus was at Chalcis, finally coming to see that all he had gained from Greece was a winter pleasantly spent in Chalcis and a disreputable marriage. He now excoriated the Aetolians for their empty promises, and he rebuked Thoas; but he was full of admiration for Hannibal, not merely as a man of sound judgment but almost as a prophet of all that was then taking place. Not to ruin his reckless endeavour further by inactivity, he sent messengers to Aetolia with instructions for the Aetolians to mobilize all their fighting men and meet him at Lamia, and he himself led to that city about 10,000 infantry (their number having been augmented by troops that had subsequently arrived from Asia) and

500 cavalry. The Aetolians who assembled here did so in considerably smaller numbers than on any previous occasion, and were represented only by their leading men and a few dependants. They claimed that they had done their best to call out as many as possible from their communities, but that their influence, their standing, and their authority all proved ineffectual against those refusing to serve. Antiochus was thus left deserted on every side—by his own men who were malingering in Asia, and also by his allies who were not providing the support which they had led him to expect when they had asked him to come—and he fell back into the pass of Thermopylae.

As Italy is divided by the chain of the Apennines, so the mountain range here splits Greece in two. Before the pass of Thermopylae are Epirus, Perrhaebia, Magnesia, and Thessaly, as well as Pthiotic Achaea and the Malian Gulf, all of them facing north. On the other side of the pass, to the south, lie most of Aetolia, Acarnania, Phocis together with Locris, and Boeotia with its adjoining island, Euboea, and the land of Attica (on a kind of promontory which juts out to sea), along with the Peloponnese, lying behind these. The range extends from Leucas and the western sea through Aetolia to the other sea which lies to the east, and at points the terrain is so craggy and precipitously steep that it is not easy for lightly equipped men, much less an army, to find paths affording a way across. The mountains at the eastern extremity are called Oeta, and the highest of these is named Callidromus. In the Callidromus valley, at the point where it approaches the Malian Gulf, there is a passage no more than sixty paces wide. This is the only road suitable for an army, a point where forces could be led through if they met no opposition. For that reason the place is called Pylae—Thermopylae by others, because there are hot-springs right within the pass—and it is renowned for the deaths of the Spartans in the struggle against Persia,* deaths more famous than the engagement which was fought there.

16. It was with feelings very different from those of the Spartans that Antiochus now pitched his camp within the 'Gates' of the place and used defence-works to make it even more impenetrable. He threw up a barricade to protect the entire position—a double rampart, a ditch, and, where required, even a wall made of the numerous stones lying around the area. Confident that the Roman army would

never force its way through this barrier, he sent some of the 4,000 Aetolians who had congregated there to serve as a garrison to secure Heraclea, which lay right before the pass, and the others he sent to Hypata. He was convinced that the consul would attack Heraclea, and many reports were already coming in of widespread raids being conducted in the area of Hypata.

The consul laid waste the fields of Hypata first, then those of Heraclea, the Aetolians providing effective assistance to neither, and then encamped within the pass itself, in a position close to the hot springs and facing the king. The two Aetolian forces barricaded themselves in Heraclea.

Before he set eyes on his enemy, Antiochus had thought the entire position was strongly enough fortified and well secured by his guard-posts. Now, however, he was overtaken by a fear that the Romans might find some paths over the hills dominating the pass that would let them through—for it was said that this was how the Spartans had once been encircled by the Persians and, more recently, Philip by these same Romans.* He therefore sent a message to the Aetolians at Heraclea, asking them at least to provide this one piece of assistance for him in the war-effort, namely to seize and occupy the mountain peaks in the vicinity, to prevent the Romans from making their way over them. When the Aetolians received the message, an argument arose amongst them. Some thought they should accede to the king's request and go. Others felt they should remain at Heraclea ready to respond to either outcome: should the king be defeated by the consul, they would have at their disposal fresh troops to bring assistance to their own cities in the vicinity and, if he were victorious, they could chase the Romans when they scattered in flight. The two sides not only remained firm in their opinions but actually acted on their views. Two thousand men stayed on at Heraclea; 2,000 others formed three groups and seized Callidromus, Rhoduntia, and Tichius, as the peaks were called.

17. When he saw that the heights were held by the Aetolians, the consul sent Marcus Porcius Cato and Lucius Valerius Flaccus, his legates of consular rank, each with 2,000 hand-picked men, to the fortified positions of the Aetolians, Flaccus to Rhoduntia and Tichius, and Cato to Callidromus. Before moving his troops ahead against the enemy, he himself summoned the men to a meeting and briefly addressed them as follows:

'Men: I see that there are among you a large number—soldiers of all ranks—who fought in this province under the leadership and auspices of Titus Quinctius. In the Macedonian war, the pass at the River Aous was more difficult to get through than this one. For here there are gates and, with the whole terrain blocked, only one naturally formed passageway, as it were, between the two seas. On that earlier occasion the defences of the enemy were more favourably situated for them, and more firmly established. That enemy army was numerically superior and also had a considerably better quality of soldier; for at the Aous there were Macedonians, Thracians, and Illyrians, all highly aggressive peoples, and here there are Syrians and Asiatic Greeks, the dregs of humanity, born to be slaves.* The king facing us then was a great warrior, who had been trained from boyhood in wars against his Thracian and Illyrian neighbours, and all the other peoples inhabiting the region. In this king you have a man who, to say nothing of the rest of his life, crossed from Asia to Europe to make war on the Roman people, and has throughout the entire period of the winter done nothing more significant than to get married for love—and to a woman from the household of an ordinary individual, and a family of no distinction even amongst her compatriots! And now he has come out to fight, a new bridegroom, almost bloated with his wedding feasts!

'Antiochus' greatest strength and hope lay in the Aetolians, a vain and fickle people, as you have learned before him and he is learning now. They have not come in large numbers; they could not be made to stay in their camp; they are arguing amongst themselves; and, after demanding that Hypata and Heraclea be defended, they failed to defend either and fled to the mountain-tops, some of them shutting themselves up in Heraclea.

'The king himself has clearly acknowledged that he cannot risk even an encampment in the open, let alone a battle on level ground. He has abandoned all that area that lay before him, which he would boast he had taken from us and from Philip, and he has buried himself amongst the rocks. And not even at the opening to the pass, as they say the Spartans once did—no, he has brought his camp back into the depths of it. In terms of showing funk, what is the difference between doing this and shutting oneself up within the walls of a city to face a siege? But Antiochus is not going to be protected by the narrow pass, nor the Aetolians by the hilltops which they have

seized. Enough care and precaution has been taken in every quarter
to see that in the battle all that you will have against you is the enemy.

'This is what you should keep at the front of your minds. You are
not simply fighting for the independence of Greece, though that
would also be a fine enterprise—to free now from the Aetolians and
Antiochus a country which you earlier freed from Philip. And it is
not only what can now be found in the king's camp that will fall to
you as your prize—you will also have as your booty all the equipment that is expected any day from Ephesus. After that you will open
up to Roman domination Asia, Syria, and all the wealthy kingdoms
stretching as far as the rising sun. How far will we be then from
having our empire, from Gades to the Red Sea, limited only by the
Ocean that embraces the world? How far from having the entire
human race revere the Roman name only after the gods? Prepare
your spirits and make them deserving of such great rewards, so that
tomorrow, with the gracious help of the gods, we may decide the
issue on the field of battle.'

18. Dismissed from the assembly, and before taking food and rest,
the men made ready their armour and weapons. At dawn the consul
displayed the signal for battle and drew up his battle-line, with a
narrow front, as was required by the limitations of the area's natural
features. When the king saw the enemy standards he also led out
his forces. Some of his light infantry he deployed in the front line
before the rampart, and then, as his mainstay, he set his powerful
'Macedonian' unit, called the 'sarisophori',* around the actual
defence-works. To support these, on the left flank, he placed a unit
of javelin-throwers, archers, and slingers, right at the foot of the
mountains, so they could put pressure on the unprotected flank of
the enemy from the higher ground. To the right of the 'Macedonians', where the fortifications actually terminated, but where the
position was blocked by marshland and bogs (making it impassable
right down to the sea), he placed his elephants, with the guard that
usually attended them. Behind these he stationed his cavalry and, a
short distance behind them, the rest of his troops in a second line.

The 'Macedonians' stationed before the rampart at first found it
easy to parry the attack of the Romans as these tried at all points to
open up a breach, and they were considerably aided by the men with
the slings on the higher ground who hurled down a veritable shower
of lead balls and arrows, as well as javelins. Then, as the enemy

pressure mounted to the point of being irresistible, they were dislodged from their position and, pulling back their ranks, retreated within their fortifications. There, from the rampart, they made what almost constituted a second rampart by extending their spears before them. In addition, the breast-work was of such limited height that, while it offered the defenders a higher position from which to fight, it also enabled them to keep the enemy within reach of their long spears. Many who recklessly ventured up to the rampart were impaled by these, and the Romans would have withdrawn in failure, or suffered heavier losses, but for Marcus Porcius. He drove the Aetolians down from the crest of Callidromus, killing most of them—he had taken them by surprise, a large number of them still sleeping—and appeared on the hill overlooking the camp.

19. (Flaccus had not met with the same success at Tichius and Rhoduntia, and had been unsuccessful in his efforts to reach these strongholds.)

At first all that could be seen in the distance was a body of men on the march, and the 'Macedonians' and the others in the king's camp assumed that these were the Aetolians, that they had seen the battle in the distance and were now coming to help. As soon as they recognized the standards and armour at close quarters, however, and their mistake was made clear to them, they were all instantly overtaken by such panic that they threw down their weapons and fled. The pursuers were impeded both by the defence-works and the narrowness of the valley through which the pursuit had to be conducted, but above all by the presence of the elephants in the enemy rear line— infantrymen found getting past them difficult, and cavalrymen found it impossible because the horses took fright,* and created greater turmoil amongst themselves than they had amongst the enemy in the battle. Plundering the camp also took a certain amount of time. Even so, on that day, they chased the enemy as far as Scarphia. On the way they inflicted heavy casualties and took many prisoners, killing not just horses and men but also elephants that they had been unable to capture. They then returned to camp. The camp had been attacked that day—while the battle was actually in progress—by the Aetolians who formed the garrison occupying Heraclea, but their ambitious enterprise had proved unsuccessful.

At the third watch of the following night the consul sent his cavalry ahead to give chase to the enemy, and at dawn moved his legions forward. The king had covered some distance, since he had not halted his headlong flight before reaching Elatia. Here he brought together those who had survived the battle and the flight, and retreated to Chalcis with a mere handful of poorly armed soldiers. The Roman cavalry did not in fact overtake the king himself at Elatia, but they did catch most of those in his column, men who stopped from fatigue, or became dispersed after losing their way, as was to be expected with people fleeing without guides on roads they did not know. In fact, not one person escaped from the entire army, with the exception of the 500 who formed the king's retinue, a tiny fraction even of a total of 10,000 soldiers, which is the number I gave above (following Polybius,*) as being that which the king brought across to Greece with him. Imagine if we accept Valerius Antias' account that there were 60,000 men in the king's army, that 40,000 of them lost their lives, and that more than 5,000 were captured, along with 230 military standards! One hundred and fifty Romans were killed actually fighting in the battle, and no more than 50 were killed defending themselves in the assault made by the Aetolians.

20. As the consul was leading his army through Phocis and Boeotia, the inhabitants of the communities in the region stood before their gates with suppliant olive-branches, conscience-stricken over their defection and fearful of being plundered as enemies. But during that entire period the Roman column marched ahead as if the countryside were pacified, and inflicted no damage at all until its arrival in the territory of Coronea. Here a statue of Antiochus that had been erected in the temple of Minerva Itonia made tempers flare, and the soldiers were given leave to lay waste the countryside around the temple. The thought then struck Acilius that savage reprisals against the territory of Coronea alone were unwarranted, since the statue had been erected by a communal decision of the people of Boeotia. The men were immediately called back, and the pillaging was stopped. The Boeotians were merely reprimanded for their ingratitude towards the Romans after all the benefits so recently conferred on them.

While the battle was actually in progress, ten of the king's ships, commanded by Isidorus, lay at anchor off Thronium in the Malian gulf. To these Alexander the Acarnanian came in his flight. He was severely wounded, and he brought news of the defeat, unnerving the fleet which, in the initial panic, headed for Cenaeum in Euboea. Here Alexander died and was buried. Three ships from Asia which had put in at the same port returned to Ephesus on hearing of the defeat of the land-army, and Isidorus crossed from Cenaeum to Demetrias, on the off-chance that the king's flight might take him there.

About this same time the admiral of the Roman fleet, Aulus Atilius, intercepted a large convoy of provisions belonging to the king which had crossed the strait close to the island of Andros. He sank some of the ships and captured others, and those at the rear turned back towards Asia. Atilius returned to Piraeus, the point from which he had set out, with his contingent of captured vessels, and distributed large quantities of grain to the Athenians as well as to other allies in the region.

21. As the consul drew near, Antiochus left Chalcis, first steering a course for Tenos, and then crossing to Ephesus. On reaching Chalcis, the consul found the gates open since the king's prefect, Aristoteles, had left the city at his approach. The other cities of Euboea also capitulated without a struggle, and a few days later, when a state of peace had been restored everywhere with no damage inflicted on any city, the army was brought back to Thermopylae—more praiseworthy for its moderation after the victory than for the victory itself.

From Thermopylae, the consul dispatched Marcus Cato to Rome so the Senate and people of Rome could be informed of the events from a reliable source. Cato made for Patrae in Achaea, setting out from Creusa,* a commercial port of the Thespians that lies in the inner reaches of the Corinthian Gulf. From Patrae he passed along the coastline of Aetolia and Acarnania as far as Corcyra, and then crossed to Hydrus in Italy. Four days later, after an overland journey conducted at a flying pace, he reached Rome. He entered the city before dawn, and headed from the gate to the praetor Marcus Iunius.

Iunius summoned the Senate at break of day. Lucius Cornelius Scipio had been sent to Rome by the consul some days before, but on his arrival he was told that Cato had outpaced him* and was now in the Senate. Scipio therefore came there himself, arriving just when Cato was giving an account of the events. The two officers were then brought before the popular assembly by order of the Senate, and here they gave the same report on events in Aetolia as they had given in the Senate. A three-day period of public prayer was decreed, and the praetor was to sacrifice forty full-grown victims to gods of his own choosing.

It was also at about this time that Marcus Fulvius Nobilior, who had set out for Spain two years earlier as praetor, entered the city with an ovation. He had 130,000 coins stamped with the *biga* carried before him and, in addition to the cash, 12,000 pounds of silver and 127 pounds of gold.

22. From Thermopylae the consul Acilius sent a message to the Aetolians in Heraclea. They now had personal experience of the king's ineptitude, he told them, and they should finally come to their senses, deliver Heraclea to him and consider asking the Senate to pardon what had been an act of folly, or an error of judgement, on their part. The other states of Greece had, in that war, also broken faith with the Romans, who had deserved well of them, said Acilius. They had reneged on their duty from confidence in the king, but after his flight they had not compounded their blunder by obstinacy, and had therefore been taken back under Roman protection. In the case of the Aetolians, they had not followed the king, but had actually invited him to Greece, and had been leaders in the war, not merely allies. But if they could bring themselves to show remorse, they too could be out of harm's way. The response to these overtures indicated no conciliatory attitude, and it was evident that military action had to be taken, and that, though the king was defeated, the war with the Aetolians was still only at its beginning. Acilius moved his camp from Thermopylae to Heraclea, and on the very same day rode around the walls on every side to ascertain how the city was laid out.

Heraclea lies at the foot of Mt. Oeta; it is in a plain itself, but possesses a citadel which rises above it on a lofty elevation, sheer on all sides. After thoroughly reconnoitring the essential features of the town, Acilius decided to attack the city at four points simultaneously. On the side of the River Asopus, where there is also a gymnasium, he gave Lucius Valerius command over the siege-works and the assault. The attack on the †citadel outside the walls† which was more densely populated than the city itself, he entrusted to Tiberius Sempronius Longus. On the side of the Malian Gulf, which did not afford easy access, he placed Marcus Baebius; and on the side of the other small river, called the Melas, and opposite the temple of Artemis, he set Appius Claudius. These men were in keen competition and within a matter of days the towers, battering-rams, and all the other machinery for besieging towns were completed. All the land around Heraclea is boggy and thickly forested with tall trees, and so offered a wealth of timber for all kinds of construction. The Aetolians, moreover, had sought refuge within their walls, and the houses which they had abandoned at the entrance to the city furnished tiles, cut stones, and rocks of various sizes, as well as beams and planks, that could be variously used by the Romans.

23. The Roman offensive against the city was being conducted more by means of siege-works than armed assault, whereas the Aetolians relied on their arms to defend themselves. When the walls were being shaken by the battering-ram, rather than resorting to the usual tactic of deflecting the blows with the use of lassos, they would make repeated counter-attacks in armed groups, some also carrying torches to throw on the siege-works. There were, moreover, vaulted arches in the wall, designed for making sorties, and when the Aetolians were building a wall to replace one that had been demolished, they would make more of these arches so that forays against the enemy could be made at a greater number of points. In the early days of the siege, while their strength was intact, they did this often and with vigour, but as the days passed they did so less often and less energetically. For while they had many problems to contend with, nothing sapped their strength more than the lack of sleep. The Romans, with their large numbers of troops, had men replacing each other on guard-duty, but because of their limited numbers the Aetolians were ground down by the unremitting hardships facing the same men day and night. For twenty-four days they were confronted with a struggle that went on day and night, with no time away from the conflict, as they faced an enemy attacking them simultaneously on four fronts.

The consul was aware that the Aetolians were now exhausted—he surmised this from the time the siege had lasted, and he also had reports to that effect from deserters—and he adopted the following plan. In the middle of the night he gave the signal to retreat and, after bringing back all his men from the assault at the one time, he kept them inactive in camp until the third hour of the day. At this point the offensive was resumed, and continued again until the middle of the night, when it was once more suspended until the third hour of the day. The Aetolians assumed that the reason for the failure to continue the assault was fatigue, which had also been causing them distress, and when the signal had been given for the Romans to retire, they would all leave their posts themselves, as if they too had been recalled by the signal. They would not reappear in arms on the walls until the third hour of the day.

24. After discontinuing the assault at midnight, the consul once more at the fourth watch mounted a fierce attack on three of the sides, ordering Tiberius Sempronius to hold his men at the ready on the one remaining side and to await his signal. Acilius was sure that, in the confusion of the night, the enemy would converge on the points from which the shouting would be heard. Some of the Aetolians had been asleep, and were now trying to rouse themselves from their slumber, exhausted as they were from their exertions and lack of sleep; the others, who had remained awake, were running in the darkness towards the noise of the fighting. Some of their enemy were attempting to clamber over the ruins where the wall had collapsed, others trying to scale the wall with ladders. The Aetolians bore down on them from all over the town to help repel the attack. The one side, the area of the buildings outside the city proper, was neither being defended nor attacked, but men ready to launch the attack were waiting for the signal, and there was no one there to defend it.

Dawn was already breaking when the consul gave the signal. Meeting no resistance, some of the men climbed over the half-demolished walls, and others used ladders to scale those that were intact. At the same time, the shout that signals the capture of a city was heard, and the Aetolians, everywhere abandoning their posts, fled to the citadel. The victors pillaged the town with the consul's leave, given not from anger or animosity, but rather so that the soldiers who had been kept in check when so many cities had been wrested from enemy hands might somewhere finally taste the fruits of their victory.

About midday Acilius recalled his soldiers and split them into two groups. One he ordered to be taken around the foot of the mountain to a cliff which was of the same elevation as the citadel, but separated from it by a sort of ravine that lay between them. The top parts of both eminences were so close to each other that weapons could be hurled at the citadel from the other height. With the second half of his men, the consul was going to ascend the citadel from the city, and he was waiting for a signal from the men who were to appear on the cliff to the enemy rear. The Aetolians on the citadel buckled before the shouts of the men who had taken the cliff, and then before the assault of the Romans from the city. Their spirit was now broken, and no preparations had been made in the spot for further resistance to the siege: women, children, and a host of others not involved in the fighting had been herded into the citadel, which could barely contain such a crowd, much less offer it protection. So it was that at the first attack the Aetolians threw down their arms and surrendered. Amongst those delivered to the Romans was the leading Aetolian, Damocritus, who, at the start of the war, when Titus Quinctius asked for the decree of the Aetolians by which they had voted to bring Antiochus to Greece, had replied that he would give it to him in Italy when the Aetolians had established their camp* there. This bluster of his made Damocritus' surrender all the more pleasing to the victors.

25. At the same time as the Romans were assaulting Heraclea, Philip, as had been prearranged, was attacking Lamia. Philip had met the consul near Thermopylae, as Acilius was returning from Boeotia—he wished to congratulate the Roman people and Acilius personally on their victory, and to explain that illness had prevented him from taking part in the war* against Antiochus. They had then set off in different directions to make their assaults on the two cities. The cities are about seven miles apart, and as Lamia is situated on a hill, and also has a clear view of the district about Oeta, the distance between the two seems very short indeed, and both are completely visible to each other.

The Romans and Macedonians were exerting themselves day and night on the siege-works or in the fighting, as though competing with each other, but it was the Macedonians who faced the harder task. The Romans were conducting their offensive with a mound, siege-shelters, and all manner of works that were above the ground; but the Macedonians were conducting theirs underground with tunnels, and in the difficult spots they were confronted with flint that could barely be penetrated by iron. The operation making little headway, the king parleyed with the leading citizens of Lamia, trying to induce them to surrender the city; for he was convinced that, if Heraclea were taken first, the Lamians would choose to capitulate to the Romans rather than to him, and the consul would win the credit for raising the siege. And Philip was not mistaken in his thinking. A message telling him to abandon the siege came to him immediately after the capture of Heraclea; it was fairer for the Roman soldiers who had fought the Aetolians in the field to have the prizes of victory, he was told. Philip accordingly withdrew from Lamia, and its inhabitants, because of the misfortunes that befell the neighbouring city, escaped a like fate themselves.

26. A few days before the capture of Heraclea the Aetolians held a council meeting at Hypata and then sent an embassy to Antiochus which included the same Thoas who had gone on the previous embassy. The envoys' instructions were to ask the king first of all to bring together once more his land- and sea-forces, and cross to Greece in person; if anything held him back, they were next to ask him to send money and military assistance. Not letting down his allies was a matter affecting his dignity and honour, they said; but making sure that the Romans, relieved of all concerns after they had destroyed the Aetolians, should not cross to Greece with all their forces also affected the security of his realm. Their observations were correct, and thus impressed the king all the more. As a temporary measure he gave the ambassadors the moneys required to defray the costs of the war, declaring that he would send them reinforcements of land- and naval forces. Of the ambassadors he detained only Thoas, and Thoas had no objection to staying behind, so that someone should be on the spot to oversee the king's commitments.

27. However, the capture of Heraclea finally broke the Aetolians' spirit. A few days after sending the embassy to Asia to recommence hostilities and bring over the king, they abandoned their plans for war, and sent spokesmen to the consul to ask for peace. The spokesmen had begun their address when the consul interrupted them. He had other things which required his attention first, he told them, and he bade them return to Hypata under a ten-day truce. He sent with them Lucius Valerius Flaccus, and instructed them to lay before Flaccus the matters they were going to discuss with Acilius himself, and any other issues they wished to raise. On reaching Hypata, the leading Aetolians held a meeting with Flaccus on the question of how they should handle matters with the consul. They were preparing to lead off with old treaty obligations, and the services they had rendered the Roman people, but Flaccus told them to steer clear of compacts which they themselves had violated and broken. An admission of culpability, and an address turning entirely on appeals for mercy, would do them more good, he said, for their hopes for safety

lay not in the strength of their case but in the clemency of the Roman people. If they †adopted a supplicatory demeanour, he said, he would help them†, both before the consul and in the Senate at Rome, where they would also have to send a delegation. It seemed to all present that the only road to safety lay in unconditional surrender to the Romans. In this way the Aetolians would ensure that the Romans would be ashamed to maltreat suppliants, and at the same time they would have no less control over their own fate if fortune offered them something better.

28. When the Aetolians appeared before the consul, the leader of the delegation, Phaeneas, launched into a long disquisition composed various turns of speech designed to soothe the victor's anger, and finally ended by saying that the Aetolians surrendered themselves and all their possessions unconditionally to the Roman people. When the consul heard this, he said: 'Men of Aetolia, consider very, very carefully what surrender on such terms means.' Phaeneas thereupon showed him the decree in which the Aetolian decision was clearly worded.

'Since you surrender on these terms, then,' said the consul, 'I demand that you immediately hand over to me your fellow-citizen Dicaearchus, the Epirote Menestas' (Menestas had gone into Naupactus with a garrison and forced the town to rebel), 'and Amynander, along with the leading Athamanians on whose advice you defected from us.' Phaeneas almost interrupted the Roman in mid-sentence. 'What we did was surrender, not put ourselves in slavery,' he said. 'And I am sure your mistake in giving us orders not in accord with Greek convention arises simply from your unfamiliarity with it.' To which the consul replied: 'Good God, I really do not much care what Aetolians consider is done in accordance with Greek convention. *I* am following Roman convention in asserting my authority over men who just now surrendered to me by their own decree, and who had earlier been defeated in war. So, if my order is not swiftly carried out, I shall have you clapped in irons.' He ordered the lictors to bring chains and stand around the Aetolian delegation. With that the bluster of Phaeneas and the other Aetolians was cut short, and they finally became aware of the predicament they were in. Phaeneas declared that he and the other Aetolians present knew that they were obliged to carry out Acilius' orders, but to ratify the conditions there had to be a meeting of the Aetolian council, and for that he was requesting that Acilius grant him a ten-day truce. Flaccus interceded for the Aetolians, the truce was accorded, and the envoys returned to Hypata. In a meeting of the select committee called the 'apocleti', Phaeneas gave an account of the orders they had received and the fate that had almost overtaken them. The Aetolian leaders lamented the situation in which they found themselves, but none the less voted to follow the victor's orders, and to summon the Aetolian people from all their towns to a general assembly.

29. However, when the entire assembly convened and heard the same report, the severity of the commands and the humiliation they entailed made the Aetolians so indignant that, had they been at peace, the surge of anger they felt could have pushed them to war. Apart from their anger, there was also the problem of the conditions imposed on them—for how on earth could they possibly deliver Amynander? They were also, by chance, offered some hope by the fact that Nicander, coming from Antiochus at that very time, filled the Aetolian commons with the mistaken belief that a war of immense proportions was being set in motion on land and sea.

Nicander had completed his mission, and returning to Aetolia put in at Phalara on the Malian Gulf, eleven days after he had first embarked. From there he brought Antiochus' money to Lamia, and he was later heading for Hypata with a retinue of light-armed men over paths which he knew when, early in the evening, he stumbled upon a Macedonian outpost, in the countryside between the Macedonian and Roman camps. He was brought to the king, who had not yet terminated his dinner-party. When Nicander's arrival was reported to him, Philip reacted as if it was a guest, not an enemy, who had come. He told Nicander to recline and take dinner, and then kept him behind after sending the other guests away. He told him not to have any fears about his own safety, and went on to criticize the ill-conceived plans of the Aetolians, which always backfired on them, for bringing first the Romans, and then Antiochus, into Greece. But he would forget the past, he said, which it was easier to criticize than to put right, and would not take any measures that would slight the Aetolians in their hour of adversity. They, too, he continued, should finally bring their animosity towards him to an end, and Nicander ought to bear in mind personally that day on which his life had been saved by Philip. The king then gave him men to escort him to a safe zone, and Nicander arrived at Hypata when the Aetolians were discussing the peace with Rome.

30. Manius Acilius sold off, or gave to his men, the booty taken around Heraclea. He was then informed that the decisions taken at Hypata were not for peace, and that the Aetolians had speedily assembled at Naupactus, where they intended to bear the full brunt of the war. He thereupon sent Appius Claudius ahead with 4,000 men to seize the heights where the mountains could, with difficulty, be crossed. Acilius himself climbed Oeta, and sacrificed to Hercules at the place called Pyra, so named because it was where the mortal body of the god was cremated.* Setting off from there with the entire army, he completed the rest of the journey with no real problems. When they arrived at Corax—the highest mountain between Callipolis and Naupactus—a large number of pack-animals plummeted from the train, along with their loads, and the men also found themselves in difficulty. The slackness of the enemy they were facing was immediately apparent, for these had not placed any kind of patrol in such a difficult pass to bar their crossing. Even as it was the army experienced severe distress. Acilius now went down to Naupactus. He established a single post opposite the citadel, and blockaded the other areas of the city, dividing his troops as the lay-out of its fortifications demanded. And besieging this town required as much effort and exertion as had the siege of Heraclea.

31. At the same time as this the siege of Messene in the Peloponnese began, mounted by the Achaeans because Messene refused to join their League. Two states, Messene and Elis, remained outside the league, sympathizing as they did with the Aetolians. After Antiochus had been chased from Greece, however, the Eleans had been more moderate in their response to the Achaean delegates; they said that, once the king's garrison was removed, they would then consider what course of action to take. The Messenians had simply dismissed the delegates without a response, and opened hostilities. Then, when their lands were burned in various places by a wide-ranging army, and when they saw an Achaean camp being established near the city, they became apprehensive of the plight in which they found themselves. They sent envoys to Titus Quinctius, the architect of their freedom, at Chalcis, to report that the Messenians were ready to open their gates and surrender their city to the Romans, but not to the Achaeans. After hearing the envoys,

Quinctius immediately set out from Chalcis, and from Megalopolis he sent a messenger to the chief magistrate of the Achaeans, Diophanes, to tell him to withdraw his army from Messene immediately, and come to see him. Obeying the order, Diophanes raised the siege and, going ahead of his column lightly equipped, met Quinctius in the neighbourhood of Andania, a small town situated between Megalopolis and Messene. When Diophanes explained the reasons for the siege, Quinctius gently reprimanded him for having embarked on an enterprise of such importance without his approval, and then instructed him to demobilize his army and refrain from disturbing a peace that had been settled for everyone's benefit. The people of Messene he ordered to recall their exiles and join the Achaean league, adding that they should come to see him at Corinth if there were points on which they demurred, or on which they wanted safeguards for the future, and he ordered Diophanes to give him an immediate audience at the council of the Achaeans.

At this meeting, Quinctius protested against the treacherous seizure of Zacynthus, and demanded it be restored to the Romans. Zacynthus had belonged to Philip of Macedon, and Philip had ceded it to Amynander as an inducement to let him take his army through Athamania to the upper reaches of Aetolia—the expedition that broke the spirit of the Aetolians and forced them to sue for peace. Amynander put Philip of Megalopolis in charge of the island but later, when Amynander joined forces with Antiochus against the Romans, he recalled Philip to serve in the war, and sent Hierocles of Agrigentum to succeed him.

32. After Antiochus fled from Thermopylae, and Amynander was driven from Athamania by Philip, Hierocles on his own initiative sent messengers to Diophanes, praetor of the Achaeans, and made a financial settlement with him by which he ceded the island to the Achaeans. The Romans believed that it was rightly theirs as a prize of war for, they said, it was not for the benefit of Diophanes and the Achaeans that the consul Manius Acilius and the Roman legions had fought at Thermopylae. In response, Diophanes at one moment tried to justify himself and his people, and at the next to discuss the legality of the transaction. A number of the Achaeans declared that they had objected to the business from the beginning, and they now reproached their praetor for his intransigence. At their suggestion it was decided that the matter be referred to Titus Quinctius.

Quinctius was hard on people who opposed him, but if one deferred to him he was also easily appeased. His voice and his expression softening, he said: 'If I considered the possession of this island to be in the interests of the Achaeans, I would recommend to the Senate and people of Rome that they allow you to keep it. But you are like the tortoise. When she is completely withdrawn into her shell, I can see that she is secure against all attacks but, when she puts forth some of her limbs, whatever she has exposed is vulnerable and weak. Similarly you, men of Achaea, enclosed as you are on all sides by the sea, can easily annex all that lies within the bounds of the Peloponnese and easily protect it once it is annexed; but once greed for further acquisitions makes you overstep those bounds, you will find that everything outside them is unprotected and exposed to all manner of attack.' The entire meeting agreed with him and, since Diophanes did not dare continue his opposition, Zacynthus was ceded to the Romans.

33. About the same time the consul was setting out for Naupactus, and Philip asked him if he wished the king to recover in the mean time the cities which had abandoned the Roman alliance. When the consul agreed to this, Philip moved his forces ahead to Demetrias, well aware of the chaotic situation in the town at the time. The people had lost all hope. They could see they had been abandoned by Antiochus, and that they had nothing to hope for from the Aetolians; and day and night they were awaiting the arrival of their enemy, Philip, or the Romans, even more implacable foes inasmuch as their anger was more justified. There was in Demetrias an unruly group of Antiochus' soldiers. At first just a few had been left in the garrison, but their numbers grew as men were brought there in flight after the defeat. These were mostly without weapons, and had neither the strength nor the spirit to face a siege. Men were therefore sent ahead by Philip, and because these indicated that the soldiers could hope for mercy, the response of Antiochus' men was that the gates were open to the king. When Philip first entered, a number of the leading citizens left the city and Eurylochus committed suicide. The soldiers of Antiochus were taken through Macedonia and Thrace to Lysimachia—for that was the bargain which they had struck—escorted by Macedonians to prevent any harm coming to them. There were also a few ships at Demetrias under the command of Isidorus, and these were also allowed to leave with their admiral.

After that Philip recovered Dolopia, Aperantia and a number of cities of Perrhaebia.

34. While Philip was involved in this, Titus Quinctius left the Achaean council, after gaining Zacynthus, and crossed to Naupactus. Naupactus had already been under siege for two months—and was now on the verge of collapse—and if it were taken by storm it looked as if the entire Aetolian nation would be facing extinction there. Quinctius had good reason to be incensed with the Aetolians. He remembered that they were the only people to have disparaged his glorious achievement* when he was liberating Greece, and that they had been swayed not one bit by his authority when he tried to deter them from their demented undertaking by warning them that they would face what had, in fact, befallen them just at that time. Even so, he believed that, after liberating Greece, he had a special responsibility to ensure that none of its peoples be totally destroyed. He therefore proceeded to walk about the walls so that he could be easily recognized by the Aetolians. He was quickly spotted by the guards of the first outposts, and word spread throughout the ranks that Quinctius was present. There was a rush to the walls from all quarters. The people all held out their hands towards him, and with cries that blended together begged Quinctius by name to help them and rescue them. He was moved to pity by these appeals, but at the time he simply indicated with a gesture of his hand that he could not help. After this, however, he came to the consul and said: 'Did you fail to see what is going on, Manius Acilius? Or do you fully realize it, but think it does not greatly bear upon the interests of the state?'

He had piqued the curiosity of the consul, who replied: 'Why not explain what you mean?' Quinctius then said: 'Do you realize that since defeating Antiochus you have been wasting your time besieging two cities, when the year of your imperium is almost over, while Philip, who has not set eyes on a battlefield or enemy standards, has annexed not merely cities but a whole host of nations—Athamania, Perrhaebia, Aperantia, and Dolopia? Do you see that, as your prize of victory, you and your men do not yet have two cities, and Philip has all those nations of Greece? And yet it is less in our interest to have the strength and resources of the Aetolians curtailed than it is to see that Philip's power does not grow inordinately.'

35. The consul agreed with these remarks, but felt ashamed to abandon the siege with his objective unattained. The decision was

then left entirely to Quinctius, and he went back once more to that part of the wall where the Aetolians had called out to him a little earlier. When they now appealed to him more urgently to pity the Aetolian people, he bade a number of them come out to him. Phaeneas himself and other leading Aetolians then immediately came forth. They flung themselves at his feet, and Flamininus said to them: 'Your unfortunate circumstances oblige me to control my temper and my words to you. What I said would happen has happened, and you are not even left the consolation of appearing to be undeserving victims. Nevertheless, I have by some stroke of fate been appointed to take care of Greece, and I shall not withhold my services even from those who do not appreciate them. Send spokesmen to the consul to request a truce long enough to enable you to send ambassadors to Rome through whom you can put your case to the Senate. I personally will be at the consul's side to defend your interests and to intercede for you.' They followed Quinctius' advice, and the consul did not reject their petition. A truce was accorded for a fixed period* so that the report from the embassy to Rome could be brought back, the siege was raised and the army was sent back to Phocis.

The consul then crossed with Titus Quinctius to the Achaean Council in Aegium. The deliberations here centred on the Elians and the return of the Spartan exiles. Neither issue was resolved because the Achaeans wished the case of the exiles shelved until they could win the credit for it, while the Elians preferred their induction into the Achaean League to be their own responsibility, rather than effected through Roman mediation. Ambassadors came to the consul from the Epirotes who, it was quite clear, had not been completely loyal in their adherence to their treaty, although they had supplied Antiochus with no troops. They were accused of having given him financial aid, and they themselves did not even deny that they had sent ambassadors to the king. They asked to be allowed to remain in their earlier alliance, to which the consul replied that he was not yet sure whether to consider them enemies or one of the nations at peace with Rome, a matter on which the Senate would decide. He was referring their case in its entirety to Rome, he said, and for that he was granting them a ninety-day truce. The Epirotes who were sent to Rome approached the Senate, but since their defence rested more on the listing of hostile acts which they had not committed, rather than clearing themselves of the charges against them, they were given a response which could suggest that they had gained a pardon, rather than that they had successfully substantiated their case.

At about this time envoys from Philip, offering congratulations on the Roman victory, were also brought before the Senate. They requested permission to offer sacrifice in the Capitol, and to set a gift in gold in the temple of Jupiter Optimus Maximus, and they were granted this by the Senate. They then made a dedication of a golden crown weighing 100 pounds. The king's envoys were not only given a courteous response but were also presented with Demetrius— Philip's son, who had been a hostage at Rome*—so he could be taken back to his father. Thus ended the war fought in Greece by the consul, Manius Acilius, against King Antiochus.

36. The other consul, Publius Cornelius Scipio, who had drawn Gaul as his province, had promised some games in a vow at the crucial stage of a battle during his praetorship in Spain. Now, before departing for the war which he was to fight against the Boii, he requested of the Senate that funds for these games be voted to him. The request was deemed irregular and unreasonable, and the Senators decreed that, since he had made a vow to hold the games on his own initiative †and without Senatorial authorization†, Scipio should finance them from any moneys he had kept back for that purpose from his spoils, or else from his own resources. These games were held by Publius Cornelius over a ten-day period.

At about the same time the temple of the Magna Mater Idaea was dedicated. This goddess had been brought from Asia in the consulship of Publius Cornelius Scipio (who was subsequently given the cognomen Africanus) and of Publius Licinius,* and had been escorted from the coast to the Palatine by the Publius Cornelius mentioned above. Construction of the temple had been contracted out, in accordance with a Senatorial decree, by the censors, Marcus Livius and Gaius Claudius, in the consulship of Marcus Cornelius and Publius Sempronius.* Thirteen years after the awarding of the contract, it was dedicated by Marcus Iunius Brutus, with games instituted to celebrate the dedication. According to Valerius Antias these were the first games with dramatic performances, and were called the *Megalesia*.*

A temple of Juventas was likewise dedicated in the Circus Maximus by the duumvir Gaius Licinius Lucullus. This had been promised sixteen years earlier in a vow by the consul Marcus Livius, on the day when the latter cut Hasdrubal and his army to pieces,* and it was Livius who, as censor, also contracted out the work for the temple, in the consulship of Marcus Cornelius and Publius Sempronius. Moreover, games were held to commemorate this dedication, and the entire event was celebrated with all the greater attention to ritual because of the threat of the new war with Antiochus.

37. At the start of the year when these events were taking place, at a point when Manius Acilius had already left for the war and the consul Publius Cornelius was still in Rome, it is recorded that two tame oxen climbed some stairs in the Carinae and came out on the tiled roof of a building. The *haruspices* enjoined that the oxen be burned alive and their ashes thrown into the Tiber. There were reports of stones having fallen as rain on a number of occasions at Tarracina and Amiternum; of the temple of Jupiter and shops around the forum having been struck by lightning at Minturnae; and of two ships consumed by fire after being lightning-struck in the river-mouth at Volturnum. In view of these prodigies, the decemvirs consulted the Sibylline books on a directive from the Senate, and reported that a fast should be instituted in honour of Ceres, to be held at five-year intervals. They further prescribed a nine-day period of sacrifice and one day of public prayer, with garlands worn for the prayers, and directed that the consul Publius Cornelius sacrifice to such gods and with such animals as the decemvirs should stipulate. Now that the gods had been placated by the appropriate fulfilment of vows, as well as by the expiation of the prodigies, the consul left for his province. Here he gave instructions to the proconsul, Gnaeus Domitius, to demobilize his army, leave the province, and return to Rome. He himself took his legions into the territory of the Boii.

38. About the same time the Ligurians raised an army under their 'sacred law,'* and launched a surprise attack at night on the camp of the proconsul Quintus Minucius. Minucius kept his men within the rampart until daybreak, drawn up ready for battle, determined not to let the enemy cross his fortifications at any point. At dawn he made a simultaneous counter-attack through two of the camp gates. The Ligurians were not routed at the first charge as he had hoped, and for more than two hours they kept the outcome of the battle in doubt. However, as company after company came rushing out, and fresh soldiers replaced the weary at the front, the Ligurians finally turned

tail, worn out as they were by lack of sleep as well as everything else. More than 4,000 of the enemy were cut down, and of the Romans and their allies fewer than 300 lost their lives.

Some two months later the consul Publius Cornelius fought a remarkable pitched battle against an army of the Boii. According to Valerius Antias' account, 28,000 of the enemy were killed and 3,400 taken prisoner, while 124 military standards, 1,230 horses, and 247 wagons were captured. Of the victors 1,484 perished. Little trust can be placed in this author where numbers are concerned,* because no one is more extravagant than he in exaggerating them, but it is clear that this was a victory of great proportions—the camp was captured, the Boii surrendered immediately following the battle, and a period of prayer for the victory was decreed by the Senate, and full-grown animals sacrificed.

39. About this time Marcus Fulvius Nobilior returned from Farther Spain and entered the city in ovation. He carried in his procession 12,000 pounds of silver, 130,000 silver coins stamped with the *biga*, and 127 pounds of gold.

After taking hostages from the tribe of the Boii, Publius Cornelius confiscated about half of their lands to enable the Roman people to send colonies there if they wished. Then he left for Rome, where he felt sure he would be awarded a triumph, and demobilized his troops, telling them to appear in Rome on the day of the triumph. The day after his arrival in the city, Cornelius convened the Senate in the temple of Bellona. He gave an account of his achievements and requested permission to ride into the city in triumph. The tribune Publius Sempronius Blaesus was of the opinion that Scipio should not be refused the honour of a triumph, but that it should be deferred. Wars fought with the Ligurians, he explained, were invariably connected with those fought with the Gauls, for the two tribes, being so close, brought assistance to each other. The war with the Ligurians could have been finished off, he continued, if Publius Scipio had either himself passed into Ligurian territory with his conquering army after defeating the Boii in battle, or if he had dispatched some of his forces to Quintus Minucius, who had already been pinned down there for two years in an inconclusive war. As it was, Scipio's men had been withdrawn from the field to make up the numbers at his triumph, when they could have rendered sterling service to the state—and could still, if, by deferring the triumph, the

Senate were prepared to restore the position that had been lost by Scipio's impatience for that triumph. They should, he continued, instruct the consul to go back to his province with his legions, and to concentrate his efforts on the subjugation of the Ligurians. Unless these were forced to accept the authority and jurisdiction of the Roman people, the Boii would not remain at peace either—it had to be either peace or war in both cases. Once he had defeated the Ligurians, Publius Cornelius would celebrate his triumph a few months later as proconsul, following the example of many who did not celebrate their triumph during their term of office.

40. In reply, the consul observed that the province he had been allotted had not been Liguria, that he had not been at war with the Ligurians, and that it was not over them that he was requesting the triumph. He was sure that Quintus Minucius would soon bring them to heel, he added, and for that would request, and be granted, a well-earned triumph. As for himself, his petition was for a triumph over the Gallic Boii. He had defeated them in battle, seized their camp, and two days after the battle had accepted the surrender of the entire tribe, taking hostages from them to secure peace in the future. But, in fact, there was a much more important point: he had in the field killed a huge number of Gauls, and certainly no general before him had faced in battle †so many† thousands of Boii. Of their 50,000 men, more than half had been killed, and many thousands had been taken prisoner—the Boii were left with only old men and children. Could anyone be surprised, then, at a victorious army coming to Rome to celebrate its consul's triumph, when it had left not one enemy in the province? And suppose the Senate wished to avail itself of the services of these soldiers in another province as well. Which of the two ways of dealing with them did the Senators think would make them readier to face another danger and fresh hardship? If the men were given recompense without equivocation for the danger and hardship already faced? Or if, instead, the Senators sent them off with hopes instead of tangible rewards, when they had already been deceived in their first hopes? For, as far as he himself was concerned, he had acquired enough glory to last a whole lifetime on the day when the Senate, judging him best man in the state, had sent him to welcome the Idaean mother. That inscription, even if neither his consulship nor a triumph were added to it, would make the bust of Publius Scipio Nasica honourable and honoured enough.

To a man the Senate not only agreed to accord Scipio the triumph, but also wielded its authority to make the tribune of the plebs withdraw his objection. Publius Cornelius then triumphed over the Boii during his consulship.

In the triumphal procession Scipio had arms, standards, and spoils of all kinds carried on Gallic carts, and he also had on display Gallic vases made of bronze, as well as high-born captives and a herd of captured horses. He had 1,471 gold necklaces carried along, plus 247 pounds of gold, 2,340 pounds of silver, some unwrought and some in the form of Gallic vases, which were not inelegantly crafted in the Gallic style, and 234,000 coins stamped with the *biga*. To each of the soldiers who followed his chariot Scipio gave 125 *asses*, double that amount to a centurion, and triple to a cavalryman.

The next day Scipio convened an assembly of his men and spoke about their achievements and the insulting conduct of the tribune who tried to make them responsible for a war that was not their concern, in order to cheat them of the rewards of their victory. He then gave the men their discharge and let them go.

41. While these events were taking place in Italy, Antiochus was at Ephesus,* quite unconcerned about the war with Rome since he assumed the Romans would not cross to Asia. This assurance was given him by most of his friends, who were either mistaken or simply wished to humour him. At this time Hannibal's influence with the king was at its peak and he alone demurred, saying that he had no doubt the Romans would come and was in fact surprised that they were not in Asia already. It was a shorter crossing from Greece to Asia than from Italy to Greece, he said; Antiochus was a much more important target than the Aetolians; and the Romans were no less powerful on the sea than they were on land. A Roman fleet had long been stationed off Malea, he added, and he was told that fresh ships and a fresh commander had recently arrived from Italy to take part in operations. Antiochus should therefore abandon any illusions he might have of peace for himself. He would shortly have to fight the Romans on land and sea, and do so in Asia and for Asia itself. And he must either wrest power from them as they aimed at world-wide dominion, or else lose his own kingdom. Hannibal alone seemed to have clear foresight and to give honest warnings of what was to come. And so the king made for the Chersonese in person, with such ships as were ready and fitted out, in order to secure the area with garrisons in case the Romans came overland. He ordered Polyxenidas to fit out and launch the rest of the fleet, and sent spy-vessels around the islands to conduct a thorough reconnaissance.

42. The commander of the Roman fleet, Gaius Livius, set off from Rome with 50 decked ships for Naples, for this was the rallying point he had designated for the open-decked ships which the allies on that coastline were obliged to provide by the terms of their treaty. He then made for Sicily. He went through the strait past Messana, took charge of six Carthaginian ships that had been sent to reinforce him, and requisitioned from Rhegium and Locri, and other allies of the same treaty-standing, the ships due from them. Then, after a purification ceremony* for the fleet at Lacinium, he put out to sea.

Arriving at Corcyra, his first port of call among the Greek states, Livius made inquiries about the progress of the war—for peace had not been established everywhere—and the location of the Roman fleet. On being told that the consul and the king were dug in at the pass of Thermopylae, and that the fleet was riding at anchor in Piraeus, he felt he should, given the whole situation, take speedy action, and he immediately set sail for the Peloponnese. He straightway laid waste Same and Zacynthus, because they had chosen to side with the Aetolians, then made for Malea and, a few days later, after a smooth voyage, reached the old fleet in Piraeus. At Scyllaeum he was met by Eumenes with three ships. Eumenes had waited a long time on Aegina, uncertain what to do, whether to return to defend his own realm (for he was receiving reports of Antiochus getting ready naval and land-forces at Ephesus), or stick close to the Romans on whose fortunes his own depended. Aulus Atilius then transferred command of 25 decked ships to his successor, and left Piraeus for Rome. Livius thereupon crossed to Delos with 81 decked ships, as well as a large number of smaller vessels which were either open-decked combat galleys or scouting ships without beaks.

43. At about that time the consul Acilius was engaged in the siege of Naupactus. Livius was detained for several days at Delos by contrary winds—in fact, the area around the Cyclades is particularly windy because of the straits which separate them, quite wide in some places, narrower in others. Polyxenidas received intelligence from reconnaissance vessels posted in different areas that the Roman fleet was riding at anchor off Delos, and he sent the news to the king.

Antiochus abandoned his operations in the Hellespont and, taking his beaked ships, returned with all possible speed to Ephesus. Here he immediately held a council of war to determine whether to risk a naval engagement. Polyxenidas kept saying that they should not delay, and that they should certainly take on the enemy before the Romans were joined by Eumenes' fleet and the Rhodian vessels. In this way, he said, they would be roughly equal in terms of numbers, but in all other respects superior, in the speed of their ships as well as the range of auxiliary forces at their disposal. For, he continued, the manœuvrability of the Roman vessels was poor anyway because of their inferior construction, but apart from that they were laden with supplies, since they were coming into enemy territory. Their own ships, on the other hand, leaving a peaceful environment all around them, would be carrying only fighting men and weaponry. Their knowledge of the sea, the coastline, and the winds would also considerably help them, said Polyxenidas, and all of this would pose problems for the enemy who lacked such knowledge.

All present were swayed by the mover of this scheme, who was also going to be the man putting it into action. After spending two days on preparations, they set sail on the third with two hundred ships—seventy decked and the rest open-decked, and all of them of quite small dimensions—and headed for Phocaea. Hearing that the Roman fleet was now approaching, the king then left Phocaea, because he did not intend taking part in the sea-battle, and withdrew to Magnesia-near-Sipylus* to assemble his land-forces. The fleet proceeded to Cissus, a port of the Erythraeans, which seemed a more convenient place to await the enemy.

As soon as the north winds, which had kept up for several days, died down, the Romans set sail from Delos to Phanae, a port of Chios facing the Aegean Sea. From there they brought their ships round to the city and, after taking provisions on board, crossed to Phocaea. Eumenes set off to join his own fleet at Elaea. He returned to Phocaea a few days later with twenty-four decked ships and a few more open-decked vessels, and rejoined the Romans who were now preparing and equipping themselves for the forthcoming naval battle. They set sail from there with a hundred and five decked and some fifty open-decked ships, and at first were driven landwards by northerly winds blowing across their bow, forcing the ships to proceed in a thin line, almost one behind the other. Then, as the force of the wind abated a little, they attempted the crossing to the port of Corycus, which lies above Cissus.

44. When he was brought the news that the enemy was approaching, Polyxenidas was delighted at having the chance to fight. He himself extended his left wing towards the open sea, and ordered his ships' captains to deploy the right towards the shore. They then advanced to do battle with a level front. Seeing this, the Roman admiral furled his sails, lowered his masts, and, stowing the tackle, awaited the ships coming up behind. There were now about thirty ships in his front line and, to make it extend as far as the enemy's left wing, he put up the foresails and proceeded towards the open sea, ordering those following behind to turn their prows towards the enemy right wing close to the shore. Eumenes was bringing up the rear but, as soon as the scramble to stow the tackle began, he also brought up his ships with as much speed as he could.

Now they were visible to all the enemy. Two Punic ships* were riding ahead of the Roman fleet, and these were met by three of the king's vessels. Because of the disparity in numbers, two of the king's craft closed in on one of the Carthaginians. First they sheared off her oars on both sides, and then armed men climbed aboard, threw off or killed the defenders, and captured the vessel. The ship which had been fighting on equal terms saw that the other had been captured, and beat a retreat back to the fleet before she could be surrounded by three at once. Livius was furiously angry, and headed into the enemy with the flagship. The two ships which had beset the single Carthaginian craft now bore down on him, hoping to repeat the success. Livius ordered the rowers to set their oars in the water on both sides to stabilize the ship and to hurl grappling-irons onto the oncoming enemy vessels. Then, when they had thus created conditions similar to a land-battle,* he bade them remember Roman courage, and not to consider the king's serfs as men. On this occasion, the single ship defeated and captured the two with much greater ease than the two had previously taken the one. By now the fleets had engaged in all sectors, and the battle raged everywhere as the ships became mired with each other. Eumenes had been the last to arrive, at a point when the battle had started, and when he saw the enemy left wing reduced to confusion by Livius, he himself attacked the right where the struggle was evenly matched.

45. Not much later the flight began, starting on the left flank. For

Polyxenidas, seeing that he was unquestionably outclassed as regards the valour of the fighting men, raised his foresails and proceeded with a headlong flight; and soon those who had engaged with Eumenes close to shore did the same. The Romans and Eumenes made a determined pursuit, as long as the rowers were able to keep going and they could hope to harass the vessels at the rear. But they could see that the enemy ships, swifter because they were lighter, were outrunning their own, which were heavily laden with supplies, making their pursuit futile, and they eventually abandoned the chase, having captured thirteen ships, complete with marines and rowers, and having sunk ten. The only loss in the Roman fleet was the Carthaginian vessel that had been beset by the two ships at the start of the engagement.

Polyxenidas did not end his flight until he reached the harbour of Ephesus. The Romans spent that day in the port from which the king's fleet had sailed out, and the following day they set off in pursuit of the enemy. They were roughly half-way into the voyage when they were joined by twenty-five decked Rhodian ships, along with their commander, Pausistratus. Taking these along with them, they pursued the enemy to Ephesus, where they rode at anchor, drawn up in battle formation, before the harbour-mouth. After they had thus wrung an admission of defeat from their enemies, the Rhodians and Eumenes were sent home, and the Romans headed for Chios. They first sailed past Phoenicus, a port of Erythrae, anchored at night, and the next day crossed to the island, and came to the city of Chios itself. After a stay of a few days, mostly to restore the strength of the rowers, they crossed to Phocaea. Leaving four quinqueremes here to protect the city, the fleet proceeded to Canae; and since winter was coming on, the ships were pulled ashore and surrounded with a ditch and a rampart.

At the end of the year elections were held at Rome. Lucius Cornelius Scipio and Gaius Laelius were elected consuls to finish the war with Antiochus—for the eyes of all were on Africanus. The next day the following were elected praetors: Marcus Tuccius, Lucius Aurunculeius, Gnaeus Fulvius, Lucius Aemilius, Publius Iunius, and Gaius Atinius Labeo.*

BOOK THIRTY-SEVEN

1. When Lucius Cornelius Scipio and Gaius Laelius entered their consulship, the very first piece of business arising in the Senate after the religious observances was the Aetolian question. The Aetolian delegates were pressing for action because the day marking the end of the truce was near, and they were also supported by Titus Quinctius, who had by now returned to Rome from Greece. The Aetolians placed more hope in the compassion of the Senate than they did in the strength of their case, and they adopted a suppliant attitude, trying to mitigate their recent offences by pointing to their former services. But while they were in the house they were from every direction plied with questions by the Senators, who were trying to squeeze from them an admission of guilt rather than genuine answers; and when they were ordered to withdraw from the Senate house, they became the subject of a vigorous debate. Anger played a greater part in their case than did compassion, for the fury of the Senators was directed at them not merely as enemies, but as a wild tribe of people incapable of making an alliance.

When the discussion had gone on for a number of days, it was finally decided that the Aetolians should be neither granted nor refused a peace-treaty. They were offered two options: either to put themselves entirely in the hands of the Senate, or else pay 1,000 talents* and accept the same friends and enemies as the Romans. The Aetolians wanted clarification of the areas in which they would be in the Senate's hands, but they were given no straightforward response. As a result, they were sent off without a peace-settlement, under orders to leave the city that very day and Italy within fifteen days.*

After this, discussion of the consular provinces began. Both consuls wanted Greece. Laelius had great influence in the Senate,* and when that body instructed the consuls either to draw lots or come to an agreement between themselves on the provinces, he said the consuls would show greater discretion if they left the matter to the judgement of the Senators rather than to the lot. Scipio's reply was that he would give some thought to the course he should take. He then discussed the question with his brother, and him alone. When he was told by his brother that he could confidently leave the matter to the Senate, Scipio then reported to his colleague that he would accept his proposal. This was a novel procedure, or else one based on precedents long forgotten, and it piqued the interest of the Senators, who were expecting a contest. Then Publius Scipio Africanus declared that, if the Senators formally assigned the province of Greece to his brother, Lucius Scipio, he would accompany him as his legate. This statement was received with great approval, and brought the contest to an end. The Senate wished to put to the test which of the two had the more reliable support—Antiochus in the defeated Hannibal, or the consul and the Roman legions in the victorious Africanus. The decision to assign Greece to Scipio and Italy to Laelius was practically unanimous.

2. The praetorian sortition which took place next went as follows:

Lucius Aurunculeius	urban jurisdiction
Gnaeus Fulvius	foreign jurisdiction
Lucius Aemilius Regillus	the fleet
Publius Junius Brutus	Etruria
Marcus Tuccius	Apulia and Bruttium
Gaius Atinius	Sicily

The consul who had been assigned Greece as his province was then allocated a supplementary force—in addition to the army of two legions which he was to assume from Manius Acilius—and this comprised 3,000 infantry and 100 cavalry of Roman citizens, plus 5,000 infantry and 200 cavalry from the allies and the Latin League. It was further decided that the consul should take his army across to Asia when he reached his province, if that seemed to be in the interests of the state. The other consul was assigned a completely fresh army composed of two Roman legions, and 15,000 infantry and 600 cavalry from the allies and the Latin League.

Since Quintus Minucius had written to say that his provincial responsibility had now been fulfilled, and that the entire Ligurian nation had capitulated, he was instructed to take his army from Liguria to the land of the Boii and turn it over to the proconsul Publius Cornelius (Cornelius was at that time conducting the Boii from the lands which he had confiscated from them after their defeat in the war). To govern Apulia and Bruttium, the praetor Marcus Tuccius was given the two urban legions which had been raised the previous year, as well as 15,000 infantry and 600 cavalry of the allies and the Latin League. Aulus Cornelius, who had been praetor the previous year, and had held Bruttium with an army, was ordered to take his legions over to Aetolia, if such was the consul's pleasure, and transfer them to Manius Acilius, if the latter wished to remain there. If Acilius preferred to return to Rome, then Aulus Cornelius was under orders to remain in Aetolia with the army. It was also decided that Gaius Atinius Labeo should take over from Marcus Aemilius the province of Sicily and its army and, if he wished, raise from the province itself a supplementary force of 2,000 infantry and 100 cavalry. Publius Iunius Brutus was instructed to raise a fresh army for service against the Etruscans—one Roman legion, and 10,000 infantry and 400 cavalry of the allies and the Latin League. Lucius Aemilius, holder of the maritime jurisdiction, was directed to take over from the previous year's praetor, Marcus Iunius, twenty warships with their crews, and to enlist 1,000 sailors and 2,000 infantry himself. With these ships and fighting men he was to set off for Asia and assume command of the fleet from Gaius Livius.* The governors of the two Spains and Sardinia saw their commands extended for a year, and the same armies assigned to them. Two tithes of grain were requisitioned from both Sicily and Sardinia that year; and orders were issued for all the Sicilian grain to be taken to the army in Aetolia, while that from Sardinia was to go partly to Rome, and partly, like the Sicilian, to Aetolia.

3. It was decided that the prodigies should be expiated by the pontiffs before the consuls left for their provinces. At Rome the temple of Juno Lucina* had been struck by lightning so violently that its roof and doors were warped, and in Puteoli several parts of the city wall as well as a gate were lightning-struck, with two men losing their lives. At Nursia it was well documented that there had been a sudden downpour on a clear day,* and that two free men were killed there, as well. The people of Tusculum reported that showers of earth had fallen in their lands, and those of Reate that a mule had given birth in theirs.

These prodigies were expiated, and the Latin Festival* was repeated because the people of Laurentum had not been given the meat due to them. Because of these divine manifestations, public prayer was also offered to deities specified by the decemvirs after they consulted the Books.* Ten free-born boys and ten girls, all with living fathers and mothers, were employed for the sacrifice, and the decemvirs offered up unweaned animals by night. Before he left, Publius Cornelius Scipio Africanus set up an arch on the Capitol, facing the road that leads up to the Capitol, with seven gilded figures and two equestrian statues, and before the arch he placed two marble basins.

At this time forty-three leading Aetolians, including Damocritus and his brother, were brought to Rome—by two cohorts which had been sent out by Manius Acilius—and were thrown into the Lautumiae.* The consul, Lucius Cornelius, then ordered the cohorts to return to the army. There also arrived from Ptolemy and Cleopatra,* king and queen of Egypt, ambassadors offering congratulations on the consul Manius Acilius' expulsion of Antiochus from Greece, and urging the Senators to send an army across to Asia. Panic had spread not just throughout Asia but throughout Syria as well, they said, and the rulers of Egypt would be ready to comply with any decision of the Senate. The king and queen were formally thanked, and instructions were issued for the ambassadors to be presented with 4,000 *asses* each.

4. After completing all that needed doing in Rome, the consul Lucius Cornelius held an assembly at which he issued instructions for all his men to muster at Brundisium on 15 July—both the supplementary troops which he had himself enrolled, and those who were in Bruttium with the propraetor Aulus Cornelius. He also appointed three officers—Sextus Digitius, Lucius Apustius, and Gaius Fabricius Luscinus—to bring together at Brundisium ships from all points along the coast. All his preparations concluded, Cornelius then set out from the city in his military cloak. As the consul was leaving, about 5,000 volunteers, Romans and allies, who had served their time under the command of Publius Africanus, presented themselves to him and enlisted for service with him.

The consul set out for the campaign on 11 July, during the Games of Apollo, and at that time the light faded during the daytime when the sky was clear, as the moon passed under the sun's orb.* Lucius Aemilius Regillus, to whom the fleet had fallen as his area of responsibility, also set out at the same time as the consul. Lucius Arunculeius was assigned the task of constructing thirty quinqueremes and twenty triremes by the Senate, because it was reported that, following the naval battle, Antiochus was rebuilding his fleet on a considerably larger scale.

When their ambassadors returned from Rome with the news that there was no hope of peace, the Aetolians seized Mt. Corax, to block the Romans' approach. All their coastline facing the Peloponnese had been laid waste by the Achaeans, but the Aetolians were thinking of their present danger rather than past losses, for they were in no doubt that the Romans would return at the start of spring to attack Naupactus. Acilius knew that this was what the Aetolians expected, and it seemed to him a better idea to try a surprise manœuvre and attack Lamia. Its people, he reasoned, had been brought to the verge of destruction by Philip and, besides, they could on that occasion be caught off-guard simply because they had no fear of such a move. Setting off from Elatia, Acilius first pitched camp in enemy territory close to the River Spercheus. From there he advanced at night, and at dawn attacked the city-walls with a military cordon.

5. There followed the great alarm and uproar that usually attends an unexpected event. Even so the inhabitants that day defended their city with greater resolve than one might have expected them to do in the face of sudden danger: the men were doing the fighting, and the women were carrying to the walls all manner of weapons, and rocks, too, even though scaling-ladders had already been set up at many points. Acilius sounded the retreat and led his troops back to camp at about midday. When the men were revived by food and rest, and before he dismissed his council of war, he made an announcement: they were to be in arms and ready to move before dawn, and he would not bring them back to camp without the city being taken. He then made his attack at several points at the same hour as he had done the previous day, and since the townspeople lacked strength, weapons, and, more than anything else, the will to resist, he took the city in a few hours.

Acilius sold some of the spoils, and distributed some amongst the troops, after which he held a council to consider his next move. No one wanted to go to Naupactus since the pass to Corax was held by the Aetolians. Acilius instead decided to attack Amphissa; he did not want the campaigning season frittered away, or for the Aetolians to enjoy, through his hesitation, a peace which they had failed to obtain from the Senate. The army was taken down from Heraclea over Oeta and, when he had established his camp before the walls of Amphissa,

Acilius used siege-works—not a military cordon, as at Lamia—for his assault on the city. Battering-rams were brought up in several places at the same time, and as the walls were being pounded the townspeople made no attempt to prepare or devise any counter-measures for this kind of apparatus. All their hopes lay in their fighting ability and courage, and with persistent counter-attacks they harried the advance posts of the enemy, and even those manning the earth-works and siege-engines.

6. The wall had, even so, been shattered at several points when Acilius was brought word that his successor had set his army ashore at Apollonia, and was now proceeding through Epirus and Thessaly. In fact, the consul was coming with †3,000† infantry and 500 cavalry, and had already reached the Malian Gulf. From here he sent men ahead to Hypata to order the inhabitants to surrender the city. The reply came back that the people of Hypata would act only on a communal decision by the Aetolians. Not to be held back by a siege of Hypata when Amphissa was still not captured, Scipio first sent ahead his brother Africanus, and then marched on Amphissa. At their approach, the townspeople abandoned the city, which by now had been largely divested of its walls, and everybody, armed men and non-combatants alike, retreated to the citadel, which they considered impregnable.

The consul encamped about six miles away. Ambassadors from Athens came to the camp to plead on behalf of the Aetolians, addressing themselves first to Publius Scipio who (as was noted above) had gone ahead of the column and, after him, to the consul. They received a more sympathetic response from Africanus. The latter was looking for a pretext to quit the Aetolian war with honour,* and had his attention focused on Asia and King Antiochus. Africanus had therefore told the Athenians to convince the Aetolians, as well as the Romans, to accept peace as a better option than war. At the prompting of the Athenians, a large delegation of Aetolians came swiftly from Hypata. They approached Africanus first, and his words also increased their hopes of obtaining peace, for he enumerated the many nations and peoples who had put themselves in his hands, in Spain first of all, and then in Africa. In every case, he said, he had left them with better reasons for remembering his clemency and generosity than his valour in battle. The problem appeared to be resolved, but when the consul was approached he made the same response with which the Aetolians had been rebuffed by the Senate. When they received this fresh blow, the Aetolians could see that the Athenian embassy and Africanus' indulgent response to them had meant nothing, and they declared that they wished to report back to their own people.

7. The delegates returned from there to Hypata, but no plan of action presented itself: there was no way of raising the 1,000-talent payment,* and the Aetolians were afraid that, if they put themselves entirely in the Senate's hands, they might be subjected to physical injury. They therefore ordered the same envoys to return to the consul and to Africanus, and to ask them either to reduce the total of the money to be paid, or else direct that complete surrender not entail physical maltreatment of citizens—that is, if they really did want to grant the Aetolians peace, and not merely give them a glimpse of it, thereby frustrating the hopes of hapless men. They failed to make the consul effect any change, and that embassy was also dismissed with nothing achieved. The Athenians followed the envoys home. The Aetolians were sickened now by all the rejections and were bemoaning the fortunes of their people with futile laments, but Echedemus, head of the Athenian delegation, revived their hopes with the suggestion that they ask for a six-month truce to enable them to send representives to Rome. The delay, he said, would not increase their current ills, which were as bad as they could be, and their present tribulations might possibly be relieved by any number of fortuitous events that could occur in the intervening period. On Echedemus' recommendation, the same delegates were sent once more. They met Publius Scipio first, and thanks to his intercession managed to gain from the consul a truce for the requisite period. The siege of Amphissa was raised, and Manius Acilius quit the province after transferring command of the army to the consul. The latter headed back to Thessaly from Amphissa in order to march into Asia by way of Macedonia and Thrace.

Africanus then spoke as follows to his brother: 'The road on which you are setting out has my approval, too, Lucius Scipio, but all depends on Philip's inclinations. If he loyally supports our authority,* he will provide us with a safe passage, provisions, and all the things that sustain and assist an army on a long march. If he deserts us, you will have no security passing through Thrace. So my feeling is that we should first test the king's disposition, and that will be best tested if the man sent catches him by surprise, when his reaction is in no way premeditated.'

Selected for this task was Tiberius Sempronius Gracchus,* by far the most dynamic young man of his time. By using horses stationed in relays, Gracchus achieved almost unbelievable speed, reaching Pella from Amphissa, his point of dispatch, in two days. The king was at dinner, and had drunk a lot of wine, and of itself this relaxed state of mind allayed all suspicion that he intended any mischief. At the time, moreover, the guest was given a warm welcome, and the next day he saw provisions that had been liberally stock-piled for the army, bridges built over rivers, and roads constructed where passage was difficult. Taking back this news as swiftly as he had come, Gracchus met the consul at Thaumaci. From here, buoyed by more positive and sanguine hopes, the army came to Macedonia to find everything prepared for them. On their arrival the king welcomed and entertained the Scipios with regal liberality. He seemed possessed of great consideration and civility, qualities that won the approval of Africanus who, an outstanding man in all other respects, was not averse to a cordiality that shunned extravagance. From there the Romans reached the Hellespont, passing through Thrace as well as Macedonia, escorted by Philip who made the preparations for every step of the journey.

8. After the naval battle at Corycus, Antiochus had spent all his free time in the winter on preparations on land and sea and, not to be completely stripped of his hold on the sea, had paid particular attention to refurbishing his fleet. It did occur to him that he had been defeated at a time when the Rhodian fleet had not been present, and that if this armament should also take part in the fighting—and the Rhodians would not make the mistake of lagging behind a second time—he would need a large number of ships to match the enemy fleet in strength and size. Accordingly, he had dispatched Hannibal to Syria to fetch Phoenician ships, and he also ordered Polyxenidas to refit his remaining vessels and to build others—and do it all the more energetically in view of his earlier lack of success. Antiochus himself spent the winter in Phrygia, calling for assistance from every quarter. He had even sent to Gallogrecia,* whose people at that time were more pugnacious—they still possessed their Gallic spirit,* since the original strain of the people had not yet died out. He had left his son Seleucus* with an army in Aeolis to keep the coastal

cities under control; these were being incited to rebellion on one side by Eumenes, from Pergamum, and on the other, from Phocaea and Erythrae, by the Romans.

The Roman fleet was wintering at Canae, as noted above, and about midwinter Eumenes arrived here with †twenty† thousand infantry and 500 cavalry. He remarked that a large amount of plunder could be taken from enemy territory around Thyatira, and by his urging prevailed upon Livius to send 5,000 men with him. The men who were sent removed a massive quantity of booty in a matter of days.

9. Meanwhile civil unrest arose in Phocaea when some people tried to win the support of the masses for Antiochus. Winter-quarters for the ships caused hardship for the Phocaeans; the tribute also caused hardship because 500 togas and 500 tunics were requisitioned from them; and even further hardship came from a shortage of grain, which prompted the fleet and Roman garrison to leave them. With this, the faction holding meetings to win the support of the commons for Antiochus was delivered from fear; and while the senate and aristocrats advocated standing by the Roman alliance, the ringleaders of the disaffection had more influence with the masses.

Compensating for their tardiness the previous summer, the Rhodians were quick to send out at the spring equinox* Pausistratus, the same admiral as before, with thirty-six ships. By now Livius had left Canae with thirty ships of his own, and seven quadriremes which Eumenes had brought with him, and was heading for the Hellespont to make the necessary preparations for the crossing of the army, which he thought would be arriving by land.

He first of all put in at the so-called 'Port of the Achaeans'.* From there he went up to Ilium where he sacrificed to Minerva* and then gave a gracious hearing to deputations from neighbouring communities—from Elaeus, Dardanus, and Rhoetcum—who put their towns under his protection. From there he sailed to the mouth of the Hellespont. He left ten ships stationed off Abydos and crossed with the rest of the fleet into Europe to launch an attack on Sestus. His soldiers were already approaching the walls when some Galli, the frenzied priests,* met them before the gate, dressed in the robes of their cult. They declared that they were the servants of the goddess, the mother of the gods, and that it was at her behest that they came to entreat the Romans to spare their walls and their city. None of them was ill-treated, and soon the senate and magistrates came forth to surrender the city.

From there the fleet crossed to Abydus. Here, after meetings to sound out the feelings of the people produced no response to suggest a peaceful settlement, the Romans readied themselves for a blockade.

10. Such were events in the Hellespont. Meanwhile, the king's officer Polyxenidas, who was an exile from Rhodes, had heard that a fleet of his countrymen had left home and that its commander, Pausistratus, had made some disparaging and offensive comments against him at a public meeting. As a result, Polyxenidas' feelings towards him had become particularly hostile, and day and night all he thought about was ways of making Pausistratus eat his disdainful words. He sent to him a man who was also known to Pausistratus to say that he, Polyxenidas, if he were allowed, could be very useful to him and to his native land—while Polyxenidas could also be restored to his country through Pausistratus' agency. Surprised, Pausistratus asked how this could be done. Polyxenidas asked him to give his word that they would see the affair through together or else keep it shrouded in silence, and Pausistratus agreed. Then the go-between explained that Polyxenidas would deliver up to him either the whole or the greater part of the king's fleet, and his asking-price for this great service was merely his restoration to his native land. So momentous was the proposition that it would permit Pausistratus neither to believe nor to disregard Polyxenidas' words. He made for Panhormus in Samian territory, and moored there to examine in detail the offer that had been made to him. Messengers came and went between the two, but Pausistratus could not be satisfied until Polyxenidas wrote out with his own hand, in the presence of Pausistratus' messenger, that he would make good his promise, and sent to him the tablets stamped with his seal. This pledge made Pausistratus think that he really had bought the traitor, for he believed a man living under a monarch would not have ventured to provide evidence against himself in his own handwriting.

After this, the scenario for the fake betrayal was put together. Polyxenidas said he would drop all preparations, and would not have a large number of oarsmen or other members of the crews attached to the fleet. He would beach some of his ships on the pretext of repairing them, and others he would send off to nearby harbours;

but he would keep a few on the open sea before the port of Ephesus, and bring those into battle if circumstances forced him to put to sea.

When Pausistratus heard that Polyxenidas was to be remiss in handling his fleet, he immediately became remiss himself. He sent some of his ships to Halicarnassus to fetch supplies, and others to the city of Samos <. . .> so as to be ready when he received from the traitor the signal to attack. Polyxenidas used some deception to delude him further: he beached a number of ships and built dock-yards to create the impression that he would beach others; and instead of bringing his oarsmen to Ephesus from their winter-quarters, he secretly assembled them at Magnesia.

11. It so happened that one of Antiochus' soldiers had come to Samos on a private matter. He was arrested as a spy and brought to the commander at Panhormus. Pausistratus asked him what was going on in Ephesus and he—whether from fear or from lack of loyalty to his own people is uncertain—told all. The fleet was anchored in the harbour drawn up ready for action, he said; all the oarsmen had been sent to Magnesia;* very few ships had been hauled ashore, and the docks were being covered over;* and never had so much effort been spent on naval matters. Pausistratus' mind was distracted by his delusion and false hope, so the man's story was not accepted as true.

His preparations complete, Polyxenidas summoned his oarsmen from Magnesia by night and hurriedly launched the ships which had been beached. He then passed the day there, less because he was preparing than because he did not want his fleet spotted as it moved out; and after sunset he set off with seventy decked ships and, facing a headwind, reached the port of Pygela before dawn. He spent the day immobile at Pygela—for the same reason as before—and at night crossed to the closest parts of Samian territory. From here he instructed a certain Nicander, a pirate chief,* to head for Palinurus with five decked ships, and then take a body of troops by the shortest route across country to Panhormus, to the rear of the enemy. Poly-xenidas himself meanwhile divided his fleet so that he could hold the harbour-mouth on both sides, and then he made for Panhormus.

At first Pausistratus was briefly stunned by this unexpected move, but then, being an experienced soldier, he quickly pulled him-self together. Concluding that the enemy could be more easily repulsed on land than on sea, he led his troops in two columns to the

promontories which form the harbour, the two spits of land
sheltering it from the sea. From there he expected that he would
easily push back the enemy †from both†. The sight of Nicander
arriving overland upset that strategy, and so, suddenly changing his
plan, he ordered them all to board the ships. Sheer pandemonium
then broke out among soldiers and sailors alike, and there was a
virtual flight to the ships when they saw that they were surrounded
on land and on sea at the same time. Pausistratus thought there was
only one route to safety, and that was if he could force a way through
the harbour-mouth and break through to the open sea. When he saw
that his men had boarded, he ordered the others to follow him and
himself took the lead, heading for the harbour-mouth with his ship
being rowed along at maximum speed. As the vessel was just passing
the entrance, Polyxenidas surrounded it with three quinqueremes.
Struck by their beaks, the ship went down and the defenders were
buried under a hail of missiles, amongst them Pausistratus, who lost
his life putting up a spirited fight. Of the other vessels some were
caught before the harbour, and others within it; some were captured
by Nicander as they tried to get away from shore. Only five Rhodian
ships along with two Coan vessels made good their escape, and did so
by opening up a path for themselves between the crowded enemy
ships by terrifying them with shooting flames; for they each carried
before themselves great quantities of fire that they had ignited in
iron bowls suspended from two poles that projected from the prow.

Some Erythraean triremes met the fleeing Rhodian ships—which
they were coming to reinforce—not far from Samos, after which
they changed course to rejoin the Romans in the Hellespont. Close
to this time Seleucus regained Phocaea, which was betrayed to him
after one of the gates was opened by the sentries. Cyme and other
cities on that coastline also defected to him out of fear.

12. While this was going on in Aeolis, Abydus had been facing its
siege for a number of days, with a garrison of the king defending the
walls. By now they were all exhausted, and their magistrates proceeded to discuss terms of surrender with Livius, with the acquiescence even of Philotas, the garrison-commander. A solution was
delayed because they failed to agree on whether the king's men were
to be released with or without weapons. They were negotiating this
when news of the Rhodian disaster arrived and took the matter
out of their hands, for Livius feared that Polyxenidas might be

encouraged by the success of such a major operation to swoop down on the fleet stationed at Canae. Accordingly, he immediately discontinued the siege of Abydus and his protection of the Hellespont, and launched the ships that had been hauled ashore at Canae. Eumenes also came to Elaea.* Livius now made for Phocaea with his entire fleet, to which he had added two Mytilenian triremes. On being told the town was occupied by a powerful royal garrison, and that Seleucus' camp was not far away, he raided the coastline, hurriedly loaded the ships with his plunder, which consisted mostly of prisoners, and waited only for Eumenes to catch up with his fleet before setting sail for Samos.

Initially, the news of the disaster caused widespread panic and grief amongst the Rhodians, for even apart from the cost in ships and manpower they had lost the best and strongest of their youth—many of their nobles had joined Pausistratus, amongst other reasons because of his prestige, deservedly great amongst his people at that time. Then the thought that they had been taken by trickery and, more than that, by one of their fellow-citizens turned their sorrow to anger. They immediately dispatched ten ships, and a few days later sent a further ten, putting Eudamus in command of all of them. In general military proficiency, he was not in Pausistratus' league, but they believed he would be a more cautious leader because he was less enterprising.

The Romans and Eumenes landed first at Erythrae, and after waiting overnight here they steered a course for the promontory of Tean Corycus the following day. Wishing to cross from there to the nearest parts of the island of Samos, they did not wait for sunrise so the helmsmen could observe the state of the weather but instead †set out† into uncertain conditions. Half-way through the journey the north-easterly wind veered due north, and they began to be buffeted by a sea roughened with waves.

13. Thinking that his enemies would head for Samos to join up with the Rhodian fleet, Polyxenidas set sail from Ephesus, and at first rode at anchor off Myonnesus. From there he crossed to the island called Macris, intending to attack any ships that strayed from the line of the enemy fleet as it passed by, or to fall on the end of the line when given the chance. After he saw that the fleet had been scattered by the bad weather, his first thoughts were that he had an opportunity to attack, but a little later the wind increased, producing even

higher waves, and he saw that he could not reach the enemy. He therefore crossed to the island of Aethalia so that he could from there pounce upon the ships the next day as they headed for Samos from the open sea. As darkness fell a small number of the Romans made it to a deserted haven in Samian territory, and the rest of the fleet, after spending the whole night storm-tossed out at sea, also sought shelter in the same harbour. Learning from peasants there that enemy ships were anchored at Aethalia, they held a meeting to decide whether to fight it out immediately or wait for the Rhodian fleet. The decision was to defer the encounter, and they crossed to Corycus, the point from which they had come. After a fruitless wait, Polyxenidas also went back to Ephesus.

As the sea was now unimpeded by the enemy, the Roman ships crossed to Samos, and the Rhodian fleet arrived at the same destination a few days later. To give the impression that this was all that they had been waiting for, the Romans immediately set sail for Ephesus, intending either to decide the contest with a battle at sea or else to wring an admission of fear from the enemy if he refused battle— something of great importance *vis-à-vis* the inclinations of the city-states. The Romans positioned themselves opposite the harbour-mouth with their vessels facing it in a line. When no one came to confront them, they divided the fleet and one part rode at anchor on the open sea opposite the harbour entrance while the other put ashore its fighting men. The latter raided the countryside far and wide and were bringing back an enormous quantity of booty when Andronicus the Macedonian, a member of the garrison at Ephesus, made a sortie against them as they were approaching the walls, stripping them of most of their plunder and driving them back to their vessels on the shore. The next day the Romans set an ambush about half-way between the two sides, and then marched in a column towards the city in order to entice the Macedonians outside their walls. However, suspicion that this very scheme was afoot deterred anyone from coming out, and so they returned to their ships. The enemy avoiding engagement on both land and sea, the Roman fleet returned to Samos, its point of departure.

The praetor* then dispatched two triremes of the Italian allies and two Rhodian triremes, under the command of the Rhodian Epicrates, to keep watch on the strait of Cephallenia. The strait was being rendered perilous by the piracy of the Spartan Hybristas* and a group of young Cephallenians, and the sea was already closed to supplies from Italy.

14. Lucius Aemilius Regillus, who was succeeding to the naval command, was met in Piraeus by Epicrates. He was told of the Rhodian defeat and, since he had no more than two quinqueremes, he took Epicrates and his four ships back to Asia with him. Some open-decked Athenian vessels also accompanied them.

†Aemilius crossed the Aegean Sea.† The Rhodian Timasicrates also reached the same harbour from Samos at dead of night with two quadriremes. Taken to Aemilius, Timasicrates said that his mission was to serve as a convoy, because the king's ships, with their repeated forays from the Hellespont and Abydus, were making that coastline hazardous for freighters. Crossing from Chios to Samos, Aemilius was joined by two Rhodian quadriremes—which had been sent to meet him by Livius—and by Eumenes with two quinqueremes. When they reached Samos, Aemilius assumed command of the fleet from Livius, duly conducted the customary sacrifice,* and called a council of war. At the meeting Gaius Livius was the first to be asked his opinion. Livius said that no one could provide more trustworthy advice than the man who encourages another to do what he himself would have done in that same situation. He had intended sailing to Ephesus with the whole fleet, he explained, taking along with him some transport vessels, heavily loaded with gravel, which he would sink in the harbour mouth. The difficulty of creating an obstruction was lessened by the fact that the harbour mouth was like a river, he said—long, narrow, and with many shallow spots. In this way he would have deprived the enemy of access to the sea and rendered his fleet useless.

15. Nobody liked the proposal,* and Eumenes asked Livius what on earth he was thinking about. 'Imagine the situation when the vessels had been sunk and the allies had blocked the harbour-mouth,' he said. When the fleet then had freedom of action, were they going to leave the harbour to help the allies and to instil terror in the enemy? Or would they continue to blockade the port with the whole fleet just the same? For, if they left, no one could doubt that the enemy would raise the submerged wrecks and open the port with less effort than it would take to block it. And if they had to stay there just the same, what was the point of closing the harbour? In fact, he said, the enemy would then have a peaceful campaigning season, enjoying a port that was absolutely secure, and the advantages of a wealthy city, with Asia providing everything they needed. The Romans meanwhile would be facing waves and storms on the open sea, short of everything, constantly on guard, and themelves more tied down and restricted with regard to all that they should be doing, apart from maintaining the blockade of the enemy.

Eudamus, admiral of the Rhodian fleet, signalled his disapproval of the plan but without expressing his own opinion on what they should do. The Rhodian Epicrates voted that they forget Ephesus for the moment and send some of their ships to Lycia to bring Patara, capital of the country, into an alliance. That would prove advantageous in two important ways, he said: with the lands facing their island on friendly terms with them, the Rhodians could bring all their strength to bear on the one war, that against Antiochus; and, secondly, the fleet being put together in Cilicia would be prevented from joining up with Polyxenidas. This was the suggestion that prevailed, but it was nevertheless decided that Regillus should sail out to the harbour of Ephesus with all his fleet to intimidate the enemy.

16. Gaius Livius was dispatched to Lycia with two Roman quinqueremes, four Rhodian quadriremes, and two open-decked vessels from Smyrna. His orders were to go to Rhodes first and formulate all his plans in concert with the Rhodians. The city-states that he passed—Miletus, Myndus, Halicarnassus, Cnidus, and Cos—zealously executed his orders, and when he reached Rhodes he explained to the Rhodians the purpose of his mission and at the same time sought out their views on it. The Rhodians were unanimously in favour of the strategy, and Livius sailed on to Patara, with three quadriremes added to the fleet he was commanding.

At first, a following wind took them towards the city itself, and they had hopes that the sudden panic would yield some result; but the wind changed direction, and the sea began to surge with waves rolling in different directions. They did manage to hold close to the land with the use of their oars, but there was no safe anchorage near the city, and they could not lie off the harbour-mouth on the open sea, either, because the waters were rough and night was coming on.

They sailed past the city walls and headed for the port of Phoenicus, which was less than two miles distant from there and which provided ships with shelter from the fury of the sea. There were, however, lofty cliffs rising above the harbour, and these were quickly seized by the townspeople, who took with them the king's soldiers whom they had in the garrison. Although the shoreline was rough and hard to negotiate, Livius sent against these his Issaean auxiliaries and his light infantry from Smyrna. At first it was a matter of skirmishing with missiles, and †light attacks† against limited numbers of the enemy, rather than full-scale battle, and during these Livius' men managed to keep up the fight. Then more people came streaming from the city, and eventually the entire population poured out, making Livius afraid that his auxiliaries might be cut off and his ships be at risk even from the shore. Accordingly, he led out into battle not just his fighting men, but the crews as well—his large contingent of oarsmen—all armed with whatever they could lay their hands on. Even then the battle remained uncertain and in addition to a number of common soldiers Lucius Apustius also fell in the disorderly fighting. Eventually, however, the Lycians were completely routed and driven back into their city, and the Romans returned to their ships with a victory won not without loss of blood.

From there they set off into the gulf of Telmessus, which washes Caria on one side and Lycia on the other, having abandoned <all thought> of a further attempt on Patara. The Rhodians were sent home, and Livius, after skirting the coast of Asia, crossed to Greece so that he could meet the Scipios, who were in the area of Thessaly at the time, and then sail to Italy.

17. Aemilius had himself been driven from Ephesus by a storm and had returned to Samos with his enterprise aborted. When he learned that the operation in Lycia had been abandoned and that Livius had left for Italy, he felt the failed attempt on Patara was a disgrace and decided to go there with his entire fleet and launch a full-scale attack on the city. He sailed past Miletus and the rest of the coastline under allied control and landed at Iasus in the bay of Bargylia. The city was held by a garrison of the king, and the Romans subjected the surrounding countryside to ruthless pillaging. Then a deputation was sent to hold discussions with the leading citizens and magistrates to sound out their inclinations and, when these replied that they were powerless to act, Aemilius led out his troops to attack the city.

There were with the Romans some exiles from Iasus. These proceeded to appeal to the Rhodians in large numbers not to let an unoffending city perish which was both their neighbour and ethnically connected to them. The reason for their own exile, they declared, was simply their loyalty to the Romans, and those remaining in the city were subject to the same duress from the king's troops that had made them exiles themselves. All the people of Iasus had but one purpose, to escape their servitude to the king. The Rhodians were touched by their entreaties, and they found a supporter in Eumenes. By pointing to their racial ties and at the same time by expressing pity at the misfortunes of a city at the mercy of a garrison of the king, the Rhodians convinced Aemilius not to attack.

With control established everywhere else, the allies left Iasus and skirted the coastline of Asia, eventually reaching Loryma, a port facing Rhodes. Here there arose some surreptitious talk in the officers' quarters, beginning among the military tribunes but then reaching the ears of Aemilius himself. It was said that the fleet was being removed from Ephesus and from its own theatre of operations so that the enemy would be left behind them, free to make all manner of attacks with impunity on the many allied cities there. This talk had an effect on Aemilius. He called the Rhodians and asked them †whether† it was possible for the whole fleet to ride at anchor in the harbour at Patara. When the Rhodians declared that impossible, he made this the pretext for abandoning the operation and took the fleet back to Samos.

18. Seleucus, Antiochus' son, had kept his army in Aeolis throughout the wintertime, partly engaged in helping his allies, and partly in conducting raids on those whom he could not inveigle into an alliance. At this time he decided to move into territory that was part of the kingdom of Eumenes, while the latter was far from home with the Romans and the Rhodians, attacking the coastal areas of Lycia. Seleucus first marched on Elaea, but then, forgoing an assault on the city, he exhaustively plundered its agricultural lands and led his army forward to attack Pergamum, the capital and citadel of the realm. Attalus at first put guard-emplacements before the city, and mounted attacks with his cavalry and light infantry, actually harassing his enemy instead of merely mounting a defence. He eventually discovered from these minor skirmishes that he was no match for his enemy in any area of his forces and withdrew within the city walls. The siege of the city thereupon commenced.

At about the same time Antiochus, who had left Apamea, established a base first at Sardis and then at the mouth of the River

Caicus, not far from Seleucus' camp. He had with him a powerful army made up of a mixture of different races, but the greatest threat resided in his 4,000 Gallic mercenaries. These soldiers, †with a few others added, he sent out† to lay waste the fields of Pergamum at many points. When this was reported on Samos, Eumenes, called away by the war in his own land, first of all sailed to Elaea with his fleet. When cavalry and light infantry became available, he used them as a protective escort and hurried on to Pergamum before the enemy became aware of his approach or made any move. There, once again, a number of sorties precipitated some light skirmishing, Eumenes clearly avoiding a decisive encounter. A few days later the Roman and Rhodian fleets reached Elaea from Samos to bring assistance to the king. Antiochus was brought the news that the allies had disembarked their troops at Elaea, and that many fleets had converged on the one harbour. About the same time he also heard that the consul was already in Macedonia with his army, and that the preparations required for the crossing of the Hellespont were under way. He now thought the time had come to discuss peace-terms, before he found himself under pressure on land and sea at the same time. He therefore seized a certain hill facing Elaea for his camp, and there left all his infantry. After this he went down with his cavalry (which numbered 6,000) into the plains beneath the very walls of Elaea, having first sent a herald to Aemilius to report that he wished to discuss terms of peace.

19. Aemilius summoned Eumenes from Pergamum, and held a meeting to which he invited the Rhodians. The Rhodians were not against peace,* but Eumenes declared it was neither honourable to discuss peace-terms at this juncture, nor possible to bring the matter to a conclusion. 'For', he said 'how shall we honourably accept so-called terms of peace when we are shut up within our walls facing a siege? Or who will consider such a peace treaty as valid when we shall have struck it without the consul, and without Senatorial authorization or the bidding of the Roman people? Suppose peace *is* made on your authority. I would like to know this—are you going to return to Italy immediately, pulling back your fleet and your army? Or are you going wait for the consul's pleasure in the matter, for the vote of the Senate, and for the order of the Roman people? Your only option is to stay in Asia, abandon the campaign, and lead back to winter-quarters your forces—to drain your allies who must provide

supplies. And then if those with the authority see fit, we must start the war all over again—though we can have it finished before winter, God willing, if we do not delay and thereby lose some of our drive in the operation.'

This was the view that carried the day, and the reply given to Antiochus was that peace-terms could not be discussed before the arrival of the consul. His attempt to gain peace a failure, Antiochus laid waste the fields of the people of Elaea first, then those of the Pergamenes. Leaving his son Seleucus there, he next marched on Adramytteum and headed for the rich land which they call the Plain of Thebe, made famous by Homer's poem.* In no other place in Asia was greater booty won by the soldiers of the king. Aemilius and Eumenes, sailing around with their ships, also came to Adramytteum in order to give protection to the city.

20. About this time it happened that 1,000 infantry and 100 cavalry reached Elaea from Achaea, all these troops commanded by Diophanes.* After disembarking from the ships they were escorted to Pergamum at night by men who had been sent by Attalus to meet them. They were all veterans with experience of armed combat, and their leader was himself a pupil of Philopoemen, the greatest general amongst all the Greeks of the time. They spent two days resting the men and horses, and also in scrutinizing the enemy outposts to see the points at which they came and went, and the times at which they did so.

The king's men would advance to a point close to the foot of the hill on which the city stands, thus leaving the land behind them clear for plundering. The townspeople had confined themselves within their walls from fear, and after that there was no sally made from the city, not even to throw spears at the outposts at long range. Now contempt for them arose amongst the king's men, followed by inattention to their duties. Most of them did not have their horses saddled or bridled. A few remained under arms and in their ranks, but the rest had slipped away and dispersed throughout the plain, a number engaging in young men's sports and fun, some eating in the shade, and others even lying asleep on the ground.

This Diophanes saw from the heights of the city of Pergamum, and he ordered his men to take up arms and hold themselves in readiness at the gate. He himself went to Attalus and explained that he intended to assault an enemy outpost. Attalus allowed this with reluctance, since he could see that Diophanes would be facing 600 cavalry with 100, and 4,000 infantry with 1,000; and Diophanes, passing through the gate, installed himself not far from an enemy outpost, waiting for his opportunity. The people in Pergamum believed this was insanity rather than daring. The enemy, too, turned their attention to them for only a short while, and when they saw no activity they made no alteration to their usual laxness, going so far as to mock the small numbers of their enemy as well. For some time Diophanes kept his men at a standstill, as if they had been brought out simply to watch. When he saw the enemy had broken ranks, he instructed the infantry to follow with all the speed they could muster. Putting himself at the head of the cavalry with his own troop, he made a sudden charge on the enemy outpost, galloping as rapidly as possible, and with the war-cry raised simultaneously by every foot soldier and horseman. Even the horses were terrified, not just the men; they burst their reins and created panic and havoc amongst their own men. A few horses stood unperturbed, but the men could not easily saddle or bridle or mount these, either, because the Achaeans struck far greater terror into them than the number of their cavalrymen warranted. The infantry, in ranks and well-prepared, attacked a foe carelessly disordered and virtually half asleep. Men were slaughtered and put to flight all through the fields. Diophanes chased the scattered enemy as far as it was safe, and then returned to service in the garrison of the city. He had won great glory for the Achaean nation, for the combat had been witnessed from the walls of Pergamum by men and women alike.

21. The next day the king's advance guards encamped a half-mile further from the city, in better order and closer formation, and the Achaeans went forward at roughly the same time and to the same place as on the previous occasion. For several hours both sides waited intently for the attack which they expected at any moment. When it was time to return to camp, not long before sunset, the king's men brought their standards together and proceeded to march off in a column organized more for marching than for fighting. Diophanes did nothing as long as they were in sight. Then he bore down on the rear of the column with the same ferocity as the day before, and once more struck such panic into them and caused such chaos that although their rear was being cut down no one halted to put up a fight. Terror-stricken and barely managing to keep their

marching column together, they were driven back to their camp. This intrepid feat of the Achaeans obliged Seleucus to withdraw his camp from Pergamene territory.

When Antiochus was told that the Romans had arrived to offer protection to Adramytteum, he at least kept clear of that city, and after laying waste the countryside he went on to storm Peraea, a colony of the Mitylenaeans. Cotton, Corylenus, Aphrodisias, and †Prinne† were taken with the first assault. From there Antiochus returned to Sardis by way of Thatira, and Seleucus remained on the coast, intimidating some and assisting others. The Roman fleet along with Eumenes and the Rhodians came to Mitylene first of all, after that returning to Elaea, their starting-point. From there, on their journey to Phocaea, they put in at the island called Bacchium which overlooks the city of Phocaea, and after brutally plundering its temples and statues, which they had previously spared and with which the island was very well endowed, they crossed to the city itself. They proceeded with the attack after distributing amongst themselves the various responsibilities involved, and it looked as if the town could be taken by assault with scaling-ladders, without the use of siege-works. However, a garrison comprising 3,000 soldiers entered the city, sent by Antiochus, and the allies immediately abandoned the attack and retreated to the island, with nothing achieved save the plundering of enemy territory around the city.

22. It was decided that Eumenes should be sent home from here and that he should undertake for the consul and the army the necessary preparations for crossing the Hellespont. The Roman and Rhodian fleets were to return to Samos and there keep watch in case Polyxenidas moved from Ephesus. The king then returned to Elaea, the Romans and Rhodians to Samos. Here Marcus Aemilius, brother of the praetor, died.

There was a report of a fleet coming from Syria and, after Aemilius' funeral, the Rhodians set off to meet it with thirteen of their own ships, one Coan quinquereme and a second from Cnidus, sailing to Rhodes where they were to remain on guard. Thirteen ships had also been sent from Rhodes under the command of Pamphilidas against the same Syrian fleet, and, two days before Eudamus came from Samos with his fleet, these linked up with four ships that had been guarding Caria and raised the siege of Daedala and a number of other fortresses in Peraea which were being blockaded by the king's troops. The decision was made that Eudamus should leave at once, and he was assigned six open-decked vessels to add to the fleet which he commanded. After setting sail he made all the speed he could and overtook the men who had gone ahead at the port called Megiste. From there they came to Phaselis in a single column, and the best idea seemed to be to await the enemy in that spot.

23. Phaselis lies on the border of Lycia and Pamphylia. Projecting far out to sea, it is the first land to be sighted by voyagers coming from Cilicia to Rhodes and it also affords a view of shipping in the distance. For that reason more than any other it was chosen as the place to meet the enemy fleet. But there was an unforeseen occurrence: because of the insalubrious locality, the time of the year (it was midsummer) and also because of an unusual stench, diseases began to attack a large number of them, especially the oarsmen. Fearing this outbreak, they left the place, and as they were sailing along the Gulf of Pamphylia they put in at the River Eurymedon,* where they were told by the people of Aspendus that the enemy were already at Side. The king's navy had made quite a slow voyage because of the Etesians,* which make this an unfavourable time of the year, one almost exclusively given over to north-westerly winds. The Rhodians had thirty-two quadriremes and four triremes, and the king's fleet comprised thirty-seven ships of larger dimensions, including three galleys with seven banks of oars and four with six banks, and ten triremes in addition to these. From a look-out tower they perceived that the enemy was at hand.

The following day both fleets moved from port at dawn, assuming they would fight that day; and before the Rhodians passed the headland projecting into the sea from Side they were suddenly spotted by the enemy whom they also sighted themselves. In the king's fleet the left wing, which was on the side of the open sea, was commanded by Hannibal, the right by Apollonius, one of the king's courtiers; and they now had their vessels drawn up in line. The Rhodians came forward in a long line, the flagship of Eudamus first, Chariclitus bringing up the rear and Pamphilidas commanding the centre part of the fleet.

When Eudamus saw the enemy line drawn up and ready to join battle, he too moved out into open water, ordering the ships that were following to form a straight line while maintaining their order. Initially, this move caused confusion: Eudamus had not sailed far enough out to permit all his ships to be deployed in a line towards the land, and being over-hasty he engaged Hannibal with a mere five vessels. The others, because they had been ordered to make a line, were not following him. At the end of the column there was no room left on the landward side, and confusion reigned amongst them while the battle with Hannibal was starting on the right wing.

24. But in a trice the quality of their vessels and their accomplished seamanship removed all fear from the Rhodians. The ships sailed swiftly into open water, each leaving behind it space on the landward side for one moving up; and if any of them collided with an enemy vessel with its beak, it would tear open its prow or shear off its oars, or else, finding an open passage between the lines, it would sail past the enemy ship and attack its stern. The greatest dismay was occasioned by the sinking, after a single impact, of a king's ship with seven banks of oars by a much smaller Rhodian craft. As a result the right flank of the enemy was quite clearly preparing for flight. On the open water Eudamus, who had by far the advantage in all other respects, was under severe pressure from Hannibal because of his ships' superior numbers. He would have been surrounded by Hannibal had not the usual signal for bringing together a scattered fleet been raised on the flagship. At this all the ships that had been victorious on the right wing hurriedly got together to assist their comrades. Then Hannibal and the ships with him also took to flight, and the Rhodians were unable to give chase because most of the oarsmen were in poor health and so more quickly fatigued.

While they were rebuilding their strength with food where they had stopped on the open sea, Eudamus watched the enemy hauling their disabled and damaged vessels with tow ropes from open-decked ships, and saw not many more than twenty moving off unharmed. He called for silence from the tower of the flag-ship. 'Get up and take in a wonderful sight,' he said. They all rose and looked at their enemy in terror-stricken flight; and with almost one voice they shouted out that they should give chase. Eudamus' own ship had been damaged by numerous collisions, but he ordered Pamphilidas and Chariclitus to follow for as long as they thought they could in safety. They did follow for a while, but after Hannibal began to approach the shore they became afraid of being pinned down by the wind on a coast held by the enemy and they returned to Eudamus. Then with difficulty they towed to Phaselis the captured ship with seven banks of oars which had been wrecked with the first collision. They returned from there to Rhodes, elation over their victory taking second place to mutual recrimination over their failure to sink or capture the entire fleet of their enemy when it had been possible to do so.

Hannibal had suffered only one defeat, but, even so, he did not venture to sail beyond Lycia, despite his eagerness to join up with king's original fleet at the earliest opportunity. Moreover, the Rhodians sent Chariclitus with twenty beaked ships to Patara and the harbour of Megiste to see that he would not have the latitude to do that. They also ordered Eudamus to return to the Romans on Samos with seven of the largest ships from amongst the fleet that had been under his command so that he could use all his diplomacy and personal authority to push the Romans into storming Patara.

25. News of the victory first of all, and after that the arrival of the Rhodians, brought great joy to the Romans; and it was evident that, if the Rhodians had been relieved of the particular concern which they had voiced, they would have had the freedom of action to provide security for all the waterways in the region. But Antiochus' departure from Sardis †prevented them† from abandoning their protective role in Ionia and Aeolis, so that the coastal cities might not fall to him. The Rhodians sent Pamphilidas with four decked ships to join the fleet off Patara.

Antiochus was in the process of bringing together the garrisons from the city-states around him, but he had also sent emissaries to King Prusias of Bithynia* with a letter of complaint about the Romans' passage into Asia. They were coming, said Antiochus, to wipe out all monarchies, so that there would be no empire left anywhere in the world but that of Rome. Philip and Nabis had been conquered and he was the third to be under attack. As each lay next to a defeated neighbour, the fire next door, as it were, would sweep through them all. After him, the Romans' next step would be into Bithynia, since Eumenes had already acquiesced in voluntary servitude.

Antiochus' words troubled Prusias, who was only diverted from such suspicions by a letter from the consul, Scipio, and more so by one from Scipio's brother, Africanus. The latter drove Prusias to make himself worthy of his friendship by referring to the enduring practice of the Roman people of bestowing all manner of honours on

allied royalty to promote their standing, and also by adducing
examples of Africanus' own record in this. He pointed to petty chieftains in Spain whom he had made his protégés and left as kings; and
to Masinissa whom he had not only set on his father's throne, but
also put on that of Syphax, by whom he had been earlier deposed—
and, as well as being by far the richest of the kings of Africa, Masinissa could match any king in the entire world in regal majesty and
power. Philip and Nabis had been enemies conquered in war by
Titus Quinctius, he continued, but even so they had been left on the
throne. Indeed, Philip had even seen payment of his tribute remitted
the previous year, and his hostage son returned to him. He had also
recovered a number of city-states outside Macedonia, with the
acquiescence of the Roman commanders. Nabis, too, would have
been held in the same regard if his own madness in the first place,
and then the treachery of the Aetolians, had not destroyed him. The
king's mind was really made up when the ambassador who came to
him from Rome was Gaius Livius, who had earlier commanded the
fleet as praetor, and when Livius explained to him how much more
certain were the Romans' hopes of victory than Antiochus', and how
much more inviolate and reliable a friendship with the Romans
would be.

26. After losing all hope of an alliance with Prusias, Antiochus left
Sardis for Ephesus to inspect the fleet, which had for a number of
months been fitted out and made ready for action. He did this more
because he could see it was impossible to resist the Roman army and
the two Scipios with his land-forces than because he had ever had
any success in naval warfare himself, or because he felt any great or
certain confidence in it at that time. For the moment, however, he
had some reason to be hopeful because he had heard that most of the
Rhodian fleet was off Patara and also that Eumenes had left for the
Hellespont with all his ships to rendezvous with the consul; and his
spirits were further raised by the piece of treacherous opportunism
that had put paid to the Rhodian fleet at Samos. His confidence
raised by these considerations, Antiochus sent Polyxenidas with the
fleet to put fortune to the test in any manner of engagement, and he
himself led the troops to Notium. This is a town belonging to Colophon, overlooking the sea and about two miles distant from old
Colophon. He wanted to have the town itself under his control—it
lay so close to Ephesus that no activity on land or sea could escape

the eyes of the Colophonians, by whom it would be immediately made known to the Romans. He was convinced that when they heard about the siege the Romans would move their fleet from Samos to bring succour to an allied city, and that would be Polyxenidas' opportunity to come to grips with them. He therefore proceeded to invest the city with siege-works. He ran parallel walls down to the sea on both sides, and on either side he brought siege-sheds and a mound up to the wall and moved up the battering-ram with its protective cover.

Cowed by the dangers facing them, the Colophonians sent spokesmen to Lucius Aemilius on Samos begging for the protection of the praetor and the Roman people. Aemilius was galled by his long period of inactivity at Samos, for the last thing he expected was that Polyxenidas, whom he had twice challenged in vain, would give him the opportunity to engage. Moreover, he thought it a disgrace that the fleet of Eumenes should be helping the consul transport the legions to Asia while he himself was tied up bringing relief to the beleaguered city of Colophon, with no idea of when the operation would end. The Rhodian Eudamus, who had also kept him at Samos earlier when he wanted to leave for the Hellespont, was now joined by all the others in pressing him to stay—much better to raise the blockade of his allies, they said, or else inflict another defeat on a navy they had already beaten once, and thereby wrest from the enemy total control of the sea. Much better that than to abandon his allies, surrender mastery of Asia on land and sea to Antiochus, and leave his own sector of the war by going to the Hellespont where the fleet of Eumenes provided sufficient service.

27. Their provisions exhausted, the Romans set off from Samos to gather supplies and were preparing to cross to Chios (this served as a granary for the Romans, and was a place to which all transport vessels sent from Italy directed their course). They sailed from the city to the other side of the island, which faces north towards Chios and Erythrae, and were preparing to make the crossing when the praetor was informed in a letter that a large quantity of grain had reached Chios from Italy, but that the ships carrying wine had been held up by bad weather. Along with this came news that the people of Teos had supplied the king's fleet with generous quantities of provisions, and had promised 5,000 jars of wine. In mid-journey Aemilius suddenly turned the fleet towards Teos, intending to take

over the supplies prepared for the enemy with the agreement of the people of Teos, or else to treat these latter as enemies. After turning their prows toward the shore, some fifteen ships appeared before them off Myonnesus, and the praetor, initially believing them to be from the king's fleet, proceeded to give chase. But it then became clear that they were cutters and skiffs of buccaneers. These had been raiding the coastline of Chios and were returning with all manner of booty; and when they saw the Roman fleet from the open sea they turned to flight. They had the advantage of speed with their lighter vessels which had been designed only for that purpose, and they were also closer to land. As a result, they made good their escape to Myonnesus before the Roman fleet could get near them. The praetor, who had no knowledge of the area, began to follow them, thinking he could force the ships out of the harbour.

Myonnesus is a promontory lying between Teos and Samos, and is actually a cone-shaped hill rising from a rather broad base to a sharp peak. On the landward side it is accessible by a narrow pathway, and on the seaward side it terminates with cliffs eroded by the waves, so that in places the overhanging rocks jut out to sea beyond the vessels that are at anchor there. The Roman ships did not venture to approach land in that area for fear of coming within weapon-range of the pirates, who were standing on the cliffs above them, and so they frittered away a day. Finally, with approach of night, they abandoned their abortive enterprise and moved on to Teos the following day. They moored their ships in the harbour behind the town—its local name is Geraesticus—and the praetor sent his men forth to pillage the countryside around the city.

28. As the pillaging went on before their eyes, the people of Teos sent spokesmen to the Roman commander with the fillets and branches of suppliants.* These attempted to exonerate their community of any hostility towards the Romans in either word or deed, but Aemilius charged them with having given assistance to the enemy fleet with all manner of provisions and drew attention to the amount of wine they had promised Polyxenidas. He added that if they provided the Roman fleet with the same quantity of supplies he would recall his men from their marauding, but that he would otherwise treat them as foes. When the envoys reported this sinister response, the people were summoned to a meeting by the magistrates to discuss the action they should take.

Polyxenidas had left Colophon with the king's fleet on hearing that the Romans had moved from Samos and were pillaging the fields of the Teians, after their pursuit of the pirates to Myonnesus, and that their ships were at anchor in the harbour of Geraesticus. On that day he happened to drop anchor in a sequestered harbour on an island opposite Myonnesus which sailors call Macris. From there Polyxenidas examined what his enemy was doing at close quarters, and at first he had high hopes of defeating the Roman fleet by the same means as he had the Rhodian at Samos, when he had blockaded the narrow exit from the harbour. The natural features of the place are not dissimilar: the harbour is so restricted by two promontories coming together that it is barely possible for two ships to make their exit at the same time. Polyxenidas' intention was to seize the harbour-mouth at night; then, with ten ships stationed off each of the two promontories to attack the enemy vessels side-on from both flanks as they came out, he would put ashore soldiers from the rest of the fleet, as he had at Panhormus, and make a simultaneous assault on the enemy by land and sea. His plan would not have gone awry had not the Romans decided, when the Teians promised to meet their demands, that it was better for the fleet to move to the harbour in front of the city in order to take the supplies on board. It is also said that the Rhodian Eudamus pointed out the shortcomings of the other port when two ships happened to break off their oars after becoming entangled in the restricted harbour-entrance; and the danger on the landward side, with Antochus encamped not far away, was also one of a number of factors that induced the praetor to transfer the fleet.

29. The fleet was brought round to the city in complete secrecy, and the soldiers and crews disembarked to distribute the supplies, the wine in particular, amongst the ships. Then, about midday, it so happened that a peasant was brought to the praetor and he reported that a fleet had been riding at anchor off the island of Macris for two days now, and that a short while ago a number of the ships appeared to be moving, as if getting ready to sail. The praetor was stunned by this unexpected news. He ordered the bugles sounded for the return of all those dispersed in the fields, and he sent the tribunes to the city to bring together the soldiers and sailors to the ships. The ensuing panic resembled that seen when a fire suddenly breaks out or a city has been captured. Some were running to the city to fetch their

comrades, others were swiftly heading back to the ships from town; and with orders confounded by the confused shouts, which themselves were being drowned out by the bugles, they finally converged on the ships. Each man could scarcely recognize his own ship, or reach it in the mêlée; and the panic could have produced a dangerous situation both on land and sea had it not been for the division of tasks made by Aemilius and by Eudamus and the Rhodian fleet. The former was the first to sail out from the port into open water with his flagship, drawing out the other ships, which followed in his wake, and then setting each ship in its place to form a line; and Eudamus and the Rhodians meanwhile stuck close to shore so that the men could board without commotion, and each ship could make its exit as soon as it was ready.

So it was that the foremost vessels formed up in line before the praetor's eyes, while the rear was brought up by the Rhodians, and the whole line advanced into open water, drawn up in order, as if they had the king's men in view. They were between Myonnesus and the promontory of Corycus when they caught sight of the enemy. The king's fleet, which was approaching in a long line, two ships abreast, also formed up facing their enemy, and extended the left wing far enough to enable it to overlap and surround the Roman right. Eudamus, who was bringing up the allied rear, saw that the Romans were unable to make their line equal to the king's and that they were on the verge of being surrounded on the right wing. Making his ships put on speed—and the Rhodian vessels were by far the swiftest in the entire fleet—he made the flank equal to the enemy's and then set his own ship in the path of the enemy flagship which had Polyxenidas on board.

30. By now battle had been joined in every quarter by the entire fleets. On the Roman side eighty ships were taking part in the engagement, twenty-two of them Rhodian. The enemy fleet comprised eighty-nine vessels, and its largest ships were three with six banks of oars and two with seven. The Romans were far superior to the Rhodians in the robustness of their vessels and the courage of their men, while the Rhodian ships had the advantage in mobility, the helmsmen's skill, and the proficiency of the oarsmen. However, the ships carrying fire before them inspired the greatest terror in the enemy, and what had proved their unique source of salvation when they were surrounded at Panhormus was what on this occasion

contributed most to their victory. Fear of the flames before them made the king's ships turn aside to avoid collision. The result was that they were then unable to strike the enemy with their beaks, and at the same time they exposed themselves to broadside ramming; and any ship that did engage was consumed by the fire that poured onto it— so they were more in dread of the flames than they were of combat.

But, as usual, what counted most in the fighting was the courage of the men. After breaking the centre of the enemy line, the Romans sailed around and made an attack from the rear on the king's ships that were engaging the Rhodians. In a moment the centre of Antiochus' line and the ships on the left flank were being surrounded and sunk. The right wing remained intact, and the sailors were more frightened by the disaster that had overtaken their comrades than by the peril they faced themselves; but when they saw the others surrounded and Polyxenidas' flagship abandoning their comrades and sailing off, they hurriedly raised their topsails and fled—and there was a following wind for the journey to Ephesus. They had lost forty-two ships in the engagement: thirteen had fallen into the hands of their enemy, and the others had been burned or sunk. On the Roman side two ships were wrecked and a number disabled, and one Rhodian vessel was captured through an extraordinary mishap. After ramming a Sidonian ship with its beak, its anchor was flung out of the ship by the actual force of the collision, and this held to the prow of the other ship with its fluke, just like a grappling iron. Panic ensued and the Rhodians backed water as they tried to break free of the enemy. The cable was dragged along, becoming entangled in the oars, and sheering them off on one side of the ship. The vessel thus disabled was then captured by the very one with which it had become entangled after ramming it. Such, by and large, was the action in the sea battle off Myonnesus.

31. The defeat alarmed Antiochus. Deprived of his mastery of the sea he had no confidence in his ability to defend his distant territories, and he ordered his garrison to be withdrawn from Lysimachia for fear of its being overrun there by the Romans. As subsequent events demonstrated, this was a foolish decision. It would have been easy for him not only to defend Lysimachia against the initial Roman offensive but also to sustain a winter-long siege and even to reduce the blockading force to utter privation by dragging out the exercise, during which time he could have taken every opportunity of exploring the prospects for peace. After the naval defeat, he not only delivered Lysimachia to his enemies but he also abandoned the siege of Colophon and retreated to Sardis. From there he sent men to King Ariarathes in Cappadocia to fetch reinforcements,* and to every other place he could to amass troops, wholly bent now on one purpose, to decide the matter on the field of battle.

After his victory at sea Aemilius Regillus set sail for Ephesus. Here he lined up his ships before the harbour and wrested from the enemy a final acknowledgement that they had ceded control of the sea. He then sailed to Chios, to which he had been headed when he left Samos before the naval battle. There he repaired the ships that had been damaged in the engagement, and sent Lucius Aemilius Scaurus to the Hellespont with thirty ships to transport the army over it. The Rhodians he instructed to return home, honouring them with a portion of the booty and with the naval spoils. Instead, they enthusiastically turned themselves to ferrying over the consul's forces, finally returning to Rhodes only after they had performed this additional task.

The Roman fleet crossed from Chios to Phocaea. This city lies deep in a bay on the coast and is of oblong shape. It is surrounded by a wall two-and-a-half miles long, and it tapers at both ends into a wedge-like shape. It is called Lampter by the local people. The bay at this point has a width of 1,200 yards, and from it a spit of land runs a mile into the sea, virtually splitting the bay down the middle like a line. At the point where it is joined to the mainland by a narrow isthmus it forms two very safe harbours on either side. The one facing south is called Naustathmos from the fact that it has the capacity to hold an extremely large number of ships, and the other is close to Lampter itself.

32. The Roman fleet occupied these safe harbours, but before employing scaling-ladders or earthworks to assault the city-walls the praetor felt he should send a delegation to sound out the feelings of the leading citizens and magistrates. When he saw that they were intransigent, he proceeded with an attack at two points simultaneously. One of these spots was not densely built-up, with temples of the gods covering much of the area. It was here that Regillus first moved up the ram and began to batter the walls and turrets. Then, when the inhabitants rushed to the spot in large numbers to defend it, a battering-ram was moved up at the other point as well, and the

walls were then being demolished in both locations. Where they collapsed, the Roman soldiers were making their attack over the debris of the fallen masonry, while others were also trying to scale the walls with ladders, but so stubbornly did the townspeople resist that it was readily apparent that they received more protection from their arms and their courage than from their fortifications.

The praetor was accordingly obliged by the danger facing his men to order the retreat to be sounded, fearful as he was of exposing his unwary soldiers to men insane with frenzied despair. Not even when the battle was suspended did the townspeople stop to rest; instead, they rushed off in every direction to strengthen the walls and fill in gaps where they had been demolished. They were engaged in this task when they were approached by Quintus Antonius, who had been sent by the praetor. Antonius castigated them for their obduracy and pointed out that the Romans were more concerned than they that the fighting not result in the destruction of the city. If they ended their insane conduct, he said, they were being offered the opportunity of surrendering on the same terms on which they had formerly capitulated to Gaius Livius.

Hearing this, the townspeople took a period of five days to deliberate. During this time they tried to ascertain if there was any prospect of help from Antiochus, but when the envoys they had sent to the king brought word that no assistance was forthcoming from him, they opened their gates on the understanding that they not be treated as enemies.

The standards were carried into the city and the praetor had announced that he wanted the people spared, since they had surrendered. Then the cry went up all over that it was a disgrace that the Phocaeans should get off scot-free when they always been implacable enemies and never loyal allies. After these words the men scattered in all directions to plunder the city as if on a signal from the praetor. At first Aemilius tried to stop them and call them back, saying that it was captured cities that were ransacked, not those which surrendered, and even then it was up to the general, not his men, to make the decision. But their rage and greed proved stronger than his authority, and he then sent heralds throughout the city to order all free men of the town to come to him in the forum to avoid mistreatment. And the praetor was true to his word in all that was subject to his control. He restored to them their city, their lands, and their self-government; and as winter was now drawing on he chose the harbours of Phocaea as the winter base for his fleet.

33. The consul had now passed through the territory of the Aenians and Maronians, and it was at about this time that he was brought word that the king's fleet had been defeated off Myonnesus and that Lysimachia had been vacated by his garrison. The latter was far more pleasing news than the naval victory, especially after they reached Lysimachia and found the city well-stocked with all manner of provisions, as if in anticipation of the army's arrival, when they had imagined themselves facing extreme privation and hardship in blockading the city. They encamped there a few days to allow the baggage to catch up with them, as well as the sick, who had been left throughout the strongholds of Thrace, exhausted by their illnesses and the long march. After recovering all of these, they resumed the march and made their way to the Hellespont through the Chersonese.* Here, thanks to the efforts of Eumenes, all the preparations for the sea passage had been made, and they made an orderly crossing to what seemed like pacified shores, meeting no opposition and with ships sailing to different parts of the coast. This actually boosted the confidence of the Romans: they could see that they had been allowed a crossing to Asia, which they had anticipated would involve heavy fighting. After this they remained in camp on the Hellespont for some time because it so happened that the days of the moving of the shields*—when there is a religious injunction against travelling—had come round. Those same days had also occasioned Publius Scipio's separation from the army—the religious obligations touched him more personally because he was a Salian priest*—and he too caused delay for the army until he caught up.

34. As it happened, Heraclides of Byzantium had at that time come to the camp as an emissary from Antiochus bearing instructions for peace-negotiations. He was led to high hopes of gaining peace by the fact that the Romans who, he had believed, would make for the king's encampment at a rapid pace as soon as they reached Asia, were in fact taking their time and delaying matters. Heraclides decided to approach Publius Scipio first, rather than the consul, and such had been his orders from the king. It was in Scipio that Antiochus had placed his greatest hopes : the man's magnanimity and the fact that he had had more than enough glory made him particularly forgiving, and, apart from that, the whole world knew the kind of

victor he had been in Spain and after that in Africa. There was also the fact that his son was a prisoner-of-war in the king's hands.

There is, as often, little agreement among the authorities on where, when and in what circumstances the son was taken prisoner. Some say that he was intercepted by the king's ships while he was making for Oreus from Chalcis at the beginning of the war. Others claim that his capture dates to a time after the crossing to Asia, when he had been sent on a reconnaissance mission towards the king's camp with a Fregellan squadron. Some enemy cavalry rushed out to meet him and, while he was beating a retreat, he fell from his horse in the mêlée and was captured with two cavalrymen and taken to the king. On one point there is general agreement: had a state of peace existed then between the king and the Roman people, and personal ties of hospitality between him and the Scipios, the young man could not have received kinder and more considerate treatment than he did.

It was for these reasons that the emissary had awaited the arrival of Publius Scipio, and when he came he approached the consul with a request that he hear the instructions he had been given.

35. A full council was convened, and the emissary was given an audience. Many delegations had previously gone to and fro in search of peace, he said, but without result; and yet he felt confident of gaining a treaty for the very reason that those previous embassies had achieved nothing. For in those conferences Zmyrna, Lampsacus, Alexandria Troas, and, in Europe, Lysimachia had been contested items. With regard to these, the king had already withdrawn from Lysimachia so that the Romans might not claim that he had possessions in Europe; and he was ready to surrender the communities in Asia, and any others they might wish to claim from the king's empire, on the grounds that they were supporters of the Roman cause. Furthermore, the king would pay the Roman people half the costs of the war.

Such were the terms of peace he put forward. The rest of his address was devoted to urging the Romans to remember the human condition, to be circumspect with regard to their own fortunes and not deal harshly with those of others. He asked them to limit their empire to Europe. It was still immense, he said, and the piecemeal acquisition of territory had been an easier matter than keeping the whole would be. But if the Romans also wished to take away a part of

Asia, he continued, the king's restraint would permit him to bend before Roman acquisitiveness, just for the sake of peace and concord—provided that the area have clearly defined limits.

What the emissary thought important concessions for obtaining peace the Romans found insignificant. Even with regard to the expenses for the war, they thought it only fair that the king cover them all since it was his fault that the war had been started in the first place; and it was not just a matter of the withdrawal of the king's garrisons from Ionia and Aeolis—as all Greece had been liberated, so too all cities lying in Asia should be liberated. And this could be done only by Antiochus ceding possession of Asia this side of the Taurus mountains.

36. The emissary began to feel that he was getting no favourable response in the council, and so he attempted to sound out Publius Scipio's feelings in private (for such had been his instructions). The very first thing he said to Scipio was that the king would restore his son without ransom. Then, having no knowledge of Scipio's personality and the Roman character, he promised him an enormous quantity of gold and partnership in Antiochus' entire kingdom—the royal title alone being excepted—if he succeeded in gaining peace through Scipio's intervention.

In reply Scipio said: 'Your ignorance of the Romans in general, and of me, the man to whom you have been sent, I find the less surprising when I see your ignorance of the fortunes of the man from whom you come. You should have retained possession of Lysimachia to stop us entering the Chersonese, or you should have opposed us at the Hellespont to prevent our crossing to Asia—that is, if you intended to seek terms of peace from a foe whom you expected to be apprehensive about the outcome of the war. But after allowing us passage into Asia and after accepting not just our reins but our yoke as well, what room has been left for negotiations on equal terms, when you have to submit to our authority? Personally, I shall regard my son as the greatest gift forthcoming from your king's generosity. As for his other presents, I pray to heaven that my circumstances never have need of them—my heart, at least, will not need them. For so great an act of generosity towards me he shall find me appreciative—if he wishes to accept reciprocity on a personal level for a personal gift. In my official capacity I shall accept nothing from him and I shall give him nothing. What I *can* give him at the moment is a piece of honest advice. Go and tell him this from me: he should give up the war and refuse no terms of peace.'

This did nothing to sway the king. He felt that war would now be a safe bet since terms were already being dictated to him as if he were defeated. For the moment he set aside talk of peace and focused all his attention on preparing for war.

37. When all had been prepared for carrying through his plans, the consul moved from his base camp and came first to Dardanus, and after that to Rhoeteum, the people of both communities pouring out to meet him. From there he advanced to Ilium, and encamped in the plain beneath its walls. He went up to the city and to its citadel, and offered sacrifice to Minerva,* protectress of the citadel. Meanwhile, the people of Ilium declared the Romans their descendants by showing them every mark of respect in their words and actions, while the Romans expressed pleasure at returning to their roots.

Setting off from Ilium, they reached the source of the River Caicus after five days' march. Eumenes also came to this area. He had attempted to bring his fleet back to Elaea from the Hellespont to pass the winter, but facing contrary winds he failed to round the promontory of Lecton during a period of several days. Accordingly, in order not to miss the early stages of the campaign, he disembarked and hurried to the Roman camp by the shortest route at the head of a small detachment. He was sent back to Pergamum from the camp to organize provisions and, after delivering grain to the people specified by the consul, he returned to the same base camp. The plan was to prepare several days' worth of rations and head out against the enemy from there before winter overtook them.

The king's camp was in the neighbourhood of Thyatira. Here Antiochus heard that Publius Scipio had fallen ill and been taken to Elaea, and he sent a delegation to take his son back to him. This was not just a gift that pleased the father's heart—Scipio's joy was good for the health of his body, too. When he had eventually embraced his son to his heart's content, he said: 'Report to the king that I thank him, but cannot reciprocate in any other way than by urging him not to take the field until he hears that I have returned to camp.'

His 60,000 infantry and a cavalry force of more than 12,000 occasionally inspired him to confidence about the impending conflict, but Antiochus was moved by the great man's authority—facing the vicissitudes of war, he had pinned all his hopes on him for assistance, come what may. He therefore withdrew and, crossing the River Phrygius, pitched camp in the area of Magnesia-near-Sipylus. To prevent a Roman assault on his fortifications if he decided to delay matters, he dug a ditch six cubits deep and twelve cubits wide around them. He then surrounded the outside of the ditch with a double rampart, and on the inner bank he raised a wall, with turrets at short intervals, by which the enemy could be easily prevented from crossing the ditch.

38. Thinking the king to be in the vicinity of Thyatira, the consul by forced marches came down to the Hyrcanian plain four days later. At the news that Antiochus had left the area, he followed in his tracks and encamped this side of the River Phrygius, four miles from the enemy. Here about 1,000 enemy cavalry crossed the river—they were Galatians for the most part, but with a number of Dahae and mounted archers from other races amongst them—and made a furious attack on the forward posts of the Romans. Since the latter were not formed up, the enemy at first threw them into confusion; but then, as the battle went on and the Roman numbers increased, with reinforcements being easily brought up from the camp nearby, the king's men tired and were unable to cope with the greater numbers. They tried to pull back, but before they could make it to the river a number of them were cut down on the riverbank by the Romans who were putting pressure on their rear.

There followed two days of inactivity, with neither side crossing the river, but on the third day the Romans all crossed in a concerted movement, pitching camp about two-and-a-half miles from the enemy. They were measuring out the camp and engaged in fortifying it when 3,000 hand-picked cavalry and infantry of the king's appeared, creating great panic and uproar. The men at the Roman forward post were considerably outnumbered, but through their own efforts, and without calling any soldiers away from fortifying the camp, they managed to keep the battle equal in its initial stages; and as the fighting intensified they drove the enemy back, killing a hundred of them and taking about a hundred prisoners. In the four-day period that followed both lines stood drawn up before their ramparts, and on the fifth day the Romans advanced to the centre of the field. Antiochus did not move his standards forward at all, so that his men at the rear were less than 1,000 feet from the rampart.

39. When the consul saw that the enemy was refusing to engage,

he called a meeting the following day to discuss what should be done if Antiochus gave them no opportunity to fight. Winter was coming on, he said, and either the troops would have to be billeted in tents or else, if he decided to retire to winter-quarters, the campaign would have to be deferred till the summer.

No enemy was ever regarded with such disdain by the Romans. The cry went up on all sides that Scipio should lead them out at once and exploit the fervour of the men—these now felt that they did not have to do battle with so many thousands of the enemy so much as slaughter that number of cattle, and they were ready to cross ditches and a rampart to reach the camp if the enemy would not come out to fight. Gnaeus Domitius was sent to inspect the route and the direction from which the enemy rampart could be approached, and after he came back with a full and reliable report, it was decided that the camp should be moved closer to the enemy the following day. On the third day the standards were advanced to the centre of the field, and the deployment of the battle-line began. Antiochus also felt he should evade the issue no longer in case his refusal to engage should weaken the morale of his men and also boost the hopes of the enemy. He, too, led out his forces, advancing so far from his camp as to make it clear that he intended to fight.

The Roman battle-line was more or less uniform in terms both of men and weaponry. There were two Roman legions, and two units of allies and members of the Latin League. Each of these bodies comprised 5,400 men. The Romans formed the centre, the Latins the wings. The front line was made up of *hastati*, after which came the *principes*, and the *triarii* brought up †the rear†. Such was the 'regular' battle formation, but apart from that the consul also set on the right flank, lined up with the legions, Eumenes' auxiliaries, some 3,000 infantrymen, combined with a number of Achaean *caetrati*. Beyond these he positioned a force of fewer than 3,000 horse, 800 of which were Eumenes' soldiers and all the others Roman cavalrymen. On the outer flank he placed the Trallians and Cretans, each group numbering 500 men. The left wing appeared not to require such an auxiliary force in position against the enemy because, on that side, cover was afforded by the river with its steep banks, but four cavalry-squadrons were stationed there just the same.

Such was the sum of the Roman troops, apart from the combined force of 2,000 Macedonians and Thracians who had come along with them as volunteers—these were left to guard the camp. The Romans placed sixteen elephants in reserve to the rear of the *triarii*. It was evident that they could not stand up to the superior number of the king's elephants (there were fifty-four of them) and apart from that African elephants are no match for Indian* elephants even when numbers are the same because they are inferior either in terms of size—the Indian animals are much larger—or in fortitude.

40. The king's line of battle was more diverse, composed as it was of many races with different weaponry and different supporting troops. There were 16,000 infantry called *phalangitae* who were armed in Macedonian fashion.* These formed the centre of the line, and were divided into ten sections in front, the sections being separated by pairs of elephants* set between them. From the front this grouping extended backwards thirty-two ranks deep. This was the strength of the king's forces, and it inspired great fear by its general appearance in the first place, but also because of the elephants towering so high amongst the soldiers. These beasts were huge themselves, and they were made the more striking by their ornaments and crests, and by towers set on their backs, with four armed men, not including the driver, standing in each of them. To the right of the *phalangitae* the king stationed 1,500 Galatian infantry, and next to them he placed 3,000 mail-clad cavalry with the native name *cataphracti*. Added to these was a squadron of some 1,000 cavalry which they called an *agema*.* These were Medes, hand-picked men, with an admixture of cavalry from many races in the same region. Flanking these, and kept in reserve, was a herd of sixteen elephants. On the same side, the wing being extended a little, was the royal company, called the *argyraspids* after the kind of arms they bore. Next came the Dahae, 1,200 mounted archers; then the light infantry, 3,000 strong, made up of Cretans and Trallians in roughly equal numbers; and attached to these were 2,500 Mysian bowmen. The end of the wing was composed of a mixture of Cyrtian slingers and Elymaean archers, totalling 4,000 men.

On the left wing the *phalangitae* were flanked by 1,500 Galatian infantry and 2,000 Cappadocians with arms similar to theirs (these had been sent to the king by Ariarathes). After these came a mixture of all kinds of auxiliary troops, totalling 2,700; then 3,000 mounted *cataphracti*, plus 1,000 other cavalrymen who formed the royal squadron (their own armour and that of their mounts were lighter, but otherwise they were fitted out like the others). These were mostly Syrian, with an admixture of Phrygians and Lydians. Before this cavalry force there were scythed chariots* and the camels called dromedaries. Riding the latter were Arab archers carrying narrow-bladed swords which were four cubits in length, to enable them to reach the enemy from their elevated position. After these came another horde equal in size to the one on the right wing: Tarentines* first of all, then 2,500 Galatian horse, followed by 1,000 Neocretans and 15,000 similarly armed Carians and Cilicians, the same number of Trallians, and 4,000 *caetrati* (Pisidians, Pamphylians, and Lycians). After these there were Cyrtian and Elymaean auxiliary forces in numbers equal to those stationed on the right wing, and sixteen elephants a short space from them.

41. The king himself was on the right wing; on the left he put in command his son Seleucus and his brother's son, Antipater.* The centre of the line was assigned to three men: Minnio, Zeuxis, and Philip,* the master of the elephants.

There was a morning mist which rose to form clouds as the day advanced and produced overcast conditions. Then a drizzle, like that brought by the south wind, dampened everything. While these factors had no adverse affects on the Romans, they were particularly disadvantageous for the king's troops. Their line being relatively short, the faintness of the light did not hamper the Romans' view in any direction and, their troops being almost exclusively heavy-armed, the drizzle did not take the edge off swords or spears. With a wide line of battle, the king's men were unable to see from the centre to the wings, and much less could the wings keep each other in sight, while the drizzle had taken the tautness out of bows, slings, and spear-thongs. In addition to this, the scythed chariots, with which Antiochus had believed he would throw the enemy line into disarray, instead brought terror to the Syrians themselves.

The chariots were fitted out much as follows. There were spikes projecting like horns on both sides of the pole at a point ten cubits from the yoke, designed to transfix anything that came in their way; and at either end of the yoke two blades protruded, the one on a level with the yoke, the other below it and pointing towards the ground— the former intended to slash through whatever met it on the sides, the latter to catch any who fell or lay beneath the chariot. There were also two blades attached in similar fashion, pointing in different directions, to the wheel-hubs on both sides. As was observed above, the king had positioned the chariots, armed in this manner, in the front line, because it would have been necessary to drive them through his own men if they had been placed at the extremities of the line or in the centre.

Eumenes saw this. He was †an experienced soldier and knew the danger inherent in† that sort of auxiliary force if one were to strike panic in the horses rather attack in a regular battle. He therefore ordered his Cretan bowmen, his slingers, and his spear-men, together with <. . .> of cavalry, to rush ahead, spread out as much as possible instead of maintaining close order, and to hurl their weapons from all sides at the same time. It was as if a storm hit the horses—the wounds dealt by the missiles hurled from every quarter on the one hand, the discordant shouts on the other—and it so terrified them that they suddenly bolted in all directions indiscriminately, as though they had no reins. The light infantry, the lightly equipped slingers, and the swift-moving Cretans would swerve to avoid them as they charged; and the cavalry were heightening with their pursuit the confusion and panic in the horses and camels, who were also caught up in the same commotion—and added to it all were the redoubled shouts from the crowd of bystanders. So it was that the chariots were driven away from the ground between the two lines, and once this ridiculous side-show was removed from the scene the signal was given on both sides and they proceeded to a regular battle.

42. Nevertheless, that futile episode soon proved to be the cause of a real calamity. For the panic and confusion amongst the chariots struck dismay into the supporting auxiliary troops who had been stationed next to them, and these took to flight, exposing the entire formation right through to the mail-armoured cavalry. When the Roman cavalry reached the latter, with their cover now dissipated they failed to resist even the first charge: some were put to flight, and others, weighed down by their protective armour and weapons, were killed. Then the entire left wing gave way and, after the auxiliary forces posted between the cavalry and the troops called *phalangitae* were thrown into disorder, the panic reached as far as the centre. The ranks in this quarter were now reduced to confusion, and the use of their long spears, called *sarisae* by the Macedonians, was obstructed by their own men fleeing through the lines, whereupon the Roman legions advanced and hurled their javelins at their disordered foe. Not even the elephants positioned amongst the enemy could unnerve the Roman soldiers who, after the African wars, were now accustomed to sidestepping the charging animal and showering javelins upon it from the side or else slashing its hamstring with the sword, if they could get close to it.

By now the centre had been almost completely brought down at the front, and the auxiliary troops had been encircled and were being cut to pieces from the rear. Then the Romans discovered that their comrades were in flight on the other side, and heard their panicking shouts close to the camp itself. In fact, Antiochus could see that on his right flank, because the Romans were trusting to the river, there were no auxiliaries apart from four squadrons of cavalry, and that the latter were leaving the bank exposed by sticking close to the main body of their comrades. He therefore launched an attack on this position from the right wing, using his auxiliary troops and mail-armoured cavalry, not merely exerting pressure on the front, but also also encircling the wing on the side of the river and driving in from the flank as well. Eventually, the cavalry were routed, and then the nearest of the footsoldiers were driven back to the camp in headlong flight.

43. In command of the camp was the military tribune Marcus Aemilius, son of Marcus Lepidus, the one who became pontifex maximus a few years after this. Aemilius hastened with his entire garrison to the point where he saw his comrades in flight, and ordered these first to stop and then to return to the fight, berating them for their panic and shameful flight. Next came threats—they were rushing blindly to their own destruction if they did not obey his command, he said—and finally he gave his men the signal to cut down the leading fugitives and use sword-thrusts to drive back into the enemy the horde that was following them. The fear this inspired was greater than the other and conquered it. The danger on both sides at first made them halt; then they returned to the fray, and Aemilius with his garrison, which comprised 2,000 stalwart men, resolutely opposed the king's vigorous pursuit. When Eumenes' brother, Attalus, saw his comrades fleeing on the left, and the commotion evolving around the camp, he made a timely appearance on the scene with 200 cavalry from the right wing where the enemy's left had been driven back with the first assault.

On seeing the men whom he had just witnessed in flight now returning to battle, as well as another horde of men streaming forward both from the camp and the battle-line, Antiochus wheeled round his horse to flee. And so the Romans, victorious on both wings, pushed forward to plunder the camp, clambering over mounds of corpses which they had piled up, especially in the centre of the line where flight had been hindered both by the vigour of the enemy's finest troops and the weight of their arms. With Eumenes' cavalry in front, and the rest of the horse following them, they pursued the enemy throughout the plain, killing those at the rear as they overtook them. But a greater handicap for the fugitives was their own disorder, caught up as they were amongst chariots, elephants, and camels. When they broke ranks they would crash into each other like blind men and were then trodden under by the charging animals. In the camp, too, there were casualties on a massive scale, almost greater than in the battle. The first men to flee had mostly headed for the camp, and the soldiers in the garrison there were encouraged by this accession of numbers to put up a more stubborn defence of the rampart. The Romans were held up at the gateways and the rampart, which they had expected to take simply with their assault, and when they eventually broke through their fury made them produce a bloodier slaughter.

44. Some 50,000 infantry and 3,000 cavalry are said to have been killed that day, with 1,400 captured along with fifteen elephants and their drivers. A number of Romans were wounded, but no more than 300 infantrymen and 24 cavalrymen lost their lives, and 25 from Eumenes' army.

On that day the victors plundered the enemy camp and returned to their own with a rich booty. The following day they proceeded to strip the bodies of the enemy dead and herd together the captives. Ambassadors now came from Thyatira and Magnesia-near-Sipylus to surrender their cities. Antiochus was in flight with a few men, but more gathered around him on the actual journey, so that he arrived at Sardis about midnight with a small group of armed men. Then, told that his son Seleucus and a number of his courtiers had gone on to Apamea, he headed for Apamea himself at the fourth watch with his wife and daughter, leaving the defence of the city of Sardis to Xenon and putting Timon in command of Lydia. The authority of these commanders was disregarded, and following an agreement struck between the townspeople and the soldiers in the citadel, a deputation was sent to the consul.

45. At about the same time envoys arrived from Tralles,* Magnesia-on-the-Maeander, and Ephesus to surrender their respective cities. After hearing about the battle Polyxenidas had left Ephesus. He came by sea as far as Patara in Lycia, but fearing the Rhodian ships stationed at Megiste he then disembarked and with a small retinue took the overland route to Syria. The communities of Asia now began to put themselves in the consul's hands and under the authority of the Roman people. The consul was by this time at Sardis, and as soon as Publius Scipio could stand the fatigue of the journey, he too came here from Elaea.

At about the same time a herald from Antiochus, using Publius Scipio as an intermediary, asked that the king be allowed to send spokesmen, a request which was granted by the consul. A few days later a former governor of Lydia, Zeuxis, and Antiochus' brother's son, Antipater, arrived. They met Eumenes first; they thought that because of their long-standing differences he would be the one most averse to a peace-treaty with the king. However, finding him more amenable than either they or the king had expected, they next approached Publius Scipio and, through the latter's intervention, the consul. At their request they were granted a full council to lay out their instructions.

'It is not so much a matter of our †having proposals† to make ourselves,' said Zeuxis. '†Rather, men of Rome, we ask of you† by what act of reparation we can make amends for the king's mistake, and gain peace and forgiveness from the victors. You have always shown the greatest magnanimity in pardoning kings and peoples you have conquered; how much more magnanimous and conciliatory should your conduct be after this victory which has made you rulers of the world? You should now lay aside the quarrels you have with any mortals whatsoever and, just like the gods, show consideration and indulgence to the human race.'

The response to be made had already been decided before the arrival of the envoys, and it was agreed that Africanus should make it. Africanus is said to have spoken more or less as follows:

'We Romans possess as a gift of the gods those things which it is in the gods' power to give; our spirit is controlled by our own will, and we have kept this, and still keep it, constant, notwithstanding the vagaries of fortune—success has not inflated it nor has misfortune diminished it. As witness to this fact, to pass over others, I might cite for you your comrade Hannibal—did I not have you yourselves to cite! After we crossed the Hellespont and before we saw the camp of the king and his line of battle, at a time when we both faced the same chances in war and the outcome of the conflict was uncertain—at that point you made overtures for peace and we put before you terms as equals to equals. Now as conquerors to conquered we are offering the same terms. Stay out of Europe, and withdraw from all of Asia lying this side of Mt. Taurus. In the next place you will pay 15,000 Euboean talents to cover the expenses of the war, 500 immediately, 2,500 when the Senate and people of Rome confirm the treaty, and then <1,000> talents annually for twelve years. It is also our pleasure that Eumenes be awarded 400 talents and the residue of the grain that was owed to his father. So that we may have confidence that you will fulfil the conditions once we have settled them, we shall have some guarantee if you give us twenty hostages chosen by us. But we shall never be sure that the Roman people can have peace where Hannibal will be found, and we demand him before all else. You will also surrender the Aetolian Thoas, instigator of the war with the Aetolians; it was he who incited you to arms against us by inspiring your confidence in them, and also incited them against us by inspiring their confidence in you. Along with Thoas you will surrender the Acarnanian Mnasilochus and the Chalcidians Philo and Eubulidas. The king will be negotiating peace from a weaker position because he is negotiating later than he might have done. If he delays now he must realize that it is more difficult to bring down the prestige of kings from the highest level to mediocrity than to precipitate it from mediocrity to the bottom.'

The envoys had been sent by the king under orders to accept any terms of peace, and it was therefore decided that ambassadors be sent to Rome. The consul distributed his forces between Magnesia-on-the-Maeander, Tralles, and Ephesus to spend the winter. A few days later the hostages from the king were delivered to the consul in Ephesus, and the ambassadors who were to go to Rome arrived as well. Eumenes also set off for Rome at the same time as the king's embassy, and they were followed by deputations from all the peoples of Asia.

46. While these events were taking place in Asia two proconsuls arrived in Rome at about the same time hoping to celebrate a triumph: Quintus Minucius came from Liguria and Manius Acilius from Aetolia. The Senate heard accounts of their exploits. Minucius was refused a triumph while Acilius was voted one by a large majority, and he rode into the city in triumph over Antiochus and the Aetolians. Borne before him in that triumph were 230 military standards, 3,000 pounds of uncoined silver, 113,000 Attic four-drachma coins, 249,000 coins stamped with the *cista*, and many embossed silver vessels of great weight. Acilius also included in his procession silver furniture that had been the king's, some splendid clothing, forty-five golden crowns that had been gifts from allied states, and all manner of booty. He had following him thirty-six important prisoners of war, officers of the Aetolians and of the king. (A few days before this, the Aetolian leader Damocritus,* who had escaped from prison by night, stabbed himself with a sword on the bank of the Tiber before the guards who were chasing him could catch him.) All that was missing were soldiers to attend his chariot; apart from that, the triumph was splendid as a spectacle and as a celebration of Acilius' achievements.

The euphoria of the triumph was curtailed by bad news from Spain. There had been a defeat in the war against the Lusitanians at the town of Lyco in the territory of the Bastetani. Fighting under the command of the proconsul Lucius Aemilius, 6,000 men of the Roman army had lost their lives and the rest had been driven in panic within the palisade of their camp. After barely managing to defend this, they were brought back by forced marches like fugitives to pacified territory. Such was the news from Spain.

Envoys from Placentia and Cremona in Gaul were ushered into the Senate by the praetor Lucius Aurunculeius. They complained about their dearth of colonists, some of whom had been lost as casualties of war, others through disease, while yet others had abandoned their colonies because they had had enough of having Gauls as neighbours. The Senate decreed that, if he agreed, the consul Gaius Laelius should enrol 6,000 households to be divided between the colonies involved, and that the praetor Lucius Aurunculeius should establish a board of triumvirs to escort the colonists. Chosen for this were Marcus Atilius Serranus, Lucius Valerius Flaccus, son of Publius, and Lucius Valerius Tappo, son of Gaius Valerius Tappo.

47. Not long after this, as the time for the consular elections was

drawing near, the consul Gaius Laelius returned to Rome from Gaul. He not only followed up the Senatorial decree, passed in his absence, by enrolling colonists to supplement the populations of Cremona and Placentia, but he also made the proposal, which the Senate ratified on his recommendation, that two new colonies be founded in what had been territory of the Boii.

At this same time a letter arrived from the praetor Lucius Aemilius. This brought news of the naval battle off Myonnesus and of the consul Lucius Scipio's transporting of his army to Asia. Public prayer lasting one day was decreed for the naval victory, with a second day added for a successful and felicitous outcome for the campaign, that being the very first time that a Roman army had pitched camp in Asia. The consul was instructed to do sacrifice with twenty full-grown animals for each of the two periods of prayer.

After that came the consular elections, which were hard fought. Marcus Aemilius Lepidus' candidacy was generally unpopular because he had left his province, Sicily, without seeking the authorization of the Senate to do so, in order to run for office. Running against him were Marcus Fulvius Nobilior, Gnaeus Manlius Vulso, and Marcus Valerius Messalla. Only Fulvius was elected consul since the others failed to win a majority of the centuries, and the next day, Lepidus being disqualified, Fulvius declared Gnaeus Manlius his colleague,* since Messalla had no support. After that the following were elected praetors: the two Quinti Fabii, Labeo and Pictor (Pictor had that year been inaugurated as *flamen Quirinalis*), Marcus Sempronius Tuditanus, Spurius Postumius Albinus, Lucius Plautius Hypsaeus, and Lucius Baebius Dives.

48. Valerius Antias records under the consulship of Marcus Fulvius Nobilior and Gnaeus Manlius Vulso that there was a rumour widely circulating in Rome, and accepted almost as fact, that the consul Lucius Scipio and, along with him, Publius Africanus, had been invited to parley with the king with a view to the recovery of the young Scipio. These had been arrested, according to the rumour, and, the generals now prisoners, a Syrian army had been immediately led to the Roman camp, which was then stormed, with the Roman troops being entirely wiped out. As a result, the Aetolians had gained some confidence, and had refused to discharge their treaty-obligations. Their leaders had left for Macedonia, Dardania, and Thrace to hire mercenary forces; and Aulus Terentius Varro and

Marcus Claudius Lepidus had been sent from Aetolia to Rome by the propraetor Aulus Cornelius to report on the situation. Claudius then appends to this piece of fiction that Aetolian envoys were interrogated on a number of matters in the Senate, including the source from which they had heard about the capture of the Roman generals in Asia by Antiochus and about the annihilation of the army. The Aetolians are supposed to have answered that their information had come from their own ambassadors who had been with the consul. Having no other source for this rumour, I feel the tale is neither to be accepted as true nor rejected out of hand.

49. When the Aetolian delegates were brought into the Senate, their case and unfortunate situation required that they admit their guilt and beg pardon on bended knee either for their wrong-doing or their mistake. Instead, they began by listing their services to the Roman people, and they adverted to their valour in the war with Philip in almost reproachful tones. They annoyed the Senators with the arrogant tenor of their address, and by harking back to things in the past long-forgotten they brought it about that the Senators began to recall the nation's misdeeds, which were considerably more numerous than its services, and men in need of compassion only succeeded in provoking anger and resentment. They were asked by one Senator whether they left the decision on their fate entirely to the Roman people, and by a second whether they would have the same allies and enemies as the Roman people, but they gave no answer to these questions and were ordered out of the temple.

The cry then arose from virtually the entire Senate that the Aetolians were still completely committed to Antiochus and that it was from hopes pinned uniquely on him that they derived their confidence. Accordingly, they said, war had to continue against these avowed enemies and their violent spirit had to be curbed. There was another factor that irritated the Senate, too: at the very same time that they were seeking a peace-treaty from the Romans, the Aetolians were making war on Dolopia and Athamania. On a motion by Marcus Acilius, who had defeated Antiochus and the Aetolians, a Senatorial decree was passed ordering the Aetolians to quit the city that day and leave Italy within fifteen days. Aulus Terentius Varro was sent to give them protection on their journey, and notice was formally served that, in the case of any future delegation coming to Rome from the Aetolians, all members would be regarded as enemies unless they came with the permission of the general governing the province and accompanied by a Roman legate. With that the Aetolians were sent on their way.

50. After that the consuls brought the matter of their provinces before the house, and it was decided that they should draw lots for Aetolia and Asia. The man drawing Asia was allocated the army then commanded by Lucius Scipio, and as supplementary forces for it he was to have 4,000 Roman infantry and 200 cavalry, plus 8,000 infantry and 400 cavalry from the allies and Latin League. With these forces he was to prosecute the war against Antiochus. The other consul was allocated the army in Aetolia, and permitted to supplement it by raising the same number of citizens and allies as his colleague. The same consul was commanded to equip and take with him the ships that had been built the year before and not merely make war on the Aetolians but also cross to the island of Cephallenia. He was further instructed to come to Rome for the elections, if he could do that without injuring the interests of the state, for apart from the need to replace annual magistrates it was also the Senate's wish that censors be elected. If anything held him back, he was to inform the Senate that he could not present himself in time for the elections. In the allotment Aetolia came to Marcus Fulvius and Asia to Gnaeus Manlius.

The result of the praetorian sortition which followed was as follows:

Spurius Postumius Albinus	urban and foreigners' jurisdictions
Marcus Sempronius Tuditanus	Sicily
Quintus Fabius Pictor, *flamen Quirinalis*	Sardinia
Quintus Fabius Labeo	the fleet
Lucius Plautius Hypsaeus	Hither Spain
Lucius Baebius Dives	Farther Spain

Sicily was allocated a single legion and the fleet then stationed in the province, and orders were given for the new praetor to requisition from the Sicilians two tithes of grain, one of which he was to dispatch to Asia, and the other to Aetolia. Orders were given for the same quantity to be levied from the Sardinians, the grain to be shipped to the same armies as that from Sicily. To supplement his forces for service in Spain, Lucius Baebius was given 1,000

Roman infantry and 50 cavalry, together with 6,000 infantry and 200 cavalry of the Latin League. For Hither Spain Plautius Hypsaeus was granted 1,000 Roman infantry, and 2,000 infantry and 200 cavalry of the allies and the Latin League. The two Spains were each to have a legion plus the aforementioned additional forces. †Of the previous year's magistrates, Gaius Laelius saw his imperium extended for a year, and he retained his army;† Publius Iunius, propraetor in Etruria, †also had his imperium† prolonged a year and he kept the army that was in the province, as did Marcus Tuccius, propraetor in Bruttium and Apulia.

51. Before the praetors could leave for their provinces, a disagreement arose between the pontifex maximus, Publius Licinius, and the *flamen Quirinalis*, Quintus Fabius, of the kind that arose in our fathers' time between Lucius Metellus and Aulus Postumius Albinus. Metellus, in his capacity as pontifex maximus, had detained Albinus, who was consul, to perform religious ceremonies just when he was setting off for Sicily to join the fleet with his colleague, Gaius Lutatius; and on this occasion the praetor Fabius was held back from his journey to Sardinia by Publius Licinius. Both in the Senate and before the people the dispute raged with acrimonious debates: authority was applied on this side and that, bonds taken, fines issued, applications made to tribunes, and then appeals to the people. Eventually religious feeling won the day, with the *flamen* being ordered to obey the pontiff and the fine on the latter cancelled by order of the people. Angry at seeing his province taken from him, Fabius attempted to resign from his office, but the Senators exercised their authority to deny him this, decreeing that he should accept jurisdiction over foreigners. After this the levies were conducted in a matter of days, few soldiers needing to be raised, and the consuls and praetors left for their provinces.

Idle and groundless gossip circulated after this about the campaign in Asia, but this was followed a few days later by some reliable news in a letter brought to Rome from the commander-in-chief. The great elation that this occasioned was not because of the recent crisis—the Romans had ceased to fear <Antiochus> after his defeat in Aetolia—but rather because of the king's reputation of old, for when the Romans entered the war he had seemed a fearsome enemy, both for his own strength and because he had Hannibal directing his campaign. Even so they did not vote for any change with regard to the consul to be sent to Asia or for any diminution of his forces, fearing as they did that they would have to fight the Gauls.

52. Not much later Lucius Scipio's officer, Marcus Aurelius Cotta, came to Rome with emissaries from Antiochus, and Eumenes and the Rhodians arrived as well. Cotta gave an account of the events in Asia, first in the Senate and afterwards, on the order of the Senators, in an assembly of the people. A three-day period of state prayer was thereupon decreed, with orders given for the sacrifice of forty full-grown animals.

After this, before all other business, Eumenes was given an audience with the Senate. He briefly thanked the Senators for delivering his brother and himself from the siege and for rescuing his kingdom from the aggression of Antiochus; and he congratulated them on their military successes on land and sea, on defeating and routing Antiochus, taking his camp from him, and driving him first from Europe and afterwards from Asia this side of the Taurus mountains. He then declared that he wanted the Romans to know of his services to them from their generals and officers rather than from his own account. There was unanimous applause for this from all the Senators who, nevertheless, told him to put aside his modesty in the matter, and state what he felt was a fair reward for him from the Senate and people of Rome—for the Senate, they said, would then act to meet his requests as far as it could, and in accordance with his deserts, all the more promptly and generously. In reply the king said that if he were being offered a choice of rewards by people other than the Romans, and if he had simply been given the opportunity of consulting the Roman Senate, he would happily have availed himself of that august body's advice, to avert the possibility of his appearing to have been too extravagant in his ambitions, or too lacking in restraint in his requests. But now it was the Romans themselves who were to make the reward, and it was all the more appropriate that they themselves be the judges of how generous they should be towards him and his brothers. The members of the Senate were not in the least put off by these comments from their insistence that he speak for himself. For some time the competition went on, with generosity evinced on the one side, and modesty on the other, as both parties tried to give in to each other with insurmountable courtesy evinced on either side; and eventually Eumenes left the temple. The Senate clung to its opinion, declaring that it was inconceivable that the king should be unaware of his aspirations and aims when he came. He himself knew what was in the interests of his kingdom, they said, and he knew Asia far better than the Senate did. He should therefore be recalled and made to reveal his wishes and thoughts on the matter.

53. The king was brought back to the temple by the praetor and told to take the floor. 'I should have continued with my silence, Members of the Senate,' he said, 'did I not know that you would soon be calling upon the Rhodian delegation and that, after you had heard them, I would be obliged to speak. To tell the truth, what I have to say is made the more difficult by the fact that their demands are going to be such that, apart from appearing not to disadvantage me, they will not even seem to be serving their own interests. For they will plead the cause of the Greek states, and will say that these should be freed. If this is granted, who can doubt but that they will deprive us not only of the states that will be liberated but also of those which have long been paying tribute to us, while they themselves will nominally have them as allies beholden to them for this great favour, but in reality as peoples subject to their rule and at their command? And, for heaven's sake, when aspiring to power of this magnitude they will pretend that there is nothing at all in it for them! They will be saying this is simply the proper course for you, one consistent with your past record! You will have to make sure that you are not hoodwinked by these arguments of theirs, and see to it that you not only avoid humbling some of your allies to an unfair and excessive degree while you overvalue others, but also that men who have born arms against you do not find themselves better off than your allies and friends.

'As far as I am concerned, I should in other situations prefer to be seen as having given in to anyone at all when I was within my rights than as having been too determined in asserting those rights. But when the competition centres on your friendship, on goodwill towards you, on the respect which a person will be accorded by you—then I cannot be at all content to be outdone. This is the greatest inheritance I received from my father, who was the very first of the inhabitants of Asia and Greece to enter into an alliance with you, an alliance which he constantly maintained with unwavering loyalty to the very end of his days. Nor was his loyalty and goodwill towards you merely a matter of feelings—he took part in all the wars that you fought in Greece, and helped you with land- and naval forces, and with all kinds of supplies, to a degree that none of your allies can possibly match in any regard. Finally, when he was encouraging the Boeotians to ally themselves with you, he collapsed in the middle of his address and breathed his last shortly afterwards. In his footsteps I have followed and, while I have in no way been able to go beyond his goodwill and enthusiasm in developing his friend-ship with you—in these areas he could not be surpassed—fortune, circumstances, Antiochus, and the war in Asia offered me the opportunity to surpass him in respect of practical assistance and services to you, and in the level of expense of our obligations. King of Asia and part of Europe, Antiochus offered me his daughter in marriage and was ready to restore immediately the city-states that had defected from us. He offered me strong assurances of later increasing my kingdom if I joined him in making war on you.

'I am not going to boast that I have in no way been derelict in my duty to you; rather I shall point to the things that are worthy of my house's long-standing friendship with you. I have aided your com-manders with land- and naval troops on such a scale that none of your allies could match me; I have supplied you with provisions by land and sea; I have taken part in all your naval battles, fought in many locations; in no place did I shrink from hardship or danger. I have experienced the worst fate in warfare, a siege—I was blockaded at Pergamum, my life and kingdom both in critical danger. Then, delivered from the siege, at a time when I had Antiochus encamped one side of the citadel of my kingdom and Seleucus on the other, I abandoned my own affairs and hurried to meet your consul Lucius Scipio at the Hellespont with my entire fleet in order to help him ferry across his army. I never left the consul's side after your army had crossed to Asia, and no Roman soldier spent more time in your camp than did I and my brothers. There was no military enterprise, no cavalry engagement in which I did not participate. In battle I took my place and defended my position where the consul wanted me to be.

'Members of the Senate, I am not going to say: "Who in this war can stand comparison with me in terms of services to you?" Of all those whom you greatly esteem, whether they be peoples or monarchs, there is none with whom I would not venture to compare myself. Masinissa was your enemy before he was your ally, and he did not come over to you with auxiliary forces when his kingdom was intact. No, he was an exile driven from his land, all his troops lost, and he fled to your camp with a squadron of cavalry. And yet because he stood by you loyally and vigorously in Africa to face Syphax and the Carthaginians you not only restored him to the kingdom of his forefathers but also made him powerful amongst the monarchs of Africa by further giving him the richest part of Syphax's kingdom. So, I ask, what reward and what honour do we deserve from you when we have never been your enemies and always been your allies? My father, I myself, and my brothers—we have borne arms for you on land and sea, and not just in Asia but far from home, too, in the Peloponnese, in Boeotia, and in Aetolia, fighting against Philip, Antiochus and the Aetolians.

'"What are you asking for, then?" someone may say. Members of the Senate, you want me to speak at all costs, and I must obey you. If in pushing Antiochus back beyond the Taurus range you had it in mind to possess those lands yourselves, there are no people I should prefer living beside me as neighbours than you, and I do not expect anything to give greater security and stability to my realm. But if you intend leaving the area and withdrawing your armies, I would venture to say that none of your allies deserves to have the territory you have taken in war more than I do. Yes, of course, it is a noble gesture to free enslaved communities. I think that myself—if the communities have taken no hostile action against you. If, however, they have sided with Antiochus, then how much more does it befit your good sense and fair-mindedness to consult the interests of allies who have served you well rather than the interests of your enemies!'

54. The Senators liked the king's speech and it was easy to see that they were ready to show generosity and favour towards him in every respect. Because some of the Rhodians were not present, a brief audience with an embassy from Smyrna was slipped into the proceedings. The Smyrnaeans were heartily thanked for the willingness they had shown to endure the extremes of suffering rather than yield to the king, and then the Rhodians were ushered in.

The leader of the delegation began with a discussion of the origins of the Rhodian alliance with the Roman people and services rendered by the Rhodians first in the war against Philip, and then in that against Antiochus. 'In all of this business we have with you, Members of the Senate,' he went on, 'nothing is more difficult and distasteful for us than the fact that our argument is with Eumenes, for he is the only king with whom our community has very close ties of hospitality, on a private level as individuals and, what causes us more concern, on a public level as well. But what separates us, Members of the Senate, is not our feelings for each other but the overwhelming facts of the situation—we are free men also advocating the freedom of others, while monarchs want to see everything enslaved and under their power. However, be that as it may, the greatest problem for us is our respect for the king—not the difficulty of the argument or the likelihood of its presenting you with complex deliberation. For if delivering free communities into slavery were the only means you had of honouring a king who was an ally and a friend, and who had deserved well of you in this very war, the rewards for which are now being discussed—in that case your deliberation would be problematical, for fear that you might either send away a friendly king without appropriate honour, or depart from your established practice and sully the glory won in the war with Philip by subjecting so many communities to slavery.

'In fact, fortune splendidly releases you from this necessity of curtailing either your gratitude to a friend or your own glory. By the favour of the gods your victory is as remunerative as it is glorious, so that it can easily deliver you from this debt, as you may call it. For Lycaonia, the two Phrygias,* all Pisidia, the Chersonese and all the regions of Europe around it are in your power. The addition of any one of these can greatly augment Eumenes' kingdom; giving all of them to him could put him on a par with the most powerful of kings. Accordingly, you have the scope to enrich your friends with the spoils of war without abandoning your principles. You can call to mind the reason you gave for your war first against Philip, and now against Antiochus; and you can remember the measures you took after the defeat of Philip, and what measures are wanted and expected of you now, as much because they befit you as because you took them before. People have different reasons for going to war, both honourable and commendable—the possession of territory, perhaps, or villages or towns, or ports and some part of the coast. In your case, you have not harboured ambitions for such possessions before having them in your control, and now that the world is in your power you *cannot* harbour them. What you have fought for is respect and prestige in the eyes of the entire human race, which has long considered your name and empire as standing next to those of the immortal gods.

'It may be that it is more difficult to protect what took great effort to obtain and acquire. You have undertaken to protect from enslavement to a king the independence of an ancient people well-known because of the fame of its achievements, and because everyone holds in esteem its culture and its arts. This defence of an entire race which you have taken under your protection and guardianship you should maintain in perpetuity. The cities on the ancient soil are no more Greek than their colonies, which left there for Asia in the past—the change of land did not change their national character or culture. All our communities have presumed to enter into respectful competition with their parents and founders in every noble art and area of excellence. Several of you have been to the cities of Greece and those of Asia; apart from our greater distance from you, we are in no way inferior to them. If one's innate make-up could be overcome by what one may term the character of the land, the people of Massilia would long ago have been brutalized by all the uncivilized tribes living around them, but we are told that they are held in as much honour and are deservedly shown as much respect by you as if they were living in the very heart of Greece. They have preserved pure and untouched by contact with their neighbours not only their spoken accent, dress, and overall appearance, but above all their culture, laws, and character.

'The limit of your empire at present is the Taurus range. Nothing short of that point ought to seem distant to you; your jurisdiction should stretch from here as far as your weapons have reached. Let the barbarians have the monarchies they love—the orders of their masters have always served in place of the rule of law for them. Greeks have their own fortunes, but your temperament. They once had an empire, too, won by their own strength, but now they want the seat of power to remain for ever where it is currently situated. They are satisfied to have their liberty protected by your arms since they cannot protect it by their own.

'Yes, it is true that some states sympathized with Antiochus. So did others earlier with Philip, and so did the Tarentines with Pyrrhus. Not to add other peoples to the list—Carthage is free with her own laws. Members of the Senate, just consider the obligation on you set by this precedent! You will then take it upon yourselves to deny to Eumenes' ambitions what you denied to your own justifiable wrath. The Rhodians †also† were in all the wars which you fought on that coast, and we leave it to you to judge how energetic and loyal we were in our assistance to you. Now, in peacetime, we are offering you this advice; accept it and everyone will consider the use to which you put your victory more splendid than the victory itself.'

The speech appeared in keeping with the greatness of Rome.

55. After the Rhodians the ambassadors of Antiochus were summoned. These followed the usual pattern of people asking for pardon: they admitted the king's error and begged the Senators to pay more heed in their deliberations to their own clemency than to the guilt of the king, who had more than paid the penalty for his actions. Finally, they asked them to ratify by their authority the peace-treaty granted by the commander Lucius Scipio, on the terms specified by him. The Senate did vote for the acceptance of the peace-treaty, and a few days later the people endorsed it. The treaty was struck on the Capitol with the head of the legation, Antipater, who was also the son of Antiochus' brother.

After that the other delegations from Asia were also heard. All were given the answer that the Senate would follow ancestral custom and send ten commissioners to adjudicate and settle affairs in Asia. However, they were informed that the essence of the settlement would be that Eumenes would be awarded the lands this side of the Taurus range that had been within the bounds of Antiochus' kingdom, with the exception of Lycia and Caria as far as the River Maeander, which would belong to the state of Rhodes. The other communities of Asia that had paid tribute to Attalus would also pay it to Eumenes, and those that had been tributary states of Antiochus would be independent and free of tax. The ten commissioners they selected were the following: Quintus Minucius Rufus, Lucius Furius Purpureo, Quintus Minucius Thermus, Appius Claudius Nero, Gnaeus Cornelius Merenda, Marcus Iunius Brutus, Lucius Aurunculeius, Lucius Aemilius Paullus, Publius Cornelius Lentulus, and Publius Aelius Tubero.

56. These commissioners were given discretionary powers to judge disputes arising locally, but the guiding principle established by the Senate was that the following go to Eumenes: all Lycaonia, the two Phrygias, and the royal forests of Mysia; Lydia and Ionia apart from those towns which had been independent on the day of

the battle with Antiochus (and Magnesia-by-Sipylus was mentioned by name); the Caria called Hydrela, and the territory of Hydrela on the Phrygian side; the strongholds and villages on the River Maeander, along with the towns apart from those which had been free before the war (Telmessus was mentioned by name and Castra Telmessium, apart from the land that had belonged to Ptolemy of Telmessus*). Orders were issued for all the afore-mentioned territories to be awarded to Eumenes. The Rhodians were given Lycia, with the exception of Telmessus, just mentioned, of Castra Telmessium, and of the territory that had belonged to Ptolemy of Telmessus (the latter was excepted both in the case of Eumenes' award and that of the Rhodians). They were also given the area of Caria beyond the Maeander and closer to the island of Rhodes, and the towns, villages, strongholds, and lands on the side of Pisidia, apart from the towns amongst them which had been free the day before the battle was fought with Antiochus in Asia.

After expressing their thanks for these gifts, the Rhodians brought up the question of the city of Soli in Cilicia. The people of Soli, like themselves, were descended from Argos, they said, and there were feelings of fraternal affection between them because of this kinship. They were now asking for a special favour, namely that the Romans exempt the community from subjection to the king. The ambassadors of Antiochus were called in, and the issue brought up with them. Nothing was gained, however, because Antipater pointed to the terms of the treaty which, he said, were being contravened by the Rhodians who had designs on Cilicia, not Soli, and were thus making inroads across the Taurus range. The Rhodians were then recalled to the Senate where the members explained to them the serious objection raised by the king's ambassador, adding that if the Rhodians believed that if this was of special concern to the prestige of their city-state the Senate would do all in its power to overcome the intransigence of the king's ambassadors. At this point the Rhodians became more fulsome in their thanks than earlier and declared that they would yield to the arrogance of Antipater rather than afford an excuse for upsetting the peace-treaty. Thus there was no change made with regard to Soli.

57. During the time covered by these events an embassy from Massilia brought the report that the praetor Lucius Baebius had been ambushed by the Ligurians as he was setting off for his province

in Spain. Most of his retinue had been killed, said the report. Baebius himself had been wounded and had fled with a few comrades
and without his lictors to Massilia, where he had died within three
days. On hearing of this the Senate decreed that Publius Iunius
Brutus, who was propraetor in Etruria, should transfer his province
and army to one of his deputies whom he thought suitable and that
he himself should set off for Farther Spain, which was now to be his
province. The senatorial decree and an accompanying letter was sent
to Etruria by the praetor Spurius Postumius, and the propraetor
Publius Iunius left for Spain. In this province Lucius Aemilius Paullus (who later won great renown for his defeat of Perseus) had the
previous year been less than successful in his military enterprises,
and some time before his successor arrived he put together a makeshift army and engaged the Lusitanians in pitched battle. The enemy
were scattered and put to flight, with 18,000 of their troops killed,
2,300 taken prisoner, and the camp taken by storm. Word of this
victory brought some tranquillity to the situation in Spain.

On 30 December of the same year the triumvirs Lucius Valerius
Flaccus, Marcus Atilius Serranus and Lucius Valerius Tappo established a Latin colony at Bononia as authorized by a Senatorial
decree. Three thousand men were taken there, and cavalrymen were
granted seventy acres each, the other colonists fifty. The land had
been captured from the Gallic Boii who themselves had driven out
the Etruscans.

The same year there were a large number of distinguished candidates for the censorship. As though it were of itself insufficient to
raise tensions, this provoked a much greater drama. Running for the
office were: Titus Quinctius Flamininus, Publius Cornelius Scipio,
son of Gnaeus Scipio, Lucius Valerius Flaccus, Marcus Porcius
Cato, Marcus Claudius Marcellus, and Manius Acilius Glabrio (who
had defeated Antiochus and the Aetolians at Thermopylae). Popular
support was inclining most towards the last-mentioned because †he
had had† considerable largesse by which he had secured the
endorsement of a large number of men. Many nobles took it ill that a
'new man' was so far ahead of them, and the plebeian tribunes Publius Sempronius Gracchus and Gaius Sempronius Rutilus arraigned
him on a charge of not carrying in his triumph, or depositing in the
treasury, a portion of the king's money and the booty that had been
taken in Antiochus' camp. The testimony of officers and military

tribunes was conflicting, and eyes fell on Marcus Cato as a witness more than anybody else, though the authority conferred on him by a career of unswerving morality was diminished by his white toga.* Cato, called to give evidence, stated that he had not seen in the triumph the gold and silver vessels that he had seen with the rest of the royal plunder when the camp was taken. In the end, mostly to provoke ill-will against Cato, Glabrio declared that he was withdrawing his candidacy, for, he said, a candidate as 'new' as he was himself was resorting to shameful perjury to attack his popularity, which the nobility accepted with silent resentment.

58. The fine that had been proposed was 100,000 *asses*. The case had been before the court twice, and since, by the third occasion, the defendant had withdrawn his candidacy, the people were unwilling to vote on the fine and the tribunes abandoned the case. The men elected censors were Titus Quinctius Flamininus and Marcus Claudius Marcellus.

In this period Lucius Aemilius Regillus, who had defeated Antiochus' admiral with his fleet, was given an audience with the Senate in the temple of Apollo outside the city. When they heard of his achievements, the size of the enemy fleets he had met in battle, and the number of ships in them he had sunk or captured, the senators voted him a naval triumph by a large majority. He celebrated the triumph on 1 February, and in it forty-nine golden crowns were carried, but nothing like as much money as a splendid triumph over a king would lead one to expect: 34,200 Attic four-drachma pieces, and 132,300 coins stamped with the *cista*. Following a senatorial decree public prayers were then offered in recognition of Lucius Aemilius' successes in Spain.

Not long after this Lucius Scipio came to the city with a request that he be named 'Asiaticus'—he did not want to be overshadowed by his brother with regard to his surname—and he gave an account of his achievements both in the Senate and in a popular assembly. There were some who claimed that the war enjoyed a greater reputation than its difficulty warranted: it had been finished off with a single notable encounter, and furthermore the battle at Thermopylae had prevented the glory of that victory from coming to bloom. But, to look at it fairly, the battle at Thermopylae was more with Aetolians than it was against the king—for it was with a fraction of his forces that Antiochus fought there. In Asia the strength of all Asia stood with him, with auxiliary troops of all its races drawn from the furthest †in† boundaries of the east.

59. There was therefore justification for the greatest possible honour being paid to the immortal gods because they had made the victory easy as well as great, and also for the commander being awarded a triumph. Scipio celebrated his triumph in the intercalary month on the day before 1 March. It was a triumph more spectacular than that of his brother Africanus, but if one considers the respective achievements, and weighs up the danger and struggle involved for both men, the comparison is as unfair as comparing the one commander with the other or comparing Antiochus as a general with Hannibal. Scipio carried in his triumph 224 military standards, 134 depictions of towns, 1,231 ivory tusks, 234 golden crowns, 137,420 pounds of silver, 214,000 Attic four-drachma pieces, 321,070 coins stamped with the *cista*, 140,000 golden Philippics, 1,423 pounds of silver vases (all with relief carvings), and 1,023 pounds of gold vases. There were also thirty-two of the king's officers (military captains and courtiers) led before the chariot. The common soldiers were each given twenty-five denarii, a centurion twice that amount, and a cavalryman three times. After the triumph, the soldiers' pay and grain-allowance was doubled—Scipio had already doubled these after the battle in Asia. He celebrated the triumph approximately a year after leaving the consulship.

60. The consul Gnaeus Manlius reached Asia at about the same time as the praetor Quintus Fabius Labeo reached the fleet. The consul was not short of motives for making war on the Gauls, but since Antiochus' defeat the sea had been in a pacified state, so that Fabius was wondering about the most suitable course of action to avoid the possibility of his provincial administration appearing lethargic. He decided the best thing was to cross to the island of Crete. The people of Cydonia had been making war on those of Gortyn and Cnossos, and it was said that a large number of Roman and Italian prisoners were enslaved throughout the island.

Fabius set sail with his fleet from Ephesus, and as soon as he landed on the coast of Crete he sent messengers around the cities ordering the citizens to terminate hostilities. Each state was to search out and restore prisoners from its respective towns and country areas, and send delegates to him so he could discuss with them matters of concern to Cretans and Romans alike. These communications did not provoke much response from the Cretans, and none of them restored prisoners apart from the Gortynians. According to Valerius Antias, 4,000 prisoners were restored from the island as a whole because of Cretan fears when they were threatened with war, and this was the reason for Fabius' successful application to the Senate for a naval triumph, though he had accomplished nothing else. Fabius returned from Crete to Ephesus, and from there dispatched three ships to the coast of Thrace bearing orders that Antiochus' garrisons be withdrawn from Aenus and Maronea, to permit these states to live in freedom.

BOOK THIRTY-EIGHT

1. While the war was in progress in Asia, the situation was not peaceful in Aetolia either, the unrest here having its origins with the Athamanian people. At this time, following the expulsion of Amynander,* Athamania was occupied by a royal garrison under officers of Philip, and the arrogant and oppressive regime of these men had made people regret the loss of Amynander. Amynander, then in exile in Aetolia, was led to hopes of recovering his kingdom by a letter from his supporters telling him how matters stood in Athamania. The men he sent back with his reply reported to the leading citizens at Argethia—the capital of Athamania—that if he could clearly discern support for himself amongst the commons he would obtain assistance from the Aetolians and come to Athamania <. . .> with the select group of men forming that people's supreme council,* and their magistrate Nicander.* Seeing them ready for any venture, he †immediately† informed his supporters of the day on which he would invade Athamania with an army.

At first the conspiracy against the Macedonian garrison comprised four people. Each of these enlisted six assistants to execute the plot, but then, anxious about their small numbers, which were better suited for keeping the operation secret than bringing it off, they added the same number again. Now fifty-two-strong, they divided themselves into four groups. One of these made for Heraclea, the second for Tetraphylia (where the royal treasury was normally kept under guard), the third for Theudoria, and the fourth for Argethia. All of them had arranged that they would at first circulate unobtrusively in the forum, as if they had come to transact private business; then, on the pre-arranged date, they would call the entire commons together to drive the Macedonian garrisons from the citadels. That day now arrived, Amynander was at the border with a thousand Aetolians, and the Macedonian garrisons were driven from the four locations at the same time according to plan. Letters were then sent in all directions to the various other towns urging them to take a stand against Philip's oppressive tyranny and restore their king to his ancestral throne that was his by right. The Macedonians were expelled in all quarters. The town of Telum withstood a siege for a few days; the letter had been intercepted by Xenon,* the garrison-commander, and the citadel was seized by the king's troops. But then this, too, was surrendered to Amynander, and all Athamania was now in his hands, with the exception of the fortress of Athenaeum which lay close to the border of Macedonia.

2. When he heard of the revolt of Athamania, Philip set off with 6,000 soldiers and swiftly reached Gomphi. Here he left most of his force—they would not have had the strength for such strenuous marches—and came with 2,000 men to Athenaeum, the only town to have been successfully held by a garrison of his. Then, probing the surrounding areas and easily recognizing that he was facing resistance everywhere else, he fell back on Gomphi and marched back into Athamania from there with all his troops. He then sent Xenon ahead with a thousand infantry, under orders to seize †Aethiopa† which was strategically placed, overlooking Argethia. When Philip saw the position occupied by his men, he himself encamped near the temple of Jupiter Acraeus.* Detained here for a day by a fierce storm, he proceeded with his march towards Argethia the following day. As the Macedonians advanced, however, the Athamanians suddenly appeared before them, making a dash for the hills that dominated the road. The leading companies came to a halt on sighting them, and there was panic and trepidation throughout the column as each man speculated on what might transpire if the column were taken into the valleys lying below the cliffs. The king wanted to get through the ravine quickly, if his men would follow him, but their discomposure forced him to recall the forward units and beat a retreat along the path by which he had come.

The Athamanians proceeded to follow him, at first at a distance and biding their time; but when the Aetolians joined them, they left these latter to put pressure on the Macedonian rear and themselves closed in on the flanks of the column. Some of them went on ahead, taking a short cut by paths that they knew, and blocked those their enemy would take. So great was the panic instilled in the Macedonians that their crossing of a river here was more like a chaotic route than an ordered march, with men and weapons left behind in large numbers.

This represented the end of the pursuit, and from there the Macedonians returned safely to Gomphi, and then from Gomphi to Macedonia. The Athamanians and Aetolians swiftly converged from all sides on †Eopa† in order to overwhelm Xenon and his 1,000 Macedonians. Having little confidence in their position, the Macedonians moved from †Eopa† to a hill that was higher, and steeper on all sides. The Athamanians, however, found a way up to them at several points and dislodged them, capturing some and killing others as they scattered and were unable to negotiate their escape over the rugged terrain and unfamiliar rocks. In panic many tumbled over the precipices, and very few were they who made good their escape to the king with Xenon. Later the Macedonians were given an opportunity to bury their dead under truce.

3. On recovering his throne, Amynander sent representatives both to the Senate in Rome and to the Scipios in Asia (these had stayed on at Ephesus after the major battle with Antiochus*). He sued for peace, made excuses for having used the Aetolians to recover his ancestral throne, and put the blame on Philip.

The Aetolians left Athamania to march against the Amphilochians, and they brought the entire people under their control and authority, with the acquiescence of the majority. After recovering Amphilochia, which had once belonged to the Aetolians, they moved on to Aperantia hoping for similar results, and this city also surrendered, without resistance for the most part. The Dolopians, who were subject to Philip and had never been under the Aetolians, at first rushed to arms; but when they heard that the Amphilochians were now on the side of the Aetolians, that Philip had been driven from Athamania and that his garrison had been massacred, they too abandoned Philip for the Aetolians. With these tribes encircling them, the Aetolians now believed themselves protected against the Macedonians on all sides, but then word came of Antiochus' defeat by the Romans in Asia. And shortly afterwards their deputation returned from Rome bringing no prospect of a peace-treaty, and bearing the news that the consul Fulvius had already made the crossing with an army. The Aetolians were terrified by the news. They first of all summoned delegations from Rhodes and Athens, hoping that through the influence of these states their entreaties which had been recently rejected might gain easier access to the Senate. Then they sent the most eminent of their people to Rome for one last hopeful attempt—though they had taken no steps to avoid war before the enemy was almost in sight.

By now Marcus Fulvius* had taken the army over to Apollonia

and was discussing with the Epirote leaders where to start the campaign. The Epirotes were in favour of attacking Ambracia which had at this time allied itself with the Aetolians. Should the Aetolians come to defend the city, they said, there were open plains round about on which to do battle; alternatively, if they declined to fight, a siege would not prove difficult. For, they explained, there was plentiful wood nearby for erecting ramparts and other siege-works; the Aratthus, a navigable river suitable for transporting the materials they needed, flowed right past the city-walls; and summer, the season for campaigning, was approaching. With these arguments they persuaded Fulvius to march through Epirus.

4. As the consul approached Ambracia he thought a siege would involve a great effort. Ambracia lies at the foot of a rugged hill, called Perranthes by the local people. Where the wall meets the plains and the river, the city is westward-facing; and the citadel, sitting on the hill, faces east. The River Aratthus rises in Athamania and flows into a gulf of the sea called the Ambracian Gulf, named after the nearby city. Apart from the protection offered by the river on one side and the hills on the other, the city was also enclosed by a stout wall with a circumference of slightly more than three miles. Fulvius placed two camps on the side facing the plain a short distance from each other, and a single fortress on the high ground facing the citadel; and he was preparing to join all three with a rampart and a ditch to prevent those shut in the city from coming out and to render it impossible to bring in any assistance from outside.

At the news of the assault on Ambracia, the Aetolians had already assembled at Stratus in response to an edict from their magistrate Nicander. Their original intention had been to come in full force to prevent the siege, but when they saw that the city was mostly fenced in by siege-works and that the camp of the Epirotes had been pitched in the plain across the river, they decided to divide their troops. Eupolemus set off for Ambracia with 1,000 light infantry and entered the city through a gap where the fortifications had not yet come together. Nicander had at first planned to launch a night attack on the Epirote camp with the rest of the force, the river between them making it difficult for assistance to come from the Romans. Later he felt the operation was risky since the Romans might get wind of it and his withdrawal might be jeopardized, and so, put off this particular plan, he turned instead to making raids on Acarnania.

5. After completing the barricades for the circumvallation of the city and the siege-engines which he was intending to move up to the walls, the consul attacked the city's defences at five points at the same time. Access from the plain was easier, and so he moved three of his engines, equidistant from each other, towards the so-called Pyrrheum;* another he advanced on the area of the temple of Aesculapius;* and one more on the citadel. He proceeded to pound the walls with the rams, and to break off the turrets with poles armed with hooks. The sight of this, and the blows on the walls with their terrifying crash, at first filled the townspeople with panic and alarm; then, seeing the walls still standing contrary to their expectations, they pulled themselves together once more and began to use swing-beams to drop weights of lead or stone, or else thick logs, on the battering-rams. They also hurled grappling irons to pull the hooks to the inside of the wall and then break the poles. In addition, they made counter-attacks on the guard emplacements for the siege-engines by night and on the advance positions by day, now themselves striking terror into the enemy.

Thus stood matters at Ambracia, and by now the Aetolians had returned to Stratus after raiding Acarnania. The magistrate Nicander then conceived the hope of raising the siege with a bold stroke, and sent a certain Nicodamus into Ambracia with 500 Aetolians. Nicander appointed a certain night, and even a point during the night, at which Nicodamus' men were to launch an attack from the city on the enemy siege-works facing the Pyrrheum, and at which he himself was to cause alarm in the Roman camp. He felt that, with the commotion in the two spots, and with the darkness heightening the panic, a sensational coup could be brought off.

Nicodamus did manage to slip by some of the sentry-posts at the dead of night, and force his way past others with a determined charge; he then surmounted the rampart and made his way into the city. In so doing he inspired the beleaguered population with the spirit to try anything, and boosted their hopes. Furthermore, as soon as the pre-arranged night arrived, Nicodamus launched his sudden attack on the siege-engines according to plan. The operation was more impressive in its theory than its outcome, because no pressure was put on from outside. Either the Aetolian praetor had been frightened off, or else it seemed a better idea to bring succour to the recently-recovered Amphilochians—for these were now facing an all-out attack from Philip's son Perseus,* who had been sent to retake Dolopia and the Amphilochians.

6. As noted above, there were Roman siege-engines at three points facing the Pyrrheum. The Aetolians attacked all three at the same time, but not with the same equipment or the same force. Some approached carrying flaming torches, others with tow, pitch and incendiary darts, and the whole line was lit up with flames. Many of the guards they overpowered at the first charge. Then, when the shouting and clamour carried to the camp and the signal was given by the consul, the Romans seized their weapons and poured out from all the gates to bring help to their comrades. †In one place the battle was fought with iron and fire. From the two† others the Aetolians withdrew with nothing accomplished, after tentatively engaging but without really committing themselves to the battle. The savage fighting thus remained centred on one spot. Here, the two commanders, Eupolemus and Nicodamus, were urging on their fighters from different quarters, and keeping up their morale with the almost certain hope that Nicander would be there at any time according to plan and would attack the enemy rear. For a time this gave the combatants encouragement but, when they did not receive the pre-arranged signal from their comrades and they saw the enemy numbers increasing, they became discouraged and slackened their efforts. Finally, they gave up the fight and, at a point when their way back was no longer very secure, were driven in flight into the city. They had burned a number of the siege-engines but with losses considerably heavier than had been inflicted by them. If the enterprise had gone according to plan, however, the siege-engines could certainly have been taken in at least one of the locations, with heavy enemy casualties. The Ambracians, and the Aetolians who were in the city, not only abandoned that night's operation but were also less ready from then on to face the perils of the war, feeling that they had been let down by their comrades. Now nobody took part in the sallies against the enemy outposts as they had before. Instead they positioned themselves on the walls and parapets from which they could fight in safety.

7. When he heard that the Aetolians were coming, Perseus abandoned the siege of the city which he was undertaking and, after merely ravaging the countryside, left Amphilochia and went back to Macedonia. The Aetolians were also diverted from there by

marauding expeditions conducted on their coastline. The Illyrian king Pleuratus had sailed with sixty light vessels into the Corinthian Gulf where he had joined the Achaean ships anchored at Patrae, and had proceeded to ravage the coastal areas of Aetolia. A thousand Aetolians were sent to combat them, and as the fleet hugged the twisting shoreline these would come to meet them by taking shorter paths.

At Ambracia the Romans had laid bare a section of the city by battering the walls at several places at once with the rams, but they still could not make their way into the town. A new wall would be thrown up as quickly as the earlier one was demolished and, in addition, armed men would stand on the ruins, forming an effective barrier. And so, since the consul found his openly conducted offensive was achieving little success, he decided to construct a secret tunnel in an area which he first covered with siege-sheds. For a time, despite working day and night, they were unobserved by the enemy both as they dug underground and as they brought out the soil. But then the rising heap of earth that suddenly appeared gave away the operation to the townspeople. Frightened that the wall might already be undermined, and a way into the city opened up, these proceeded to dig a ditch within the wall in the direction of the work covered by the siege-sheds. When they reached a point as deep as the floor of the tunnel could possibly be, they remained silent, placed their ears to the soil at several points, and tried to catch the sound of the enemy digging. When they heard this, they proceeded to open a path straight into the tunnel. This did not take much effort; in no time they came through to an open place where the wall was supported by †forked props† by the enemy. The two works meeting at this point, with a path now open from the ditch into the tunnel, the diggers at first clashed with the actual tools which they had used for the work, but then armed soldiers quickly appeared as well, to engage in a subterranean battle hidden from view. The fighting then became less intense since the defenders would quickly block the tunnel wherever they wished, stretching screens or doors* across it.

They also devised a novel countermeasure, requiring little effort, against the men in the tunnel. They made a hole in the bottom of a barrel such that a small tube could be inserted into it, and they also fashioned an iron tube and an iron lid for the barrel, the lid itself pierced with several holes. The barrel they filled with down, and placed it with its mouth facing the tunnel. Through the holes in the lid projected some of the long spears called *sarisae* to keep the enemy at bay. They then set a small spark in the down and fanned it with a smith's bellows, inserted into the end of the tube, until the down caught fire. As a result the whole tunnel was filled with thick smoke which, moreover, was all the more objectionable because of the foul odour of burnt feathers, and scarcely anyone could bear to remain inside.

8. While matters stood thus at Ambracia, Phaeneas and Damoteles, who had been vested with full discretionary powers by their people, came to see the consul. The Aetolian praetor could see Ambracia under siege on one side, their shores under attack from enemy vessels on another, and Amphilochia and Dolopia being raided by the Macedonians on a third; and he realized that the Aetolians had not the resources to prosecute three wars at the same time on different fronts. He had therefore summoned a council meeting and put to the leading †Aetolian† citizens the question of the action to be taken. The opinions of all coincided on one point: peace was to be sought, on favourable conditions if possible, and failing that on conditions they could bear. It was because of their confidence in Antiochus that the war had been undertaken, they said, and now that Antiochus had been defeated on land and sea and driven practically from the whole world to a point beyond the Caucasus* range, what hope was there of keeping up the war? Phaeneas and Damoteles should negotiate an agreement in the interests of the Aetolians, taking account of the situation and following their conscience. For, they asked, what strategy or what choice of action had fortune left them?

Sent with this mandate, the envoys begged the consul to spare their city and pity a people which had once been an ally and which had been driven to insanity by the misfortunes, not to say the injustices, she had suffered. As for their deserts, the harm the Aetolians had done in the war with Antiochus, they said, was not greater than the good they had done in fighting against Philip, and just as they were not liberally recompensed on that occasion, so they should not be too harshly punished on this. In reply the consul observed that the Aetolian requests for a peace-treaty were more frequent than they were sincere. In seeking a treaty, he said, they should follow the lead of Antiochus, whom they had dragged into the war—Antiochus had relinquished not just a handful of cities whose independence was disputed, but a rich empire comprising all of Asia this side of the Taurus range. He would listen to the Aetolians' plea for peace only if they were disarmed, he continued. They first had to hand over their weapons and all their horses, and then deliver to the Roman people a thousand talents, half the sum payable immediately, if they wanted to have peace. In addition to these terms he would add to the treaty a further clause stipulating that they were to have the same friends and enemies* as the Roman people, he said.

9. The conditions were harsh, and the envoys knew the wild and capricious disposition of their people. They therefore made no reply and returned home so that, with no commitment made, they could urgently press their praetor and leading citizens for an answer on what should be done. They were met with shouts and jeers, asked how long they were going to drag out the business, and told to bring back a peace on any terms. As they were returning to Ambracia, however, they were caught in an ambush set near the road by the Acarnanians, with whom they were at war, and taken to Thyrreum for imprisonment. This delayed the peace-making process, and at this time deputations from the Athenians and Rhodians, who had come to plead for the Aetolians, were now with the consul. The king of the Athamanians, Amynander, had also come to the Roman camp with a safe conduct, more concerned for the city of Ambracia, where he had spent the greater part of his exile, than for the Aetolians. When the consul was informed by these people of what had befallen the Aetolian delegates, he had the latter brought from Thyrreum, and after they arrived the peace negotiations began.

Amynander worked hard to get the people of Ambracia to surrender, that being his principal concern. He approached the town wall for discussions with the leading citizens, but met with little success. Finally, with the consul's permission, he went into the city where, by argument as well as entreaty, he convinced the citizens to put themselves in the hands of the Romans. For their part, the Aetolians received distinguished service from Gaius Valerius Laevinus, half-brother of the consul* (both were born of the same mother), and son of the Laevinus who had first struck a treaty of friendship with that people. After first making a pact to send out Aetolian auxiliaries in safety, the Ambracians opened their gates. Then <. . .> they were to pay 500 Euboean talents, 200 immediately, and 300 in equal instalments over six years; they were to surrender prisoners-of-war and deserters to the Romans; they were to claim jurisdiction over no city which, since the date of Titus Quinctius' crossing to Greece, had been either taken by force by the Romans or had voluntarily entered into an alliance with them; and the island of Cephallenia was to be exempted from the provisions of the treaty.

The terms were somewhat milder than the Aetolian delegates had expected, but they nevertheless asked, and were granted, permission to take them back to their council. There was a slight dispute over the cities which had formerly been under Aetolian jurisdiction, and which they were reluctant to have torn from their body, as it were; but to a man they urged the acceptance of the peace. The people of Ambracia presented the consul with a 150-pound crown of gold.* All their bronze and marble statues and all their pictures were removed and taken off—Ambracia was more richly endowed with such art-works than other cities in the region because it had been the site of Pyrrhus' palace—but nothing else was touched or violated.

10. The consul now left Ambracia for the interior of Aetolia, and pitched camp at Amphilochian Argos, which is twenty-two miles from Ambracia. The Aetolian envoys eventually arrived there, the consul meanwhile wondering what was delaying them. When told that the Aetolian council had approved the peace-treaty, the consul bade the envoys go to the Senate in Rome. He also gave permission for both the Rhodians and the Athenians to go there to plead on the Aetolians' behalf, and had his brother Gaius Valerius accompany them. After this, he himself crossed to Cephallenia.

The envoys found that the ears and minds of the important people at Rome had already been swamped with charges levelled by Philip. The king had been complaining through embassies and letters that Dolopia, Amphilochia, and Athamania had been filched from him, and that his garrisons and, to cap it all, even his son Perseus, had been driven from Amphilochia. In this way Philip had made the Senate reluctant to hear the pleas of the Aetolians. Nevertheless, the Rhodians and the Athenians were heard in silence. It is even said that a member of the Athenian delegation, Leo, son of Cichesias, impressed them with his oratory. Using a well-known simile he compared the Aetolian populace to a calm sea whipped up by the winds, and said that when the Aetolians had faithfully abided by their alliance with Rome they remained at peace, demonstrating the tranquillity natural to them as a people. But when Thoas and Dicaearchus began to blow like winds from Asia, and Menestas and Damocritus from Europe, he said, that was the beginning of the tempest that had driven them on to Antiochus as if onto a reef.

11. The Aetolians were kept in torment for a long time, but at last they succeeded in gaining an accord on the peace-terms. The terms were as follows:

'The Aetolian people are to respect the power and sovereignty of the Roman people with complete integrity. They are not to permit any army that is being led against the Romans' allies or friends to pass through their territory, or help it in any way. They are to have the same enemies as the Roman people, to bear arms against these enemies and wage war on them along with the Romans. Deserters, fugitives, and prisoners of war they are to return to the Romans and their allies, exception being made for captives who were captured a second time, after they had returned to their homes, and for those who were taken prisoner by the Aetolians from people who were enemies of Rome, at the time when the Aetolians were among the supporters of the Romans. Any others coming to light are to be delivered within a hundred days to the magistrates of the Corcyreans in good faith; and those not found are to be delivered as soon as each is discovered. The Aetolians are to surrender to the Romans forty hostages acceptable to the consul, all between the ages of twelve and forty, and excluding any praetor, or cavalry commander, public secretary, and anyone who has earlier been a hostage amongst the Romans. Cephallenia is to be exempted from the provisions of the treaty.'

(No change was made to the agreement reached with the consul regarding the sum of money the Aetolians were to pay and its instalments, but it was decided that they should be allowed to pay in gold instead of silver if they preferred, provided that one gold piece be worth ten pieces of silver.)

'The Aetolians are to renounce any intention of reclaiming cities, lands or persons that were formerly under their jurisdiction but which came into the control of the Roman people either by military conquest or their own volition in or after the consulship of Lucius Quinctius and Gnaeus Domitius.* Oeniadae, both the city and its agricultural lands, are to belong to the Acarnanians.'

Such were the terms of the treaty struck with the Aetolians.

12. Not just that same summer, but almost during the very days that these actions were taken in Aetolia by the consul Marcus Fulvius, the other consul, Gnaeus Manlius, fought a war in Galatia, an account of which I shall now begin.

At the beginning of spring the consul arrived at Ephesus. He took over command of the army from Lucius Scipio, conducted a purification of the troops, and delivered an address to the men. In this Manlius commended them for their courage in terminating the war with Antiochus in a single battle, and encouraged them to undertake a fresh campaign, this time against the Gauls. The latter, he said, had assisted Antiochus with auxiliary forces, and were of such a recalcitrant nature that Antiochus' removal to a point beyond the Taurus range would prove futile unless the power of the Gauls were smashed. He finished with a few remarks on himself, which were neither untrue nor exaggerated. The men heard the consul's words with elation, frequently punctuating them with applause. They believed the Gauls to have been no more than a division of Antiochus' strength; with the king defeated they thought the Gallic troops would be no effective force on their own.

The consul believed Eumenes' absence*—he was then in Rome—an untimely nuisance: Eumenes knew the terrain and the people, and crushing the power of the Gauls was in his interest. Manlius therefore summoned Eumenes' brother, Attalus, from Pergamum, and encouraged him to join him in prosecuting the war; and when Attalus promised his personal support and that of his people, Manlius sent him home to make preparations. A few days later, after his departure from Ephesus, the consul was met at Magnesia by Attalus, who came at the head of 1,000 infantry and 500 cavalry. Attalus had instructed his brother Athenaeus to follow behind with the rest of his forces, and had left the protection of Pergamum in the hands of men he believed loyal to his brother and his regime. The consul commended the young man and advanced with the entire force to the Maeander. He pitched camp because the river could not be forded and ships had to be brought together to take the army across. After crossing the Maeander they came to Hiera Come.

13. In Hiera Come there is a revered temple and oracle of Apollo where the priests are said to make prophetic utterances in verse of some refinement. From here, two days later, they reached the River Harpasus. There ambassadors came to Manlius from Alabanda requesting that he use his authority, or armed force, to bring back into its former allegiance a stronghold which had recently defected from them. There, too, Athenaeus, brother of Eumenes and Attalus, came to Manlius, along with the Cretan Lensus and Corragus the Macedonian. These brought with them 1,000 infantry of various races and 300 horse. The consul took the stronghold by force, sending a military tribune with a modest contingent against it, and after capturing it he returned it to the people of Alabanda. He did not personally depart from his route, and pitched camp at Antioch on the River Maeander.

The sources of this river are at Celaenae. The city of Celaenae was once the capital of Phrygia, but the people moved from there to a point not far from old Celaenae, and the new city was given the name Apamea, after Apama, sister of Seleucus.* The River Marsyas, which rises not far from the headwaters of the Maeander, also flows into the Maeander, and the story goes that it was at Celaenae that Marsyas* had his pipe-playing contest with Apollo. The Maeander rises at the top of the citadel of Celaenae, flows down through the town-centre and passes through Caria and Ionia before issuing into a gulf of the sea between Priene and Miletus. At Antioch Seleucus, son of Antiochus, came to the consul's encampment to deliver grain to the army in accordance with the treaty made with Scipio. There was a slight argument regarding Attalus' auxiliaries, Seleucus maintaining that Antiochus had agreed to supply grain only to the Roman soldiery. That too was brought to an end by the firm resolve of the consul who sent a tribune with orders for the Roman soldiers not to accept their supply until Attalus' auxiliaries had received theirs.

The army then advanced to a place called Gordiutichos, and from there came three days later to Tabae. This city lies on the borders of Pisidia, in the region towards the Pamphylian sea. The military strength of the region was as yet untouched and it possessed pugnacious warriors. On this occasion, too, the cavalry charged out against the Roman column, causing considerable disarray with the initial assault. Later, when it became clear that they were no match for the Romans either in numbers or fighting ability, they were pushed back into the city, and they proceeded to beg pardon for their error, ready to surrender the city. They were ordered to pay 25 talents of silver and 10,000 *medimni* of wheat, and their surrender was accepted on these terms.

14. On the third day out from Tabae the Romans reached the River Casanes. Leaving there, they headed for the city of Eriza, which they took with their initial assault. They then came to the fortress of Tabusion which overlooks the River Indus, so-named from an Indian who was flung into it from his elephant. They were not far distant from Cibyra, but there was no sign of a delegation from that city's tyrant, Moagates, a man untrustworthy and lacking civility in all his dealings. To sound out Moagates' feelings, the consul sent Gaius Helvius ahead with 4,000 infantry and 500 cavalry. When this column was actually entering Moagates' territory it was met by envoys bringing word that the tyrant was ready to meet the Romans' demands. They begged Helvius to enter their territory in peace and keep his men from plundering their farmlands, and they brought 15 talents in the form of a golden crown. Helvius undertook to safeguard their lands from pillage, and told the envoys to proceed to see the consul.

When they gave the consul the same message, he replied: 'First, we Romans have no indication from your tyrant of good-will towards us and, secondly, everyone is well aware that his character is such that we should be thinking about punishing him rather than making an alliance with him.' The envoys were disturbed by this remark, and asked for nothing more than that he accept the crown and grant the tyrant permission to come to him, and the opportunity of speaking to him and exonerating himself.

With the consul's permission the tyrant came into the camp the following day. His dress and retinue were barely up to the standard of a moderately wealthy man, and his speech was submissive and halting as he played down his personal fortune, and deplored the poverty of the cities under his control. In fact, however, apart from Cibyra, Sylleum and the city called 'ad Limnen' were also subject to him. From these he promised—but almost as if he did not believe he could—to raise 25 talents, though this would be stripping his own and his subjects' resources.

'No,' said the consul, 'this charade cannot be tolerated any further. It is not enough that you felt no embarrassment at staying away and using your envoys to toy with us—now, present with us, you persist in the same impudence. Will 25 talents drain your kingdom? If you do not pay up 500 talents in three days you can expect to see your fields pillaged and your city blockaded.' Though alarmed by this threat, Moagates still persisted with his stubborn pretence of poverty. Gradually, by niggardly additions, and over quibbles which he alternated with entreaties and crocodile tears, he was brought up to 100 talents, to which 10,000 *medimni* of grain was added. The total amount was collected within six days.

15. From Cibyra the army was taken through the territory of the Sindensians and encamped after crossing the River Caulares. The following day the column was led along the banks of the Marsh of Carallites, and halted at Madamprus. As they advanced from here, the inhabitants of the next city, †Lacus†, fled in panic, and the Romans plundered a town that was deserted and copiously supplied with all manner of commodities. From there they advanced to the headwaters of the River Lysis, and the next day to the River Cobulatus.

The people of Termessus were at that time blockading the citadel of the Isiondenses, having captured the city. Since they had no other hope of assistance, the beleaguered townspeople sent representatives to the consul to beg for his support. They were imprisoned in their citadel with their wives and children, they said, and with every day that passed they were awaiting death, either by the sword or from starvation. The consul was thus offered the pretext he wanted for making a detour into Pamphylia.

Manlius' coming raised the siege of the Isiondenses, and he granted peace to Termessus for a price of 50 talents of silver (he made the same arrangement with the Aspendians and the other peoples of Pamphylia). On his return journey from Pamphylia he encamped at the River Taurus on the first day and at the place called Xyline Come the next. Setting out from Xyline Come he reached the city of Cormasa by continuous marches. The next town, Darsa, was deserted by its panic-stricken inhabitants, and Manlius found it replete with all manner of provisions. As he advanced along the marshes, envoys from Lysinoe came to him offering the surrender of their town. After that the army reached the territory of Sagalessus which is fertile and rich in crops of all kinds. It is inhabited by Pisidians, by far the best soldiers in the region, and this superiority, together with the fertility of their land, the size of their population, and their position as one of the few fortified cities in the area, gave them confidence. Because no delegation had come to meet him at the border, the consul dispatched raiding parties into the fields, and it was only when the Pisidians saw their property carried away and driven off that their determination was broken. Sending envoys they were granted peace when they agreed to pay 50 talents, 20,000 *medimni* of wheat, and 20,000 *medimni* of barley.

Moving on from there to the Rhotrine Springs, Manlius pitched camp at a village called Aporidos Come, and to this place Seleucus came from Apamea the following day. Manlius sent the sick and the baggage for which he had no use to Apamea and, setting off with guides supplied to him by Seleucus, he reached the plain of Metropolis that same day, and Dyniae, in Phrygia, the next. From Dyniae he came to Synnada, where he found all the towns round about deserted from fear. He was now trailing along a column weighed down with loot from these towns, and after barely covering a distance of five miles in an entire day he arrived at Beudos (the so-called 'Old Beudos'). He next bivouacked at Anabura, the following day at the Springs of †Alexander†, and the third day at Abbasium. At Abbasium he maintained a camp for a number of days because they had reached the territory of the Tolostobogii.

16. The Gauls, led by Brennus,* had come into Dardania in a large body, either because they were short of land or from the hope of plunder. They had also believed that none of the peoples through whom their route lay were a match for them in battle. In Dardania a rift took place, and some 20,000 men, with the chieftains Lonnorius and Lutarius, broke with Brennus and turned off into Thrace. Fighting all who resisted them and imposing tribute-payments on those who sued for peace, these reached Byzantium, and for a time they settled on the coast of the Propontis, where they levied taxes on the cities of the region. They were then overtaken by a desire to cross to Asia, for now that they were close to it they heard reports of the great fertility of its soil. They therefore took Lysimachia by subterfuge, occupied the whole of the Chersonese by military force, and went down to the Hellespont. When they saw that it was only a narrow strait that separated Asia from them, this greatly whetted their appetite to make the crossing, and they sent messengers to Antipater, the governor of the coast,* to negotiate the passage. But the negotiations were more drawn out than they had anticipated, and a fresh quarrel erupted among the chieftains. Lonnorius retraced his steps to Byzantium with most of the men. Lutarius commandeered two decked ships and three light vessels from some Macedonians

who were ostensibly on a diplomatic mission but who had really been sent out by Antipater to spy on them; and with these, by making repeated crossings by day and night, he shipped all the troops across in a matter of days. Not long afterwards, Lonnorius, assisted by King Nicomedes* of Bithynia, crossed over from Byzantium. The Gauls then reunited and lent their support to Nicomedes in his war against Ziboetes, who controlled part of Bithynia. Thanks largely to their assistance, Ziboetes was defeated and all Bithynia came under the sway of Nicomedes.

Leaving Bithynia, the Gauls had next come into Asia. Although no more than 10,000 of their total force of 20,000 were under arms they nevertheless instilled such terror in all the peoples living this side of the Taurus that these totally submitted to their authority, whether they were attacked or not, the farthest situated and nearest of them alike. Eventually, since they comprised three tribes—the Tolostobogii, the Trocmi, and the Tectosages—the Gauls made a tripartite division of Asia into the taxation districts for each of their constituent peoples. To the Trocmi was assigned the shore of the Hellespont; the Tolostobogii were allotted Aeolis and Ionia, and the Tectosages the interior of Asia. While they wrested payment from the whole of Asia this side of the Taurus, they themselves chose to settle on the banks of the River Halys. Such was the terror inspired by their name, and especially after their numbers had been increased by vigorous reproduction, that even the kings of Syria eventually did not refuse to pay tribute. The first of the inhabitants of Asia to refuse payment was Attalus,* father of Eumenes. Contrary to everyone's expectations, fortune smiled on his audacious move, and he proved superior in pitched battle. Attalus did not, however, so demoralize the Gauls as to make them abandon their domination, and their strength remained unchanged down to the war of Antiochus with the Romans. Even then, after the defeat of Antiochus, they had had high hopes that the Roman army would not reach them because they were living far from the sea.

17. Such was the enemy that the Romans had to fight, one so fearsome to all in the region. The consul therefore addressed the men at an assembly, speaking roughly as follows:

'I am not unaware, men, that of all the tribes that live in Asia the Gauls have the pre-eminent reputation in warfare. They are a fierce tribe that has wandered virtually throughout the world doing battle—and they have chosen to settle amongst the most docile race of people. The Gauls have tall frames, hair long and red, huge shields, and long swords. Then there are their chants as they go into battle, their yells and war-dances, and the frightening clash of arms as they strike their shields, following some sort of tradition—all of this deliberately contrived to instil terror. But let Greeks, Phrygians, and Carians be frightened by such practices, of which they have no knowledge or experience. We Romans are used to the wild antics of the Gauls and we know their futile tricks. On one occasion long ago, when the two first met in battle at the Allia,* our ancestors fled before them; but in the two hundred years since that time our sol-diers have been cutting them down or putting them to flight, stam-peding them like animals, and more triumphs have been celebrated over the Gauls, it is almost true to say, than over the rest of the world put together. And this is a fact we have learned from experience: just face their initial onslaught, which they mount with burning fervour and blind rage, and their limbs become flaccid with sweat and fatigue, and the weapons slip from their hands. Soft in physique and, once their anger subsides, soft in spirit, they are brought down by the sun, the dust and thirst, without one needing to draw a weapon on them.

'We have put them to the test not only fighting legion against legion, but also engaging them man to man. Titus Manlius and Marcus Valerius* have demonstrated the superiority of Roman val-our over Gallic rage. Marcus Manlius* faced an army on his own and flung down the Gauls as they climbed the Capitol.

'Besides, those ancestors of ours had genuine Gauls to deal with, men born in their own land. These are a lesser breed, mongrels aptly named "Gallograeci."* It is the same in the vegetable and animal world: the seeds have not the power to preserve the strain to the extent that the natural qualities of the soil, and the climate in which they grow, can change it. Macedonians inhabiting Alexandria in Egypt, or Seleucia* and Babylonia and other colonies scattered throughout the world have degenerated into Syrians, Parthians, and Egyptians. Massilia, situated amongst the Gauls, has derived some of its character from its neighbours. What do the people of Taren-tum have left of their tough and rugged Spartan discipline? What-ever grows in its own natural surroundings is of superior quality. Planted in foreign soil its nature changes and it declines to the level of its environment. And so it is Phrygians bearing Gallic weapons that you will be cutting down, a conquering nation cutting down a conquered nation—just as you did in the battle-line of Antiochus.

'My fear is that there will be too little glory coming of it, not that there will be too tough a fight. Attalus has often scattered them and put them to flight. Animals freshly captured at first retain that savage woodland nature of theirs, but then they become tame after prolonged feeding from human hands. Do not imagine that nature does not do the same in softening the fierceness of men. Do you think these Gauls are the same as their fathers and grandfathers were? The latter were exiles because they were short of land. Leaving home, they travelled along the rugged coastline of Illyricum, and then through Paeonia and Thrace, fighting with the wildest tribes, before settling in these lands. Toughened and brutalized by all their hardships, they were received by a land that could sate them with all manner of commodities. Fertile soil, a mild climate, natives of gentle disposition—these mollified all that fierceness with which they had arrived. And, by Hercules, you men of the war-god, you must see that from the very start you shun and avoid the delights of Asia—such power have these foreign pleasures to wipe out the vitality of one's personality, and so strong is the effect of exposure to the manners and culture of the natives. But there is one fortunate outcome of this. While the strength they have to wield against you is useless, they still enjoy amongst the Greeks a reputation as great as they had earlier, when they arrived, and as victors you will bask in the same glory amongst your allies as if you had defeated them when they still had their courage of old.'

18. Manlius broke up the assembly and sent envoys to Eposognatus who was the only one of the chieftains to have stood by his treaty with Eumenes and to have refused to send Antiochus military assistance against the Romans. He then struck camp. On the first day they reached the River Aladrus, and on the next a village called Tyscos. There he was met by ambassadors from Oroanda seeking a treaty. A price of 200 talents was demanded of them and they were granted their request to take the demand home.

The consul next led the army to †Plitendum†, and then encamped at Alyatti. The men sent to Eposognatus returned to him at Alyatti, and with them were representatives of the chieftain who begged him not to attack the Tectosages. Eposognatus would visit that tribe in person, they said, and would persuade them to follow Manlius' instructions. The chieftain was granted his request, and the army moved on from there through the land called Axylos.* It is appropriately named: not only does it bear no wood, but it does not even have brushwood or anything else to fuel a fire. The inhabitants use cow dung for this instead of wood.

The Romans were encamped at Cuballum, a fortress of Galatia, when enemy cavalry appeared with a great commotion. With their sudden attack they not only threw the Roman outposts into disarray but also killed a number of men. The noise of the uproar carried to the camp, and suddenly Roman cavalry came pouring from all the camp-gates. These scattered and drove off the Gauls and killed some of them as they fled. The consul could now see that he had reached the enemy and from that point on he proceeded only after reconnoitring and with his column carefully arranged. He now came to the River Sangarius by uninterrupted marches, and because the river was nowhere fordable he proceeded to construct a bridge.

The Sangarius flows from Mt. Adoreus through Phrygia and joins the River Tymbris at the Bithynian border. Flowing with greater volume, its waters now doubled, it runs through Bithynia and empties into the Propontis, remarkable less for its size than for the enormous quantities of fish it provides for people in the area. On the completion of the bridge the Romans crossed the river, and while they proceeded along the bank they were met by Galli of the Magna Mater* from Pessinus. Dressed in their ceremonial robes, these uttered prophesies in inspired chants, to the effect that the goddess was opening up a road in the war for the Romans and granting them victory and dominion in the region. The consul declared that he accepted the omen, and he encamped right on the spot.

The next day Manlius reached Gordium. This is not a large town, but is a more populous and busy commercial centre than is usual for the interior. It has three seas at roughly the same distance* from it: the Hellespont, the sea at Sinope, and that off the shores opposite Sinope, where the coastal Cilicians live. Besides this, it also borders on a large number of great nations, and their interrelationship focused trading mostly on this spot. At this time the Romans found that the inhabitants had fled, leaving it deserted, but that it was amply stocked with goods of all kinds. While they were encamped there, the envoys returned from Eposognatus with the news that the latter's journey to the Gallic chieftains had yielded no favourable result. The Gauls, they said, were moving in large numbers from their villages and farms in the plains. They were taking their wives and children and driving before them and carrying everything they could; they were heading for Mt. Olympus* where they intended using their arms and the natural features of the place to defend themselves.

19. An embassy from Oroanda subsequently brought more reliable information: the Tolostobogian people had seized Mt. Olympus; the Tectosagi had taken a different path and headed for another mountain, called Magaba; and the Trocmi had left their wives and children with the Tectosages and taken the decision to march under arms to assist the Tolostobogii.

At that time the chieftains of the three peoples were Ortiago, Combolomarus, and Gaulotus. They had adopted this plan of campaign because they believed that, by occupying the highest mountains in the area and transporting there all kinds of supplies in quantities sufficient for an indefinite period, they would wear down and tire out their enemy. The Romans would never venture to climb such precipitously steep terrain, they thought; and if they did try they could be stopped or hurled down even by a small group of men, and they would not tolerate cold and deprivation sitting inactive at the foot of these icy mountains. The very height of the position offered the Gauls protection, but they also ran a ditch and other defence-works around the peaks they had occupied. They paid very little attention to providing themselves with weapons for throwing, believing as they did that the rough ground would itself furnish them with a plentiful supply of stones.

20. The consul had surmised that the battle would entail long-range attacks on the enemy positions rather than hand-to-hand fighting, and he had therefore prepared a huge quantity of javelins, skirmishing spears, and arrows, as well as lead balls and smallish stones that could be shot with a sling. Armed with this array of missiles he led his men towards Mt. Olympus, pitching camp about five miles from it. The next day he advanced with Attalus and 400 cavalry to examine the natural features of the mountain and the position of the camp of the Gauls, but enemy cavalry in numbers twice his own poured from the camp and chased him off, even killing a few of the fleeing Romans and wounding more.

On the third day Manlius set off with all his cavalry to examine the position, and because none of the enemy ventured beyond their defences he rode safely around the mountain. He noticed that to the south the hills had a good covering of soil and a gentle gradient up to a certain point, and that to the north there were cliffs that were sheer and almost perpendicular. He also observed that there were only three viable means of access, all others being impossible: one up the centre of the mountain, where the surface had a covering of soil, and two difficult approaches, on the south-east and north-west sides respectively. After taking note of these, Manlius encamped that day right at the foot of the mountain. The next day he sacrificed and, gaining favourable omens with the first victims, proceeded with his advance on the enemy, his army split into three sections.

Manlius himself went up with most of the troops along the path where the mountain afforded the easiest access. He instructed his brother, Lucius Manlius, to climb the south-east slope as far as the terrain would allow and as far as he could in safety—if he were faced with ground that was dangerous and precipitous, he was not to combat the difficulty of the land, or battle against insuperable obstacles, but cut obliquely across the mountain towards him and join up with his column. Gaius Helvius he ordered to move gradually around the lower slopes of the mountain with the third part of the force, and then bring his column up on the north-western side. Manlius also divided Attalus' auxiliaries into three sections of equal size, and ordered the young man to accompany him. He left his cavalry and elephants* on the plain close to the hills, and commanded his officers to watch carefully the developments in every location and ensure that they could bring support wherever the situation required it.

21. Convinced that their position was inaccessible on the two other sides, the Gauls wanted to block access from the southern side with an armed force. They therefore sent some 4,000 men under arms to seize a hillock overlooking this route, less than a mile from their camp, thinking they could employ the hillock as a defensible position to bar the enemy's advance. Seeing this, the Romans prepared themselves for battle. The skirmishers went ahead, at a short distance before the standards, along with the Cretan archers and slingers (which Attalus had provided), the Tralles, and the Thracians. The companies of infantry were taken along at a slow pace, as they were moving over steep ground, and they held their shields

before them for the sole purpose of warding off missiles, since there seemed little chance of their actually coming to grips with the enemy.

The action commenced with missiles hurled at long range, and at first the fighting was even, the Gauls advantaged by their position, the Romans by the diversity and quantity of their weapons. As the contest proceeded this evenness disappeared. The Gauls received inadequate protection from their shields which were long but not wide enough for their large physique, and which were also flat. They also had no weapons other than their swords, and these were of no use to them since the enemy was not engaging them hand-to-hand. They did make use of stones, but not the smaller ones, since they had not stockpiled them, but just what came into the hands of each man as he frantically groped for them, and being inexperienced in this mode of fighting they had neither the skill nor the strength to assist the throw. From every direction they were receiving un-expected blows from arrows, sling-projectiles, and javelins. Blinded by rage and panic, they could not see what they were doing, and they were caught up in a kind of fighting for which they had very little aptitude. When fighting at close quarters the Gauls receive and inflict wounds by turns, and anger fires their courage; but when they are receiving wounds from light weapons coming from unseen points far off and they have no object against which to rush in their blind fury, they charge into their own comrades like speared animals. Their wounds were exposed to view because they fight in the nude, and also because their torsos are flabby and pale from never being unclothed, except for battle. As a result blood flowed more copiously from the mass of flesh, with the wounds appearing all the more horrific and the pallor of their bodies all the more streaked with dark gore. But Gauls are not so worried by open cuts. Sometimes, when the skin is lacerated and the gash is wide rather than deep they think that this adds distinction to their fighting. But when they feel the burning pain of the point of an arrow or sling-projectile that is deeply embedded in a seemingly minor wound, and the barb will not emerge despite attempts to extract it, they succumb to fits of rage and shame at so slight an affliction bringing them destruction and fling themselves to the ground †. . .†. Others were rushing into the enemy and receiving wounds from every side, and when they came to close quarters they were slaughtered by the swords of the skir-mishers. This type of soldier carries a three-foot shield and, in his right hand, some spears which he uses at long range, and he has a Spanish sword at his side. If he has to engage in hand-to-hand fighting, he transfers the spears to his left hand and draws the sword.

By now there were few Gauls left alive, and these could see that they had been bested by the light-armed troops and that the legionary forces were bearing down on them. They broke into headlong flight and headed back to their camp, which was already full of panic and confusion, this being where the women, children, and other non-combatants had been brought together. Deserted by the fleeing enemy, the hills were taken over by the victorious Romans.

22. At about this time Lucius Manlius and Gaius Helvius had made the ascent as far as the rising ground of the hills permitted.* Reaching the impassable spots, they both changed course towards the only area of the mountain which afforded a way up and, as if by prearranged plan, proceeded to follow the column of the consul, keeping a short distance from each other. And so pressure of circumstances compelled them to execute a manœuvre that would have been the best to follow in the first place. For, on such difficult terrain, supporting units have often proved invaluable: if the forward troops happen to be beaten back, they can form a second front which can both protect their routed comrades and also take up the fight with fresh vigour.

When the leading companies of the legions reached the hills taken by the light infantry, the consul told his men to take a break and rest for a while. At the same time he indicated to them the bodies of the Gauls strewn over the hills. When the light-armed troops had fought a battle like that, what, he asked, could be expected of the legions, what of regularly armed troops, what of the courage of his bravest men? They now had to capture the camp of the Gauls, he said, where the enemy was cowering, driven there by the light infantry. Even so Manlius ordered the light infantry to take the lead. These had not wasted their time while the column was at a halt, but had spent it gathering weapons on the hills so as to have an adequate supply of missiles.

The Romans were now approaching the camp, and the Gauls, fearing that their defences might provide insufficient protection, had taken up a position, in arms, before the rampart. They were now buried under a hail of weapons of all kinds, and the more numerous and closely packed they were, the less likely it was that any weapon fell ineffectually. In a moment they were driven within the rampart, leaving strong guards only at the actual approaches to the gates. Missiles were then hurled in enormous quantities at the mass of people driven back into the camp, and the cry that went up, mingled with the lamentations of women and children, indicated that many were receiving wounds. The forward troops of the legions hurled their javelins at the Gauls forming the guard-posts for the gates. While these were not wounded by the weapons, a number of them became entangled and caught up with each other when their shields were pierced right through, and they no longer withstood the Roman assault.

23. The gates now lay open, but before the victors could burst in the Gauls fled in all directions from their camp. They rushed blindly ahead, roads or no roads. No precipices, no cliffs stood in their way—it was only their enemy they feared. As a result many fell headlong to their deaths from enormous heights †or† were maimed.

The camp taken, the consul kept his men from pillaging it for booty, ordering them to follow him as quickly as best each could, to press their advantage and add panic to the enemy's dismay. The second column under Lucius Manlius also arrived on the scene, and he did not allow these men to enter the camp, either. He sent them immediately in pursuit of the enemy, and shortly afterwards he followed himself, leaving his military tribunes to guard the captives. He thought that if he killed or captured as many as possible while they were in that state of panic the war would be at an end. After the consul left, Gaius Helvius arrived with the third column, but he could not stop his men from looting the camp, and by a cruel stroke of fate the booty fell to men who had taken no part in the fighting. The cavalry long remained at a standstill, unaware of the engagement and their comrades' victory, and then they, too—as far as their horses could negotiate the hills—chased the Gauls, now dispersed in flight, around the foot of the mountain, killing them or taking prisoners.

The number of the fallen could not be determined easily because the chase and the killing went on throughout the winding valleys in the mountains, with many falling from impassable cliffs into deep canyons, and others being slaughtered in woods and undergrowth. Claudius records that there were two battles on Mt. Olympus and puts the number of dead at 40,000, but Valerius Antias, who is usually more prone to gross exaggeration of numbers, puts it at no more than 10,000. There is no doubt that the number of prisoners reached 40,000 because the Gauls had hauled along with them a multitude of people of all kinds and all ages, more like men moving home than going to war.

The consul burned the arms of the enemy in a single heap and ordered all his men to gather together the rest of the booty. He then sold the part that had to be converted to cash for payment into the public treasury, and carefully divided the rest amongst his soldiers so that shares should be as even as possible. In addition, the men were all given a public commendation at an assembly, and rewarded according to their individual merits—Attalus more than anyone else, to universal approval. For the young man's courage and indefatigability in the face of all the hardship and danger had been remarkable, as also had been his modest demeanour.

24. War with the Tectosages, as yet unstarted, still remained. The consul proceeded against them, and on the third day of his march reached Ancyra, a city famous in that area. The enemy were a little more than ten miles distant. When Manlius was encamped here, a remarkable exploit was brought off by a female captive.

The wife of the Gallic chieftain Ortiago* was one of a number of prisoners. She was a very attractive woman, and charged with guarding her was a centurion with the sexual appetite and the greed of a soldier. This man at first attempted to seduce her, but seeing that consensual sex was abhorrent to her, he assaulted her person, which fortune had enslaved to him. Later, to temper the humiliation of the assault, he gave the woman hope that she might return to her people, but even that was not offered free of charge, as by a lover. The centurion negotiated the payment of a certain amount of gold and, not to have any of his men privy to his dealings, he allowed the woman to send any one of her fellow-prisoners she wished as a messenger to her people. He picked a spot near the river to which no more than two of the prisoner's kinsmen were to come to fetch her the following night, bringing the gold. It so happened that a slave actually belonging to the woman was amongst the prisoners in custody with her. This man was chosen as the messenger, and the centurion took him out at dusk beyond the guard-outposts.

The next night the woman's two relatives came to the appointed place and the centurion also came with the prisoner. Here they were showing the centurion the gold, which amounted to a full Attic talent—the price that he had negotiated—when the woman told them in her own language to draw their swords and dispatch him while he was weighing the gold. After they killed him she cut off his head, wrapped it in her dress and came with it to her husband Ortiago who had made good his escape home from Olympus. Before she embraced him she threw the centurion's head at his feet. Ortiago was wondering whose head this was and what was the meaning of such unfeminine conduct, and she openly confessed to her husband the sexual assault and the retribution she had taken for the violation of her honour. And it is said that by the moral purity and propriety she showed in the rest of her life she maintained to the end the esteem she won by this act of a decent woman.

25. Spokesmen of the Tectosages came to the consul at his base at Ancyra with a request that he not strike camp before parleying with their chieftains. Any conditions of peace would be better than war, they said. The rendezvous was fixed for the following day at a spot that appeared very close to half-way between the camp of the Gauls and Ancyra. The consul arrived on time at the place with an escort of 500 horsemen, but there was not a Gaul to be seen and he returned to camp. Then the same spokesmen reappeared to explain that, because of some religious impediment, the chieftains were unable to come, but that leading members of their tribe would attend and the business could just as effectively be transacted by them. The consul said that he would on his side send Attalus to represent him, and this meeting was attended by both sides.

Attalus brought with him 300 horsemen as a bodyguard, and discussion of peace-terms began. No conclusion could be reached in the absence of the commanders-in-chief, however, and it was agreed that the consul and the chieftains should meet in that spot the following day. The prevarication of the Gauls had a double purpose. First, they wanted to waste time until they could transport across the River Halys the property they did not want put at risk, along with their wives and children; and, secondly, they were in the process of laying a trap for the consul himself, who took insufficient precautions against treachery at the meeting. For the deed they selected from their entire force 1,000 horsemen of proven enterprise, and their treacherous action might have succeeded had not fortune stood on the side of international law, which the Gauls had determined to violate.

Roman foragers and wood-gatherers were brought into the area where the meeting was to take place. The tribunes had thought these would enjoy greater security because they would have the consul's escort, and the consul himself, serving as a protective outpost against the enemy. Even so, they established another outpost of their own, made up of 600 cavalrymen, closer to the camp.

When Attalus assured him that the chieftains would be coming and the business could be concluded, the consul left the camp and advanced about five miles, taking the same cavalry escort as on the previous occasion. He was not far from the rendezvous when he suddenly saw the Gauls galloping towards him with a warlike charge. Manlius halted the column, and told his horsemen to prepare their weapons and their spirit. He faced up to the initial onslaught with resolve and did not give ground, but when the enemy numbers overwhelmed him he began to give way little by little, without allowing the ranks to break formation. Finally, there was more danger in delaying the inevitable than there was safety in maintaining the ranks, and they all scattered in indiscriminate flight.

At this point the Gauls proceeded to press ahead and cut down the scattered Romans, most of whom would have lost their lives but for the arrival on the scene of 600 horsemen, the escort of the foragers. When these heard the distraught shouting of their comrades in the distance, they made ready their weapons and mounts and, fresh in the field, took up the battle which had turned against the Romans. Fortunes were immediately reversed, and the panic was transferred from the conquered to the conquerors. The Gauls were scattered at the first assault; the foragers came running to the spot from the fields; and the Gauls were faced by their enemy on every side. The result was that even flight was not easy or safe, because the Romans had fresh horses and were pursuing exhausted men. Few of the Gauls made good their escape, no prisoners were taken, and the large majority paid with their lives for violating the safe conduct guaranteed to a parley. Fired with anger, the Romans came to the enemy with all their forces the next day.

26. The consul spent all of two days examining the topography of the mountain for himself so as not to miss a single detail. On the third day, he attended to the auspices and offered sacrifice, and then brought out his troops split into four sections. Two he would lead up the centre of the mountain, and two he would send up each side

against the flanks of the Gauls. The enemy's main strength, that is the Tectosages and the Trocmi, formed the centre of their line with 50,000 men. Since they could not make use of their horses on the rocky, uneven terrain, they placed their cavalry, dismounted, on the right wing, a force of 10,000 men. Ariarathes' Cappadocians and Morzus' auxiliaries, totalling approximately 4,000 men, were on the left wing.

As at Mt. Olympus, the consul put his light-armed troops in the front line, making sure that they had an equally great supply of weapons of all kinds available. When they approached each other, all was the same on both sides as in the previous battle—except for their morale. In the victors this was buoyed up by their success; in the enemy <it was low> because, while they had not been conquered themselves, they took the defeat of men who were members of their own race as a defeat for them. So it was that, after a similar beginning, the engagement had the same result. The Gallic line was covered with what seemed to be a cloud of light missiles discharged against it. No one had the temerity to run forward from the ranks for fear of exposing his body to weapons thrown from all sides, and the closer together they stood the more wounds they received, being thus a fixed target for their enemies' projectiles. Seeing the Gauls already in such confusion, the consul thought they would all immediately take to their heels if he simply showed them the legionary standards, and so, taking the skirmishers and the rest of the auxiliaries back into the ranks, he moved his line forward.

27. The Gauls were terrified as they recalled the defeat of the Tolostobogii; they moved about with weapons piercing their bodies; and they were exhausted from making their stand as well as from their wounds. Thus they failed to resist even the first assault and shout of the Romans. They fled towards the camp, but few managed to enter the fortifications, the majority passing by to the right and the left as they ran off in whatever direction each was swept by his headlong flight. The victors followed them as far as the camp, cutting down the hindmost, but then, greedy for plunder, they remained in the camp, and none continued the pursuit. The Gauls on the flanks stood their ground longer because the Romans were later reaching them, but then they failed to withstand even the first volley of missiles. Unable to drag the men who had entered the camp away from their pillaging, the consul sent those on the wings in

immediate pursuit of the enemy. They followed the Gauls for some distance, but killed no more than 8,000 men in the rout—there was no battle as such—and the rest made it across the River Halys.

Most of the Romans remained in the enemy camp that night, and the consul took the others back to his own. The following day Manlius made an inventory of the captives and the spoils, which were as great as a rapacious tribe could have amassed after many years of military occupation of the whole area this side of the Taurus. The Gauls gathered together in one spot after scattering in random flight, most of them wounded or without weapons, and stripped of all their possessions, and they sent spokesmen to the consul to sue for peace. Manlius ordered them to come to Ephesus. He himself was in a hurry to leave the region which was chilled by the proximity of the Taurus range—for it was already mid-autumn—and he led his victorious army back to winter-quarters on the coast.

28. There was peace in the other provinces during the time of these events in Asia. At Rome the censors Titus Quinctius Flamininus and Marcus Claudius Marcellus reviewed the membership of the Senate. Publius Scipio Africanus was selected to be *princeps senatus* for the third time, and only four men were rejected,* none of them having held a curule office. The censors were also very lenient in reviewing the list of *equites*.* They put out for contract the building of a foundation on the Aequimaelium on the Capitol, and the paving with flint of the road between the Porta Capena and the temple of Mars. The people of Campania consulted the Senate on where they should be registered for the census and it was decided that this should be Rome. There were huge floods that year, and the Tiber twelve times inundated the Campus Martius and the lower areas of the city.

When the war with the Gauls in Asia had been finished off by the consul Gnaeus Manlius, the other consul Marcus Fulvius, who had by now defeated the Aetolians, crossed to Cephallenia. He sent deputies around the states on the island to ask whether they wanted to surrender to the Romans or else take their chances in war. In all cases fear prevailed, and they surrendered. They delivered the hostages demanded of them, the poor peoples according to their strength <... the Pronnaei>, but the Cranians, Palensians, and Samaeans each giving twenty. The rays of an unexpected peace had shone on Cephallenia when suddenly, for some unknown reason, one state,

Same, revolted. Because the city was strategically situated, the people of Same claimed that they had been afraid that they would be compelled by the Romans to move from home. But whether this was an imaginary fear they conjured up for themselves, with a dormant malaise awoken through groundless panic, or whether the suggestion really had been discussed among the Romans and then reported back to the Samaeans, is not certain. What *is* known is that after they had already surrendered the hostages the Samaeans suddenly closed their gates and were unwilling to abandon their course of action even after entreaties from their own people—for the consul had sent a number of them up the walls to rouse the sympathies of parents and fellow-countrymen. When no answer suggested a peaceful resolution, the siege of the city got under way. Fulvius had with him the whole battery of slings and siege-engines that he had brought across from the siege of Ambracia, and his men energetically completed the works that were needing to be built. Battering-rams were therefore moved forward at two points and these proceeded to pound the wall.

29. Nothing that could obstruct the siege-works or the enemy offensive was overlooked by the people of Same. They had, however, two main means of resistance: first, they would without fail erect a new and strong defensive-wall close by on the inside to replace one that was demolished; and, secondly, they made sudden counter-attacks, either on the enemy siege-works or their outposts, and they usually had the upper hand in these encounters.

One method of checking these attacks was devised, though it does not sound very impressive. A hundred slingers were brought in from Aegium, Patrae, and Dymae. These men had from boyhood received what amounted to the routine training of their people, shooting out to the open sea by means of a sling the round pebbles which are usually found strewn, mixed with sand, along the beaches. Thus they had a longer range using that weapon than does the Balearic slinger, and a more accurate and powerful shot. (Furthermore, the sling is not made up of a single thong like the Balearic sling and that of other peoples. Instead, it has three strips which are reinforced by seams at close intervals so that the missile is not sent forth from a strap that has no tautness at the moment of propulsion but, sitting well-balanced in the sling, it is discharged as though it were shot from a bowstring.)

Since they were accustomed to hitting circles of small circumference at long range, these slingers would inflict wounds not only to the heads of the enemy but to any part of the face which they made their target.

These slings curbed the frequency and the boldness of the Samaean counter-attacks, so much so that the townspeople entreated the Achaeans from their walls to withdraw for a short time and simply watch their engagements with the Roman outposts, without taking part.

Same withstood the siege for four months. Few at the start, they also suffered daily casualties, either dead or wounded, and the survivors were physically and mentally drained. Then the Romans crossed the wall at night in the area of the citadel called †Cyatides†, so-named because the city slopes down to the sea and faces westwards, and reached the forum. Realizing that part of their city had been taken by the enemy, the Samaeans fled to the larger citadel with their wives and children. The following day they surrendered, the city was sacked, and they were all sold into slavery.

30. After settling affairs in Cephallenia, and installing a garrison at Same, the consul crossed to the Peloponnese, for the people of Aegium, in particular, and of Sparta, too, had long been pressing him to come. Since the beginning of the Achaean League, the plenary meetings of the nation had always been convened at Aegium, and this could be attributed either to the city's importance or its convenient location. This year, for the first time, Philopoemen attempted to undermine the tradition, and was preparing to propose a law that the meetings be held in turn in all the member-states of the Achaean League. Shortly before the arrival of the consul the *damiurgi* of the member-states (that is, their chief magistrates) called a meeting at Aegium, but Philopoemen, who was then praetor of the League, pronounced Argos the venue. When it became clear that nearly all members would make an appearance here, the consul also came to Argos, despite his support for the cause of the people of Aegium. A discussion of the issue arose here, and the consul, seeing the case of the people of Aegium was lost, abandoned his initial support for them.

After this the Spartans drew his attention to their disagreements. The city had been having the severest problems with its exiles, most of whom lived in the maritime strongholds and cities on the Laconian coastline. All of these territories had been taken from Sparta.

The Spartans were aggrieved at this—they wished to have free access to the sea at some point for sending embassies to Rome or elsewhere, and also to have a market and a haven for foreign merchandise to meet urgent needs. They therefore took by a surprise assault a coastal village called Las, attacking it by night. The villagers and resident exiles were initially daunted by the unexpected blow, but then as dawn approached they mustered and drove out the Spartans with a minor skirmish. Even so panic spread all along the coast, and all the fortresses, villages, and exiles in residence in the area sent a joint embassy to the Achaeans.

31. The Achaean praetor Philopoemen had from the beginning espoused the cause of the exiles, and he had always recommended to the Achaeans the curtailment of Spartan power and influence. Now he granted an audience to the complainants. On his proposal the following decree was then passed: that whereas Titus Quinctius and the Romans had transferred to the protection and custody of the Achaeans the strongholds and villages of the Laconian seaboard, and whereas the village of Las had been attacked, and blood had there been shed although the Spartans were bound by their treaty not to interfere with these places, the treaty would be considered broken unless the perpetrators of the deed and their accomplices were delivered to the Achaeans. Envoys were immediately dispatched to Sparta to demand the surrender of the culprits. The order struck the Spartans as so high-handed and unfair that, had their state enjoyed its ancient standing, they would certainly taken up arms forthwith. They were particularly agitated by the fear that, once they accepted the yoke by complying with the first commands, Philopoemen would carry through the scheme he had long been working on and deliver Sparta to the exiles. So, in a paroxysm of rage, they murdered thirty men of the party which had been connected with the policies of Philopoemen and the exiles, and decided that the pact with the Achaeans should be revoked. They further decided that envoys should be sent immediately to Cephallenia to surrender Sparta to the consul Marcus Fulvius and the Romans, and beg the consul to come to the Peloponnese to take the city of Sparta under the protection and authority of the Roman people.

32. When the envoys brought back this news to the Achaeans, war was declared on Sparta, with the unanimous agreement of the states at the council meeting. Winter prevented immediate commencement

of hostilities, but the territory of the Spartans was subjected to minor incursions, more like piracy than warfare, and not just over land but with naval attacks from the sea as well. The disorder brought the consul to the Peloponnese. At his behest a meeting of the council was called at Elis and the Spartans were invited to argue their case. This went beyond being a great debate to become a great shouting-match. Although the consul had been showing favour to both sides and making diplomatically evasive remarks, he brought closure to the matter with a single command, that they eschew military action until they had sent envoys to the Senate in Rome.

A deputation was sent to Rome by both parties, and the Spartan exiles joined their case and their deputation with those of the Achaeans. The leaders of the Achaean delegation were Diophanes and Lycortas, both of Megalopolis. These were political opponents and on this occasion, too, had very few points of agreement in the speeches they delivered. Diophanes advocated leaving everything to the discretion of the Senate who, he said, would be the best to settle the differences between the Achaeans and the Spartans. Lycortas, who had been briefed by Philopoemen, insisted that the Achaeans should have the right under the treaty and their laws to put their decrees into effect, and that they be granted unrestricted exercise of the freedom which the Romans had themselves vouchsafed to them. At that time the Achaean people were very influential with the Romans, but even so the decision reached was that there should be no change in regard to the Spartans. However, so cryptic was the Roman answer that the Achaeans took it as permission to act in the case of Sparta, while the Spartans on their side interpreted it as not giving the Achaeans a completely free hand. The Achaeans were extreme and high-handed in their use of this power.

33. Philopoemen's magistracy was renewed. At the beginning of spring he mobilized an army, pitched camp in Spartan territory and sent envoys to demand the surrender of the men responsible for the sedition. He promised that their city-state would have peace if the Spartans complied with the order, and that the guilty parties would receive no punishment without a hearing. The others remained silent from fear, but the men whom Philopoemen had named in his demand agreed to go since they had the assurance from the envoys that they would receive no violent treatment before they pleaded their case. Other prominent men went along with them, both to

support them as private individuals, and also from the belief that their case was important to the interests of the state. The Achaeans had never taken Spartan exiles with them into Spartan territory, because there was evidently nothing as likely to offend the feelings of the citizen body; but on this occasion the exiles virtually represented the vanguard of the entire army. These formed a column and met the Spartans as they arrived at the gate of the camp. At first they taunted them with abusive comments. Then a wrangle ensued and, as tempers flared, the most hot-blooded of the exiles attacked the Spartans. The Spartans appealed to the gods, and to the guarantee given by the envoys, and both the envoys and the praetor tried to drive back the crowd, to shield the Spartans, and to push away a number of men who were already in the process of shackling them. The crowd swelled after the disturbance broke out. At first the Achaeans swiftly converged on the spot to see what was happening. Then the exiles loudly proclaimed their past sufferings and begged for assistance, claiming they would never have such an opportunity again if they let this one slip. The treaty, they said, had been solemnly ratified on the Capitol, at Olympia, and on the Athenian acropolis, and this had been abrogated by these men; so they should punish the guilty before they were restricted once more by another treaty. The crowd were roused to anger by these words and, when one man cried out that they should give the Spartans a thrashing, they proceeded to hurl stones. So it was that seventeen of the Spartans who had been shackled in the fracas lost their lives. The next day a further sixty-three were arrested. These the praetor had protected against violent treatment, not because he wanted them unharmed but because he did not want them put to death without a hearing. They were now thrown to the angry mob. After uttering a few words that fell on deaf ears they were all condemned and handed over for execution.

34. The Spartans, terrified by this episode, were first of all ordered to tear down their walls. Next they were told that all foreign auxiliary troops who had been mercenaries under the tyrants should quit Laconian territory, and then that slaves freed by the tyrants—and there were large numbers of these—should leave before a certain date, with the Achaeans having the right to seize, take away, and sell any who remained. They were also ordered to repeal the legislation and system of Lycurgus and acclimatize themselves to Achaean laws

and institutions. In this way they would become a united body and find it easier to reach agreement on everything, they were told.

No condition did the Spartans fulfil with more readiness than the demolition of their walls, and none more reluctantly than the recall of the exiles. The decree relating to their restoration was passed in a full council of the Achaeans in Tegea. It was also noted at the meeting that the foreign auxiliaries had been dismissed and that the 'newly enfranchised Spartans', as they called the men freed by the tyrants, had left the city and scattered into the countryside. It was decided that, before the demobilization of the army, the praetor should go at the head of the light infantry and arrest men in this situation and sell them under the law pertaining to plunder. Many were arrested and put on sale, and a portico at Megalopolis which the Spartans had destroyed was rebuilt from the proceeds, with the agreement of the Achaeans. In addition, the territory of Belbina, which had been unlawfully seized by the tyrants of Sparta, was returned to that state under an old statute passed during the reign of Philip, son of Amyntas.* The state of Sparta was virtually drained of her strength by these measures and was long subject to the Achaeans, but nothing was so harmful to them as the removal of the discipline of Lycurgus to which they had accustomed themselves over a period of eight hundred years.

35. Marcus Fulvius left the council in which the debate between the Achaeans and Spartans had taken place before the consul and came to Rome for the elections, the year being now at an end. There he supervised the election of Marcus Valerius Messala and Gaius Livius Salinator as consuls, after rejecting the candidacy of his enemy Marcus Aemilius Lepidus, who was also seeking election that year. The following were then elected praetor: Quintus Marcius Philippus, Marcus Claudius Marcellus, Gaius Stertinius, Gaius Atinius, Publius Claudius Pulcher,* and Lucius Manlius Acidinus. The elections finished, it was decided that the consul Marcus Fulvius should return to his province and to his army, and both he and his colleague, Gnaeus Manlius, had their commands extended for a year. In the temple of Hercules a statue of the god was that year erected at the direction of the decemviris, and a six-horse chariot overlaid with gold was set up by †Gnaeus† Cornelius* on the Capitol, with an inscription stating that it was donated by the consul. Twelve gilded shields were also set up on

the Capitol by the curule aediles, Publius Claudius Pulcher and Servius Sulpicius Galba, paid for from fines they imposed on grain-merchants for hoarding grain-supplies. In addition, the plebeian aedile, Quintus Fulvius Flaccus, erected two statues overlaid with gold after the conviction of a single defendant, the aediles having brought independent prosecutions (his colleague, Aulus Caecilius, succeeded in prosecuting nobody). The Roman Games were repeated in their entirety three times, the Plebeian Games five times.

After entering their consulship on 15 March, Marcus Valerius Messala and Gaius Livius Salinator consulted the Senate on civic affairs, and on the provinces and the armies for them. No change was made with regard to Aetolia and Asia, and one of the consuls was assigned Pisae and the Ligurians as his province, the other Gaul. They were instructed to settle the allocation between themselves, or by lot, and to raise for themselves two armies, each comprising two legions, and to requisition from the allies and the Latin league 15,000 infantry for each army as well as a total of 1,200 horse. The Ligurians fell to Messala, and Gaul to Salinator. The praetorian sortition after this went as follows:

Marcus Claudius	urban jurisdiction
Publius Claudius	foreign jurisdiction
Quintus Marcius	Sicily
Gaius Stertinius	Sardinia
Lucius Manlius	Hither Spain
Gaius Atinius	Farther Spain

36. The following decisions were reached with respect to the armies. The legions formerly under the command of Gaius Laelius were to be transferred from Gaul to the propraetor Marcus Tuccius for service in Bruttium. The army in Sicily was to be disbanded, and the propraetor Marcus Sempronius was to bring back to Rome the fleet in that province. The Spanish provinces were each allocated the single legion already stationed in them, and each of the praetors was given the authority to requisition from the allies and take with him a supplementary force of 3,000 infantry and 200 cavalry. Before the new magistrates set out for their provinces, a three-day period of public prayer was imposed at all the crossroads in the name of the college of decemvirs because darkness had fallen between roughly

the third and fourth hours of daylight. A nine-day sacrifice was also proclaimed after a shower of stones on the Aventine.

Following a Senatorial decree of the previous year, the censors had obliged the Campanians to register for the census at Rome, since it had not been clear earlier where they should register. The Campanians now requested that they be allowed to take wives who were Roman citizens and that any who had already taken them be permitted to keep them; and they also asked that any children born to them before that date be considered as legitimate and able to inherit. Both requests were granted.

The tribune of the plebs, Gaius Valerius Tappo, promulgated a bill relating to the townspeople of Formiae, Fundi, and Arpinum which gave these peoples the right to vote, for up to that time they had held citizenship without voting rights. Four tribunes of the plebs vetoed the proposal on the ground that it did not have the approval of the Senate, but when they were told it was the people's prerogative to bestow the right of suffrage as they wished, and not the Senate's, they withdrew their initial objection. A law permitting the people of Formiae and of Fundi to vote in the Aemilian tribe, and the people of Arpinum in the Cornelian tribe, was then passed; and this was the first occasion on which these peoples were registered in these tribes in accordance with Valerius' resolution. After besting Titus Quinctius in the drawing of lots, the censor Marcus Claudius Marcellus performed the closing ceremony for the census. The citizens registered in the census numbered 258,318. When the closing ceremony was done, the consuls left for their provinces.

37. During the winter of these events at Rome, Gnaeus Manlius was in his winter-quarters in Asia. Deputations came to him, first in his capacity as consul, and subsequently as proconsul, and they came from every quarter, from all the states and peoples living this side of the Taurus range. And while victory over Antiochus was more prestigious and glorious in Roman eyes than the Gallic victory, for the allies that over the Gauls was a greater source of joy than the victory over Antiochus. Submission to the king had been easier to bear than the barbarous savagery of the Gauls and the daily incertitude and fear of where their pillaging would descend like a tempest.

These people, then, had been granted freedom by the defeat of Antiochus, and peace by the subjugation of the Gauls; and they had not just come to Manlius to offer congratulations, but had also brought him crowns of gold varying in value according to the resources of each. Envoys also arrived from Antiochus and even from the Gauls to have peace-terms dictated to them; and some came from Ariarathes, king of Cappadocia, to ask for pardon and to pay compensation for the wrong the king had done in giving Antiochus military assistance. Ariarathes was ordered to pay 600 talents of silver, and the reply given to the Gauls was that Manlius would give them his terms when Eumenes came. The deputations from the city-states were sent away with courteous replies and even happier than when they arrived. The envoys of Antiochus were instructed to take money and grain to Pamphylia in accordance with the pact made with Lucius Scipio, and were informed that Manlius would proceed there with his army.

At the beginning of spring Manlius set out after the ritual purification of his army, and came to Apamea seven days later. He encamped there for three days, and with a further three days' march from Apamea reached Pamphylia, where he had ordered the king's representatives to take the money and the grain. Here, 2,500 talents of silver were taken in and transported to Apamea, and the grain was distributed amongst the troops. Manlius then marched to Perga, the only place in the area occupied by a garrison of the king. As he drew near, he was met by the commander of the garrison who asked for a moratorium of thirty days in which to consult Antiochus about the surrender of the city. Granted the time, the commander left with the garrison on the specified date. The consul sent his brother Lucius Manlius from Perga to Oroanda with 4,000 men to collect the remainder of the money which the people of Oroanda had agreed to pay. Since he had been told that Eumenes and the ten commissioners had arrived in Ephesus from Rome, Manlius himself led the army back to Apamea, ordering Eumenes' representatives to follow him.

38. At Apamea a treaty with Antiochus was drawn up on the recommendation of the ten commissioners, worded roughly as follows:

There is to be peace between Antiochus and the Roman people on the following terms and conditions:

The king is not to permit to pass through his lands, or those of peoples who shall be subject to him, any army intending to make war on the people of Rome or their allies, or to help it with provisions, or give it any other form of assistance. The Romans and their allies are to make the same commitment to Antiochus and those who shall be subject to his rule.

Antiochus is not to have the right to make war on the peoples of the islands, or to cross to Europe.

Antiochus is to withdraw from the cities, territories, villages, and strongholds this side of the Taurus range as far as the River Tanais, and from the valley of the Taurus to the heights where the range slopes towards Lycaonia.

From the towns, territories, and strongholds from which he withdraws, Antiochus is to take away nothing apart from his weaponry, and anything he has removed he is to return to where it belongs.

Antiochus is not to take any soldier or any other person from the kingdom of Eumenes. With regard to citizens of those cities separating from Antiochus' empire who are with Antiochus and within the bounds of his realm, these are all to return to Apamea by a fixed date. Any people now with the Romans or their allies, but who are subjects of Antiochus, are to have the right to leave or to stay. The king is to return to the Romans and their allies slaves, whether runaways or prisoners-of-war, and all free men, whether prisoners or deserters.

Antiochus is to surrender all his elephants and not acquire others. He is also to surrender his warships with their equipment, and retain in his possession no more than ten passenger vessels, none of them propelled by more than thirty oars, nor †smaller than that† for a war in which he will be on the offensive. He is not to sail beyond the promontories of Calycadnus or Sarpedonium,* except when a ship will be carrying tribute-payment, envoys or hostages.

Antiochus is not to have the right to hire mercenaries from the peoples in the power of the Roman people, or accept volunteers from them.

Houses and buildings belonging to Rhodians or Rhodian allies within the bounds of Antiochus' kingdom shall remain the property of these Rhodians and allies on the same legal basis as before the war. In the case of financial debts, these may be called in; and the right to search for, identify, and recover any property that has been removed shall also obtain.

Antiochus is also to remove his garrisons from any cities which are due to be surrendered and which are held by people on whom he conferred them, and he is to ensure that these are properly handed over.

Antiochus is to pay 12,000 Attic talents of unadulterated silver in equal instalments within a period of twelve years—with a talent to weigh not less than 80 Roman pounds—and 540,000 measures of wheat. He is to pay King Eumenes 350 talents within a five-year period, as well as the 127 talents in lieu of grain, as had been assessed.

He is to give the Romans twenty hostages, changing them every three years, none of them being younger than eighteen or older than forty-five.

In the case of military aggression against Antiochus by any of the allies of the Roman people, he is to have the right to fend off force with force, provided that he neither hold in subjection any city under the rules of war nor accept any in an alliance.

The two parties are to settle their differences by legal and judicial procedure or, if both agree, by war.

There was also a clause included in the treaty about the surrender of the Carthaginian Hannibal, the Aetolian Thoas, the Acarnanian Mnasilochus, and the Chalcidians Eubulidas and Philo, and another stating that any additions, removals, or modifications subsequently negotiated could be made without invalidating the treaty.

39. The consul took an oath to observe the treaty, and Quintus Minucius Thermus and Lucius Manlius, who happened to come back from Oroanda just at that time, left to demand an oath of compliance from the king. The consul also wrote to Quintus Fabius Labeo, commander of the fleet, ordering him to leave for Patara immediately and break up and burn any of the king's ships that were docked there. Leaving Ephesus, Labeo smashed or burned fifty decked ships, and on the same expedition he accepted the surrender of Telmessus whose inhabitants were terror-stricken by the sudden approach of the fleet. Ordering the troops left at Ephesus to follow, he immediately crossed from Lycia to Greece by way of the islands and, after spending a few days in Athens to allow the ships to reach Piraeus from Ephesus, he brought the whole fleet back from there to Italy.

Gnaeus Manlius made a gift to Eumenes of all the elephants he received from Antiochus—these were amongst the various items he was supposed to receive from the king. He then looked into the concerns of the city-states, many of which were in turmoil as a result of the changed conditions. Thanks to the intervention of Eumenes, to whom he had at this time betrothed his daughter, Ariarathes was excused payment of half the money demanded of him, and was accepted as a friend of Rome. After examining the cases they presented, the ten commissioners made various dispositions for the various states. They granted tax-exemption to those which had been paying tribute to Antiochus, and had sided with the Roman people, but ordered all those who had supported Antiochus, or had paid tribute to Attalus, to pay taxes to Eumenes. In addition, they made special grants of tax-exemption to the Colophonians living in Notium, to the Cymaeans, and the Mylasenians. To the people of Clazomenae they made a gift of the island of Drymussa, in addition to exemption from taxes; to the Milesians they restored the so-called 'sacred territory'; and to the people of Ilium they also made a gift of Rhoeteum and Gergithus, less because of any recent services on their part than from consideration of the Romans' ancestry. The same reasons lay behind the liberation of Dardanus. They also made gifts of land to the Chians, the Smyrneans, and the Erythraeans in recognition of their exemplary loyalty in the war, according them every mark of honour. The Phocaeans had the territory which they possessed before the war restored to them, and they were also granted the right to live under their ancient laws. The people of Rhodes were given confirmation of what they had been granted by the earlier decree: they were accorded Lycia and Caria as far as the River Maeander, with the exception of Telmessus. To Eumenes' realm the commissioners added, in Europe, the Chersonese and Lysimachia, and the strongholds, villages, and lands that had been within the territory held by Antiochus; and in Asia they restored to him both Phrygias—the one called Hellespontine Phrygia, and the other Greater Phrygia—as well as Mysia (which Prusias had filched from Eumenes), Lycaonia, Milyas, and Lydia, the cities of Tralles, Ephesus, and Telmessus being specifically mentioned by name. There was a dispute between Eumenes and the representatives of Antiochus over Pamphylia because part of it lies this side of, and part beyond, the Taurus, and the whole matter was referred to the Senate.

40. After issuing these terms and decrees, Manlius set off for the Hellespont with the ten commissioners and the entire army. There he called to him the chieftains of the Gauls and specified the terms under which they were to keep peace with Eumenes. He informed them that they were to discontinue their practice of armed migrations and keep within the boundaries of their own lands. He then brought together ships from all along the coast, and had Eumenes' fleet brought there from Elaea by the king's brother, Athenaeus. With these he transported all his troops over to Europe. Then, at the head of a column weighed down with booty of all kinds, he proceeded by short marches through the Chersonese and established a base at Lysimachia—he wanted to have his pack-animals in as fresh and vigorous a condition as possible for embarking on the march into Thrace, the journey through which the men mostly contemplated with dread.

On the day he left Lysimachia, Manlius reached the river they call 'The Melas',* and the day after that he reached Cypsela. After Cypsela he faced a narrow, broken road for approximately ten miles through a wooded area, and the difficulty this stage of the journey presented made him split the army in two. He ordered one part to go on ahead and the other to leave a large interval before bringing up the rear, and he set between these two the baggage, which comprised carts loaded with public money and other rich booty. As the Romans were marching in this formation through a pass, a band of Thracians, numbering not more than 10,000 and drawn from four tribes—the Asti, the Caeni, the Maduateni, and the Coreli—blocked the road right at the neck of the defile. It was thought that this did not happen without the complicity of Philip of Macedon. It was believed that Philip knew that the only route the Romans would take for their return journey lay through Thrace, and that he also knew how much money they were transporting.

The commander was at the head of the column, and he was worried about the difficulty of the terrain. The Thracians made no move until the armed troops went by; but when they saw that the vanguard was past the neck of the defile, and that the troops at the rear were still not close, they pounced upon the baggage-train. They killed the guards, and some of them pillaged the contents of the wagons while others dragged away the pack-animals together with their loads. The shouts from this action first reached those following behind who had now entered the pass, and then carried to the front of the column as well. There was a rush to the centre from each end, and haphazard fighting broke out at several places at the same time. The booty itself exposed the Thracians to carnage: they were encumbered by their loads and most were without weapons, so as to have their hands free to seize the plunder. It was the difficulty of the terrain that hurt the Romans since the barbarians used paths which they knew to fall upon them and sometimes concealed themselves in ambush in the deep hollows. The loads and wagons themselves, adversely positioned for one side or the other as chance would have it, also obstructed the combatants. In one sector the looter fell, in another the man defending that loot. The fortunes of the battle varied according to whether the lie of the land was favourable or unfavourable for this side or that; according to the spirit of the fighters; and according to the numbers involved—for some had met numbers superior, and others numbers inferior, to their own. There were heavy casualties on both sides. Night was already coming on when the Thracians left the battle, not running to avoid wounds or death but because they had sufficient booty.

41. The leading companies of the Roman column bivouacked in an open area outside the pass, near the temple of Bendis.* The rest remained within the pass, surrounding themselves with a double palisade, to guard the baggage. The following day they reconnoitred the pass before striking camp and then joined the first contingent.

In that battle, fought as it was at several points virtually all along the pass, some of the baggage and some camp-followers were lost as well as a number of fighting men, but the most serious setback was the death of Quintus Minucius Thermus, a courageous and energetic man.

That day the Romans reached the River Hebrus, after which they crossed the frontier of the Aenians close to the temple of Apollo, whose local title is Zerynthius. They were faced with another gorge, no less rugged than the earlier one, near a place called Tempyra, but because there is no woodland in the area it does not offer hiding-places for an ambush. On this spot the Trausi, also a Thracian people, converged with similar hopes of plunder, but since the tree-less valleys rendered them visible as they were blocking the pass there was less panic and consternation amongst the Romans. For despite the unfavourable terrain it was nevertheless a regular engagement that had to be fought, with lines out in the open and troops deployed. The Romans approached in close formation. With a shout they attacked, at first dislodging the enemy and then driving them back. Now began the flight and slaughter, the Thracians being obstructed by the narrowness of the terrain which they had themselves chosen. The victorious Romans pitched camp near a village of the Maroneans called Sale.

The following day a march along an open road brought them to the Priatic plain where they stayed for three days provisioning themselves with grain. (Some of this was provided by the Maroneans from their own fields, and some came from the Romans' ships which followed them loaded with all manner of supplies.) From the camp it was a day's march to Apollonia, and from here they came through the land of Abdera to Neapolis. This part of the route, thanks to the presence of the Greek colonies, was completely peaceful, but after that the journey through central Thrace, though without event, was day and night fraught with anxiety until they reached Macedonia. The same army, led by Scipio along the same route, had not found the Thracians so aggressive for the simple reason that there had been less booty to invite an attack—although even on that occasion, according to Claudius, some 15,000 Thracians confronted Muttines the Numidian* when he was reconnoitring ahead of the main column. (Claudius states that the Numidian force consisted of 400 cavalry and a few elephants, and that Muttines' son broke through the enemy centre with 100 hand-picked horsemen. Setting his elephants in the centre and deploying his cavalry on the wings, Muttines engaged the enemy, and in a short while the son caused panic in the enemy ranks with an attack from the rear. The Thracians were thrown off balance by this furious cavalry charge and failed to reach the column of infantry.)

Gnaeus Manlius led the army through Macedonia and into Thessaly. He continued from there through Epirus to Apollonia, and spent the winter in Apollonia, for he did not have such little regard for the sea in winter as to risk a crossing.

42. It was close to the end of the year when the consul Marcus Valerius came to Rome from Liguria to see to the appointment of the new magistrates, though he had achieved nothing of note in his province to provide a reasonable excuse for his arriving later than usual for the elections. The consular elections were held on 18 February, and at these Marcus Aemilius Lepidus and Gaius Flaminius were chosen. The next day the following were designated praetors: Appius Claudius Pulcher,* Servius Sulpicius Galba, Quintus Terentius Culleo, Lucius Terentius Massaliota, Quintus Fulvius Flaccus, and Marcus Furius Crassipes.

At the conclusion of the elections, the consul brought before the

Senate the question of the provinces to be assigned to the praetors. The Senators decided that two jurisdictions should be at Rome for legal administration; two, Sicily and Sardinia, should be outside Italy; and two, Tarentum and Gaul, within Italy. The praetors designate were also instructed to draw lots for these before entering office. The sortition went as follows:

Servius Sulpicius	urban jurisdiction
Quintus Terentius	foreigners' jurisdiction
Lucius Terentius	Sicily
Quintus Fulvius	Sardinia
Appius Claudius	Tarentum
Marcus Furius	Gaul

That year, on the order of Marcus Claudius, the urban praetor, Lucius Minucius Myrtilus and Lucius Manlius* were handed over to ambassadors by the fetial priests and taken off to Carthage because they had allegedly beaten some Carthaginian envoys.

There was talk of a major war in Liguria which was said to be growing more serious every day. Accordingly, on the day on which the new consuls raised with them the matter of the provinces and the state of the republic, the Senators formally assigned Liguria to both of them as their province. The consul Lepidus tried to block the Senate's decision, claiming that it was outrageous for the two consuls to be confined to the valleys of Liguria when Marcus Fulvius and Gnaeus Manlius had spent two years in Europe and Asia respectively, ruling like monarchs and virtually replacing Philip and Antiochus. If it was necessary to secure those provinces with armies, it should be the consuls who commanded them, not individuals without office. Those men had been roaming around spreading the fear of war amongst tribes on whom war had not been declared, he said, and charging a price for peace. If those provinces needed to be secured by armies, then just as Manius Acilius had been replaced by the consul Lucius Scipio, and then Lucius Scipio by Marcus Fulvius and Gnaeus Manlius when they became consuls, so Fulvius and Manlius should have been replaced by the consuls Gaius Livius and Marcus Valerius. The Aetolian war was over, he said; Asia had been recovered from Antiochus; and the Gauls had been defeated. Now surely either the consuls should be sent to the consular armies or the legions there should be brought home and finally restored to the state. After listening to these arguments, the Senate remained firm in its judgment that Liguria should be the province of the two consuls, but decided that Manlius and Fulvius should quit their provinces, withdraw the armies from them, and return to Rome.

43. There was no love lost between Marcus Fulvius and the consul Marcus Aemilius. In particular, Aemilius supposed that it was because of Marcus Fulvius' devices that his consulship had been retarded two years. Accordingly, to provoke antipathy towards Fulvius, Aemilius brought before the Senate some Ambracian envoys whom he had primed with accusations. These protested that they had been subject to aggression despite the fact that they had been at peace with Rome, had done the bidding of the former consuls and had been ready to show the same compliance to Marcus Fulvius. First of all their lands had been plundered, they said, and their city faced with the dreadful prospect of pillage and massacre, fear of which compelled them to shut their gates. Then they had been blockaded, attacked, and subjected to every form of treatment meted out in war, with massacres, burning, and the destruction and plundering of the city. Their wives and children had been dragged off into slavery, their property had been taken from them and—what distressed them more than anything else—their temples had, throughout the entire city, been stripped of their ornaments.* The statues of the gods—no, the gods themselves—had been torn from their dwellings and carried off, and all that the Ambracians had been left for their worship, and for their offerings of prayers and supplications, were bare walls and doorposts. While the envoys made these complaints the consul followed a pre-arranged plan, questioning them in an accusing manner and thus appearing to entice from them more than they would have said on their own.

The Senators were impressed by this, but the other consul, Gaius Flaminius, came to the defence of Marcus Fulvius. The Ambracians had taken an old and outmoded course, he said—for such were the charges brought earlier against Marcus Marcellus* by the Syracusans, and against Quintus Fulvius* by the Campanians. So why should the Senators not allow that line of attack against Titus Quinctius by King Philip, he asked, or against Manius Acilius and Lucius Scipio by Antiochus? Or against Gnaeus Manlius by the Gauls, and against Marcus Fulvius himself by the Aetolians and the peoples of Cephallenia?

'Ambracia was attacked and captured,' Flaminius continued. 'Statues and art-works were taken from it, and other things occurred that are normally associated with the capture of cities. Do you think that I will deny this on Marcus Fulvius' behalf, Members of the Senate, or that Marcus Fulvius himself will deny it—when he is going to request of you a triumph for these actions, and will bear before his chariot, and affix to his door-posts, conquered Ambracia, the statues which they charge him with taking from there, and all the other spoils from that city? The Ambracians have no reason to disassociate themselves from the Aetolians—the Ambracian cause and the Aetolian cause are the same. Accordingly, my colleague should vent his hostility in some other cause or, if he prefers to concentrate especially on this one, let him keep his Ambracians here until Marcus Fulvius arrives. For my part, I am not going to allow any decision to be made on either the Aetolians or the Ambracians in the absence of Marcus Fulvius.'

44. Aemilius now attacked the cunning and the spite of his political opponent, suggesting that it was something of which all were aware, and claiming that Fulvius would stall and draw out the time so as not to come to Rome while his enemy was still consul. Two days were spent on the struggle between the consuls, and it appeared that no decision could be taken while Flaminius was present. However, the Senate took advantage of a moment when Flaminius happened to be absent through illness, and passed a decree on a motion from Aemilius that the Ambracians should have all their property restored. They were also to be independent and live under their own laws, and gather whatever tariffs they wished on goods carried by land and sea, provided that the Romans, their allies, and members of the Latin League be exempted. As for the statues and other works of art which the Ambracians complained had been removed from their holy shrines, the Senate decided that the matter should be referred to the college of priests on Marcus Fulvius' return to Rome, and that the college's decisions be put into effect. Not content with this, the consul subsequently capitalized on a poorly attended session of the house to add a Senatorial decree which stated that it did not appear that Ambracia had been taken by force.

After this, by decree of the decemvirs, public prayers were offered for three days on behalf of the health of the people because a deadly plague had been taking a heavy toll in the city and the countryside.

Then the Latin Festival took place. When they were freed from these religious duties and had completed the muster of the troops—for both preferred to employ new recruits—the consuls set off for their province, where they demobilized all the veterans.

After the departure of the consuls, the proconsul Gnaeus Manlius came to Rome. Granted an audience with the Senate at the temple of Bellona by the praetor Servius Sulpicius, Manlius gave an account of his achievements and demanded that, in view of these, the immortal gods be appropriately honoured and he be permitted to ride in triumph into the city. His request was opposed by a majority of the ten commissioners who had been with him, and especially by Lucius Furius Purpureo and Lucius Aemilius Paullus.

45. These said that they had been assigned as commissioners to Gnaeus Manlius in order to make peace with Antiochus and finalize the terms of the pact initially formulated with Lucius Scipio. Gnaeus Manlius had done everything he could to jeopardize that peace-treaty, they said, and to catch Antiochus in a trap, if the king gave him the chance. But Antiochus had recognized the consul's duplicity, and though Manlius had tried to lure him with numerous requests for conferences he had avoided not only meeting him but even setting eyes on him. Manlius wanted to cross the Taurus range, and it was only with difficulty that he was restrained by the combined entreaties of all the commissioners from putting to the test the prediction of disaster made in the Sibylline verses for those who passed those fatal bounds. He brought up his army even so, and encamped almost on the crest, at the point where the waters divide. Finding no pretext for opening hostilities here, since the king's people kept the peace, he brought the army around against the Galatians, a tribe on which he made war without Senatorial authorization or a directive from the people. Who, they asked, had ever presumed to take this action on his own authority? The most recent wars were with Antiochus, Philip, Hannibal, and the Carthaginians, they said, and in every case there had been a resolution of the Senate and a directive from the people; restitution had been formally demanded by means of embassies, and finally men had been sent with the declaration of war.

'Which of these protocols was followed in your case, Gnaeus Manlius,' they continued, 'to lead us to believe that that war of yours was one officially fought by the people of Rome and not a piece of private buccaneering on your part? But of course you were satisfied with your procedure, and you then took your army by a direct route against the enemies you had made your target! Or did you rather take all the circuitous routes, stopping at cross-roads, so that you, a money-grubbing consul, could follow with a Roman army wheresoever Eumenes' brother, Attalus, directed his column? And did you make your way into all the nooks and crannies of Pisidia, Lycaonia, and Phrygia, collecting your cash from tyrants and occupants of lonely fortresses? For what do you have to do with the people of Oroanda, or with other similarly inoffensive peoples?

'As for the war itself—the war for which you are requesting a triumph—how did you conduct it? Did you have favourable ground for the battle, and a time of your choosing? You are quite correct in demanding that the immortal gods be shown due honour. First of all they did not want the army to pay for the recklessness of its commander, whose campaign was in flagrant contravention of international conventions; and, secondly, they set before us beasts instead of soldiers.

46. 'Do not think that it is just the name of the Gallogrecians that is a mongrel.* Long before they received that name their physique and character showed the effects of interbreeding and contamination. If they really were the Gauls with whom we had a thousand encounters in Italy with mixed success, do you think, considering your commander, that even a messenger would have returned from there? Twice he fought with them; twice he attacked them on unfavourable terrain, bringing his fighting-line up almost beneath the feet of the enemy in a valley below them. They could have crushed us without hurling their weapons at us from above—they only had to throw their naked bodies at us. So what was the result? Great is the fortune of the Roman people, great and awesome its reputation. The recent defeat of Hannibal, Philip and Antiochus had left the Gauls almost stupefied. For all their massive physique, they were thrown into panic-stricken flight by slings and arrows. Not a sword was bloodied in the fighting—in a battle with Gauls! They flew off like flocks of birds at the first sound of our projectiles. But, my word! We were the same force that was cut down, put to flight, and robbed of its baggage when we fell among Thracian bandits on the return journey—and fortune reminded us of what would have happened had we faced a *real* enemy. Along with many other brave men Quintus Minucius Thermus met his end, a loss much more serious than if Gnaeus Manlius had perished, the man whose recklessness had precipitated that débâcle. The army bringing back the spoils of Antiochus was broken up into three pieces, the vanguard in one place, the rear in another, and the baggage in a third; and it spent a night hiding in the bushes in the lairs of wild animals.

'Is it for this that a triumph is requested? Even if no defeat or ignominy had been incurred in Thrace, who are the enemies over whom you would be requesting your triumph? Those, I suppose, whom the Senate or Roman people had specifically assigned to you as enemies. This was how a triumph came to be awarded over Antiochus to Lucius Scipio here, and to Manius Acilius before him; and over Philip a little earlier to Titus Quinctius; and over Hannibal, the Carthaginians, and Syphax to Publius Africanus. And even after the Senate had voted for war, the most minor details were *still* investigated. To whom was the declaration of war to be made? Was it to be declared to the kings themselves, or was an announcement to some outpost good enough?

'Do you want this entire protocol degraded and destroyed? Fetial rights removed and the fetial priests done away with? Heaven forgive me for saying so, but let religious observances be discontinued, and let forgetfulness of the gods seize your hearts—you still do not wish that consultation of the Senate in the case of war also be abandoned, do you? That the question of whether they 'wish and command' a war to be fought with the Gauls not be put to the people? It is true that the consuls recently wanted Greece and Asia, but when you insisted on assigning them Liguria as their province they accepted your decision. They will thus be justified in seeking a triumph from you if the war is successful, since it is by your authorization that they will have fought it.'

47. Such was the address presented by Furius and Aemilius. Manlius, I have gathered, replied more or less as follows:

'Members of the Senate: it was the tribunes of the plebs who would in the past oppose applications for a triumph. I now give my thanks to the tribunes. They have granted, either to me personally, or to the greatness of my achievements, the distinction of not only approving by their silence the honour which I seek, but also of appearing ready to propose it, if need be. It is amongst the ten commissioners, for heaven's sake, that I find my opponents—a board assigned to generals by your ancestors to regulate and distribute the honours of victory. Lucius Furius and Lucius Aemilius are trying to stop me from mounting the triumphal car, and to snatch the crown of honour from my head—and these are men whom I should have called as witnesses of my achievements if the tribunes now stood in the way of my triumph.

'I certainly begrudge no man his meed of honour, Members of the Senate, and you yourselves recently used your authority to discourage some brave and energetic plebeian tribunes who were trying to block the triumph of Quintus Fabius Labeo. Labeo had his triumph, despite his opponents' contention, not that he had fought an unauthorized campaign, but that he had not set eyes on the enemy at all. In my case, I fought many a pitched battle with 100,000 of our most fierce enemies, captured or killed more than 40,000 men, stormed two of their camps, and left everything this side of the Taurus range more peaceful than the land of Italy. And I am not only being cheated of my triumph, but am pleading my case before you in person, Members of the Senate, with my own commissioners pressing the charges.

'As you observed, Members of the Senate, their line of attack was twofold. They said I should not have fought a war with the Gauls, and then that the war was fought in a foolhardy and reckless fashion. "The Gauls were not our enemies," they said, "but you assaulted them when they were at peace and doing our bidding". Members of the Senate, I am not going to ask you to apply to your thinking about the Gauls who live in Asia what you generally know about the brutality of the Gallic race, and their rancorous hatred for the Roman name. Set aside the ill-fame attaching to the race as a whole and the loathing felt for it, and consider these Gauls on their own. I wish that Eumenes and all the cities of Asia could be present, that you could hear their complaints rather than my accusations! Come now, send delegations around all the cities of Asia and ask them which was the heavier servitude from which they were delivered—was it from Antiochus when he was pushed back beyond the Taurus range, or from the Gauls when they were brought to heel? Let them tell you how often their lands were devastated, how often they were pillaged—at a time when they barely had the means to ransom their prisoners and when they were told of human sacrifices and the immolation of their own children. Be assured that your allies had been paying tribute to the Gauls and, if I had remained inactive, that they would have been paying it even now when, thanks to you, they have been freed from the king's rule.

48. 'The further Antiochus had been driven back, the more despotic Gallic dominion in Asia would have been, and all territory this side of the Taurus range you would have been adding to the empire of the Gauls, not to your own. All right, you will say, be that as it may—the fact is that at one time the Gauls had pillaged Delphi, oracle shared by the human race and navel of the world, and the Roman people did not declare war on them or make war on them for that. Yes, indeed, but I used to think that, with respect to your control and supervision of activities in those territories, there was a difference between that earlier period, when Greece and Asia were as yet not under your jurisdiction and authority, and this one, when you have fixed the Taurus range as the boundary of Roman dominion—a time when you grant independence and tax-exemption to communities, add territories to some, take land from others, impose taxes on yet others, a time when you augment, diminish, give, and remove kingdoms, and consider it your responsibility to ensure these peoples have peace on land and sea. If Antiochus had not withdrawn his garrisons you would not now consider Asia liberated even if those garrisons had remained at peace within their citadels, would you? And if the armies of the Gauls were now wandering far and wide, would the gifts you made to Eumenes, or the independence you granted to the city-states, be secure?

'But why am I using this line of argument, as if I made the Gauls my enemies and did not receive them as such? I appeal to you, Lucius Scipio—it was to have your courage and success alike that I prayed (and not in vain!) to the immortal gods, when I succeeded to your command—and to you, Publius Scipio, who had the legal position of legate but the eminence of colleague, both in the eyes of your consul brother and those of the troops. I ask you to tell us if you know that there were legions of Gauls in Antiochus' army; if you saw them in the line of battle, located on both flanks, evidently representing his greatest strength; if you fought with them as with a regular enemy, killed them, and brought back spoils from them. And yet, it will be said, it was with Antiochus and not the Gauls that the Senate had decreed, and the people enjoined, that there be war. But in my view what they had decreed and enjoined was also directed against those in Antiochus' camp. Of these, all who bore arms against us on behalf of Antiochus were still our enemies—all apart from Antiochus, with whom Scipio had concluded a peace-treaty and with whom you had expressly directed that an accord be reached. More than anyone, the Gauls were in this category, along with a number of petty kings and tyrants. Even so, I took it upon myself to negotiate peace with the others (after forcing them to atone for their wrong-doings, as the dignity of your empire required), and to probe the feelings of the Gauls, in the hope that their native brutality could be modified. It was only after I saw that they were wild and unrelenting that I concluded that force of arms was required to bring them to heel.

'Since the charge of starting the war has been disposed of, I must now account for my conduct of it. Here, I would feel confidence in my case even if it were not before the Roman Senate that I was appearing but the Senate of Carthage where, they say, commanders are crucified* for poor strategy in a campaign, even if it is successful. Now, in fact, I am appearing in the state which brings the gods into the commencement and conduct of all its enterprises for the very reason that it subjects to no man's critical remarks actions which have received divine approval; in the state which, in its formulaic language authorizing public thanksgiving or a triumph, includes the expression: "Inasmuch as he has well and successfully performed public business." Suppose I were reluctant to vaunt my military prowess; suppose I thought it overweening and presumptuous to do this, but that I still requested that due honour be paid to the immortal gods only for my own good fortune and that of my army, in defeating such a great tribe with no casualties amongst our soldiers. And suppose I asked also that I myself should climb in triumph to the capitol, the place from which I set off after the formal declaration of my vows. Would you, in this state, deny this to me, and to the immortal gods, as well?

49. 'You would, you say—I fought on unfavourable ground. Tell me, then, on what more favourable ground could I have fought? The enemy had seized a hill and were in a fortified position. Obviously, if I wanted to defeat them, I had to go to that enemy. Well, just suppose they had a city in that spot and were keeping to their walls. Obviously they would need to be attacked. So, did Manius Acilius fight with Antiochus on "favourable ground" at Thermopylae? Why, was

not Philip in a similar position, occupying the heights overlooking the River Aous, when he was dislodged by Titus Quinctius? In fact, I have been so far unable to work out what conception my opponents have of this enemy or how they wish you to imagine him. If it is as one degenerate and corrupted by the delights of Asia, what danger was there in facing him even on "unfavourable ground"? If it is as an enemy fearsome for his barbarous character and physical strength, do you then refuse a triumph for a victory of such magnitude? This is blind jealousy, Members of the Senate, which knows only how to disparage acts of courage and sully the honours and rewards that accrue from them. So I ask for your indulgence, Members of the Senate, if my address to you has been rather protracted—not through any desire on my part to sing my own praises, but from the need to defend myself against these charges.

'Another point. On the journey through Thrace, could I have broadened passes that were narrow? Levelled high ground? Made cultivated areas out of wild forests? Could I have ensured that Thracian bandits were nowhere skulking in lairs known only to them, that no piece of baggage be filched, and no pack-animal taken from a column of such length? That no one be wounded, and that the valiant and stalwart Quintus Minucius not die of his wound? They focus on this unhappy accident, which made us lose a citizen of such qualities. The fact is that the enemy attacked us in a difficult pass in unfamiliar territory, but two battle-lines of ours, from the front and rear of the column respectively, simultaneously encircled the barbarian force which stuck close to the baggage, and killed or captured many thousands that very day, and many more a few days later. Even if they say nothing about this, can they believe that you are not going to know about it when the whole army is witness to what I say? Had I not drawn my sword in Asia, had I not set eyes on the enemy there, I should still have been entitled to a triumph for the two battles in Thrace. But I have said enough. In fact, Members of the Senate, I should like to request and be granted your indulgence for tiring you with an address longer than I would have wished.'

50. On that day the accusations would have prevailed over the defence, had not the Senate drawn out the debate into the evening. When the house broke up the feeling was that the Senate was going to refuse the triumph. But the following day the relatives and friends of Gnaeus Manlius exerted great pressure on his behalf and the

authority of the senior members also carried weight. The latter claimed that there was no known precedent for a commander entering the city without the triumphal carriage and laurel wreath, as a private citizen denied his meed of honour, when he had crushed an enemy, fulfilled his allotted assignment, and brought home his army. Embarrassment prevailed over spite, and a crowded Senate authorized the triumph.

After this, all discussion and recollection of the debate were eclipsed by a more momentous confrontation involving a man of greater stature and distinction. According to Valerius Antias, Publius Scipio Africanus was impeached* by the two Quinti Petillii,* an event to which people reacted according to their various inclinations. Some had harsh words, not for the plebeian tribunes but for the entire community for being able to tolerate such a thing. The two greatest cities in the world were found, virtually at the same time, guilty of ingratitude towards their most prominent citizens, they said, but Rome's ingratitude was the greater in that it was a defeated Carthage that had driven a defeated Hannibal into exile, whereas a victorious Rome was in the process of driving out a victorious Africanus. Others opined that no one citizen should have such preeminence as to be above legal investigation—nothing fostered the impartial application of justice as much as the requirement that all the most powerful people defend themselves in court. Without accountability, can anyone be entrusted with anything at all, much less the governance of the state? Force could be legitimately used on anyone unable to accept the impartiality of justice, they argued.

Such were the arguments put forward in conversation until the day of the trial arrived. Nobody before that time, not even Scipio himself during his consulship or censorship, had been escorted to the forum by a greater crowd of people of all stations than was the defendant on that day. Instructed to plead his case, he made no reference to the charges but launched into a discourse on his own career so stirring that it was generally agreed that no one had ever received a more eloquent eulogy or one closer to the truth. For in the statement of his achievements he revealed the same spirit and character as when he accomplished them, and he did not offend the ears of his listeners because these were brought up when he was at risk in court, not as self-advertisement.

51. To lend credibility to the present charges, the plebeian tribunes

resurrected the old ones relating to the extravagance of Scipio's winter-quarters in Syracuse and the troubles caused by Pleminius at Locri.* They then accused Scipio of misappropriation of funds, using circumstantial rather than hard evidence. His son, who had been taken prisoner, was released without ransom, they noted, and in everything else Scipio had been cultivated by Antiochus in a way that suggested that in his hands alone rested the decision on peace or war with the Romans. In the province he had behaved as a dictator rather than a legate towards the consul, they said. His sole reason for going there had been to make clear to Greece, Asia, and all the potentates and peoples lying to the east, something of which Spain, Gaul, Sicily, and Africa had long been persuaded, namely, that one man was the head and mainstay of the Roman Empire, and that the state that ruled over the entire world lay in the shadow of Scipio, whose nod had the force of Senatorial decrees and directives from the people. A man untouched by scandal they hounded with all the malice of which they were capable. The speeches dragged out till nightfall, and the session was adjourned to another day.

When that day arrived, the tribunes took their seats on the Rostra at dawn. The defendant was summoned, and he approached the Rostra through the midst of the crowd with a large column of friends and clients attending him. Silence fell, and Scipio declared: 'Tribunes of the people and citizens of Rome: this was the day on which I fought a pitched battle with Hannibal and the Carthaginians in Africa, and did so meritoriously and successfully. It is therefore proper to avoid litigation and strife today. I shall go forthwith from this place to the Capitol to pay my respects to Jupiter Optimus Maximus, to Juno, to Minerva, and to the other deities who protect our Capitol and citadel. I shall thank them for having granted me the will and the occasion to render outstanding service to my state both on this very day and on many other occasions. You, too, go along with me, citizens—those of you for whom it is convenient—and ask the gods in your prayers for men like me as your leaders, but do so only if, from the time I was seventeen up to my old age, you have continually conferred your honours upon me before the due time, and if I for my part have shown myself by my record to be in advance of these honours of yours.'

From the Rostra he climbed to the Capitol. At the same time the whole gathering turned and followed Scipio, in such numbers that in the end even the clerks and messengers left the tribunes, with whom there now remained nobody apart from their retinue of slaves and the herald who, from the Rostra, used to summon the defendant. Scipio, attended by the people of Rome, did the rounds of all the temples of the gods throughout the city, and not just on the Capitol. The public acclamation he then received, and the genuine appreciation expressed for his greatness, almost made that day more famous than the one on which he rode into the city in triumph over Syphax and the Carthaginians.

52. This was the last brilliant day to shine on Publius Scipio. After it he could see that what he had in prospect was malicious wrangling with the tribunes, and when the case was adjourned for a lengthy period he retired to his estate at Liternum, determined not to make an appearance to defend himself. His spirit and personality were too great, and wedded to fortunes too great, for him to be able to stand trial and put himself in the demeaning position of pleading a case in court. When the trial-date arrived and the summons went out for the absent defendant, Lucius Scipio adduced illness as the reason for his brother's non-appearance. The tribunes responsible for the indictment refused to accept this plea. Scipio's failure to appear in his defence, they said, was motivated by the same pride which had earlier made him quit his trial, the tribunes of the people, and the assembly   the time when he had been attended by the people whom he had deprived of the right and freedom to judge him, and when, taking these along as his prisoners, he had celebrated a triumph over the Roman people and orchestrated on that day a secession to the Capitol away from the tribunes of the people.

'So you have the reward for that injudicious move,' they said. 'You have yourselves been abandoned by the man who led and incited you when you abandoned us. And day by day our resolution has weakened to this point: whereas seventeen years ago, when Scipio commanded an army and a fleet, we had the nerve to send plebeian tribunes and an aedile to Sicily to arrest him and bring him back to Rome, now when he is a private citizen we have not the nerve to send men to pull him from his country estate to defend himself in court.'

When an appeal was made to the tribunes of the plebs by Lucius Scipio, these made the following decree: if illness were adduced as the reason for the defendant's failure to appear, their wish was that this reason be accepted and the trial-date be held over by their colleagues.

One of the plebeian tribunes at this date was Tiberius Sempronius Gracchus, who had a personal feud going on with Publius Scipio. Gracchus refused to have his name added to his colleagues' decree, making everyone expect an even more severe judgment from him. Instead he made the following pronouncement. Lucius Scipio's plea of sickness on his brother's behalf he found satisfactory, he said, and he would not permit any accusation of Publius Scipio to proceed before the latter's return to Rome. Even at that point, he continued, if Scipio appealed to him, he would help him avoid a court appearance. Through his achievements and the honours granted him by the Roman people, Publius Scipio had, by the agreement of gods and men, reached such a high standing that for him to stand as a defendant beneath the Rostra and give ear to the abusive comments of the young was a greater disgrace for the people of Rome than for the man himself.

53. Gracchus added angry words to his official pronouncement: 'Tribunes, is he going to stand at your feet—Scipio, the famed conqueror of Africa? Is this why he defeated and drove back four of the Carthaginians' most renowned commanders in Spain, and four armies? Why he captured Syphax and vanquished Hannibal? Why he made Carthage pay tribute to us and pushed back Antiochus to the far side of the Taurus range (for Lucius Scipio recognized his brother as his partner in this glorious achievement)? All this so that he should grovel before the two Petillii and see you seek the palm branch of victory over Publius Africanus? Will no services that they have performed, no honours that you have bestowed, citizens, ever allow men of distinction to reach a bastion secure and virtually sacrosanct, that permits their advancing years finally to come to rest free from attack, if not with respect?'

Gracchus' formal pronouncement and the words appended to it had an effect not just on the others present but even on Scipio's accusers. They stated that they would consider their legal rights and duties. After this the assembly of the people was adjourned and the Senate went into session. At the meeting Tiberius Gracchus was profusely thanked by the entire Senatorial order, but especially by the consular and senior members, for having set the interests of the state above private squabbles; and the Petillii were showered with abuse for having tried to gain a reputation by inciting hatred against another, and for looking for spoils from a triumph over Africanus.

No more was heard of Africanus after that. He lived out his life at Liternum and did not miss the city. They say that on his deathbed he gave instructions that he be buried in that same spot in the country and his tomb be set up there so that his funeral not take place in his ungrateful native region. He was a remarkable man, but more remarkable for his military rather than his peace-time capabilities. The early part of his life was <more distinguished> than his final years because in his youth there was incessant warfare, whereas with old age his career also lost its bloom and no scope was offered to his talents. His second consulship cannot stand comparison with his first, even if one adds the censorship. Then there was his position of second-in-command in Asia, rendered inconsequential by ill-health and sullied by his son's mishap, as well as by the need to face trial, after his return, or else to quit both the trial and his native region at one and the same time. But no war fought by the Romans was greater and more fraught with danger than the Punic War, and he above all took the greatest share of the glory for bringing it to an end.

54. With the death of Africanus the morale of his opponents improved. Chief amongst these was Marcus Porcius Cato who, even during Scipio's lifetime, made a habit of carping at the man's eminence. It is thought that Cato was responsible for the Petillii commencing their suit against Africanus while he was alive, and introducing their bill after his death. The bill was worded much as follows: 'Citizens, with regard to the portion of the moneys captured, removed, and exacted from Antiochus and those under his command, and which was not delivered to the public purse, is it your wish and command that the urban praetor, Servius Sulpicius, put to the Senate the question of which of the current praetors it wishes to investigate the matter?'

At first, Quintus and Lucius Mummius tried to veto the bill, expressing the view that it was only fair that it be the Senate that investigate any case of moneys not paid into the public purse, as had invariably been done in the past. The Petillii proceeded with an attack on the prestige of the Scipios and their dominant position in the Senate. Lucius Furius Purpureo, a consular who had been one of the ten commissioners in Asia, opined that the scope of the enquiry should be broadened to include moneys taken from other kings and peoples, not merely Antiochus—targeting thereby his enemy Gnaeus Manlius. Lucius Scipio came forward to oppose the bill, evidently more with a view to defend himself than to attack the proposal. Scipio protested that it was the death of his brother Publius Africanus—a man of superlative bravery and distinction—that had occasioned the proposal. It was not enough that there was no eulogy for Africanus at the Rostra after his death—he had to be denounced as well. Even the Carthaginians had been content with Hannibal being sent into exile, he said, but the Roman people could not be satisfied even with the *death* of Publius Scipio—no, the man's reputation was to be torn to shreds while he lay in the grave and his brother, too, was to be sacrificed, a further victim of envy. Marcus Cato spoke in favour of the bill—his speech 'On the Money of King Antiochus' still survives—and used his influence to deter the Mummii, the tribunes, from opposing it. Accordingly, when these withdrew their veto, all the tribes voted in favour of the bill.

55. Servius Sulpicius then raised the question of whom the Senators wished to conduct the enquiry specified by the Petillian law, and they designated Quintus Terentius Culleo. This praetor was so friendly with the Cornelian family, according to those people who claim that Publius Scipio's death and funeral took place in Rome— for there is also a report of this—that he preceded the bier in the funeral ceremony wearing a freedman's cap, just as he had done at Scipio's triumph, and distributed mulled wine at the Porta Capena to those who attended the funeral. Culleo did this, they say, because he had been amongst the prisoners delivered from enemy hands in Africa by Scipio. Alternatively, Culleo is said to have been on such *bad* terms with the family that he was the one particularly selected by the anti-Scipio faction to conduct the enquiry, because his animosity was well-known. At all events, it was before this praetor—too favourably or too unfavourably disposed to him—that Lucius Scipio was immediately arraigned. At the same time the names of Aulus and Lucius Hostilius, Scipio's officers, were brought forward and accepted for indictment, as was that of Scipio's quaestor, Gaius Furius Aculeo. To make it look as if everything was tainted with corruption by association, even two secretaries and an attendant were indicted. Lucius Hostilius, the secretaries, and the attendant were acquitted before Scipio's case came to court, but Scipio, his officer Aulus Hostilius, and Gaius Furius were found guilty. The verdict was that Scipio had received 6,000 pounds of gold and 480 pounds of silver more than he deposited in the treasury for Antiochus to be granted a more favourable peace-treaty, while Aulus Hostilius had taken 80 pounds of gold and 403 of silver, and Furius the quaestor 130 pounds of gold and 200 of silver.

Such are the amounts of gold and silver which I found in the work of Antias. In Lucius Scipio's case I should prefer to assume a scribal error rather than misrepresentation on the author's part with respect to the amounts of gold and silver. It is more plausible for there to have been a greater quantity of silver than gold, and for the fine to have been set at four million rather than 24 million sesterces. This is made all the more probable because there is a report that a justification of just such a sum had been asked of Publius Scipio himself in the Senate. This account has it that Scipio told his brother Lucius to bring to him his ledger and then tore it to bits with his own hands before the eyes of the Senate, furious that he was being asked to account for four million when he had brought 200 million to the treasury. He demonstrated the same self-confidence, they say, when the quaestors dared not break the law by drawing money from the treasury: he asked for the keys and said that he would open the treasury because it was he who had been responsible for its being closed.

56. There are many other conflicting stories in the tradition that focus especially on the latter days of Scipio, his trial, death, funeral, and tomb, so that I cannot decide on which anecdotal or literary account to accept. There is no agreement on who it was that accused him—some authors say that Marcus Naevius arraigned him, others the Petillii. No agreement again on the date of his arraignment, the year of his death, or the location of his death and funeral—some say he died and was buried at Rome, others at Liternum. Cenotaphs and statues are to be seen in both places. There was at Liternum a cenotaph with a statue set upon it, and this statue, which had been shattered by a storm, I recently saw for myself. There are also at Rome three statues on the cenotaph of the Scipios outside the Porta Capena, and two of these are said to be those of Publius and Lucius Scipio, the third that of the poet Quintus Ennius.

The discrepancy in accounts is not confined to historians, either. The speeches of Publius Scipio and Tiberius Gracchus—provided that those which are in circulation are authentic—are also at variance with each other. The title-tag of Publius Scipio's oration contains the name of Marcus Naevius, the plebeian tribune, but the oration itself lacks the name of Scipio's accuser, referring only to 'the reprobate' or, elsewhere, 'the dilettante'. Even the speech of Gracchus makes no mention of the Petillii as prosecutors of Africanus, or of his arraignment.

A completely new scenario needs to be established that accords with Gracchus' speech, and we must follow those authors who report that Africanus was a member of a diplomatic mission in Etruria at the time that Lucius Scipio was accused and found guilty of taking money from the king. According to them, †there† Africanus abandoned the delegation after news was brought of his brother's misfortunes, and hastened to Rome. Apprised that his brother was being imprisoned, he went straight from the city-gate to the forum, pushed the attending officer from his brother, and, when the tribunes tried to hold him back, assaulted them, with more thought for family loyalty than his role as a citizen. This behaviour is precisely what forms the substance of Tiberius Gracchus' complaint—the power of the tribunes being violated by a private citizen—and eventually, when he promises his assistance to Lucius Scipio, Gracchus adds that to give the impression that the tribunician power and the whole state have been undermined by a tribune of the people rather than by a private individual was a more acceptable precedent. But Gracchus' vituperation of Scipio's single instance of uncontrolled violence is done in such a way that, in reproaching him for having so fallen short of his own standards, he compensates for his immediate criticism by augmenting the praise heaped upon him in the past for his restraint and self-discipline. For he states that the people were reprimanded by Scipio for wishing to make him consul and dictator without term; that he forbade statues to be set up to him in the comitium, on the Rostra, in the Senate-house, on the Capitol, and in the shrine of Jupiter; and that he opposed a decree authorizing a portrait of him exiting from the temple of Jupiter Optimus Maximus, dressed for the triumph,

57. Even set in a eulogy such statements would bear witness to a tremendous greatness of spirit, which restricted honours to constitutional norms; and they were uttered by an opponent in the course of criticism.

It was to this Gracchus, it is generally agreed, that the younger of

Scipio's two daughters was married (the elder was certainly betrothed by her father to Publius Cornelius Nasica). What is not so sure is whether the girl was betrothed and married to him after her father's death, or whether the well-known anecdotes on the matter are true. According to these, when Lucius Scipio was being taken to prison and none of Gracchus' colleagues came to his aid, Gracchus swore that his earlier feud with the Scipios was still alive and his actions were not designed to curry favour with them, but that he would not have the brother of Africanus taken to that prison into which he had seen Africanus take enemy potentates and commanders. The story continues that the Senate happened to be dining on the Capitol that day, and that the members rose up together and requested that Africanus betroth his daughter to Gracchus during the dinner. The betrothal thus took place at this public occasion, and when Scipio went home he told his wife, Aemilia, that he had arranged the engagement of their younger daughter. Aemilia, just like a woman, was angry at his complete lack of consultation about a daughter who belonged to them both, and went on to say that the girl's mother should not have been left out of the decision even it were Tiberius Gracchus to whom he was betrothing her. Scipio was reportedly delighted with the correspondence of their opinions and replied that this was the very man to whom she was engaged. In view of the stature of the man, it was incumbent on me to report these differing versions in the anecdotal accounts as well as the literary records.

58. At the conclusion of the trials, which were presided over by the praetor Quintus Terentius, Hostilius and Furius were found guilty, and on that same day they gave the urban praetors their sureties. Scipio, however, insisted that all the money he had received was in the treasury, and that he was in possession of no public funds, whereupon imprisonment proceedings were begun.

Publius Scipio Nasica appealed to the tribunes and delivered a speech filled with valid tributes, not just to the Cornelian *gens* as a whole, but to his branch of it in particular. His own father, and the father of Publius Africanus and Lucius Scipio—the man now being imprisoned—had been Gnaeus and Publius Scipio, men of great distinction, he said. These had, over a number of years, enhanced the reputation of the Roman people in the struggle against a large number of Punic and Spanish commanders and armies, and not just by their campaigns but also by giving those peoples an illustration of Roman self-discipline and reliability. Eventually both had met their end fighting for the state. It would have been enough for their descendants to maintain the glorious reputation of these men, said Nasica, but instead Publius Africanus had so far eclipsed the exemplary record of his father as to make people believe that his blood-line was not human but that he was of divine lineage. As for Lucius Scipio, the man now under discussion, one could pass over his achievements in Spain and in Africa as his brother's officer. As consul he had †been considered† by the Senate worthy of being assigned the province of Asia and direction of the war with Antiochus, without sortition, and his brother—who had held two consulships and the censorship, and had celebrated a triumph—thought enough of him to accompany him to Asia as his legate. In that province a fortuitous event saw to it that the grandeur and eminence of the legate did not eclipse the merits of the consul—on the day that Lucius Scipio vanquished Antiochus in pitched battle at Magnesia, Publius Scipio lay sick at Elaea, a number of days' journey away. And the army of Antiochus was no smaller than the army of Hannibal which the Romans had faced in Africa—that same Hannibal who had been the commander-in-chief in the Punic War was in fact only one of the king's many officers. The war, too, had been fought in such a way that nobody could even find fault with his luck. It was in the peace-treaty that grounds for criticism were sought—this, it is said, was put on sale. On this score the ten commissioners are also incriminated, because it was on their advice that the peace was concluded. Some of the ten commissioners had emerged to accuse Gnaeus Manlius, but that denunciation had not enough weight even to delay his triumph, let alone inspire confidence in the charge.

59. But, heavens above, Nasica continued, in Scipio's case the allegation was that the peace-terms themselves looked suspiciously favourable to Antiochus. His kingdom was left untouched: he had, in defeat, everything that he had possessed before the war; and though he had had a large amount of gold and silver, none of it had been made public property, but all of it had gone into private hands. In fact, though, at Lucius Scipio's triumph, had not as much gold and silver as in ten other triumphs put together been carried before the eyes of the whole population?

'What am I to say about the bounds of Antiochus' kingdom?'

Nasica continued. Antiochus had held the whole of Asia and the parts of Europe next to it. How much of the world this covers, extending as it did from the Taurus range all the way into the Aegean Sea, the number of peoples and not just towns it encompasses—everybody is aware of this. This area, which was more than thirty days' journey in length and ten days' in width between the two seas, and which extended as far as the heights of the Taurus range—this was taken from Antiochus who was driven to the farthest corner of the world. What more could have been taken from him if the peace-settlement had cost him nothing? The conquered Philip had been left Macedonia, and Nabis had been left Sparta, but no indictment was sought against Quinctius. No, because he had not had Africanus as a brother, a man whose brilliant reputation should have helped Lucius Scipio, who was instead harmed by the jealousy felt for his brother.

According to the judgement, as much gold and silver had been taken into Lucius Scipio's home as could not be raised by the sale of all his property. So where was the king's gold, where the many legacies Scipio received? A pile of newly acquired wealth should have come to light in a house that expenses had not drained. And of course Lucius Scipio's enemies were now going to take from his body and his back, by hounding and insulting him, what could not be raised from his property. Their aim was to have a man of great distinction locked in a prison amongst thieves of the night and foot-pads, to have him breathe his last in a dark gaol, and then thrown out naked before the prison. That would be less scandalous for the family of the Cornelii than it would for the city of Rome, he concluded.

60. In response, the praetor Terentius read out the bill of the Petillii, the decree of the Senate, and the verdict passed on Lucius Scipio. Unless the fine imposed by the sentence of the court were paid into the treasury, said Terentius, he had no option but to order the convicted man arrested and taken to prison. A little later, after the tribunes had withdrawn to confer, Gaius Fannius declared that he and all his colleagues apart from Gracchus were agreed that the tribunes not veto the praetor in the exercise of his authority. Tiberius Gracchus made the following pronouncement. He did not veto the collection of the fine prescribed by the sentence from the property of Lucius Scipio, he said. But Lucius Scipio was a man who had vanquished the richest king in the world, and advanced the rule of the Roman people to the farthest limits of the earth; he had put Eumenes, the Rhodians, and many other cities of Asia under obligation through services rendered them by the Roman people; and he had led along in his triumphal procession, and then imprisoned, a large number of enemy generals. So he, Gracchus, was not going to let Lucius Scipio sit in chains in prison amongst the enemies of the Roman people, he said, and he ordered his release.

Gracchus' decree was met with such universal approval, and people were so happy to see Scipio released that it hardly seemed possible the verdict had been passed in the same community. After this the praetor sent the quaestors to see to the public confiscation of the property of Lucius Scipio. So far from there being any trace of the king's money, the amount raised was nowhere close to the sum he had been sentenced to pay. So much money was raised for Lucius Scipio by his relatives, friends and clients that accepting it would have left him richer than he had been before the tragedy struck. But he took nothing. What he needed for basic living was bought back for him by his closest family, and the resentment felt for the Scipios recoiled on the praetor, his board of advisors, and the prosecutors.

BOOK THIRTY-NINE

1. While these events were taking place at Rome—if, in fact, this was the year* in which they did take place—the two consuls* were at war in the territory of the Ligurians. This was an enemy almost made for sustaining Roman military discipline in the breaks between the major wars, and no other province did more to hone the soldiers' valour. Asia offered captivating towns, ample commodities from land and sea, a spineless enemy, and the wealth of kings, thus enriching armies rather than tempering them. Discipline was particularly lax and slipshod under Gnaeus Manlius' command, which was why the slightly harder journey in Thrace and a better-trained foe proved a chastening experience that resulted in heavy casualties.

In Liguria there was everything to energize the soldiers: a mountainous and forbidding terrain where gaining ground themselves and dislodging the enemy from already-occupied positions were both a challenge; roads that were difficult and narrow, and fraught with the danger of ambush; a lightly equipped, mobile, and unpredictable enemy who allowed them to rest or feel secure at no time and in no place; fortified strongholds, which had to be attacked, entailing hardship and risk at the same time; and an impoverished landscape that obliged the men to live frugally and offered little in the way of booty. As a result, there were no camp-followers with them, and no long line of pack-animals to draw out the column. There was nothing but arms, and men who placed all their hopes in those arms. And an occasion or motive for war with the Ligurians was never lacking because the poverty of their own homeland prompted them to raid their neighbours' territory. Even so, the fighting was not bringing a final resolution of the conflict.

2. The consul Gaius Flaminius fought several successful battles with the Ligurian Friniates in their territory, accepting their surrender and disarming them. Under punishment for failing to make an honest surrender of their arms, the Friniates abandoned their villages and sought refuge on Mt. Auginus, swiftly followed by the consul. But scattering once more, and most of them without weapons, they fled headlong over rugged country and steep cliffs where the enemy could not follow, and in this way made good their

escape over the Apennines. Those who had stayed in camp were surrounded and overwhelmed.

After this the legions were taken across the Apennines. Here the enemy briefly succeeded in defending themselves, thanks to the height of a mountain they had seized, but they soon capitulated. At this time a more thorough search of their weapons was instituted and they were totally disarmed.

The theatre of war was then transferred to the Ligurian Apuani, whose incursions into the farmlands of Pisae and Bononia had rendered cultivation there impossible. The Apuani were also brought to heel, and the consul bestowed peace on their neighbours. And having now stabilized the province after the hostilities, he built a road from Bononia to Arretium in order not to have his men kept idle.

The other consul, Marcus Aemilius, burned and pillaged the fields and villages of the Ligurians who lived in the plains and valleys, while these people themselves occupied two mountains, Ballista and Suismontium. Aemilius then attacked the men on the hills, at first grinding them down with skirmishes and eventually forcing them into a regular engagement and defeating them in pitched battle. During this battle he also vowed a temple to Diana. After crushing all the Ligurians this side of the Apennines, Aemilius next attacked those beyond the mountains, including those Ligurian Friniates whom Gaius Flaminius had not invaded. He brought them all to their knees, disarmed them, and moved them *en masse* from the mountains to the plains.

With Liguria pacified, Aemilius led his army into Gallic territory and constructed a road from Placentia to Ariminum to join up with the Flaminian Way. In the last pitched battle in which he clashed with the Ligurians he made a vow of a temple to Queen Juno. Such were that year's operations in Liguria.

3. In Gaul, the praetor Marcus Furius had been looking for a pretext for war in the midst of peace, and had disarmed the inoffensive Cenomani. The Cenomani lodged a grievance about this before the Senate at Rome, and were referred to the consul Aemilius, to whom the Senate had entrusted the responsibility of examining and judging the dispute. After a heated argument with the praetor, the Cenomani won their case, and the praetor was instructed to restore their arms and leave the province.

An audience with the Senate was then granted to ambassadors

from the allies of the Latin League who had come together there in great numbers from all points of Latium. These complained that a large portion of their citizens had moved to Rome and been placed on the census-list in the city. The praetor Quintus Terentius Culleo was assigned the duty of tracing these people, and of forcing any who had been shown by the allies to have been enrolled with them, or to have had a father enrolled, in or after the censorship of Gaius Claudius and Marcus Livius,* to return to their original place of census. Following this investigation 12,000 Latins went back to their homes—even by that time the large number of foreigners was becoming burdensome for the city.

4. Before the consuls returned to Rome, the proconsul Marcus Fulvius also returned from Aetolia. In a session of the Senate in the temple of Apollo, Fulvius gave an account of his achievements in Aetolia and Cephallenia* and requested of the members that—if they deemed it warranted—they give the order for the gods to be honoured in view of his capable and successful management of the state's interests. He also requested that they officially sanction a triumph for him. The plebeian tribune Marcus Aburius indicated that he would veto any decision reached on the question before the arrival of the consul Marcus Aemilius. Aemilius wanted to speak against the proposal, he said, and, on his departure for his province, had instructed Aburius to see that discussion of the issue not be broached before his arrival. For Fulvius, he added, it was simply a matter of loss of time—the Senate would follow its own inclinations in the vote even in the consul's presence.*

Then Fulvius declared that if people had been unaware of Marcus Aemilius' feud with him or of the extent to which Aemilius kept up that quarrel with an obsessive and almost tyrannical passion—even then, he said, it would have been intolerable for an absent consul to obstruct the respect to be paid to the immortal gods and also delay a triumph well and truly deserved. It would even then have been intolerable for a general, who had conducted a superlative campaign, and his victorious army to be kept standing before the city-gates with their plunder and prisoners-of-war until the consul—who was stalling for this very reason—should choose to come back to Rome. As it was, said Fulvius, his feud with the consul was a matter of common knowledge. So, he asked, what fair play could anyone expect from a man who had brought to the treasury a decree of the

Senate furtively passed at a poorly-attended session—a decree which stated that 'Ambracia had apparently not been taken by force'? This although that city had been attacked with earth-works and siege-sheds; even when fresh siege-works had been constructed after the original ones were burned; when there had been fifteen days of combat around the city-walls, above and below ground; when our soldiers had been long engaged in an undecided battle from the crack of dawn, when they scaled the walls, right until nightfall; and when more than 3,000 of the enemy had been hacked down! Furthermore, what were these slanderous criticisms that he brought before the priests about the sacking of the temples of the immortal gods in the captured city? Or perhaps it was morally acceptable for Rome to be embellished with art-works from Syracuse and other captured cities—whereas only in the capture of Ambracia were the rules of war not applicable! He was appealing to the Senate, he said, and asking the tribune, not to let him become an object of ridicule to a supercilious personal enemy.

5. The Senators assailed the tribune from every quarter, some with entreaties, some with abuse; but what moved him most of all was the address of his colleague, Tiberius Gracchus. Gracchus argued that even to engage in one's personal vendettas while holding public office did not set a good precedent; but that a tribune of the plebs should be a spokesman in other people's quarrels was a disgrace, and an affront to the authority and sacred laws of the college of tribunes. A man should follow his own judgement in disliking or liking people, and in approving or disapproving measures; he should not be hanging on another's expression or nod of the head, or be led around by the prompting of someone else's sentiments. And a tribune of the people should not be bolstering the anger of a consul; he should not remember a private assignment that Marcus Aemilius gave to him but forget the tribuneship conferred on him by the Roman people—an office conferred to assist and protect the interests of individual citizens, not the personal power of a consul.* Aburius, he said, did not even see that the historical record passed on to posterity would show that of the two tribunes of the plebs—men who were of the same college—one had renounced his own personal feud in the interests of the state while the other had become embroiled in a feud consigned to him by a third party.

Overawed by such censure, the tribune left the temple; and on the proposal of Servius Sulpicius a triumph was formally awarded to Marcus Fulvius. After expressing his gratitude to the Senators, Fulvius added that he had vowed great games to Jupiter Optimus Maximus on the day of his capture of Ambracia, and that he had received a contribution of 100 pounds of gold for that purpose from the cities. He now requested that the Senate authorize that this gold be separated from the money which he was going to deposit in the treasury after carrying it in his triumphal procession. The Senate ordered that the question of whether the entire quantity of gold needed to be spent on the games be put to the college of pontiffs and, when the pontiffs stated that the amount spent on the games had no religious significance, the Senate permitted Fulvius to decide how much to spend, provided that he not exceed the sum of 80,000 sesterces.

Fulvius had decided to hold the triumph in the month of January. He then heard that the consul Marcus Aemilius had received a letter from Marcus Aburius on the withdrawal of his veto, that Aemilius was himself coming to Rome to block the triumph but that had stopped on the way because of illness. Fulvius therefore brought forward the date so as not to face more conflicts over the triumph than he had in the war. He celebrated his triumph over the Aetolians and Cephallenia on 23 December. Golden crowns* weighing 112 pounds were carried before his chariot along with the following: 83,000 pounds of silver, 243 pounds of gold, 118,000 Attic four-drachma pieces, 12,322 Philippics, 785 bronze statues, 230 marble statues, a great quantity of armour, spears, and other spoils from the enemy, as well as catapults, ballistae, and all kinds of artillery. There were also in the procession some twenty-seven officers, either Aetolian and Cephallenian or royal officers left behind by Antiochus. Before riding into the city, Fulvius that day presented military decorations in the Circus Flaminius to a large number of tribunes, prefects, cavalrymen, and centurions, both Romans and allies. He distributed 25 denarii from the booty to each of the infantrymen, twice that amount to each centurion, and three times to each cavalryman.

6. The time of the consular elections was now drawing near. Marcus Aemilius, who had been allotted responsibility for them, was unable to attend, and so Gaius Flaminius came to Rome. Flaminius presided over the election to the consulship of Spurius Postumius Albinus and Quintus Marcius Philippus, and then the following were elected praetor: Titus Maenius, Publius Cornelius Sulla,

Gaius Calpurnius Piso, Marcus Licinius Lucullus, Gaius Aurelius Scaurus, and Lucius Quinctius Crispinus.

It was on 5 March—at the year's end and after the election of the magistrates—that Gnaeus Manlius Vulso celebrated his triumph over the Gauls living in Asia. There was a reason for his postponement of the triumph. He wanted to avoid defending himself under the Petillian law before the praetor Quintus Terentius Culleo, and being consumed in the flames of litigation directed against someone else, which had resulted in Lucius Scipio's condemnation.* In fact, he felt the jury would be all the more hostile to him than they had been to Scipio because of the rumour that Vulso had, in succeeding him, undermined by all manner of laxity the military discipline that Scipio had strictly maintained. And his reputation was sullied not only by stories of what went on in the province, far from the eyes of the citizens—there was also, and more important, what could every day be seen amongst his soldiers. For foreign luxury was originally brought to the city by the army that had been in Asia. These were the men who first introduced into Rome bronze couches, expensive bed-covers, tapestries, and other woven materials, and—things then regarded as furniture of high fashion—pedestal tables and sideboards. This was when girls playing harps and lutes made their appearance at dinner-parties, together with other entertainments to amuse the guests; and more attention and expenditure also began to be devoted to the dinners themselves. This was the period when the cook, the lowest slave for ancients in terms of his worth and manner of employment, began to be prized, and what had been menial labour to be regarded as an art. And yet the things that began to appear in those days were no more than the seeds of the luxury yet to come.

7. Borne in the triumphal procession by Gnaeus Manlius were the following: 212 golden crowns; 220,000 pounds of silver; 2,103 pounds of gold; 127,000 Attic four-drachma coins; 250,000 coins stamped with the *cista*; 16,320 gold Philippics. There were also large quantities of Gallic arms and spoils carried on wagons, and fifty-two enemy officers were led before the triumphal car. Manlius distributed 42 denarii to each of his infantrymen, double to each centurion, and three times the amount to each cavalryman; and he also doubled their pay. Many men from all ranks, who were awarded military decorations, followed the car. And the songs that were sung by the

soldiers to their general were such that it was readily apparent that they were addressed to an undemanding leader who courted popularity, and that the triumph was more warmly welcomed by the troops than by civilians. But Manlius' friends had the influence to win over the support of the people, too, and under pressure from these a Senatorial decree was passed to the effect that some of the money carried in the triumph be used to discharge the as-yet unpaid portion of the taxes contributed to the state by the people. The urban quaestors were scrupulously careful in paying twenty-five-and-a-half *asses* on each thousand imposed.

At about the same time two military tribunes came from the two Spains with a letter from the provincial governors, Gaius Atinius and Lucius Manlius. From this letter it was ascertained that the Celtiberians and Lusitanians were under arms and raiding the territory of Roman allies. Consideration of the issue the Senate left entirely to the new magistrates.

The Roman Games that year were staged by Publius Cornelius Cethegus and Aulus Postumius Albinus. At them a poorly secured beam in the circus fell on the statue of Pollentia and knocked it over. Disturbed by this sign from heaven, the Senators voted for a day's extension for the games and also for the setting up of two statues in place of the one, with the new one overlaid with gold. The Plebeian Games were also renewed for one day by the aediles Gaius Sempronius Blaesus and Marcus Furius Luscus.

8. The following year saw the consuls Spurius Postumius Albinus and Quintus Marcius Philippus turning their attention from the army, and from the sphere of military and provincial affairs, to disciplinary measures against an internal conspiracy. The provincial sortition for the praetors was as follows:

Titus Maenius	urban jurisdiction
Marcus Licinius Lucullus	citizens/foreigners' jurisdiction
Gaius Aurelius Scaurus	Sardinia
Publius Cornelius Sulla	Sicily
Lucius Quinctius Crispinus	Hither Spain
Gaius Calpurnius Piso	Farther Spain

Both consuls were assigned the task of investigating clandestine seditious activity.*

It began with the arrival in Etruria of a Greek of no importance.

He was endowed with none of those many accomplishments which that most erudite of peoples* has brought to us for our intellectual and physical betterment—he was a mere priest and oracle-monger. And he was not the type who would delude people's minds while practising his religion openly, and overtly proclaiming his business and his precepts—rather, he was the leader of a secret cult that operated at night. There were rites of initiation which were at first limited to a few but which subsequently spread more widely amongst men and women. To rouse the interest of a greater number of people, the pleasures of drinking and feasting were also made part of the religious ceremonies. When the drink <had roused> passions, and the darkness and the fact that men and women, older and younger, were intermixed had eliminated all moral judgement,* every kind of depravity began to emerge; for they all had laid on for them the instant gratification of any sexual desire to which they were inclined by nature. Nor was the immorality confined to promiscuous sex between freeborn men and women. There was also perjured testimony in court, forged seals and wills, and manufactured evidence, all emanating from the same workshop; and from there, too, came cases of poisoning and murders within families, sometimes with the bodies not even coming to light to make burial possible. Many offences involved swindles, and most of them violence. The violence was kept hidden, however, because, amid the fornication and bloodshed, no scream of protest could be heard above the shouting and the beating of drums and cymbals.

9. This pernicious scourge made its way from Etruria to Rome like a spreading infection. At first the size of the city—being larger it was also more tolerant of such immorality—kept the cult's practices hidden. But eventually word of them reached the consul Postumius, in a manner more or less as follows.

Publius Aebutius,* whose late father had served in the cavalry with a horse supplied by the state, had been left a ward. Then, when the guardians died, he had been brought up in the care of his mother Duronia and his stepfather Titus Sempronius Rutilus. The mother was totally committed to her husband, and the stepfather, whose guardianship of the boy had been such that he could not provide a financial account, wanted his ward eliminated, or else to have some kind of hold on the boy as would put him at his mercy. The Bacchanalia provided one way of corrupting him. The mother approached the young man and told him that she had made a vow for him when he had been ill. She had promised to initiate him in the rites of Bacchus as soon as he recovered, she said. She was duty-bound to fulfil the vow, thanks to heaven's kindness, and now she wanted to discharge it. There was need of a ten-day period of abstinence, she continued, and on the tenth day Aebutius would dine and ritually purify himself, after which she would take him to the shrine.

There was a well-known prostitute, a freedwoman called Hispala Faecenia.* She was too good for that occupation, which she had taken up as slave-girl, but she had continued to keep herself by the same line of work even after her manumission. A sexual relationship with Aebutius arose from their being neighbours, but this in no way damaged the young man's finances or his reputation—it was he who was the object of Hispala's affections and it was he who had been sought out by her, and while his own family was niggardly in every respect towards him he was actually supported by the harlot's generosity. In fact, her affair with him had taken Hispala even further: since, on her patron's death, she was under nobody's legal authority, she petitioned the tribunes and the praetor for a guardian, made a will and appointed Aebutius her sole heir.

10. Such were the ties of affection between the two, and they kept no secrets from each other. The young man then jokingly told Hispala not to be surprised if he slept apart from her for a few nights. He explained that, for religious reasons—namely, to be released from a vow made for his recovery from illness—he wished to be initiated in the rites of Bacchus. Hearing this the woman became very emotional and exclaimed: 'Heaven forbid!' Death was preferable to doing that, both for him and for her, she said, and she was calling down curses and plague on the heads of those who had suggested it. The young man was shocked at her words and her agitation, and he told her to spare her curses—it was his mother who had instructed him to do it, and with his stepfather's approval. 'Then,' said Hispala, 'by this action your stepfather is speedily bringing on the destruction of your good character, your reputation, your prospects, and your life—for perhaps it would not be right to blame your mother.'

Aebutius was all the more taken aback at this remark, and asked what she meant. Hispala asked for the grace and indulgence of the gods and goddesses if affection for him obliged her to divulge matters that should be kept secret, and then explained that, when she was a slave-girl, she had gone into that shrine along with her mistress, though she had never visited it since being free. She said she knew it to be a breeding-ground for all manner of vice, and that it was a matter of common knowledge that for two years no one above the age of twenty had been initiated there. As each newcomer was brought in, he was passed on to the priests like a sacrificial victim. These priests took him to a place resounding with shrieks, and where instruments were playing and cymbals and drums beating, all intended to render inaudible the voice of anyone protesting when he was being sexually assaulted. Hispala then begged and entreated Aebutius to find some way to end the business and not throw himself into a situation where he first had to suffer, and then inflict on others, all manner of unspeakable abuse. And she did not let him go until the young man gave his word to have nothing to do with these rites.

11. When Aebutius came home, his mother brought up the subject of the steps involved in the rites which he had to follow that day and on the following days. Aebutius replied that he would follow none of them, and that he had no intention of being initiated. His stepfather was party to the conversation. The woman immediately exclaimed that Aebutius could not go without sleeping with Hispala for ten days, that it was because he had been infected by that bitch's poisonous wheedling that he had no respect for his mother, his stepfather or for the gods. Pouring reproaches on him from both sides, mother and stepfather drove him from the house with four slaves. The young man went from there to his aunt Aebutia, and he related to her why he had been thrown into the street by his mother. Then, at Aebutia's suggestion, he reported the affair the following day to the consul Postumius, in a private conversation. The consul sent him off after telling him to come back in two days, and himself asked his mother-in-law Sulpicia, a dignified lady, whether she knew an old woman from the Aventine called Aebutia. Sulpicia answered that she knew her and that she was a decent woman with traditional values. The consul said that he needed to meet her—Sulpicia should send her a message asking her to come.

Aebutia came to Sulpicia when she was summoned; and shortly afterwards the consul, dropping in as if by chance, broached with her the topic of her brother's son, Aebutius. Tears welled up in the woman's eyes and she proceeded to lament the young man's fate. He had, she said, been despoiled of his assets by those who should have been the last people to do this, and he was now at her house. He had been thrown out by his mother because, decent young man that he was, he refused to be initiated in what were rumoured to be disgusting rites (and she prayed heaven to forgive her for calling them so!).

12. The consul felt he had probed sufficiently to see that Aebutius was not an unreliable informant, and after letting Aebutia go he asked his mother-in-law to send for Hispala, a freedwoman who was also from the Aventine and not unknown in the quarter. He had certain questions to put to her as well, he explained.

On receiving the message, Hispala was frightened—without knowing why, she was being summoned to the presence of a woman of great distinction and dignity—and when she caught sight of the lictors in the forecourt, and then the consul's retinue and the consul himself, she almost fainted. She was taken to the interior of the house. Here, with his mother-in-law present, the consul informed Hispala that she had no reason to be alarmed if she could bring herself to tell the truth—on this she could take the word of such a lady as Sulpicia, or indeed of himself. He then bade her divulge to him what usually went on at the nocturnal rite of the Bacchanalia in the grove of †Simila†.* When she heard this, the woman was overtaken by such panic, and such trembling seized all her limbs, that she was long unable to open her mouth. Finally, pulling herself together, she said that she had undergone initiation with her mistress when she was a very young slave-girl, but for several years now, ever since her manumission, she had had no idea of what went on there.

At this point the consul commended her for not having denied that she had been initiated, but he pressed her to make a full disclosure of everything else, on the same assurance as before. Hispala said she knew no more, at which the consul declared that she would not receive the same indulgence or favour if she were refuted by the testimony of another as she would if she made a clean breast of it herself. And he concluded by saying that the man who had got the story from her had told him everything.

13. Convinced that it was Aebutius who had given away her secret (as was, indeed, the case), the woman threw herself at Sulpicia's feet. At first she began to beg her not even to take seriously, and certainly not turn into a capital charge, the words spoken by a freedwoman to her lover—it was only to scare Aebutius that she had said these

things, not because she really knew anything. At this Postumius flew into a rage. Hispala evidently thought she was even then exchanging pleasantries with her lover Aebutius, he said, instead of conversing in the home of a lady of great dignity, and with a consul. Sulpicia raised up the frightened woman, offering her words of encouragement while simultaneously calming her son-in-law's anger. Eventually Hispala pulled herself together and, after a long tirade against the disloyalty of Aebutius for thus repaying her for her devoted services to him, she declared that she greatly feared the gods whose secret rites she would expose, but much more did she fear the men who would tear her apart with their own hands for informing on them. As a result, she said, she had this appeal to make to Sulpicia and to the consul, that they remove her to some place outside Italy where she could live out the rest of her life in safety; but the consul told her to cheer up and said that he would personally see to it that she should live safely in Rome.

Now Hispala disclosed how the rites began. Initially, she said, that shrine had been limited to women, with no male accepted there. They had set aside three days a year for initiation in the Bacchic rites, a daylight ceremony, and it was the practice for married women to be appointed to the priesthood in turns. It was Paculla Annia, a priestess from Campania, who had made the radical changes, seemingly at the prompting of the gods. She was the first to have initiated males (her own sons, Minius and Herennius Cerrinius) and she had made it a night-time as opposed to a daylight ceremony, with five days of rites per month instead of three in the year. Ever since the rites were integrated, with men mixed with women, and with darkness giving participants freedom of action, there was no crime and no shameful act omitted at them. There were more sexual assaults inflicted on the men by other men than on the women, continued Hispala, and any who showed reluctance to submit to abuse, or hesitated to engage in crime, became sacrificial victims. To consider nothing sinful—amongst them that was the essence of religion, she said. Men who appeared deranged would utter prophesies with a furious shaking of their bodies. Married women wearing the dress of Bacchants, and with streaming hair, would run to the Tiber carrying blazing torches; they would plunge these in the water and draw them out again, the flames still burning because of the mixture of live sulphur and calcium on them. They would tie people to a crane and whisk them out of sight into hidden caverns; these individuals were said to have been 'taken by the gods', and were those who refused to join the conspiracy, participate in crimes, or submit to sexual abuse. The number of participants was by now enormous, virtually amounting to a second city-population, and included a number of men and women from the nobility. In the past two years, Hispala said, it had been made a rule that no one above the age of twenty be initiated—people of an age susceptible to corruption and sexual abuse were the targeted group.

14. After finishing her statement the woman once more fell at their feet and repeated her entreaties that Postumius banish her. Instead, the consul asked his mother-in-law to make space in part of her house for Hispala to move in. Hispala was given a loft above the house, with the stairs from it to the exterior sealed off and access to the loft brought inside the building. All of Faecenia's belongings were promptly carried over, and her slaves summoned; and Aebutius was told to move to the home of a client of the consul's.

Having both informants at his disposition, Postumius now brought the affair before the Senate, with all the details laid out in order, from the initial reports down to his own enquiries. The Senators were gripped by terrible panic. In their official capacity they feared that these intrigues and nightly meetings might precipitate some covert sedition and state of emergency; and privately they each feared for their own relatives, in case one of them should be party to the villainy. However, the Senate voted that the consul be thanked for having made his enquiries into the affair with extraordinary diligence and without causing alarm. The Senators then gave the consuls the supplementary assignment of investigating the Bacchanalia and the nightly rites. They ordered them to make sure that the informants Aebutius and Faecenia came to no harm as a result of the affair, and to offer rewards to attract others to lay information. The priests of the cult, whether male or female, were to be tracked down, not just in Rome but throughout the country towns and administrative centres, so that they should be at the disposition of the consuls. A proclamation was also to be made in the city of Rome, with edicts sent out the length of Italy, forbidding anyone who had been initiated in the Bacchic rites to hold religious gatherings or assemblies, or perform any divine ceremony of this kind. Above all there was to be an investigation conducted into those people who had gathered or conspired to perpetrate an immoral or shameful act. Such were the decisions of the Senate.

The consuls instructed the curule aediles to hunt down all the priests of the cult, apprehend them, and keep them under house-arrest for the investigation; and they told the plebeian aediles to ensure that there be no clandestine celebration of the rites. The *triumviri capitales** were charged with the task of posting of sentries through the city, of seeing that there were no gatherings at night and of taking precaution against arson. The *triumviri* were to be assisted by the quinquevirs each of whom, on both sides of the Tiber, was to keep watch on the buildings in his district.

15. With the officers sent off to perform these duties, the consuls mounted the Rostra and convened a meeting of the people. After completing the formulaic recitation of the prayer usually uttered by magistrates before they address the people, the consul began to speak as follows:

'Citizens, never has there been a meeting for which this formulaic invocation of the gods has been so appropriate and, more than that, so necessary. For it reminds you that these are the deities whom your ancestors ordained that you should venerate, worship, and address in prayer—not those that besot men's minds with depraved foreign beliefs, and use infernal stimuli to drive them to all manner of criminal and immoral acts.

'Frankly, I cannot tell what I should suppress or how openly I should speak. If you are kept unaware of anything, I fear I may leave room for you to become indifferent, and if I make a full disclosure I am afraid I might cause you excessive alarm. Whatever I say, you must realize that my words fail to match the heinous nature and seriousness of the situation. But we shall do our best to take ample precautions.

'I am sure that you know that Bacchic rites have long been prac-tised throughout Italy and are now being practised at many locations in the city, and that you have heard this not simply from rumour but also from the noise and shrieking at night that resounds throughout the city. But I am also sure that you are ignorant of just what is involved, some of you thinking that this is a form of divine worship, others that it is a lawful form of entertainment and amusement, and that, whatever its nature, membership is limited to a few. As regards numbers, you cannot fail to be terrified if I say that there are many thousands of people involved—unless I further explain who and what sort of people these are. First of all, then, most are women, and they are the source of this plague; then there are males closely resembling women, who submit to and in turn inflict sexual abuse, frenzied characters, men in a stupor from lack of sleep, from drinking, and from the nightly hullaballoo and shouting. As yet the conspiracy has no strength, but it is gaining strength on an enormous scale because its members become more numerous every day.

'Your ancestors opposed even *your* engaging in random and irregular gatherings. Meetings were limited to occasions when the army was led out for an election, with the flag raised on the citadel, or when the tribunes proclaimed a meeting of the plebs, or one of the magistrates called an assembly; and they believed that, wherever a crowd gathered, there should be a duly appointed crowd-marshal in attendance. What sort of meetings do you think we have here— meetings which are held at night and which are also attended by men and women together? If you knew the age of initiation for males, you would feel shame as well as pity for them. When young men have taken *this* oath of initiation, citizens, do you think they should be employed as soldiers? Are weapons to be put in the hands of men drawn from this disgusting shrine? Bedaubed with their own and others' depravity, will they fight with the sword for the honour of your wives and children?

16. 'It would not be so bad if their immoral behaviour had merely made them effeminate—that would have been largely a matter of their own personal dishonour—and if they had kept their hands free of crime and their minds free of subversive activity. Never has villainy of such proportions existed in the state, touching so many people and so many aspects of society. You must realize that all the iniquity of the past few years—all the depravity, treachery, and criminal behaviour has emanated from the one shrine. These people have not as yet made public all the criminal acts they have conspired to commit; for their unholy conspiracy, not yet having the strength to bring down the state, has so far been confined to crimes against individuals. The mischief is growing and infiltrating society each day—it is already too large to be contained by the resources of an individual, and it seeks to engulf the whole state. Unless you take precautions, my fellow-citizens, their nocturnal assembly will soon be able to rival this daylight meeting which has been legitimately

convened by a consul. At present they are individuals standing in fear of your unity; soon, when you have slipped away to your homes and farms, and they have assembled, they will be discussing saving themselves and destroying you—and then it is *their* assembled number that *you* as individuals will have to fear. So each and every one of us should pray that all our relatives have shown good sense. If lechery or folly has swept any of them into that maelstrom, we must each consider that that man belongs not to us but to those people with whom he conspired to commit all manner of crime and villainy.

'Citizens, I am not convinced that none of you will falter and go astray; for nothing is more deceptively alluring than a depraved cult. When the will of the gods is used as a screen for criminal activities, one is overtaken by fear that in punishing human wrongdoings we may be violating some divine law fused into them. To free you from such concern for religious propriety you have countless decrees of the priests, resolutions of the Senate, and, indeed, responses from our soothsayers. In the days of our fathers and grandfathers, how many were the occasions on which the magistrates were charged with the responsibility of outlawing the practice of foreign rites; of excluding minor priests and prophets from the Forum, the Circus, and the city; of ferreting out and burning books of oracles;* and of expelling every sacrificial practice apart from those conforming with Roman custom! In fact, the greatest experts in all divine and human law judged that nothing served to destroy our religion as much as sacrifice performed according to foreign rather than our native ritual.

'I thought you should be apprised of this in advance in case some superstitious misgivings assail your minds when you observe us putting a stop to the Bacchanalia and breaking up its unholy gatherings. All that we shall do will have the sanction and endorsement of the gods. It is they who, from anger at the defilement of their divine power by criminal and immoral acts, brought these activities into the light of day from darkness and obscurity; and their desire to have them exposed was not so that they should go unpunished, but so that they should be penalized and suppressed. The Senate has assigned to my colleague and me the supplementary task of investigating the affair. We shall with vigour carry out what we ourselves must do, and we have vested the minor magistrates with responsibility for surveillance at night throughout the city. It is only fair that you, too, should vigorously perform your respective duties, doing what you are commanded to do in your various stations, and that you should make every effort to prevent any danger or unrest arising from the subversive activities of the guilty parties.'

17. The consuls then had the Senatorial decrees read aloud, and they posted a reward for any informer bringing an offender before them, or denouncing him in his absence. They said they would establish a time-limit for anyone who fled on being reported; if the party failed to answer the summons by the specified date, he would be condemned in his absence. They added that in the case of an accusation brought against any of those outside Italy at that time, they would grant greater leeway in the deadline for his appearance to answer the charge. After this they proclaimed an edict outlawing sales or purchases made for the purpose of fleeing justice, and forbidding anyone to harbour, conceal, or use any means to help fugitives.

At the adjournment of the meeting there was great trepidation throughout the city. Nor did this did stop at the walls or within the bounds of Rome; panic began to spread the whole length of Italy as letters were received from friends on the subject of the Senatorial decree, the meeting, and the edict of the consuls. During the night that followed the day of the exposure of the affair at the meeting, a large number of fugitives were caught and brought back by the triumvirs who had posted guards at the gates; and many were reported by informers. Several of these committed suicide, both men and women. More than seven thousand men and women were said to have been party to the conspiracy, but the ringleaders, it was established, were Marcus and Gaius Atinius from the Roman plebs, a Faliscan Lucius Opicernius, and a Campanian Minius Cerrinius. All the criminal and immoral activity was believed to have started with these men, who were the high priests and founders of the cult. Every effort was made to have them arrested at the earliest opportunity, and when they were brought before the consuls they confessed their own guilt and did not hesitate to furnish information.

18. In fact, so great had been the exodus from the city that the cases and proceedings of many litigants were invalidated, obliging the praetors Titus Maenius and Marcus Licinius* to use the authority of the Senate to adjourn cases for a thirty-day period until the investigations could be completed by the consuls. This massive departure from the city also forced the consuls to do the rounds of

the country towns, and undertake investigations and trials there, because in Rome the people who were denounced failed to answer their summons and could not be found.

Some of the prisoners had merely been initiated, and had followed ritual formulas, dictated by a priest, to make prayers that related to the unholy conspiracy to commit all the criminal and shameful acts; they had not actually perpetrated against themselves or others any of the acts to which they had been bound by their oaths. These the consuls left in prison. Those who had dishonoured themselves by degenerate behaviour or by murder they condemned to capital punishment, as they did those who had degraded themselves by giving false testimony, counterfeiting seals, forging wills, and by other fraudulent activities. More were put to death than were imprisoned, but there were a large number of men and women in both categories. They delivered condemned women to their relatives or those acting as their legal guardians so these people could inflict the punishment on them in private, but in the absence of a suitable person to exact it the penalty was applied publicly.

The consuls were then assigned the task of demolishing all centres of Bacchic worship, first in Rome and then throughout Italy, excepting only those where an ancient altar or statue had been consecrated to the god. Any celebration of the rites of Bacchus, in Rome or Italy, was thereafter forbidden by Senatorial decree. In the event of anyone considering such a rite to be an essential part of his religious observance which he could not renounce without a guilty conscience and acts of expiation, this person was to make a declaration before the urban praetor and the praetor was to consult the Senate. If he were granted permission by a Senate with a quorum of a hundred, he was to hold the rite with no more than five participants at the sacrifice, and with no common funds, no master of ceremonies, and no priest.

19. After this, on the motion of the consul Quintus Marcius, a further Senatorial decree was passed, and attached to this one. By this the entire question of those used as informers by the consuls was to be referred to the Senate when Spurius Postumius returned to Rome at the conclusion of his investigations. The Senators voted that the Campanian Minius Cerrinius be sent to Ardea for imprisonment, and that the magistrates of the Ardeans be warned to keep a particularly close watch on him, not simply to prevent his escape but also to remove any opportunity for suicide. Some time

later Spurius Postumius came to Rome. He proposed to the Senate that Publius Aebutius and Hispala Faecenia be rewarded since it was thanks to them that the affair of the Bacchanalia had been brought to light, and a Senatorial decree was passed declaring the following:

1. that the city quaestors pay each of the two 100,000 *asses* from the treasury;

2. that the consul discuss with the plebeian tribunes the matter of taking to the people at the earliest opportunity a proposal that Publius Aebutius' military service be considered fulfilled;* that he not do army service against his will, and that the censor †. . .† not assign him a public horse;

3. that Faecenia Hispala have the right to convey her property, or draw on it; to marry outside her *gens*; and to choose a guardian, just as if a husband had granted her that privilege in a will;

4. that she be permitted to marry a free-born man, and that whosoever married her* suffer thereby no prejudice or loss of status;

5. that current and future consuls and praetors see to it that the woman come to no harm and that she live in security.

Such, the decree continued, was the will of the Senate, which considered it just that these steps be taken. All the measures were brought before the people, and all were enacted in accordance with the decree of the Senate. The consuls were left to decide on impunity and rewards for the other informers.

20. By this time Quintus Marcius was preparing to set off for his province of Liguria, the investigations in his area being completed. He had been given as a supplementary force 3,000 Roman infantry, plus 150 cavalry, along with 5,000 infantry and 200 cavalry of the Latin League. Marcius' colleague was also assigned that same province and the same number of infantry and cavalry. The two took command of the armies led the previous year by the consuls Gaius Flaminius and Marcus Aemilius. They were further instructed by Senatorial decree to raise two new legions; and they levied from the allies and members of the Latin League 20,000 infantry and 800 cavalry, and enrolled 3,000 Roman infantry and 200 cavalry. It was decided that this entire armament, the legions excepted,* should be taken to reinforce the army in Spain. The consuls therefore put Titus Maenius in charge of the mobilization of the troops while they were tied up with their investigations.

On the completion of the investigations, it was Quintus Marcius who set out first, making for the Ligurian Apuani. Pursuing these deep into some secluded forests, which had always served as a place of retreat and shelter for the Apuani, Marcius found himself on difficult ground, cut off in a pass which his enemy had occupied ahead of him. Four thousand men were lost; and three standards of the second legion, as well as eleven banners of the allies and Latin League, fell into enemy hands, together with a large quantity of weapons which had been thrown away at various points because they impeded the Romans' flight along the woodland paths. The Ligurians gave up the chase before the Romans did their flight; and as soon as he emerged from enemy lands, the consul demobilized his army in pacified territory so that the magnitude of his troop-losses would not be evident. He could not even so erase the infamy of the débâcle, for the wood from which the Ligurians had driven him was given the name the Marcian Wood.

21. Just after this news from Liguria was made public, dispatches from Spain were read out which brought a mixture of joy and sadness. Gaius Atinius, who had left for that province as praetor two years earlier, had engaged the Lusitanians in pitched battle in the territory of Hasta. Some 6,000 of the enemy had been killed, and the rest were scattered and put to flight, with their camp taken from them. Following this, Atinius took his legions forward to assault the town of Hasta, capturing this, too, with no greater a struggle than he had the camp. But as he approached the city-walls with insufficient caution he was struck by a weapon, and died from the wound a few days later. When the letter reporting the death of the propraetor was read out, the Senate voted to send a man to overtake the praetor Gaius Calpurnius at the port of Luna and advise him that the Senate thought it appropriate that he should advance the date of his departure so that the province should not be without a governor. The man who was sent reached Luna three days later, but Calpurnius had left a few days before that.

There was also action in Hither Spain where Lucius Manlius Acidinus, who had gone to his province at the same time as Gaius Atinius, clashed with the Celtiberians. The combatants parted with the victory still undecided—the only result being that the Celtiberians moved their camp from there the next night, giving the Romans the opportunity both to bury their dead and also scoop up spoils from their enemy. The Celtiberians then put together a larger army and a few days later went on the offensive against the Romans at the town of Calagurris. No explanation has been left on record as to what it was that made them weaker when their numbers were increased. They were defeated in the field, some 12,000 men were killed, and more than 2,000 taken prisoner, and the Romans captured their camp. In fact, had Acidinus' successor not by his arrival eased the pressure exerted by the victor, the Celtiberians would have been brought to heel. The new praetors both led their armies into winter-quarters.

22. At about the time that this news arrived from Spain, the Taurian Games* were held over a two-day period for religious reasons. †Then, for ten days and with great ceremony,† Marcus Fulvius* staged the games which he had vowed during the Aetolian War. A large number of artists came from Greece to honour him, and this was also the first occasion on which competitive athletics were put on as a spectacle for the Romans. A lion and panther hunt was also staged, and the show was held on a scale and with a variety of events almost matching today's. After this there was a nine-day religious observance because of a shower of stones in Picenum that lasted three days, and especially because of the reports of fires breaking out in the sky in numerous places and setting light to the clothes of several people when there was a light breeze. In accordance with a decree of the pontiffs, a single day of public prayer was added because the temple of Ops on the Capitol had been struck by lightning. The consuls used the full-grown victims for expiation and ritually purified the city. In the same period news came from Umbria of the discovery of a hermaphrodite* of about twelve years of age, and feelings of abhorrence at this prodigy led to the consuls ordering it to be kept from Roman soil and put to death as soon as possible.

That same year some Transalpine Gauls crossed into Venetia, without looting or hostile action, and occupied a spot for founding a town not far from the present site of Aquileia. When Roman envoys were sent across the Alps to enquire into the matter, they were given the answer that the migrants had set out without the authorization of their people, who were ignorant of what they were doing in Italy.

At this time Lucius Scipio staged over a period of ten days the games which he said he had promised in a vow during the war with Antiochus, and for them used money that had been contributed for the purpose by various kings and city-states.* According to Valerius

Antias, Scipio had been sent as an ambassador to Asia in the period following his conviction and the sale of his property, in order to settle the disputes between Antiochus and Eumenes. Antias says that it was at this time that the funds were awarded to him, and performers also brought together throughout Asia. Scipio, he claims, had omitted to mention the games in the period following the war in which he said he made the vow promising them, and it was only after the embassy that discussion of them was finally raised by him in the Senate.

23. As the year drew to a close, Quintus Marcius was still absent from the city and was on the point of leaving office. Accordingly, Spurius Postumius, who had now terminated his investigations (which he conducted with the utmost integrity and diligence), dealt with the elections. The consuls elected were Appius Claudius Pulcher and Marcus Sempronius Tuditanus. The next day the following were appointed as praetors: Publius Cornelius Cethegus, Aulus Postumius Albinus, Gaius Afranius Stellio, Gaius Atilius Serranus, Lucius Postumius Tempsanus, and Marcus Claudius Marcellus.

The consul Spurius Postumius had earlier reported that his investigations had taken him along both coasts of Italy, and that he had found two colonies abandoned: Sipontum on the Adriatic and Buxentum on the Tyrrhenian Sea. Thus, at the end of the year, in accordance with a Senatorial decree, a board of triumvirs was set up by the urban praetor Titus Maenius to enrol colonists for these places. The board consisted of Lucius Scribonius Libo, Marcus Tuccius, and Gnaeus Baebius Tamphilus.

War with Perseus and the Macedonians was now imminent. The causes of the war were not those now generally accepted and did not lie with Perseus himself. Its true origins go back to Philip, who would in fact have fought the war himself had he lived longer. There was one thing that particularly galled him when conditions were imposed on him after his defeat: he had been deprived by the Senate of the right to take punitive measures against those Macedonians who had defected from him during the war; and he not been without hope of being granted this because Quinctius had, in drawing up of the peace-terms, left the entire matter in abeyance. Later on, when Antiochus had been beaten in the field at Thermopylae, there had been a division of responsibilities, with the consul Acilius attacking Heraclea and Philip attacking Lamia at the same time. But Philip had then been incensed because, on the capture of Heraclea, he had been ordered to withdraw from the walls of Lamia,* and the town had been surrendered to the Romans. The consul had calmed his wrath: in his haste to reach Naupactus, the town to which the Aetolians had retreated after their flight, he allowed Philip to make war on Athamania and Amynander, and to annex to his kingdom the cities which the Aetolians had taken from the Thessalians. It had taken no great effort to drive Amynander from Athamania and to recover a number of cities; and, in addition, Philip brought under his sway Demetrias—a strong city that was strategically positioned in every respect—and the people of Magnesia. After this he also acquired a number of cities in Thrace that were in chaos because of feuding amongst their leading citizens—for which their recently acquired independence, to which they were unaccustomed, was to blame—and he did so by allying himself with the sides that were losing these internal struggles.

24. The king's rancour towards the Romans was for the time being appeased by these acquisitions. However, he never took his mind off amassing in peacetime resources to use in time of war, whenever the occasion should arise. He augmented the income of his kingdom not just by agricultural produce and harbour dues, but also by reopening old, abandoned mines and by starting new ones in many places. In order to restore earlier population levels after the losses brought about by military defeats, he proceeded to establish a new generation of his people by forcing everyone to produce and rear children; and in addition to this he had transplanted large numbers of Thracians in Macedonia. In this way he had taken advantage of the temporary cessation of hostilities to devote all his attention to augmenting the resources of his realm.

Then a state of affairs once more arose to reawaken his resentment towards the Romans. There had been protests from the Thessalians and Perrhaebians over the occupation of their cities by Philip, and from ambassadors of Eumenes about the forceful seizure of Thracian towns and the transfer of population to Macedonia. These grievances had been given such an attentive hearing that it was quite clear that they were not being rejected. Of particular concern to the Senate had been a report that Philip was attempting to seize Aenus and Maronea—they were less concerned about the Thessalians. Athamanian representatives also came before them, and their complaints were not about being dispossessed of some part of their lands or about territorial losses, but rather about the fact that all of Athamania had fallen under the control and authority of the king. †There were, in addition,† Maronean exiles who had been driven from home for championing the cause of freedom against the king's garrison, and these brought word that Aenus, and not just Maronea, was also in Philip's hands.

Representatives had come from Philip, too, in order to clear him of these charges. The king had taken no action without the authorization of the Roman commanders, they claimed. They argued that the Thessalian, Perrhaebian, and Magnesian city-states, and the Athamanian people, along with Amynander, had been in the same position as the Aetolians. After defeating Antiochus, the consul had been preoccupied with attacking the cities of Aetolia, and had sent Philip to recover the states in question; brought into subjection by force of arms, their populations were now subject to the king. To avoid taking a decision in the absence of the king, the Senate dispatched Quintus Caecilius Metellus, Marcus Baebius Tamphilus, and Tiberius Sempronius* as its representatives to resolve the disputes, and on their arrival in Thessalian Tempe a meeting was called for all those city-states which had differences with the king.

25. At the meeting the Romans took their seats as judges, the Thessalians, Perrhaebians, and Athamanians quite clearly as the prosecution, and Philip as the defendant who was to hear the charges against him; and all the heads of the various delegations dealt with him harshly or leniently, according to their own inclinations, and according to whether they were on terms of friendship or enmity with him. The debate centred on Philippopolis, Tricca, Phaloria, Eurymenae, and other towns in the vicinity. Had these been forcibly taken and occupied by the Aetolians at a time when <they were> under Thessalian control—for that Philip had taken them from the Aetolians was not in question—or had the towns belonged to the Aetolians in the distant past? For, it was argued, Acilius had ceded them to the king on the premiss that they belonged to the Aetolians, and that they had joined the Aetolians of their own free will and not after military coercion. The argument over the Perrhaebian and Magnesian towns went along the same lines; for by seizing them as the opportunities arose the Aetolians had confused the legal claims to all of them.

In addition to these matters of dispute there were also complaints lodged by the Thessalians to the effect that, if the towns were restored to them now, Philip would hand them over looted and deserted. For, apart from the losses occasioned by the vicissitudes of war, Philip had taken off to Macedonia five hundred of their most prominent young men, and was maltreating them by putting them to work on servile tasks. Furthermore, all that he had been obliged to return to the Thessalians he had taken care to return in an unusable condition. Thebes in Pthiotis, they said, had formerly been the Thessalians' one flourishing and prosperous coastal market. The king had there seized merchant vessels which could bypass Thebes and make for Demetrias, and had thereby diverted all maritime trade to the latter port. And now he did not even stop short of violating ambassadors, who were sacrosanct under international law—he had set an ambush for them when they were going to see Titus Quinctius. The result was that all Thessalians had been thrown into such panic that nobody dared open his mouth in his own community, or in the communal meetings of the nation. The Romans, authors of their freedom, were far off, and they had a stern master sticking close to them, preventing them from profiting from the benefits provided by the Roman people. What was the use of being free if they had no freedom of expression, they asked. Even on this occasion, when they felt confidence in, and were protected by, their position as ambassadors, they were uttering laments rather than speaking out. Unless the Romans made some provision for diminishing the fear of those Greeks living close to Macedonia, and curbing the audacity of Philip, his defeat and their liberation had both been pointless. The king, they said, was like an obstinate horse; if he did not obey he should be chastened with harsher reins. Such were the bitter words of those who spoke last, while the earlier speakers had been more conciliatory, soothing Philip's anger by asking him to pardon them for speaking up for their freedom, and requesting that he renounce the severity of an overlord, accustom himself to acting as their ally and friend, and emulate the Roman people, who preferred to win allies for themselves by affection rather than intimidation.

When the Thessalians had been heard, the Perrhaebians made the claim that Gonnocondylus—renamed Olympias by Philip—belonged to Perrhaebia, and requested its return to them; and the same petition was made for Malloea and Ericinium. The

Athamanians asked for the restoration of their independence, and of the fortresses of Athenaeum and Poetneum.

26. To appear as accuser rather than defendant, Philip also began with grievances. He protested that the Thessalians had used military force to storm Menelais in Dolopia, which had formed part of his realm, and likewise that Petra in Pieria had been taken by the Thessalians and Perrhaebians. They had also annexed Xyniae, which was clearly an Aetolian town; and Parachelois, which had been under the rule of Athamania, had been unlawfully made subject to the Thessalians. As for the charges brought against him—ambushing envoys, and ports being frequently used or abandoned—the one, that he be accountable for harbours which merchants and sailors made for, was absurd, while the other was out of line with his character. For years now embassies had been incessantly bringing charges against him, either before the Roman commanders or before the Senate in Rome, but which of them, he asked, had ever been mistreated by him, even verbally? It was said that they had been ambushed once on their way to Quinctius, but details of what happened to them were not supplied. These, he claimed, were accusations laid by men looking for trumped-up charges because they had no legitimate complaint. The Thessalians were impudently and grossly taking advantage of the kindness of the Roman people—drinking down too greedily the cup of undiluted freedom, as it were, for which they had been long thirsting. Like slaves suddenly and unexpectedly set free, they were testing the limits of freedom of speech and expression, and showing off by hurling abusive insults at their masters.

Then, in a fit of temper, Philip added that the sun had not yet set on all his days, a threat which the Romans, as much as the Thessalians, took as directed against themselves. Uproar followed his remarks. When this eventually subsided, Philip then made his reply to the envoys of the Perrhaebians and Athamanians. All the city-states they were discussing were in the same situation, he told them. The consul Acilius and the Romans had granted these to him, as being cities of the enemy. If those who had made the gift wished to withdraw it, he knew he had to comply, but they would only be wronging a better and more loyal friend to please allies who were fickle and worthless. For, the king concluded, nothing produced gratitude of shorter duration than did the granting of freedom, especially in the case of people who would spoil it by misuse.

When the hearing concluded, the Roman commissioners announced their decision: the Macedonian garrisons were to be withdrawn from the cities in question, and Philip's kingdom was to be limited to the old boundaries of Macedonia. On the matter of the wrongs forming the basis of the two sides' complaints against each other, the commissioners declared a legal procedure would have to be established for resolving the contentious issues between the peoples involved and the Macedonians.

27. Having seriously offended the king, the commissioners left Tempe for Thessalonica to consider the case of the cities of Thrace. Here, spokesmen of Eumenes told them that, if the Romans wanted Aenus and Maronea to be free, their sense of decency forbade them to say more than that they advised the commissioners to leave these cities truly, and not just nominally, free, and not allow their gift to them to be filched by another. If, however, the Romans were less concerned about the states located in Thrace, then there was greater justification for Eumenes rather than Philip to have as prizes of war the lands that had belonged to Antiochus. This was justified by the services of Eumenes' father, Attalus, during the war which the Roman people fought against Philip himself, or else by Eumenes' own services, as he had shared in all the hardships and perils of the war with Antiochus on land and on sea. Besides, added the spokesmen, Eumenes actually had an advance judgement of the ten commissioners on the issue: since they had granted him the Chersonese and Lysimachia, they had evidently also granted him Maronea and Aenus, these being so close to the region as to be virtually appendages to the main award. For in Philip's case, what service towards the Roman people or what territorial right justified his imposition of garrisons on these city-states, when they were so far removed from the boundaries of Macedonia? The commissioners should have the Maroneans summoned, they said—from these they would gain more reliable information on everything to do with the situation of the cities in question.

When the representatives of the Maroneans were summoned, they stated that the king's garrison did not occupy just one spot in the city as in other communities, but several spots at the same time, and that Maronea was full of Macedonians. As a result, they said, the king's 'yes-men' had control; they were the only ones permitted to speak either in the Senate or at meetings, and these either took for themselves, or conferred on others, all the public offices. All men of worth, men who cared about liberty and the laws, were living in exile, having been driven from their country, or else they were holding their tongues, disrespected, and at the mercy of their inferiors. The delegates also added a few remarks about territorial rights. When Quintus Fabius Labeo had been in the region, they said, he had established as Philip's boundary the old royal road leading to Parorea in Thrace, which at no point went down to the sea; but Philip had later made a new road that veered off to take in the cities and farmland of the Maroneans.

28. Responding to these remarks, Philip took a very different approach from the one he had just used in dealing with the Thessalians and Perrhaebians. 'My argument is not with the Maroneans or with Eumenes,' he declared. 'It is now with you, Romans, for I have long been aware that I am getting no fair treatment from you. Restoration to me of the Macedonian communities that had defected from me during the truce I considered only fair. Not that these would have been a great addition to my realm—they are small towns and they also lie on our most remote frontiers—but it was an important precedent for keeping the other Macedonians under control. My request was denied.

'In the Aetolian war I was ordered by the consul Manius Acilius to attack Lamia where, over a long period, I was drained of strength constructing siege-works and fighting battles. Then, as I was actually scaling the walls, I was called back from an almost captured city by the consul who made me withdraw my troops. As consolation for this slight, I was allowed to recover a number of what were strongholds rather than cities in Thessaly, Perrhaebia, and Athamania. Those very strongholds, Quintus Caecilius, you took away from me again a few days ago.

'A short while ago the envoys of Eumenes took it as an indisputable fact (for heaven's sake!) that it was fairer for Eumenes than for me to have Antiochus' former possessions. I have a very different view on this. You see, Eumenes could not have remained in his kingdom if the Romans had not undertaken the war in the first place, and not simply won it. Thus he owes you a favour, not you him. As for my own kingdom, so far from any part of it being at risk, I in fact rejected the overtures of Antiochus who, to bribe me into an alliance, actually came to me with a promise of 3,000 talents, fifty decked ships, and all the city-states of Greece that I had formerly held. I chose to be his enemy even before Manius Acilius brought his army over to Greece. With that consul, moreover, I took on whatever part he assigned me in the war, and when the succeeding consul, Lucius Scipio, decided to take his army to the Hellespont by land, I did not simply grant him passage through my kingdom but even built roads, constructed bridges, and provided supplies for him. And I did this not just throughout Macedonia, but also throughout Thrace, where, apart from everything else, I was forced to establish peace with the barbarians. In view of my support—let me not say "my services"—for you, which course should you have followed, you Romans? Should you have done something to increase and extend my kingdom, or should you have stripped from me what I held either by my own right or through your beneficence—which is exactly what you are doing now? The city-states of the Macedonians which you admit were part of my realm are not being restored to me. Eumenes is coming to plunder me as if I were Antiochus, and (for heaven's sake!) is using the decree of the ten commissioners as a cover for his shameless perversion of justice—when it is by this that he can be most effectively refuted and shown to be in the wrong. For there is an absolutely explicit and clear statement in it that the Chersonese and Lysimachia are awarded to Eumenes, but where on earth are Aenus, Maronea, and the city-states of Thrace added? Will Eumenes gain from you what he did not even presume to ask of them, on the pretext that he was granted it by them?

'It is important to know where I stand with you. If you are set on harassing me as a private enemy and as an enemy of your people, carry on with the actions you have begun; but if you have some respect for me as an ally and as a king well-disposed to you, I beg you not to judge me deserving of such ill-treatment.'

29. The king's words made a considerable impression on the commissioners who accordingly made a non-committal response that left the matter unresolved. If the states in question had been granted to Eumenes by decree of the ten commissioners, they said, they were not altering anything; and if Philip had captured them in war he would have them as the prize of victory under the rules of war. If neither condition obtained, their decision was that judgement of the issue be reserved for the Senate, and that the garrisons

stationed in the cities involved be withdrawn, so that everything should remain open for discussion.

Such were the circumstances that particularly set Philip against the Romans; so one can see that war was not fomented by his son Perseus from a new set of motives, but was, for the reasons given, handed down from the father to the son.

At Rome there was no thought of war with Macedon. The proconsul Lucius Manlius had returned from Spain. In the temple of Bellona he requested a triumph of the Senate, and the extent of his achievements lent weight to his petition. What stood in the way was precedent: ancestral custom had established that nobody should triumph who had not brought his army home, unless he had passed on to his successor a province that had been totally subdued and pacified. Manlius was none the less granted the compromise honour of entering the city in ovation. His procession included 52 golden crowns as well as 132 pounds of gold and 16,300 pounds of silver. He also announced in the Senate that his quaestor Quintus Fabius* was bringing 10,000 pounds of silver and 80 pounds of gold, and that he would deposit this in the treasury, too.

There was a dangerous slave revolt in Apulia that year. Tarentum was the province of Lucius Postumius, who conducted a strict inquiry into a conspiracy of shepherds whose banditry had made roads and public pasture lands unsafe. He convicted some 7,000 men. Many of them fled and many were put to death. After being long delayed in the city conducting troop-levies, the consuls eventually left for their provinces.

30. In Spain, at the beginning of spring of that same year, the praetors Gaius Calpurnius and Lucius Quinctius brought their troops from winter-quarters and joined up in Baeturia. They then advanced into Carpetania, the site of the enemy camp, ready to prosecute the war together with a shared plan of action. Not far from the cities of Toletum and Dipo fighting broke out amongst the foragers. These were given support from their camps on both sides, and gradually all the troops were brought out into the line of battle. In this irregular encounter both the home ground and the nature of the fighting favoured the enemy. The two Roman armies were routed and forced back into their camp, but the enemy failed to press their advantage against the demoralized Romans. The Roman praetors feared the camp would be attacked the next day, and so, in the still of

the night that followed, they gave a silent signal and led the army away. At first light the Spaniards ordered their line of battle and advanced to the rampart. Entering a camp which was unexpectedly deserted, they pillaged the things that the Romans had left behind in the confusion of the night. They then returned to their own camp and spent a few days of inaction at their base. About 5,000 Romans and allies were killed in the battle and the retreat. The enemy armed themselves with the spoils taken from the dead and set off from there towards the River Tagus.

The Roman praetors meanwhile spent all this time bringing together auxiliary forces from the allied Spanish communities, and rebuilding the confidence of the men who were terrified after the defeat. When they were satisfied with the strength of their force, and the men were also demanding to take on the enemy to wipe out their earlier disgrace, they set off and encamped twelve miles from the River Tagus. Breaking camp at the third watch, they came in square formation from there to the banks of the Tagus, which they reached at dawn. The enemy camp was on a hill on the other side of the river. The river presented shallows at two points, and the praetors immediately took the army across at these, Calpurnius on the right and Quinctius on the left. The enemy made no move, amazed at the sudden arrival of the Romans, and they proceeded to discuss the situation at a time when they could have been striking panic into their adversaries, now apprehensively crossing the river. In the mean time, the Romans brought over all their baggage, which they concentrated in one spot; then, seeing that the enemy were now starting to move and that they themselves had no time to fortify a camp, they drew up a line of battle. Calpurnius' fifth legion and Quinctius' eighth were set in the centre, and this constituted the major strength of the entire army. They had before them an open plain as far as the enemy camp, with no fear of ambush.

31. When the Spaniards saw the two columns of Romans on their bank of the river, they suddenly poured out of their camp and came running to the fight in order to catch them before they could come together and form up. It was a furious engagement at the outset. The Spaniards were in high spirits after their recent victory, and the Roman soldiers were spurred on by the disgrace which was unfamiliar to them. The fiercest clash was at the centre where the two strongest legions were in action. When the enemy became aware

that these could be pushed back by no other means, they proceeded to fight with a wedge-configuration, putting pressure on the centre with more and more men in tighter formation. The praetor Calpurnius saw that his line was in difficulties, and he swiftly dispatched his officers Titus Quinctilius Varus and Lucius Iuventius Thalna to encourage each of the legions. He told them to explain and make clear to the troops that all their hopes of victory and of holding Spain lay with them, and that if they gave ground no member of the army would ever again see the far bank of the Tagus, let alone Italy. Taking the cavalry of the two legions, Calpurnius himself rode a short distance around the field and made a side-on charge at the enemy wedge that was pressing the centre. Quinctius attacked the other enemy flank with †his† cavalry. But Calpurnius' cavalry were putting up a far more determined fight, and the praetor more than the others. He was the first to strike an enemy, and he threw himself with such vigour into the thick of the fray that one could hardly tell to which side he belonged. The cavalry were inspired by the praetor's conspicuous valour, and the infantry by that of the cavalry.

Humiliation descended on the senior centurions at the sight of their praetor amidst the weapons of the enemy. Each of them urged on the standard-bearers, telling them to carry forward the standards and ordering the men to follow swiftly. A shout once more went up from the whole line, and it was now as if their assault were being made from higher ground. Just like a torrent, they swept away and smashed the panic-stricken enemy. Resistance was impossible as they surged forward in successive waves. The cavalry chased the fleeing Spaniards to their camp and, merging with the enemy horde, forced their way inside the rampart. There the fight was renewed by the men left to guard the camp, and the Roman cavalry were obliged to dismount. As the cavalry entered the fray they were joined by the fifth legion, and then other troops poured in as they were able. Spaniards were being cut down throughout the camp, and no more than 4,000 men made good their escape. About 3,000 who had held on to their weapons then occupied a nearby hill; another 1,000, half-armed at best, wandered through the fields.

The enemy had numbered more than 35,000, and this tiny fraction was all that survived the battle. One hundred and thirty-two standards were captured. Not many more than 600 Romans and allies fell, plus some 150 provincial auxiliaries, but the loss of five military tribunes and a few Roman horsemen made the victory appear particularly bloody. The Romans remained in the enemy camp because they had not had time to fortify their own. At an assembly the following day the cavalry were praised by Gaius Calpurnius and presented with decorations for their mounts. Calpurnius declared that it was thanks mostly to them that the enemy had been routed, and the camp occupied and taken by storm. The other praetor, Quinctius, presented his own cavalry with ornamental chains and clasps. Presentations were also made to a large number of centurions from the armies of the two praetors, particularly those who held the centre.

32. On the conclusion of the troop-levies and their other duties in Rome, the consuls led the army against the Ligurians, their sphere of command. Sempronius set off from Pisae against the Ligurian Apuani and, by laying waste their fields, and burning their villages and fortresses, he opened up the pass all the way to the River Macra and the port of Luna. The enemy occupied a hill that had been the ancient seat of their ancestors, but the difficulty of the terrain was overcome and they were forcefully dislodged from there, as well. Moreover, amongst the Ligurian Ingauni, Appius Claudius emulated the attainments and courage of his colleague, fighting a number of successful engagements. In addition, he stormed six towns of the Ingauni, taking many thousands of prisoners and beheading forty-three men who were responsible for the war.

The time for the elections was now at hand. Because his brother Publius Claudius was standing for the consulship, Claudius reached Rome before Sempronius, who had been assigned by lot the supervision of the elections. Publius' rivals among the patricians were Lucius Aemilius, Quintus Fabius,* and Servius Sulpicius Galba. These were seasoned candidates who, after earlier defeats, were now seeking an office they felt to be all the more rightfully theirs because it had been initially refused them. The race between the four candidates was made even closer by the fact that election of more than one patrician was not permitted.* There were influential plebeian candidates, as well: Lucius Porcius, Quintus Terentius Culleo, and Gnaeus Baebius Tamphilus. After earlier defeats these, too, were now hoping to gain at last an office that had been long in coming to them. The one new candidate amongst all of them was Claudius. The general belief was that the men destined for office were Quintus

Fabius Labeo and Lucius Porcius Licinus. But the consul Claudius was dashing around the whole forum with his brother, and without his lictors, despite protests from opponents and most of the Senate. These told him that he should remember that he was first and foremost a consul of the Roman people and only after that the brother of Publius Claudius. Why, they asked, could he not simply take his place on the tribunal as an umpire of the elections, or else as a silent observer? But Claudius could not be deterred from his active canvassing. In addition, the elections were on a number of occasions disrupted by quarrels among the plebeian tribunes—who were either fighting against the consul or else in support of his cause—until Appius eventually succeeded in bringing about Fabius' defeat and his brother's election. Publius Claudius Pulcher was elected, contrary to his and everyone else's expectations. Lucius Porcius Licinus gained his office because amongst the plebeians the competition was characterized by moderation, rather than Claudian violence, on the part of supporters.

The praetorian elections followed, and in these Gaius Decimius Flavus, Publius Sempronius Longus, Publius Cornelius Cethegus, Quintus Naevius Matho, Gaius Sempronius Blaesus, and Aulus Terentius Varro were elected. Such were events on the home and military front in the year of the consulship of Appius Claudius and Marcus Sempronius.

33. Quintus Caecilius, Marcus Baebius, and Tiberius Sempronius had been sent to mediate disputes in which Philip was embroiled with Eumenes and the Thessalian city-states; and at the start of the following year, after these men reported the findings of their mission, the consuls Publius Claudius and Lucius Porcius also brought into the Senate representatives of those kings and of the cities. There was a restatement by both parties of the arguments that had been presented to the commissioners in Greece, and the Senators thereupon decreed that a second, newly constituted commission, led by Appius Claudius, be sent to Macedonia and Greece to check on whether the Thessalians and Perrhaebians had indeed had their cities returned to them. The commissioners had the further mandate of ensuring the withdrawal of the garrisons from Aenus and Maronea, and the liberation of the entire Thracian coastline from Philip and the Macedonians. They were also instructed to go to the Peloponnese, which the earlier commissioners had left in a

more unsettled state than if they had not come in the first place. Apart from everything else, they had been sent off with no reply to their queries, and had not been granted their request for a meeting with the Achaean council. Quintus Caecilius lodged a stern protest about this, and at the same time the Spartans complained that their walls had been destroyed, their common people deported to Achaea and sold into slavery, and the laws of Lycurgus, which had been the basis of their state up to that time, repealed. The Achaeans sought in particular to answer the charge of having refused to call a meeting of the council, and did so by reading out a law which precluded convening the council except on questions of peace and war, or when representatives came from the Senate with a letter or written instructions. To prevent such a plea being used in future, the Senate pointed out to them that they had a duty to ensure that Roman delegates always had the opportunity of meeting the council of their people, just as the Achaeans were granted an audience with the Senate any time they wished.

34. After the embassies were dismissed and Philip was notified by his representatives that he was obliged to vacate the cities and withdraw his garrisons, he was incensed with everyone, but it was on the Maroneans that he vented his wrath. He instructed Onomastus, his commander of the coast, to put to death the leaders of the faction opposed to him. Employing a certain Cassander, one of the king's party and a long-time resident of Maronea, Onomastus let some Thracians into the town at night and produced carnage such as when a city is taken in war. The Roman commissioners protested against such ruthless action against the unoffending Maroneans and such high-handed behaviour towards the Roman people—men being butchered as enemies when the Senate had voted that they should have their independence restored—but the king's response was to deny the least involvement on the part of himself or any of his supporters. The Maroneans, he said, had been fighting amongst themselves after political dissension, with some trying to bring the state to support him, and others to support Eumenes. The Romans could easily establish this—they should question the Maroneans themselves (Philip was in no doubt that the Maroneans were all terror-stricken after the recent blood-bath and that no one would dare open his mouth against him). Appius replied the case was open and shut and required no investigation as though it were in doubt. If Philip

wished to exculpate himself, he added, he should send to Rome Onomastus and Cassander, the alleged perpetrators of the deed, so the Senate could interrogate them. This suggestion at first so shook the king that his colour drained and he could not control his expression. At last he composed himself and said that, if that really was the commissioners' wish, he would send Cassander, who had been at Maronea but, he added, he wondered how Onomastus could be implicated when he had not even been anywhere near Maronea, much less in it. In fact, Philip was more inclined to have Onomastus spared. He had more respect for him as a friend, and he also feared him much more as a potential informer—he had personally discussed the affair with him and had used him as an intermediary and confidant in many operations of this kind. It is also thought that when men were sent to escort him through Epirus to the sea, Cassander was poisoned to prevent any possibility of his information leaking out.

35. In leaving their meeting with Philip the commissioners made clear their dissatisfaction with the entire situation, and Philip was left in no doubt that he had to go to war again. His strength was not yet sufficient for this, and so to gain time he decided to send his younger son, Demetrius, to Rome both to clear him of the charges against him, and at the same time to allay the anger of the Senate. The king was confident that Demetrius would, despite his youth, make something of an impression, for he had given an indication of possessing the character of a king while he was a hostage at Rome. Meanwhile, Philip set off on an expedition, ostensibly to assist the people of Byzantium but really to strike fear into the Thracian chieftains. He defeated the latter in a single battle and took the chieftain Amadocus prisoner. He then returned to Macedonia, after sending men to incite the barbarians living along the River Hister* to invade Italy.

In the Peloponnese, too, people were awaiting the arrival of the Roman commissioners—they had been instructed to proceed to Achaea from Macedonia—and the praetor Lycortas called a session of the council so that the Achaeans would have arguments formulated in advance with which to meet them. At the meeting, the Spartan question was discussed. Enemies before, the Spartans had now become their accusers, it was said, and there was a danger of their being more to be feared in defeat than they had been when they were at war. For the Achaeans had had the Romans as their allies in the war, they reasoned; but at that moment those same Romans looked more favorably on the Spartans than they did on the Achaeans. Even Areus and Alcibiades,* both of them exiles who had been restored by the good offices of the Achaeans, had gone on a mission to Rome against the Achaean people, who deserved well of them for the favour they had received; and they had employed such vindictive language as to give the impression of having been driven from their country rather than restored to it!

The cry went up on every side that Lycortas should present a motion mentioning these men by name; and since all the proceedings were guided by anger and not reason, the two were condemned to death. A few days later the Roman commissioners arrived and were granted a meeting with the council at Clitor in Arcadia.

36. Before they could conduct any business, the Achaeans were panic-stricken at the thought of how one-sided the debate was going to be, for they could see in the commissioners' company Areus and Alcibiades, the men whom they had condemned to death at the last session of the council. Not one of them dared open his mouth. Appius now revealed the Senate's displeasure over the grievances brought to it by the Spartans. First there was the murder at Compasium of the men who had come to defend themselves after being summoned by Philopoemen. Then, after this barbarous treatment of the victims, the Achaeans would not allow their savagery to let up anywhere—they had torn down the walls of a renowned city, repealed laws of the greatest antiquity, and removed the Lycurgan system that was famous the world over.

After these comments from Appius, Lycortas made the following reply, partly in his capacity as praetor but also because he belonged to the party of Philopoemen, who had been responsible for all that had happened in Sparta:

'Speaking before you, Appius Claudius, is more difficult than speaking, as we recently did, before the Senate in Rome. For on that occasion it was a case of responding to the accusations of the Spartans; on this occasion you, the judges before whom we must present our case, are yourselves our accusers. We accept this unfair situation in the hope that you will hear us from the viewpoint of an arbitrator, setting aside the impassioned rhetoric with which you spoke a moment ago. At all events, when, a little while back, you repeated the complaints which the Macedonians made here at an earlier date before Quintus Caecilius, and subsequently in Rome, I began to think that my response was not being made to *you*, but to *them* before you.

'You charge us with the murder of the men who were killed after being summoned to plead their case by the praetor Philopoemen. This is an accusation, Romans, which I feel should not have even have been made against us *before* you, much less made *by* you. Why? Because it was stipulated in your treaty that the Lacedaemonians were to keep their hands off the maritime cities. They took up arms and by an attack at night seized the cities which they had been told to avoid. If Titus Quinctius and a Roman army had been in the Peloponnese, as they had been earlier, it is with them that these captured and oppressed populations would certainly have sought refuge. Since you were a long way off, with whom would they seek refuge but with us, your allies? They had earlier seen us bringing assistance to Gythium, and attacking Sparta along with you and for the same reason. Thus it was on your behalf that we undertook a just and righteous war. Others applaud this action; even the Lacedaemonians cannot condemn it; and the gods themselves approved it by giving us the victory. So how can acts that conform to the rules of war be called into question?

'In fact, most of what happened has nothing to do with us. Our responsibility is limited to having called to account men who had incited the masses to arms, stormed and pillaged the coastal towns, and murdered their leading citizens. But as for their being killed when they were entering our camp, that is your fault, Areus and Alcibiades—you who are accusing us, for heaven's sake—not ours. The Spartan exiles, including these two, were with us at that time, and they believed themselves to be under attack because they had chosen the coastal towns as their abode. It was they who launched the attack—on the men whom they angrily perceived as being responsible for their banishment from their country, and for depriving them now even of a secure old age in exile. So it was Lacedaemonians, not Achaeans, killing Lacedaemonians, and it is beside the point to argue about the justice or injustice of their deaths.

37. 'Ah, but those other acts are your responsibility, men of Achaea, you will say: you repealed the ancient laws and system of Lycurgus, and tore down the walls. How can these two charges be

brought against us by the same people? For the walls of Sparta were not built by Lycurgus; they were raised a few years ago for the purpose of quashing the Lycurgan system. It was the tyrants who put them in place in recent times to be a bastion and fortification for themselves, not for the state; and should Lycurgus arise from the dead today, he would be pleased with their destruction, and would say he now recognized his homeland and the Sparta of old. You should not have waited for Philopoemen or the Achaeans; you yourselves, men of Sparta, should have dismantled and demolished with your own hands all these vestiges of tyranny. For these stood as the ugly scars of your enslavement. Though you had been free and without walls for almost eight centuries, and at times had been the leaders of Greece,* you were slaves for a hundred years, imprisoned by walls that were thrown around you like shackles. As for the abolition of the legal system, I personally think that it was the tyrants who deprived the Spartans of the ancient laws. We did not take their laws from them—they did not have them at that point—but gave them ours. Nor do I think we did badly by their state, since we made them part of our league and combined them with us so that the whole Peloponnese should be a unified body and one confederation. In my opinion, if we ourselves were living under one set of laws and had imposed another set on them, then they could complain and be indignant at being unfairly treated.

'I realize, Appius Claudius, that the language I have employed thus far is not that used by allies to allies, nor indeed that used by an independent people; really it is the language of slaves arguing before masters. For if they were not just empty words that the herald used when you bade the Achaeans to be the first to accept their freedom, if the treaty was ratified, and if our alliance and friendship are based on equality—then why do I not ask what you Romans did after capturing Capua since you demand a reckoning of what we Achaeans did after defeating the Spartans in war? Say some of them were killed by us. So what? Did you not behead Campanian senators? We tore down their walls. In your case it was not merely the walls of Capua that you took, but the city and lands as well.

'The treaty, you say, only appears to be on equal terms; in fact, on the Achaean side there is only freedom dependent on others' favour, while on the Roman side there is real power. I recognize this, Appius, and I do not feel aggrieved if that is what is expected of me.

But whatever the power-differential between the Romans and the Achaeans, I beg you not to let men who are your enemies and ours be as well-placed—no, better-placed!—in your regard as we, your allies. For we put them on an equal footing with us when we conferred our laws on them and made them members of the Achaean League. But what satisfies the victors is insufficient for the vanquished, and your enemies are asking for more than what your allies have. Things that have been hallowed and sanctified by the taking of oaths and by the creation of written records carved on stone, to provide a record for all time—these things they are preparing to remove, thus making us into perjurers. And while we have respect for you, Romans, and even fear, if that is what you want, we have more respect and fear for the immortal gods.'

Lycortas was heard with applause by most of his audience, and everyone felt that his speech was in keeping with the dignity of his office. It was thus readily apparent that the Romans could not maintain their dignity by treading softly. At this point Appius declared that he strongly advised the Achaeans to try to enter the Romans' good graces while they could still act according to their own inclinations; later they might be doing this against their wishes and under compulsion. Appius' remark was received with a groan from all present, but it filled them with fear of refusing to carry out his orders. Their one request was that the Romans undertake such modifications as they thought appropriate *vis-à-vis* the Spartans, and not trammel the Achaeans with a religious difficulty of invalidating what they had sanctioned by oath. The sole measure repealed was the recent condemnation passed on Areus and Alcibiades.

38. When the allocation of consular and praetorian provinces was discussed in Rome at the beginning of that year, the consuls were assigned the Ligurians because there were no hostilities elsewhere. The praetorian sortition was as follows:

Gaius Decimius Flavus	urban jurisdiction
Publius Cornelius Cethegus	citizens/foreigners
Gaius Sempronius Blaesus	Sicily
Quintus Naevius Matho	Sardinia (and also investigation into poisonings)
Aulus Terentius Varro	Hither Spain
Publius Sempronius Longus	Farther Spain

It was about this time that the legates Lucius Iuventius Thalna and Titus Quinctilius Varus arrived from these latter two provinces. They explained to the Senate that a war of great proportions had been decisively concluded in Spain, and at the same time requested that honour be paid to the immortal gods for such great success in the campaign and that the praetors be allowed to bring back their armies. A two-day period of public thanksgiving was decreed, but the Senators ordered the question of bringing back the legions to be held over until the armies of the consuls and praetors should be discussed. A few days later the consuls were each assigned a pair of legions—those which had been commanded by Appius Claudius and Marcus Sempronius—for service against the Ligurians.

A bitter quarrel over the armies in Spain arose between the new praetors and the friends of the absent ones, Calpurnius and Quinctius. Each side had plebeian tribunes and a consul supporting it. One party threatened to veto the decree if the Senate voted to bring home the armies, the other to allow no further decision to be taken if the veto were so used. Eventually the influence of the absent men was overcome, and a Senatorial decree was passed authorizing the praetors to enlist 4,000 Roman infantry and 400 cavalry to take with them to Spain, as well as 5,000 infantry and 500 cavalry from the allies and the Latin League. After distributing these men amongst the four legions, the praetors were to demobilize men according to how far the complement of 5,000 infantry and 300 cavalry was surpassed in each legion They were to let go first the men who had completed their terms of service, and then those individuals whom Calpurnius and Quinctius had found to have performed most gallantly in the field.

39. This dispute settled, another immediately arose with the death of the praetor Gaius Decimius. Candidates for the office were the previous year's aediles Gnaeus Sicinius and Lucius Pupius, the *flamen Dialis** Gaius Valerius, and Quintus Fulvius Flaccus. The last campaigned without the white toga because he was curule aedile designate,* but did so with greater vigour than all of them, making it a race between him and the *flamen Dialis*. In the early stages Flaccus seemed to be running level with his rival, and then even to overtake him, at which point some of the plebeian tribunes maintained that his candidacy should not be recognized because it was not possible for one person to assume or hold two offices concurrently, especially

curule offices. Others were of the opinion that he should be freed of the legal restrictions so that the people should have the opportunity to elect whomsoever they wished as praetor.

The consul Lucius Porcius from the start held the view that he should not accept Flaccus' candidacy. Then, to have Senatorial authorization for his action, he convened a meeting of the Senators and told them he was putting the matter to them. He did this, he said, because there was no constitutional sanction, or precedent acceptable in a free state, for a curule aedile designate campaigning for the praetorship; and unless they had other views he intended holding the election in accordance with the law. The Senators decreed that Lucius Porcius, the consul, should discuss the matter with Quintus Fulvius so that the latter would not impede the holding of a legally constituted election of a praetor to replace Gaius Decimius. When the consul had the discussion, in accordance with the decision of the Senate, Flaccus replied that he would do nothing that was beneath his dignity.

By this evasive response Flaccus had raised hopes in the minds of people who made the remark fit in with their wishes that he would defer to the authority of the Senate. As for the election, however, he campaigned even more vigorously than before, charging that the gift of the Roman people was being taken out of his hands by the consul and the Senate. Antipathy towards him was being fomented over the double tenure of office, he said, as if it were not obvious that he would immediately relinquish the aedileship on becoming praetor elect. Seeing the candidate's determination growing, and public favour veering more and more towards him, the consul suspended the election and convened the Senate.

A well-attended session decided that since the authority of the Senators had had no effect on Flaccus, the question should be raised with him before the people. An assembly was called, and the consul brought up the issue. Not even at that point was Flaccus dissuaded from his purpose. He thanked the Roman people for their enthusiastic support for his election to the praetorship on every occasion that they had been given the opportunity to express their wishes, and said that he had no intention of betraying that support from his fellow citizens. So determined a comment inspired such enthusiasm for him that he would certainly have become praetor had the consul been willing to entertain his nomination. The tribunes then engaged in a bitter altercation, both amongst themselves and with the consul, until the Senate was convened by the consul. At this meeting the following decree was passed: since a legally constituted election to replace a praetor was being impeded by the obstinacy of Quintus Flaccus and the misguided support he was receiving from the people, the Senate was of the opinion that the number of praetors was sufficient. They further decided that Publius Cornelius should hold both jurisdictions in the city and supervise the games for Apollo.

40. The election was thus suspended through a judicious and courageous decision of the Senate, but a second now came up which was marked by more intense competition, the position being more important and the candidates more numerous and powerful. There was fierce rivalry amongst the candidates for the censorship—the patricians Lucius Valerius Flaccus, Publius and Lucius Scipio, Gnaeus Manlius Vulso, and Lucius Furius Purpureo, and the plebeians Marcus Porcius Cato, Marcus Fulvius Nobilior, Tiberius Sempronius Longus, and Marcus Sempronius Tuditanus. Although these were patricians and plebeians from the most eminent families, Marcus Porcius stood head and shoulders above them all. In this man there was such strength of intellect and character that it was obvious that he would have achieved success for himself whatever station he had been born to. He lacked none of the expertise appropriate to the conduct of private business or of affairs of state, and was equally adept in affairs of the city and of the farm. Some men have been promoted to the highest offices by their legal expertise, others by rhetorical ability or by a distinguished military record; but Cato's versatile talents covered all fields so evenly that one might say that whatever he was currently engaged in was the specialization for which he had been born. In combat he was a valiant soldier with a brilliant record in many famous battles, and he was also an outstanding general after he reached the higher offices. In peacetime, too, he was extremely well-informed if consulted on the law, and displayed great eloquence if he had to plead a case. Nor was he simply one of those who, though his eloquence bloomed while he was alive, left no record of his speaking ability; in fact, his eloquence remains alive and vigorous, immortalized in all manner of written texts. There are numerous extant speeches written in defence of himself and others, and many prosecuting other people. He ground down his enemies

not simply by prosecuting them but also in the process of making his own defence. The vendettas mounted against him—and which he mounted against others—were all too numerous, and you could not easily say which was the greater, the pressure put on him by the nobility, or his baiting of the nobility. He was undoubtedly a fractious personality with a sharp and over-free tongue; but he was possessed of a character immune to the base appetites and of a strict integrity, and he had no regard for influence or wealth. In frugality and ability to face hardship and danger, he was physically and mentally almost hard as iron, and was not even crushed by old age which breaks down everything. At eighty-six he defended himself in court, delivering in person a speech of his own composition, and in his ninetieth year he arraigned Servius Galba before the people.

41. Running for office at this time, Cato had the nobility against him, as he did throughout his life. All the candidates—with the exception of Lucius Flaccus, his colleague in the consulship—had formed a cabal to prevent his election to office. This was not merely to increase their chances of attaining the position themselves, or because they objected to seeing a 'new man' as censor. They also anticipated that his censorship would be strict and would endanger the reputation of many, for he had been harmed by a number of people and was eager to inflict harm himself. Even during his campaign at this time he was making threats, charging that opposition to him came from such men as feared a forthright and tough censorship. At the same time he also gave his support to Lucius Valerius, maintaining that only with him as his colleague could he chasten the new wave of vice and revive traditional morality. People were fired by his words, and over the objections of the nobility they not only elected Marcus Porcius censor but also gave him Lucius Valerius Flaccus as his colleague.

After the election of the censors, the consuls and praetors set off for their provinces, with the exception of Quintus Naevius. The latter's departure for Sardinia was delayed for no less than four months by his investigations into cases of poisoning, most of which he conducted outside Rome in the towns and market-centres, as had seemed more convenient. If one chooses to believe Valerius Antias, Naevius found some 2,000 people guilty. In addition, the praetor Lucius Postumius, who had been allotted Tarentum as his province, punished some widespread conspiracies by shepherds, and also painstakingly mopped up what remained of the Bacchanalian investigation. There were large numbers of people in hiding in that area of Italy after failing to appear in response to their summons, or after forfeiting their bond. Some of these Postumius adjudged guilty and others he arrested and sent to the Senate in Rome. These were all incarcerated by Publius Cornelius.

42. There was peace in Farther Spain following the crushing defeat of the Lusitanians in the most recent hostilities. In Hither Spain, Aulus Terentius, operating amongst the Suessetani, took the town of Corbio using siege-sheds and earthworks, and sold off the prisoners. After that the closer province also enjoyed a tranquil winter. The erstwhile praetors Gaius Calpurnius Piso and Lucius Quinctius returned to Rome where both were accorded a triumph with the enthusiastic approval of the Senate. Gaius Calpurnius celebrated his triumph over the Lusitanians and the Celtiberians first, and in his procession carried 83 golden crowns and 12,000 pounds of silver. A few days later Lucius Quinctius Crispinus also triumphed over the Lusitanians and Celtiberians, with the same quantity of gold and silver transported in the triumphal procession.

The censors Marcus Porcius and Lucius Valerius revised Senate membership in an atmosphere of suspense mingled with apprehension. They ejected seven from the body, including one man well-known both because of his noble birth and the offices he had held: the ex-consul Lucius Quinctius Flamininus. It is said that the practice of the censors affixing the mark of infamy to the names of those removed from the Senate dates to a period within the memory of those Senators. Now while there are extant other vitriolic speeches by Cato against men whom he either expelled from the Senate or deprived of their horses, by far the most scathing is the speech he made against Lucius Quinctius; and had Cato delivered this as a prosecutor before the use of the mark of infamy, instead of as censor after its employment, keeping Lucius Quinctius in the Senate would have been impossible even for his brother Titus Quinctius had he been censor at the time!

Amongst the charges made against Quinctius by Cato was one of having induced the Carthaginian Philip, a famous male prostitute and a favourite of Quinctius, to come from Rome to his province of Gaul, by holding out to him the hope of substantial gifts. Cato claimed that the boy, in playful banter, would often scold the consul for taking him away from Rome right before a gladiatorial show to provide his lover with his paid services. According to Cato the two happened to be having dinner and were already flushed with wine when word was brought to them at table that a Boian nobleman had come as a deserter with his children, and that he wished to meet the consul to have a guarantee of protection from him in person. The Boian was brought into the tent where he proceeded to address the consul by means of an interpreter. As the man was speaking, Quinctius said to the catamite: 'You missed your gladiatorial show. Do you want to see this Gaul dying now?' The boy nodded to him, only half-seriously, and at the nod of a catamite the consul drew his sword, which was hanging up above his head, and first of all landed a blow on the head of the Gaul while he was still talking. Then, as the man fled, all the time begging for the protection of the Roman people and of those who were present, Quintius thrust the sword into his side.

43. Not having read Cato's speech, and since he had accepted uncorroborated hearsay, Valerius Antias presents another version, though it has similarities in the sex and brutality involved. At Placentia, according to Antias, a woman of some notoriety, with whom Quinctius was completely infatuated, had been invited to dine with him. At the dinner, Quinctius was showing off to the whore, and in the course of his remarks he commented on the severity with which he had handled his court-cases, and on the large number of condemned men he then had in irons and whom he intended to behead. The woman, who was reclining below him on the couch, observed at that point that she had never seen anyone conduct a beheading, and that was something she really would like to see. The indulgent lover thereupon gave orders for one of the poor wretches to be dragged before him, and then beheaded him with an axe.

This was a ruthless and heinous crime, whether it was perpetrated in the manner alleged by the censor or as described by Valerius: a human victim sacrificed, and a table bespattered with blood, to provide a spectacle for a shameless whore lying in the consul's arms! And that taking place in a setting of drinking and feasting when it was the custom to make libations to the gods and offer prayers of benediction! At the end of Cato's speech, a proposal is made to Quinctius. If he denied the incident happened, and rejected all the other charges against him, he should put down a security in his defence; but if he admitted the charges, why should he think anyone would feel sympathy for his disgrace when he had made a party-game out of a man's life-blood while he was deranged with drink and lust?

44. In the review of the equestrian class Lucius Scipio Asiagenes* had his horse taken from him.* Cato's censorship was also rigorous and severe on all classes in census assessments. Tax officials were instructed to assess at ten times their market value decorative articles, women's dresses, and carriages worth more than 15,000 *asses*.* Slaves under twenty years of age who had fetched 10,000 *asses* or more since the last *lustrum* he likewise ordered to be assessed at ten times their market value. All these items were to be taxed at a rate of three *asses* per thousand.

The censors shut off all public water supplied to any private building or private land; and structures owned by private individuals that had been built or erected on public land they demolished within thirty days. They next contracted out works that were to be financed by moneys officially designated for the purpose: the paving of cisterns with stone, the cleaning of sewers where necessary, and the construction of new ones on the Aventine and other areas where none yet existed. They also completed projects independently of each other, Flaccus building a causeway at the Neptunian waters to provide a public footpath, and a road across the hill at Formiae; and Cato purchasing for public use two auction rooms in the Lautumiae, the Maenian and Titian, and four shops, and also constructing there a basilica which was called the Porcian Basilica. Furthermore, they charged the highest rates in contracting out tax-collection, and paid the lowest to creditors for commissioned works. When the Senate was moved by the tearful entreaties of the *publicani** to order that these contracts be revoked and new ones issued, the censors issued an edict that removed from the bidding those who had not taken seriously their original contracts, and then placed all the same works at only slightly reduced figures. It was a remarkable censorship, full of controversies that hounded Marcus Porcius throughout his life, since it was to him that its stringent character was attributed.

That same year saw the establishment of two colonies: Potentia in the territory of Picenum, and Pisaurum in Gallic territory. Colonists were each granted six acres. The land was distributed and the colonies established by the same triumvirs, Quintus Fabius Labeo,

Marcus Fulvius Flaccus and Quintus Fulvius Nobilior. The consuls of that year achieved nothing of note in either the domestic or military sphere.

45. They oversaw the election as consuls for the following year of Marcus Claudius Marcellus and Quintus Fabius Labeo.

On 15 March, the day of their entry into the consulship, Marcus Claudius and Quintus Fabius raised the question of their own provinces and those of the praetors. The praetors who had been elected were Gaius Valerius (the *flamen Dialis* who had also run for the office the previous year), Spurius Postumius Albinus, Publius Cornelius Sisenna, Lucius Pupius, Lucius Iulius, and Gnaeus Sicinius. The consuls were assigned Liguria as their province, with the same armies which Publius Claudius and Lucius Porcius had commanded. The Spanish provinces, along with their armies, were retained for the praetors of the previous year without use of the lot. A sortition was authorized for the praetors, with the condition attached that the *flamen Dialis* be assigned as his sphere one of the jurisdictions at Rome (and he drew the one concerning foreigners).

The others received:

Cornelius Sisenna	urban jurisdiction
Spurius Postumius	Sicily
Lucius Pupius	Apulia
Lucius Iulius	Gaul
Gnaeus Sicinius	Sardinia

Lucius Iulius was instructed to hasten his departure; as noted above, some Transalpine Gauls had crossed into Italy by a hitherto unknown route through the mountain passes, and were building a city in what is now the territory of Aquileia. The praetor's orders were to stop them, but without military force, as far as that was possible. If armed intervention were required to restrain them, Iulius was to inform the consuls, one of whom, the Senate had decided, was to lead the legions against the Gauls.

At the end of the previous year an election had been held to appoint an augur to replace the late Gnaeus Cornelius Lentulus, and Spurius Postumius Albinus had been elected.

46. At the beginning of this year the pontifex maximus Publius Licinius Crassus died. Marcus Sempronius Tuditanus was co-opted as pontiff in his place, and then Gaius Servilius Geminus was elected to the position of pontifex maximus. A public sacrificial feast was held for Publius Licinius' funeral, and there was a contest involving 120 gladiators, funeral games lasting three days and a banquet following the games. During the banquet, dining-furniture had been set out all over the Forum, but a storm blew up with high winds, and this obliged a large number of people to pitch tents in the Forum. Shortly afterwards, with the return of fine weather everywhere, the tents were again taken down. The word then went around that the people had fulfilled the prophecy that soothsayers had pronounced as one of the decrees of fate, namely that tents had to be pitched in the Forum. Relieved of this religious scruple, they were immediately faced with another—a shower of blood had lasted for two days in the precinct of the temple of Vulcan. To expiate this prodigy a period of public prayer †had been† enjoined by the decemvirs.

Before setting out for their provinces, the consuls brought before the Senate delegations from overseas. Never before had there been in Rome so many people from these parts. Word had spread amongst the peoples living close to Macedonia that serious consideration was being given by the Romans to charges and grievances lodged against Philip, and that many had found it worth their while to lodge a complaint. Since that time all the various communities and peoples had come to Rome to represent themselves, and individuals had also come to raise their private concerns (for Philip was a difficult neighbour for all of them), either hoping for relief from the wrongs inflicted on them, or at least to have some consolation from deploring them. There was also a delegation from Eumenes which included Eumenes' brother Athenaeus. The delegation came to lodge a twofold complaint: the garrisons were not being withdrawn from Thrace, and also reinforcements for Prusias' campaign against Eumenes had been sent to Bithynia by Philip.

47. All these complaints had to be addressed by Demetrius who was at the time no more than a boy. It was not easy for him to remember all the charges that were being made, or the appropriate responses to them, not just because of their number but also because several of them were utterly trivial, dealing as they did with border disputes, the abduction of individuals and the theft of farm-animals, court decisions made arbitrarily or not made at all, and judicial verdicts reached under duress or through corruption. The Senate could see the impossibility of Demetrius offering any clarification of

these issues, and of their gaining explicit information from him, but members were at the same time moved by the young man's inexperience and unease. They accordingly had the question put to him whether he had been given any written brief on these matters by his father. Demetrius replied that he had, and it was then decided that the highest priority and precedence be given to the king's replies to each of the charges. They forthwith demanded the scroll be produced and then allowed Demetrius to read it out.

It contained, however, only summary arguments against the individual charges, with Philip claiming that in some instances he had followed the commissioners' directives, and that in others responsibility for his failure to do so lay not with himself but with the very people accusing him. He had punctuated it with complaints about the unfairness of the directives, commenting on how partial the debate before Caecilius had been, when the king had been subjected to scandalous and unwarranted abuse by all present. The Senate saw these remarks as indications of the king's resentment, but then the young man tried to explain some of Philip's actions and gave his assurance that others in future would meet the specific wishes of the Senate. At this the members voted that Demetrius be given the answer that none of his father's actions had been more correct or more in line with the Senate's wishes than Philip's decision to have his past undertakings, whatever they had been, justified to the Romans by his son Demetrius. The Senate, they said, could overlook and forget, and simply put up with, much of Philip's past behaviour, and they also had confidence in Demetrius. For even if they returned him physically to his father, they said, they still held his spirit hostage, and they knew that he was as great a friend of the Roman people as duty to his father would allow. As a token of their respect for him, they continued, they would send a delegation to Macedonia to see that any of the conditions not adequately fulfilled now be met, with no redress for past omissions. They also wanted Philip to be aware, they concluded, that it was thanks to the good offices of his son Demetrius that his entire relationship with the Roman people remained intact.

48. These measures had been taken to boost Demetrius' prestige; instead they brought the young man instant unpopularity, and soon even precipitated his downfall.

The Spartans were next brought in. A large number of minor

issues were broached, but the most important centred on the question of whether or not the men condemned by the Achaeans should be sent home, and whether the killing of those whom they had killed was wrong or justified. †There was also the matter of† whether the Spartans should remain in the Achaean League or be the only state in the Peloponnese to have a separate constitution as they had had earlier. The decision reached was that the men should be repatriated, with the sentences set aside, and Sparta was to remain in the Achaean League. This enactment was to be written down and signed both by the Spartans and by the Achaeans.

Quintus Marcius was sent as a commissioner to Macedonia, and was also given orders to examine the situation of the allies in the Peloponnese. In this area, too, unrest still lingered after the quarrels of the past, and in addition the Messenians had seceded from the Achaean League. But to recount what started this war and how it developed would be to disregard my decision not to touch upon foreign affairs except where they were connected with Roman history.

49. A noteworthy result of the campaign was that, although the Achaeans were victorious in the war, their general Philopoemen was taken prisoner. Philopoemen had entered a dangerous valley in order to gain Corone ahead of the enemy, who were making for the town, and here he was taken by surprise along with a few cavalrymen. They say that he could himself have escaped with the help of the Thracians and the Cretans, but shame at abandoning the cavalry, the élite of his people and men recently hand-picked by himself, held him back. He was trying to provide a means of escape from the pass for these, bringing up the rear in person, but as he parried the attacks of the enemy his horse stumbled. He was almost killed by the fall itself and also by the weight of the horse falling on top of him—for he was now seventy years old, and considerably weakened by a lingering disease from which he was at that time just recovering. As he lay on the ground the enemy poured over him and overpowered him. When they recognized him, their respect for him and the recollection of his distinguished record prompted them to pick him up and revive him, just as if he were their own leader. They then brought him from the remote valley to the main road, scarcely believing their own eyes in the flush of unexpected joy; and some of them sent messengers ahead to Messene to say that the war was over and that Philopoemen was being brought in as a prisoner.

Initially, the report was so far beyond belief that the news was considered to be not just groundless but senseless. Then, as one man after another kept coming in, all of them saying the same thing, the story was finally believed; and even before they could be sure that Philopoemen was approaching the city all the Messenians came pouring out to look at him, free men and slaves, and children, too, along with the women. As a result, a crowd had blocked the entrance-gate, each person apparently unwilling to accept the truth of such startling news without the evidence of his own eyes; and the men bringing in Philopoemen were barely able to push aside those in their way and get through the gate. A crowd just as dense had obstructed the rest of the route and, since most people were excluded from the spectacle, they swiftly filled the theatre, which lay next to the road, and with a single voice kept demanding that Philopoemen be brought there to be seen by the public. The magistrates and leading citizens feared that compassion for a man of such stature in their midst would lead to disorder. Some would be abashed at the contrast between his former grandeur and his present misfortune, others moved by the recollection of his outstanding services. And so they set him at a distance but within view, and then swiftly whisked him out of sight, the praetor Dinocrates claiming that the magistrates wished to interrogate him on matters germane to the overall conduct of the war. They then took him away to the Senate house, where the Senate was convened and the matter brought under discussion.

50. By now it was growing dark and, apart from everything else, they were not even reaching agreement on where Philopoemen could be securely guarded for the oncoming night. They were paralysed by the magnitude of his erstwhile fortune and valour, not daring to take him into custody in their own homes, and yet not prepared to entrust his custody to any one of their number. Then some of them made the observation that they had an underground public treasury with a wall of dressed stones. Philopoemen was lowered into this in chains, and a huge rock was winched into place over it, blocking access. Deciding thus that his custody was better entrusted to a place than any one person, they awaited the approach of dawn.

The next day the commons, who recalled his former services to the state, were all agreed that Philopoemen's life should be spared and that through him they should seek ways to remedy their present ills. But those responsible for the secession, the men in whose hands the government now rested, held secret discussions and were unanimously agreed on putting him to death. There was, however, disagreement on whether they should do it quickly or defer it. The group more eager to punish him won the day and a man was sent to bring him poison. The story goes that, when he took the cup, Philopoemen's only words were to ask if Lycortas (the other commander of the Achaeans) and the cavalry had made good their escape. On being told that they were safe, he said 'that's good', fearlessly drained the cup, and died shortly afterwards.

Joy over Philopoemen's death was not of long duration for those responsible for the barbaric act. Defeated in the war, Messene surrendered the guilty parties at the demand of the Achaeans. The bones of Philopoemen were returned, and his funeral was attended by the entire Achaean council, with all manner of human tributes being paid to him, to the point that he was not denied even divine honours. This man is shown so much respect by Greek and Latin historians that it is recorded by a number of them, as a way of signalling this year as exceptional, that three distinguished commanders died in the course of it: Philopoemen, Hannibal, and Publius Scipio. These authors have gone so far as to put him on a par with the greatest generals of the two strongest peoples in the world.

51. Titus Quinctius Flamininus came as an ambassador to Prusias. The king was looked upon with suspicion by the Romans both because he had given shelter to Hannibal after the flight of Antiochus, and also because he had made war on Eumenes. It is possible that Prusias was there reprimanded by Flamininus for, among other things, harbouring at his court the man who was the greatest living enemy of the Roman people, one who had first of all pushed his own country, and then, when his country's resources were shattered, Antiochus into war with the people of Rome. Or perhaps Prusias himself adopted a plan of killing Hannibal, or putting him in Flamininus' hands, in order to gratify the Romans and Flamininus while the latter was present at his court. At all events, after the king's initial conversation with Flamininus, soldiers were immediately dispatched to keep watch on Hannibal's house.

Hannibal had always imagined that his life would end thus: he could see the implacable hatred of the Romans for him, and he had no confidence at all in the word of royalty. In fact, he had already had experience of Prusias' fickleness; and Flamininus' arrival, which he saw as sealing his fate, had sent a shudder through him. Faced with danger on every side, he had constructed seven exits from the house so that he would always have an escape-route at the ready, and some of these were concealed so that they would not be blocked by guards. But the despotic power of monarchs sees to it that nothing they want investigated fails to come to light. Prusias' men threw a cordon of guards around the perimeter of the entire building, making it impossible for anyone to slip out. When Hannibal was brought word that the king's men were in his forecourt, he tried to flee by a well-sequestered back door that permitted departure in total secrecy. Discovering that this, too, was sealed off by a blockade of soldiers, and that the entire neighbourhood was surrounded by guard-emplacements, he called for the poison which he had prepared well in advance and was holding in reserve for such an occasion.

'Let us free the people of Rome from their lingering anxiety,' he said, 'since they find it too long a process to wait for an old man's death. But it is a victory neither great nor notable that Flamininus shall win over a man unarmed and the victim of treachery. Today will at least show how far the character of the Roman people has changed. These men's ancestors forewarned Pyrrhus, an enemy under arms with an army in Italy, to be on his guard against poison; but *these* have sent an ex-consul as an envoy to incite Prusias to the heinous act of murdering a guest.' Then, bringing down curses on Prusias' head and his kingdom, and calling upon the gods of hospitality to witness the king's breach of faith, he drained the cup. So ended the life of Hannibal.

52. The accounts of both Polybius and Rutilius* assign Scipio's death to this year. I am in agreement neither with them nor with Valerius. Not with Polybius and Rutilius because, according to my findings, the man elected leader of the Senate during the censorship of Marcus Porcius and Lucius Valerius was the censor Lucius Valerius himself, whereas Africanus had been in that position during the previous two *lustra*; and nobody else would have been elected leader in his place during his lifetime, unless Africanus had been removed from the Senate, a disgrace recorded by no one. As for Antias, his version is refuted by the tribune of the plebs, Marcus Naevius, who appears as the accused in the title of a speech of Publius Africanus. This Naevius comes up in the books of the

magistrates as tribune of the plebs in the consulship of Publius Claudius and Lucius Porcius, but he commenced his tribunate on 10 December in the consulship of Appius Claudius and Marcus Sempronius. From that date it is three months to the Ides of March (the 15th), when Publius Claudius and Lucius Porcius began their consulship. It therefore appears that Scipio was alive in the tribunate of Naevius, who could have been arraigned by him, but that he died before the censorship of Lucius Valerius and Marcus Porcius.

The deaths of three of the most illustrious men of their respective nations evidently merit comparison not so much because of their occurring at the same time as because none of the men had an end appropriate to the distinction of his life. In the first place, the deaths and burials of all three took place outside their native soil. Hannibal and Philopoemen were done away with by poison; Hannibal died an exile and betrayed by his host, Philopoemen in prison and in chains. Scipio was not an exile and was not condemned; but failing to appear to face prosecution, and having his name called out in his absence, he brought down not just on himself but also on his funeral a penalty of voluntary exile.

53. Such were events in the Peloponnese, from which my digression began. In the mean time, the return to Macedonia of Demetrius and his embassy had provoked various reactions in different quarters. The Macedonian commons, terrified at the alarming prospect of a war coming from the Romans, looked on Demetrius with great favour as a peace-maker, and at the same time they fully expected that he was marked out for the throne on his father's death. For, although he was younger than Perseus, they reasoned that he was the son of a legally married mother while Perseus was the son of a concubine, and that while the latter, born of a whore,* had no physical characteristic clearly recalling his father, Demetrius bore a remarkable likeness to Philip. Apart from this, they imagined that the Romans would install Demetrius on his father's throne, but that Perseus carried no weight with them.

Such was the common talk. As a result, Perseus was tortured by the worrying thought that age alone would not tell sufficiently in his favour, his brother having the advantage in everything else; and Philip himself, believing that the decision of whom to leave as heir to the throne would hardly be left to him, kept saying that his younger son was for him, too, more of a worry than he would like. Sometimes he resented the numbers of Macedonians milling around Demetrius, and was indignant that a second court existed while he was still alive. Furthermore, the young man himself had quite clearly come back rather full of himself, his ego boosted by the Senate's estimation of him and by the concessions made to him that had been denied his father. And every reference he made to the Romans, while raising his standing with the rest of the Macedonians, only served to generate as much animosity against him, not just from his brother, but from his father as well. This was especially the case after a fresh delegation of Romans arrived, and Philip was obliged to quit Thrace, withdraw his garrisons, and take other actions in compliance with the decisions of the earlier commissioners or a new resolution of the Senate. But despite his distress and complaints—intensified by seeing his son spending almost more time with the Romans than with him—Philip was even so punctilious in meeting all the Romans' demands, in order not give them reason to open hostilities against him right then. He also felt he should divert their thoughts from any suspicion of his harbouring such designs,* and so he led his army through the middle of Thrace on a campaign against the Odrysae, Dentheleti, and Bessi. He took Philippopolis, whose inhabitants had fled and retreated with their families to the neighbouring hill tops, and accepted the surrender of the barbarian plainsmen after ravaging their territory. Then, leaving a garrison at Philippopolis—it was shortly afterwards expelled by the Odrysae—he proceeded to found a city in an area of Paeonia called Derriopus, close to the Erigonus, a river which flows from Illyricum through Paeonia and empties into the River Axius not far from the ancient city of Stobi. He had the new city named Perseis as a mark of honour for his elder son.

54. While this was going on in Macedonia, the consuls left for their provinces. Marcellus sent a message ahead to the proconsul Lucius Porcius ordering him to move his legions forward to the town newly built by the Gauls. On the consul's arrival the Gauls surrendered to him. They totalled 10,000 armed men, most of them holding weapons which they had seized in the countryside. To their chagrin, they were deprived of these arms along with the other items which they had appropriated in pillaging the country districts, or which they had brought with them. The Gauls sent representatives to Rome to protest against these measures. Brought into the Senate by Gaius Valerius, the representatives explained that it was shortage

of land and poverty arising from overpopulation in Gaul that had compelled them to cross the Alps in search of a home, and that, without doing harm to anyone, they had settled in what they saw to be an uncultivated stretch of land in an unpopulated area. Moreover, they said, they had begun the construction of a town as a way of showing that they had not come to bring force against any country district or any city. Recently, they continued, Marcus Claudius had sent them a message saying that he would open hostilities against them if they refused to surrender, and they, preferring a certain, if not creditable, peace to the vagaries of war, had entrusted themselves to the good faith of the Roman people rather than fall under their sway. A few days later they had been told to quit both the town and the district, and they had intended slipping away quietly to whatever parts they could. Then they were deprived of their arms and, in fact, of all their goods and chattels. They implored the Senate and people of Rome not to be more severe in dealing with guiltless men who had surrendered than they were with their enemies.

The Senate ordered this petition to be answered in the following way. While the Gauls had acted improperly in coming into Italy, and in attempting to build a town in another's land without authorization from any Roman magistrate in charge of that province, the Senate was still not pleased to dispossess men who had surrendered. Accordingly, the Senators would send a deputation with them to the consul to order the return of all their possessions to those who returned to their place of origin, and to make an immediate journey over the Alps to warn the Gauls to keep their teeming population at home. The Alps, they said, lay between them as a virtually impassable frontier, and they certainly would have no more success than the Gauls who originally made their way over them. The deputation sent comprised Lucius Furius Purpureo, Quintus Minucius, and Lucius Manlius Acidinus. After all the goods which they possessed without cost to anyone had been restored to them, the Gauls left Italy.

55. The Transalpine peoples were courteous in their response to the Roman deputation. Their elders took the Roman people to task for being too soft-hearted in letting off scot-free men who had, without the authorization of their people, attempted to settle in the territory of the Roman empire and build a town on land belonging to others. A heavy penalty should have been fixed for their effrontery, they

said, and they feared that others might be encouraged to similar presumptuous acts by the Romans' excessive leniency in also restoring their property to them. The elders made gifts to the delegates both in welcoming them and in bidding them farewell.

After driving the Gauls from his province, the consul Marcus Claudius next began to engineer a war with the Istrians, but he first sent a letter to the Senate to ask permission to take his legions across to Istria. The Senate opposed this. They were in the midst of discussions on the establishment of a colony at Aquileia, and were not agreed on whether the colonists should be Latins or Roman citizens. Eventually the Senators voted for the establishment of a Latin colony, and the triumvirs elected for it were Publius Scipio Nasica, Gaius Flaminius, and Lucius Manlius Acidinus.

The same year saw the founding of Mutina and Parma as colonies of Roman citizens. Two thousand people were settled at each of the two colonies, in territory that had most recently belonged to the Boii and before that the Etruscans. Each colonist received eight iugera at Parma, or five at Mutina. The founding triumvirs were Marcus Aemilius Lepidus, Titus Aebutius Parrus, and Lucius Quinctius Crispinus. Saturnia was also established as a colony of Roman citizens in Caletranian territory, the founding triumvirs being Quintus Fabius Labeo, Gaius Afranius Stellio, and Tiberius Sempronius Gracchus. Settlers here were each given ten iugera.

56. That same year the proconsul Aulus Terentius fought some successful engagements with the Celtiberians in Ausetanian territory, not far from the River Ebro, and he also took by storm a number of towns which the Celtiberians had fortified in that region. Farther Spain was at peace that year: the proconsul Publius Sempronius was stricken with a lingering sickness, and having no aggressor the Lusitanians, fortunately, remained inactive. And no action worthy of note was taken by the consul Quintus Fabius amongst the Ligurians, either.

On being recalled from Istria, Marcus Marcellus demobilized his army and returned to Rome for the elections, at which he declared Gnaeus Baebius Tamphilus and Lucius Aemilius Paullus consuls. Paullus had been curule aedile with Marcus Aemilius Lepidus, and it was now four years since the consulship of Lepidus, even though he had himself become consul only after two defeats. The praetors elected after this were: Quintus Fulvius Flaccus, Marcus Valerius

Laevinus, Publius Manlius (a second term), Marcus Ogulnius Gallus, Lucius Caecilius Denter, and Gaius Terentius Histra.

At the end of the year there was a period of public prayer because of some prodigies: there was widespread belief that there had been two-day shower of blood in the precinct of the temple of Concord, and there was a report of a new island, one that had not been in existence earlier, rising from the sea not far from Sicily. Valerius Antias records Hannibal's death in this year after delegates were sent to Prusias to bring it about. The delegates were—apart from Titus Quinctius Flamininus, whose name is well known in the episode— Lucius Scipio Asiaticus and Publius Scipio Nasica.

BOOK FORTY

1. At the beginning of the following year the consuls and praetors drew lots for their provinces, with the Ligurians as the only responsibility to be assigned to the consuls. The urban jurisdiction fell to Marcus Ogulnius Gallus, that of citizens and foreigners to Marcus Valerius. Of the Spains, Hither went to Quintus Fulvius Flaccus, and Farther to Publius Manlius, while Sicily went to Lucius Caecilius Denter and Sardinia to Gaius Terentius Histra.

The consuls were instructed to raise troops. Writing from Liguria, Quintus Fabius had reported that the Apuani were considering insurrection, and that there was a risk of their launching an attack on Pisan territory. The Senators were also aware that, of the Spanish provinces, Hither Spain was up in arms and a war was being conducted against the Celtiberians, while in Farther Spain military discipline had become slack from easy living and inertia, because of the praetor's chronic illness. These were the reasons for the decision to raise fresh armies. There were to be four legions to face the Ligurians, and each was to comprise 5,200 infantry and 300 cavalry, with a supplementary force of 15,000 infantry and 800 cavalry from the allies and the Latin League. These would constitute the two consular armies. The consuls were also instructed to enlist 7,000 infantry and 400 cavalry from the allies and the Latin League, and to send these into Gaul to Marcus Marcellus, whose imperium had been extended after his consulship. There were also orders for the enrolment of troops which were to be led to the two Spains: 4,000 infantry and 200 cavalry made up of Roman citizens, and 7,000 infantry plus 300 cavalry from the allies. Furthermore, Quintus Fabius Labeo saw his imperium in Liguria extended for a year, and he retained command of his army there.

2. It was a stormy spring that year. About midday on the day before the Parilia* there arose a terrible storm with squalls, which caused severe damage at many spots, both sacred and secular. It toppled bronze statues on the Capitoline; it tore a door off the temple of Luna on the Aventine, carried it along and left it lodged against the rear walls of the temple of Ceres; it overturned other statues in the Circus Maximus along with the pedestals on which

they stood; and it ripped the ornamentation off the roofs of a number of temples and reduced it to an ugly debris. As a result, the storm was taken to be a prodigy, and the *haruspices* prescribed expiatory ceremonies. Expiation was also made at this time following a report of the birth of a three-footed mule at Reate, and another report from Formiae that the temple of Apollo at Caieta had been struck by lightning. As a result of these prodigies twenty full-sized victims were sacrificed and there was a single day of public prayer.

It was about this time that news arrived in a letter from the propraetor Aulus Terentius that Publius Sempronius* had died in the further province after a sickness lasting more than a year. The praetors were therefore instructed to hasten their departure for Spain.

After this, embassies from overseas were ushered into the Senate. The first of them were from the kings Eumenes and Pharnaces,* and from the Rhodians, who deplored the disaster that had overtaken the people of Sinope. There arrived at about the same time envoys from Philip, from the Achaeans, and from the Spartans. Before responses were made to these the Senate first heard Marcius* who had been on a mission to examine the situation in Greece and Macedonia. The answer given to the kings of Asia and to the Rhodians was that the Senate would send an embassy to examine the items in question.

3. The Senate's uneasiness with regard to Philip had been increased by Marcius. He maintained that the manner in which the king had complied with the Senate's wishes made it quite clear that he would not continue to do so any longer than was necessary. And Philip was making no secret of the fact that he would restart the war, said Marcius—all his actions and statements pointed in that direction. First of all, he had removed practically the entire citizen population of the coastal cities, together with their families, to what is now called Emathia (formerly it was named Paeonia); and he had then presented these cities to Thracians and other barbarians as their homes, thinking that these sorts of people would be more loyal to him in a war with Rome. This undertaking of Philip's had caused a great commotion throughout Macedonia. Few were the men who kept silent their resentment as they left their homes with their wives and children, and curses on the king could be heard in the columns of those departing as their hatred for him overwhelmed their fear. Such reactions infuriated Philip, who began to suspect all men in all places and at all times. Eventually, he began to declare openly that he

could have no real security unless he arrested the children of the men he had put to death, kept them under guard, and eliminated them at different times.

4. Such brutality was repulsive in itself, but the tragedy befalling one household rendered it more repulsive still. Many years before, Philip had executed Herodicus, a leading Thessalian, and he went on to put to death Herodicus' sons-in-law as well, leaving the daughters as widows, each of them with one small son. The names of these women were Theoxena and Archo. Though many sought her hand, Theoxena rejected the idea of further marriage. Archo married a certain Poris, by far the most prominent of the Aenian people, but died after bearing him several children, leaving all of them quite young. To have the upbringing of her sister's children in her own hands, Theoxena married Poris, and she had the same affection towards her own son and the sons of her sister as if she had herself given birth to all of them. When she heard of an edict of the king ordering the arrest of the children of men who had been executed, she thought that these would be subjected not only to insulting treatment by the king but to sexual abuse by the guards as well. She therefore turned her thoughts to a gruesome plan, and ventured to say that she would kill them all with her own hands rather than see them fall into Philip's power. Horrified at the suggestion of such an appalling act, Poris said he would take the children to some loyal friends in Athens and would himself accompany them in their exile.

They left Thessalonica for Aenea to attend a traditional sacrifice which the citizens of the town celebrate each year with great ceremony to honour their founder Aeneas. At Aenea they spent a day over the ritual feast and then, about the third watch, when all were asleep, boarded a ship that had been made ready in advance by Poris, ostensibly to return to Thessalonica. In fact, their intention was to cross to Euboea. But, struggling vainly against a head wind, they were still close to land when dawn came upon them, and the king's men who were responsible for guarding the port sent an armed clipper to take the ship in tow, with strict orders not to return without it.

As these men now bore down on him, Poris focused all his efforts on encouraging his oarsmen and sailors, occasionally raising his hands to heaven and begging the gods to help. Meanwhile, the fearsome lady turned her thoughts back to the heinous act she had contemplated long before, and she mixed poison and brought forth weapons. Setting the cup in the children's sight and drawing the swords she said: 'Death is the only way to claim our freedom. These are the paths to death; use whichever method you please to escape the king's tyrannical behaviour. Come, my children, older ones first—take the sword or, if you want a slower death, drain the cup.' The enemy were approaching, and at the same time the instigator of death was urging them on. Carried off by one means or the other, they were thrown from the vessel in their death throes, and Theoxena herself, embracing her husband who shared her end, then hurled herself into the sea. The king's men took possession of a ship vacated by its owners.

5. The barbarous nature of this event served to add new flames to the resentment felt for the king, bringing curses from the common people on Philip himself and on his children. In a short while these maledictions were heard by all the gods, who made the king vent his savagery on his own flesh and blood.

Perseus could see that Demetrius' popularity and esteem with the Macedonian public, and his influence with the Romans, were increasing by the day. He now thought that only by crime could he hope to gain the throne, and it was to this that he therefore turned all his thoughts. But he did not believe that he had sufficient strength on his own even for this product of his unmanly imagination, and he proceeded to test the feelings of friends of his father's, one by one, by dropping ambiguous remarks. Now at first some of these gave him the impression of opposing such a move because they had more confidence in Demetrius' cause. But Philip's antipathy towards the Romans increased with every day that passed, as Perseus nursed it and Demetrius did his best to check it, and they foresaw the undoing of the young man who was unguarded against his brother's duplicity. And so, believing they should help along what was bound to happen anyway, and foster the aspirations of the stronger, they attached themselves to Perseus.

The other matters they put off till the appropriate time; for now they decided that all their energy should be directed to inciting the king against the Romans and pushing him into making plans for war, to which he had already turned his thoughts in any case. At the same time, to make Demetrius more suspect every day, they contrived to bring their conversation round to †the aspirations† of the Romans.

At that point some would ridicule Roman customs and institutions, and others Roman achievements; some would mock the appearance of the actual city—which had not yet undergone refurbishment of either its public or private areas—and others individual Roman leaders. The young man was off-guard, and his love of the Roman people and his conflict with his brother rendered him suspect to his father and an easy target for recriminations as he defended the Romans on all counts. Consequently his father excluded him from all discussions of Roman affairs. Turning exclusively to Perseus, he would night and day discuss with him his reflections on the Roman question.

It so happened that representatives whom Philip had sent to the Bastarnae* to solicit aid had now returned and had brought back from the area some young noblemen, a number of them of royal birth. One of the latter promised his sister in marriage to a son of Philip, and a prospective tie with this people had piqued the king's interest. 'What good is that?' asked Perseus. 'Protection furnished by help from abroad does not at all compensate for the danger from treachery at home. We have in our bosom—I don't want to say "a traitor", but at least "a spy". After his time as a hostage in Rome, the Romans gave his body back to us, but they have retained his heart. The eyes of almost all the Macedonians are focused on him, and they are saying they will have no other king than the one the Romans give them.' The old man's already diseased mind was chagrined by these remarks, and he began to take these allegations to heart without revealing it in his expression.

6. As it happened, the time now came for the ceremonial purification of the army.* The rite for this proceeds as follows. The head and fore section of a bitch that has been cut in two are placed on the right side of the road, the rear and intestines on the left. The troops are then led in arms between the members of the severed victim. Ahead of the foremost column are carried the armour and emblems of all the kings dating back to the earliest beginnings of Macedonia, and then the king follows in person, along with his children. Next comes the royal company and the king's bodyguards, and then the rear of the army is brought up by the Macedonian rank and file.

On each side of the king were his two young sons: Perseus who was now in his thirtieth year and Demetrius who was five years his junior. Perseus was at the acme of his youth, Demetrius at the flowering of his—grown children of a lucky father, were his mind but sound! Once the ritual purification was finished, it was the custom to hold military exercises, at which the army, divided into two battle lines, would clash in a mock engagement.* The young princes were appointed leaders in this war-game. But it was no simulated fight; they clashed as if the throne were in question, and there were numerous wounds inflicted by the wooden stakes.* All that was lacking to give it the appearance of a real battle was the cold steel. The group under Demetrius' command was by far the stronger. This angered Perseus, but his forethinking friends were happy; this episode would itself furnish them with grounds for incriminating the young man, they said.

7. On that day the two princes each hosted a separate banquet for the comrades who had taken part in the exercises with him, since Perseus had refused an invitation to dinner from Demetrius. It was a holiday, and the cordial invitations and the high spirits of youth led both parties to drink. During the drinking there were recollections of the mock engagement, and light-hearted quips were made against the respective adversaries, which not even the leaders themselves were spared. One of Perseus' guests was sent as a spy to eavesdrop on these remarks, but being rather careless in his movements he was caught and manhandled by some young men who happened to be leaving the dining-room. Demetrius was unaware of this. 'Why do we not go and drink at my brother's?' he said, 'and with our openness and good cheer soothe any resentment lingering from the fight?' The whole company cried out that they would go—apart from those who feared immediate retribution for having beaten the spy. When Demetrius insisted on dragging these along, too, they concealed swords under their clothing for self-defence in the event of a violent confrontation.

There can be no secrets in domestic conflict. Both houses were full of spies and traitors. An informer ran ahead to Perseus bringing word that four of the young men coming with Demetrius were armed with swords. The reason for this was self-evident—Perseus had been told that his dinner-guest had been beaten by these men— but to make a scandal of the incident he ordered his door to be locked, and from the windows that faced the street in the upper part of the house he forbade the merrymakers to approach the door, pretending that they were coming to kill him. For a short while

Demetrius drunkenly bawled out his protests at being shut out and then returned to his banquet, unaware of what was really going on.

8. As soon as he had an opportunity of seeing his father the next day, Perseus entered the palace and, a look of anxiety on his face, stood in silence at some distance from him, but within view. 'Are you all right?' asked his father, who then inquired why he was so downcast.

'You must realize that you are lucky that I am alive,' Perseus told him. 'It is no longer in secret that plots are being engineered against me by my brother. He came to my house with armed men during the night to kill me; I closed my doors and used the shelter of my walls to protect myself from his rage.' Having inspired in his father a mixture of dread and surprise, he added: 'But if you can give me your attention, I shall see that you have a clear account of the matter.' Philip replied that he would certainly hear him out, and gave orders for Demetrius to be called immediately; and he also summoned to use as advisers Lysimachus and Onomastus,* two older friends of his who had played no part in the youthful quarrels between the brothers because they were now rarely at court. During the time that his friends were coming, Philip paced up and down on his own, turning over many things in his mind, while his son stood at a distance. When he was brought word of their arrival, he retired to the inner part of the palace with his two friends and the same number of bodyguards, and he allowed each of his sons to bring in with him three unarmed men.

Here the king took his seat and said: 'I sit here a very unhappy father, acting as a judge between my two sons, one bringing a charge of fratricide, the other accused of it; and within my family I shall make the shameful discovery of a crime that has either been trumped up or actually committed. I had long feared this gathering storm, seeing the anything-but-brotherly looks that passed between you two, and hearing some of your language. But the hope would occasionally come to me that the flames of your anger could subside, and your suspicions be cleared away. Even enemies, I mused, had put down their weapons and made peace, and the private feuds of many men had been brought to an end. I thought that at some stage you would remember that you are brothers, and would recall the candid relationship you had as boys and, indeed, the things I taught you— though I fear these lessons may have been fruitless and have fallen on deaf ears. How often in your hearing have I expressed my abhorrence at the idea of brothers quarrelling and recounted the terrible results—how they completely destroyed themselves and their families, their homes and their kingdoms! I also produced for you better examples on the other side: the harmonious partnership between the two kings of Sparta, which provided security for them and their fatherland for many generations, and the overthrow of that same state when the practice of individuals seizing personal tyranny grew up. Then I pointed to the brothers Eumenes and Attalus, whose beginnings were so modest that one was almost embarrassed to use the title "king".* With nothing more than brotherly concord these built a kingdom to rival mine, and that of Antiochus or any other king of this age. I did not forgo even Roman examples which I had either seen or heard about: Titus and Lucius Quinctius who fought a war against me; Publius and Lucius Scipio who defeated Antiochus; and the father and the uncle of these two whose unfailing rapport in life was maintained even in death.* But the wickedness of the Spartans,* with the results appropriate to that wickedness, could not deter you from your insane bickering, nor could the wisdom and good fortune of these others bring you to your senses.

'While I still live and breathe, you have through your unconscionable ambition and greed already entered into your inheritance from me. You want me alive only to the point when, surviving just one of you, I make the other the uncontested king at my death. You cannot stand to have either a brother or a father. Nothing is dear, nothing sacred to you. Everything has been supplanted by your insatiable craving for one thing—the throne. Come on, then, befoul your father's ears, and with your accusations try to decide what you will soon decide with the sword. State openly whatever truths you can find and whatever lies you wish to fabricate. My ears are open, but after today they will be closed to the recriminations you make behind each other's backs.' After Philip uttered these words in a fit of raging temper, tears came to everyone's eyes, and a gloomy silence long hung in the air.

9. Then Perseus began: 'Of course I should have opened my door last night. I should have let in the armed merry-makers, and put my throat to their swords. For the crime is not believed unless it has been carried through, and though I was the target of a plot I face the same verbal abuse as a footpad or conspirator. The people who say that

your only son is Demetrius and that I am a bastard son of a whore*
have a point. For if I had with you the standing of, and the affection
accorded to, a son, your fury would be directed not against me when
I protest about the conspiracy which has been uncovered, but
against its perpetrator; and you would not think my life of so little
account as to be unmoved by the peril which I have already faced,
and will face in future if the conspirators get off scot-free. So if I
must die without saying a word, let me keep silence, praying only
that the crime which started with me also ends with me, and that a
weapon is not being aimed at you through me. But, when men are
waylaid in deserted spots, nature herself prompts them to cry out for
protection from people whom they have never seen. So, when I see a
sword drawn against me, if I too am permitted a cry for help, then I
beg you as my father—and you have long been aware of which of the
two of us reveres that title more—to hear me now just as if you had
been woken by my cries and lamentations in the dark, and had come
in response to my appeals for help, to catch Demetrius with his
armed men in my courtyard at the dead of night. What I would have
cried out in terror then in my hour of danger—that forms the
substance of my protest now, the day after.

'Brother, we have had no interest in socializing †with each other†
for a long time now. You want to be king at all costs; but my age
stands in the way of this ambition of yours, as does international
convention, the ancient practice of Macedonia,* and, in fact, the
decision of our father, as well. Such impediments you can surmount
only by shedding my blood. All your efforts and undertakings have
had this end, but so far either my vigilance or my good luck has
thwarted your murderous aims. Yesterday, at the purification ceremony, with its manœuvres and the mock-battle—a piece of fun—you
almost staged a deadly contest, and all that saved me from death was
my permitting myself and my side to be defeated. You then tried to
lure me to dinner from that fight between enemies as if it had been a
game between brothers. Father, do you think I was going to be sitting
at dinner in unarmed company, when men visited me with weapons
for after-dinner drinks? Do you think I would have been facing
no danger from swords at night when they almost killed me with
wooden stakes as you looked on? Why come at this time of night?
Why come as an enemy to an angry man, and why accompanied by
young men with swords at their sides? I did not dare entrust myself

to you as a guest—was I going to welcome you for after-dinner drinking with your armed companions? Had my door been open, father, you would at this moment at which you are hearing my protests be preparing my funeral.

'I am not proceeding like a prosecutor, using defamation and building a flimsy case on inference. Look: does he deny that he came to my door with a mob, or that there were men with him armed with swords? Call in the men I name! The people who presumed to do this can dare to do anything—but they will not dare deny this. If I were bringing them before you after I had arrested them carrying weapons within my threshold, you would consider it an open-and-shut case. So, since they confess, consider them so arrested.

10. 'All right, curse regal aspirations, and conjure up the spirits that set brothers at odds. But to ensure that your curses are not blindly directed, father, you must make distinctions. You must tell the plotter from the victim of the plot, and you must target the guilty party. Let the one who was intending to murder his brother feel the wrath of his father's gods; and let the one who was to die through his brother's heinous act find a haven in his father's compassion and justice. For where else am I to seek refuge, when I have no security at the ritual purification of the army, or in military manœuvres, or at home, or at dinner, or at night, which is vouchsafed to mortals by nature's gift to give them repose? If I accept the invitation and go to my brother, I must die; if I welcome my brother within my door for after-dinner drinking, I must die. Go or stay, I cannot avoid the trap.

'Where am I to turn? Only the gods and you have I venerated, father. I do not have the Romans to turn to—they want me dead for the pain I feel over your injuries, for my resentment at their taking from you all those cities and all those nations, and now the coast of Thrace. They have no hope of Macedonia being theirs while either you or I remain. But if I am eliminated by my brother's criminal act and you by old age—and they may not even wait for that—they know that the king and kingdom of Macedonia will be theirs. Had the Romans left you with any possession outside Macedonia, I could believe that this was also left as a place of refuge for me.

'But, some might say, I have enough protection in the Macedonians. You saw the soldiers attacking me yesterday—what did they lack but steel? And what they lacked in the daytime, my brother's guests took up at night. Why mention the majority of our leading citizens, who have placed all their hopes of advancement and prosperity in the Romans, and in the man who is all-important to the Romans? My God, they do not just prefer that fellow to me, his elder brother, but they almost prefer him to you yourself, his king and father. For it is thanks to him that the Senate waived your punishment; it is he who now protects you from Roman arms and who thinks that you in your old age should be beholden and indebted to him, young as he is. The Romans are on his side; all the cities freed from your dominion are on his side; the Macedonians who are happy to have peace with Rome are on his side. Apart from you, father, what hope or protection do I have anywhere?

11. 'What do you think is the point of that letter recently sent to you by Titus Quinctius—the letter in which he states that you looked after your own interests well in sending Demetrius to Rome, and in which he encourages you to send him back again with a larger delegation, and also with leading Macedonian citizens? Titus Quinctius is now that man's champion as well as his teacher in everything. Demetrius has rejected you as his father and replaced you with Quinctius. Most importantly, it is at Rome that the secret designs against you have been hatched. When Quinctius tells you to send more representatives and leading Macedonians with Demetrius, what is being sought is supporters for these designs. Men go to Rome from here upright and honest, believing Philip to be their king; they come back from there tainted and corrupted by the seductive words of the Romans. For them Demetrius, and he alone, is everything, and they are already calling him king while his father still lives.

'If I am angry about this, I must immediately face the charge—not just from others but from you, too, father—of coveting the throne. Now if this charge is made in general against us both, I for my part do not admit it. For whom am I pushing from his rightful position in order to gain his position myself? Only my father stands ahead of me, and I pray God he may long do so. If I survive him—and I hope I may, provided that I am worthy of *his* wishing that I do so—then I shall accept the throne as my inheritance, if my father passes it to me. The man who covets the throne, and villainously covets it, is the one who hastens to infringe the order of priorities established by age, nature, the custom of the Macedonians, and international convention. "My elder brother stands in my way," Demetrius says. "The

throne belongs to him by right, and also by the wish of my father.
Let us get rid of him; I shall not be the first to have sought a throne
by murdering a brother. My father, old and alone, will be too afraid
for his own safety to exact retribution for the son's killing. The
Romans will be happy and will approve of and defend the act.'

'These hopes of his are forlorn, father, but not entirely without
foundation. This is how matters stand. You are now able to ward off
the danger to my life by punishing those who took up the sword to
assassinate me; but if their criminal design meets with success, you
will not then be able to avenge my death.'

12. When Perseus finished speaking, the gaze of all present was
fixed on Demetrius in the expectation that he would respond
immediately. But there followed a long silence, during which it
became clear to everyone that he was bathed in tears and could not
speak. Finally, when ordered to respond, the pressure of his circumstances overcame his anguish, and he began as follows:

'Father, all the means of assistance previously available to men
accused have been seized in advance by my accuser. Shedding false
tears for the purpose of destroying his adversary, he has led you to
suspect my genuine tears. Ever since my return from Rome he has
been holding clandestine meetings with his supporters, and plotting
against me day and night; and he has actually made me out to be not
just a conspirator but an out-and-out brigand and murderer. He
frightens you by his claim to be in danger, so that through you he can
the more quickly destroy his guiltless brother. He claims to have no
place of refuge anywhere in the world, his purpose being to ensure
that *I* have no shred of hope left with you. I am cut off, isolated, and
helpless, and he puts on me the heavy opprobrium of having influence abroad (which is more a hindrance than a help). And then how
like a prosecutor he was, putting his accusation relating to last night
along with general criticism of my way of life! His purpose in this
was to make this event—and the true nature of it you will learn in a
moment—look suspicious against the background of the rest of my
life, and also to bolster the flimsy charges of my ambition, my wishes,
and my designs by means of this night-time scenario that he has
devised and scripted.* He had this other motive, too: to give the
impression that his accusation was a spur-of-the-moment and
unpremeditated reaction, arising (naturally!) from his fright and
sudden trepidation last night. But, Perseus, if I was a traitor to my

father and the realm, and if I had entered into plots with the Romans and other enemies of my father, then you should not have waited for last night's drama—you should have accused me of treason earlier. But if that particular accusation—separated now from this episode—was groundless, and likely to demonstrate your resentment towards me rather than criminal behaviour on my part, in that case, too, you should today either have omitted it or deferred it to a later date. This would then allow an independent examination of the question of whether I plotted against you or whether you, with a novel and unprecedented venom, plotted against me.

'For my part, in this distress that has suddenly engulfed me, I shall do my best to disentangle the questions that you have jumbled together, and bring into the open the trap set this night, whether it was laid by you or me. Perseus wants to make it look as if I hatched a plot to assassinate him; the motive, of course, was that by removing my elder brother—who would gain the crown by international convention, Macedonian custom, and even, he says, by your wishes—I, the younger brother, would take the place of the man I had killed. So what is the point of the second part of his speech, with his claim that the Romans were cultivated by me and that I had come to entertain regal aspirations through my reliance on them? For if I thought the Romans so influential as to be able to impose their choice of king on Macedonia, and if I was also so confident of the weight I carried with them, why was murder necessary? So I could don a crown dripping with a brother's blood? So I should be cursed and hated by the very people with whom I have by my integrity (be it genuine or at least affected) gained whatever influence I happen to have. Or perhaps you believe that Titus Quinctius—the man by whose wishes and advice you say I am guided—pushed me to kill my brother, despite the degree of his loyalty to *his* brother? Along with my influence with the Romans, Perseus also brought up the judgment of the Macedonians and the almost unanimous agreement of gods and human beings—all of which made him believe that he would be no match for me in a struggle for the throne. Yet that same man accuses me of having resorted to crime—my final hope—since I was inferior to him in all other respects. Is this the guiding principle you want to see followed in this case: the one who fears that the other may appear more worthy of the throne is to be judged guilty of having planned to eliminate his brother?

13. But no matter how trumped up it is, let us see how this charge develops. Perseus claims that he was the object of numerous attacks, and all my methods of trapping him he has brought together into the space of a single day. I wanted to assassinate him in the daytime during our contest following the purification, and, my God, on the actual day of the purification ceremonies! When I invited him to dinner, I wanted to kill him—with poison, presumably. When men wearing swords came with me for after-dinner drinks, I wanted to murder him with the sword. You can see the sort of time chosen for the fratricide: sports, a banquet, a drinking-session. And what sort of day are we talking about? The day on which the army was purified, when the royal arms of all the kings of Macedon who ever lived were carried ahead and we two, father, alone, rode at each side of you between the severed victim, while the main body of the Macedonians followed us. Even had I been previously guilty of some deed that required atonement, I was purified and cleansed by that rite. And after that, at the very time that I looked upon the victim set each side of our path, was I really pondering in my mind assassination, poisoning, and swords prepared for the drinking-session? Yes, so I should need to purify my mind polluted with all manner of crime—and by what further sacred rituals?

'But Perseus' mind is blindly set on incrimination, and in trying to cast suspicion on everything he has got things confused. For if I wanted to dispose of you with poison at dinner, what was less to the purpose than to make you angry by putting up a stiff fight when we met in competition, which would lead to your rejecting my invitation to dinner, as indeed you did. But when you had angrily refused, what should I have done next? Concentrated on placating you so I could find another such occasion, now that I had the poison prepared? Or jumped, as it were, from one plan to another, to killing you with a sword, and on that very day, too, as I pretended to drink with you? But then, if I believed you had avoided my dinner from fear of assassination, how did I think you were not going to avoid a drinking-party from the same fear?

14. 'Father, I have no reason to feel embarrassment if I went too deeply into the wine with my comrades on a feast day. I would actually like you to ask about the cheerfulness and merriment with which last night's dinner was held at my house, the occasion heightened by the elation—improper elation, perhaps—of our not coming off worse in the young men's competition in arms. The present misfortune and my fear have easily shaken off my hangover. But for these, we "plotters" would be flat out on our beds. If I intended taking your house by storm, and killing its master after taking it, would I not have kept away from drink for one day, and made my men abstain, too? And so that I would not be alone in making a defence with excessive candour, my brother, too—without a trace of malice or suspicion—has himself said: "I know nothing, and make no allegation, except that they came to drink bearing swords." Should I ask you how you know this for a fact, you will have to admit either that my house was full of your spies or that those men of mine were so open in taking up their weapons that everybody saw it. Then, to avoid the impression of having made prior inquiries himself, or of now making slanderous allegations, he kept telling you to ask the men he named whether they had carried a sword so that—as if the matter were actually in question!—they could be regarded as guilty when you had interrogated them about what they freely admit. Why do you not rather have them asked whether their purpose in taking up the weapons was to kill you, and whether I was behind it and aware of it? You want the latter to *appear* to be so, despite what they say and what is clearly the case. †And† they say they took them up for self-protection; whether they were right or wrong in so doing, they will themselves account for their action. Do not confuse my case with that—it has nothing to do with what they did. Or else explain to us whether together we were going to attack you openly or covertly. If it was openly, why did we not *all* have weapons? Why did no one have them apart from those who manhandled your spy? If it was covertly, what was the programme? When I had left the drinking that followed the break-up of our banquet, would four men have stayed behind to attack you in your sleep? How would they have escaped detection? They were strangers, they were my men, and they were particularly suspect after being involved in a fight shortly before. How were they going to get away themselves after killing you? Could your residence have been captured and taken by storm with four swords?

15. 'Why do you not drop this story of the night-time escapade and get back to what really galls you and burns you up with jealousy? "Why on earth was there talk of you succeeding to the throne, Demetrius? Why is it that some people find you more deserving of

our father's position than I? Were it not for you, my aspirations would be assured—why do you render them uncertain and worrisome?" These are Perseus' feelings, even if he does not voice them; this is what makes that man my enemy and my accuser. This is what fills your home and kingdom with accusations and suspicion. Perhaps, father, it is not proper for me to entertain hopes of succession now, or ever to raise the question, because I am the younger son and you wish me to defer to the elder; but likewise it was not and is not proper for me to make myself appear †to everybody to be unworthy of you†. For in that case I should be obtaining the position by my shortcomings, not by my modesty in deferring to a man with human and divine right on his side.

'You reproach me with the Romans, and what should be a credit to me you twist into a denunciation. *I* did not ask to be turned over to the Romans as a hostage or to be sent as a spokesman to Rome, but I did not refuse to go when sent by you. On both occasions I regulated my behaviour so that I would bring no disgrace on you, the kingdom, or the Macedonian people. And so, father, it was you who were responsible for my friendship with the Romans. As long as they are at peace with you, so long will my influence with them continue. If war breaks out, I, the man who was not without his uses for his father, as a hostage and an ambassador—I shall also be their fiercest enemy. I do not ask today that my influence with the Romans stand in my favour; my plea is merely that it not count against me. It did not begin in wartime, and has not been kept up for the purposes of war. I was a surety of peace, and I was sent as a ambassador to maintain the peace. Let neither role bring me either credit or recrimination.

'Father, if my behaviour towards you has been in any way disloyal, and if I have committed any crime against my brother, I seek to avoid no punishment. If I am innocent, I beg that I not be consumed in the flames of envy, when I cannot be touched by a criminal charge. Today is not the first time my brother has accused me, but today is the first time he has done so openly, though I have done nothing to him to deserve it. If my father were angry with me, it would be your duty, as the elder brother, to intercede with him on behalf of the younger, and to gain indulgence for my youthful inexperience and folly. Where I should have found a safeguard, there I face destruction. I was rushed from a dinner and a drinking-party almost half-asleep to answer a charge of murder, and am obliged to present my own case without the benefit of counsellors or legal representatives. If I had to speak on another's behalf, I would have taken the time to reflect on and formally compose my address—and in that situation what would I be risking apart from my reputation for my ability? Not knowing why I had been summoned, I heard your angry orders for me to defend myself, and I heard my brother's accusations. He delivered a speech against me that was prepared and rehearsed well in advance; I had only the time in which I faced his charges to find out what was afoot. Was I to use that brief space of time listening to my accuser or working out my defence? Stunned by the sudden and unexpected blow, I could barely comprehend the charges—and much less do I know how to defend myself. What hope would I have, did I not have my father judging the case? For even if I take second place to my elder brother in his heart, I should not at least take second place in his pity when I am on trial. *I* am begging you to save me for your sake as well as mine; *he* is demanding that you kill me to make his position secure. What do you think he will do to me when you have passed your throne to him, seeing that he even now thinks it right to indulge himself with my blood.'

16. As Demetrius said this, tears stifled both his breath and his voice. Philip dismissed his sons and after a brief discussion with his friends announced that he would not make a decision on their case based on what they had said in a single hour's debate. He would decide rather through an inquiry into the life and character of each, and by considering what they had said and done in situations of greater and lesser importance. This made it clear to everybody that the accusation relating to the previous night had been unequivocally refuted, but that Demetrius was still under suspicion because he was too popular with the Romans. Such, one may say, were the seeds of the Macedonian War which had to be fought †mostly† with Perseus, and they were sown during Philip's lifetime.

The two consuls left for Liguria, which was at that time the sole consular province; and because of their success there, a decree was passed authorizing a single day's public devotions. Some 2,000 Ligurians came right to the border of the province of Gaul where Marcellus had his camp, and asked to be taken into his charge. Marcellus instructed the Ligurians to remain in place and by letter asked the Senate for guidance. The Senate ordered the praetor

Marcus Ogulnius to write back to Marcellus that <guidance> would more properly have been sought from the consuls charged with the province than from them; and also that on this occasion it was the Senate's decision that the Ligurians not be taken into his charge unless by surrender. They added that the Senate considered it appropriate that if they were taken into his charge they be disarmed and sent to the consuls.

The praetors Publius Manlius and Quintus Fulvius Flaccus arrived in their provinces at this same time, Manlius in Farther Spain, which he had also received as his province in his previous praetorship, and Flaccus in Hither Spain, where he took over command of the army from Aulus Terentius. Farther Spain had been without imperium since the death of the proconsul Publius Sempronius.

As Fulvius Flaccus was laying siege to a Spanish town called Urbiaca, the Celtiberians launched an attack on him, and a number of hard-fought battles took place there in which large numbers of Roman soldiers were either wounded or killed. Fulvius prevailed through his determination; he could be diverted from the siege by no show of force, and the Celtiberians left exhausted after a number of battles of mixed success. This support removed, the city was captured within a matter of days and pillaged, and the praetor surrendered the plunder to his men. When this city was taken, Fulvius led his army to winter-quarters, as did Manlius, who merely brought together his scattered army and achieved nothing else of note.

Such were that summer's operations in Spain. Terentius, who had left that province, entered the city in ovation, carrying in his procession 9,320 pounds of silver, 82 pounds of gold, and 67 golden crowns.

17. The same year Roman arbitrators were on the spot to mediate a territorial dispute between the Carthaginian people and Masinissa. Gala, father of Masinissa, had captured the land in question from the Carthaginians, but Syphax had driven Gala from it and had later made a gift of it to the Carthaginians to ingratiate himself with his father-in-law Hasdrubal.* This year Masinissa had driven out the Carthaginians. The issue was debated before the Romans with a clash of wills as ferocious as had been the fight on the battlefield. The Carthaginians kept asking for the restoration of what had belonged to their ancestors and had later come to them from Syphax.

Masinissa maintained that he had recovered territory that had belonged to his father's realm; that his occupation of it was sanctioned by international law; and that he was the stronger claimant both in terms of his case and by virtue of possession. In the dispute, he said, his only fear was that the decency of the Romans might do him harm—they might be afraid of appearing to have favoured a king who was an ally and a friend over men who were enemies common to themselves and to him. The ambassadors made no change in the title to the land, and referred the whole issue untouched to the Senate in Rome.

There were no further developments in Liguria. The Ligurians had first of all fallen back to some remote forests, and then, demobilizing their army, had slipped away to their villages and strongholds. The consuls also wished to demobilize their armies, and they consulted the Senate on the matter. The Senators' instructions were that one of them should disband his army and return to Rome to hold the election of the magistrates for the coming year; the other was to winter at Pisae with his legions. There was a rumour that the Transalpine Gauls were arming men of military age, but it was not known into which part of Italy the horde would pour. The consuls accordingly arranged between them that it should be Gnaeus Baebius who would proceed to the elections, because his brother Marcus Baebius was standing for the consulship.

18. The elections of the consuls were then held, and Publius Cornelius Lentulus* and Marcus Baebius Tamphilus were elected. The following were then elected praetor: the two Quinti Fabii, Maximus and Buteo, Tiberius Claudius Nero, Quintus Petillius Spurinus, Marcus Pinarius Rusca, and Lucius Duronius. The sortition of provinces for these when they entered office was as follows:

The consuls	the Ligurians

The praetors:

Quintus Petillius	urban jurisdiction
Quintus Fabius Maximus	foreigners' jurisdiction
Quintus Fabius Buteo	Gaul
Tiberius Claudius Nero	Sicily
Marcus Pinarius	Sardinia
Lucius Duronius	Apulia

Duronius was given the added responsibility of the Istrians because the people of Tarentum and Brundisium reported that their coastal districts had been rendered unsafe by piracy conducted by vessels from overseas. The people of Massilia lodged the same complaint about Ligurian ships. The armies were then formally assigned, and the consuls were given four legions (each of which was to have 5,200 Roman infantry and 300 cavalry) and 15,000 infantry and 800 cavalry from the allies and the Latin League. In the Spanish provinces the old praetors had their imperium extended and retained command of their armies; and they were also assigned a supplementary force of 3,000 Roman citizens, together with 200 cavalry, as well as 6,000 infantry and 300 cavalry from the allies and Latin League. Naval affairs were not neglected, either. The consuls were ordered to organize the election of duumvirs to supervise these, and the duumvirs were to see to the launching of twenty ships, to be manned by crews of Roman citizens who had been slaves, but with command restricted to the free-born. Defence of the coastline was divided between the duumvirs, each commanding ten of the ships; the promontory of Minerva would serve as a line between them, and from this one of them was to stand guard over the area to the right as far as Massilia, and the other over the left as far as Barium.

19. That year there were many dire prodigies witnessed at Rome and also reported from elsewhere. Blood fell as rain in the precincts of Vulcan and Concord; and the pontiffs announced that the spears had moved, and that also the statue of Juno Sospita at Lanuvium had shed tears. There was a plague of such virulence in the countryside, in the rural towns and administrative centres, and in the city, that the burial facilities could scarcely cope with the funerals. Disturbed by these prodigies and natural disasters, the Senators issued a decree that the consuls should offer full-grown victims to the gods they thought fit and also that the decemvirs should consult the books. Following a decree of the decemvirs, a one-day period of devotions at all the couches in Rome was enjoined, and, again at the dictate of the decemvirs, the Senate decreed—and the consuls issued a declaration to the effect—that a three-day period of prayer and holiday be held throughout Italy. Because of a revolt by the Corsicans and a war fomented in Sardinia by the Ilienses the Senate had voted that 8,000 infantry and 300 cavalry be mobilized from the allies and Latin

League, and that the praetor Marcus Pinarius should take these across to Sardinia with him. However, so virulent was the plague that the consuls reported that the dead and the sick were everywhere too numerous for such a total to be reached. The praetor was then ordered to make up the difference in strength from the troops of the proconsul Gnaeus Baebius, who was wintering at Pisae, and then cross to Sardinia.

The praetor Lucius Duronius, to whom Apulia had fallen as his province, was assigned the additional responsibility of investigating the Bacchanalia;* for during the previous year some residual outgrowths, as it were, from the earlier mischief had already come to light, and the inquiries conducted before the praetor Lucius Pupius had, in fact, only been started rather than brought to a conclusion. The Senators ordered the new praetor to cut this evil back to prevent it spreading once more. In addition, on the authority of the Senate, the consuls brought before the people a law against corruption.

20. After this, the consuls brought some delegations into the Senate, the first being those of the kings Eumenes, Ariarathes of Cappadocia, and Pharnaces of Pontus. The response these were given was no more than a promise that the Senate would send representatives to examine and decide upon their disputes. After this, representatives of the Spartan exiles and the Achaeans were shown in, and the exiles were given the hope that the Senate would write to the Achaeans to recommend their return. The Achaeans' account of the recovery of Messene and the settlement made there elicited applause from the Senators. Two spokesmen, Philocles and Apelles, also came from Philip of Macedon. These were not charged with making a request of the Senate, but had been sent rather to act as spies and ask questions about conversations that Perseus had accused Demetrius of holding with the Romans, and especially with Titus Quinctius—conversations concerning the throne and directed against his brother. The king had sent these two in the belief that they were impartial and supporters of neither brother; but in fact they too were henchmen and confederates in Perseus' schemes against his brother.

Demetrius was aware of nothing apart from the recent furore arising from his brother's villainy, and at first he did not entertain sanguine hopes—but he was not without hope either—that his father could be reconciled to him. But every day he felt less and less sure about his father's feelings when he saw Philip's ears beset by his brother. He therefore watched what he said and did in order not to heighten anyone's suspicions, and he especially avoided any mention of, or contact with, the Romans, not even wanting them to write to him because he felt that his father was particularly incensed by aspersions of this kind.

21. So that his soldiers should not lose their edge through inactivity, and at the same time to avert suspicion that he had a war with Rome on his mind, Philip ordered the army to muster at Stobi in Paeonia, and then proceeded to lead it into Maedica.* An urge had taken him to climb to the peak of Mt. Haemus;* for he had accepted the popular belief that the Pontus, the Adriatic Sea, the River Danube, and the Alps could all be seen from there, and he thought this panorama laid out before his eyes would have no little impact on his designs for war with Rome. He made enquiries about the climbing of Haemus of men who knew the area, and discovered that there was general agreement that there was no path for an army, but that †there was a very difficult way up† for a small group of lightly armed men. Philip had decided not to take his younger son with him, and he now wished to soothe his feelings with a tête-à-tête. He first asked Demetrius whether he should persist with his enterprise, given the extreme difficulty of the proposed journey, or drop the idea. If he went ahead with the expedition, he said, he could not in such circumstances forget the example of Antigonus.* Antigonus had once had all his family with him in the same ship when he was overtaken by a violent storm, and he was said to have instructed his children to remember for themselves, and pass on the lesson to their descendants, that nobody should venture to put himself in jeopardy in perilous situations when accompanied by his entire family. Having Antigonus' lesson in mind, said Philip, he would not put his two sons at risk together in the venture that lay ahead; and since he was taking his elder son with him, he would send the younger back to Macedonia to safeguard his hopes for the future and to protect the realm.

Demetrius was not unaware that he was being marginalized so that he would not attend the meeting when Philip, examining the geographical features, would be considering the question of the most direct routes to the Adriatic Sea and Italy and the strategy to be adopted for the war. But he was obliged not only to obey his father but actually to express approval, in order to avoid suspicion that he was obeying reluctantly. To assure Demetrius a safe journey to Macedonia, however, Didas, one of the king's officers who was governor of Paeonia, was ordered to attend him with a small escort. Perseus had recruited this man in the plot to destroy his brother, as he had the majority of his father's friends—ever since doubt had begun to fade from everyone's mind on who was to inherit the throne, given the king's preference. For the moment Perseus' instructions to Didas were to use all manner of obsequious behaviour to worm his way into as close a relationship with Demetrius as possible, so as to be able to elicit from him all his secrets and monitor his innermost thoughts. So it was that Demetrius went off with an escort that put him in greater danger than if he were travelling alone.

22. Philip first crossed Maedica, and then the deserted areas between Maedica and the Haemus range, reaching the foot of the mountain on the seventh day of the march. He spent a day there to select the men he would take with him, and started on the journey on the third day after his arrival. There was little strain at first, in the foothills, but the higher they went the more they were faced with forest and ground that was for the most part impenetrable. They then reached a pathway so thickly shaded that the sky was barely to be seen through the dense cover of the trees with their intertwining branches. And when they were approaching the crest there was such a blanket of mist over the whole area—a rare phenomenon at high altitudes*—that they were hampered as much as on a night-march. Finally, on the third day, they reached the top.

On their descent they did not discredit the popular belief, more, I think, to avoid ridicule for a wasted journey than because the widely separated seas, mountains, and rivers could really be seen from the one spot. They were all in pain from the rigours of the expedition, the king more so than the others because of the heavier burden of his age. He sacrificed on the two altars consecrated there to Jupiter and the Sun, and then in two days came down the path he had taken three to climb. For he was particularly afraid of the cold at night which was, even though it was the time of the rising of the dog-star, like the cold of winter.

After contending with many difficulties during those days, Philip found the situation no brighter in the camp, where there was an extreme dearth of provisions, as was to be expected in a region surrounded on all sides by wastelands. Accordingly, after waiting only a single day to rest the men he had taken with him, the king swiftly crossed to the Dentheleti on a march that was more like a flight. The Dentheleti were allies, but the Macedonians, because of their shortages, plundered their lands like those of an enemy. At first they destroyed scattered farmhouses with their raids, and then certain villages as well, not without a deep feeling of shame on the part of the king when he heard the voices of his allies vainly appealing to the gods who oversee alliances, and calling out his name.

Taking grain from the area, Philip drew back into Maedica and launched an attack on a town which they call Petra. He himself pitched camp where the city is approached from the plain, and sent his son Perseus around with a small force to attack the town from higher ground. With fearful pressure being exerted on them from every side, the townspeople for the moment gave hostages and surrendered; but, after the army retreated, they forgot about their hostages, abandoned the town and sought refuge in fortified areas and the mountains.

Philip had exhausted his men with all manner of hardship and had achieved nothing; and his suspicions of his son had been increased by the machinations of his officer Didas. He therefore returned to Macedonia.

23. Didas, as noted above, had been sent to accompany Demetrius. By flattery, and by voicing indignation over Demetrius' plight, he worked on the naïvety of the unsuspecting young man, who was understandably incensed with his family. Freely offering his help in everything, and giving him assurance of his loyalty, Didas winkled his secrets out of him. Demetrius was considering flight to the Romans, and it looked as if a heaven-sent helper for his project had been offered him—the governor of Paeonia, through whose province he had conceived the hope of being able to escape in safety. This plan was promptly betrayed to Demetrius' brother, and at the latter's instigation to the father as well. A letter was first of all brought to Philip during his siege of Petra. After this Herodorus, the best friend of Demetrius, was thrown in prison, and orders were issued for Demetrius to be kept discreetly under surveillance.

Coming on top of everything else, these events cast gloom over the king's return to Macedonia. He was deeply disturbed by the latest charges, but he still felt that he should await the return of the men whom he had sent to Rome to make a full investigation. He had for some months been tortured by these anxieties when his delegates eventually returned—but these had earlier worked out, in Macedonia, the report they would make from Rome. In addition to their other nefarious acts, they also brought the king a forged letter to which was affixed a counterfeit seal of Titus Quinctius. The letter contained an apology for any dealings the young man, led astray by lust for the throne, had had with him. Demetrius, he said, would not harm any of his family, and Scipio himself was not a person who could be thought likely to support any dishonourable plan. This letter furnished confirmation for Perseus' charges. As a result, Herodorus was immediately subjected to lengthy torture; but he died in agony without revealing anything.

24. Perseus once more denounced Demetrius to his father. The escape that he had been preparing through Paeonia was used against him, along with his having bribed some men to escort him on the journey; but it was the forged letter from Titus Quinctius that did the most damage. So that he could be furtively eliminated, however, no harsh judgement was formally passed on him; and this was not out of consideration for Demetrius, but so that his penalty would not bring to notice Philip's plans against the Romans.

Philip himself was to travel from Thessalonica to Demetrias. He sent Demetrius, again in the company of Didas, to Astraeum in Paeonia, and Perseus he sent to Amphipolis to receive hostages from the Thracians. As Didas left him, Philip is said to have given him instructions about his son's murder. Didas either held or pretended to hold a sacrifice; Demetrius was invited to participate, and for it he came from Astraeum to Heraclea. At the dinner, it is said, poison was given to him. After drinking the cup Demetrius realized what was afoot. Soon the pains commenced; and he left the table and retired to his bedroom. Here, in agony, he deplored his father's cruelty, and denounced his brother's murderous act and Didas' villainy. Then a certain Thyrsis from Stuberra and Alexander of Beroea were sent into the room, and these pulled the coverlets over his head and mouth and smothered him. Thus was the murder of the guiltless young man effected, with his enemies not even satisfied with a single form of death for him.

25. While this was happening in Macedonia, Lucius Aemilius, who had had his imperium extended, †led his troops† against the Ligurian Ingauni at the beginning of spring. As soon as he pitched

camp in the territory of the enemy, some envoys came to him, ostensibly to seek peace but really to gather intelligence. When Paullus said he negotiated peace only with those who surrendered, the men did not reject this out of hand but rather claimed that, their countrymen being peasants, they needed time to bring them round. Given a ten-day truce to do this, the envoys then requested that the Roman soldiers not cross the mountains next to the camp in search of forage and wood, since these were the cultivated areas of their territory. When they were granted this request, the Ligurians brought together their entire army behind the very mountains from which they had kept their enemy clear and, with huge numbers of men, suddenly launched an attack on the camp of the Romans, assaulting all the gates simultaneously. They kept up the attack with extreme violence throughout the day, not even giving the Romans enough time to bear out the standards or enough room to deploy their line. Packed into the gateways, the Romans defended their camp more by obstructing the enemy than fighting them.

The enemy withdrew at sunset. Paullus then sent two riders to the proconsul Gnaeus Baebius at Pisae bearing a letter in which he asked Baebius to come to his assistance as soon as possible since he was under siege during a time of truce. Baebius had passed his army on to the praetor Marcus Pinarius who was then on his way to Sardinia, but he informed the Senate by dispatch that Lucius Aemilius was under siege from the Ligurians. He also wrote to Marcus Claudius Marcellus, whose province was closest to Aemilius, with the request that Marcellus should, if he concurred, take his army from Gaul to Liguria and free Lucius Aemilius from the siege. This assistance was going to arrive too late. The Ligurians returned to the Roman camp the following day, and though Aemilius knew they would be coming, and though he could have led his men out to battle-stations, he instead kept them within the rampart in order to drag out the engagement until such time as Baebius could get there with his army from Pisae.

26. In Rome, Baebius' dispatch caused great consternation, and this was made all the greater because, when Marcellus arrived in Rome a few days later, he had already turned his army over to Fabius and thus removed any hope of the army stationed in Gaul possibly being transferred to the Ligurian theatre. Marcellus explained that this was because a war was going on with the Istrians, who were

blocking the establishment of the colony at Aquileia; Fabius had set out for the region, he said, and could not return since hostilities had already commenced

There remained only one way of bringing succour, and that was slower than the emergency required, namely if the consuls brought forward their departure to their province. All the Senators loudly proclaimed that this was what they should do. The consuls, however, said they would not go before the troop levies were concluded, and it was not their inactivity that was to blame for the late completion of this but the virulence of the disease that was circulating. Nevertheless, they could not resist the collective will of the Senate, and they did set off in their military cloaks, giving the soldiers whom they had already conscripted a day on which they were to gather at Pisae. The consuls were permitted to enrol emergency troops summarily along their route and take these with them. The praetors Quintus Petillius and Quintus Fabius were also given their orders: Petillius was to enlist two emergency legions of Roman citizens and to administer the military oath to all men under fifty, and Fabius was to conscript 15,000 infantry and 800 cavalry from the allies and the Latin League. Gaius Matienus and Gaius Lucretius were elected naval duumvirs,* and vessels were equipped for them. Matienus, whose administrative sphere extended to the Gallic gulf, was ordered to take his fleet to the Ligurian coastline at the earliest possible opportunity in the hope that he might be able to be of service to Lucius Aemilius and his army at any point.

27. When no assistance appeared from any quarter, Aemilius assumed his riders had been intercepted and he felt he should no longer delay putting his own fortunes to the test. The enemy's conduct of the siege was somewhat remiss and desultory, and before they arrived back on the scene he deployed his troops at the four camp gates* so they could simultaneously charge out on every side once given the signal.

To the four supplementary cohorts Aemilius attached a further two, putting his legate Marcus Valerius in command of them and ordering them to make their charge from the praetorian gate. At the main gate on the right he deployed the *hastati* of the first legion, and placed the *principes* of that same legion in reserve; the military tribunes Marcus Servilius and Lucius Sulpicius were given command of these troops. The third legion was drawn up at the main gate on the left, the only change here being that the *principes* were set in front and the *hastati* in reserve; the military tribunes Sextus Iulius Caesar and Lucius Aurelius Cotta were given command of this legion. The lieutenant Quintus Fulvius Flaccus was stationed at the quaestorian gate with the right auxiliary division, and two cohorts plus the *triarii* of the two legions were instructed to stay back to protect the camp.

The commander went around all the gates in person to deliver his exhortation, using all the taunts he could to rouse the anger of his men. At one moment he would denounce the treachery of an enemy who sued for peace, were granted a truce, and then took advantage of the very time of that truce to come to attack their camp, violating international convention; at another he would make it clear to them how much shame was involved in a Roman army facing a siege by Ligurians, who were bandits rather than a real enemy.

'If you get away from here through the assistance of others rather than by means of your own valour,' he said, 'what expression will each of you have on his face when he meets his fellow-soldiers—I do not mean those soldiers who defeated Hannibal, Philip, and Antiochus, the greatest kings and generals of our day, but those who have on many occasions chased down and cut to pieces like animals these very Ligurians as they ran through their trackless forests? What Spaniards would not dare to do, or Gauls, Macedonians, or Carthaginians, our Ligurian enemy is now doing—approaching the Roman rampart, actually besieging and attacking it, and this an enemy that we had difficulty finding earlier as he lurked in hiding and we beat remote forests for him!'

In answer to these words a cry went up in unison from the men. The soldiers were not to blame, they said, since no one had given them a signal to charge out. Let him give the signal—he would learn that both the Romans and the Ligurians were the same as they had been before!

28. There were two Ligurian camps on the Roman side of the mountains, and during the early days of the siege the enemy would all advance together from these at dawn, well-ordered and ready for combat. By now, however, they were taking up arms only after gorging themselves with food and wine, and they would come forth poorly organized and out of formation, like men almost convinced their enemy would not advance their standards beyond their palisade.

They were advancing out of formation like this when the Romans burst out against them from all the gates at the same time, with everybody in the camp, servants and camp-followers included, raising the war-cry together. The move so surprised the Ligurians that they were as panic-stricken as if they had been caught in an ambush. For a brief moment there was some semblance of a battle; then there was only disordered flight and everywhere the massacre of fleeing Ligurians, for the cavalry had been given the signal to mount up and allow none to escape. The Ligurians were to a man driven into their camps in a frenzied rout, and then the camps were also taken from them. More than 15,000 Ligurians were killed that day, and 2,500 prisoners were taken. Three days later the whole nation of the Ligurian Ingauni gave hostages and capitulated. The pilots and crews †which had manned† their pirate-ships were hunted down and all thrown in prison. Thirty-two such ships were captured by the duumvir Gaius Matienus on the Ligurian coast.

Lucius Aurelius Cotta and Gaius Sulpicius Galus were sent to Rome to report on this and deliver dispatches to the Senate. At the same time they were to request permission for Lucius Aemilius to quit his sphere of command, its duties having been discharged, and to bring back and demobilize his men. Both requests were granted by the Senate which also authorized a three-day period of thanksgiving at all the couches. Instructions were issued to the praetors as well; Petillius was to demobilize the city legions, and Fabius to terminate his conscription amongst the allies and Latin League. The urban praetor was to inform the consuls in writing that the Senate thought it appropriate that the emergency troops raised to meet the uprising be disbanded at the earliest possible moment.

29. The colony of Gravisca was founded that year in Etruscan territory that had earlier been captured from the people of Tarquinii. Five acres of land were granted to each settler, and the founding triumvirs were Gaius Calpurnius Piso, Publius Claudius Pulcher, and Gaius Terentius Histra. The year was exceptional for its drought and crop failures, and it is recorded that for six months no rain fell anywhere.

This same year some farm-workers were digging the soil at a greater than usual depth on the land of the clerk Lucius Petillius below the Janiculum, when two stone chests were unearthed. These were about eight feet long and four feet wide, and had lids fastened down with lead. Each chest bore an inscription in Greek and in Latin which stated that Numa Pompilius, son of Pompo and king of the Romans, was buried in the one, and that the books of Numa Pompilius were in the other. On the advice of his friends, the landowner opened the chests. The one with the inscription claiming that the king was buried in it was found empty, with no trace of a human body or of anything else; the decomposition of so many years had removed everything. In the other chest were two bundles tied with a wax cord, each containing seven scrolls which were not only in one piece but even appeared of recent date. Seven, in Latin, dealt with pontifical law; the other seven, in Greek, dealt with a branch of philosophy that might have been in vogue in the period of Numa. Valerius Antias adds the detail that they were Pythagorean, and by a plausible piece of fiction lends support to the popular view that Numa had been a student of Pythagoras.

The books were initially read by Petillius' friends who were on the spot. Later, as the number of readers increased and they became better known, the urban praetor Quintus Petillius was eager to study the books, and he borrowed them from Lucius Petillius. (In fact, the two men were acquainted, for Quintus Petillius had, as quaestor, selected Lucius as a clerk on his staff.) On a general perusal of the contents, the praetor noticed a number of things tending to undermine Roman religion, and he told Lucius Petillius that he intended to burn the books. Before doing so, however, he said he was giving Lucius the opportunity to avail himself of any legal recourse or public assistance at his disposal for recovering the books, and that he would not lose the praetor's friendship by doing this. The clerk went to see the plebeian tribunes, and the matter was referred by the tribunes to the Senate. The praetor declared that he was ready to swear that the books should not be read or preserved, and the Senate voted that the praetor's undertaking to swear to this should be deemed sufficient, and that the books should be burned in the comitium at the earliest opportunity. They added that the owner should be reimbursed for the books to an amount determined by the praetor Quintus Petillius and a majority of the tribunes. The clerk refused payment, and the books were burned in the comitium before the eyes of the people in a fire lit by the sacrificial assistants.

30. A major war broke out in Hither Spain that summer. The Celtiberians had mustered some 35,000 men, a number almost

unprecedented before that time. Quintus Fulvius Flaccus, governor of the province, had heard that the Celtiberians were putting their men of military age under arms, and had himself mobilized as great a force of auxiliaries as he could from the allies, but he came nowhere near his enemy in terms of numbers. At the beginning of spring Flaccus led his army into Carpetania and encamped near the town of Aebura after installing a garrison in it. A few days later the Celtiberians pitched camp about two miles from him at the foot of a hill. When the Roman praetor became aware of their arrival, he dispatched his brother Marcus Fulvius with two squadrons of allied cavalry towards the enemy camp on a reconnoitring expedition. Fulvius was told to approach the enemy rampart as closely as possible in order to inspect the dimensions of the camp, but to avoid combat and to fall back if he saw the enemy cavalry making a sortie.

Fulvius followed his instructions and for a number of days there was no action apart from these two squadrons making an appearance and then retreating whenever the enemy cavalry charged out of the camp. Eventually, the Celtiberians left their camp with all their infantry and cavalry forces at the same time, and took up a position in battle-formation mid-way between the two camps. The plain was completely level and well-suited for combat. The Spaniards stood here, waiting for their enemy, but the Roman commander kept his men within his rampart. For four days in succession the Spaniards kept their line deployed in the same spot and no move was made by the Romans. After this, since they were given no opportunity to engage, the Celtiberians remained inactive in their camp. Only the cavalry rode out to mount guard, so as to be ready in the event of any enemy movement. Both sides would go behind their camps to forage and gather wood, neither trying to obstruct the other.

31. When he was satisfied that so many days of inactivity had led his enemy to expect that he would not initiate the action, the Roman praetor ordered Lucius Acilius to take the left division and 6,000 provincial auxiliaries and move around the hill that lay to rear of the enemy. When, from this position, he heard a shout, Acilius was to swoop down on the enemy camp.

The force set off at night to avoid detection. At dawn, Flaccus sent a commander of the allies, Gaius Scribonius, to the enemy rampart at the head of the supplementary cavalry of the left division. When the Celtiberians saw them coming closer than they usually did, and in larger numbers, their cavalry came pouring *en masse* from their camp, and at the same time the signal to march out was given to the infantry. Following his instructions, Scribonius wheeled round his horses as soon as he heard the noise of the enemy cavalry, and headed back to camp. This prompted an even more reckless pursuit by the enemy. First came the cavalry, and soon after them came the infantry-line, confidently expecting that they would take the camp by storm that day. They were now no more than half a mile from the rampart. Flaccus had deployed his force within the rampart and, when he judged that the enemy had been sufficiently drawn away from the shelter of their camp, he burst forth with his troops from three points at the same time, raising a war-cry which was intended not merely to fire enthusiasm for the fight, but also to be heard by the men in the hills. The latter, following their orders, did not hesitate to swoop down on the camp, where the guard that had been left numbered no more than 5,000 men. These were panic-stricken by the paucity of their own numbers, by the size of the enemy's, and by the suddenness of the attack; and the camp was taken almost without a fight. †The camp taken† Acilius set it on fire at the point that could most easily be seen by the combatants.

32. It was the Celtiberians at the rear of their battle line who first spotted the flames. Word then spread throughout the line that the camp was lost, and was burning at that very moment. What filled the Celtiberians with terror also served to boost the morale of the Romans; the cries of their triumphant comrades came to them at one moment, and at the next the blazing camp of the enemy appeared before their eyes. For an instant the Celtiberians wavered in uncertainty. But retreat was impossible if they were defeated, and their only hope lay in the fight; and so they rejoined the battle with greater determination. At the centre of the line they were under severe pressure from the fifth legion. However, they moved forward more confidently against the left wing, on which they saw the Romans had positioned the provincial auxiliaries from their own people. The Roman left wing now faced defeat, and would have suffered it but for aid brought by the seventh legion. At that same moment the men who had been left to garrison Aebura arrived from the town, at the point when the battle was at its hottest, and Acilius also appeared to the rear of the enemy. For a long time the Celtiberians were cut to pieces between them; and the survivors fled and

scattered in all directions. The cavalry, sent after them in two sections, inflicted heavy casualties. Some 23,000 of the enemy were killed that day and 4,700 were captured, along with more than 500 horses and 88 military standards. It was a great victory but not a bloodless one. From the two legions slightly more than 200 Roman soldiers lost their lives, along with 830 allies and members of the Latin League, and some 2,400 foreign auxiliaries. The praetor led his triumphant army back to their camp, and Acilius was ordered to remain in the camp that he had captured. The following day the spoils were gathered together from the enemy, and the men who had shown outstanding valour in the battle were rewarded at an assembly.

33. The wounded were then transported to the town of Aebura, and the legions were marched through Carpetania to Contrebia. When this town was besieged, it sent for assistance from the Celtiberians. The Celtiberians were slow to arrive—not from any hesitation on their part but because they were detained after leaving home by roads made impassable by incessant rain and by swollen rivers. The people of Contrebia thus lost hope of receiving aid from their friends and surrendered. Flaccus, who was also at the mercy of the foul weather, was compelled to bring his entire army into the town.

The Celtiberians had left home unaware of the surrender. As soon as the rains let up, they finally crossed the rivers and reached Contrebia; but when they saw no camp outside the walls they assumed that it had been taken to the other side of town, or else that the enemy had retreated. Accordingly, they advanced on the town in a careless and disorganized fashion. The Romans charged out at them from two gates, attacking and putting to flight a disordered enemy. The circumstance that prevented the Celtiberians from resisting and putting up a fight, namely that they were not approaching in a single column or massed around the standards, also proved to be the salvation of most of them, and permitted escape. For they were scattered and dispersed all over the plain, and at no point did the enemy catch them grouped together. Even so about 12,000 men were cut down, and more than 5,000 prisoners were taken, along with 400 horses and 62 military standards. The stragglers who reached home after the rout turned back a second army of Celtiberians coming to the fight by telling them of the surrender of Contrebia and of their own defeat. They all then immediately slipped away to their villages and strongholds. Leaving Contrebia, Flaccus conducted his legions on a marauding expedition through Celtiberia, assaulting large numbers of strongholds, until most of the Celtiberians surrendered.

34. Such were that year's operations in Hither Spain. In the further province the praetor Manlius fought a number of successful battles against the Lusitanians.

The Latin colony of Aquileia was founded that year in Gallic territory. Three thousand infantry each received fifty acres, with centurions each receiving a hundred and cavalrymen a hundred and forty. The founding triumvirs were Publius Cornelius Scipio Nasica, Gaius Flaminius, and Lucius Manlius Acidinus. Two temples were dedicated in the course of the year. One was the temple of Venus Erycina at the Porta Collina which the duumvir Lucius Porcius Licinus, son of Lucius, dedicated and which had been promised in a vow by Lucius Porcius as consul during the Ligurian War. The other was the temple of Pietas in the vegetable market. This shrine was dedicated by the duumvir Manius Acilius Glabrio who erected there a gilded statue—the very first gilded statue set up in Italy—of his father Glabrio. It was the latter who had promised the temple in a vow on the day of his decisive engagement with Antiochus at Thermopylae; and he had contracted out the work in accordance with a decree of the Senate.

It was during the period of the dedication of these temples that the proconsul Lucius Aemilius Paullus celebrated his triumph over the Ligurian Ingauni. He carried in his procession 25 golden crowns, but apart from this no gold or silver was borne in that triumph. Large numbers of captive Ligurian chieftains were led along before his chariot. Paullus distributed three hundred *asses* to each of his men. To add to the brilliance of this triumph, Ligurian ambassadors came with a request for an abiding peace—the Ligurian people, they said, had resolved never again to take up arms except at the command of the Roman people. The reply given to the Ligurians by the praetor Quintus Fabius, who spoke to them at the behest of the Senate, was that there was nothing new in the Ligurian declaration; what was most in their interest said Fabius, was to assume a new attitude that matched that declaration. He told them to approach the consuls and follow the orders they gave, adding that the Senate would accept only the consuls' word on whether the Ligurians were sincere in making peace. There was now peace in Liguria.

There was a clash with the Corsicans in Corsica, where the praetor Marcus Pinarius killed some 2,000 in battle. The defeat obliged the Corsicans to give hostages and 100,000 pounds of wax. The army was then taken to Sardinia where there were successful engagements with the Ilienses, a tribe that is not even today completely pacified. The same year a hundred hostages were returned to the Carthaginians, and the Romans guaranteed them peace not only with themselves but also with Masinissa, who was occupying the disputed territory with an armed force.

35. The consuls had a province free of trouble. Marcus Baebius was recalled to Rome for the elections, and he returned as consuls Aulus Postumius Albinus Luscus and Gaius Calpurnius Piso. The following were then elected praetors: Tiberius Sempronius Gracchus, Lucius Postumius Albinus, Publius Cornelius †Mamercus†,* Tiberius Minucius Molliculus, Aulus Hostilius Mancinus, and Gaius Maenius. All of these took up their appointments on 15 March.

At the start of the year of the consulship of Aulus Postumius Albinus and Gaius Calpurnius Piso, the legate Lucius Minucius* and two military tribunes, Titus Maenius and Lucius Terentius Massaliota, were brought into the Senate by the consul Aulus Postumius. These had come from Quintus Fulvius Flaccus in Hither Spain. They brought word of the two successful battles, the surrender of Celtiberia and the completion of the mission assigned to Fulvius. They added that the payment normally sent to the province and the grain transported to the army were not needed that year. They made two requests of the Senate, first that the immortal gods be honoured in the light of the successful operations, and secondly that Quintus Fulvius be permitted to take with him, when he left the province, the army of whose gallant service both he and many praetors before him had availed themselves. Apart from being the correct procedure, this was almost an unavoidable one, they said. The soldiers were so set on leaving that keeping them any longer in the province appeared impossible, and they would go without authorization if they were not demobilized, or would break into a catastrophic mutiny if coerced into staying.

The Senate ordered that Liguria be the province of the two consuls, and the ensuing praetorian sortition went as follows:

Aulus Hostilius	urban jurisdiction
Tiberius Minucius	foreigners' jurisdiction
Publius Cornelius	Sicily
Gaius Maenius	Sardinia

The Spanish provinces were drawn by Lucius Postumius (Farther) and Tiberius Sempronius (Hither). The latter was to succeed Quintus Fulvius, and he was afraid of his province being robbed of its veteran army. 'I put this question to you, Lucius Minucius,' he said, 'since you report on "the completion of the mission". Do you think the Celtiberians will always remain loyal, so that the province can be administered without an army? If you cannot give us any assurance or guarantee about the loyalty of the barbarians, and you think an army has to be maintained there in any case, which course of action would you recommend to the Senate? Sending supplementary forces to Spain so that only those soldiers whose service is complete can be demobilized, and having new recruits integrated with veterans? Or withdrawing the veteran legions, and raising and sending new ones there—when disdain for inexperienced recruits could incite to rebellion barbarians even less aggressive than these? Subduing a naturally fierce and recalcitrant province is easier said than done. Few cities—or so I am told—have come under our control and authority, and these were kept in check mostly by the proximity of our winter-quarters. The more remote cities are up in arms. That being so, Senators, I make this declaration right now. I will perform the duties of state with the army that is now there; and if Flaccus takes his legions away with him, I shall select a pacified area for my winter-quarters and will not expose inexperienced soldiers to our most ferocious enemy.'

36. In response to the questions put to him, the legate said that neither he nor anyone else could guess what the Celtiberians had in mind now, or would have in future. He could not, therefore, deny that it was more judicious for an army to be sent to a province where the barbarians, pacified though they were, were not yet sufficiently habituated to being ruled. But whether it should be a new or veteran army, that was for that man to say who could be sure how faithfully the Celtiberians would keep the peace, and who at the same time knew for certain that the soldiers would acquiesce if they were further detained in the province. If their sentiments had to be gauged

from their conversations with each other, or from the tenor of their shouts when harangued by the commander, they had openly and loudly proclaimed that they would either keep the commander in the province or come to Italy with him.

A motion made by the consuls interrupted the dispute between the praetor and the legate; it was their opinion that their provinces should be dealt with before the praetor's army was discussed. An entirely new army was formally assigned to the consuls: two Roman legions for each, with the appropriate cavalry, and the regular number of allies and members of the Latin League, that is 15,000, infantry and 800 cavalry. With this army the consuls were ordered to make war on the Ligurian Apuani. Publius Cornelius and Marcus Baebius had their imperium extended and were instructed to govern their provinces until the arrival of the consuls, at which point their orders were to demobilize the armies under their command and return to Rome.

Discussion of Tiberius Sempronius' army followed. The consuls were instructed to mobilize a new legion for him consisting of 5,200 infantry and 400 cavalry, with an additional force of 1,000 Roman infantry and 50 cavalry. They were also to conscript for him 7,000 infantry and 300 cavalry from the allies and members of the Latin League. This was the army with which it was decided that Tiberius Sempronius was to proceed to Hither Spain. Quintus Fulvius was permitted to take with him from the province, if he so decided, the soldiers—Roman citizens and allies—who had been transported to Spain before the consulship of Spurius Postumius and Quintus Marcius.* He could also take men whose valiant service he had relied on in the two battles against the Celtiberians, up to the number by which the complement of the two legions (10,400 infantry, 600 cavalry, plus 12,000 infantry and 600 cavalry of the allies and Latin League) was exceeded when the supplementary forces were added. Furthermore, periods of public thanksgiving were proclaimed in honour of Fulvius' sterling service to the state. The other praetors were also sent off to their provinces, and Quintus Fabius Buteo had his imperium extended in Gaul. It was decided that there should be a total of eight legions that year, apart from the veteran army in service in Liguria which anticipated discharge in the near future. And because of the epidemic which had already been ravaging the city of Rome and Italy for two years, it was only with difficulty that the complement of this force was attained.

37. The praetor Tiberius Minucius died at this time, and not long after him so did the consul Gaius Calpurnius and many other distinguished men of all classes. Eventually the calamitous death-toll became regarded as a portent. The pontifex maximus, Gaius Servilius, was ordered to look into ways of appeasing the anger of the gods, while the decemvirs were to consult the books and the consul was to offer vows of gifts and present gilded statues to Apollo, Aesculapius, and Salus (and he did indeed offer the vows and make the presentation). The decemvirs proclaimed a two-day period of public devotions for the return of the country's health, to be held not just in Rome but throughout the country towns and administrative centres, and all people over twelve years of age offered these prayers wearing garlands and holding laurel boughs in their hands.

The suspicion that some human villainy was at work had also wormed its way into people's minds, and the praetor Gaius Claudius, who had been elected to replace Tiberius Minucius, was charged by Senatorial decree with investigating cases of poisoning that had taken place in the city, or within ten miles of it; cases in the country towns and rural centres beyond the tenth milestone were to be the responsibility of Gaius Maenius before he made the crossing to his province of Sardinia. The consul's death aroused greatest suspicion—it was said that he had been murdered by his wife, Quarta Hostilia. In fact, it was when her son, Quintus Fulvius Flaccus, was declared consul to replace his stepfather that Piso's death began to develop into a somewhat greater scandal. Witnesses came forward to attest that, after Albinus and Piso had been declared consuls in an election in which Flaccus had been defeated, Flaccus had been reproached by his mother for having now been three times a losing candidate for the consulship. She had added that he should prepare to run for the office again—that she would see to his becoming consul within two months. There were many other pieces of evidence relevant to the case but it was this comment, proven all too true by what followed, that secured Hostilia's conviction.

At the beginning of this spring, army recruitment detained the new consuls at Rome, and the death of one of the consuls, and election of a consul to replace him, produced a delay in all affairs of state. Meanwhile, Publius Cornelius and Marcus Baebius, who had done nothing worthy of note in their consulship, led their army against the Ligurian Apuani.

38. The Ligurians had not been expecting a war before the arrival of the consuls in the province, and they were taken by surprise and defeated. Some 12,000 surrendered. Cornelius and Baebius, who had first consulted the Senate on the matter by letter, decided to bring these down from their hills into land on the plains, far from their home. Their purpose was to deprive them of any hope of returning; for they thought that before that was done there was no way of ending the Ligurian War. There was some public land belonging to the Roman people in Samnite territory that had formerly been the property of the Taurasini. <. . .> This was where the consuls wished to relocate the Ligurian Apuani, and so they issued an order for them to come down from the hills with their wives and children, and bring with them all their possessions. The Ligurians made numerous appeals through spokesmen, begging not to be forced to leave their household gods, the place where they had been born and the tombs of their forefathers; and they promised to surrender their arms and give hostages. Their appeals were of no avail, but they had not the strength to fight, and so they obeyed the order. Some 40,000 free men, along with their wives and children, were relocated at public expense, and were given 150,000 sesterces for the purchase of necessary items for their new homes. Charged with the division of land and distribution of money were Cornelius and Baebius, the same men who had carried out the relocation, but at their own request these were given an advisory board, comprising five men, by the Senate.

The business complete, Cornelius and Baebius led the veteran army back to Rome where they were accorded a triumph by the Senate. They were the very first men to celebrate triumphs without having fought a war. Only the sacrificial animals were led before the chariot, because in their triumphs there was nothing to be carried, no captives to be led, and nothing to be distributed to the soldiers.

39. In Spain that same year the proconsul Fulvius Flaccus' successor was slow to arrive in his province. Flaccus therefore led his troops from winter-quarters and proceeded to lay waste the more distant territory of Celtiberia, where the natives had not surrendered. By this move he provoked rather than cowed the spirit of the barbarians, who covertly mobilized their forces and blockaded the Manlian Gorge, through which they well knew the Roman army would pass.

Now when his colleague, Lucius Postumius Albinus, was leaving for Farther Spain, Gracchus had charged him with instructions for Quintus Fulvius to bring the army to Tarraco, where Gracchus wished to discharge the veterans, distribute the supplementary troops, and generally reorganize the army. Flaccus was also notified of the day on which his successor was to arrive, and this was close at hand. The arrival of this news obliged Flaccus to abandon the project on which he had already embarked and lead the army swiftly from Celtiberia. The barbarians were unaware of his reason for doing this. They supposed he had got wind of their uprising and the covert mobilization of their troops, and had lost his nerve. They were accordingly all the more vigorous in blockading the gorge. When the Roman column entered the pass at break of day, the enemy suddenly rose up on both sides at the same time and attacked the Romans.

Seeing this, Flaccus calmed the initial commotion in the column by issuing instructions through his centurions for all to stay where they were and make ready their weapons. He then brought the baggage and pack-animals to one spot and, either in person or else by means of the legates and military tribunes, deployed all the troops as the emergency and terrain required, and without a hint of panic. All the time he reminded them that their engagement was with men who had twice surrendered; that the new qualities these men had found were villainy and duplicity, not courage or fortitude; and that they had done the Romans the favour of turning a lacklustre return to the fatherland into a glorious and memorable one. They would, he said, be carrying back for the triumph swords spattered with the fresh gore of the enemy, and spoils dripping with blood. Time did not permit a longer address; the enemy were rushing to the attack and there was already fighting at the extremities of the field. Then the lines clashed.

40. It was a ferocious battle in all quarters, but fortunes varied. The legions put up a magnificent fight, and the two divisions were no less energetic. The foreign auxiliaries, under pressure from enemy counterparts similarly armed but a better class of soldiers than they, could not hold their ground. When the Celtiberians realized that they were no match for the legions in ordered battle with lines drawn up against each other, they made an assault with a wedge-formation, a manner of fighting in which they are so strong that resistance is impossible at any point at which they have directed their charge. On this occasion, too, the legions were thrown into disarray, and the line almost broken. When he saw the panic this caused, Flaccus rode up to the legionary cavalry and said: 'Unless you can provide some assistance, this army of ours is done for.' From all sides they loudly asked him simply to tell them what action he wanted taken—they would not be half-hearted in carrying out his orders.

'You cavalry of the two legions,' he said, 'double up your squadrons. Turn your steeds on the enemy wedge at the point where they are bearing down on our men. You will have more force in your charge if you drive the horses into them at full gallop—we are told that Roman cavalry have often won great glory by such a manœuvre.'

The men obeyed his command and, dropping the reins, twice ran back and forth through the ranks of the enemy, causing great loss of life and shivering all their spears. The Celtiberians' hopes had all been pinned on their wedge-formation; with this now broken up they panicked and, virtually abandoning the fight, looked around for a way to flee. Witnessing the notable coup brought off by the Roman cavalry, the allied cavalry were inspired by their courage and, without an order from anyone, themselves directed their horses against an enemy already in disarray. At that point the Celtiberians all scattered in flight and the Roman commander, looking upon the routed enemy, made a promise in a vow of a temple for Fortuna Equestris, and games for Jupiter Optimus Maximus. Celtiberians were cut down throughout the pass as they dispersed in flight. It is said that 17,000 of the enemy were killed that day, with †more than 3,200 taken alive† and 77 military standards and almost †1,100 horses† captured. That day the victorious army remained †in the enemy camp†. The victory was not without loss of men: 472 Roman soldiers fell, and 1,019 allies and members of the Latin League, along with 3,000 auxiliary troops.

And so the triumphant army, which had recovered its earlier glory, was led to Tarraco. The praetor Tiberius Sempronius, who had arrived two days earlier, came to meet Fulvius on his arrival and congratulated him on his outstanding service to the state. They were in perfect agreement on which soldiers to discharge and which to retain. Fulvius then embarked his demobilized men on ships and left for Rome, and Sempronius led the legions into Celtiberia.

41. The two consuls led their armies against the Ligurians in different regions. Postumius laid siege to Mt. Ballista and Mt. Letum with the first and third legions. He put pressure on the enemy with a blockade of their narrow passes, thus cutting their supply-lines, and brought them to heel by depriving them of all provisions. With the second and fourth legions, Fulvius launched an attack from the direction of Pisae on the Ligurian Apuani living on the banks of the River Macra. Accepting the surrender of about 7,000 of them, he put them on ships and had them transported along the shore of the Tuscan Sea to Neapolis. From there they were taken to Samnium where they were given land amongst their compatriots. The vines of the mountain Ligurians were cut down and their grain burned by Aulus Postumius until they were finally forced by all the military defeats they had suffered to capitulate and surrender their arms. Postumius then advanced by ship to reconnoitre the coastline of the Ligurian Ingauni and Intemelii.

Before these consuls reached the army which had been instructed to assemble at Pisae, Aulus Postumius was in command. The brother of Quintus Fulvius, Marcus Fulvius Nobilior, was military tribune of the second legion, and during his months of command he disbanded the legion, making the centurions swear an oath to convey the moneys involved to the quaestors for deposit in the treasury. When word of this was brought to Aulus at Placentia—to which, by chance, he had proceeded—he set off in pursuit of the demobilized soldiers with some light horse. Those whom he was able to overtake he reprimanded and took back to Pisae, and he informed the consul about the others. On the consul's motion, a Senatorial decree was passed that Marcus Fulvius be exiled to Spain, to a point beyond New Carthage, and he was also given a letter to take to Publius Manlius in Farther Spain. The soldiers were directed to return to service, and it was decreed that the legion, as a mark of disgrace, be given only six month's pay for that year. In the case of any soldier failing to return to the army, the consul was ordered to sell him and his possessions.

42. The same year Lucius Duronius, who had been praetor the previous year, returned from Illyricum to Brundisium with ten ships. Leaving his fleet in the harbour, he proceeded from Brundisium to Rome. He gave an account of his actions in Illyricum, during which he squarely fixed the blame for all the piracy on the seas on

Gentius, king of the Illyrians. Gentius' kingdom, said Duronius, was the source of all the ships that had ravaged the coastline of the Adriatic; Duronius had sent representatives to him on these matters, but they had not been given an opportunity to meet the king.

Ambassadors from Gentius had already come to Rome to say that when the Romans had come for an audience with him, the king had by chance been ill in the farthest reaches of his kingdom. Gentius, they said, asked the Senate not to believe the trumped-up charges his enemies had brought against him. In his reply Duronius added that many Roman citizens, allies, and members of the Latin League had been maltreated in Gentius' kingdom, and it was said that Roman citizens were being forcibly detained on Corcyra. The Senate's decision was that all these people be brought to Rome and that the praetor Gaius Claudius conduct an investigation into the matter, with no response given to King Gentius and his representatives before the investigation.

Many people were carried off by the epidemic of that year, and a number of priests were amongst the dead. The pontiff Lucius Valerius Flaccus died, and Quintus Fabius Labeo was selected to replace him. The *triumvir epulo** Publius Manlius, who had recently returned from Farther Spain, was also a casualty, and Quintus Fulvius, son of Marcus,* was co-opted as triumvir in his place while still wearing the toga praetexta.* On the question of the appointment of a *rex sacrificulus** to replace Gnaeus Cornelius Dolabella, there was a dispute between the pontifex maximus Gaius Servilius and the naval duumvir Lucius Cornelius Dolabella. The pontiff ordered Dolabella to resign from his office so that he could install him in the priesthood. The duumvir refused, and was fined for his refusal by the pontiff. When Dolabella appealed, the issue was debated before the people.

Most of the tribes had already been called in to vote, and their decision was that the duumvir should obey the pontiff and that the fine should be waived if he resigned from his office. At that point, however, an unfavourable sign came from the sky to interrupt the proceedings. After this the pontiffs felt there was a religious impediment to inaugurating Dolabella, and they installed Publius Cloelius Siculus, who had the second-place nomination, instead.

The end of the year also saw the death of the pontifex maximus Gaius Servilius Geminus, who was a *decemvir sacrorum** as well.

Quintus Fulvius Flaccus was co-opted by the college to replace Servilius as pontiff, and after this Marcus Aemilius Lepidus was elected pontifex maximus from a wide field of distinguished candidates. Quintus Marcius Philippus was co-opted as a *decemvir sacrorum* to replace the same Servilius. The augur Spurius Postumius Albinus also died, and the augurs co-opted Publius Scipio, son of Africanus, to replace him.

That year, the people of Cumae were granted their request to make Latin their official language, and their auctioneers were granted the right to do business in Latin.

43. When the people of Pisae offered land for the foundation of a Latin colony, they were thanked by the Senate, and Quintus Fabius Buteo and Marcus and Publius Popillius Laenas were elected as the triumvirs to establish the colony. A letter was also brought from the praetor Gaius Maenius, who been allotted Sardinia as his province but who had been given the further responsibility of investigating cases of poisoning that occurred more than ten miles from the city. Maenius wrote that he had already condemned 3,000 people and that his investigation was growing, thanks to evidence brought by informers. He should either abandon the investigation or forfeit his province, he said.

Quintus Fulvius Flaccus returned to Rome from Spain where his achievements had won him great renown. While he waited for his triumph outside the city he was elected consul along with Lucius Manlius Acidinus; and he entered the city in triumph a few days later with the soldiers whom he had brought back from Spain. He bore along in the triumph 124 golden crowns and in addition 31 pounds of gold and <. . . of silver>, and 173,200 coins minted at Osca. From the booty he bestowed on each of his soldiers 50 denarii, with double that amount going to centurions and triple to cavalrymen, and the same amounts accorded to allies and members of the Latin League. All were given double pay.

44. That year a proposal was made for the first time—by the plebeian tribune Lucius Villius—to specify the age for candidacy for, and the holding of, the various magistracies. As a result, Villius' family were accorded a cognomen 'Annalis'. For the first time in many years four praetors were elected under the Baebian Law, which stipulated that four should be elected in alternate years. Those attaining office were Gnaeus Cornelius Scipio, Gaius Valerius

Laevinus, and Quintus and Publius Mucius Scaevola, sons of
Quintus Scaevola.

The consuls Quintus Fulvius and Lucius Manlius were assigned
the same province as their predecessors, with the same number of
troops in terms of both infantry and cavalry, citizens and allies. In
the two Spains, Tiberius Sempronius and Lucius Postumius had
their imperium extended and retained command of their armies; and
the consuls were instructed to raise supplementary forces: approximately 3,000 Roman infantry, and 300 Roman cavalry, plus 5,000
infantry and 400 cavalry from the allies and the Latin League. Publius Mucius Scaevola was allotted the urban jurisdiction as well as
responsibility for the inquiry into cases of poisoning in the city and
within a ten-mile radius; Gnaeus Cornelius Scipio received the
foreigners' jurisdiction, Quintus Mucius Scaevola Sicily, and
Gaius Valerius Laevinus Sardinia.

The consul Quintus Fulvius stated that, before undertaking any
official business, he wished to free himself and the state of a religious
obligation by repaying his vows. On the day of his final battle with
the Celtiberians, he explained, he had vowed to hold games for Jupiter Optimus Maximus and to construct a temple for Fortuna Equestris. Money for these projects had been contributed to him by the
Spaniards, he said. Authorization was given for the games and for
the appointment of duumvirs to put the construction of the temple
out for contract. A limit was set on expenditure—the cost of the
games was not to exceed the amount allocated to Fulvius Nobilior
when he staged games after the Aetolian War. Moreover, the consul
was not to solicit, appropriate, or accept funds for the games, or in
any way contravene the Senatorial decree on games passed in the
consulship of Lucius Aemilius and Gnaeus Baebius. This decree had
been passed by the Senate because of the inordinate expenditure on
games by Tiberius Sempronius when he was aedile; this had proved
a hardship not just for Italy, the allies and members of the Latin
League, but for the provinces abroad as well.

45. Winter was harsh that year, with snow and all manner of
storms; after blighting all trees vulnerable to the cold, †it was also†
considerably longer than in other years. A consequence was that the
Latin festival was interrupted on the mountain by the sudden arrival
of darkness and a devastating storm, and was repeated by decree of
the pontiffs. The same storm also toppled several statues on the

Capitol, and caused lightning-damage to a number of locations—the temple of Jupiter at Tarracina, and the White Temple and Roman gate at Capua, where parapets were torn off the wall at several points. In the midst of these prodigies there was also a report from Reate of the birth of a three-footed mule. Because of these events the decemvirs were ordered to consult the books. The decemvirs then made a pronouncement on which gods should be given sacrifices and the number of victims to be offered, and they also prescribed a day of public devotions. After this, the votive games of the consul Quintus Fulvius were held, with great ceremony, over a ten-day period.

Election of the censors followed. Elected in these were the pontifex maximus, Marcus Aemilius Lepidus, and Marcus Fulvius Nobilior, who had triumphed over the Aetolians. Between these men there was a notorious feud, made public on many occasions in numerous bitter quarrels both in the Senate and before the popular assembly. The elections over, the censors followed the ancient tradition of seating themselves on their curule chairs at the altar of Mars in the Campus Martius. Suddenly the leading Senators and a crowd of citizens appeared at this spot. Amongst them was Quintus Caecilius Metellus, who spoke as follows:

46. 'Censors: we have not forgotten that a short time ago you were put in charge of our morals by the entire people of Rome, and that it is we who should be admonished and directed by you, not you by us. Even so, we must point out to you what it is about you that irritates all loyal citizens, or at least what modification they would prefer to see in your behaviour.

'Marcus Aemilius, Marcus Fulvius: when we look at you as individuals, we find no-one in the state today whom we would wish to see put ahead of you if we were recalled to take the vote. But when we look at you together, we cannot but fear that you are a bad combination, and that the fact that we all like you enormously might do the state less good than your dislike for each other might do it harm. For many years you have continued a fierce and implacable vendetta against each other, and there is a danger that from today this may be more prejudicial to us and to the republic than to you. I have many thoughts on the reasons for this fear of ours, and I could adduce these if implacable rage has not taken control of your minds.

'We are united in requesting that you terminate your quarrelling today, and in this holy place; and that you allow the men whom the

Roman people have linked together by their votes also to be linked by us in a spirit of reconciliation and friendship. Be of one mind and one purpose in choosing the Senate, reviewing the *equites*, conducting the census, and performing its purification. See to it that it is a sincere and heartfelt wish that you utter in the formula that you will use in almost all your prayers—"May this matter turn out well and successfully for my colleague and me"—and make us humans also believe that your prayers to the gods reflect your own wishes. Titus Tatius and Romulus ruled in harmony in the city where they had as enemies clashed in a battle in the midst of the forum. Wars, not just quarrels, come to an end; and after being bitter enemies men often become loyal allies, and sometimes even fellow-citizens. When Alba was destroyed the Albans were brought to Rome; and Latins and Sabines were welcomed into our state. That well-known saying that "friendships should be immortal and feuds mortal" became a proverb because it was true.'

A buzz of assent arose. Then the voices of the entire crowd, all making the same request, blended into unison and cut off his words. At this point Aemilius made a number of complaints, particularly about being twice rejected from the consulate by Marcus Fulvius when his election was a certainty. Fulvius for his part complained about relentless provocation from Aemilius, and the legal challenge launched to discredit him. Even so, each suggested that he would follow the bidding of so many of the state's leading citizens, if the other also agreed. At the urging of all present, they shook hands and pledged to resolve and bring to an end their mutual animosity. Then, to general applause, they were escorted to the Capitol. Both the solicitude of the leading citizens over such an issue and the ready acquiescence of the censors were warmly commended and praised by the Senate. The censors then requested that a sum of money be allocated to them to be used on state projects, and for this they were formally assigned a year's revenues.

47. That same year Lucius Postumius and Tiberius Sempronius, the propraetors in Spain, came to an agreement between themselves that Albinus should go through Lusitania on an offensive against the Vaccaei, but that he would return to Celtiberia if the war there should escalate. Gracchus, meanwhile, was to march into the furthest reaches of Celtiberia. Gracchus first took the city of Munda by assault, launching a surprise attack at night. After accepting hostages and installing a garrison, he proceeded to attack strongholds and burn agricultural land until he reached another powerful town which the Celtiberians call Certima. When he was already in the process of bringing up siege-engines, delegates came to him from the town. Their language was blunt in the old-fashioned manner, and they made no secret of their readiness to fight if they had the strength. For the request they had to make of Gracchus was permission to go to the camp of the Celtiberians to solicit assistance. If they failed to gain this aid, they said, they would consider their position without taking account of the Celtiberians. Gracchus gave them permission and they left, only to bring back with them another ten delegates a few days later.

It was midday, and the very first thing these men asked of the praetor was that he issue orders for them to be given a drink. Their first cups drained, the delegates asked for others, provoking considerable mirth amongst the onlookers by their uncouth character and lack of refinement. Then the eldest of them said: 'We have been sent by our nation to ascertain what on earth gives you the nerve to attack us.' Gracchus answered the question by saying that he had come because he had confidence in his fine army, and if they wanted to see this for themselves he would give them the opportunity, so that they could take more reliable intelligence back to their people. He then commanded the military tribunes to order all the infantry and cavalry to equip themselves and manœuvre under arms. Dismissed after this display, the delegates discouraged their people from bringing help to the beleaguered city. The townspeople raised fires on their watchtowers at night—the agreed signal—but to no avail; and after losing their one hope of assistance they surrendered. The sum of 2,400,000 sesterces was taken from them, plus 400 knights from the best families. These latter were not termed hostages, since they were ordered to serve in the army, but in fact they were to be a guarantee of loyalty.

48. From Certima Gracchus next marched to the city of Alce, site of the Celtiberian camp from which the delegates had recently come to him. For several days he harassed the enemy with minor skirmishes, sending light-armed troops to attack their outposts; then, each day, he extended the fighting in order to draw them all from their fortifications. When he felt this objective adequately reached, he ordered the commanders of the auxiliary forces to join battle and

then suddenly to turn tail as if they were outnumbered, and to run in disorder for the camp. Gracchus himself marshalled his troops at all the gates within the rampart.

Not much time elapsed before he caught sight of the column of his men in flight, as planned, with the barbarians in disordered pursuit behind them. Gracchus now had his line deployed within the rampart to meet this very situation. Waiting only long enough to permit his own men to flee unimpeded back into camp, he raised the shout and sallied forth from all the gates at the same time. The enemy failed to stem the unexpected charge, and men who had come to attack the camp were unable even to defend their own. They were immediately scattered and routed; soon they were herded in panic within their palisade, and finally robbed of their camp. That day 9,000 of the enemy were killed, and 320 taken alive, along with 112 horses and 37 military standards. Losses in the Roman army numbered 109.

49. From this battle Gracchus took his legions forward to pillage Celtiberia. As he carried and drove off all manner of booty, whole populations bowed to his yoke, some of their own volition and others from fear. In a matter of days he accepted the surrender of a hundred and three towns and took possession of massive quantities of plunder. He then turned the column back towards its starting-point, Alce, and proceeded to assault the town. The townspeople withstood the initial attack of the enemy, but later, when they found themselves under attack from siege machinery as well as weapons, they lost confidence in their town's defences and all withdrew to the citadel. Finally, they even sent spokesmen from there and put themselves and all their possessions in the power of the Romans. This was a source of great booty, and many noble prisoners fell into Roman hands, including two sons and a daughter of Thurrius. Thurrius was the chief of these tribes and by far the most powerful of all the Spaniards. When he heard of the blow that had struck his family, he came to Gracchus, having first sent emissaries to request a safe conduct to come to the camp to see him. Thurrius' first question was whether Gracchus would spare him and his family their lives. The praetor replied that he would, and Thurrius next asked if he could be permitted to fight alongside the Romans. When Gracchus also granted this request, Thurrius declared: 'I shall follow you against my old allies since †. . .†.' He thereafter followed the Romans, and in

many places provided stalwart and loyal support for Roman undertakings.

50. After this the famous and powerful city of Ergavica threw open its gates to the Romans, fearful after the destruction that had befallen other peoples in the area. The surrender of these towns was not made in good faith, according to certain authors. These sources record the following version of events. There was an immediate resumption of hostilities in the area from which Gracchus had withdrawn his legions, and he subsequently fought a fierce engagement with the Celtiberians at Mt. Chaunus, where a pitched battle lasted from daybreak to the sixth hour,* with many casualties on both sides. The Romans did not produce any other major feat to make one believe them the victors—unless one counts harassing the enemy the next day while the latter remained within their rampart. The Romans spent the whole day gathering spoils. On the third day the two sides clashed again in a greater battle, and this time the Celtiberians were at last definitively beaten, with their camp taken and plundered. Twenty-two thousand of the enemy were killed on that day, with more than 300 captured, and roughly the same number of horses, plus 72 military standards. With that, the war was terminated, and the Celtiberians made a true peace and not with vacillating loyalty as before.

The same summer, these same authors also tell us, Lucius Postumius fought two magnificent battles with the Vaccaei in Farther Spain where he killed some 35,000 of the enemy and stormed their camp. It is closer to the truth to state that Postumius' arrival in the province was too late for him to have had the opportunity to campaign that summer.

51. The censors kept their word to co-operate with each other in revising membership of the Senate. The censor and pontifex maximus, Marcus Aemilius Lepidus, was himself chosen *princeps senatus*. Three men were expelled from the house, and a number were retained on the list by Lepidus after being omitted by his colleague. The following were the public works which the censors completed from the moneys which were allocated to and divided between them:

Lepidus built a causeway at Tarracina, a construction that brought him no thanks because he had estates there, and he had included private charges in the public account. He also contracted out the building of a theatre seating-area and a stage at the temple of

Apollo, and the cleaning and whitening of the temple of Jupiter on the Capitol and the pillars around it. In addition, Lepidus removed from these pillars statues which seemed to be inappropriately mounted before them, and took from the columns shields and all manner of military standards attached to them.

Marcus Fulvius put out for contract a larger number of works, which were also more functional: a harbour and pillars for a bridge on the Tiber (a few years later the censors Publius Scipio Africanus and Lucius Mummius* contracted out the work of setting arches on these pillars); a basilica to the rear of the new banking-houses, and a fish-market surrounded by shops which Fulvius sold for private enterprise; and a forum and colonnade outside the Trigemina Gate, and other colonnades behind the dock-yards, at the temple of Hercules, behind the temple of Hope on the Tiber-bank, and at the temple of Healing Apollo.

The †praetors† also had moneys for joint projects, and from these they together put out for contract the building of an aqueduct and its arches. The work was blocked by Marcus Licinius Crassus who would not let it be taken across his land. The same censors also put in place numerous harbour-dues and taxes. In addition, they had a number of shrines and public places that had been appropriated by individuals restored to their former religious and public status, and saw that they were again open to the people. They reformed electoral procedure and designated the tribes by region on the basis of birth,* social status, and income.

52. One of the censors, Marcus Aemilius, also asked the Senate for funds to be allocated to him to stage games for the dedication of temples of Queen Juno and Diana which he had promised in a vow in the Ligurian War eight years earlier. The Senators allocated him 20,000 *asses*. Aemilius then dedicated the temples, both of them in the Circus Flaminius district, putting on three days of theatrical performances after the dedication of the temple of Juno, and two after that of the temple of Diana. He also staged a day's games in the Circus on each occasion. In addition, he dedicated a temple of the Lares of the Sea in the Campus Martius; this had been promised in a vow eleven years earlier by Lucius Aemilius Regillus during the sea-battle against the commanders of Antiochus. Above the temple-doors a plaque was affixed bearing the following inscription: †"To Lucius Aemilius, son of Marcus Aemilius† for finishing a great war

and subjugating kings †the source of obtaining peace† under his auspices and command, and through his good fortune and leadership, the erstwhile undefeated fleet of King Antiochus was scattered, smashed, and routed between Ephesus and the islands of Samos and Chios, while Antiochus himself, and all his army, cavalry, and elephants looked on. And there on that day forty-two warships were captured with their entire crews. When that battle had been fought Antiochus and his realm <were completely crushed>. For that engagement he made a vow of a temple to the Lares of the sea.'

A plaque with the same text was placed above the doors in the temple of Jupiter on the Capitol.

53. Two days after the censors reviewed membership of the Senate, the consul Quintus Fulvius set out against the Ligurians. After negotiating difficult hills, valleys, and passes with his army, he engaged the enemy in pitched battle and not only vanquished him in the field but also captured his camp on the same day. Enemy losses numbered 3,200, and that whole area of Liguria surrendered. The consul led those who had surrendered down to the lowlands and stationed garrisons on the hills. A letter swiftly <. . .> reached Rome from the province. A three-day period of public thanksgiving was proclaimed for these successes, and the praetors sacrificed forty full-grown victims during this thanksgiving. No noteworthy operation was mounted in Liguria by the other consul, Lucius Manlius. Some Transalpine Gauls, 3,000 in number, crossed into Italy, but without any act of aggression, and requested land of the consuls and Senate so that they could live in peace under the rule of the Roman people. The Senate ordered the Gauls to leave Italy, and instructed the consul Quintus Fulvius to track down and punish the leaders and instigators of this crossing of the Alps.

54. That same year Philip of Macedon died, exhausted from old age and melancholy after the death of his son. He had been wintering at Demetrias, tortured by grief for his son and also by regret for his own heartless behaviour. He was, moreover, vexed by the other son, who now clearly saw himself as king, and was so seen by others, with everybody's attention focused on him; and he was aggrieved to see himself abandoned in his old age, with some people awaiting his death and others not even bothering to wait. This all served to increase his distress, which was shared by Antigonus, son of Echecrates. Antigonus was named after his uncle, the Antigonus who had

been the guardian of Philip—a man of regal presence who was also famous for his celebrated battle against the Spartan Cleomenes.* The Greeks gave the older Antigonus the title 'Guardian' to distinguish him by that sobriquet from the other kings bearing the name. The younger Antigonus was the son of this man's brother, and was the only one of Philip's honoured circle of friends to have remained uncorrupted. Such loyalty had made Perseus—no friend of his anyway—a deadly enemy. Antigonus could foresee the danger he faced by the throne passing to Perseus as his inheritance. As soon as he perceived the king having second thoughts, and sometimes lamenting the loss of the son, he would be at his side, lending an ear, or even prompting him to bring up the act of folly he had committed, and would add his own laments to Philip's. And, as usual, the truth began to emerge through various indications of it; and Antigonus did everything he could to accelerate full disclosure of the facts. The men most under suspicion as perpetrators of the crime were Apelles and Philocles: these had been the ambassadors to Rome and had brought the letter, ostensibly from Flamininus, which had proved fatal to Demetrius.

55. The rumour that ran rife in the palace was that this was a spurious document, tampered with by a scribe, and that the seal was a forgery. This was a matter of conjecture rather than hard fact, but then Xychus* happened to cross paths with Antigonus, who arrested him and brought him to the palace. Leaving him to the guards, Antigonus went on ahead to Philip.

'From my many conversations with you,' Antigonus said to the king, 'I think I have come to realize that you would set great store by knowing the whole truth about your sons, specifically which one was the victim of the other's perfidious machinations. The one man able to solve this knotty problem is in your power—Xychus. He fell into my hands by chance and has been brought to the palace. †Have him summoned†.'

Brought to the king, Xychus was so hesitant in his denials that it was apparent that with a little intimidation he would be ready to turn informer. He fell to pieces at the sight of the torturer and his whips, and divulged all the details of the crime of the ambassadors, step by step, and the part he played himself. Men were immediately dispatched to arrest the two ambassadors. They caught Philocles who was still in town; but Apelles had been sent to hunt down a certain

Chaereas and when he heard about Xychus' disclosures he crossed to Italy. As for Philocles, no reliable information came into circulation. Some say that at first he confidently denied the charges, but that when Xychus was brought into his sight he held out no longer; others say that he kept up his denials even under torture. Philip's distress was renewed and intensified, and he felt that his unhappy lot with regard to his children was all the more distressing because the other one †had perished†.*

56. Perseus was told that all had been revealed, but he was now too strong now to feel that flight was necessary. He simply took care to keep his distance, ready to protect himself against the blazing anger of Philip for as long as the latter remained alive. Philip had now lost hope of laying his hands on Perseus to punish him, and all he could do was focus his attention on seeing that his son did not profit from the crime in addition to escaping punishment. He therefore called Antigonus to him. Philip owed him a debt of gratitude for having brought the murder to light, and he thought the Macedonians would have no reason to feel embarrassed or displeased with him as king in view of his uncle Antigonus' prestige in the recent past.

'Antigonus,' he said, 'I have reached the stage of having to consider the loss of a child, which others find abhorrent, as something desirable. Accordingly, it is my intention to pass on to you the kingdom which I received from your uncle, a kingdom which he watched over, and even extended, as a valiant as well as a loyal caretaker. You are the one person I have whom I consider worthy of the throne. If I had nobody, I would prefer to see my realm destroyed and wiped out rather than become Perseus' prize for his heinous treachery. I shall believe that Demetrius has been raised from the dead and brought back to me if I leave you as his replacement—you alone shed tears over the guiltless boy's death and my unhappy mistake.'

After this interview, Philip never stopped promoting Antigonus with all sorts of honours. During Perseus' absence in Thrace, he went about the Macedonian towns recommending Antigonus to the leading citizens; and had longer life been granted him Philip would doubtless have left him in possession of the throne. After quitting Demetrias he had spent a long time at Thessalonica. When he came from there to Amphipolis he was struck with a serious malady. It is clear, however, that the illness had mental rather than physical origins. His death came from anxiety and insomnia, haunted as he was time and again by the spectre of the innocent son he had killed, and he died uttering terrible curses on his other son. Even so, Antigonus could have been ensconced on the throne, if either <he had been there himself> or the king's death had been immediately brought to public notice. The doctor Calligenes who was in charge of Philip's treatment did not wait for the king's death. At the first signs that the situation was hopeless, he followed a pre-arranged plan, sending messengers to Perseus by horses posted in relays, and concealing the king's death from all outside the palace until the prince's arrival. 57. As a result, Perseus caught them all off-guard and ignorant of the situation, and ascended a throne won by crime.

Philip's death came at an opportune moment for delaying hostilities with Rome and withdrawing some forces from them.* For, a few days later, the Bastarnian people left their homes, as they had long been encouraged to do, and crossed the Danube with a large force of infantry and cavalry. Antigonus and Cotto then went ahead to make a report to the king. Cotto was a Bastarnian nobleman, and †Antigonus had been sent as an envoy with this same Cotto to incite the Bastarnae to arms†. Not far from Amphipolis they were first met by a vague rumour, then definite reports, that the king was dead, and this threw into confusion the entire scenario that they had planned. It had been agreed that Philip would give the Bastarnae a safe passage through Thrace and provisions for the journey. To be able to do this Philip had used gifts to gain the support of the chieftains of those regions, giving his word that the Bastarnae would pass by peacefully in an orderly column. Philip's plan had been to destroy the Dardanian people, and give the Bastarnae settlements in their territory. A two-fold advantage would derive from this: the removal of the Bastarnae, a race ever hostile to Macedonia and lying in wait for occasions when its kings were in difficulties; and the possibility of the Bastarnae, who would have left their wives and children in Dardania, being sent to pillage Italy. Philip knew that a route to the Adriatic and Italy lay through the territory of the Scordisci, and that there was no other way of taking an army across. The Scordisci, he thought, would readily grant the Bastarnae a passage—there were no great linguistic or cultural differences between the two peoples—and would themselves join their venture when they saw that the aim of the journey was to plunder a nation of great riches. After that the king's strategy was formulated to accommodate any eventuality.

Should the Bastarnae be slaughtered by the Romans, he could still console himself with the fact that the Dardanians had been eliminated, that there would be spoils to take from what was left of the Bastarnae, and that he would have uncontested possession of Dardania. If the Bastarnae were successful, he would recover his lost possessions in Greece while the Romans' attention was diverted to a war with the Bastarnae. Such had been Philip's plans.

58. At first the Bastarnae did enter the country peacefully in a tranquil column. Then, with the departure of Cotto and Antigonus, and the rumour of Philip's death coming soon after, the Thracians were less amenable to trading, while the Bastarnae could not remain content merely with what they bought, or be kept in line and prevented from going off the road. This led to violations on both sides, and as these increased by the day war broke out. Finally, unable to cope with the violence and superior numbers of the enemy, the Thracians abandoned their villages on the plains and withdrew to a mountain of enormous height, called Donuca. The Bastarnae wanted to climb this, but as they vainly attempted to approach the peaks a storm overtook them like the one by which the Gauls are said to have been crushed when they were plundering Delphi.* They were overwhelmed with a torrential downpour, followed by densely falling hail, while the sky roared deafeningly with thunderclaps and flickered with blinding lightning; and on top of that there were thunderbolts that flashed on every side, making it look as if it were their bodies that were the targets, and striking and bringing down the leaders as well as the rank and file. The Thracians pounced on the shattered Bastarnae while they were being struck down or were rushing to destruction, blindly seeking headlong flight over towering cliffs; but the Bastarnae themselves claimed that it was the gods who were responsible for their rout, and that the heavens were falling in on them. Dispersed by the storm, most of them returned to the camp from which they had come with half their weapons lost, like men emerging from a shipwreck, and discussions began on what to do next. Then disagreement arose; some were for going back, others for pushing on into Dardania. Some 30,000, under Clondicus' leadership, reached the destination for which they had set out; the rest of the troop headed back to †Apollonia the southern region† on the road by which they had come.

On gaining the throne Perseus had Antigonus put to death and, until he could establish his position, he sent envoys to Rome to renew the treaty made with his father and to request that he be accorded the title of king by the Senate. Such were that year's events in Macedonia.

59. One of the consuls, Quintus Fulvius, celebrated a triumph over the Ligurians, but it was generally agreed that it was Fulvius' influence rather than the greatness of his achievements that was to be thanked for it. He carried in the procession a large quantity of enemy weapons, but absolutely no money. However, he did distribute thirty *asses* to each soldier, with double the amount going to centurions and triple to cavalrymen. The most remarkable feature of that triumph was the fact that Fulvius happened to celebrate it on the very day that he had triumphed after his praetorship the previous year.

After the triumph Fulvius announced the elections, and at these Marcus Iunius Brutus and Aulus Manlius Vulso were elected consuls. A storm interrupted the election <. . .> of the praetors which followed, after three had been elected. The next day, 12 March, the other three were appointed:* Marcus Titinius Curvus, Tiberius Claudius Nero, and Titus Fonteius Capito. The Roman Games were repeated by the curule aediles, Gnaeus Servilius Caepio and Appius Claudius Centho, because a number of prodigies had occurred. There was an earthquake; in the public shrines, during the holding of the *lectisternium*, the heads of the gods on the couches turned away, and the dish and its covering that had been placed in front of Jupiter fell from the table; and the mice had taken a taste of the olives, and this was also regarded as a prodigy. All that was done by way of expiation was the renewal of the games.

APPENDIX 1

LIST OF VARIATIONS FROM THE TEUBNER TEXT

Briscoe		OWC
34.12.1	sic	sic omitted
37.6.3	habent	habebant
37.59.5	duces regii praefecti purpurati	duces regii, praefecti et purpurati
38.37.10	praesidio	cum praesidio
39.49.1	†in†	inita
40.9.7	per te patriumque nomen	per te patrium nomen
40.12.17	†virtute†	voluntate
40.16.8	†ut hic nam†	Urbiacam
40.45.2	†mox†	nox
40.46.6	fueritis	furores
40.46.15	mittere vere	remittere se
40.58.1	†digressi sunt pacato agro†	Primum ingressi sunt pacato agmine, digressu deinde

There are also a few misprints in Briscoe's text. In the hope that it may be of some use to those following the Latin, I note those which I have detected: 31.6.4 tribunis (for tribunus); 31.10.1 nihi (nihil); 31.14.5 Anticho (Antiocho); 33.31.3 Chalicis (Chalcis); 34.58.11 suspectum (susceptum); 35.1.1 creba (crebra); 35.26.6 notus (motus); 40.15.10 fratem (fratrem); 40.21.11 obsequia (obsequium). To these should be added the following, communicated to me by letter by Dr Briscoe: 31.8.8 praesidii (praesidio); 35.41.7 Bruttii (Bruttii prouincia); 37.22.5 pregressos (praegressos); 38.1.4 delectis (delectis Aetolorum); 38.17.15 homanis (humanis); 38.33.10 saxas (saxa); 38.50.3 prounicia (prouincia); 40.9.9 ominia (omnia); 40.12.11 quae re<re>tur (quaere<re>tur); 40.12.20 consilum (consilium).

APPENDIX 2

CONSULS (CENSORS) AND PRAETORS 200–179 BC

200 *consuls*: P. Sulpicius Galba and C. Aurelius Cotta
praetors: Q. Minucius Rufus, L. Furius Purpureo, Q. Fulvius Gillo, C. Sergius Plautus

199 *consuls*: L. Cornelius Lentulus and P. Villius Tappulus
censors: P. Cornelius Scipio Africanus, and P. Aelius Paetus
praetors: L. Quinctius Flamininus, L. Valerius Flaccus, L. Villius Tappulus, Cn. Baebius Tamphilus

198 *consuls*: T. Quinctius Flamininus and Sex. Aelius Paetus Catus
praetors: L. Cornelius Merula, M. Claudius Marcellus, M. Porcius Cato, C. Helvius

197 *consuls*: C. Cornelius Cethegus and Q. Minucius Rufus
praetors: (increased to six): L. Manlius Vulso, C. Sempronius Tuditanus, M. Sergius Silus, M. Helvius, M. Minucius Rufus, L. Atilius

196 *consuls*: L. Furius Purpureo and M. Claudius Marcellus
praetors: Q. Fabius Buteo, Ti. Sempronius Longus, Q. Minucius Thermus, M'. Acilius Glabrio, L. Apustius Fullo, C. Laelius

195 *consuls*: L. Valerius Flaccus and M. Porcius Cato
praetors: Cn. Manlius Vulso, Ap. Claudius Nero, P. Porcius Laeca, C. Fabricius Luscinus, C. Atinius Labeo, P. Manlius

194 *consuls*: P. Cornelius Scipio Africanus and Ti. Sempronius Longus
censors: C. Cornelius Cethegus and Sex. Aelius Paetus
praetors: P. Cornelius Scipio Nasica, Cn. Cornelius Merenda, Cn. Cornelius Blasio, Cn. Domitius Ahenobarbus, Sex. Digitius, T. Iuventius Thalna

193 *consuls*: L. Cornelius Merula and Q. Minucius Thermus
praetors: L. Cornelius Scipio, M. Fulvius Nobilior, C. Scribonius, M. Valerius Messalla, L. Porcius Licinus, C. Flaminius

192 *consuls*: L. Quinctius Flamininus and Cn. Domitius Ahenobarbus
praetors: L. Scribonius Libo, M. Fulvius Centumalus, A. Atilius Serranus, M. Baebius Tamphilus, L. Valerius Tappo, Q. Salonius Sarra

191 *consuls*: P. Cornelius Scipio Nasica and M'. Acilius Glabrio
praetors: L. Aemilius Paullus, M. Aemilius Lepidus, M. Iunius Brutus, A. Cornelius Mammula, C. Livius Salinator, L. Oppius Salinator

190 *consuls*: L. Cornelius Scipio and C. Laelius
  praetors: M. Tuccius, L. Aurunculeius, Cn. Fulvius, L. Aemilius
  Regillus, P. Iunius Brutus, C. Atinius Labeo

189 *consuls*: Cn. Manlius Vulso and M. Fulvius Nobilior
  censors: T. Quinctius Flamininus and M. Claudius Marcellus
  praetors: Q. Fabius Labeo, Q. Fabius Pictor, M. Sempronius
  Tuditanus, Sp. Postumius Albinus, L. Plautius Hypsaeus,
  L. Baebius Dives

188 *consuls*: M. Valerius Messala and C. Livius Salinator
  praetors: Q. Marcius Philippus, M. Claudius Marcellus,
  C. Stertinius, C. Atinius, P. Claudius Pulcher,[1] L. Manlius Acidinus

187 *consuls*: M. Aemilius Lepidus and C. Flaminius
  praetors: Ap. Claudius Pulcher,[1] Ser. Sulpicius Galba,
  Q. Terentius Culleo, L. Terentius Massaliota, Q. Fulvius Flaccus,
  M. Furius Crassipes

186 *consuls*: Sp. Postumius Albinus and Q. Marcius Philippus
  praetors: T. Maenius, P. Cornelius Sulla, C. Calpurnius
  Piso, M. Licinius Lucullus, C. Aurelius Scaurus,
  L. Quinctius Crispinus

185 *consuls*: Ap. Claudius Pulcher and M. Sempronius Tuditanus
  praetors: P. Cornelius Cethegus, A. Postumius Albinus,
  C. Afranius Stellio, C. Atilius Serranus,
  L. Postumius Tempsanus, M. Claudius

184 *consuls*: P. Claudius Pulcher and L. Porcius Licinus
  censors: L. Valerius Flaccus and M. Porcius Cato
  praetors: C. Decimius Flavus, P. Sempronius Longus, P. Cornelius
  Cethegus, Q. Naevius Matho, C. Sempronius Blaesus,
  A. Terentius Varro

183 *consuls*: Q. Fabius Labeo and M. Claudius Marcellus
  praetors: C. Valerius Flaccus, Sp. Postumius Albinus, P. Cornelius
  Sisenna, L. Pupius, L. Iulius Caesar, Cn. Sicinius

182 *consuls*: L. Aemilius Paullus and Cn. Baebius Tamphilus
  praetors: Q. Fulvius Flaccus, M. Valerius Laevinus, P. Manlius,
  M. Ogulnius Gallus, L. Caecilius Denter, C. Terentius Histra

181 *consuls*: P. Cornelius Cethegus and M. Baebius Tamphilus
  praetors: Q. Fabius Maximus, Q. Fabius Buteo,
  Ti. Claudius Nero, Q. Petillius Spurinus, M. Pinarius Rusca,
  L. Duronius

---

[1] Livy may have reversed the order of the praetorships of Publius and Appius Claudius
(see note to p. 391).

180   *consuls*: A. Postumius Albinus Luscus and C. Calpurnius Piso
        (Q. Fulvius Flaccus *suff.*)
        praetors: Ti. Sempronius Gracchus, L. Postumius Albinus,
        P. Cornelius Mammula,[2] Ti. Minucius Molliculus, C. Claudius
        Pulcher,[3] A. Hostilius Mancinus, C. Maenius

179   *consuls*: L. Manlius Acidinus Fulvianus and Q. Fulvius Flaccus
        censors: M. Aemilius Lepidus and M. Fulvius Nobilior
        praetors: Cn. Cornelius Scipio Hispallus, C. Valerius Laevinus,
        P. Mucius Scaevola, Q. Mucius Scaevola.

[2] See Explanatory Note to p. 516 on the crux over this name.
[3] Tiberius Minucius Molliculus died after taking office and was replaced by
C. Claudius Pulcher (40.37).

EXPLANATORY NOTES

Abbreviations used:

Briscoe, *Comm.* John Briscoe, *A Commentary on Livy: Books XXXI–XXXIII*, and *Books XXXIV–XXXVII* (Oxford, 1973, 1981)

Polyb.   Polybius

BOOK THIRTY-ONE

3 *I too am happy*: just as the Roman people were happy to see the end of the Hannibalic War.

end of the Punic War: Livy devoted the third decade of his work (Books 21–30) to the Second Punic (or 'Hannibalic') War (218–201 BC).

sixty-three years: by inclusive reckoning the time from the beginning of the First Punic War in 264 until the end of the second in 201 would be sixty-*four* years. Either Livy is counting from 264 to the battle of Zama in 202 or he uses exclusive reckoning.

four hundred and eighty-eight years: the MSS actually read CDLXXVIII (478), but since Livy normally regards the foundation date of Rome as 751 (not the Varronian date of 753), the text is perhaps rightly emended to '487'.

Appius Claudius: Appius Claudius Caudex (consul 264).

Asia: Asia Minor.

ten years earlier: the so-called 'First Macedonian War', which actually began in 215. According to Livy 26. 24, the Aetolians joined the war in 211.

discontinued for three years: the war ended with the Peace of Phoenice in 205 (Livy 29. 12).

cause of both war and peace: the Aetolian agreement with Philip V, reached without consulting the Roman people, played no small part in bringing the First Macedonian War to a conclusion.

military and financial assistance: cf. Livy 30. 26 (4,000 men under the command of Sopater); 30. 33 (a 'legion' from Macedonia): also 30. 40, 42; 34. 22; 45. 2. But Polybius says nothing of Macedonian troops at Zama, and we may be dealing with an invention of the annalistic tradition. Some Macedonians may, however, have fought as mercenaries.

the Athenians: they were party to the Peace of Phoenice (Livy 29. 12).

4 *his former inclinations towards the Roman people*: there existed between the two states at this time a political friendship (*amicitia*) which had been

concluded during the reign of Ptolemy II Philadelphus in 273 BC (Livy, *Periochae* 14) and renewed by Ptolemy IV Philopator in 210 (cf. Livy 27. 4).

4 *in Gaul*: here, and elsewhere, Cisalpine Gaul. The Boii were located in the Apennine region between the River Po and Umbria. The campaign was conducted in the summer of 201.

Boii: a Gallic tribe occupying the territory around modern Bologna, where they had settled already in the late fifth century BC.

Ligurian Ingauni: the Ingauni were one of several tribes of the Ligurians (for the other important tribe, the Apuani, see 39. 32; 40. 1), an Italic people who lived north of Etruria and along the Italian riviera. The Romans fought numerous wars with them in the late third and early second centuries BC.

5 *imperium*: supreme military authority. Only dictators, consuls, and praetors, or those whose offices were extended by prorogation (proconsuls and propraetors), could exercise imperium, which gave them the power to impose the death penalty within the army as well as supreme authority over the Roman civilian population. The latter were, however, protected by the right of appeal (*provocatio*). The magistrate's imperium was furthermore symbolized by the lictors who attended him and carried the *fasces*. See note below, *propraetorian*; cf. also note to p. 299. *our authority*.

cross with it to Macedonia: to Illyria, where the Romans had allies. Macedonia itself did not have an Adriatic coastline.

propraetorian: it was Roman practice, both because of the shortage of qualified leaders and in order to preserve continuity of command, to extend the imperium of praetors and consuls. The process is known as prorogation.

Marcus Valerius Laevinus: he had commanded the Roman troops that fought against Philip V in the years 215–211.

Marcus Aurelius: Marcus Aurelius Cotta had been one of three ambassadors sent to Philip V in 203 (Livy 30. 26). Probably *not* identical with the plebeian aedile in 216 and decemvir for sacrifices from 204 onwards, whose death is recorded in chap. 50 below.

Pyrrhus: king of Epirus. His grandmother, Troas, was the aunt of Alexander the Great. After a brief attempt to occupy the throne of Epirus, which ended in 302, Pyrrhus was firmly established in his ancestral kingdom by his father-in-law, Ptolemy I Soter, in 297. Between 280 and 275, he campaigned in Italy and Sicily, initially at the invitation of the Tarentines. He defeated the Romans at Heraclea and Asculum, but his 'pyrrhic' victories soon forced him to abandon his schemes in the west and return to Greece, where he became embroiled in the affairs of the Peloponnese (see note to p. 8 below).

land that was . . . public property: public land (*ager publicus*) had a long history. It was normally land confiscated from conquered peoples or rebellious allies and rented by Roman citizens from the state. This land, however, tended to be occupied by the wealthy and as early as the Licinian-Sextian legislation of 367 limits were put on how much public land an individual could occupy. In this case, the land in question had been confiscated from those in southern Italy who had defected during the Hannibalic war.

a further period of two days: in the event of incorrect practices, all or a portion of the Roman Games had to be repeated (cf. the repetition of the Latin Festival in 198 on procedural grounds, Livy 32. 1). Since the *Ludi Romani* (held in September) lasted four days, this represents a partial repetition. The Roman Games were originally known as the Great Games (*ludi magni*) and are associated in tradition with the fifth king, Tarquinius Priscus (Livy 1. 35). In 366, when the curule aediles were instituted, the games were held annually. Theatrical performances were added in 240, upon the conclusion of the First Punic War. Not all repetitions or extensions of games were ascribable to incorrect procedure, however, since they provided useful diversions in times of war and opportunities for aediles to put on the games in order to win the goodwill of voters, who might be expected to remember them when they ran for higher political office.

asses: the *as* was the basic unit of coinage, originally weighing one Roman pound (324.75 g). By the Second Punic War this weight was halved and, in the first half of the second century, an *as* equalled one-sixth of a pound. The silver denarius was equal in value to ten bronze *asses*, the relative value of silver being 120 times that of bronze.

6 *Plebeian Games*: held in November and presided over by the plebeian aediles. Just as the Roman Games, which were the responsibility of the curule aediles (see 32. 7; 33. 25), were associated with Capitoline Jupiter, so the Plebeian Games were held in honour of Ceres. The Games may have been instituted in 220 when Gaius Flaminius built the Circus Flaminius; they are first attested in 216 and were held annually.

five hundred and fifty-first year after the founding of the city: 200 BC. Cf. note to p. 3, *four hundred and eighty-eight years*. The MSS reading is again ten years short at '541'.

the day on which one began the consulship at that time: until 153 BC, 15 March (the Ides of March) marked the beginning of the consular year; thereafter it was set at 1 January. But, for problems with the Roman calendar, see Briscoe, *Comm.* ii 17–26, esp. the table on p. 25.

triumph: the triumph was a celebration of Roman victory, in which the victorious commander paraded from the Campus Martius to the Capitoline. Certain conditions had to be met before a triumph was awarded: the defeat of a foreign army, with at least 5,000 enemy dead, by a magistrate endowed with imperium. Lesser victories might be awarded an 'ovation' (on which see chap. 20 below). But the triumph had at least one downside: generals eager to earn triumphs recklessly exposed their troops to danger and risked the welfare of the Roman state in the process.

6 *the consul who received responsibility*: the Latin word used is 'provincia', which denotes an area of responsibility. At this time, Macedonia was an independent kingdom.

7 *King Philip and the Macedonians*: this was the correct formula; cf. Polyb. 7. 9. 7. (where the treaty with Hannibal was made by 'King Philip and the Macedonians'). Probably in the time of Antigonus Doson the Macedonian 'league' or *koinon* came into being.

praetorian sortition: the assignment of the most important provinces was reserved for the consuls and often determined before the actual elections. The Senate decided which provinces should be set aside for the praetors and these (including the urban and foreign jurisdiction) were drawn by lot by the elected praetors.

centuries: the basic voting groups of the Comitia Centuriata. Roman assemblies generally used 'block' voting, each unit casting a single vote that was determined by the majority of votes within that unit. The Comitia Centuriata was organized by centuries—based on groupings within the state that were responsible for supplying a hundred men (century) each for military purposes—but the distribution of centuries was originally such that the two highest property-classes (the equites and the first property class) contributed 98 of 193 centuries. Hence the assembly was weighted in favour of the rich, and a decision could be reached before the middle and lower classes even had the opportunity of voting. After the First Punic War the Comitia Centuriata was reformed (apparently by reducing the centuries of the first property class from 80 to 70 and by distributing these amongst the 35 tribes) in such a way as to give some power to the middle class. But the assembly was never intended to be purely democratic.

Quintus Baebius: Quintus Baebius and Licinius Crassus, the pontifex maximus (chap. 9 below), both attempted to stall the Senate's 'Eastern' policy, of which it appears Publius Scipio Africanus, with whom they were allied, disapproved. The obstructions occurred, one immediately before, the other right after, the second vote on the war was taken.

Saguntum: a city in Spain said to have been founded by Greeks from Zacynthus. The Romans made Hannibal's attack on it a *casus belli*, claiming that the city was allied to Rome. This appears not to have been the case, and the city was well south of the River Ebro, which the Romans had established as the northern frontier of Carthaginian expansion in Spain in their treaty with Hasdrubal. Hannibal first laid siege to Saguntum in Spring 219; the city fell eight months later.

8 *Pyrrhus' death*: Pyrrhus was killed in the streets of Argos in 272, after a woman struck him with a roof-tile.

an allegiance to a common language and lineage: unlike Hannibal, who came to Italy as a foreign invader, Philip V, like Pyrrhus before him, could attract the Greeks of southern Italy to his side as a 'compatriot'.

9 *their couches*: possibly a reference to the *lectisternium*, on which see the note to p. 249.

fetial priests: the *fetiales* formed a college of twenty priests, responsible for the declaration of war and the sanctioning of treaties. In accordance with fetial law, two priests carried the demand for satisfaction to the enemy and, if this was not met (within a space of 30 or 33 days), they made a formal declaration of war (*indictio belli*) and cast a spear into his territory, thus both signifying the outbreak of hostilities and establishing the war as 'just'. This and other passages (cf. chap. 9 below) illustrate the Roman preoccupation with procedural correctness.

allies and members of the Latin League: Livy's terminology is imprecise. He appears to conflate the Italian allies (*socii*) with the Latins (*nomen Latinum*), of whom the latter had a restricted form of Roman citizenship. In fact, the term as it appears in the Latin, 'allies of the Latin League', is merely a variant of 'allies and members of the Latin League', as our translation indicates.

11 *college of priests*: the pontifical college consisted at this time of nine priests, whose concern was religious law and custom in general and whose head was the pontifex maximus. By contrast, the functions of *flamines* were tied directly to a specific god. Collegiality was a feature of Roman priesthoods, though the *haruspices* provide a notable exception, apparently a sign of their non-Roman (Etruscan) origin.

Great Games: the *ludi magni*. See note to p. 5, *a further period of two days*, above.

a former member of Hasdrubal's army: Hasdrubal was Hannibal's younger brother. In 207 he brought a second army from Spain to Italy, only to be defeated and killed at the Metaurus river (see Livy 27. 36–51).

12 *it was unclear*: this uncertainty about Hamilcar's background is undoubtedly due to conflicting evidence in Livy's primary sources. At chap. 21 below Livy records Hamilcar's death near Cremona, but at 32. 30 he records his capture in 197 BC (cf. 33. 23).

13 *a purple toga . . . a curule chair*: cf. the gifts given by Scipio to Masinissa in 203 (Livy 30. 15). These were the accoutrements of triumphant generals and curule officials, and thus amongst the highest 'political' status symbols.

Proserpina: Persephone.

Pleminius' crime: Quintus Pleminius, propraetor in 205, had robbed the treasures of Proserpina (Livy 29. 8); for his imprisonment and death see 34. 44.

14 *consulship of Gaius Claudius and Marcus Livius*: Gaius Claudius Nero and Marcus Livius Salinator (the latter's second consulship), 207 BC. For the prodigy see Livy 27. 37; for discovery of a hermaphrodite in 186 see 39. 22.

14 *the Sibylline books*: collections of oracles, preserved in hexameter verse, thought to be utterances of the Sibyl of Cumae. Their keeping and interpretation was entrusted to the *duoviri sacris faciundis* (cf. Livy 5. 13), but this body was increased to ten (*decemviri*) in 367; by 51 BC there were fifteen (*quindecemviri*).

Livius: the poet Lucius Livius Andronicus, a Greek captured at Tarentum (272 BC). He became the slave of Livius Salinator but was later freed.

16 *Ptolemy's death*: Ptolemy IV Philopator had died in 204/3, leaving the throne of Egypt to his young son, Ptolemy V Epiphanes.

rites of Eleusis: these celebrations, in honour of Demeter and Persephone, were held in September and provide one of the anchors for the chronology of the outbreak of the war.

Piraeus: the port of Athens.

17 *ten ancient tribes*: the ten tribes, each named for an eponymous hero, were instituted in 508/7 with the establishment of the Cleisthenic democracy. After Demetrius Poliorcetes' capture of Athens in 307, two new tribes, Demetrias and Antigonis, were added, but these were later abolished.

18 *that witnessed at Saguntum*: the story is told in Livy, Book 21.

19 *the formulae of execration*: that is, curses against anyone failing to carry out the deed.

wearing fillets: normally, headbands of wool (*infulae*), worn as symbols of surrender: cf. Livy 45. 26. 3 and 30. 36. 4, where they are hung from a Carthaginian ship which carried ambassadors seeking peace. Cf. note to p. 320 below.

21 *ovation*: a scaled-down version of the triumph (see note to p. 6, above) the ovation was reserved for victories over a lesser foe or those which failed to kill the requisite number of enemies, or for victorious generals who did not meet certain necessary conditions (cf. 39. 29).

the 5,000 allies and members of the Latin League: for these troops see chap. 11 above.

legates: legates (*legati*) appear frequently in Livy's account and take essentially two forms: ambassadors sent to other states and military appointees. The latter formed part of the commanding general's staff and could lead troops and attend war councils. It was in this capacity that Scipio Africanus later accompanied his brother Lucius Cornelius to Greece and Asia (cf. note to p. 299 *our authority*).

22 *Vediovis*: an ancient deity worshipped on the Capitoline (see *Oxford Latin Dictionary* s.v. 'Veiovis').

as noted above: at chap. 14.

24 *these are called 'day-runners' by the Greeks*: 'hemerodromos'. Livy is explaining a term found in his Greek source, probably Polybius. Livy,

however, appears to have confused the *hemerodromos/hemerodromes* ('messenger': as in Herodotus 6. 105, used of Philippides at the time of the Marathon campaign) and *hemeroskopos* ('scout' or 'spy').

Athenian praetor: that is, one of the ten annually elected 'generals' (*strategoi*), of whom this one was the foremost. When Livy uses the term *praetor* (here and elsewhere) of a non-Roman official, it is usually in reference to a magistrate whom the Greeks termed *strategos*.

26 *Philopoemen*: Livy's first mention of the famous Achaean *strategos*, whom Polybius greatly admired. For his career see, especially, Plutarch, *Philopoemen*; for his death see 39. 49–50.

27 *with their two arms*: these are the so-called 'Long Walls', built during the Periclean age (fifth century BC), which allowed Athens to withstand sieges from the land and import food and supplies through the port of Piraeus. The walls had been demolished after Athens' defeat in 404 but were rebuilt in the early fourth century.

29 *'Friends'*: a group of high-ranking officials that had its origin in the aristocratic entourage of the Macedonian kings (cf. note to p. 36, and also 34. 33). These men served both as officers and advisors of the Hellenistic kings. The term 'Friends' (*philoi*; Latin *amici*) had replaced the word 'Companions' (*hetairoi*), used of the Macedonians of Philip II and Alexander, already in the time of the Successors (323–281 BC).

council of the Aetolians, which they call 'Panaetolian': the autumn meetings of the Aetolian league, held on this occasion, as we are informed below, at Naupactus. For Livy's confusion regarding the spring meetings at Thermum see note to p. 34, *Pylaic*, below.

axes and rods: carried by the lictors of Roman magistrates with imperium (see note to p. 5), the axes symbolized the official's power of life and death, the rods his right to compel obedience.

32 *illicitly took possession of the city*: this occurred after Pyrrhus' departure from Italy; the Campanian mercenaries were defeated and punished in 270. But principle did not, five years later, prevent the Romans from supporting the Mamertines at Messana who had imitated the actions at Rhegium.

foreign tyrants: Hippocrates and Epicydes, who were agents of Hannibal and the Carthaginians.

a three-year land- and sea-offensive: between 214 and 211. Syracuse went over to the Carthaginians after the death of their king ('tyrant'), Hieron II in 215. The city's defence against the Romans was aided by the ingenious machines devised by Archimedes; but it was captured by Marcus Claudius Marcellus.

at war with the Samnites for almost seventy years: the Samnites occupied the mountainous area north of Lucania and between Campania and Apulia. The Romans subdued them in the course of three Samnite wars (the first in the 340s, the second 326–304, the third 298–290).

33 *extermination of family members*: apparently an anachronistic reference to the murder of his son, Demetrius, in 182 (on which see Livy 40. 5–16, 20–4, 54–5). Although the charge may be a general one—elimination of family rivals had a long tradition in Macedonia—the murder of Demetrius contrasts unfavourably with the harmonius nature of relations within the Antigonid dynasty before Philip V (Plutarch, *Demetrius* 3).

Aetolian praetor: the *strategos* of the Aetolian League. For the use of *praetor* to designate a Greek elected 'general' (*strategos*) cf. note to p. 24, *Athenian praetor*, above. Damocritus held the *strategia* in 200/199 and then again in 193/2.

34 *Pylaic*: Livy appears to be confused. The Aetolians met in council at two different sittings: the spring meetings were called *Panaitolika* and were convened at various sites; the *Thermaika*, held in the autumn, were so called because the council met at Thermum, which Livy has mistaken for Thermopylae.

his son Perseus: Perseus was to rule Macedon 179–168. At this time he was only 12 or 13 years old. Such early exposure to the battlefield has ample precedent in Macedonian history: one thinks especially of Demetrius II, father of Philip V, who as a mere boy defeated Alexander II of Epirus.

35 *instead afflicted them with fear and misgiving*: Plutarch (*Flamininus*, 7. 4) relates a story about the Macedonians' demoralization at the sight of the dead, but this occurs before Cynoscephalae and differs in other respects.

and the kind of men they had to face: Harris (*War and Imperialism in Republican Rome, 327–70 BC* (Oxford, 1979), 52 (with n. 5)) rightly draws attention to the Roman fondness for warfare and killing, adding that this passage makes it clear that it was not merely the Spanish swords that were responsible for the mutilation but the men who took pleasure in wielding them. Polybius may indeed have been more critical of the Roman lust for blood, but the troops and their general will have understood something about the psychology of terror.

36 *belonging to barbarians*: the same anecdote is told of Pyrrhus by Plutarch.

as I have noted elsewhere: cf. 27. 32; cf. also 33. 4; 37. 39; 38. 21.

one of his courtiers: that is, one of his 'Friends' (see note to p. 29). For the Latin phrase, 'uno ex purpuratis', cf. Curtius 3.12.7, where virtually the same phrase is used, denoting Alexander's 'Friend', Leonnatus.

peltasts: light-armed troops, named for the crescent-shaped shield (*pelte*) they carried.

37 *captured during the Punic War*: Livy mentions the capture of elephants by the Romans at various points in his account of the Hannibalic War, but the majority were handed over by Carthage as part of the peace settlement. For elephants at the battle of Cynoscephalae see Livy 33. 9.

40 *Macedonian phalanx*: see the note on the phalanx, note to p. 69 below.

by their lances: 'rumpiae' = long spears used by Thracians.

tortoise-formation: the Romans, when attacking under or near city walls or any other position which allowed the enemy to bombard them from above, formed their shields into a tortoise-like protecting shell (the *testudo*).

43 *maniple*: Livy inaccurately applies Roman terminology to the Macedonian army. Such divisions did not exist in the army of Philip V, and it was precisely the rigidity and inflexible nature of the Macedonian phalanx that led to its demise. The Roman army too was originally a rigid phalanx, with the troops carrying an oval-shaped shield; this shield was replaced by a longer, semi-cylindrical one and the organization of the legion made more flexible by the creation of smaller units, called maniples (literally, 'handfuls', they comprised two centuries), which could act independently. Later three maniples were joined together to form a cohort. The smaller and more manageable maniples could exploit gaps in the Macedonian phalanx and played no small part in the Roman victories at Cynoscephalae and Pydna.

45 *all decrees enacted in the past against the Pisistratids*: against Hippias, who was expelled in 510 (his brother Hipparchus had been assassinated in 514); possibly also Thessalus.

46 *light craft*: 'lembi' (Greek: *lemboi*). These were open-decked ships, fast and consequently used by pirates.

47 *having been attacked in the past*: in 208 BC, by Attalus and Sulpicius Galba, who captured it briefly (through the defection of Philip's officer, Plator) during the First Macedonian War (Livy 28. 5–6).

48 *the autumn equinox was drawing near*: mid-September 199.

Euboean gulf known as Coela: the so-called 'Hollows of Euboea' were the scene of a famous shipwreck during the Persian Wars (480 BC); cf. Herodotus 8. 12–13. See also Strabo 10. 445 C, who locates the 'Hollows' between the Euripus and the southern tip of Euboea, that is, between Attica and Euboea.

50 *confided to the family of the Furii*: Marcus Furius Camillus had been appointed dictator in c.386 BC and reputedly inflicted a defeat on them after their infamous 'sack of Rome' (Livy 5. 49); but the story may be face-saving propaganda. Lucius Furius Camillus was victorious over the Gauls in 349 (Livy 7. 25–6).

pieces of silver: something may have dropped out of the text here: normally Livy designates coined silver as 'stamped with the *biga*' (cf. 33. 37; 34. 10, 46; 36. 21, 39–40). The *biga* or two-horse chariot was commonly found on the *denarius*. Hence, these references to 'pieces of silver' could safely be translated as *denarii*.

51 *flamen of Jupiter*: the position of the *flamen Dialis* was restricted to members of the Patrician order. There were strict regulations concerning his lifestyle and actions; particularly, he was not permitted to leave the city of Rome. Hence, when Gaius Valerius Flaccus was later elected to

the praetorship of 183, his province could not be determined by normal sortition. Only the urban and foreigners' jurisdictions were open to him, and he drew the latter (see 39. 39, 45).

52 *after many years of service*: Lucius Manlius Acidinus had gone to Spain in 206 and shared command there as propraetor with Lucius Lentulus (Livy 28. 38). See also 32. 7 for his return.

Gnaeus Cornelius Lentulus: this is apparently an error for Cornelius Blasio. At 33. 27 Livy mentions the return of Cornelius Blasio at the end of 197 and an ovation, which is confirmed by the lists of Roman magistrates known as the *Fasti*.

BOOK THIRTY-TWO

53 *Ides of March*: see note to p. 6, above.

the distribution of land to soldiers . . . Spain, Sicily and Sardinia: cf. 31. 49. They were to receive two iugera each. The task was originally entrusted to decemvirs, who appear to have passed the matter on to Sergius. In 31. 49, Livy mentions only troops who had served in Spain and Sicily. Whether service in Sardinia was subsequently added, or if Livy merely omitted Sardinia in his earlier notice, is unclear.

Sergius . . . Minucius: for the election of Sergius Plautus and Quintus Minucius Rufus see 31. 6. For the strange goings-on in Bruttium see 31. 12.

Latin Festival: held in April (cf. 37. 3).

54 *first payment in silver of the tribute*: according to the terms of the peace that ended the Second Punic War 10,000 talents were to be paid in equal annual instalments over 50 years (Livy 30. 37); cf. 30. 44 for the Carthaginian difficulties in raising the initial payment.

the return of their hostages: the conditions of the peace that terminated the Hannibalic War included the surrender of 100 hostages to be chosen by Scipio Africanus from men between the ages of 14 and 30 (Livy 30. 37; see 40. 34 for their return).

Narnia: a Latin colony founded in 299 on the site of the Umbrian fortress of Nequinum. In 209, Narnia was one of twelve colonies that claimed they could not provide men and money to the Roman war effort (Livy 29. 9). This appears to be an effort to remedy the situation.

55 *Pylae*: Thermopylae.

Thaumaci gets its name: the Greek word *thauma* means 'wonder' or 'marvel'.

56 *Winter was also now approaching*: winter 199/8.

founding of Megalopolis: established in 370, after the Theban victory at Leuctra (370), as a check on Spartan resurgence, Megalopolis was built by the Arcadians, though Theban forces were present to prevent Spartan disruption of the work. It joined the Achaean league in 235.

58 *elections for the censorship*: two censors were elected every five years and held office for a term of eighteen months. In that time, censors were responsible for maintaining the citizenship rolls and overseeing finances. They could expel unworthy members from the Senate and deprive unsuitable *equites* of their horses (cf. 38. 28, and 39. 42, 44). The office was instituted in 443 or 435. Like the consuls, at least one of the elected censors (beginning in 351) had to come from the Plebeian Order.

Acidinus had been granted that honour by the Senate: at 31.50, Livy says that he was allowed to leave Spain, but there is no mention of an ovation.

the elections: for 198 BC.

the ladder of successive offices: the essential offices of the *cursus honorum* were those of quaestor, praetor, and consul. The aedileship was not included, nor, of course, the office of plebeian tribune, since patricians were barred from it. In 180 the *lex Villia Annalis* (see 40. 44), introduced by Lucius Villius (tribune of the plebs), sought to remedy abuses and regulate the system by establishing minimum ages and compulsory waiting-periods between the holding of offices.

59 *Servius and Gaius Sulpicius Galba*: these pontiffs were brothers (cf. Livy 30. 26, 39), and probably brothers of Publius, the consul for 200 BC. Servius reappears in 39. 32, where he stands unsuccessfully for the consulship of 184; he never attained the office.

Gnaeus Cornelius Scipio: Scipio Hispallus (consul 176), brother of Publius Cornelius Scipio Nasica.

67 *dismissed Gaius Livius*: Livius Salinator had been praetor in 202, but his career in the years that followed appears to have been somewhat unspectacular (hence Livy's failure to mention his activities before he was replaced by Lucius Quinctius). In the elections of 193 (i.e. for the consulship of 192), he was defeated by the plebeian candidate Gnaeus Domitius Ahenobarbus. Subsequently, he secured a second praetorship in 191, served again with the fleet (before handing it over to Aemilius Regillus; whether he celebrated a naval triumph is uncertain) and attained the consulship for 188.

Same: on Cephallenia.

68 *nummi*: coins, apparently *drachmae* (possibly *denarii*). For the relationship of the two see the notes to pp. 187 and 188 below.

69 *the Macedonian wedge, called the 'phalanx' by the Macedonians themselves*: At 31. 39, Livy mentions the phalanx without explaining the Greek word to his Roman audience (cf. his reference to 'hemerodromos' at 31. 24). The description of the phalanx as a wedge, however, recalls Curtius 3. 2. 13: 'wedges of tough, densely-packed soldiers. The Macedonians call it a phalanx.'

74 *On the last occasion*: in the First Macedonian War.

his host at Cyparissia, Chariteles: Cyparissia is in Messenia, and the incident must have occurred in 214/13. Chariteles and his death are otherwise unknown.

74 *Sicyonian father and son, both called Aratus*: for the poisoning of the elder Aratus (in 213 BC), through the agency of Taurion, see Plutarch, *Aratus* 51–2 and Polybius 8.12. 2–6; cf. Pausanias 2. 9. 4. Aratus' son is said to have been driven mad, again from taking Philip's poison (*Arat.* 54). Cf., of course, Philip's role in the murder of his own son Demetrius.

carting off to Macedonia the son's wife: this was Polycratea (see Livy 27. 31), who became the mother of Perseus. But Livy, following Polybius, who surely knew the truth, later (39. 53 and 40. 9) refers to Perseus' mother not only as a 'concubine' but as a 'whore'.

75 *Antigonus*: Antigonus III Doson, who ruled from 229 to 221 BC.

76 *damiurgi*: ten *damiurgi* and the *strategos* 'seem to have formed a board which probably acted as the standing government' of the Achaean League (R. M. Errington, *Philopoemen* (Oxford 1969), 6).

77 *Macedonian kings were descended from them*: the Argead royal house traced its descent from the Heraclidae, in particular, Temenus of Argos.

78 *titled 'Acraea'*: *akra* in Greek are heights or headlands.

81 *urban praetor, Lucius Cornelius Lentulus*: the urban praetor, as Livy tells us at chap. 7 above, was Lucius Cornelius Merula. The mistake is perhaps due to the fact that Livy mentioned the proconsul, Lucius Cornelius Lentulus, at the beginning of this chapter.

82 *elected consuls*: for the year 197.

for the first time, six praetors were elected: there had previously been four praetors, but in 197 two more were added for the administration of the two new Spanish provinces. The office was instituted in 367, with the creation of the *praetor urbanus*; in 242 the *praetor peregrinus* was added, and subsequent praetors were created as Rome acquired provinces. In Sulla's time the number had grown to eight.

were plebeian aediles: that is, they were plebeian aediles for 198, and now praetors for 197. Quintus Minucius Thermus and Tiberius Sempronius Longus were curule aediles for 198, not for 197, as one might mistakenly assume from Livy's phrasing.

85 *Hamilcar, the general of the Carthaginians*: at 31. 21, Livy says he died in battle. It appears that we have conflicting versions in the sources, which Livy did not reconcile. At 33. 23 he says that Hamilcar graced Gaius Cornelius' triumph; but note that here he adds that 'some say' this was the case.

86 *Xenophon*: apparently, Xenophon of Aegae (on whom see Polyb. 18. 10. 11; 28. 19. 3), whose father was probably Euryleon, *strategos* of the Achaean League in 211/10. The list of delegates repeats that given by Polybius (18. 1. 2–4); on Philip's side, however, Polybius names the Macedonians, Apollodorus and Demosthenes, along with Brachylles of Boeotia in addition to Cycliadas the Achaean.

88 *clear even to a blind man*: cf. Antigonus I, the 'One-Eyed', Philip V's ancestor, who was said once to have remarked that a dispatch was written in letters 'large enough for a blind man to read'.

92 *his daughters in marriage to the sons of Nabis*: Briscoe (*Comm.* i. 243) takes the plural literally. Probably it is used to indicate a general offer, with no particular individuals specified—we might say 'one of my daughters to one of your sons'. Whether such a marriage actually came about is uncertain: 34.32 is ambiguous.

94 *his wife*: for the story cf. Polybius 18. 17. Her name is given by Polybius (13. 7. 6) as Apega; perhaps she is a daughter of Aristippus of Argos, and thus well placed to carry out the crime imputed to her. The woman's family becomes more complicated if the sister of Pythagoras is the same wife of Nabis (see note to p. 163 below).

BOOK THIRTY-THREE

95 *At the beginning of spring*: 197 BC.

hastati of a legion, numbering 2,000 men: the normal structure of a legion of 4,200 was 1,200 *hastati*, 1,200 *principes*, 600 *triarii*, and 1,200 *velites*, but legions larger than 4,200 existed, and Livy mentions some of 6,000 (42. 31; 43. 12; 44. 21) and 6,200 (29. 24; 35. 2). Hence, a single legion could easily contain 2,000 *hastati*, since the number of *triarii* remained fixed at 600. The *principes* appear to have fought originally in the front line and to have used swords; the *hastati* were named for the spear (*hasta*) they carried. But both units were rearmed with the *pilum* (a heavy javelin about 2 m. in length), and the *hastati* now formed the front fighting rank. The *triarii*, as their name implies, formed the third rank, a reserve of veterans. The soldiers of these three ranks were distinguished by seniority.

Antiphilus, praetor of the Boeotians: possibly the *strategos* of the Boeotian League; less likely is his identification with the League's *archon*.

lictor: the singular is unusual, since the proconsul was attended by twelve lictors. Perhaps Livy refers to the lictor at the head of the group. Lictors were attendants of those magistrates who exercised imperium (dictators, consuls, praetors; also proconsuls and propraetors). They carried bundles of rods (*fasces*) symbolizing their power to chastise the disobedient and axes which denoted their power over life and death (cf. note to p. 5, *imperium*).

too old and frail: he was now 71 (cf. chap. 21 below for his age and death).

96 *Aristaenus, praetor of the Achaeans*: Aristaenus was the *strategos* for 199/8. By Livy's own account (32. 39), Nicostratus was now *strategos*. Nevertheless, we should not correct Aristaenus to Nicostratus, since Livy (chaps. 14–15 below) makes it clear that the latter was active in the Peloponnese in 197. Aristaenus spoke on behalf of the Achaeans, but not as their *strategos*. As *strategos* in 196/5, he was again allied with Flamininus, this time against Nabis (Livy 34. 24–25, 30).

97 *at Atrax*: cf. 32. 15, 17. For the defeat at the Aous see 32. 11.

99 *Cynoscephalae*: literally, dog's heads, named for their appearance (cf. Plutarch, *Flamininus* 8. 1). The hills are due west of Pherae in Thessaly.

101 *to lay down their spears . . . and fight with their swords*: many of Livy's errors in the military sphere derive from his lack of experience. Here he has, however, misunderstood Polybius' Greek—mistaking Polybius' observation that the Macedonians 'lowered' (i.e. levelled) their spears for 'laying them down'—and attempted to make sense of this procedure by dismissing the *sarissae* as encumbrances and providing the phalanx with swords. As he understood Polybius' account, the Macedonians after discarding their spears went into battle unarmed!

103 *Claudius' account*: Claudius Quadrigarius. See Introduction, p. xxviii.

Polybius: one of only four references (by name) to the historian who was Livy's main source for this decade (cf. 34. 50; 36. 19; 39. 52).

104 *appropriating . . . credit for the victory*: a contemporary poem by Alcaeus of Messene, quoted by Plutarch (*Flamininus* 9. 2), gives the Aetolians priority over the Romans for the victory at Cynoscephalae.

106 *on the very same day*: such synchronisms were popular in Greek historiography. The best known is perhaps the simultaneous defeat of 'barbarian' armies by Greeks in 480, at Salamis and at Himera, on the same day; also, the father of Agis III, Archidamus III, who died fighting in Italy on the same day, indeed, at the very hour of the battle at Chaeronea in 338 BC.

108 *shield-bearers*: these were élite troops, a development from the hypaspists of Alexander the Great. In Hellenistic Macedonia we find both Silver Shields (*argyraspides*) and Golden Shields (*chrysaspides*).

113 *treaty concluded in days of old*: a reference to famous 'Peace of Callias', which is generally dated by those who accept its historicity to 449 BC. By the terms of this peace, the Persian fleet was prohibited from sailing west of the Cheilidonian *islands*. Livy's words, 'kings of Persia'—if the plural is significant—may refer to a renewal upon the accession of Darius II in 424 BC.

114 *ancient bonds*: there is no surviving evidence of close ties between Rhodes and Antiochus' ancestors, though this does not preclude their existence.

his recent delegation to Rome: probably over the winter 198/7, in response to Roman concerns over Antiochus' attacks on Pergamene territory (cf. 32. 8). Attalus had threatened to withdraw his forces from Greece to meet the danger from Antiochus. The fact that he did not suggests that either Roman diplomacy was effective or Attalus feared repercussions for abandoning Rome.

uncertain how the war with Philip would turn out: Rome was quick to take a hard line with Antiochus, once peace with Philip V had been secured.

age of seventy-one . . . rule of forty-four years: Attalus had succeeded Eumenes I in 241.

fit for a throne: he was, in fact, the first of the Attalid rulers to use the title *basileus* ('king'); Eumenes I had termed himself *dynastes* and, like the founder of the dynasty, Philetaerus, had maintained at least a nominal allegiance to the Seleucid rulers.

115 *four of whom survived him*: in addition to the two who ruled (see below), two other sons are known: Philetaerus and Athenaeus.

lasted to the third generation: Attalus was succeeded by his sons Eumenes II (197–159) and Attalus II (159–138). The kingdom came to an end with the death of Attalus III (son on Eumenes II) in 133; it became the Roman province of Asia.

citizens and foreigners: Livy has slipped here. Marcus Sergius Silus was the urban praetor (see 32. 28).

116 *on the Alban mount*: for other examples of triumphs on the Alban mount see Livy 26. 21 (Marcellus) and 42. 21 (Gaius Cicereius); Publius Cornelius Scipio may have celebrated a private triumph here on his return from Spain, but this hardly supports Livy's comment about consular prerogatives, since Scipio had been in Spain as *privatus cum imperio*.

Hamilcar: at 31. 21, Livy claims that Hamilcar died in battle; but this picks up the version of 32. 30 that he was captured. That Hamilcar graced Gaius Cornelius' triumph smacks of embellishment by a Roman annalist and, because it brings credit to the Cornelii, must be treated with suspicion.

with freedman caps: the *pilleus* was a soft cap worn by ex-slaves upon being granted their freedom (manumission). The image is obvious, but the representatives from Cremona and Placentia have just told the Senate that 'he [Gaius Cornelius] had also delivered them from slavery when they were in the hands of the enemy'. Cf. the Roman prisoners-of-war who had been freed from slavery in Greece, who marched with shaved heads in Flamininus' triumph (34. 52).

biga: see note to p. 50 above.

117 *consulship of Publius Cornelius and Tiberius Sempronius*: the year is 218, the beginning of the Second Punic War. Publius Cornelius Scipio is the father of Africanus; his colleague's cognomen was Longus. Their sons held the consulship jointly in 194 (cf. 34. 42). The Sempronii were political friends of the Cornelii; Africanus' daughter, Cornelia, married the elder Tiberius Sempronius Gracchus (soon after her father's death) and won fame as the 'mother of the Gracchi'.

Roman Games: held in September, they were the responsibility of the curule aediles. See also 31. 50; 32. 7, 27; 33. 42; 34. 44, 54; 38. 35; 39. 7; 40. 59.

119 *A Roman knight*: *eques* here probably refers to a member of the 18 cavalry centuries, rather than a man of the Equestrian Order, though the separation of business and politics had already been spelled out by the *lex Claudia* of 218.

120 *who fought on the king's side*: Brachylles is named by Polybius (18. 1) as one of Philip's supporters at the conference at Nicaea.

three Italians and three Aetolians: the composition of the band of assassins is taken from Polybius (18. 43. 12), but this is as close as Livy comes to indicating that both Flamininus and the Aetolians were behind Brachylles' murder (Polyb. 18. 43. 10 claims that Flamininus said he would not 'participate in the deed but would not prevent those who wished to do it'). Polybius also tells us that Alexamenus, who later murdered Nabis (35. 35–6), was responsible for the assassination of Brachylles.

122 *peace on the following terms*: Livy's terms agree fundamentally with those recorded by Polybius (18. 44), except that the latter makes clear that cities garrisoned by Philip would come under Roman control— particularly the so-called 'fetters of Greece': Demetrias, Chalcis, and Acrocorinth (cf. Plutarch, *Flamininus* 10. 1). Livy may have misunderstood Polybius, but it is more likely that he omitted the occupation of the 'fetters' in order to depict the Romans and Flamininus as true liberators.

123 *Demetrius*: he was paraded in triumph by Flamininus (34. 52); for his release see 36. 35.

Lemnos, Imbros, Delos, and Scyros: this provision (not found in Polybius) was apparently added by Valerius Antias.

127 *the Pylaic Council*: Livy again mistakes the Aetolian council at Thermum for the Amphictyonic council at Thermopylae (cf. notes to pp. 29 and 34 above).

128 *Marsian cohort*: the Marsians were of Italic stock, dwelling in the centre of the peninsula near the Fucine Lake. In 304 they became allies of the Romans.

132 *strengthened by family ties*: a reference to the impending marriage of Antiochus' daughter, Cleopatra, to Ptolemy V Epiphanes (for which see 35. 13, with note).

Lysimachus: Lysimachus, son of Agathocles, had been a Somatophylax ('Bodyguard') and general of Alexander the Great. Upon the latter's death, he became first *strategos* of Thrace, which he carved into a kingdom of his own, and later ruled Macedonia. In 281, he was defeated by Seleucus I Nicator at Corupedium in Asia Minor. But Seleucus, when he crossed into Europe, was killed by Ptolemy Ceraunus, the dispossessed half-brother of Ptolemy II Philadelphus.

his son Seleucus: the future Seleucus IV.

a rumour: Polybius knows nothing of this, but it is recorded also by Appian, *Syrian Wars*, 4. 14.

133 *triumviri epulones*: the *triumviri epulones* formed a priesthood, founded in 196 BC and concerned with public games and the feast of Jupiter. Since the games and feast were administered by magistrates, the role of the *triumviri* was apparently to prevent extravagant displays by the aediles, who used such occasions as platforms for election to higher office.

134 *Gaius Atinius Labeo*: named as a praetor for 195 (the name is confirmed in chap. 43), Gaius Atinius Labeo reappears as a praetor in 190 (36. 45; cf. 37. 2); furthermore, a Gaius Atinius holds the praetorship in 188 (38. 35). The last may be identical with the military tribune named at 34. 46, but the relationship of the praetors of 195 and 190 is less certain; for it is doubtful that they are the same man.

and his father: the elder Gaius Flaminius (consul 223) had been the first governor of the new Roman province of Sicily. During his second consulship (217) he was defeated and killed at Lake Trasimene in the first great Roman disaster of the Hannibalic War.

135 *during the consulship of Gnaeus Servilius and Gaius Flaminius*: in 217, the second year of the Hannibalic War (for the episode see 22. 9). A Sacred Spring (*ver sacrum*) involved dedicating to the gods (for sacrifice) every living animal born in the spring of that year. Earlier, particularly in times of famine, the ritual made a virtue of necessity, stipulating also that all humans born at that time would upon maturity be required to leave home and settle elsewhere.

137 *the order of judges*: these numbered 104. They formed an aristocratic council similar to the Athenian Areopagus, but Aristotle (*Politics* 2. 11) likens them to the Spartan ephors.

praetor: one of the two chief officers known as *sufetes*. The use of 'quaestor' in the same sentence is, of course, another example of applying Roman terminology to foreign offices and refers to a financial officer.

140 *incited to do so by Hannibal*: a pact had been made between Hannibal and Philip in 215, as a consequence of the Roman disaster at Cannae in 216 (cf. Polyb. 7. 9, and Introduction, p. xii with n. 17).

founders of Carthage: according to legend, Carthage was founded by the Tyrians, led by Queen Dido. This, in Virgil's *Aeneid*, is contemporary with the fall of Troy. But even the traditional date of 814/13 (Dionysius of Halicarnassus, *Roman Antiquities* 1. 74; cf. Justin 18. 6. 9, '72 years before the founding of Rome') appears too early: archaeological evidence suggests a foundation date in the mid-to-late eighth century.

Daphne: a suburb of Antioch, where there was a sacred precinct of Apollo. Antiochus' son is not the future Antiochus IV Epiphanes but rather an older son of that name whom Antiochus left in Syria in 193 (for news of his death see 35. 15). The games appear to have been celebrated every two years, and the fact that games were known to have been held in 197 helps to date this episode to 195 (Appian, *Syrian Wars*, 4 and Nepos, *Hannibal* 7 incorrectly place it in 196).

their original treaty: see chap. 13 above for the case of Pharsalus in Thessaly. For Aetolian dissatisfaction with the Senate's provisions, see Polybius 18. 45.

BOOK THIRTY-FOUR

141 *Oppius*: the *lex Oppia* is his only claim to fame. Apart from his tribune-ship in 215, nothing is known about him; even his praenomen is given in different MSS as Gaius, Gnaeus, and Marcus.

consulship of Quintus Fabius and Tiberius Sempronius: 215 BC. Quintus Fabius is Fabius Maximus Cunctator, Tiberius Sempronius was an ancestor of the famous Gracchi, Tiberius and Gaius. Sempronius Grac-chus held the consulship again in 213, this time with another Quintus Fabius, the son of the dictator, but the law clearly belongs in 215, for Livy later (chaps. 6 and 8 below) remarks that it had been passed twenty years before 195.

multi-shaded clothes: the law appears to have specified that women were not to wear purple. For a discussion see R. Bauman, *Women in Politics in Ancient Rome* (London, 1992), 31–4.

Porcius Cato: Marcus Porcius Cato (consul 195, for his election see 33. 42), whom J. P. V. D. Balsdon, (*Roman Women* (London, 1962), 32) describes as 'that self-confident and boorish embodiment of austere moral rectitude'. The speech that follows is fabricated, and not based on any text of Cato's actual speech; whether it is the creation of Livy himself or of Valerius Antias is not certain, but it does contain anachronisms and slight inconsistencies with what Livy has reported in earlier books (see the notes that follow).

wife: the Latin is *materfamilias*, that is, the matron or mistress of the house.

142 *a female cabal*: a reference to the legend of the Lemnian women, who at some point before the arrival of the Argonauts, had put their menfolk to death.

144 *the Idaean mother*: the 'Great Mother' (Magna Mater) or Phrygian Cybele. The bringing of the goddess (in the form of the black stone from Pessinus) from Asia Minor occurred in 205, when consultation of the Sibylline Books led the Romans to believe that the invader would be driven from Italy if Cybele's cult were introduced (Livy 29. 10, 11, 14). See also note to p. 207 below.

Pyrrhus used his envoy Cineas: for Cineas see Plutarch, *Pyrrhus*, 14ff. For gifts brought to individual Romans, their wives and children, see *Pyrrhus*, 18. The attempted bribery of the Romans occurred after one of Pyrrhus' victories in Italy, either Heraclea (280) or Asculum (279).

the Licinian law of the 500 iugera: Livy refers to the Licinian-Sextian legislation of 367, which controlled the amount of public land (*ager publicus*) that could legally be occupied by Roman citizens (cf. Livy 6. 35). But this probably specified a figure lower than 500; the latter represents an increase legislated in the second century (cf. Appian, *Civil War*, 1. 8. 33). The abuse of these restrictions played no small part in the Gracchan reforms of 133. Since Cato's speech, as given by Livy, is not strictly historical the reference to 500 iugera in 195 may be anachronistic.

Cincian law: introduced, perhaps, in 204, the year in which Marcus Cincius Alimentus (possibly a relative of the annalist Lucius Cincius Alimentus) was tribune. Details are known only from Tacitus (*Annals*, 11. 5; 13. 42; 15. 20), who says it prohibited payments to advocates.

146 *your own Origins*: an obvious anachronism. Cato had not yet composed this work, which Nepos (*Cato* 3. 3) describes as a work of his later years.

married women running between the two lines: that is, the Sabine women (Livy 1. 13).

the legions of the Volsci, led by Marcius Coriolanus: 488 BC. See Livy 2. 40 for the women's intervention; cf. Plutarch, *Coriolanus*, 33–6.

147 *When the city had been taken by the Gauls*: c.386 (see Livy 5. 48–50).

In the last war: a reference to the Hannibalic War (214 BC; cf. Livy 24. 18), though, strictly speaking, the Second Macedonian War was more recent.

a law of the kings: that is, a law from the regal period (753–509), or perhaps merely an old law of uncertain date or authorship.

Twelve Tables: the codification of Roman law established by two successive boards of ten (*decemviri*), appointed in 451–450. It was still being memorized by schoolboys in Cicero's time.

148 *victorious at Cannae*: in 216 BC.

Slaves were being bought up to be put under arms: Livy 22. 57 speaks of the arming of 8,000 slaves after Cannae. These were purchased from their masters at public expense, and Livy says nothing at this point of deferring the payment until the war's end; indeed, at 22. 61 he says that the Senate had already put the money for their payment aside and refused to use these funds to ransom prisoners from Hannibal.

149 *toga praetexta*: the toga worn by the curule magistrates, apparently of Etruscan origin. The *toga praetexta* was worn also by the sons of nobles (they are sometimes referred to as *praetextati*) before they assumed the *toga virilis* at the age of 18. Cf. note to p. 524 below.

as a coverlet for your bed: or 'as a covering garment' (Briscoe, *Comm*. ii. 61). (Translator's note.)

150 *the law was withdrawn*: Valerius Maximus (9. 1. 3) regards this move as a mistake on the part of the Romans.

151 *mother country also of the Massiliots*: modern Marseilles, founded c.600 BC by the Phocaeans from Asia Minor; Emporiae (mod. Empúries) in Spain was founded either by the Phocaeans themselves or the Massiliots.

152 *According to Valerius' account*: although Livy normally cites Valerius Antias in order to discredit him (cf. chap. 15 below), here he refrains from criticism, perhaps for want of better evidence.

biga: see note to p. 50 above.

152 *another man's auspices . . . another man's province*: cf. 31. 20, where Lucius Cornelius Lentulus is denied a triumph but granted an ovation for the same reasons.

154 *boundary of their empire*: the infamous Hasdrubal or Ebro treaty (226 BC), which stipulated that the River Ebro (Iber) should be the northeastern limit of Carthaginian expansion in Spain (cf. Polyb; 2. 13. 7). By the terms of this treaty, Saguntum fell into the Carthaginian sphere, and Roman apologists were hard-pressed to justify Rome's ultimatum to Hannibal and Carthage.

156 *principes and hastati*: see note to p. 95 above.

does not underestimate his own achievements: cf. Plutarch, *Cato* 19: 'no man ever did more to heap praises upon himself' (in *Plutarch: The Makers of Rome*, trans. Scott-Kilvert (Harmondsworth, 1965), 141).

[Cato . . . the standards]: the lines are bracketed by most editors, including Briscoe, as being spurious. (Translator's note.)

157 *Turduli*: i.e. the Turdetani.

159 *Saguntia*: probably Segontia (mod. Siguenza) thus the reading of the Teubner text (defended by Briscoe, *Comm.* ii. 82, who suspects confusion with Saguntum; cf. Livy 26. 20).

162 *cheated out of Echinus and Pharsalus*: cf. 33. 49.

163 *Pythagoras . . . brother of his wife*: cf. chap. 32 below. Livy's details are vague, but if the wife of Nabis referred to here is Apega (thus Polyb. 13. 7. 6), and she in turn is the daughter of Aristippus of Argos, then Pythagoras would also be an Argive and brother of Aristippus. The friendship was sealed by a double marriage-alliance, which saw Pythagoras himself marry a daughter of Nabis. The relationship (both son-in-law and brother-in-law) is attested also in the case of Alexander I of Epirus and Philip II of Macedon.

166 *the Ilotae*: a reference to Helots, the only one of two in Latin literature. (The other is Nepos, *Pausanias* 3. 6.) But Livy appears not to understand who these people are: 'a country people, living in fortified towns from early times' misses the point. Helots were state slaves or serfs, drawn primarily from the pre-Dorian population of Laconia and, later, from the conquered territory of Messenia. By providing for the needs of everyday life, they freed the Spartan citizen (*homoios* = 'equal') to devote his time and energies to military training. The Helots' position was in many respects similar to that of the New World Indians in relation to the Spanish *encomenderos*.

Antigonus . . . fought a pitched battle with . . . Cleomenes: the battle of Sellasia took place in 222 BC. The Macedonian king is Antigonus III Doson, Philip V's immediate predecessor.

167 *in whom he had placed all his confidence*: he did not doubt the fighting qualities of his Spartans, but rather distrusted their loyalty to him.

170 *Our lawgiver*: Lycurgus (cf. chap. 32 below). Sparta's political and social institutions developed gradually, and some were not in place until after the Second Messenian War in the late seventh century BC. Nevertheless, tradition ascribed Sparta's laws to the legendary Lycurgus, whose date and career are far from certain. See esp. Plutarch, *Lycurgus*, and Xenophon, *Constitution of the Lacedaemonians*.

171 *our native succinctness*: a reference to the famed Laconic brevity, of which Herodotus (3. 46; 7. 226) and Xenophon (*Hellenica* 1. 1. 23) provide notable examples (but cf. also Plutarch's *Sayings of the Spartans*).

172 *to establish a family bond*: cf. 32. 38.

174 *pass on to his successor a military victory*: aristocratic *cupido gloriae* often inclined commanders to put their own interests ahead of the state, but in Flamininus' case, his conduct of both the Second Macedonian War and the war with Nabis was influenced by concerns about whether he would be replaced.

177 *only recently had the tyrants erected a defensive-wall*: Sparta had remained unwalled until the late fourth century (cf. also 39. 37).

180 *first year of the Second Punic War*: 218 BC.

181 *Sacred Spring*: see note to p. 135 above.

182 *as the princeps senatus the consul Publius Scipio*: the *princeps senatus* had the honour of speaking first in any Senatorial debate. Scipio held that rank for fifteen years.

   crimes that he had committed . . . at Locri: cf. 31. 12.

183 *Lucius Aemilius Paullus*: Scipio Africanus' brother-in-law (Scipio was married to Aemilia, daughter of the elder Lucius Aemilius who died at Cannae in 216). He held his first consulship in 182, and a second in 168, when he commanded Roman forces in the Third Macedonian War and became famous as the conqueror of Perseus. The younger of Lucius Aemilius' sons by his first (divorced) wife Papiria was adopted by Publius Cornelius (Africanus' son, on whom see 40. 42), taking the name Publius Cornelius Scipio Aemilianus.

184 *Gaius Atinius*: probably not identical with Gaius Atinius Labeo, but perhaps the praetor of 188 BC.

187 *Roman citizens in slavery*: these details are also given by Plutarch (*Flamininus* 13), though he treats their liberation as a 'gift' from the Greeks.

   Polybius' comment: this portion of Polybius' *Histories* has not survived. Livy, probably following Polybius, treats the Roman denarius as the rough equivalent of the Greek *drachma*. One talent comprised 6,000 *drachmae* (hence 600,000 *drachmae* = 100 talents). Nevertheless, he records (chap. 52 below) that the four-drachma coin was worth only three *denarii*.

188 *'tetrachms'*: the form appears elsewhere (cf. 37. 46, 58, 59; 39. 7, though the term is translated 'four-drachma pieces [or coins]'). The correct form is, however, *tetradrachmae*.

189 *Publius Sempronius Sophus*: an individual of this name was consul in 268 and censor in 252; if Livy's comment about the dedication made during the Hannibalic war is correct, the man in question must be Publius Sempronius Tuditanus (consul 204). Tuditanus' censorship, however, belongs to 209, and he could not have acted upon a vow he had not yet made!

190 *the first to stage dramatic performances at the Megalesia*: at 36. 36 Livy (following Valerius Antias) appears to have forgotten what he records here. At least, he does not bother to refute Antias' claim.

195 *as noted above*: see 33. 45–9 for Hannibal's flight from Carthage.

196 *the Barca faction*: the supporters of the Barca family, to which Hamilcar, Hasdrubal, and Hannibal belonged. Carthage, like Rome, was dominated by powerful aristocratic élites, and the generalship was both a sign of political ascendancy and a means of maintaining it. In the past the Magonids had been particularly powerful, but in the Punic War era the Barcids had emerged as a major force, and it was their influence that saw Carthage carve out an empire in Spain and provoke the Second Punic War. Predictably, the Barcids also had numerous enemies at home.

sufetes: for these officals and the Carthaginian government see note to p. 137.

198 *the Bursa*: the citadel of Carthage (known today as the Hill of St Louis, after the famous crusading king, Louis IX); *bursa* means ox-hide in Greek.

BOOK THIRTY-FIVE

199 *As propraetor*: upon expiration of his term as praetor, his office was extended by prorogation.

204 *Marcus Claudius had written personal letters*: the Claudii were bitter political opponents of the Cornelii, and the charges made will have been politically motivated without regard for Cornelius' true military worth. The fact that the letters were unofficial and written to 'most of the Senators' (chap. 8) reveals their tendentious nature.

Feralia: a festival of the Dead, held on 21 February.

206 *census-purification*: The *lustratio* was an official purification of the people (citizens) who gathered in the Campus Martius; see Livy 1. 44.

Publius Cornelius Scipio (son of Gnaeus Scipio): Publius Cornelius Scipio Nasica. Although he failed on this occasion, he gained the consulship for 191 (see chap. 24, below, and 36. 1).

patricians seeking the same seat: as a result of the Sextian-Licinian legislation of 367, only one of the consuls could be a patrician (though in the period 355–343 this was not strictly observed); in 172, for the first time, both consuls were plebeians.

brothers of the candidates: Titus Quinctius was Lucius' brother, Africanus was actually Scipio Nasica's cousin. The term *fratres* includes brothers and cousins.

207 *with a Cornelius presiding over the election as consul*: the presiding consul could declare candidates ineligible and was thus able to help his own 'faction' or harm opponents. See the action of Marcus Fulvius, rejecting the candidacy of Marcus Aemilius Lepidus (38. 35).

to welcome the Idaean mother . . . from Pessinus: the story of the bringing of Phrygian Cybele (Magna Mater) to Italy is told by Livy (29. 10–11, 14), but only Livy (followed by Silius Italicus) claims that the Sibylline Books prophesied that Hannibal would be driven out of Italy if the goddess's image were brought to Rome. The Romans were also instructed to receive the sacred stone representation hospitably, sending the 'best man' (*vir optimus*) to receive it. Publius Cornelius Scipio Nasica was selected— one suspects that it may have been a posthumous honour bestowed upon his father Gnaeus—to receive the statue, which had been conveyed by ship from Pessinus in Phrygia to the mouth of the Tiber, and pass it on to the matrons who accompanied him, of whom the most celebrated for her virtue (*castissima*) was Claudia Quinta. The ceremony thus brought together representatives of two of Rome's most powerful rival families, the Cornelii and Claudii. Celebration of the cult soon developed into the annual *Ludi Megalenses*. E. S. Gruen, *Studies in Greek Culture and Roman Policy* (Leiden, 1990), chap. 1, believes the cult came from Ida in the Troad via Pergamum, that it had reinforced Roman links with Troy, and that the story of the cult stone's coming from Pessinus is mistaken (see note to p. 375 below).

The aedileship of that year: the curule aedileship. At chap. 23 below Livy names one of the plebeian aediles, Lucius Oppius Salinator, in a different context.

208 *disaster of the Caudine Forks*: a notable disaster during the Second Samnite War (321 BC), after which the Roman army endured the humiliation of 'going under the yoke' of enemy spears.

210 *gave his daughter in marriage*: this was Cleopatra I, whose son Ptolemy VI took the title 'Philometor'. The location of the marriage, at Raphia, must have been significant; for it was here in 217 BC that Ptolemy IV Philopator had defeated Antiochus III in an earlier battle (cf. John Whitehorne, *Cleopatras* (London, 1994), 81, comparing it to 'Hitler forcing the defeated French to sign the 1940 armistice in the same railway carriage in which the German high command had been compelled to accept the Treaty of Versailles.').

211 *his son Antiochus*: see the note to p. 140, *Daphne*, above; for his death see chap. 15 below.

212 *Apamea*: Seleucid foundations, especially those of Seleucus Nicator and his son Antiochus I, were commonly named for Nicator's parents (Antiochea and Laodicea) or his barbarian wife, Apame (Apamea); others were simply Seleucea. This Apamea, where the Peace of 188 was concluded, was in Phrygia and had been formed by transferring the inhabitants of Celaenae to the site (cf. 38. 13). Just like Antigonea in Syria, which was

reconstituted nearby as Antioch, Celaenae had been an administrative centre of Antigonus the One-Eyed.

213 *Minnio, who was his leading courtier*: he reappears in a military capacity at 37. 41.

214 †*and the country of Sparta*†: these words appear to be an explanatory gloss. Nabis 'own country' *was* Sparta.

215 *asked the Spartans for earth and water*: in the time leading up to Xerxes' invasion of Greece in 480 BC. Earth and water were the symbols of submission to Persian authority.

216 *never to be a friend of the Roman people*: Livy 21. 1 tells the story (taken over from Polybius 3. 11, and there are numerous versions of it in later sources) that when Hannibal was only nine years old, his father, before setting out with him for Spain, made him swear, with his hand on the sacrificial victim, that he would be the enemy of Rome.

219 *plebeian aedile the year before*: Lucius Oppius Salinator was tribune of the plebs in 197 (32. 28). Livy (chap. 10, see note to p. 207 above) mentions only the curule aediles for 193. Oppius' colleague was perhaps Marcus Iunius Brutus.

220 *Gaius Livius . . . Salinator*: Livius' career merits comment. Unsuccessful in his bid for the consulship of 192, he was elected praetor for a second time; his first term as praetor was in 202. Second praetorships were abnormal, usually involving individuals who had been expelled from the Senate and were seeking reinstatement as a result of holding the office (this, at least, was the case in the first century BC). But it is unlikely that Livius would have been a candidate for the consulship in the previous year if he had been expelled from the Senate. Furthermore, by the terms of the *lex Gennucia*, Livius, though eligible for the consulship, was actually barred from running for the praetorship of 192. Since the number of praetors had recently increased from four to six, Livius must have thought that his chances of winning the praetorship (and a province) were greater than those of a second bid for the consulship. Indeed, he may have been encouraged to stand for the lower office on the understanding of support for the consulship at a later date; for the Scipionic group was clearly backing the *novus homo*, Manius Acilius Glabrio.

new magistrates were to draw lots for their provinces: the results of the sortition are delayed until 36. 2.

222 †*eighty years*†: that is, in 272. Plutarch (*Philopoemen* 14) says that the event occurred forty years earlier, which is impossible, since the individuals in question (either Craterus or his son, Alexander; see below) would no longer have been alive in 232, and Alexander's widow, Nicaea, had married Demetrius, son of Antigonus Gonatas in the 240s. Briscoe (*Comm.* ii. 183) believes the text should perhaps read 'sixty'. This, though somewhat arbitrary, does at least provide a plausible historical context. Certainty is impossible.

Nicaea, wife of Craterus: Craterus was the son of Alexander's famous general of the same name and Phila, daughter of Antipater the Regent. After the elder Craterus' death, Phila married Demetrius the Besieger and the son was brought up together with his half-brother, Antigonus II Gonatas, who ruled Macedon from 276 to 239 BC. Nothing is known of his marriage, or of the identity of Nicaea. On the other hand, Craterus' son Alexander did have a wife named Nicaea, who after her husband's death married Demetrius II.

223 *caetrati*: bearing the *caetra*, a small Spanish shield (cf. chap. 28 below and 37. 39).

the Camp of Pyrrhus: dating from the time of Pyrrhus' attack on Sparta in 272 BC.

224 *in whom he had most confidence*: repeating the sentiments of 34. 28.

the so-named Tarentine cavalry: a type of cavalry, perhaps named for their weapons, though the origin of the name is not certain. Livy mentions them again at 37. 40 in the army of Antiochus III. They were not men from Tarentum in Italy. 'Tarentines' are already attested in the early age of the Successors, serving in the army of Antigonus the One-Eyed. That the Tarentines had two horses each is nowhere else attested and, unless Livy has made a slip, may be true on this occasion only.

225 *Lycortas*: the father of the historian Polybius, who was serving as *hipparch* of the Achaeans.

231 *from a camp pitched on the bank of the Tiber*: the remark would come back to haunt the Aetolians in general and Damocritus in particular (cf. note to p. 275, below).

243 *cataphracti*: cf. 37. 40, where they are used by Antiochus III at Magnesia (cf. Polybius 16. 18. 6, 30. 25. 9).

244 *turned their horses in flight*: cf. Plutarch, *Crassus* 24; and also Horace, *Odes* 1. 19. 11, with the note in the edition of Nisbet and Hubbard (Oxford, 1970).

247 *which the Greeks call 'asyla'*: that is, 'freedom from violence'. The abstract noun is rather *asylia*.

BOOK THIRTY-SIX

249 *lectisternium*: in this ritual—instituted in 399 BC, when the ceremony lasted eight days (Livy 5. 13)—the statues of the gods (Apollo and his mother Latona (Leto), Hercules and Diana, Mercury, and Neptune) were brought out and offered lavish meals.

250 *double jurisdiction*: he exercised the office of both the *praetor urbanus* and the *praetor peregrinus* (cf. 25. 3). The years 201–198 (to consider only the years from the conclusion of the Second Punic War) saw the offices combined, and the creation of two additional praetors in 197 appears to have addressed this problem. But the military situation in 191 (perhaps, also Roman apprehensions about Hannibal's participation) must account

for the temporary sharing of functions by Marcus Iunius Brutus, thus freeing up one more praetor for the defence of the state. A separate *praetor peregrinus* reappears in 190.

252 *they had already declared*: see 31. 8.

253 *500 cavalry plus elephants*: these appear to have been sent, under the command of the Numidian Muttines (cf. note to p. 400 below).

254 *the assassination of Brachylles*: for this episode see 33. 28. Though Livy omits Polybius' charge that Flamininus countenanced Brachylles' murder, his talk of 'pretexts' should not be taken as a denial of Roman involvement. Livy prefers to ascribe Boeotian support for Antiochus to a flaw in their collective character.

discipline . . . had already been in decline: Livy is contrasting the Boeotians of the early second century with those of the 370s and 360s, no doubt, with Epaminondas in particular.

257 *Cynoscephalae*: for the casualties at Cynoscephalae see 33. 10. Philip certainly fled from the battlefield, leaving the dead unburied, but 33. 11 shows that he sent an ambassador to Flamininus at Larisa to arrange a truce for their burial.

260 *the daughter of Cleoptolemus*: Antiochus was 50 at the time. The comparison with Philip II's final marriage, to the young Cleopatra, is obvious. Although Cleoptolemus is described by Polybius as a leading man of Chalcis, he is otherwise unknown and we have no reason to doubt that the primary motive for the marriage was infatuation. Polybius adds that Antiochus renamed her 'Euboea' upon marriage (her maiden-name is not recorded), again recalling Philip II's practice. Antiochus was already married to Laodice, daughter of Mithridates II (who had himself married a daughter of Antiochus II) and mother of Seleucus IV and Antiochus IV. Whether she was officially divorced is neither stated nor certain. An inscription from Susa shows that she was still alive in 177/6, long after Antiochus' own death in 187.

263 *saluted as a king*: a sarcastic reference to the Megalopolitan's claim to have descended from Alexander the Great (cf. 35. 47).

265 *deaths of the Spartans . . . against Persia*: the famous '300 Spartans' who died, with their king, Leonidas, in defence of the pass in 480 BC (Herodotus 7. 222–8).

266 *more recently, Philip by these same Romans*: see 32. 11–12.

267 *Syrians and Asiatic Greeks, the dregs of humanity, born to be slaves*: cf. 37. 39, where Livy compares them to cattle ready for the slaughter: 'No enemy was ever regarded with such disdain by the Romans.'

268 *the 'sarisophori'*: the so-called 'Macedonians' (although these may have contained men of Macedonian origin, resident in the Seleucid kingdom, which was dotted with military colonies or *katoikiai*), take their name from their weapons and style of fighting. *Sarisophori* means, literally, lance-bearers. They are not to be confused with the cavalry unit found in

the time of Alexander the Great, who fought from horseback, armed with a special, shorter, *sarisa*. At 37. 40, in his description of the battle of Magnesia, Livy speaks of the *phalangitae* 'who were armed in Macedonian fashion'.

269 *the horses took fright*: the natural fear of elephants (and camels) by horses is well documented in the ancient sources.

270 *following Polybius*: Polyb. 20. 8. 6.

271 *Creusa*: more commonly 'Creusis', the Boeotian port on the Gulf of Corinth.

Cato had outpaced him: cf. Plutarch *Cato* 14. For his rivalry with the Cornelii Scipiones, especially Lucius, see *Cato* 15, 18. It is nowhere explained why it was necessary for Acilius Glabrio to send two messengers with the news. Acilius, who was supported by the Scipionic faction, probably allowed Lucius Cornelius to return to Rome in order to stand for the consulship; Cato, who had played no small part in circumventing the troops who were blocking Thermopylae, was presumably given the honour of carrying the message home. Whether there was any petty intrigue, or if this is simply another case of Cato's thirst for glory (he was not standing for political office in the upcoming election), is not clear.

275 *when the Aetolians had established their camp*: Damocritus had made this boast as *strategos* of the Aetolian League in 192 (cf. 35.33: 'from a camp pitched on the bank of the Tiber'). For Damocritus' fate see 37. 3, 46.

prevented by illness from taking part in the war: although the excuse may have been valid, it was a notorious ploy of kings to plead illness in order to avoid involving themselves in delicate (or unpopular) situations. Philip may, in fact, have been awaiting the outcome of the first action between the Romans and Antiochus before committing himself.

279 *the mortal body of the god was cremated*: that is, only the mortal part. Thereafter, Hercules was translated to Olympus, where he married Hebe, the daughter of Zeus and Hera, a sign of his reconciliation with the latter.

282 *the only people to have disparaged his glorious achievement*: cf. note to p. 104 above.

283 *for a fixed period*: this period is described at 37. 1 as about to expire. Perhaps the Aetolians like the Epirotes were granted ninety days.

284 *a hostage at Rome*: this had been part of the peace treaty that ended the Second Macedonian War (33. 30). See also 34. 52 for his appearance in Rome, and Books 39–40 for his later career and fate.

consulship of Publius Cornelius Scipio . . . and of Publius Licinius: in 205, during Africanus' first consulship; his colleague was Publius Licinius Crassus Dives. The statue arrived in Ostia in 204.

consulship of Marcus Cornelius and Publius Sempronius: 204 BC. The consuls were Marcus Cornelius Cethegus and Publius Sempronius Tuditanus; the censors, Marcus Livius Salinator and Gaius Claudius Nero.

284 *Megalesia*: or *ludi Megalenses*. This is another of the rare instances where
     Livy appears to accept Valerius' testimony. Nevertheless, his details may
     be wrong and Livy contradicts his own testimony (34. 54) that the first
     dramatic performances at the *Megalesia* occurred in 194.

285 *when the latter cut Hasdrubal and his army to pieces*: in 207 Hasdrubal
     brought reinforcements from Spain to his brother, Hannibal, in Italy. He
     was, however, intercepted and defeated at the River Metaurus; his
     severed head was delivered to Hannibal in the south (see 27. 39–51, esp.
     47–9 with no mention of Marcus Livius Salinator's vow).

     their 'sacred law': it was a widespread practice among the Italian peoples
     to deprive those who refused military service of both life and property.
     For examples see 4. 26; 9. 39; 10. 38.

286 *Little trust . . . where numbers are concerned*: cf. Antias' numbers for Antio-
     chus' casualties at Thermopylae (chap. 19 above).

288 *Antiochus was at Ephesus*: Ephesus had become a favourite residence for
     the Seleucids (cf. 33. 38, 41, 49; 35. 13–16; 21 above). The eastern and
     western capitals of the empire were Antioch, on the Orontes in Syria,
     and Seleucia-on-the-Tigris. In the time leading up to the Laodicean or
     Third Syrian War (*c*.246), Antiochus II's divorced wife Laodice resided
     in Ephesus.

289 *purification ceremony*: conducted also by Aemilius Regillus when he took
     over the fleet from Gaius Livius (see 37. 14). Cf. the ceremony and
     Scipio's prayer at 29. 27.

290 *Magnesia-near-Sipylus*: the site of the forthcoming, decisive, battle
     between Antiochus and the Romans. There were two important towns in
     Asia Minor that bore the name Magnesia. This one, by the River Hermus
     and closer to Pergamene territory, is the site of the battle with Antiochus
     and is to be distinguished from Magnesia-on-the-Maeander, south of
     Ephesus. See also the note to p. 303, *Magnesia*.

291 *Two Punic ships*: of the six that Carthage had contributed (chap. 42 above;
     cf. Appian, *Syrian Wars*, 22), no doubt to avert Roman suspicion that
     they were in sympathy with Antiochus, at whose court Hannibal now
     resided.

     created conditions similar to a land-battle: this was the purpose of the
     Roman *corvus* (Gk. *korax*), but the use of the so-called 'crow', which had
     served the Romans well in the naval battles of the First Punic War, seems
     to have been abandoned in favour of grappling-irons. Cf. the use of these
     devices, with the same aim (i.e. creating the conditions of land warfare),
     in the battle in the harbour of Syracuse in 413 (Thucydides, 7. 62).

292 *Gaius Atinius Labeo*: see note to p. 134 above.

BOOK THIRTY-SEVEN

293 *pay 1,000 talents*: this is the same amount that Philip V was required to pay at the end of the Second Macedonian War (33. 30), and it appears that, on this occasion, the Romans were deliberately offering the Aetolians impossible conditions. Eventually they made peace on the condition of paying 500 talents (38. 11).

leave the city that very day and Italy within fifteen days: presumably so that they could not lobby Roman politicians, but also as a sign of the Senate's disfavour. For the same period of days see chap. 49 below. The time-limits varied, however: Perseus' ambassadors were given a mere eleven days (42. 36) in 171 BC.

Laelius had great influence in the Senate: Laelius was plebeian and a *novus homo*. It is doubtful that Scipionic support for his candidacy did not involve some kind of understanding that the conduct of the war against Antiochus should be awarded to Lucius Cornelius. The fact that there was discussion of the issue and deviation from the practice of sortition supports this view. In normal circumstances, consuls drew lots for their provinces—after the election until 123 BC, when a *lex Sempronia* prescribed that sortition should precede it—and Cicero (*Philippics* 11. 17) claims that Lucius had actually obtained Asia (which in this case included Greece) by lot, but the Senate had misgivings about his military abilities, which were laid to rest by his brother's offer to serve as his legate.

295 *assume command of the fleet from Gaius Livius*: for Livius' naval activities see 36. 42–5. His successor, Aemilius Regillus, was another adherent of the Scipionic group.

Juno Lucina: like her Greek counterpart, Hera, a goddess of marriage and child-birth.

a sudden downpour on a clear day: or, possibly, 'storm clouds had gathered on a clear day' (see Briscoe, *Comm.* ii. 293). (Translator's note.)

Latin Festival: held in April (cf. 32. 1).

the Books: the so-called Sibylline Books, which contained collections of oracles and were kept and interpreted by the *decemviri sacris faciundis* (on whom see the note to p. 14, *the Sibylline books*).

296 *Lautumiae*: the stone-quarries on the slope of the Capitoline hill, where prisoners-of-war were kept. Similar facilities served also for the Spartans captured at Pylos in 424 BC (Thucydides, 4. 41) and the Athenians taken in Sicily (Thucydides, 7. 86–7).

Ptolemy and Cleopatra: Ptolemy V Epiphanes and Cleopatra I (for their marriage see note to p. 210 above).

the moon passed under the sun's orb: this eclipse occurred on 14 March 190, and it is a valuable anchor for the chronology of the period. At this point, the pre-Julian calendar was 119 days out of alignment.

298 *pretext to quit the Aetolian war with honour*: if Lucius Cornelius was to win
glory, and a triumph, he would need to deal with the Aetolians quickly
and confront Antiochus in Asia. Acilius Glabrio had already defeated
him at Thermopylae and driven him from Greece (a fact that was used
against Lucius when he later claimed a triumph). One suspects that
the Senate's 'peace terms' to the Aetolians (cf. note to p. 293 above)
were perhaps intended to harden their resistance and keep the Scipionic
commanders (whether Acilius Glabrio or Lucius Cornelius) preoccupied
in Greece.

299 *1,000-talent payment*: see chap. 1 above.

our authority: *imperio nostro*. In his commentary, Walsh says: 'Strictly
speaking, only the consul wielded *imperium*.' It is not, however, certain
that Publius is claiming imperium for himself. Perhaps he is merely referring to *Roman* authority, to which Philip V was subject by virtue of his
alliance.

300 *Tiberius Sempronius Gracchus*: although he had a distinguished career, this
man is best known as the father of Tiberius and Gaius, who between 133
and 121 inaugurated the period of political strife (between *optimates* and
populares) that was to destroy the Republic. He was to become Africanus'
son-in-law, though apparently after Scipio's death. Briscoe (*Comm.* ii.
302) assumes that Livy's praise of Gracchus derives from Polybius.

Gallograecia: Galatia, the form used in the translation henceforth.

still possessed their Gallic spirit: for Livy the inhabitants of the East have
become soft and effeminate. Livy's apparently ambiguous attitude concerning the manliness of the Galatians merely reflects two contemporary
depictions of them, one intended to enhance the achievement of Manlius
Vulso, the other to cheapen it. See note to p. 373 below.

Seleucus: the later Seleucus IV Philopater (who ruled from 187 to 175);
cf. note to p. 132 above.

301 *spring equinox*: 190 BC

'Port of the Achaeans': that is, the harbour of Troy, where the 'Achaean'
ships were sheltered. The refounded city was known as Ilium.

he sacrificed to Minerva: for the famous temple of Athena at Troy, and
Alexander's sacrifice there see Arrian 1.11.7; cf. Cicero, *Pro Archia* 24.
Xerxes had, of course, sacrificed there in 480 (Herodotus 7.43), and the
fact will have influenced Alexander's actions. In Scipio's case, there may
be an element of *Alexandri imitatio* as well.

Galli, the frenzied priests: two only in Polybius (21. 6. 7). They were the
priests of Phrygian Cybele, whose frenzied rites culminated in self-
castration. Interest in them would have been great at this point, since the
temple of Magna Mater was officially dedicated in 191. In Rome the
Galli were permitted to parade only during the festival in April, being
sequestered the remainder of the time.

303 *Magnesia*: the MSS add *ad Sipylum*, which is clearly a misinformed gloss.

The place in question is Magnesia-on-the-Maeander. Magnesia ad Sipylum, the site of the decisive battle with Antiochus III lies about 90 miles from Ephesus.

covered over: see Briscoe, *Comm.* ii. 308 on the reading. (Translator's note.)

Nicander, a pirate chief: piracy was an age-old, and often honourable, profession (Odysseus could make the claim proudly when he returned to Ithaca in disguise). Like the modern privateers from the Elizabethan period through to (and beyond) the American Civil War, pirates performed useful services not only by preying on enemy shipping but by acting as naval allies. See the excellent discussion in H. Ormerod, *Piracy in the Ancient World* (London, 1924).

305 *Elaea*: the port of Pergamum, not to be confused with Elaeus on the Hellespont (chap. 9 above; cf. 31.16).

306 *the praetor*: Gaius Livius.

Hybristas: Hybristas means 'Arrogant' and is perhaps a nickname: it is otherwise unattested in Sparta but Briscoe (*Comm.* ii. 313) draws attention to the Aetolian *strategos* (165/4) of the same name.

307 *conducted the customary sacrifice*: see the note to p. 289 above.

Nobody liked the proposal: the rejection by Eumenes of the advice proffered by Gaius Livius can scarcely have been flattering to the Roman commander, and it is hard to see why Livy includes the story.

311 *Rhodians were not against peace*: perhaps an early indication of the developing rift between Eumenes and the Rhodians.

312 *the plain of Thebe, made famous by Homer's poem*: Homer, *Iliad* 6. 397. Hector's wife Andromache came from here.

Diophanes: the high profile of Diophanes of Megalopolis is doubtless attributable to the work of his compatriot Polybius.

315 *River Eurymedon*: famous as the scene of Cimon's great victory over Persia in the early 460s (the date is uncertain but often given as 469 or 468).

Etesians: these 'unfavourable' winds occur in July and August. They stranded Caesar's forces in Alexandria in the summer of 48 BC.

317 *King Prusias of Bithynia*: ruled *c.*230–*c.*180 BC. His neutrality in the war with Antiochus (of which the king complains) bought him no favours from Rome: Mysia was taken from him and returned to Eumenes II (see 38. 37). Prusias later gave refuge to Hannibal.

320 *with the fillets and branches of suppliants*: cf. note to p. 19 above. The branches of suppliants are *velamenta*, olive-branches covered with wool (cf. 35. 34).

324 *Ariarathes . . . to fetch reinforcements*: Ariarathes IV; he ruled Cappadocia from 220 to 164 BC. Ariarathes had married Antiochis, daughter of Antiochus III and Laodice; he was himself the grandson of Antiochus II Theos, whose daughter Stratonice had married Ariarathes III. He sent

some 3,500 troops to Antiochus at Magnesia (see chap. 40 below) and later supplied forces to oppose Manlius Vulso (38. 26).

326 *Chersonese*: the Thracian Chersonese (i.e. the Gallipoli peninsula).

the moving of the shields: the twelve sacred (figure-eight) shields (*ancilia*: Livy 1. 20), which were housed in the Regia, were taken out during the festival of Mars by the Salian priests, who danced through the streets, striking them with their spears. The twelve shields comprised one original that according to legend had fallen from heaven and eleven imitations.

because he was a Salian priest: during the festival of Mars the Salian priests could not change their dwelling places. The Salii were twenty-four priests (apparently two groups of twelve, the second group vowed by Tullus Hostilius, Livy 1. 27) who performed ritual dances to Mars at the beginning and end of the campaigning season.

329 *offered sacrifice to Minerva*: cf. chap. 9 above.

332 *African elephants are no match for Indian*: although the well-known modern African elephant is larger than that found in India, the African variety used by the Romans was the smaller, forest elephant.

phalangitae who were armed in Macedonian fashion: many of them would have been Greeks or Macedonians, but it was the armour (particularly the *sarissa*, see chap. 42 below) that marked them out as *phalangitae* or *Macedones*.

separated by pairs of elephants: similar to the arrangement used by Porus, with equal lack of success, at the Hydaspes in 326.

agema: the élite corps of cavalry in Macedonian armies was called the *agema* and was perhaps originally under the leadership of the king himself. The strength of the unit (1,000) may go back to Alexander the Great's military reforms, which saw the introduction of 'chiliarchies' (perhaps on the Persian model) later in his campaign.

333 *scythed chariots*: these were used with equal lack of effect by Artaxerxes II at Cunaxa (401) and Darius III at Gaugamela (331). Like elephants they were often mere 'status symbols', presenting a greater danger to their own troops than to the enemy, as Livy himself notes in chap. 41 below.

Tarentines: see note to p. 224 above.

his brother's son, Antipater: cf. Polyb, 21. 16–17, 24 and elsewhere. His brother's name is nevertheless unknown.

Minnio, Zeuxis, and Philip: for Minnio see note to p. 213 above. Philip had done lengthy service under Antiochus III; he is attested as elephantarch at Raphia in 217 (Polyb. 5. 82). Zeuxis is the best known of these three Seleucid officials. He appears to have served Antiochus III faithfully throughout his reign, though primarily in an administrative capacity.

337 *Tralles*: a town in Asia Minor (southeast of Ephesus), not to be confused with the Tralles who are an Illyrian people (see 31. 35; 33. 4).

339 *Damocritus*: the *strategos* of the Aetolian League in 192, who boasted that the Aetolians would discuss peace-terms with the Romans on the banks of the Tiber. Perhaps Livy intended his death there to be viewed as ironic.

340 *Fulvius declared Gnaeus Manlius his colleague*: but for the disqualification of Marcus Aemilius Lepidus, Gnaeus Manlius would have failed in three successive bids for the consulship. If no candidate gained a majority of the centuries, a second election was necessary. There is, however, considerable debate about whether Livy is right in stating that Fulvius 'declared Gnaeus Manlius his colleague' (accepting the emendation of the text to *dixit*) and whether this means that Fulvius selected him as his colleague on the strength of the previous day's voting or presided over the second election. Both interpretations present difficulties, but the latter appears more likely.

348 *the two Phrygias*: see 38. 39.

351 *Ptolemy of Telmessus*: apparently the grandson of Ptolemy, the son of Lysimachos and Arsinoë II, who escaped from his treacherous stepfather Ptolemy Ceraunus.

353 *white toga*: the *candida toga* was worn by candidates for office.

BOOK THIRTY-EIGHT

356 *the expulsion of Amynander*: see 36. 32.

that people's supreme council: the *apocleti*, on whom see 35. 34.

Nicander: Nicander, son of Bithes, was *strategos* of the Aetolian league in 190/89. For his earlier activities see 35. 12 and 36. 29.

357 *Xenon*: an officer of Philip V and, hence, to be distinguished from the Seleucid official entrusted with the defence of Sardis at 37. 44.

Jupiter Acraeus: the temple is otherwise unknown. The epithet is applied to Juno (Hera) at 32. 23 (see note to p. 78).

358 *the major battle with Antiochus*: the battle of Magnesia (see 37. 37–45).

Marcus Fulvius: Marcus Fulvius Nobilior, consul for 189; his colleague was Gnaeus Manlius Vulso (see 37. 47).

360 *Pyrrheum*: the palace of Pyrrhus I of Epirus (cf. chap. 9).

Aesculapius: the healing god.

361 *Perseus*: see note to p. 34 above.

362 *doors*: another mistranslation of Polybius (21. 28. 11). Livy mistakes the word *thyreous* ('shields') for *thyras* ('doors').

363 *to a point beyond the Caucasus*: this is deliberate hyperbole; in the following paragraph, Livy shows that he is aware that Antiochus had been pushed beyond the *Taurus* range.

364 *same friends and enemies*: cf. 37. 1, 49. The notions of political (state) friendships were merely extensions of those on a personal level.

Gaius Valerius Laevinus, half-brother of the consul: he was half-brother of Marcus Fulvius Nobilior, whose mother had subsequently married Marcus Valerius Laevinus (consul. 210).

365 *150-pound crown of gold*: that is, a crown worth 150 talents of gold.

366 *the consulship of Lucius Quinctius and Gnaeus Domitius*: 192 BC. The manuscripts read *T. Quinctius*. It is easier to emend the *praenomen* than to assume a more serious error on Livy's part.

367 *Eumenes' absence*: he was in Rome; cf. 37. 52–4.

368 *Apama, sister of Seleucus*: Apama, daughter of Spitamenes (a noble adversary of Alexander the Great) married Seleucus (later known as Nicator) at Susa in 324. She was the mother of Antiochus I Soter. 'Sister' was a title used by the Seleucids to indicate the king's chief consort.

Marsyas: the springs of the River Marsyas are at Celaenae, the old capital of Greater Phrygia, where the Persian king, Xerxes, had a palace (Xenophon, *Anabasis*, 1. 2. 7–8). The story is told that the satyr Marsyas challenged Apollo to a musical competition, only to be defeated and flayed alive by the god. Either his blood or the tears of the other satyrs gave rise to the river.

371 *Brennus*: the Gauls led by Brennus formed a second wave that had irrupted into northern Greece *c*.279/8. Earlier the Gallic chieftain Belgius (or Bolgius) had killed in battle Ptolemy Ceraunus, the son of Ptolemy I Soter who had murdered Seleucus I Nicator after the battle of Corupedium (282/1) and seized the kingdom of Macedon. Brennus' Gauls pushed southward into central Greece but were repelled near Delphi (cf. Livy's allusion at 40. 58) by the Aetolians.

Antipater, the governor of the coast: this man is otherwise unknown, unless Livy refers to Antipater 'Etesias', the nephew of Cassander, who ruled Macedonia briefly in the chaotic period (279–277) which saw a succession of ephemeral rulers between the death of Ceraunus and the establishment of the Antigonid kingdom by Antigonus Gonatas.

372 *Nicomedes*: Nicomedes I, king of Bithynia (*c*.279–255).

The first . . . to refuse payment was Attalus: actually, Antiochus I had resisted the Galatians, winning his famous 'Elephant Victory' (*c*.269), for which he gained the epithet 'Soter'. Attalus I's victory over the Galatians occurred *c*.237, by which time the Seleucid kingdom had been weakened by the strife of the Laodicean and Fraternal wars. As a consequence, Attalus was the first of his dynasty to take the title 'King' (*basileus*); he was also accorded the title 'Soter'.

373 *battle at the Allia*: following the Gallic sack of Rome, which occured, according to the Varronian chronology, in *c*.386 (but 387 is more likely).

Titus Manlius and Marcus Valerius: Titus Manlius Torquatus and Marcus Valerius Corvus. See Livy 7. 9, 26.

Marcus Manlius: see Livy 5. 47; cf. Virgil *Aeneid* 8. 652–70. Gnaeus Manlius characteristically places emphasis on the accomplishments of his ancestors.

mongrels aptly called "Gallograeci": ethnic slurs of this sort are common in Livy: 'in Athens, rabble-rousing tongues are never in short supply' (31. 44; cf. 34. 23: '[the Athenians were] once the leading advocates and champions of independence but now traitors to their common cause by virtue of their self-seeking obsequiousness'); the Gauls are described as 'physically soft and weak, with little tolerance for thirst' (34. 47); at 34. 51, Livy comments on 'the turbulent character of [the Thessalian] race'; eunuchs are, of course, universally despised—they are 'individuals who endear themselves to monarchs by performing such criminal services' (35. 15); and cf. 36. 17 for negative comments on Syrians and Asiatic Greeks, and, a few sentences later, on the Aetolians.

Seleucia: Seleucia-on-the-Tigris, founded by Seleucus Nicator. It soon replaced Babylon as the eastern capital of the Seleucid kingdom.

375 *Axylos*: 'without wood'.

Galli of the Magna Mater: see note to p. 207 above. Pessinus was firmly entrenched in Roman minds as the seat of the cult of Magna Mater (a fact emphasised by Manlius Vulso's encounter with the Galli), and this may have led to the mistaken view that the black aerolite (cult stone) that was transported to Rome came from Pessinus and not Mt. Ida, via Pergamum: see Gruen, *Studies in Greek Culture and Roman Policy*, 19.

three seas at roughly the same distance: for this view of Gordium as the *omphalos* (navel) of Asia Minor cf. Curtius 3. 1. 12, perhaps going back to Herodotus 2. 34. For a similar, peculiar and equally erroneous, geographic concept see 40. 21–2 (on the view from Mt. Haemus).

376 *Mt. Olympus*: there were numerous mountains of this name in the Hellenized world, apart from the famous one in southern Macedonia. This particular one is to be identified with Ala-Dagh, north-east of Gordium.

377 *elephants*: the Romans had sixteen elephants at Magnesia, though these were never used on account of the superior numbers (fifty-four) in the Seleucid army (37. 39), and captured another fifteen from the enemy (37. 44).

379 *as far . . . permitted*: this is the usual interpretation of *colles obliqui* (*Oxford Latin Dictionary* obliquus 1A). However, Walsh may be right in interpreting the phrase as 'the hills across their path'. (Translator's note.)

381 *wife of the Gallic chieftain Ortiago*: her name was Chiomara, according to Polybius (31. 38), who claims to have met her in Sardis. Walsh, in his commentary (on 38. 35), considers it 'characteristic of Livy to omit such a foreign name as being of little interest to his reader'. This may not have been his motive for omitting the name, though he certainly omits some foreign names that can be recovered from other sources. Livy may have

considered the name unpleasant or excessively barbarous, thus detract-
ing from the story's moral value. Nameless, she is not unlike a Virginia or
a Lucretia.

385 *only four men were rejected*: in the previous review (194, during the censorship of Gaius. Cornelius Cethegus and Sextus Aelius Paetus) three
were expelled. Even the notorious hard-liner, Cato, expelled only seven
members from the Senate—though one was the ex-consul Lucius Quinctius Flamininus; furthermore, Lucius Scipio had his horse taken from
him. It is interesting to note that during Scipio Africanus' censorship
(with Publius Aelius Paetus) there was no recorded rejection.

reviewing the list of equites: this involved a ceremony held in the forum at
which each knight was required to display his horse before the censors.

391 *during the reign of Philip, son of Amyntas*: during Philip II's settlement of
Greek affairs after his victory at Chaeronea in 338 BC.

Publius Claudius Pulcher: there are good reasons for believing that Livy
has confused the praetorships of the brothers, Appius and Publius Claudius Pulcher. A few lines below, he remarks that Publius was curule aedile
in 189, which makes his holding of the praetorship in the following year
unprecedented. In all other cases, at least one year intervened between
the completion of the curule aedileship and the praetorship (though it
was not at all uncommon for plebeian aediles to hold the praetorship in
the following year). Livy, however, names Appius Claudius as praetor for
187. Since Appius held the consulship in 185 and Publius in the succeeding year, there is a strong likelihood that Appius was praetor in 188 and
Publius in 187.

†*Gnaeus*† *Cornelius*: the *praenomen* is troublesome. There is no Gnaeus
Cornelius who can be termed consular at this time. Gnaeus Cornelius
Blasio had been praetor in 194; Gnaeus Cornelius Merula was consul in
193; and Gnaeus Cornelius Scipio Calvus, father of Scipio Nasica, even
earlier (222). The most recent Cornelian consulship was that of Lucius
Scipio in 191.

395 *promontories of Calycadnus and Sarpedonium*: Sarpedonium is a promontory; the Calycadnus, however, is a Cilician river, famous in the Middle
Ages as the stream in which the Emperor Frederick Barbarossa died in
1190.

398 '*The Melas*': i.e. the Black.

399 *Bendis*: Mendis, a Thracian goddess identified with Artemis and Cybele.

400 *Muttines the Numidian*: presumably the leader of the force of 500 cavalry
and thirty elephants sent by Masinissa (see 36. 4).

Appius Claudius Pulcher: the *praenomen* should probably be corrected to
Publius. See note to p. 391 above.

401 *Lucius Minucius Myrtilus and Lucius Manlius*: both individuals are other-
wise unknown. Lucius Manlius can be identified with neither Lucius
Manlius Vulso, brother of the consul Gnaeus Manlius, nor with Lucius
Manlius Acidinus.

402 *stripped of their ornaments*: see chap. 9 above.

    Marcus Marcellus: Marcus Claudius Marcellus. The reference is to his siege of Syracuse during his consulship in 211.

    Quintus Fulvius: Quintus Fulvius Flaccus; he had been consul in 237, 224, and 212 (with a praetorship in 215). During his third consulship he captured Capua, which had gone over to Hannibal.

405 *Do not think . . . just the name of the Gallogrecians . . . is mongrel*: Livy's description of the Galatians at chap. 17 above is echoed by Manlius' opponents at this point, in order to cheapen his victory over them and to deny him a triumph. A more favourable view of the Galatians is given at 37.8.

409 *Carthage where . . . commanders are crucified*: see for example Polyb. 1. 11 (for Hanno at Messana in 264); 1. 24 (Hannibal in Sardinia, also during the First Punic War); an earlier example in Justin 18. 7. 15.

411 *Publius Scipio Africanus was impeached*: for the 'trials of the Scipios' see Introduction, pp. xxv–xxvi.

    Quinti Petillii: tribunes of the plebs in 187, they were apparently cousins, rather than brothers, since they sport the same praenomen. According to Gellius they were supporters, and agents, of Marcus Porcius Cato, for whose hostility to Africanus see Plutarch, *Cato* 18. One of them is probably Quintus Petillius Spurinus, who held the praetorship in 181 (see 40. 18) and the consulship in 176.

412 *Pleminius at Locri*: see 31. 12 with note to p. 13, and 34. 44.

BOOK THIRTY-NINE

423 *if, in fact, this was the year*: Livy is relating the events of 187 BC. Scipio Africanus' trial belongs in 184. See the Introduction for a full discussion of the trials of the Scipios.

    the two consuls: Marcus Aemilius Lepidus and Gaius Flaminius, consuls for 187. For their election see 38.42.

425 *the censorship of Gaius Claudius and Marcus Livius*: Gaius Claudius Nero and Marcus Livius Salinator held the censorship in 204 BC.

    achievements in Aetolia and Cephallenia: for details of this campaign see 38. 28–30.

    would follow . . . the consul's presence: an alternative rendering would be 'would vote in accordance with Fulvius' wishes even if the consul were present'. (Translator's note.)

426 *protect the interests of individual citizens, not the personal power of a consul*: one of the original functions of the tribune was to protect the common citizen from abuse at the hands of a magistrate.

427 *Golden crowns*: Livy, and apparently the earlier annalists, translated the Greek word *stephanos* (which Polybius uses merely to indicate gifts of precious metal) literally as 'crown'.

428 *Lucius Scipio's condemnation*: see Introduction, pp. xxv–xxvi.

429 *clandestine seditious activity*: for a thorough discussion of the Bacchanal-ian episode see Gruen, *Studies in Greek Culture and Roman Policy*, 34–78, who regards it as evidence of 'the increasing tension between private assimilation of Hellenism and public distancing from it' (p. 78). The suppression of the Bacchanalia reflects the typical paranoia on the part of governments concerning so-called 'secret societies'. But there must have been an element in Rome that had a genuine (albeit self-righteous) concern for public morality and the restricting of the behaviour of women (cf. the arguments in favour of preserving the *lex Oppia;* see also Bauman, *Women and Politics in Ancient Rome*, 36). Furthermore, the Bacchanalia represented the encroachment of 'dangerous' eastern practices on Roman life.

430 *that most erudite of peoples*: Livy's comments on Greeks and other foreigners are not often so positive.

men and women ... intermixed ... eliminated all moral judgement: such apprehensions about immoral conduct are expressed already in Euripi-des' *Bacchae*. More significant perhaps, is the fact that one of the themes of Roman comedy was the young woman raped at nocturnal ceremonies

Publius Aebutius: consanguinity with Titus Aebutius Carrus (*pr.* 178) is possible, but any mature paternal relative ought to have assumed the guardianship of young Publius; Aebutia, the father's sister (see chap. 11), would not have had rights of guardianship under Roman law.

431 *Hispala Faecenia*: Faecenia was the name she took upon manumission.

433 †*Simila*†: there is a textual problem. *Simila* is probably incorrect. Per-haps one should read *Stimula*, a minor deity identified with Semele (see Walsh's commentary on this passage). (Translator's note.)

436 *triumviri capitales*: also known as *triumviri nocturni*, they formed a small 'police commission', responsible for prisons and prisoners, punishments, and executions. The quinquevirs directed their attentions against incen-diaries and are attested for the first time in 186.

438 *burning books of oracles*: cf. 40. 29 for the fate of the books (of Numa) discovered by Lucius Petillius.

439 *the praetors Titus Maenius and Marcus Licinius*: the *praetor urbanus* and *praetor peregrinus* respectively, to whom such matters were of primary concern.

441 *that Publius Aebutius' military service be considered fulfilled*: this was no small concession since the minimum term of military service was six years; for an *eques* the maximum was probably ten years.

whosoever married her: apparently not Aebutius; cf. Balsdon, *Roman Women*, 42, remarking on the absence of the 'storybook ending'. Despite the fact that Faecenia exhibits many of the characteristics of the cour-tesan of New Comedy, the historicity of the episode and its conclusion need not be doubted.

excepted: possibly 'in addition to'. See Walsh's commentary on this passage. (Translator's note.)

443 *the Taurian Games*: these games to the 'infernal gods'—apparently of Etruscan origin—were held every five years in late June.

Marcus Fulvius: Nobilior (consul. 189).

a hermaphrodite: cf. 31. 12, recording two hermaphrodites, one of whom had reached the age of 16. The prodigy-list for 186 is, unusually, given at the end rather than the beginning of the account of the year's activities. Nor does Livy link the prodigies with the Bacchanalian affair.

used money that had been contributed for the purpose by various kings and city-states: Livy has earlier recounted the trial of Lucius Scipio (187 BC) and reported that Scipio could not pay the fine imposed upon him except through the generosity of his friends. Hence, it is necessary to explain how, in the following year, he could afford to put on such lavish games. Haywood (*Studies on Scipio Africanus* (Baltimore 1933), 96) surmises from Lucius Scipio's healthy financial picture in 186 that the trial and the fine belonged instead to 184. On the other hand, if the charges against Lucius concerned the money from Antiochus for which Quintus Petillius and Terentius Culleo demanded an accounting in 187, it is unlikely that the matter was postponed until 184.

445 *ordered to withdraw from the walls of Lamia*: see 36. 25.

446 *Tiberius Sempronius*: possibly Tiberius Gracchus. Polybius (22. 6. 6) calls this commissioner Tiberius Claudius (Nero?), but Tiberius *Sempronius* recurs in chap. 33 below.

452 *quaestor Quintus Fabius*: probably one of the praetors of 181: either Quintus Fabius Maximus or Quintus Fabius Buteo (see 40. 18).

455 *Lucius Aemilius, Quintus Fabius*: Lucius Aemilius Paullus (apparently) and Quintus Fabius Labeo. Neither was successful, but Labeo won the consulship for 183 and Paullus for 182. Servius Sulpicius Galba was also unsuccessful and never attained the consulship.

election of more than one patrician was not permitted: according to the Sextian-Licinian legislation of 367; cf. note to p. 206 above, *patricians seeking the same seat*.

458 *the barbarians living along the River Hister*: the Bastarnae (cf. 40. 5), a Germanic tribe that had appeared north of the Danube (= Hister) shortly before.

459 *Areus and Alcibiades*: Areus may have been of royal descent; Alcibiades is otherwise unknown.

461 *leaders of Greece*: both in the war against Xerxes (480/79) and after the defeat of Athens in the Peloponnesian War; though Sparta could have claimed leadership in Greece by virtue of her hegemony over the Peloponnesian League. Sparta's fortunes declined rapidly after the defeat of

Leuctra in 371 and the liberation of Messenia by Epaminondas; Agis III's war was crushed by Antipater in 331/o.

463   *flamen Dialis*: see note to p. 59, *flamen of Jupiter* above.

curule aedile designate: in fact, his term of office had already begun.

469   *Lucius Scipio Asiagenes*: Lucius Cornelius, in emulation of Africanus, had taken the title Asiaticus (37. 58; cf. chap. 56 below); Asiagenes is a Greek form meaning 'born in Asia' or 'sprung from Asia'. His expulsion from the *equites* was possibly the result of being unfit for service—he was not expelled from the Senate, as was Lucius Veturius. Nevertheless, it was not the way to treat the 'conqueror of Antiochus'.

had his horse taken from him: one of the censors' functions was to conduct the *recognitio equitum*. At this public ceremony the horse of a knight who had received equipment from the state was inspected. Failure to maintain one's equipment properly or an unsatisfactory record resulted in the removal of the horse. In this case, Cato perhaps dismissed Lucius Cornelius on account of his age. This he was entitled to do, but for a man of Scipio's stature and family it was a public insult.

women's dresses and carriages worth more than 15,000 asses: Cato, who prided himself on the simplicity of his life, had failed to block the rescinding of the *lex Oppia* (cf. 34. 1–8). This was clearly an attack on the same 'evil'.

publicani: Roman businessmen who made bids for public contracts. Perhaps the most notorious and despised were the so-called 'tax-farmers'.

476   *Rutilius*: Publius Rutilius Rufus was a friend of Scipio Aemilianus, with whom he campaigned at Numantia in 133; he later served with Metellus in Numidia. He held the consulship of 105 but was later prosecuted for extortion and spent his retirement writing history.

477   *born of a whore*: Plutarch (*Aratus* 54) calls Perseus' mother a seamstress named Gnathaenion (the name was one commonly used by prostitutes). She was, in fact, Polycratea (Livy 27. 31), whom Philip had taken from the younger Aratus (see note to p. 74 above, *carting off to Macedonia the son's wife*), but the charge is repeated at 40. 9. The name of Demetrius' mother is not known.

478   *designs*: that is, of a war with Rome. Livy has abbreviated his source too abruptly.

BOOK FORTY

482   *Parilia*: an agricultural festival, the importance of which was enhanced by the fact that it fell on 21 August, the day of Rome's founding in 753 BC.

483   *Publius Sempronius*: Publius Sempronius Longus served as praetor in 184. For his illness see also 39. 56; for his death cf. also chap. 16 below.

Pharnaces: Pharnaces I of Pontus, who ruled *c*.185–*c*.159.

Marcius: Quintus Marcius Philippus, consul in 186.

486 *Bastarnae*: see note to p. 458 above.

ceremonial purification of the army: Curtius (10. 9. 12) describes this practice in the weeks after the death of Alexander the Great; cf. Justin 13. 4. 7. Herodotus (7. 39–40) tells a bizarre story, which he does not explain, of the Persian army marching between the severed body of Pythius' eldest son—Pythius had asked Xerxes that his sons be spared military service. This is perhaps a macabre or insulting re-enactment of the same practice in Persia (cf. Genesis 15: 10–17).

487 *clash in a mock engagement*: compare the mock battle in Alexander's camp in 331 (Plutarch, *Alexander* 31).

wooden stakes: some editors, including Walsh, prefer Gronovius's emendation *rudibus*, which would translate as 'practice-swords'. (Translator's note.)

488 *Lysimachus and Onomastus*: the former is unknown, but the latter is apparently identical with Philip's 'commander of the coast' in 39. 34.

489 *Eumenes and Attalus . . . embarrassed to use the title "King"*: Eumenes II and Attalus II, two of the four attested children of Attalus I. The dynasty originated with the eunuch treasurer Philetaerus of Tius, who had transferred his allegiance from Lysimachus to Seleucus I Nicator in the days before the battle of Corupedium (281 BC). His successor Eumenes I minted coins with the head of Philetaerus and used the title *dynastes*; Attalus I was the first to term himself 'king' (*basileus*).

maintained even in death: Publius Cornelius Scipio (father of Lucius and Publius Scipio Africanus) and Gnaeus (father of Publius Scipio Nasica) were killed twenty-nine days apart (Livy 25. 36).

of the Spartans: the text actually reads 'of the former' and refers back to the Spartan tyrants mentioned above.

490 *bastard son of a whore*: see note to p. 477 above.

ancient practice of Macedonia: what this means is not entirely clear. Perseus seems not to refer to rules of primogeniture which were not strictly enforced in Macedonia, though the first-born son generally inherited the kingdom. The king needed the support of the leading aristocrats, the 'first of the Macedonians', whose choice was normally acknowledged by the army.

493 *His purpose . . . scripted*: Briscoe, following the previous Teubner editors (Weissenborn and Müller), makes this a question. I prefer to treat it as an exclamation. (Translator's note.)

499 *Hasdrubal*: son of Gisgo. His daughter Sophonisba married Syphax. See Livy 30. 12–15 for the bizarre story of her dealings with Masinissa and her fate.

500 *Publius Cornelius Lentulus*: Livy is mistaken about the *cognomen*, having

recorded Lentulus' death shortly before (39. 45). The consul for 181 and colleague of Marcus Baebius was Publius Cornelius Cethegus.

502 *investigating the Bacchanalia*: see 39. 8–19.

503 *Maedica*: the Maedi were enemies of Macedon. Alexander the Great had campaigned successfully against them in 340, when he was only 16 (Plutarch, *Alexander*, 9).

Mt. Haemus: in Thrace.

the example of Antigonus: in his commentary Walsh assumes that the reference is to Antigonus I 'the One-Eyed'. But the only known occasion when Monophthalmus was at sea with his entire family was in 322/1, when he was still satrap of Phrygia and had fled to Greece under threats from Perdiccas. If the reference is indeed to Monophthalmus, there is a certain irony in the story, since Antigonus and his son Demetrius were celebrated for their loving relationship (Plutarch, *Demetrius* 3, where Philip V is actually singled out as the only member of the dynasty to kill his own son). The story may equally refer to Antigonus II Gonatas, who firmly established the Antigonids on the throne of Macedon.

504 *a rare . . . altitudes*: Walsh may be right in accepting Weissenborn's supplement of *haud* (not) at this point: 'not a rare phenomenon at high altitudes.' (Translator's note.)

508 *naval duumvirs*: this office was created in 311 BC, and the duumvirs were elected by the comitia tributa.

four camp gates: our knowledge of the layout of the Roman camp comes primarily from Polybius 6. 27–32. The four gates comprised the *porta praetoria* (located behind the commander's headquarters, the *praetorium*, to the side of which we find also the *quaestorium*); the *porta decumana*; and two *portae principales*. The last two were located at the left and right ends of the *via principalis*, which ran through the camp between the *praetorium* and the tents of the troops, and were known as the *porta principalis sinistra* and *porta principalis dextra*.

516 *Publius Cornelius †Mamercus†*: 'Mamercus' does not appear to be correct. There is no attested Cornelian family with this *cognomen*. An Aulus Cornelius Mammula held the praetorship in 191 (35. 24), and it appears that Mammula may in this case be the proper *cognomen*.

Lucius Minucius: the only Lucius Minucius mentioned by Livy up to this point is Lucius Minucius Myrtilus, who was extradited by the Carthaginians to be tried for beating their ambassadors (38. 42). Calpurnius Piso's legate appears to be Lucius Minucius Thermus, who reappears as a legate in 178 (41. 8).

518 *consulship of Spurius Postumius and Quintus Marcius*: Spurius Postumius Albinus and Quintus Marcius Philippus, 186 BC.

524 *triumvir epulo*: see note to p. 133 above.

Quintus Fulvius, son of Marcus: in the absence of a *cognomen*, the identification is uncertain, but it is likely that the father was Marcus Fulvius Nobilior (consul 189).

still wearing the toga praetexta: he had not yet reached manhood.

rex sacrificulus: identical with the *rex sacrorum* who, during the Republic, fulfilled many of the religious functions that had been exercised by the King.

decemvir sacrorum: that is, one of the *decemviri sacris faciundis*. These are discussed in the note to p. 14, *the Sibylline books*.

531 *to the sixth hour*: the Romans divided the period of daylight into twelve 'hours'.

532 *the censors Publius Scipio Africanus and Lucius Mummius*: Publius Cornelius Scipio Aemilianus, the younger Africanus and conqueror of Carthage in the Third Punic War, and Lucius Mummius (consul 146), who sacked Corinth, were censors in 142 BC.

on the basis of birth: that is, free or servile.

534 *a man of regal presence ... famous for his celebrated battle against the Spartan Cleomenes*: Antigonus III Doson became guardian of Philip V in 229, upon the death of Demetrius II, whose widow Phthia (Philip's mother) he married. In 227 he actually took the royal title and in 222 he defeated Cleomenes at Sellasia (on which see note to p. 166). Doson was a son of Demetrius 'the Fair' and thus a grandson of Demetrius Poliorcetes. Echecrates, the father of Antigonos, was apparently Doson's brother.

Xychus: this individual appears without introduction or adequate explanation and is known only from this passage in Livy. He was apparently an agent of Philocles and Apelles, and we may surmise from Antigonus' claim that he was the 'one man able to solve this knotty problem' and the later reference to his part in the affair that he was the scribe who forged the letter 'from Flamininus'.

535 *because the other one †had perished†*: the reading *superesset* advocated by Walsh is attractive: 'because the second of them was still alive.' (Translator's note.)

536 *withdrawing from them*: reading *subtrahendas* with Briscoe. But the manuscript reading *contrahendas* could be correct; see Walsh's note. (Translator's note.)

537 *when they were plundering Delphi*: on the Gauls and their leader see note to p. 371, *Brennus*.

538 *the other three were appointed*: the three not named by Livy were Titus Aebutius Parrus, who received Sardinia, Gaius Cluvius Saxula (Sicily), and Marcus Titinius (urban praetor). Marcus Titinius Curvus served in Spain and cannot therefore be identical with the *praetor urbanus* whom Livy (41. 6) later calls Marcus Titinius. The coincidence of two magistrates named Marcus Titinius is unusual but not unique. Cf. the tribunes of 187, amongst whom there were two named Petillius, both with the

praenomen Quintus. On the other hand, Livy may have confused the *praenomina* of the *praetor urbanus* and his colleague. Marcus Titinius Curvus appears to have been tribune of the plebs along with Gaius Titinius.

INDEX OF PERSONAL NAMES

The following abbreviations occur:

cos.	consul	*mil. trib.*	military tribune
cos. suff.	consul suffectus	*pl. aed.*	plebeian aedile
cur. aed.	curule aedile	*pr.*	praetor
iiivir	triumvir	*regn.*	*regnavit* (reigned)
iivir	duumvir	*trib. pl.*	tribune of the plebs

Marcus ADURIUS: **39.** 4–5 (*trib. pl.* 187)

Acesimbrotus (Rhodian admiral): **31.** 46–7; **32.** 16, 32

ACIDINUS, *see* MANLIUS

Lucius ACILIUS: **40.** 30, 32

Manius ACILIUS Glabrio (*cos.* 191): **31.** 50 (replaces Marcus Aurelius Cotta as *decemvir*); **33.** 24 (*pr.* 196), 25–6, 36 (deals with slave rebellion in Etruria); **35.** 10 (candidate for consulship of 192), 24 (elected consul); **36.** 1–4, 20, 22, 24–5, 27–8, 30, 32, 34–7, 43; **37.** 2–7, 46; **38.** 42–3, 46, 49; **39.** 23, 25–6, 28; **40.** 34 (father of Manius, below)

Manius ACILIUS Glabrio (*cos.* 154): **40.** 34 (*iivir*)

Gaius ACILIUS (historian): **35.** 14

Aebutia (aunt of Publius Aebutius): **39.** 11–12

Publius AEBUTIUS: **39.** 9–14, 19

Titus AEBUTIUS Parrus: **39.** 55 (*iiivir*)

Publius AELIUS: **34.** 59

Publius AELIUS Paetus: **31.** 2–4, 8; **32.** 2, 7 (censor)

Sextus AELIUS Paetus Catus (*cos.* 198): **31.** 50 (*cur. aed.* 199); **32.** 2, 7–9 (*cos.*), 26–7; **34.** 44 (censor, 194); **35.** 9

Publius AELIUS Tubero: **37.** 55

Quintus AELIUS Tubero: **34.** 53 (*trib. pl.*); **35.** 9 (*iiivir*); **37.** 55

Aemilia (wife of Scipio Africanus): **38.** 57

Marcus AEMILIUS Lepidus (*cos.* 187): **31.** 2, 18; **32.** 7; **35.** 10 (*cur. aed.* 192; cf. **39.** 56), 24 (*pr.* 191); **36.** 2; **37.** 2, 43, 47; **38.** 35 (candidacy for consulship of 188 rejected by M. Fulvius Nobilior), 42

(elected consul for 187), 43–4, 47; **39.** 2–6, 20, 55 (*iiivir*), 56; **40.** 42 (elected pontifex maximus), 45 (censor 179), 46, 51–2

Marcus AEMILIUS Lepidus (son of the above): **37.** 43

Lucius AEMILIUS Paullus (*cos.* 182): **34.** 45 (*iiivir*); **35.** 10 (*cur. aed.* 192), 24 (*pr.* 191); **36.** 2; **37.** 46, 55, 57; **38.** 44; **39.** 32, 56 (*cos.*); **40.** 25–8, 34, 44

Lucius AEMILIUS Regillus: **36.** 45 (*pr.* 190); **37.** 2, 4, 14–15, 17–19, 26–9, 31–2, 47; **40.** 52

Marcus AEMILIUS Regillus: **37.** 22 (brother of Lucius; died at Samos)

Marcus AEMILIUS Regillus (father of Lucius and Marcus, above): **40.** 52

Lucius AEMILIUS Scaurus: **37.** 31

Aenesidemus (Achaean, from Dymae): **32.** 25

Gaius AFRANIUS: **33.** 22 (*trib. pl.* 197)

Gaius AFRANIUS Stellio: **39.** 23 (*pr.* 185), 55 (*iiivir*)

Agesipolis: **34.** 26

AHENOBARBUS, *see* DOMITIUS

Alcibiades (Spartan): **39.** 35–7

Alexamenus (Aetolian): **35.** 34–5, 37

Alexander the Great: **35.** 14, 47 Alexander (Epirote 'master of the horse'): **32.** 10

Alexander (Aetolian): **32.** 33–4; **34.** 23

Alexander (Acarnanian): **35.** 18; **36.** 11, 20 (his death)

Alexander (of Megalopolis): **35.** 47 (claimed descent from Alexander the Great)

Alexander (son of Alexander of Megalopolis): **35.** 47

Alexander of Beroea: 40. 24

Gaius AMPIUS: 31. 2.

Amynander (king of the Athamanians):
31. 28, 41–2; 32. 13–14, 32, 36; 33. 3,
12; 35. 47; 36. 6–10, 14, 28–9, 31–2; 38.
1, 3, 9; 39. 23

Amyntas (III), father of Philip II: 38. 34

Androcles (Acarnanian): 33. 16
(supporter of Philip V)

Andronicus (Macedonian): 37. 13

Androsthenes (Macedonian, garrison
commander of Corinth): 32. 23; 33.
14–15

ANTIAS, see VALERIUS

Antigonus (Macedonian king): 40. 21 (for
his identity see note)

Antigonus III Doson (regn. 229–221): 32.
21–2, 34; 34. 28 (battle of Sellasia)

Antigonus, son of Echetrates: 40. 54–6
(cousin of Philip V)

Antigonos (Macedonian): 40. 57–8

Antiochus III: 31. 14; 32. 8, 27; 33. 13,
18–20, 27, 31, 34–5, 38–41, 45, 47, 49;
34. 25, 33, 37, 43, 57–60, 62; 35. 12–13,
15–20, 22–3, 25, 31–5, 40–3, 46, 48–51;
36. 1–3, 5–17, 20–1, 25–6, 29, 31–6,
41–3, 45; 37. 1, 3–4, 6, 8–9, 11, 15,
18–19, 21, 25–6, 28, 30–2, 34–9, 42–6,
48; 38. 3, 8, 10, 12–13, 16–18, 37–9,
42–3, 45–9, 51, 53–5, 58–9; 39. 22–4,
27–8, 51; 40. 8, 27, 34, 52

Antiochus (son of Antiochus III): 33. 49;
35. 13, 15 (his death)

Antipater (Macedonian commander of
the early 3rd cent.): 38. 16.

Antipater (nephew of Antiochus III): 37.
41, 45

Antiphilus (Boeotian leader): 33.1

Quintus ANTONIUS: 37. 31

Apama (wife of Seleucus I Nicator): 38.
13 (see note)

Apama (wife of Amynander): 35. 47
(daughter of Alexander of
Megalopolis)

Apelles (courtier of Philip V): 40. 20,
54–5

Apollodorus: 35. 50

Apollonius (courtier of Antiochus III):
37. 23

Apthir (Numidian): 34. 62

Lucius APUSTIUS Fullo: 31. 4, 27, 44,
46–7; 32. 16; 33. 24 (pr. 196), 26; 34.

53 (iiivir) 35. 9 (iiivir); 37. 4, 16 (his
death)

Aratus the Elder: 32. 21

Aratus the Younger (his wife was carried
off by Philip V): 32. 21.

Archelaus (Acarnanian): 33. 16
(pro-Roman)

Archidamus (Aetolian): 32. 4; 35. 48–9

Archippus (Argive): 34. 40

Archo: 40. 4

Ardys: 33. 19

Areus (Spartan): 39. 35–7

Ariarathes (king of Cappadocia): 37. 31,
40; 38. 26, 37, 39; 40. 20

Aristaenus (strategos of the Achaeans): 32.
19–21, 32; 33. 2; 34. 24–6, 30, 33

Aristo: 34. 61–2

Aristoteles: 36. 21 (Antiochus' officer at
Chalcis)

Armenes (son of Nabis): 34. 52

Athenaeus (son of Attalus I; brother of
Eumenes II and Attalus II): 38. 12–13,
40; 39. 46

Athenagoras (officer of Philip V): 31. 27,
35–6, 43; 32. 5; 33. 7

Lucius ATILIUS: 32. 27 (pr. 197)

Aulus ATILIUS Serranus: 34. 54 (cur. aed.
193); 35. 10 (pr. 192), 20, 22–3, 37; 36.
2, 11–12, 20, 42; 37. 46

Gaius ATILIUS Serranus: 39. 23 (pr. 185)

Marcus ATILIUS Serranus: 37. 46 (iiivir),
57

Gaius ATINIUS: 39. 17

Marcus ATINIUS: 39. 17

Gaius ATINIUS (pr. 188): 34. 46 (mil.
trib.); 38. 35 (pr.); 39. 7, 21

Marcus ATINIUS: 34. 47 (killed by Gauls)

Gaius ATINIUS Labeo (pr. 195): 32. 29
(trib. pl. 197); 33. 22, 25, 42 (elected
praetor; see note), 43

Gaius ATINIUS Labeo: 36. 45 (pr. 190);
37. 2

Attalus I of Pergamum: 31. 1, 14–18, 24,
28, 33, 44–7; 32. 8, 16, 19, 21, 23, 27,
32–5, 39–40; 33. 1–2, 21 (his death), 30
(father of Eumenes); 38. 16–17, 39

Attalus II of Pergamum (son of Attalus I):
35. 23 (brother of Eumenes II), 37. 18,
20, 43; 38. 12–13, 20–1, 23, 25, 45; 39.
27; 40. 8

Lucius AURELIUS: 33. 42 (quaestor)

Marcus AURELIUS: 31. 3, 5

Gaius AURELIUS Cotta (*cos.* 200): 31. 4–6, 11–12, 22, 47, 49; 32. 1, 7

Lucius AURELIUS Cotta: 40. 27–8 (*mil. trib.*)

Marcus AURELIUS Cotta: 31. 50 (*decemvir*), his death

Marcus AURELIUS Cotta: 37. 52 (officer of Lucius Scipio)

Gaius AURELIUS Scaurus: 39. 6 (*pr.* 186), 8

Lucius AURUNCULEIUS: 36. 45 (*pr.* 190); 37. 2, 4, 46, 55

Quintus BAEBIUS: 31. 6

Gnaeus BAEBIUS Tamphilus (*cos.* 182): 31. 49 (*pr.* 199), 50 (*pl. aed.* 200); 32. 1, 7; 39. 23 (*iiivir*), 32, 56 (*cos.*); 40. 17, 19 (proconsul), 25–6, 44

Marcus BAEBIUS Tamphilus (*cos.* 181): 34. 45 (*iiivir*); 35. 10 (*pr.* 192), 20–1, 23–4; 36. 1, 8, 10, 13, 22; 39. 24, 33; 40. 17–18, 36–8

Lucius BAEBIUS Dives: 37. 47 (*pr.* 189)

Baesadines (Spanish commander): 33. 44

Bato (son of Longarus, Dardanian): 31. 28

Bianor (Acarnanian): 33. 16 (pro-Roman)

Bilistages (chieftain of the Ilergetes): 34. 11–12

BLASIO, *see* CORNELIUS

Boiorix (Gallic chieftain): 34. 46

Brachylles (Boeotarch): 33. 27 (served with Philip V), 28 (murdered by pro-Roman party); 35. 47; 36. 6

Brennus (Gallic chieftain of the early 3rd cent.): 38. 16

BRUTUS, *see* IUNIUS

Budares (Spanish commander): 33. 44

BUTEO, *see* FABIUS

Aulus CAECILIUS: 38. 35 (*pl. aed.* 189)

Lucius CAECILIUS Denter: 39. 56 (*pr.* 182); 40. 1

Quintus CAECILIUS Metellus: 31. 4; 35. 8; 39. 24, 28, 33, 36, 47; 40. 45

Marcus CAECILIUS (Metellus?): 31. 21

CAESAR, *see* IULIUS

Calligenes: 40. 56

Callimedes: 31. 16

Lucius CALPURNIUS: 32. 19

Gaius CALPURNIUS Piso (*cos.* 180): 39. 6 (*pr.* 186), 8, 21, 30–1, 38, 42; 40. 29 (*iiivir*), 35 (*cos.*), 37

CATO, *see* HOSTILIUS

CATO, *see* PORCIUS

CENTHO, *see* CLAUDIUS

Herennius CERRINIUS: 39. 13

Minius CERRINIUS: 39. 13, 17, 19

Chaereas: 40. 55

Chariclitus (Rhodian): 37. 23–4

Chariteles (Messenian, murdered by Philip V): 32. 21

Charops (Epirote leader): 32. 6, 11, 14

Cichesias (Athenian): 38. 10 (father of Leo)

Marcus CINCIUS: 34. 56

Appius CLAUDIUS: 31. 1

Appius CLAUDIUS: 32. 35 (*mil. trib.*), 36; 33. 29; 34. 10, 28, 50; 36. 10, 13, 22, 30

Publius CLAUDIUS: 33. 36 (*mil. trib.*, fell in battle with the Boii in 196)

Appius CLAUDIUS Centho: 40. 59 (*cur. aed.* 179)

Gaius CLAUDIUS Centho: 31. 14, 22–3

Marcus CLAUDIUS Lepidus: 37. 48

Marcus CLAUDIUS Marcellus (*cos.* 222): 31. 13; 38. 43

Marcus CLAUDIUS Marcellus (*cos.* 196): 31. 49 (*cur. aed.* 199); 32. 7–8 (*pr.* 198), 27; 33. 24–5 (*cos.*), 36 (wages war on the Boii), 37 (celebrates triumph), 42 (becomes pontiff, replacing C. Sempronius Tuditanus; conducts elections), 47 (envoy to Carthage); 35. 5–6, 8; 38. 28 (censor), 36

Marcus CLAUDIUS Marcellus (*cos.* 183): 38. 35 (*pr.* 188); 39. 45 (*cos.*), 54–6; 40. 1, 16, 25–6

Marcus CLAUDIUS Marcellus (*pr.* 185): 39. 23

Appius CLAUDIUS Nero (*pr.* 195): 33. 42 (elected praetor), 43; 34. 17 (commander in Farther Spain); 37. 55

Gaius CLAUDIUS Nero: 31. 2, 12; 36. 36; 39. 3 (censor 204)

Tiberius CLAUDIUS Nero: 40. 18 (*pr.* 181)

Tiberius CLAUDIUS Nero: 40. 59 (*pr.* 178)

Appius CLAUDIUS Pulcher (*cos.* 212): 33. 44 (father of Gaius Claudius Pulcher (*cos.* 177))

Appius CLAUDIUS Pulcher (*cos.* 185): 38. 42 (*pr.* 188 or 187? see note); 39. 23 (*cos.*), 32–4, 36–8, 52

Gaius CLAUDIUS Pulcher (*cos.* 177): 33. 44; 40. 37 (*pr.* 180, replacing Tiberius Minucius), 42

Publius CLAUDIUS Pulcher (*cos.* 184): 38. 35 (*pr.* 188 or 187?); 39. 32–3 (*cos.*), 52; 40. 29 (*iiivir*)

CLAUDIUS Quadrigarius (historian): 33. 10, 30, 36; 35. 14; 37. 48; 38. 23, 41

Cleomedon (representative of Philip V): 32. 21

Cleomenes (Spartan tyrant): 34. 26 (his death), 28 (battle of Sellasia); 40. 54

Cleopatra I (daughter of Antiochus III, wife of Ptolemy V): 37. 3

Cleoptolemus (Chalcidian): 36. 11 (Antiochus III marries his daughter)

Clitus (Acarnanian): 36. 11–12

Publius CLOELIUS Siculus: 40. 42

Clondicus: 40. 58

Combolomarus (Galatian chieftain): 38. 19

Gnaeus CORNELIUS: 31. 50 (*cur. aed.*)

Gnaeus CORNELIUS: 38. 35 (see note)

Gnaeus CORNELIUS Blasio (*pr.* 194): 33. 27 (governor of Hither Spain 199–197); 34. 42–3 (*pr.* 194)

Gaius CORNELIUS Cethegus: 31. 49–50; 32. 7 (*cur. aed.*), 27–8 (*cos.* 197), 30; 33. 22–3 (his triumph); 34. 44 (censor, 194), 53, 62; 35. 9

Marcus CORNELIUS Cethegus: 33. 42 (pontiff, dies and is replaced by L. Valerius Flaccus); 36. 36.

Publius CORNELIUS Cethegus (*cos.* 181): 39. 7 (*cur. aed.* 187), 23 (*pr.* 185), 32, 38 (*pr.* 184), 39, 41; 40. 18 (*cos.*; see note), 36–8

Gnaeus CORNELIUS Dolabella: 40. 42 (*rex sacrificulus*).

Lucius CORNELIUS Dolabella: 40. 42 (naval *iivir*)

Gnaeus CORNELIUS Lentulus: 31. 14, 50; 32. 2; 39. 45 (his death)

Lucius CORNELIUS Lentulus: 31. 20, 49; 32. 1–2, 7–8 (*cos.* 199), 26, 39 (sent by Senate to settle dispute between Ptolemy and Antiochus), 41

Publius CORNELIUS Lentulus Caudinus (*pr.* 203): 33. 35, 39 (*decemvir*); 37. 55

Aulus CORNELIUS Mammula (*pr.* 217): 33. 44 (his vow fulfilled)

Aulus CORNELIUS Mammula: 35. 24 (*pr.* 191); 36. 2; 37. 2, 4, 48

Publius CORNELIUS Mammula (*pr.* 180): 40. 35 (with note)

Gnaeus CORNELIUS Merenda (*pr.* 194): 34. 42–3; 37. 55

Lucius CORNELIUS Merula (*cos.* 193): 32. 7–8 (*pr.* 198); 34. 45 (*iiivir*), 54 (elected consul), 55–6; 35. 4–6, 8, 20

Gnaeus CORNELIUS Scipio Calvus (*cos.* 222); father of Nasica: 31. 49; 35. 1, 10, 24; 36. 1; 38. 58; cf. 40. 8

Gnaeus CORNELIUS Scipio Hispallus (*cos.* 176): 32. 7 (pontifex); 40. 44 (*pr.* 179)

Lucius CORNELIUS Scipio (*cos.* 190): 34. 54 (*pr.* 193), 55; 35. 24 (candidate for consulship of 191); 36. 21, 45 (elected consul for 190); 37. 1, 3–4, 6–7, 25–6, 47–8; 38. 3, 12–13, 37, 41–3, 45–6, 48, 52–3, 55–60; 39. 6, 22, 28, 40, 44, 56 (embassy to Prusias); 40. 8

Publius CORNELIUS Scipio (*cos.* 218): 33. 24; 38. 58; cf. 40. 8

Publius CORNELIUS Scipio Africanus (*cos.* 205): 31. 4, 8, 49; 32. 7 (censor 199); 33. 47; 34. 42–3 (second consulship, 194), 48, 54, 56, 62; 35. 1, 2 (stragglers from his army in Africa), 10 (supports Nasica's bid for consulship); 14, 36, 45; 37. 1, 3–4, 6–7, 16, 25–6, 33–4, 36–7, 45, 48; 38. 3, 28 (*princeps senatus*); 46, 48, 50–8; 39. 50; 40. 8, 42 (father of Publius, below)

Publius CORNELIUS Scipio (son of Africanus): 40. 42 (augur)

Publius CORNELIUS Scipio Africanus Aemilianus: 40. 51 (censor in 142)

Publius CORNELIUS Scipio Nasica (*cos.* 191): 31. 49; 33. 25 (*cur. aed.* 196); 34. 42–3 (*pr.* 194); 35. 1, 10, 24 (second bid for consulship successful); 36. 1–3, 36–7, 39–40; 37. 2, 16; 38. 57–9; 39. 40, 55, 56 (embassy to Prusias); 40. 34 (*iiivir*)

Publius CORNELIUS Sulla: 39. 6 (*pr.* 186), 8

Publius CORNELIUS Sisenna (*pr.* 183): 39. 45

Corolamus (chieftain of the Boii): 33. 36

Corragus (Macedonian): 38. 13

Corribilo (Spanish chieftain): 35. 22

COTTA, *see* AURELIUS

Cotto: 40. 57–8

Craterus (half-brother of Antigonus II Gonatas): 35. 26

Culchas (Spanish chieftain): 33. 21

Manius CURIUS: 32. 7 (*trib. pl.* 199)

Cycliadas (*strategos* of the Achaeans): 31. 25; 32. 19, 32

Cydas (Cretan commander): 33. 3

Damocles (Argive): 34. 25

Damocritus (Aetolian): 31. 32, 40–1, 43; 35. 12, 33, 35; 36. 24; 37. 3, 46 (commits suicide); 38. 10

Damoteles (Aetolian): 38. 8

Gaius DECIMIUS Flavus (*pr.* 184): 39. 32, 38 (*praetor urbanus*), 39 (his death)

Demetrius II (father of Philip V): 31. 28

Demetrius (younger son of Philip V): 33. 12; 34. 52 (cf. 35. 31); 36. 35; 39. 47–8, 53; 40. 5–9, 11–12, 15–16, 20–1, 23–4, 54, 56

Dexagoridas (Spartan commander at Gytheum): 34. 29 (killed by Gorgopas)

Dicaearchus (Plataean; Boeotarch?): 33. 2

Dicaearchus (Aetolian, brother of Thoas): 35. 12; 36. 28; 38. 10

Sextus DIGITIUS (*pr.* 194): 34. 42–3 (elected praetor); 35. 1–2; 37. 4

Didas (Macedonian governor of Paeonia): 40. 21–4

Dinocrates (officer of Philip V): 33. 18

Dinocrates (Messenian magistrate): 39. 49

Diocles (Aetolian): 35. 34

Dionysodorus (legate of Attalus I): 32. 32

Diophanes (Achaean): 36. 31–2; 37. 20–1; 38. 32

Dioxippus: 31. 24

Gnaeus DOMITIUS Ahenobarbus (*cos.* 192): 33. 42 (*pl. aed.* 195); 34. 42–3 (*pr.* 194), 53; 35. 10 (elected consul), 20–2, 40; 36. 37; 37. 39; 38. 11

Dorulatus (Gallic chieftain): 34. 46

Duronia (mother of Publius Aebutius): 39. 9

Lucius DURONIUS: 40. 18 (*pr.* 181), 19, 42

Echedemus (Acarnanian): 33. 16 (supporter of Philip V)

Echedemus (Athenian): 37. 7

Echetrates (brother of Antigonus Doson): 40. 54

Quintus ENNIUS (poet): 38. 56

Epicrates (Rhodian): 37. 13–15

Eposognatus (Galatian chieftain): 38. 18

Eubulidas (Chalcidian): 37. 45; 38. 38

Eudamus (Rhodian): 37. 12 (succeeds Pausistratus), 15, 22–4, 26, 28–9

Eumenes II of Pergamum (son of Attalus I): 33. 30; 34. 26, 29–30, 35, 40; 35. 13, 17, 23, 39, 50–1; 36. 42–5; 37. 8–9, 12, 14–15, 17–19, 21–2, 25–6, 33, 37, 39, 41, 43–5; 38. 12–13, 16, 18, 37–40, 45, 47–8, 60; 39. 22, 24, 27–9, 33–4, 46, 51; 40. 2, 8, 20

Eunomus (Thessalian): 35. 39

Euphanes (Cretan): 36. 5

Eupolemus (Aetolian): 38. 4, 6

Eurylochus (Thessalian): 35. 31–2, 34, 37, 39, 43; 36. 33

Euthymidas (Thessalian): 35. 37–8

Quintus FABIUS Buteo: 33. 24 (*pr.* 196), 26

Quintus FABIUS Buteo: 40. 18 (*pr.* 181), 36, 43

Quintus FABIUS Labeo (*cos.* 183): 33. 42 (quaestor); 37. 47 (*pr.* 189); 38. 39, 47; 39. 27, 32, 44 (*iiivir*), 45 (*cos.*), 55 (*iiivir*), 56; 40. 1, 42

Quintus FABIUS Maximus 'Cunctator': 34. 1, 6

Quintus FABIUS Maximus: 33. 42 (augur, dies at a young age)

Quintus FABIUS Maximus: 40. 18 (*pr.* 181), 26, 28, 34

Quintus FABIUS (nephew of Titus Quinctius' wife): 32. 36

Quintus FABIUS Pictor: 37. 47 (*pr.* 189)

Quintus FABIUS (Buteo or Maximus?): 39. 29 (quaestor 188)

Gaius FABRICIUS Luscinus (*pr.* 195): 33. 42–3; 37. 4

Faecenia, *see* Hispala

FALTO, *see* VALERIUS

Gaius FANNIUS: 38. 60

FLACCUS, *see* FULVIUS

FLACCUS, *see* VALERIUS

FLAMININUS, *see* QUINCTIUS

Gaius FLAMINIUS (*cos.* 223): 33. 42

Gaius FLAMINIUS (*cos.* 187): 33. 42, 54 (*pr.* 193), 55–6; 35. 2, 7, 20, 22; 36. 2; 38. 42 (*cos.*), 43–4; 39. 2, 6, 20, 55; 40. 34 (*iiivir*)

Titus FONTEIUS Capito: 40. 59 (*pr.* 178)

FULLO, *see* APUSTIUS

Marcus FULVIUS: 32. 7 (*trib. pl.* 199)

Marcus FULVIUS Centumalus (possibly identical with M. Fulvius above): 35. 10 (*pr.* 192), 20–2, 24

Marcus FULVIUS Flaccus: 31. 4; 39. 44
(*iiivir*); 40. 30

Quintus FULVIUS Flaccus (*cos.* 237): 38.
43 (reference to his third consulship in
212)

Quintus FULVIUS Flaccus (*pr.* 187): 38. 35
(*pl. aed.* 189); 38. 42 (*pr.*)

Quintus FULVIUS Flaccus (*cos. suff.* 180;
cos. 179): 39. 39, 56 (*pr.* 182); 40. 1, 16,
27, 30–1, 33, 35, 37 (stepson of Gaius
Calpurnius Piso), 39–45, 53, 59
(identical with Q. Fulvius 32. 28 and
perhaps 36?)

Quintus FULVIUS Gillo: 31. 4, 6, 8

Marcus FULVIUS Nobilior (*cos.* 189): 33. 42
(*cur. aed.* 195); 34. 54 (*pr.* 193), 55–6;
35. 7, 20, 23; 36. 2, 21, 39; 37. 47
(elected consul), 48; 38. 3–4, 12; 28, 31,
35, 42–4; 39. 4–5, 22, 40; 40. 44, 45–6
(censor), 51

Marcus FULVIUS Nobilior: 40. 41 (*mil.
trib.*, see note)

Quintus FULVIUS Nobilior: 39. 44 (*iiivir*)

Quintus FULVIUS Nobilior (son of
Marcus): 40. 42 (*triumvir epulo*)

Gnaeus FULVIUS (*pr.* 190): 36. 45; 37. 2

Quintus FULVIUS: 32. 28 (*trib. pl.*)

Quintus FULVIUS (legate): 32. 36

M. FUNDANIUS: 34. 1 (*trib. pl.* 195)

Gaius FURIUS Aculeo: 38. 55, 58

Marcus FURIUS: 31. 21

Marcus FURIUS Crassipes (possibly
identical with M. Furius above): 34. 53
(*iiivir*); 35. 40 (*iiivir*); 38. 42 (*pr.* 187);
39. 3

Marcus FURIUS Luscus: 39. 7 (*pl. aed.* 187)

Lucius FURIUS Purpureo (*cos.* 196): 31. 4,
6, 8, 10–11, 21, 29, 47–9; 33. 24–5
(*cos.*), 37 (fights Boii and Ligurians);
34. 53; 35. 41; 37. 55; 38. 44, 47, 54; 39.
40, 54

GALBA, *see* SULPICIUS

Gala (father of Masinissa): 40. 17

Gaulotus (Galatian chieftain): 38. 19

Gentius (Illyrian king): 40. 42

Marcus GENUCIUS: 35. 5 (*mil. trib.*)

GILLO, *see* FULVIUS

GLABRIO, *see* ACILIUS

Gorgopas (Spartan commander at
Gytheum): 34. 29

GRACCHUS, *see* SEMPRONIUS

Hamilcar (father of Hannibal): 35. 19

Hamilcar: 31. 10–11, 19, 21 (his death);
32. 30 (allegedly captured); 33. 23
(graces Gaius Cornelius' triumph)

Hannibal: 31. 1, 7, 18, 31; 32. 3, 23; 33.
12, 45–9; 34. 43, 50, 60–1; 35. 10, 12,
14, 18–19, 42–3, 48; 36. 6–8, 15, 41; 37.
1, 8, 23–4, 45, 51, 59; 38. 38, 45–6,
50–1, 53–4, 58; 39. 50–2, 56; 40. 27

Hasdrubal (brother of Hannibal): 31.
10–11; 36. 36 (defeat at the Metaurus)

Hasdrubal (son of Gisgo): 40. 17
(son-in-law of Syphax)

Hegesianax (envoy of Antiochus III): 34.
57–9

Gaius HELVIUS: 32. 7–9 (*pr.* 198), 26; 38.
14, 20, 22–3

Marcus HELVIUS: 32. 27–8 (*pr.* 197), 33.
21; 34. 10, 45 (*iiivir*)

Heraclides: 31. 5, 16, 33, 46

Heraclides of Byzantium: 37. 34–5

Herodicus (Thessalian): 40. 4

Herodorus (Thessalian): 35. 37–8

Herodorus (Macedonian): 40. 23 (friend
of Demetrius)

Hierocles (of Agrigentum): 36. 32

Hilernus (Spanish chieftain): 35. 7

Hippolochus (Thessalian): 36. 9

Hispala Faecenia: 39. 9–14, 19

Aulus HOSTILIUS Cato: 31. 4; 38. 55, 58

Lucius HOSTILIUS Cato: 31. 4; 38. 55,
58

Aulus HOSTILIUS Mancinus: 40. 35 (*pr.*
180)

Hybristas (Spartan pirate): 37. 14

Isidorus: 36. 20, 33

Lucius IULIUS (*pr.* 183): 39. 45

Gaius IULIUS Caesar (*cos.* 59): 34. 9

Sextus IULIUS Caesar: 40. 27 (*mil. trib.*)

Decimus IUNIUS Brutus: 34. 45 (*iiivir*)

Marcus IUNIUS Brutus (*cos.* 178): 34. 1
(*trib. pl.* 195); 35. 24 (*pr.* 191); 36. 2, 21,
36; 37. 2, 55; 40. 59

Marcus IUNIUS Pennus (*pr.* 201): 31. 4
(urban praetor)

Publius IUNIUS Brutus (*pr.* 190): 34. 1
(*trib. pl.* 195); 35. 41 (*cur. aed.* 192); 36.
45 (elected praetor); 37. 2, 57

Marcus IUNIUS Silanus: 33. 36 (killed in
battle with the Boii in 196)

Titus IUVENTIUS: 33. 22 (*mil. trib.*; killed)

Lucius IUVENTIUS Thalna: 39. 31, 38
Titus IUVENTIUS Thalna (*pr.* 194): 34.
   42–3 (elected praetor)

LABEO, *see* FABIUS
Laconicus (Spartan): 35. 36
LAECA, *see* PORCIUS
Gaius LAELIUS (*cos.* 190): 33. 24 (*pr.* 196),
   25–6; 35. 10 (candidate for consulship
   of 192); 36. 45 (elected consul for 190);
   37. 1, 25, 46–7; 38. 36
Gaius LAETORIUS: 31. 21; 34. 45 (*iiivir*)
LAEVINUS, *see* VALERIUS
Lensus (Cretan): 38. 13
LENTULUS, *see* CORNELIUS
Leo (son of Cichesias, Athenian): 38. 10
Leon: 35. 50
Publius LICINIUS Crassus (pontifex
   maximus): 31. 9; 34. 44; 36. 2, 36; 39.
   46 (his death)
Marcus LICINIUS Crassus: 40. 51
Gaius LICINIUS Lucullus: 33. 42; 36. 36
Marcus LICINIUS Lucullus: 39. 6 (*pr.*
   186), 8, 18
Publius LICINIUS Tegula: 31. 12
Gnaeus LIGURIUS: 33. 22 (*mil. trib.*)
Gaius LIVIUS Salinator (*cos.* 188): 32. 16
   (hands the fleet over to Lucius
   Quinctius); 35. 5, 10 (candidate for
   consulship of 192), 24 (*pr.* 191); 36.
   2–3, 42–4; 37. 2, 8–9, 12, 14–17, 32; 38.
   35 (*cos.*), 42
Marcus LIVIUS Salinator (*cos.* 219): 31.
   12; 36. 36; 39. 3 (censor 204)
LIVIUS Andronicus (poet): 31. 12
Longarus (Dardanian; father of Bato):
   31. 28
Lonnorius (Gallic chieftain of the early
   3rd cent.): 38. 16
Gaius LUCRETIUS: 40. 26 (naval duumvir)
Spurius LUCRETIUS: 31. 11
LUCULLUS, *see* LICINIUS
Lutarius (Gallic chieftain of the early 3rd
   cent.): 38. 16
Luxinius (Spanish chieftain): 33. 21
Lycortas (father of Polybius): 35. 29; 38.
   32; 39. 35, 37
Lycurgus (lawgiver): 34. 32; 38. 34
Lycurgus (tyrant): 34. 26
Lysimachus (general and successor of
   Alexander the Great): 33. 40; 34. 58
Lysimachus ('Friend' of Philip V): 40. 8

Gaius MAENIUS: 40. 35 (*pr.* 180), 37, 43
Titus MAENIUS (*pr.* 186): 39. 6, 8, 18, 20,
   23; 40. 35 (*mil. trib.*)
Mago: 31. 11
Aulus MANLIUS: 34. 53 (*iiivir*)
Lucius MANLIUS: 38. 42 (see note)
Publius MANLIUS (*pr.* 195 and again in
   182): 33. 42–3; 34. 17, 19; 39. 56; 40. 1,
   16, 34, 41, 42
Lucius MANLIUS Acidinus (*cos.* 179): 31.
   50; 32. 7; 38. 35 (*pr.* 188); 39. 7, 21, 29,
   54–5; 40. 34 (*iiivir*), 43–4 (*cos.*), 53
Titus MANLIUS Torquatus: 38. 17
Aulus MANLIUS Vulso (*cos.* 178): 35. 9
   (*iiivir*); 40. 59 (*cos.*)
Gnacus MANLIUS Vulso (*cos.* 189): 33. 25
   (*cur. aed.* 196); 33. 42 (*pr.* 195); 35. 10
   (patrician candidate for consulship of
   192), 24 (second unsuccessful bid for
   consulship); 37. 47 (elected consul), 48;
   38. 12–13, 15, 18, 20, 22, 24–5, 27–8,
   35, 37, 39–47, 50, 54, 58; 39. 1, 6–7, 40
Lucius MANLIUS Vulso: 32. 27–8 (*pr.*
   197); 38. 20, 22–3, 37, 39, 42
Publius MANLIUS (*pr.* 195): 33. 42–3 (*pr.*
   and *iiivir epulo*); 34. 17, 19 (his
   command in Spain); 39. 56 (second
   praetorship, 182 BC); 40. 1, 16, 34, 41–2
   (second command in Spain)
MARCELLUS, *see* CLAUDIUS
Marcus MARCIUS: 35. 5 (*mil. trib.*)
Quintus MARCIUS: 35. 5 (*mil. trib.*)
Quintus MARCIUS Philippus (*cos.* 186):
   38. 35 (*pr.* 188); 39. 6 (*cos.*), 8, 19–20,
   23, 48; 40. 2–3, 36, 42 (*decemvir
   sacrorum*)
Quintus MARCIUS Ralla: 33. 25 (*trib. pl.*);
   34. 53 (*iivir*); 35. 41 (*iivir*)
Lucius MARCIUS Septimus: 32. 2
Masinissa (Numidian king): 31. 11, 19;
   32. 27; 33. 47; 34. 61–2; 36. 4; 37. 25;
   40. 17
Gaius MATIENUS: 40. 26 (naval duumvir),
   28
Memnon (of Pellene, son of Pisias): 32. 22
Menestas (Epirote): 36. 28; 38. 10
Menippus (envoy of Antiochus III): 34.
   57, 59; 35. 32, 50–1; 36. 10–11
METELLUS, *see* CAECILIUS
Micythio (Chalcidian): 35. 38, 46, 50–1
Minnio (courtier of Antiochus III): 35.
   15–16; 37. 41

Lucius MINUCIUS Myrtilus: 38. 42

Tiberius MINUCIUS Molliculus: 40. 35 (*pr.* 180), 36 (his death), 37

Marcus MINUCIUS Rufus: 32. 27–8 (*pr.* 197); 34. 53 (*iiivir*); 35. 40

Quintus MINUCIUS Rufus (*cos.* 197): 31. 4, 6, 8, 11–13; 32. 1, 27–8 (*cos.* 197), 31; 33. 22–3; 37. 55; 39. 54

Lucius MINUCIUS Thermus: 40. 35 and note (legate)

Quintus MINUCIUS Thermus (*cos.* 193): 32. 27 (*cur. aed.* 198, see note), 29 (*iiivir*); 33. 24 (*pr.* 196), 26; 34. 10, 17, 45 (*iiivir*), 54 (elected consul), 55–6; 35. 3, 6, 20–1; 36. 38–40; 37. 2, 46, 55; 38. 39, 41 (his death), 46, 49

Publius MINUCIUS: 35. 5 (*mil. trib.*)

Quintus MINUCIUS: 35. 5 (*mil. trib.*)

Mithridates: 33. 19

Mnasilochus (Acarnanian): 36. 11–12; 37. 45; 38. 38

Moagetes (tyrant of Cibyra): 38. 13

Morzus: 38. 26

Publius MUCIUS Scaevola (*cos.* 175): 40. 44 (*pr.* 179)

Quintus MUCIUS Scaevola (*cos.* 174): 40. 44 (*pr.* 179)

Quintus MUCIUS Scaevola (father of Publius and Quintus, above): 40. 44

Lucius MUMMIUS (*trib. pl.*): 38. 54

Lucius MUMMIUS (*cos.* 146): 40. 51 (censor in 142)

Quintus MUMMIUS (*trib. pl.*): 38. 54

Muttines (Numidian): 38. 41

Nabis (tyrant of Sparta): 31. 25; 32. 19, 21, 38–40, 45; 34. 22–4, 27–30, 33, 35, 37, 39, 41, 43, 48–9, 52; 35. 12–13, 17–18, 25–7, 29, 31, 35–6; 37. 25; 38. 59

Marcus NAEVIUS: 38. 56; 39. 52

Quintus NAEVIUS: 34. 53 (*iiivir*); 35. 40 (*iiivir*)

Quintus NAEVIUS Matho: 39. 32, 38 (*pr.* 184), 41

Nicaea (wife of Craterus): 35. 26

Nicander (Aetolian): 35. 12; 36. 29; 38. 1, 4–6

Nicander (pirate leader): 37. 11

Nicodamus (Aetolian): 38. 5–6

Nicanor ('Friend' of Philip V): 33. 8

Nicomedes (I), king of Bithynia: 38. 16

Nicostratus (Achaean *strategos*): 32. 39–40; 33. 14–15

Numa Pompilius (Roman king): 40. 29

Gnaeus OCTAVIUS (*pr.* 205): 31. 3, 11; 34. 45 (*iiivir*); 35. 23; 36. 12

Marcus OGULNIUS: 33. 36 (military tribune, killed in battle with the Boii in 196)

Marcus OGULNIUS Gallus: 39. 56 (*pr.* 182); 40. 1, 16

Onomastus ('Friend' of Philip V): 39. 34; 40. 8

Lucius OPICERNIUS: 39. 17

Gaius OPPIUS (introduced the lex Oppia in 215, otherwise unknown): 34. 1

Lucius OPPIUS Salinator: 32. 28 (*trib. pl.* 197); 35. 23, 24 (*pr.* 191); 36. 2

Ortiago (Galatian chieftain): 38. 19, 24 (wife raped by Roman centurion)

Paculla Annia: 39. 13

Pamphilidas (Rhodian): 37. 22–5

Pausanias (Epirote general): 32. 10

Pausanias (Thessalian): 36. 9

Pausistratus (Rhodian general): 33. 18; 36. 45; 37. 9–12

Pelops (Spartan): 34. 32

Perseus (son of Philip V): 31. 28, 33; 38. 5, 7, 10; 39. 23, 29, 53; 40. 5–9, 12–13, 15–16, 20–4, 54, 56–8

Lucius PETILLIUS: 40. 29

Quintus PETILLIUS: 38. 50 (*trib. pl.* 187), 53–4, 56, 60

Quintus PETILLIUS Spurinus: 38. 50 (*trib. pl.* 187), 53–4, 56, 60; 40. 18 (*pr.* 181), 26, 28–9

Phaeneas (Aetolian leader): 32. 32–4; 33. 3, 12–13; 35. 44–5; 36. 28, 35; 38. 8

Pharnaces (king of Pontus): 40. 2, 20

Philip II (son of Amyntas): 38. 34

Philip V of Macedon: 31. 1–3, 5–9, 11, 14–18, 23–6, 28, 30–4, 38–42, 44–7; 32. 4–5, 9–10, 13, 15–16, 19–23, 25, 32–9; 33. 3–4, 6–8, 10–14, 16, 18–21, 24–5, 27, 30–3, 39–40, 44, 49; 34. 23, 26, 31–2, 41, 48, 52, 57–8; 35. 12–13, 16, 18, 31–2, 35, 47–9; 36. 3–4, 7–8, 10, 13–14, 16–17, 25, 29, 31–5, 37.7, 25; 38.1–3, 5, 8, 10, 40, 42–3, 45–6, 49, 59; 39. 23–9, 33–5, 42, 46–7, 53; 40.2–5, 8, 11, 16, 20–4, 27, 54–8

Philip (son of Alexander of Megalopolis): 35. 47; 36. 8, 13–14, 31

Philip (*elephantarch* of Antiochus III): 37. 41

Philip (Carthaginian male prostitute): 39. 42, 46–7, 53

Philo (Chalcidian): 37. 45; 38. 38

Philocles: 31. 16, 26; 32. 16, 23, 25, 38, 40; 34. 32; 40. 20, 54–5

Philopoemen (Achaean): 31. 25; 35. 25–30, 37, 47; 37. 20; 38. 30–1, 33; 39. 37, 49– 50

Philotas (garrison commander of Abydus): 37. 12

Marcus PINARIUS Rusca: 40. 18 (*pr.* 181), 19, 25, 34

Pisias (of Pellene, father of Memnon): 32. 22

Pisistratus (Boeotian): 33. 27 (pro Roman), 28 (involved in murder of Brachylles), 29 (executed)

Piso (of Patras): 35. 26

Lucius PLAUTIUS Hypsaeus: 37. 47 (*pr.* 189)

PLAUTUS, *see* SERGIUS

Quintus PLEMINIUS: 31. 12; 34. 44 (executed); 38. 51

Pleuratus (Illyrian, son of Scerdilaedus): 31. 28, 34, 40; 33. 34; 38. 7

Polybius (historian): 33. 10; 34. 50; 36. 19; 39. 52

Polyxenidas: 35. 50; 36. 8, 41, 43–5; 37. 8, 10–13, 15, 22, 26, 28–30, 45

Gnaeus POMPEIUS (*cos.* 70): 34. 9

Pompey, *see* POMPEIUS

Pompo (father of Numa Pompilius): 40. 29

Marcus POMPONIUS: 31. 12

Marcus POPILLIUS Laenas: 40. 43 (*iiivir*)

Publius POPILLIUS Laenas: 40. 43 (*iiivir*)

Marcus PORCIUS Cato (*cos.* 195): 32. 7–8 (*pr.* 198); 33. 42 (elected consul) 43; 34. 1–4, 13–18, 20, 27, 42–4, 46; 35. 1, 9; 36. 17–18, 21; 38. 54; 39. 40–4 (censor 184), 52

Publius PORCIUS Laeca (*pr.* 195): 32. 7 (tribune); 33. 42 (*pr.*), 43

Lucius PORCIUS Licinus (*cos.* 184): 34. 54 (*pr.* 193), 55; 39. 32–3, 39, 52, 54; 40. 34 (father of Lucius, below)

Lucius PORCIUS Licinus: 40. 34 (*iivir*)

Poris (Aenian): 40. 4

Aulus POSTUMIUS Albinus Luscus (*cos.* 180) 36. 12; 39. 7 (*cur. aed.* 187), 23 (*pr.* 185); 40. 35, 39–41

Lucius POSTUMIUS Albinus: 40. 35 (*pr.* 180), 37, 39, 44, 47, 50

Spurius POSTUMIUS Albinus (*cos.* 186): 37. (*pr.* 189), 57; 39. 6 (*cos.*), 8–9, 11, 13–14, 19, 23, 45 (augur), 40. 36, 42 (his death)

Spurius POSTUMIUS Albinus (*cos.* 174): 39. 45 (*pr.* 183)

Lucius POSTUMIUS Tempsanus (*pr.* 185): 39. 23, 29, 41

Lucius POSTUMIUS Tympanus: 34. 47 (quaestor; killed by Gauls)

Prusias (king of Bithynia): 33. 30; 37. 25–6; 38. 39; 39. 46, 51, 56

Ptolemy III Euergetes: 33. 40

Ptolemy IV Philopator: 31. 14; 32. 33 (his death); 35. 16

Ptolemy V Epiphanes: 31. 2, 9, 16, 43; 32. 33; 33. 19, 39–41; 35. 13; 36. 4; 37. 3

Lucius PUPIUS: 39. 39 (*cur. aed.* 185), 45 (*pr.* 183); 40. 19

Pyrrhias (Aetolian): 31. 46

Pyrrhus I of Epirus: 31. 3, 7, 31; 32. 13 (Camp of Pyrrhus; cf. 35. 27); 35. 14; 38. 9 (his palace in Ambracia); 39. 51

Pythagoras (son-in-law of Nabis): 34. 25, 29–30, 32, 39–41; 35. 29

Pythagoras (Greek philosopher): 40. 29

Quarta Hostilia: 40. 37 (wife of Gaius Calpurnius Piso and mother of Quintus Fulvius Flaccus)

Titus QUINCTILIUS Varus: 39. 31, 38

Lucius QUINCTIUS Crispinus: 39. 6 (*pr.* 186), 8, 30–1, 38, 42, 55 (*iiivir*)

Lucius QUINCTIUS Flamininus (*cos.* 192): 31. 4, 49 (*pr.* 199); 32. 1, 16, 19, 23, 28, 39; 33. 16–17; 34. 26, 29 (attacks Gytheum from the sea), 30 (negotiates with Nabis), 40, 50; 35. 1 (elected consul) 20–2, 40–1; 36. 1–3, 12; 38. 11; 39. 42–3; 40. 8

Titus QUINCTIUS Flamininus (*cos.* 198): 31. 4, 49 (*iiivir*); 32. 6–11, 14–15, 18, 21, 24, 28, 32, 35–7, 39–40; 33. 1–3, 5–6, 9–13, 24–5, 27, 29–32, 34, 41, 45, 49; 34. 22, 24–6, 28–31, 33–5, 38–43, 48–52, 57–8; 35. 10 (supports Lucius' bid for consulship), 13, 15, 23, 25, 31–4, 37, 39, 45, 48–51; 36. 6, 17, 24,

31–2, 34–5; 37. 1, 25; 38. 9, 28 (censor), 31, 36, 43, 49, 59; 39. 23, 25–6, 42, 51, 56; 40. 8, 11–12, 20, 23–4, 54

Romulus: 40. 46
RUFUS, *see* MINUCIUS
Publius RUTILIUS Rufus (historian): 39. 52

SALINATOR, *see* LIVIUS
Gaius SALONIUS: 34. 45 (*iiivir*)
Quintus SALONIUS Sarra: 35. 10 (*pr.* 192), 20
Scerdilaedus (father of Pleuratus): 31. 28
SCIPIO, *see* CORNELIUS
Scopas (Aetolian): 31. 43
Gaius SCRIBONIUS: 40. 31 (commander of allies in Spain)
Gaius SCRIBONIUS Curio: 33. 42 (*pl. aed.* 195); 34. 53, 54 (*pr.* 193), 55; 35. 6
Lucius SCRIBONIUS Libo: 34. 54 (*cur. aed.* 193); 35. 10 (*pr.* 192), 20–1; 39. 23 (*iiivir*)
Seleucus I Nicator: 33. 40; 34. 58; 38. 13 (see note)
Seleucus IV (son of Antiochus III): 33. 40–1, 35. 15; 36. 7; 37. 8, 11–12, 18–19, 21, 41, 44; 38. 13, 15
Gaius SEMPRONIUS Blaesus: 39. 7 (*pl. aed.* 187), 32, 38 (*pr.* 184)
Publius SEMPRONIUS Blaesus: 36. 39 (*trib. pl.* 191)
Tiberius SEMPRONIUS Gracchus (*cos.* 215): 34. 1, 6
Tiberius SEMPRONIUS Gracchus (*cos.* 177), father of the famous Gracchi: 37. 7; 38. 52–3, 56–7, 60; 39. 5, 55 (*iiivir*); 40. 35 (*pr.* 180), 36, 39–40, 44, 47–50
Titus SEMPRONIUS Gracchus: 33. 36 (killed in battle with the Boii in 196)
Publius SEMPRONIUS Longus: 39. 32, 38 (*pr.* 184), 56 (proconsul); 40. 1 (his illness and death), 16
Tiberius SEMPRONIUS Longus (*cos.* 218): 33. 24
Tiberius SEMPRONIUS Longus (*cos.* 194): 31. 20 (*trib. pl.*); 32. 27 (*aed. cur.* 198; see note), 29 (*iiivir*); 33. 24 (*pr.* 196), 26; 34. 42–3 (elected consul), 45 (*iiivir*), 46, 56; 35. 5, 8; 36. 22, 24; 39. 40
Titus SEMPRONIUS Rutilius (stepfather of Publius Aebutius): 39. 9
Publius SEMPRONIUS Sophus: 34. 53

Gaius SEMPRONIUS Tuditanus: 32. 27–8 (*pr.* 197); 33. 25 (proconsul, killed in Spain), 26, 42 (replaced as pontiff by M. Claudius Marcellus).
Marcus SEMPRONIUS Tuditanus (*cos.* 185): 35. 7 (*trib. pl.* 192); 37. 47 (*pr.* 189); 38. 36; 39. 23 (consul), 32, 38, 40, 46 (interim pontifex maximus), 52
Publius SEMPRONIUS Tuditanus: 31. 2; 36. 36
Publius SEMPRONIUS: 34. 47 (killed by Gauls)
Tiberius SEMPRONIUS: 39. 24, 33 (Gracchus or Longus? See note)
Gaius SERGIUS Plautus: 31. 4, 6; 32. 1
Marcus SERGIUS Silus: 32. 27–8 (*pr.* 197), 31; 33. 21, 24
Gnaeus SERVILIUS: 33. 47 (ambassador to Carthage); 35. 23
Marcus SERVILIUS: 40. 27 (*mil. trib.*)
Publius SERVILIUS: 31. 4
Gnaeus SERVILIUS Caepo: 40. 59 (*cur. aed.* 179)
Marcus SERVILIUS Geminus: 31. 4; 32. 29 (*iiivir*); 34. 45 (*iiivir*)
Gaius SERVILIUS Geminus: 31. 4; 34. 53 (*iivir*); 39. 46 (pontifex maximus); 40. 37, 42
Gnaeus SICINIUS: 39. 39 (*cur. aed.* 185), 45 (*pr.* 183)
Sopater (Acarnanian): 31. 23
Sosilas (Rhodian): 34. 30
Gaius STERTINIUS (*pr.* 188): 38. 35
Lucius STERTINIUS: 31. 50 (governor of Farther Spain), 33. 27 (returns to Rome), 35 (legate), 39 (goes to Antiochus at Lysimachia)
Stratonidas (Boeotian): 33. 28 (friend of Zeuxippus)
Sulpicia (mother-in-law of Spurius Postumius Albinus): 39. 11–13
Lucius SULPICIUS: 40. 27 (*mil. trib.*)
Gaius SULPICIUS Galba: 32. 6–7
Publius SULPICIUS Galba (*cos.* 200): 31. 4–8, 14, 27, 33, 40; 32. 1, 21, 28; 33. 8, 24; 34. 59; 35. 13–14, 16–17
Servius SULPICIUS Galba (*pr.* 187): 32. 7, 24; 34. 44; 38. 35 (*cur. aed.* 189), 42 (*pr.*), 44, 54–5; 39. 5, 32 (candidate for consulship of 184), 40
Gaius SULPICIUS Galus: 40. 28
Syphax: 31. 11; 37. 25; 38. 46, 51, 53; 40. 17

TAMPHILUS, *see* BAEBIUS
Titus TATIUS: 40. 46
TEGULA, *see* LICINIUS
Telemnastus (Cretan): 35. 29
Quintus TERENTIUS Culleo (*pr.* 187): 33.
47 (envoy to Carthage in 195); 38. 42
(*pr.*), 55, 58, 60; 39. 3, 6, 32
Gaius TERENTIUS Histra: 39. 56 (*pr.* 182);
40. 1, 29 (*iiivir*)
Lucius TERENTIUS Massaliota (*pr.* 187):
31. 50 (*pl. aed.* 200); 33. 35 (member of
10-man commission), 39 (goes to
Antiochus); 38. 42 (*pr.*); 40. 35 (*mil.*
trib.)
Aulus TERENTIUS Varro: 37. 48; 39. 32, 38
(*pr.* 184), 42, 56 (proconsul); 40. 2, 16
Gaius TERENTIUS Varro: 31. 11, 49
Theoxena: 40. 4
Theoxenus (Achaean): 33. 18
Thoas (Aetolian): 35. 12, 32 4, 38, 42, 45;
36. 7, 15, 26; 37. 45; 38. 10, 38
Thurrius (Celtiberian chieftain): 40. 49
Thyrsis of Stuberra: 40. 24
Timasicrates (Rhodian): 37. 14
Timocrates (of Pellene): 34. 29, 40
Timon (prominent citizen of Pthiotic
Thebes): 33. 5
Timon (officer of Antiochus III): 37. 44
Gaius TITINIUS: 35. 8 (*trib. pl.*)
Marcus TITINIUS: 35. 8 (*trib. pl.*)
Marcus TITINIUS Curvus (possibly
identical with the above): 40. 59 (*pr.*
178)
Publius TITINIUS: 31. 21
Marcus TUCCIUS (*pr.* 190): 35. 41 (*cur.*
aed. 192); 36. 45 (elected praetor); 37.
2; 38. 36; 39. 23 (*iiivir*)

Marcus VALERIUS Corvus: 38. 17
Marcus VALERIUS Falto: 31. 8
Gaius VALERIUS Flaccus: 31. 50; 32. 7
(*cur. aed.* and *flamen* of Jupiter); 39. 39,
45 (*pr.* 183)
Lucius VALERIUS Flaccus (*cos.* 195): 31.
4, 21, 49 (*pr.* 199), 50; 32. 1; 33. 42
(replaces M. Cornelius Cethegus as
pontiff), 42 (elected consul 195), 43;
34. 22 (victory against the Boii), 42, 44,
46; 36. 17, 19, 22, 27–8; 37. 46, 57; 39.
40–2 (censor 184), 44, 52; 40. 42
Publius VALERIUS Flaccus: 37. 46 (father
of Lucius, the consul of 195)

Gaius VALERIUS Laevinus (*cos. suff.* 176):
38. 9–10 (half-brother of Marcus
Fulvius Nobilior); 40. 44 (*pr.* 179)
Marcus VALERIUS Laevinus (*cos.* 210): 31.
3, 5, 7, 13, 50 (his death); 38. 9 (father
of Gaius)
Marcus VALERIUS Laevinus: son of
Marcus (above): 31. 50
Publius VALERIUS Laevinus: son of
Marcus: 31. 50
Marcus VALERIUS Laevius (*pr.* 182): 39.
56; 40. 1, 27
Marcus VALERIUS Messala (*cos.* 188): 34.
54 (*pr.* 193), 55; 37. 47 (candidate for
consulship of 189); 38. 35 (*cos.*), 42
Gaius VALERIUS Tappo: 37. 46 (father of
Lucius *below*), 57; 38. 36
Lucius VALERIUS Tappo: 34. 1–2, 5 (*trib.*
pl.); 35. 10 (*pr.* 192), 20, 23; 36. 2; 37.
46, 57
VALERIUS Antias (historian): 32. 6; 33. 10,
30, 36; 34. 10, 15; 35. 2; 36. 19, 36, 38;
37. 48; 38. 23, 50, 55; 39. 22, 41, 43, 52,
56; 40. 29
VARRO, *see* TERENTIUS
Vermina (son of Syphax): 31. 11, 19
Quintus VICTORIUS (centurion): 34. 46
Lucius VILLIUS 'Annalis': 40. 43 (*trib. pl.*
180, *lex Villia Annalis*)
Publius VILLIUS Tappulus (*cos.* 199): 31.
4, 49; 32. 3, 6, 9, 28; 33. 24, 35, 39 (sent
to Antiochus); 34. 33, 59; 35. 13–14,
19, 23, 39
Lucius VILLIUS Tappulus (*pr.* 199): 31.
49; 32. 1
Publius VILLIUS (equestrian, struck by
lightning 196): 33. 26
VULSO, *see* MANLIUS

Xenoclides (Chalcidian): 35. 38, 50–1
Xenon (officer of Antiochus III): 37. 44
Xenon (officer of Philip V): 38. 1–2
Xenophon (Achaean): 32. 32
Xychus: 40. 55

Zeno (Thessalian): 35. 31–2
Zeuxippus (Boeotian): 33. 27
(pro-Roman); 28–9 (involved in
murder of Brachylles)
Zeuxis (Acarnanian leader): 33. 16
Zeuxis (officer of Antiochus III): 37. 41, 45
Ziboetes (ruler of Bithynia): 38. 16

GENERAL INDEX

Abbasium 371

Abdera 400

Abydus 15, 18–19, 32, 74, 87, 123, 130, 302, 304, 307

Academy 24

Acanthus 46

Acarnania 16, 70, 94, 110, 261–2, 265, 271, 359, 360

Acarnanian/ns 16, 23, 30, 107, 109, 215, 223, 260, 261–2, 270, 338, 364, 366, 396

Achaea 26, 32, 56, 72–3, 79, 91, 107, 109, 112, 122, 180, 187, 243, 265 (Pthiotic Achaea) 271, 281, 312, 457, 458, 460

Achaean League 25, 279, 283, 387, 462, 473, 552, 554

Achaeans 25–6, 56, 70–3, 76–8, 80, 86–7, 89, 90, 93 4, 96, 106 7, 111, 122, 124–5, 126 (Pthiotic Achaeans) 162–3, 167, 180, 186–7, 209–10, 221–3, 226–7, 232, 243–7, 253–5, 279–80, 283, 297, 301, 313, 387–91, 457–62, 473, 475, 483, 502, 555

Acharrae 65

Acraephia 122

Acriae 222

Acrocorinth 124, 186–7, 558

Acylla 139

Adoreus, Mt. 375

Adramytteum 312, 314

Adriatic 444, 503, 524, 536, 544

Aebura 512–14

Aefula 83

Aegae 554

Aegean Sea 290, 307, 421

Aegina 16, 17, 25, 28, 34, 92, 123, 289

Aeginium 66, 262

Aegium 222, 283, 386–7

Aenea 484

Aenians 326, 399; see also 96

Aenus 17, 32, 355, 445, 449, 451, 456

Aeolis 130, 194, 300, 304, 310, 317, 328, 372

Aequimaelium 96

Aesculapius 360, 519, 575

Aethalia 306

Aetolia 17, 31, 43, 70, 88, 110, 209, 219, 229–30, 232, 246, 252, 261–2, 264–5, 271, 277–8, 280, 295, 339, 341–3, 347, 356, 362, 365, 367, 392, 425, 446, 579

Aetolians 3, 17, 28–31, 33–4, 41–3, 47, 55, 65–6, 74, 86–90, 96, 99–100, 103–6, 109, 120, 123–4, 126–7, 135–6, 140, 161–3, 176, 180–1, 186, 209–10, 215, 220, 227, 229–36, 240–7, 252, 255–7, 260–1, 264, 266–70, 272–4, 276–83, 288–9, 293, 296–9, 318, 338–42, 347, 352–3, 356–61, 363–6, 385, 402–3, 427, 445–6, 527, 543, 550, 556, 558–9, 569, 572–3, 575–7

Africa 3, 5, 6, 8, 9, 12, 13, 15, 20, 50, 51, 55, 60, 139, 195, 198, 200, 215, 239, 251, 256, 298, 318, 327, 347, 412, 414, 416, 420

Agraei 88

Agrianes 111

Agrigentum 251, 280

Alabanda 111, 368

Aladrus 374

Alba, Mt. 53, 528

Alban mount 116, 557

Albans 528

Alce 529 30

Alexandria (in Egypt) 19, 44, 373

Alexandria Troas 239, 327

Aliphera 56

Allia 373, 576

Alopeconnesus 18

Alps 443, 479, 503, 533

Alyatti 374

Amarynthis (Diana) 235

Ambracia 66, 264, 359–60, 362–5, 386, 403, 426–7

Ambracian Gulf 66, 359

Ambracians 361, 402–3

Ambryssus 70

Amiternum 218, 285

Amphictyonic council 558

Amphilochi 88

Amphilochia 358, 361, 363, 365

Amphilochian Argos 365

Amphilochia/ns 358, 360–1

Amphipolis 506, 535–6

Amphissa 297–300
Amyclae 167
Anabura 371
Ancyra 381–2
Andania 280
Andrians 46
Andros 17, 45–7, 67, 271
Anemurium 113
Angeiae 65
Anthedon 121
Anticyra 70, 92, 94, 124
Antigonea (in Chaonia) 56
Antigonea (in Syria) 565
Antioch (in Syria) 113, 133, 140, 210, 559, 570
Antioch (on the Maeander) 368
Antipatrea 28
Antium 251
Aous 56–7, 61, 65, 73, 97, 267, 410, 556
Apamea 212, 310, 336, 368, 371, 394–5, 565
Apelaurum 107
Apennines (mountains) 265, 424, 544
Aperantia 282, 358
Aphrodisias (in Cilicia) 113
Aphrodisias (in Aeolis) 314
apocleti 242, 278
Apodoti 88
Apollo 53, 79, 94, 181, 247, 261, 296, 353, 367–8, 399, 425, 465, 483, 519, 532
Apollonia 20, 22, 27, 41, 97, 220, 298, 359, 400, 537
Aporidos Come 371
Apsus, River 27
Apuani 424, 442, 455, 482, 518–20, 523, 544
Apulia/n 5, 294, 343, 452, 470, 500, 502, 550
Aquileia 443, 470, 480, 508, 515
Arabs (archers) 333
Aradians 244
Aratthus 359
Arcadia/ns 459, 552
Ardea 53, 60, 440
Areopagus 559
Argenta 65
Argethia 356–7
Argives 76, 80, 92–3, 164, 168, 171, 179
Argos 8, 25, 79, 87, 89–94, 136, 161–4, 168, 170–3, 175, 180, 215, 351, 387, 546, 554–5
Argos (Amphilocian) 365

Aricia 206
Ariminum 11–12, 21, 49, 53, 183, 218, 424
Arpini 183
Arpinum 393
Artemis 272
Asculum 544, 560
Asia 3, 4, 28, 48, 67, 87, 111–15, 122–6, 128, 130–3, 140, 144, 192–4, 213–14, 229–30, 241, 244, 255, 257, 264, 267–8, 271, 276, 284, 288, 294–6, 298–9, 307–12, 317, 319, 326–8, 337–8, 340–7, 349–54, 356, 358, 364, 366, 371–2, 374, 385, 392–3, 397, 401, 406–8, 410, 412, 415, 420–3, 428, 444, 483, 548, 572
Asia Minor 543
Asnaus (mountain) 56–7
Asopus 272
Aspendians 370
Aspendus 315
Asti 398
Astraeum 506
Astragos 111
Ateaum 35
Atalante (island) 235–6
Athamania/ns 28, 41, 42–3, 65–6, 91, 104, 243, 254, 260, 262–3, 277, 280, 282, 341, 356–9, 364, 365, 445–6, 448, 450
Athenaeum 357, 448
Athenians 3, 6, 10, 16–17, 22, 24–5, 27, 29–31, 44–5, 71, 122–3, 162, 229–30, 271, 298–9, 364–5, 544, 577
Athens 6, 8, 10, 15–17, 22–4, 27, 44, 67, 113, 122, 144, 227, 235–6, 246, 298, 358, 396, 484
Atrax 67, 68, 97, 259, 262, 556
Attica 551
Auginus, Mt. 423
Aulis 235, 247
Ausetani 159
Aventine 150, 206, 393, 432–3, 469, 482
Axius, River (Vardar) 478
Axylos 375, 577

Babylon 577
Babylonia 373
Bacchanalia 430, 433, 435, 438, 441, 502, 580–1, 584
Bacchants 434
Bacchium 314
Baebian law (180 BC) 525

Baeturia 115, 452
Ballista, Mt. 424, 523
Bardo 115
Bargylia (bay of) 309
Bargyliae 87, 90, 112, 123, 127, 131, 171
Barium 501
Bastarnae 486, 536–7, 583
Bastetani 339
Belbina 391
Bellona 49, 115, 117, 286, 404, 452
Bendis 399, 578
Bergistani 157, 160
Bergium 160
Bessi 478
Beudos 371
Bevus, River 34
biga 116, 130, 152, 183, 272, 286, 288
Bithynia 123, 317, 372, 375, 471, 573, 576
Boebe (marsh) 42
Boeotia/ns 24, 27, 46, 68, 70, 78, 95–6,
    107, 119, 121–2, 243, 246, 247, 254–5,
    260, 265, 270, 275, 346, 347, 568
Boii 4, 11, 84–5, 115–16, 128–30, 134,
    160, 180, 183, 185, 192, 201, 203–4,
    209, 218, 237, 249, 284–8, 294, 340,
    352, 480, 544
Bologna 544
Bononia 352, 424
Books, the 206, 295
Brixia 84
Bruanium 40
Brundisium 15, 61, 188, 219–20, 250,
    252, 296, 501, 523
Bruttians 8
Bruttium 7, 9, 13, 53–4, 189, 217, 219,
    238, 250, 294, 296, 343, 392, 552
Bursa 198, 564
Buxentum 84, 181–2, 444
Byllis 256
Byzacium 139
Byzantium 87, 326, 371, 458

Cadusians 244–5
Caeni 398
Caicus, River 311, 329
Caieta 483
Calagurris 443
Caletranian territory 480
Callias (Peace of) 556
Callidromus, Mt. 265–6, 269
Callipolis (Chersonese) 18
Callipolis (Aetolia) 279

Callithera 65
Calycadnus 395, 578
Calydon 261
Campania/ns 9, 30, 32, 182, 385, 393,
    402, 434, 549
Campus Martius 7, 58, 207, 385, 527,
    532, 545, 564
Canae 292, 301, 305
Canastraeum 46
Cannae 148, 563
Capena 119, 385, 416–17
Capitol 59, 81, 83, 118, 141, 146, 183,
    189, 191, 218, 238, 284, 296, 350, 385,
    390, 391, 412–13, 418–19, 527–8,
    532–3
Capitoline 15, 129, 482, 545, 571
Capitoline Jupiter 545
Cappadocia/ns 324, 332, 384, 394, 502
Capua 30, 32–3, 58, 60, 148, 206, 461,
    527, 579
Carallites 370
Caria/ns 111, 113, 123, 309, 314, 333,
    350–1, 368, 373, 397
Carinae 85
Carmo 115
Carpetania 452, 512, 514
Carthage 3, 7, 12, 29, 33, 137–40, 171,
    195–6, 198, 349, 401, 409, 411, 414,
    523, 550, 559, 562, 564, 579, 585
Carthaginians 3, 4, 6, 8, 12, 20, 32, 54,
    80, 85, 105, 113, 136, 138, 140, 154,
    161, 169, 195–8, 251–2, 291, 347, 404,
    406, 412–14, 416, 499, 509, 516, 546,
    548–9, 552, 554, 562, 564
Caryae 165, 223
Carystus 46, 67–8, 73, 127, 235
Casanes, River 369
Cassandrea 46
Castra Telmessium 351
Castrum Frentinum 206
Castrum Novum 251
Castrum Salerni 82–3
cataphracti 243, 567
Caucasus 363, 575
Caudine Forks 208, 565
Caulares, River 370
Caunus 114
Cea 17
Celaenae 368, 566
Celathara 65
Celeiates 84
Celetrum 41

Celines 11

Celtiberia/ns 152, 157–8, 205, 429, 442, 467, 480, 482, 499, 511–18, 520–2, 526, 528, 529, 530, 531

Cenaeum 271

Cenchreae 68, 70, 73, 77, 94

Cenomani 11, 84–5, 115–16, 424

Cephallania/ns 261–2, 306, 307, 342, 365–6, 385, 387–8, 402, 425, 427, 579

Cerceii 80–1

Cercina 139

Cercinium 42

Cerdiciates 84

Ceres 16, 31, 48, 118, 148, 285, 482

Cermalus 119

Certima 529

Chaeronea 242, 260–1, 556 (battle of, 338 BC)

Chalcioecus (temple of Minerva) 234

Chalcis 22–4, 26, 67–8, 91, 124, 162, 186–7, 214, 227, 231, 235–6, 242, 245–7, 252, 253, 254, 256, 258, 260, 262, 264, 270–1, 279, 327, 558

Chaonia 56

Chaunus, Mt. 531

Chelidoniae 113, 133, 556 (islands)

Chersonese 18, 130, 132, 288, 326, 328, 348, 371, 397–8, 449, 451

Chians 397

Chios 87, 290, 292, 307, 319, 324, 533

Chyretiae 42, 259, 262

Cibyra 369, 370

Cierium 66

Cilicia/ns 113, 211, 308, 315, 333, 351, 375

Cincian law 144, 561

Circus Flaminius 427, 532, 545

Circus Maximus 119, 284, 482

Cisalpine Gaul/s 83, 256, 544

Cissus 290–1

Cithaeron 26

Cius 88, 123, 235

Clastidium 84–5

Clazomenae 397

Cleonae 107–8, 163

Clitor 459

Cnidus (Dassaretian) 28

Cnidus (in Asia) 28, 308, 314

Cnossos 354

Cobulatus 370

Codrion 28

Coela 48; 'Hollows of Euboea' 48, 551

Coele Syria 113

Coele Thessaly, see Hollow Thessaly

Colline Gate, see Porta Collina

Colophon/ians 318–19, 321, 324, 397

Comenses 130

Comitia Centuriata 546

Compasium 459

Comum 128–9

Concord 481, 501

Contrebia 514

Coracesium 113

Corax 279, 297

Corbio 467

Corcyra 20, 22, 44, 48, 57, 61, 66–7, 78, 93, 109–10, 256, 271, 289, 524

Corcyreans 366

Coreli 398

Corinth 8, 22, 25–6, 68, 70, 77–9, 87, 89, 90–1, 94, 106–8, 124, 127, 144, 161–2, 185, 188, 214, 222, 231, 236, 280, 585

Corinthian Gulf 70, 271, 362

Corinthians 77, 107, 125

Cormasa 370

Corone 473

Coronea 122, 254, 270

Corsicans 501, 516

Corupedium (battle of) 558, 576, 583

Corycus 113, 291, 300, 305–6, 322

Corylenus 314

Cos 308

Cosa 54, 117

Cotton 314

Cranians 385

Crannon 259, 264

Cremaste 48, 106

Cremona 11, 21, 80, 116, 161, 339–40

Cretans 36, 40, 107, 331–4, 354, 473

Crete 97, 165, 175, 222, 354

Creusa 271, 569 (Creusis)

Croton 183

Ctimene 65

Cuballum 375

Cumae 525, 548

cursus honorum 553

Cusibi 219

Cyatides 387

Cybele 560, 565, 572, 578

Cyclades 165, 289

Cydonia 354

Cylarabis 164

Cymaeans 397

Cyme 304
Cynosarges 25
Cynoscephalae 99, 109, 111, 114, 257,
    550–1, 556, 568
Cyparissia 74, 553
Cyphaera 65
Cyprus 133
Cypsela 18, 398
Cyrene 197
Cyrtians 332–3
Cythnus 46
Cyzicus 18

Daedala 314
Dahae 244–5, 330, 332
damiurgi 76, 554
Danube 503, 536
Daphne 140, 559
Dardania/ns 28, 34–5, 39, 41, 44, 112,
    340, 371, 536–7
Dardanus 301, 329, 397
Darsa 370
Dassaretii 34, 41, 61
Daulis 70
decemvir sacrorum 524
decemviri 285, 295, 391, 403, 544, 548,
    571, 585
Delium 46, 247, 254
Delos 123, 289, 290, 558
Delphi 261, 408, 537, 585
Demeter 548
Demetrias 24, 34, 47, 86, 91, 124, 162,
    186, 188, 214, 227–8, 231–2, 235, 236,
    239–40, 242–3, 245, 252, 254, 260, 264,
    271, 281, 445, 447, 506, 533, 535
Dentheleti 478, 505
Derriopus 478
Dialis (flamen) 463, 470
Diana 18, 235 (Amarynthis) 424, 532
Dictynneum 177
Dipo 452
Dipylon 24
Dium 96
Dolopia/ns 65, 126, 282, 341, 358, 361,
    363, 365, 448
Donuca, Mt. 537
Doriscus 18
Dromos 166
Drymussa 397
duoviri sacris faciundis 548
Duronia 430
Dymae 75–6, 79, 386

Dyniae 371
Dyrrachium 27

earth and water 215, 566
Ebro, River 154, 157, 159, 199, 480, 546,
    562
Ebro (treaty) 562
Echinus 88, 106, 162, 562
Egypt/ians 4, 16, 44, 87, 132, 133, 136,
    210, 252, 296, 373, 548
Elaea 211, 290, 305, 310–12, 314, 329,
    337, 398, 420, 573
Elaeus 18, 301
Elatia 70, 73, 78, 86, 92, 95–7, 119, 122,
    124, 163, 180, 185, 187, 270, 297
Eleusis 16, 25–6, 31
Elians 283
Elimia 41
Elis 56, 279, 389
Elymaeans 244–5, 332–3
Emathia 483
Emporiae 150, 152, 154, 156
encomenderos 562
Eordaea 40–1, 101
Ephesus 130, 133, 140, 195, 211–13, 268,
    271, 288–90, 292, 303, 305–10, 314,
    318, 323–4, 337–8, 354, 358, 367, 385,
    394, 396–7, 533, 570
Epirotes 61, 66, 223, 253, 283, 359
Epirus 8, 20, 56, 61, 64, 66–7, 73–4, 87,
    97, 101, 110, 187–8, 220, 253, 256, 265,
    298, 359, 400, 458, 544, 550
Eretria 64, 67, 73, 99, 124, 127, 187, 235
Ergavica 531
Ericinium 262, 447
Erigonus 40, 478
Eriticium 183
Eriza 369
Erythrae/ans 290, 292, 301, 305, 319, 397
Esquiline Gate 119
Etruria 12, 21, 48–9, 128, 192, 218, 256,
    294, 343, 352, 418, 429–30, 544
Etruscans 295, 352, 480
Euboea 23, 26, 47, 67, 73, 91, 125, 188,
    235, 247–8, 255–6, 265, 271, 484, 551
Euhydrium 64
Euripus 22, 24, 235, 236, 242, 246–7,
    256, 258, 551
Euromus 87, 123
Europe 3, 106, 122, 124, 126, 132, 136,
    173, 181, 193–5, 209, 215, 230, 232,
    239, 242–3, 252, 255, 267, 301, 327,

Europe (*cont.*)
338, 344, 346, 348, 366, 395, 397–8,
401, 421
Eurotas 166–7, 226, 233
Eurymedon 133, 315, 573
Eurymenae 446

fasces 544
feast of Jupiter 6, 59
Felsina 129
Feralia 204, 564
Ferentinum 54
Feronia 119
fetial priests 9, 547
fillets 19, 320, 548, 573
flamen Dialis 463, 470, 551, 582
Formiae 53, 83, 218, 393, 469, 483
Fortuna 119, 522, 526
Fortuna Equestris 522, 526
Fortuna Primigenia 189
Fraternal War 576
Fregellan squadron 327
Fregenae 83, 251
Friniates 423
Frusino 14, 83
Fundi 393

Gades 54, 268
Galatia 300, 367, 375
Galatians 330, 404, 579
Galli 301, 375, 572, 577
Gallic Gulf 150
Gallograecia/ns 300, 405, 572, 577, 579
Gaul 4, 7, 9, 11–12, 21, 22, 49, 53, 58–9,
61, 80, 82, 84–5, 116, 134–5, 160, 171,
183, 190–1, 217, 256, 284, 339, 340,
382, 392, 401, 412, 424, 467, 470, 479,
482, 498, 500, 507, 518
Gauls 4, 21, 50–1, 58, 85, 105, 111, 114,
128–9, 147, 160, 183–4, 201–2, 208,
286–7, 339, 344, 354, 367, 371–85, 393,
397, 401–2, 405–8, 428, 443, 470,
478–80, 500, 509, 533, 537, 551, 576
Gaurion 45
Genoa 84
Geraestus 46
Gergithus 397
Gerrunium 28
Gomphi 42, 65–6, 262, 357
Gonni 260
Gonnocondylus 447
Gordium 375

Gordiutichos 368
Gortyn/ians 97, 354, 355
Gravisca 510
Great Games 11, 182, 545
Greater Greece 8
Greater Phrygia 397
Greece 10, 12, 17, 24, 27, 31, 80, 82,
87–8, 90, 91, 95, 100, 103–6, 109, 113,
115, 123–8, 136, 144, 161–3, 171–4,
180, 185–7, 192, 194–5, 206, 209–10,
214–15, 218–19, 228–32, 239–42, 244,
249–51, 253, 255–7, 260, 264–5, 268,
270, 272, 275–6, 278–9, 282–4, 288,
293–4, 296, 309, 328, 345, 349, 365,
396, 406, 408, 412, 443, 451, 456, 461,
483, 537, 548, 557, 566, 571, 576, 584
Greeks 24, 30, 35, 45–6, 56, 78, 98, 105,
124, 136, 151, 161, 183, 187, 194, 237,
247, 267, 312, 349, 373–4, 447, 534,
563
Gulf of Pamphylia 315
Gyrton 259
Gythium 168, 169, 173, 177, 209, 210,
221, 222, 223, 235, 460

Hadria 183
Hadrumetum 139
Haemus, Mt. 503–4, 584
Halicarnassus 114, 303, 308
Halys 372, 382, 385
Hannibalic War 543, 545, 550, 552, 559,
561, 564
Harpasus 367
haruspices 285, 483, 547
Hasta 442
hastati 95, 156, 331, 508, 555
Hebrus, River 399
Hellespont 17, 87, 130, 220, 243, 290,
300–2, 304–5, 307, 311, 314, 318–19,
324, 326, 328–9, 338, 346, 371–2, 375,
397, 451, 573
Helo 219
hemerodromos 549
Hephaestia 127
Heptagoniae 177
Hera 571
Heraclea 47, 96, 266, 267, 269, 272, 275,
276, 279, 297, 356, 444, 506
Heraclea (in Italy) 544, 560
Heraea 56, 127
Hercules 25, 53, 60, 79, 279, 374, 391,
532

Hermione 44–5
Himera (battle of) 556
Hister 458
Hollow Thessaly 55
Hyampolis 70
Hydaspes, River 574
Hydrela 351
Hydrus 271
Hypata 264, 266–7, 276, 278–9, 298–9
Hyrcanian plain 330

Iasus 87, 90, 123, 171, 309, 310
Icus 46
Ida 565, 577
Idaean Mother 144, 560
Ides of March 6, 53, 134, 477
Ilergetes 152–3
Ilienses 501, 516
Iliturgi 152
Ilium 240, 301, 329, 397, 572
Ilotae (Helots) 166, 562
Illyria/ns 35–6, 41, 97, 105, 107, 267,
    524, 544
Illyricum 87, 90, 374, 478, 523
Ilvates 11, 84, 85
Imbros 123, 240
imperium 5, 10, 52, 118, 135, 158, 205,
    213, 216–17, 219, 250, 282, 343, 482,
    499, 501, 506, 518, 526, 544
India 229, 332
Indian 369
Indian elephant 332
Indus 369
Ingauni 4, 455, 506, 510, 515, 523, 544
Insubres 11, 84, 85, 115–16, 128–30, 134,
    183
Intemelii 523
Ionia 130, 194, 213, 317, 328, 350, 368,
    372
Isiondenses 370
Issa 46
Isthmian Games 123, 126
Istria/ns 480, 501, 507
Italy 7–8, 10, 12, 30, 53, 55, 59, 74, 82–4,
    115, 118, 120, 132, 134, 136, 148,
    161–2, 181, 186–8, 195, 200, 204, 212,
    216–17, 231, 238, 249–50, 253, 256,
    265, 271, 275, 288, 293–4, 307, 309,
    311, 319, 341, 396, 401, 405, 407,
    434–6, 439, 440, 443–4, 454, 458, 467,
    470, 476, 479, 500–1, 503, 515, 518,
    526, 533, 535–6, 544, 547, 571

Juno Lucina 295, 571
Juno Sospita 14, 85, 501
Jupiter 10, 31, 51, 53, 57, 59, 60, 79, 129,
    162, 189, 199, 207, 238, 250, 284, 285,
    357, 412, 418, 427, 504, 522, 526–7,
    532–3, 538, 575

Lacedaemon/ians 26, 94, 170–2, 179,
    232, 234, 460
Lacetani 159
Lacinium 289
Laconia/n 26, 209, 387–8, 390
Laevi 129
Lamia 55, 240, 245, 246, 264, 275, 278,
    297, 298, 444, 450, 581
Lampsacus 130, 213, 214, 239, 327
Lampsus 65
Lampter 324
Lanuvium 14, 60, 206, 501
Laodicean War 570, 576
Larisa 32, 48, 67, 79, 88, 90, 98, 103, 106,
    257–60, 262–4, 568
Las 388
Latin Festival 545, 571
Latin League 6, 9, 11, 21, 83, 134, 157,
    191, 192, 216–17, 238, 250, 252, 294–5,
    441, 442, 463, 482, 501, 502, 508, 510,
    514, 518, 522, 524–6, 548
Laudiceni 111
Laurentum 295
Lautumiae 296, 469, 571
Lechaeum 77–8
lectisternium 249, 547
Lecton 329
Lemnos 123
Lensus 368
Letum, Mt. 523
Leucae 222
Leucas 66, 109–10, 126, 140, 165, 262,
    265
Leuctra 552, 582
lex Claudia 557
lex Oppia 580, 582
lex Sempronia 571
lex Villia Annalis 553
Liber 118
Libera 118
Libui 129
Licabrum 219
Licinian law 144, 545 (Licinian-Sextian
    legislation) 560, 564
lictors 544, 549, 555

Ligures 135, 191, 533
Liguria 191, 203, 216, 218, 256, 287, 294,
    339, 400, 401, 406, 423, 424, 441, 442,
    470, 482, 498, 500, 507, 515, 516, 518,
    533
Ligurian/s 4, 11, 12, 84, 85, 116, 129,
    150, 185, 191–2, 200–1, 207–8, 218,
    237, 285–7, 294, 351, 392, 423–4,
    442, 455, 462–3, 500–1, 506–10,
    515, 518–20, 523, 532, 538,
    544
Ligynae 65
Lilybaeum 29
Limnaeum 263
Litana 160, 180
Liternum 182, 413, 415, 417
Locri/ans 13, 14, 53, 125, 127, 171, 182,
    289, 412, 579
Locris 70, 73, 86, 91, 265
Long Walls 549
Loryma 310
Lucanian 8, 14, 549
Ludi Magni 545
Ludi Megalenses 565, 570
Ludi Romani 545
Luna 150, 191, 442, 455, 482
Lusitania/ns 199, 352, 429, 442, 467,
    480, 515, 528
Lycaonia 348, 350, 395, 397, 405
Lyceum 25
Lychnidus 127
Lycia 113, 133, 308, 309, 310, 315, 317,
    337, 350–1, 396, 397
Lydia 336–7, 350, 397
Lyncus 34, 61, 64
Lysimachia 88, 131–3, 192, 193, 195,
    212, 256, 261, 281, 323, 326–8, 371,
    397–8, 449, 451
Lysinoe 370
Lysis, River 370

Macedon 3, 4, 7, 11, 19, 55, 66, 82, 97,
    101, 104, 105, 171, 211, 243, 257, 280,
    398, 452, 495, 502, 533, 567, 576, 584
Macedonia 5, 7–8, 10, 15–16, 20, 27–8,
    33, 35, 39, 41, 47, 53–4, 56–7, 59, 61,
    64, 74, 82–3, 86, 103, 105, 112, 115,
    117–18, 123, 126, 128, 135, 172, 181,
    185, 209, 215, 217, 219, 244, 249, 256,
    260, 281, 299–300, 311, 318, 340, 357,
    361, 400, 421, 445, 447, 449, 451, 456,
    458, 471–3, 477–8, 483, 486, 490–1,

494, 503–6, 536, 538, 543, 558, 576,
    583
Macedonian War 15, 498; First 543, 551,
    553; Second 561, 563, 569, 571; Third
    563
Macedonians 3, 7–8, 17, 23, 26, 29–31,
    35, 37–9, 41, 44, 46–7, 56, 64, 66, 68–9,
    71, 73, 77, 79, 87, 97–103, 107–8, 111,
    117, 125, 165, 235, 255, 257, 267–9,
    275, 281, 306, 331, 334, 356–8, 363,
    372–3, 444, 449–51, 456, 460, 478, 486,
    491–2, 494–5, 505, 509, 535, 543, 550–1
Macra 65, 455, 523
Macris 305, 321
Madamprus 370
Maduateni 398
Madytus 18, 131
Maeander 337–8, 350–1, 367–8, 397
Maedica 503–4, 584
Maenian (auction room) 469
Magaba, Mt. 376
Magna Mater 284, 375, 560, 565, 572,
    577
Magnesia/ns 125–6, 227–8, 236, 240,
    265, 290, 303, 330, 336–8, 351, 367,
    420, 445, 567, 570, 572–5, 577
Magnetarch 228, 240
Malacini 115
Malea 44, 48, 176, 288–9
Maleum 67, 172
Malian Gulf 47, 55, 86, 235, 240, 261,
    264–5, 270, 272, 278, 298
Malloea 42, 259, 262, 447
Mamertines 8, 549
manumission 557, 580
Marathon (battle of) 549
Maronea/ns 17, 32, 355, 400, 445,
    449–50, 451, 456, 457
Mars 206–7, 385, 527
Marseilles 561
Marsian cohort 128, 558
Marsyas 368, 576
Massilia 349, 351, 373, 501
Massiliots 151, 561
Medes 244–5
Medion 261–2
Megalesia 190, 284, 564, 570
Megalopolis 56, 76, 234, 243, 257, 263,
    280, 389, 391, 552, 573
Megara 22, 25
Megiste 315, 317, 337
Melambium 99

Melas 272, 398
Meliboea 262
Mendaeum 46
Mendis 578
Menelais 448
Menelaus, Mt. 167
Meropus, Mt. 56–7
Messana 29, 289, 549
Messene 32, 74, 172, 279, 473, 475, 502
Messenia/ns 175, 279, 473, 474, 582
Metaurus, River 547, 570
Metropolis 65, 66, 259, 263, 371
Milan (Mediolanum) 183
Milesians 397
Milyas 397
Minerva 31, 234, 240, 270, 301, 329, 412,
    501, 572, 574
Minturnae 251, 285
Mitylenaeans 314
Mitylene 31, 314
Mniesutae 111
Molottis 64
Moneta 119
Munda 528
Mutilum 4, 129
Mutina 201, 203, 480
Mycenica 93
Mylasenians 397
Myndus 114, 308
Myonnesus 305, 320–3, 326, 340
Myrina 123
Mysia 350, 397
Mysteries 16

Nar 183
Narnia (Nequinum) 54, 552
Naupactus 29, 41, 209, 222, 261, 277,
    279, 281–2, 289, 297, 445, 549
Neapolis 400, 523; Naples 523
Nemea (stream) 107
Nemean Games 179
Neocretans 333
Nicaea 86, 89, 557
Nicephorium 87
Noliba 219
Norba 54, 80
Notium 318, 397
Numidia 12, 20, 138, 198, 251
Nursia 295

Ocean 268
Odrysae 478

Oeniadae 366
Oenus 166; River 166
Oeta, Mt. 265, 272, 275, 279, 297
Old Beudos 371
Olympia 390
Olympias 447
Olympus, Mt. 376, 380, 384, 577
Onchestus 99
Oppian law 141, 144, 145, 148, 150
Ops 443
Orchomenos 56
Orestae 126
Orestis 41
Oreus 26, 41, 47, 48, 124, 127, 187, 327
Orgessus 28
Oricum 187–8
Oroanda 374, 376, 394, 396, 405
Osca 525
Osphagus, River 40
Ostia 53, 251, 569
Otolobus 37, 41
ovation 21, 58, 119, 152, 272, 286, 452,
    499

Pachynus 251
Paeonia 112, 374, 478, 483, 503–6
Palensians 385
Palinurus 303
Pallene 46, 107
Pamphylia 133, 244, 315, 370, 394, 397
Panaetolian Council 29, 34, 229, 549
Panhormus 302–3, 321–2
Parachelois 448
Parilia 482, 582
Parma 480
Parorea 450
Paros 17, 32
Parthenium, Mt. 165
Parthians 373
Parthini 127
Patara 133, 308–10, 317–18, 337, 396
Patrae 222, 271, 362, 386
Pedasa 123
Pelagonia 29, 34–5, 40
Pelinnaeum 263
Pelion 41
Pella 300
Pellene 76, 107, 108, 168, 179
Peloponnese 8, 26, 70, 74, 127, 136, 161,
    163, 209, 215, 253, 265, 279, 281, 289,
    297, 347, 387–9, 456, 458, 460–1, 473,
    477

Peloponnesian League 581
Peloponnesian War 581
peltasts 36, 97, 101, 108
Peneus, River 67
Peraea 87, 89, 90, 111, 112, 314
Perga 394
Pergamenes 312
Pergamum 47, 114, 123, 211, 213, 301,
 310–12, 329, 346, 367, 565, 573, 577
Perinthus 87, 123
Perranthes 359
Perrhaebia/ns 42, 67, 125, 126, 259, 262,
 265, 282, 446–8, 450
Persephone 547–8
Persia/ns 113, 215, 265
Pessinus 144, 207, 375, 560, 565, 577
Petillian law 416, 428
Petra 448, 505
Phacium 64, 262
Phaeca 65
Phalara 240, 278
Phaloria 66, 263, 446
Phanae 290
Phanotea 70
Pharae 227
Pharcadon 42
Pharsalus 88, 90, 106, 126, 140, 162, 259,
 264, 559, 562
Phaselis 315–16
Phaustus 262
Pherae 65, 98, 257–9, 264, 556
Pherinium 65
Philippopolis 446, 478
Phlius 107, 108
Phocaea 151, 290, 292, 301, 304–5, 314,
 324, 326
Phocaeans 301, 325, 397, 561
Phocians 125, 127, 171
Phocis 70, 73, 78, 86, 91, 95, 242, 260,
 262, 265, 270, 283
Phoebeum 177
Phoenice (Peace of) 543–4
Phoenicia 210
Phoenician ships 139, 300
Phoenicus 292, 308
Phrygia/ns 144, 300, 333, 368, 371,
 373–4, 375, 397, 405, 576, 584
Phrygias 348, 350, 397, 575
Phrygius, River 330
Phthian Thebes 106
Phthiotis 447
Picenum 183, 217, 443, 469

Pieria 448
pilleus 557
pilum 555
Piraeus 16, 22–3, 25, 27, 31, 45, 48, 67,
 78, 246, 271, 289, 307, 396, 548
Pisae 135, 191, 200–1, 203, 392, 424, 455,
 500, 502, 507–8, 523, 525
Pisaurum 469
Pisidia/ns 211, 333, 348, 351, 368, 370,
 405
Pisuetae 111
Placentia 11, 22, 80, 116, 161, 185, 192,
 339, 340, 424, 468, 523
Plataean 96
Plebeian Games 6, 51, 59, 118, 134, 392,
 429, 545
Plebeian Order 553
Pleiae 222–3
Plitendum 374
Pluinna 40
Po, River 11, 84, 115, 128–9, 161, 183,
 192, 544
Poetneum 448
pontifex maximus 10
Pontus 502–3, 582
Port of the Achaeans 301, 572
Porta Caelimontana 206
Porta Capena 119
Porta Collina 515
Potentia 469
praetorian sortition 546
Priatic plain 400
princeps senatus 385, 531
principes 156, 331, 508, 555
Privernum 14
Pronnaei 385
Propontis 371, 375
propraetorian 544
prorogation 544
Proserpina 13, 547
provocatio 544
Pteleon 48
Pthiotic Thebes 97, 126
Pthiotis 47, 125
Public Villa 117, 182
publicani 469
Punic War 3, 8, 33, 37, 187, 189, 415;
 First 543, 549, 579; Second 545, 552,
 557; *see also* Hannibalic War
Puteoli 58, 83, 181–2, 295
Pydna 551
Pygela 303

Pylaic Council 34, 127, 558
Pylos 571
Pyra 279
Pyrenaeus 150
Pyrrheum 360–1, 575

Raphia 210, 565, 574
Reate 295, 483, 527
Regia 574
Rhegium 30, 32, 213–14, 289, 549
Rhoda 150
Rhodes 17, 18, 23, 28, 72, 113–14, 165,
    302, 308, 310, 314–15, 317, 324, 350–1,
    358, 397
Rhodians 3, 15–17, 19, 23, 48, 70–1, 77,
    87, 89, 90, 96, 111–12, 114, 123, 174,
    179, 292, 300–1, 305, 308–11, 314–17,
    322–4, 344, 347, 350–1, 364–5, 395,
    422, 483, 573
Rhoduntia 266, 269
Rhoeteum 301, 329, 397
Rhotrine Springs 371
Roman Games 51, 59, 117, 134, 182, 190,
    392, 429, 538, 545
Romans 3–6, 10–13, 17, 20, 22–5, 28–31,
    33–41, 44–5, 47–8, 60–3, 65, 67–75,
    77–9, 84–90, 96–110, 113–14, 120–3,
    125, 127–9, 131–3, 136, 138–40, 153–8,
    160–4, 166, 168–9, 172–5, 177–80,
    184–7, 192–5, 198–9, 201, 203, 209–11,
    213–16, 218, 222, 227–32, 235–6,
    239–48, 252–6, 258, 263–4, 266, 268,
    270, 272–81, 286, 288–90, 292–3,
    296–8, 300–2, 304–6, 308–10, 314,
    317–23, 325–33, 335–7, 341, 343–4,
    351, 354, 358–9, 361–2, 364, 366,
    368–70, 372–9, 383–5, 387–9, 394,
    395–400, 403, 412, 415, 420, 427,
    442–3, 445–50, 452–4, 457, 459–62,
    471–2, 475, 477–8, 480, 485–6, 491–4,
    497–9, 502–3, 505–7, 509–14, 516, 521,
    524, 530–1, 537, 543–86 *passim*
Rome 4, 6–8, 10–11, 13, 15, 17, 19–20,
    22, 26, 29, 33, 44, 49–50, 53–4, 56, 58,
    60, 70, 73–7, 80–3, 85, 90–1, 96, 106,
    109, 113–15, 117, 119–20, 122, 124–8,
    130–1, 133–4, 140, 146, 148–9, 151–2,
    159, 163, 175, 180–1, 183, 185, 188,
    193, 195–8, 200, 203, 205, 209–12, 214,
    216–18, 220–1, 229–30, 235–7, 240–2,
    249–53, 255, 260–1, 263, 271, 277, 279,
    281, 283–9, 292–3, 295–7, 299, 317–18,

337–44, 350, 358, 365–7, 385, 388–9,
    391–4, 397, 400–4, 411–14, 416–18,
    421, 423–5, 427, 428, 430, 434–5,
    439–40, 448, 452, 455, 458–9, 462,
    466–7, 470–1, 475–6, 478, 480, 483,
    486, 492–3, 497, 500–1, 503, 505, 507,
    510, 516, 518–20, 522–5, 527–8, 533–4,
    536, 538, 543–86 *passim*

Sabines 14, 146, 528
Sacred Mount 150
Sacred Spring 135, 181–2, 563
Sagalessus 370
Saguntia 159, 562
Saguntum 7, 8, 18, 20, 153, 546, 562
Salamis (battle of) 556
Sale 400
Salernum 181, 182
Salian priest 326, 574
Salus 519
Samaeans 385, 387
Same 67, 289, 386–7
Samnite/s 5, 8, 32, 520, 549
Samos 32, 114, 303–7, 309–11, 314,
    317–21, 324, 533
Sancus 53
Sangarius, River 375
Sardinia 10, 53, 59, 82, 118, 135, 181,
    191, 217, 238, 250–1, 256, 295, 342–3,
    392, 401, 429, 462, 466, 470, 482,
    500–1, 507, 516–17, 519, 525–6, 552,
    579
Sardis 113, 310, 314, 317–18, 324, 336–7,
    577
sarisophoroi 268, 568
Sarpedonium 395, 578
Sarus 133
Saturnia 480
Scarphea 96
Sciathus 29, 46–7
Scordisci 536
Scotusa 99, 258, 264
Scyllaeum 44, 289
Scyros 123
Second Messenian War 563
Second Samnite War 565
Sedetani 50, 159
Segestica 158
Seleucia 133, 373, 570, 577
Selinus 113
Sellasia 166
Selymbria 131

Senate 4–7, 9–15, 20, 49–51, 53, 55, 60, 67, 81, 83, 86, 90–1, 105–6, 114–18, 123, 125, 127, 130–1, 134–5, 138–40, 144, 148, 152, 163, 171, 180–2, 188–90, 192, 194, 196–8, 200, 203–5, 207, 217, 219–21, 230, 237–8, 249–52, 271–2, 277, 281, 283–8, 293, 296–7, 299, 311, 338–47, 349–53, 355, 358, 365, 385, 389, 392–3, 397, 401–4, 406–10, 414–15, 417–21, 424–7, 429, 435, 438–42, 444–6, 448–9, 451–2, 456–9, 463–5, 467, 469–72, 474, 476, 478–80, 483, 492, 498, 500–2, 507–8, 510–11, 515–17, 520, 524–8, 531–3, 538
Serrheum 18
Sestus 87, 131, 301
Setia 80–1
Sexetani 115
Sibylline (books) 14, 285, 404, 548, 560, 571
Sicily 5, 7, 9, 29, 32, 53, 55, 59, 82, 118, 134, 135, 181, 191, 200, 213, 217, 219, 220, 238, 250, 289, 294–5, 340, 342, 343, 392, 401, 412–13, 429, 462, 470, 481, 482, 500, 517, 526, 552, 559, 571
Sicyon 71, 77–8, 92–4, 107, 108, 221
Side/tans 211, 244, 315
Sidon 244; Sidonian ship 323
Signia 54
Siguenza 562
Silana 262
Simila 433
Sindensians 370
Sinope 375, 483
Sinuessa 14, 60, 251
Sipontum 183, 444
Sipylus 290, 330, 336, 351
Smyrna/eans 213–14, 239, 308–9, 347
Soli 113, 351
Spain 8, 20, 50–1, 53, 58, 60, 82, 113, 115, 118–19, 134–5, 152, 154, 157–8, 160, 161, 180–1, 191, 199–200, 204–6, 217, 238, 250, 272, 284, 286, 298, 318, 327, 339, 342, 352–3, 392, 412, 414, 420, 429, 441–3, 452, 454, 462–3, 467, 480, 482, 483, 499, 511, 515–18, 520, 521, 523, 524, 525, 528, 531, 552, 561, 566
Spaniards 50, 119, 151, 155–8, 199, 209, 453, 454, 509, 512, 526, 530
Sparta/ns 26, 92, 94, 165, 168, 171–5, 177, 179, 180, 186, 214–15, 223, 226–7,

231–4, 387–9, 391, 421, 459–61, 473, 489, 566, 568 ('300 Spartans') 581, 583
Spercheus 264, 297
Sperchiae 65
Springs of †Alexander† 371
Stobi 112, 478, 503
strategos 549–50, 554–5, 569, 573
Stratonicea 111–12, 123
Suessa 53, 60
Suessetani 159, 467
Suismontium, Mt. 424
Sunium 22–3, 68
Sylleum 369
Synnada 371
Syracusans 32, 402
Syracuse 29, 32, 144, 213, 412, 426, 549, 579
Syria 16, 113, 131, 136, 211–13, 268, 296, 300, 314, 337, 372
Syrians 245, 267, 333, 373, 568, 577
Syrtis (minor) 197

Tabae 368, 369
Tabusion 369
Tagus 219, 453, 454
Tanagra 121, 247
Tanais 395
Tarentines 224, 333, 349, 567, 574
Tarentum 8, 30, 148, 213–14, 219, 250, 373, 401, 452, 466, 501, 567
Tarmiani 111
Tarracina 285, 527, 531
Tarraco 157, 521, 522
Taurasini 520
Taurian Games 443, 581
Taurus 210, 328, 338, 344, 347, 349–50, 351, 364, 367, 370, 372, 385, 393, 395, 397, 404, 407, 408, 414, 421
Taurus Mountains 344, 575
Taygetus, Mt. 167
Tectosages (Tectosagi) 372, 374, 376, 381–2, 384
Tegea 165, 223, 234, 391
Telmessus 309, 351, 396, 397, 575
Telum 356
Tempe 67, 103, 105, 127, 260, 446, 449
Tempsa 183
Tempyra 399
Tendeba 111
Tenos 271
Teos 319, 320
Termessus 370

Terracona 157
Tetraphylia 356
Teuma 65
Thapsus 139
Thasos 32, 123, 127, 131
Thatira 314
Thaumaci 55, 65, 264, 300, 552
Thebans 106, 121, 552
Thebe 312
Thebes 88, 90, 95–8, 106, 114, 121, 126, 235–6, 254, 447
Thera 111
Theraei 111
Thermopylae 24, 96, 127, 265, 271–2, 275, 280, 289, 352–3, 409, 444, 515, 550, 558, 569, 572
Thermum 549–50, 558
Thespians 271
Thessalians 62, 65–7, 107, 125, 171, 188, 227, 236, 255, 257–8, 263, 445–8, 450, 456
Thessalonica 113, 449, 484, 506, 535
Thessaly 34, 42, 48, 55, 64–6, 70, 74, 88, 91, 98, 106, 112, 117, 126–7, 187–8, 227, 257, 258, 262, 265, 298–9, 309, 400, 450, 556, 559
Thetidcum 99
Theudoria 356
Third Syrian War 570
Thrace 17, 127, 131–2, 193, 256, 281, 299–300, 326, 340, 355, 371, 374, 398, 400, 406, 410, 423, 445, 449–51, 471, 478, 491, 535–6, 558
Thracians 26, 40, 80, 88, 97, 100, 105, 107–8, 131, 193, 267, 331, 377, 398–400, 445, 457, 473, 483, 506, 537, 550
Thronium 90, 96, 235–6, 270
Thurii 189
Thyatira 301, 329–30, 336
Thyrreum 261, 262, 364
Thyrsis 506
Tiber 206 7, 218, 231, 238, 285, 339, 385, 434, 436, 532
Tichius 266, 269
Tifata, Mt. 58
Titian (auction room) 469
toga praetexta 13, 133, 149, 524, 561
Toletum 205, 219, 452
Tolostobogii 371–2, 376, 384
Torona 46
Tralles 36, 97, 337–8, 397, 575

Trallians 331, 332, 333, 377
Trasimene 559
Trausi 399
triarii 555
Tribus Sapinia 4
Tricca 64, 262, 446
Triphylia 56, 64, 127
Tripolis (Spartan): 223
Tripolis (Perrhaebian): 259
triumph 6, 20, 49, 50–1, 115–17, 119, 130, 144, 152, 183, 188, 205, 207, 249, 286–8, 339, 352–5, 403–7, 409, 410, 413, 415–16, 418, 420, 425, 427–9, 452, 467, 515, 520, 521, 525, 538
triumvir epulo 133, 524, 558
triumvirs 81, 84, 182, 206, 237, 352, 439, 469, 480, 510, 515, 525
Troad 565
Trocmi 372, 376, 384
Troy 565, 572
Turda 135
Turdetani/a 157–9, 562
Turduli 157, 562
Tuscan Sea 523
Tymbris 375
Tyre 139, 140, 196–7, 244
Tyrrhenian Sea 444
Tyscos 374

Umbria 4, 443, 544
urban jurisdiction 7, 118, 470, 482, 526
Urbiaca 499

Vaccaei 205, 528, 531
Vediovis 22, 548
Veii 60
Velitrae 53, 60
Venetia 443
Venus 87, 89, 515
Venus Erycina 515
Venusia 50
Vescelia 219
Vettones 205, 219
Vibo 5, 237
Vicus Tuscus 119
Volsci 146
Volternum 182
Volturnum 285
Vulcan 83, 183, 471, 501

White Temple 60, 527

Xyline Come 370
Xyniae 65, 96, 448

Zacynthus 280–2, 289, 546

Zelasium 47
Zephyrium 113
Zerynthius 399
Zmyrna 130, 327

The Oxford World's Classics Website

www.worldsclassics.co.uk

- Information about new titles
- Explore the full range of Oxford World's Classics
- Links to other literary sites and the main OUP webpage
- Imaginative competitions, with bookish prizes
- Peruse *Compass*, the Oxford World's Classics magazine
- Articles by editors
- Extracts from Introductions
- A forum for discussion and feedback on the series
- Special information for teachers and lecturers

www.worldsclassics.co.uk

American Literature

British and Irish Literature

Children's Literature

Classics and Ancient Literature

Colonial Literature

Eastern Literature

European Literature

History

Medieval Literature

Oxford English Drama

Poetry

Philosophy

Politics

Religion

The Oxford Shakespeare

A complete list of Oxford Paperbacks, including Oxford World's Classics, OPUS, Past Masters, Oxford Authors, Oxford Shakespeare, Oxford Drama, and Oxford Paperback Reference, is available in the UK from the Academic Division Publicity Department, Oxford University Press, Great Clarendon Street, Oxford OX2 6DP.

In the USA, complete lists are available from the Paperbacks Marketing Manager, Oxford University Press, 198 Madison Avenue, New York, NY 10016.

Oxford Paperbacks are available from all good bookshops. In case of difficulty, customers in the UK can order direct from Oxford University Press Bookshop, Freepost, 116 High Street, Oxford OX1 4BR, enclosing full payment. Please add 10 per cent of published price for postage and packing.